Robin Horton is a thinker whose ideas have influenced not only many of his fellow anthropologists but also philosophers and others interested in the study of religions and world-views. These ideas, however, are to be found in scattered articles rather than in book form. In this selection of some of his major theoretical essays, produced over a thirty-year period, with specially written introduction and postscript, readers will for the first time be able to get an overall view of his approach to the comparative study of human thought-systems.

The essays take off from an attempt to understand African religious thought. But they also deal with broader issues in the history and sociology of thought, such as secularization and intellectual modernization. Essays in the first part of the book undertake critical assessments of two established interpretative approaches, the Symbolist and the Theological. Those in the second part propose an alternative, 'Intellectualist' approach, which emphasizes the similarities of structure and process between religious and scientific thinking. The postscript appraises the Intellectualist approach in the light of recent theorizing about religions and world-views.

PATTERNS OF THOUGHT IN AFRICA AND THE WEST

PATTERNS OF THOUGHT IN AFRICA AND THE WEST

Essays on magic, religion and science

Robin Horton

University of Port Harcourt
Rivers State
Nigeria

CAMBRIDGE
UNIVERSITY PRESS

.b1939324

.0104024 8

54224024

Published by the Press Syndicate of the University of Cambridge
The Pitt Building, Trumpington Street, Cambridge CB2 1RP
40 West 20th Street, New York, NY 10011-4211, USA
10 Stamford Road, Oakleigh, Melbourne 3166, Australia

First published 1993

Reprinted 1994   1995

First paperback edition published 1997

Printed in Great Britain at the University Press, Cambridge

A catalogue record for this book is available from the British Library

Library of Congress cataloguing in publication data

Horton, Robin.
Patterns of thought in Africa and the West: essays on magic, religion, and
science / Robin Horton.
    p.   cm.
ISBN 0 521 36087 0 (hard)
1. Africa – Religion.   2. Knowledge, Sociology of.
3. Religion and science.
I. Title.
BL2400.H67   1993
299.6 – dc20   92-23089   CIP

ISBN 0 521 36087 0 hardback
ISBN 0 521 36926 6 paperback

CE

For Sokari and Winnie

Contents

Acknowledgements

First of all, I should like to thank those colleagues, both late and living, who gave me the precious hours of discussion, suggestion and constructive criticism which made these essays possible; those who gave me the moral support that an incurable armchair theoretician, particularly one working against the forbidding background of British anthropological empiricism, so badly needed in his many moments of discouragement; and those who gave me a marvellous combination of both. Since it would be invidious to be either more specific or more quantitative, let me simply say a big thank-you to: Jacob Ajayi, 'E. J.' Alagoa, Anthony Appiah, Raymond Apthorpe, Michael Crowder, Mary Douglas, Dorothy Emmet, Daryll Forde, Ernest Gellner, Jack Goody, Barry Hallen, Mary Hesse, Steven Lukes, John Middleton, Ade Obayemi, Tunji Oloruntimehin, John Peel, John Skorupski, and Godwin Sogolo.

I should also like to express my gratitude to some thirty intakes of undergraduates at the Universities of Ibadan, Ife and Port Harcourt who attended such courses as 'Theories of Religion' and 'Tradition and Modernity'. Despite the notorious 'dryness' of these courses and the equally notorious harsh marking of the lecturer, those who endured them gave me, year after year, a lively critical response, a constant insistence on clarification, and on top of these a surprisingly warm appreciation. If the essays in this volume have any cogency or clarity, much of the credit must go to this long succession of students. Since it would be invidious even to mention names here, let me just thank them all and wish them every success in their struggle to survive these hard times.

Again, I must express my gratitude to three editors at the Cambridge University Press. To Patricia Williams, for honouring me with the original proposal. To Susan Allen-Mills, for renewing the proposal when I had so ungraciously disregarded it the first time round, and for having enough faith in my work to secure me a very generous contract. And, last but not least, to Jessica Kuper, for her great patience; and for a judicious combination of stick and carrot without which the project might never have come to fruition.

Yet again, I must thank Jill Mcleod, Jane Ambrose and Okoro John for their painstaking labours on the manuscript.

Finally, let me thank Marigold Acland, Sandy Anthony and Jayne Matthews, also of the Cambridge University Press, for dressing up some very ordinary content in some very well-tailored clothes.

The author thanks the editors and publishers of the following books and journals in which some of the papers collected in the volume have previously appeared:
1: *Journal of the Royal Anthropological Institute*, Volume 90, part 2, 1960. 2: *Man*, N.S., Volume 3, no. 4, 1968. 3: R. Horton and R. Finnegan (eds.), *Modes of Thought*, Faber & Faber, London, 1970. 5: *European Journal of Sociology*, Volume 17, 1976. 6: *Cahiers d'Etudes Africaines*, Volume 96, nos. 24–4, 1984. 7: *Africa*, Volume 37, nos. 1–2, 1967. 8: *Philosophy of the Social Sciences*, Volume 3, nos. 3–4, 1973. 9: M. Hollis and S. Lukes (eds.), Blackwell, Oxford, 1982.
Paper 4 is a revised and expanded version of the 1987 Frazer Lecture.

Introduction

I

When I originally decided on the title of this book, it seemed to me to have two virtues: first, accurate indication of the book's contents; and second, absence of the flashy gimmickry so prevalent amongst modern social-anthropological book titles. Now, looking through the eyes of a sceptical would-be reader, I feel less easy with it. It has overtones of a somewhat nutty attempt to make sense of everything under the sun. So perhaps the best way to introduce the book is with an apologia for its title.

As regards the 'Africa' part of the title, little needs to be said. The train of thought pursued in these essays was triggered, in the first instance, by two periods of ethnographic fieldwork in Africa: an early and relatively short period in Nike in northern Igboland; and a later and much longer (indeed still continuing) period in Kalabari in the eastern Niger Delta.[1] In both areas, I was drawn, for a variety of reasons, to the religious aspect of the life of the peoples I encountered. Reflection on my fieldwork findings led me in two directions. First, to comparative reading in the religious ethnography of sub-saharan Africa, guided by the aim of establishing the representativeness or otherwise of my fieldwork materials. Second, to the search for a theoretical framework which would be adequate to the interpretation of the religious life of the peoples of my fieldwork areas and of other parts of the continent. This search, in turn, led on the one hand to disappointment with existing theoretical frameworks, and on the other to the quest for something more promising. The critical and the constructive essays in this book represent, respectively, the disappointment and the more positive quest that accompanied it.

So much for 'Africa'. What of 'the West'? Here, I think, a somewhat more extended explanation is required. For the reader will surely want some solid reasons as to why the West was dragged into the title of a book whose alleged primary inspiration was the religious life of Africa. In what follows, I shall offer three principal reasons.

First of all, in both my critical and my constructive work, I had to take account of the basic realities of the comparative study of human thought-systems. Particular thought-systems of particular peoples had to be brought to the notice of the widest possible audience. And comparisons between such thought-systems required a standard, universally-current medium. Both of these considerations dictated that the thought-systems of the various peoples of the world be translated into terms of a 'world' language. And for the time being, 'world' language meant Western language.

Now since translation involved finding equivalences of intention and structure between source-language and target-language, it followed that the scholar in quest of the appropriate translation instruments for African religious thought had to be prepared to enquire deeply into the intentions and structures embodied in various areas of Western discourse. This meant his spending a lot of time and effort in activities which were similar to or even indistinguishable from those of the analytic philosopher whose primary concern was with Western discourse.[2]

Here, then, is one reason why, in several of the papers in the present volume, the reader will find, as an integral part of the discussion of how to develop an appropriate framework for the interpretation of African religious thought, a searching scrutiny of various types and aspects of Western discourse.

A second aspect of my enquiry which forced me to reflect on Western thought and life was the quest for contrast cases. The purpose of this quest was two-fold. First, to sort out what was common to African and perhaps all thought-systems, from what was distinctive of Africa. Second, to help test my answers to the explanatory question: given the pervasive importance of certain features of content and mode of thought in African cultures, what factors in the technological, economic and socio-political context contribute to sustaining these features?

Now the besetting sin of many writers on African thought-systems has been to treat as unique many features which in fact are much more widely shared or even universal. And the besetting sin of many modern social anthropologists has been the tendency to set up elaborate explanatory frameworks on the base of monographic studies of single cultures or regional groups of cultures, without due concern for the kind of wider comparisons which might at least begin to test these frameworks. These were sins of which I became aware at an early stage of my induction into African Studies and Social Anthropology, and which I was determined to avoid. As I said earlier, although I started out from a mere two bodies of ethnographic findings, I quickly embarked on a programme of comparative reading which gave me an Africa-wide perspective. At that stage, however, I had no clear idea of what African thought-systems shared with the rest of the world, and what, if anything, was unique to them. Only extra-African contrast cases could throw light on this matter. Again, although my initial explanatory hunches had received encouraging confirmation from my broader reading, I was still dealing only with parallel cases involving similar manifestations of thought conjoined with similar contextual backgrounds. And as all those with scientific pretensions have recognized since John Stuart Mill, the accumulation of confirmatory parallel cases needs to be supplemented by a determined search for contrast cases, in which the phenomena to be explained are absent, and of which one must ask whether or not the contextual features alleged to constitute their causal backgrounds are also absent.[3] It was the search for such cases that drove me, once again, to the thought-world of the West.

With its highly secularized world-view and its modernistic mode of thought, the West, at first glance, stood in spectacular contrast with a spiritual and traditionalistic Africa. What could have been a more promising setting in which to clarify one's ideas about universals and uniqueness? What more promising setting in which to test one's hunches about cause and context? In the event, the exercise did throw useful if unexpected light on the question of universals and peculiarities. Further, the element of genuine contrast in content and mode of thought was revealed as being accompanied by some equally striking contextual contrasts; and this finding did at least something to corroborate my initial explanatory hunches. The exercise also had a fruitful spin-off as regards understanding of the West. For, by corollary, some features of Western thought often taken for granted by scholars were highlighted when viewed against the African background. Again, some relations between the content, mode and context of this thought, which might otherwise have remained in shadow, stood out dramatically when so viewed.

A third factor which drew me into reflection on modern Western thought was my curiosity about the roots of the theories of scholars engaged in this field. As someone fired with curiosity as to *why* people thought as they did, I moved easily from pondering the influence of socio-cultural context on the creators and sustainers of African systems of thought to pondering the influence of this context on those who theorized about such systems. Following this path, I came to think of socio-cultural and personal background as exercising its influence upon scholars in two ways.

First, it determined the translational resources which a scholar brought to his task. Philosophers such as Quine had tended to talk as though the would-be translator had at his beck and call an infinity of resources with which to embark on his task, and as though his problem was one of an *embarras de richesses*.[4] In fact, however, it seemed that the situation was rather the reverse of this. For the typical would-be translator in the real world had a decidedly limited array of resources with which to work, and had to make the best use he could of this limited array. The limits to the means at his disposal, of course, were set not only in a general way by the culture out of which he operated, but also more specifically by his personal position within this culture and by his personal educational history.

Secondly, the factor of background exerted its influence through the ideology with which it endowed the scholar. Ideology had long been defined as ideas in the service of wishes. And an important component of an individual's ideology was what he wanted to believe about the relation between other cultures and his own. Once again, moreover, what he wanted to believe in this area was shaped by the culture out of which he operated and by his position in this culture.

To avoid misunderstanding, I should perhaps stress here that I always saw the background factor as something that should be taken into account in trying to understand not only theories that were obviously at variance with the phenomena, but also those that seemed to accord well with them. I found it generally accepted that obviously inadequate theories could be explained by pointing out how, whilst the phenomena pulled in one direction, the scholar's background pulled more strongly in another. What was less generally accepted, but to me equally true, was that, even in explaining the vogue of an apparently fruitful theory, we still needed to bring in the background factor; for without this factor working in such a way as to reinforce the pull of the phenomena, the theory would not have come to accord with the latter in the way it did.

Now in the case of enquiries into African religion, it was evident that the socio-cultural and personal background of *all* of us engaged in them had a strong Western component. For not only had people born and brought up as Westerners predominated until recently in this field. The African scholars now coming to the fore in the field were also the products of an Afro-Western elite culture in which the Western component loomed large. (Even where, as they frequently did, they reacted with deep resentment against the more ethnocentric effusions of Western theorists, it was still in a sense the West that was calling their tune.) Hence, if we were fully to understand *both* the mistakes *and* the insights of researchers in this field, whether they were Westerners or Africans, we had to delve deeply into the Western element in their background. This, then, is a further reason why several of the essays in this volume move to and fro between African thought and its Western counterpart.

Here I rest my case, hoping I have persuaded the reader that the conjunction between 'Africa' and 'the West' in the title of this book not only provides an accurate indication of the content of the essays included in it, but also reflects a coherent and broadly worthwhile set of intellectual preoccupations.

II

Let me turn next to the arrangement and content of the individual essays included in this volume.

Under the first sectional heading, *Beginnings*, I have put a single early paper: 'A Definition of Religion, and Its Uses'.[5] In retrospect, I see this as a rather loosely-organized and meandering piece. Nonetheless, there are a number of reasons for including it.

First of all, it records my initial struggle to find a theoretical framework adequate to my fieldwork materials, and so may throw some light on my subsequent theoretical endeavours.

Secondly, it proposes a definition of religion which has been implicit in my subsequent work: a definition which, following Tylor's, emphasizes belief in extra-human personal beings and action in relation to such beings.

Thirdly, it contains a number of insights which I see as flowing from this definition, some of which I discuss at greater length in later essays and in the postscript. Here, I should like to pick out one such insight for special mention: that regarding the two major aspects of religious life, which I refer to in this paper as 'manipulation' and 'communion'. By 'manipulation', I refer to that aspect of a social relationship in which one partner treats the other as a means to achieving an ulterior end. By 'communion', I refer to that aspect in which one partner treats the other as an end in himself or herself. I show that, in religious as in purely human relationships, there is a wide range of variation between these two poles, with more or less pure 'manipulation' at one extreme, more or less pure 'communion' at the other, and a great many combinations lying between them. I also conduct a brief but wide-ranging exploration of the causes of such variation.

The distinction between 'manipulation' and 'communion' foreshadows my later (and I think more satisfactory) distinction between 'explanation/prediction/control' and 'communion'. In this later distinction, 'explanation/prediction/control' refers to religion as a system of theory and associated practice directed to the comprehension and practical control of events in the everyday space-time world, whilst 'communion' refers to it as a set of personal relationships with the being or beings postulated by the theory – relationships which are entered into by the human partners as ends in themselves.

Despite all the other schemes for the division of religious life into aspects which have been proposed in recent years, I continue to see this division as the most fundamental. In several of the later essays in this volume, indeed, I touch on its usefulness in elucidating some of the salient differences between African and Western religious life, and in helping us to understand modern developments in Western religious life. However, although my overall interpretative framework has continued to stress this two-aspect character of religious life, much of my actual work subsequent to this early paper has stressed the 'explanation/prediction/control' aspect to the relative neglect of the 'communion' aspect. This has been due, not to a change of mind about the importance of the latter, but rather to the fact that, from the point of view of theory development, I have seen my way ahead more clearly with respect to the former. Nonetheless, this neglect has given a certain lopsidedness to my interpretative efforts. To use recent terminology, it has led to an emphasis on the 'cold' side of religion at the expense of the 'hot'.

I shall return to this important topic in the postscript. Meanwhile, the fairly extended treatment of the 'communion' aspect in this early piece provides a reminder that, even in my notoriously Intellectualist interpretative framework, the 'cold' side of religion is not the only one to receive recognition.

Under the next heading, *Mainly Critical*, I have put five papers. As the heading suggests, these are devoted above all to criticism of the more fashionable interpretative frameworks associated in recent times with the study of African religions, and indeed of religions generally. These pieces, I hope, will soften up the reader and prepare him to look favourably on my own framework, which gets its full presentation in the following section.

Here, I single out for treatment two principal frameworks, which I call respectively the 'Symbolist' and the 'Theological'. (In the essays, I refer to adherents of the 'Theological' framework as 'The Devout Opposition'. But I now think it makes for greater clarity to refer to the framework as 'Theological' and to its adherents as 'the Theologians'.)

The Symbolist approach divides human thought and discourse into two great categories: the expressive, which involves the production of symbolic imagery as an end in itself; and the instrumental, which involves the use of literal, discursive thought and language to achieve the ulterior end of practical control of the world. Into the first category fall art, magic and religion; whilst into the second fall common-sense, technological and scientific thinking. Although both expressive and instrumental categories are within the compass of all human minds and are to be found in all human cultures, the expressive is said to predominate over the instrumental in African and other non-Western cultures, and the instrumental to predominate over the expressive in the modern West. In practice, so far as the interpretation of African magical and religious thought is concerned, what this implies is a strategy in which the scholar assimilates magic and religion to art, and in which he tries his best to translate African and/or other religious discourse into terms of Western aesthetic discourse.[6]

Three papers in this section exemplify my critique of the Symbolists. These are: 'Neo-Tylorianism: sound sense or sinister prejudice?', 'Lévy-

Bruhl, Durkheim and the Scientific Revolution', and 'Back to Frazer?'.[7] In all three papers, I point out the basic inadequacy of the Symbolist approach to African magical and religious discourse, and indeed to magical and religious discourse generally.

One major objection to the Symbolist approach arises from its assertion that, when African or other religious thinkers talk about the presence and activity of the gods, they intend their statements, not literally, but rather as figurative representations of purely earthly realities. Like any assertion that things are not what they seem, this Symbolist pronouncement would require strong supporting evidence to carry conviction. Its producers, however, fail dismally to furnish us with any such evidence. In the absence of the latter, we are bound to take African and other religious assertions as literally intended.

A second and related objection is that Symbolists, by insisting that the real, underlying intention in these areas of discourse is the production of symbolic imagery as an end in itself, dismiss both the explanation/prediction/control and the communion aspects of religion as matters of superficial and deceptive appearance. Here, they would seem to be guilty of flouting the evidence on a grand scale.

In these papers, I contend that an interpretative approach so far removed from the realities of magical and religious thought can be understood only in terms of the Western educational and ideological background of the scholars concerned. In this regard, I make two suggestions.

The first suggestion is that the whole approach is conditioned by an unbalanced endowment of Western translational resources: an endowment strongly loaded in favour of aesthetic discourse and weak in respect of both religious and scientific discourse. Those concerned have to make do with the translational resources they have got; and the latter are simply inappropriate to the task on hand.

The second suggestion is that the approach is conditioned by an ideology in which liberal scrupulousness is combined with romanticism. Most Symbolists accept that non-Western world-views, *if* considered as systems for explanation, prediction and control, and *if* measured as such against the yardstick of modern Western science, emerge as markedly inferior to the latter. By denying that explanation, prediction and control are the *real* aims of non-Western religious discourse, Symbolists are able to avoid imputations of inferiority to this discourse, and so to satisfy their liberal scruples. Again, by imputing to such discourse concerns quite other than those of the sciences, they are able to see it as at least a partial fulfilment of the romantic dream of a world from which the heartless concerns of these latter are largely absent.

Let us turn now from the Symbolist to the Theological framework. Here, we have an approach which is not only very different from that of the Symbolists, but is also frankly opposed to it. Thus to the Theologians, the Symbolist assertion that talk about the gods or about God is just figurative talk about earthly things is anathema.

The essence of the Theological approach is two-fold. First, it insists that modern Western religious discourse provides the sole legitimate 'world-language' translation instrument for other systems of religious discourse. In its portrayals of these other systems, it thereby gives universal prominence to the idea of God and to the communion aspect of religious life. Secondly, it insists that the ultimate explanation of all religious thought and action is the self-revelation of a Judaeo-Christian type God to all men at all times and places.

So far as the study of African religions is concerned, the Theological approach represents, in a sense, an alternative orthodoxy to that of the Symbolists. Amongst social anthropologists, it is true, exponents of this approach have tended to be in a minority (though some eminent Africanists such as Evans-Pritchard and Victor Turner have been numbered amongst them). In Departments of Comparative Religion and Religious Studies, however, they have tended to be in a majority. On the African continent, where most studies of African religious life are carried out nowadays by Religious Studies personnel rather than by social anthropologists, sociologists or historians, exponents of the Theological approach have come to enjoy a virtual monopoly of interpretation.[8]

In this section, my critique of the Theological theorists is represented by two essays: 'Professor Winch on safari', in which I discuss a philosopher's intervention that has found favour with some members of this school; and 'Judaeo-Christian spectacles: boon or bane to the study of African religions?', in which I take on the school more directly and as a whole.[9]

In these essays, I make two main critical points.

My first point is that the Theological approach leads to distortion at the level of translational understanding. Thus, by stressing the centrality in all religions of a single creator/sustainer of the universe who is male in sex and wholly good in moral terms, it travesties several at least of the religious systems of Africa and many in the world at large. Again, by stressing the communion aspect of religious life and underplaying the explanation/prediction/control aspect, it travesties virtually every one of the religious systems of Africa and most of those in the world at large.

My second point is that the Theological theorists' ultimate explanation of the flourishing of religious thought and discourse, in terms of the universal self-revelation of a Judaeo-Christian type God, is, when judged in terms of its observational consequences, simply worthless. For what we see in the world's religions is not just a great diversity of ideas about a supreme being, but the absence in many religions of the idea of such a being, and even the absence in some milieux of any idea of spiritual beings of any kind. As far as doing justice to the phenomena goes, then, the Theological theorists' explanation is a non-starter.

As with the Symbolists, so with the Theological theorists I have tried to supply not just a critique but also a diagnosis. Once again, I suggest that the failure of these theorists stems from a combination of inappropriate Western translation resources and obfuscating Western ideology.

With regard to translation resources, the basic trouble with the Theologians seems to be the same as that with the Symbolists. They start with an unbalanced endowment, and then go on to make their desperate best of it. Thus where the Symbolists are strong on aesthetic discourse but weak on religious and scientific discourse, the Theologians are strong on the religious but weak on the scientific and the aesthetic. So instead of pushing the claims of aesthetic discourse and neglecting those of religious and scientific discourse they push the claims of the religious and neglect those of the scientific and the aesthetic.

Unfortunately for the Theologians, modern Western religious discourse is virtually unique in confining itself to the communion aspect of religious life, whilst leaving the explanation/prediction/control aspect to the sciences. Even in the earlier West, religious discourse dealt with both aspects. In virtually all other religious traditions, moreover, such discourse not only always has dealt with both aspects, but continues to do so. It follows that, *used by itself*, modern Western religious discourse is not an adequate instrument for the translation, either of earlier Western religious discourse, or of non-Western religious discourse generally. Rather, in order that justice be done to the explanation/prediction/control aspect dealt with by these other systems, its resources need to be complemented by those of the theoretical discourse of the sciences. Here, I am calling for the re-amalgamation, for the purposes of translation, of areas of discourse which have become separated during the course of Western history. This operation, of course, is going to be an extremely tricky one; and I for one cannot be sure of mastering it. But the Theologians, in so far as they seldom command the resources of scientific discourse, can scarcely even hope to begin.

With regard to ideology, I suggest that the Theologians suffer from a conflict between the liberal, anti-racist egalitarianism which they share with the Symbolists, and the feeling they have as Christians that people who adhere to a religion whose cosmology is remote from that of Christianity are somehow inferior and indeed damned. They try to resolve this conflict by a 'Christianizing' of other religions, hoping thereby to remove the need to pass invidious judgements on their adherents. This ideological stratagem combines with their translational bias to carry them far away from the realities of religious life outside the modern West.

Despite their obvious differences, Symbolist and Theological frameworks nonetheless share some quite important features. Notable among these are: a view of the relation between the religious and the scientific which stresses a radical constrast between the guiding intentions of these two areas of thought and discourse; and an underlying desire to rescue religion, religious people and religious cultures from the disrepute into which they were cast by nineteenth- and early twentieth-century theorists. This is why, in recent lectures on Theories of Religion, I have labelled adherents of both frameworks 'Rehabilitators', and their immediate predecessors 'Denigrators'.

A further feature common to both Symbolists and Theologians is a high degree of complacent self-congratulation over the advances they have allegedly made on the thought of their predecessors. In fact, however, as I argue most explicitly and circumstantially in 'Back to Frazer?', this assumption of theoretical progress is quite unjustified. The sad truth is that, in turning from Denigrators to Rehabilitators, we see no real progress, but only the replacement of one set of errors by another. In the light of what I have said in this section, there is nothing mysterious about this depressing situation. It is simply that during the last hundred or so years, changes of theory in this area have been responses, not primarily to the massive influx of new and richer cross-cultural data which has been one of the most exciting features of the period, but rather to changes in the socio-cultural backgrounds and personal preoccupations of the theorists.

Should we then despair of theory in our field? I think not. First, since theory of one kind or another guides even those of our efforts which appear most purely descriptive and monographic, we can scarcely do without it. Secondly, once we realise that the fashionable scoffing at the ideal of objectivity in our field is little more than an excuse for the continuation of some of the subtler forms of ethnocentric indulgence to which I have been pointing, we shall feel free to try and clarify this vital ideal and make the clarified version into a beacon guiding our work. Thirdly, once we have realised the extent to which the influence of our social settings and personal preoccupations continues to detract from objectivity in this field, we can start to watch out for this influence and fight its effects on our own theoretical work.

It is with these considerations very much in mind that I have struggled to elaborate my own theoretical framework, and have offered it as an improvement on both the Symbolist and the Theological frameworks.

Under the third heading, *Mainly Constructive*, I have put three essays whose principal concern, despite some critical side-swipes at rival frameworks, is to expound my own approach. These essays are: 'African traditional thought and Western science'; 'Paradox and explanation'; and 'Tradition and modernity revisited'.[10]

As I said earlier, I took the West as a contrast case, to sort out what in African thought was shared with other non-African cultures from what was distinctive, and to test hunches about its technological, economic and socio-political context. What emerged in the first instance from the resulting African-Western comparison was a body of ideas about features of cognitive life that were common to both Africa and the West and probably universal. Hence ideas about such common or universal features loom large in these pieces.

One such feature is the existence of two levels of human cognitive interaction with the environment. In the two earlier essays, I characterized the first of these levels by means of such terms and phrases as 'observational', 'commonsense', 'everyday', and 'material-object language', and the second by means of the term 'theoretical'. In the later essay, by contrast, I characterize the first level as 'primary theory' and the second as 'secondary theory'. The change is easily explained. Briefly, it stemmed from my realization that the concepts of 'everyday material-object language' were neither more nor less 'theoretical' than those commonly dignified with this label. Thus, like other theoretical concepts, they were embedded in a usually implicit though intermittently explicit scheme of causal regularities, which in turn was shaped by a particular pattern of human activities and interests. In what follows, therefore, I shall use the later terminology.

Primary theory gives us the world of 'middle-sized dry goods' of which the Oxford philosophers used to be so fond of talking: the world of people, animals, sticks, stones, rocks, rivers, and so on. The entities which it posits are experienced as directly given. It is to be understood in the context of socially-cooperative exploitation of the environment, mediated by language and manual technology. I see it as coeval with Man himself; as the product of the period of accelerated gene-culture coevolution: and as having at least a partially innate basis. More certainly, it develops first in the life-course of every individual.[11]

Secondary theory I see as developing later, both in the history of the species and in the life-course of the individual. It comes in to make up for the cognitive deficiencies of its primary counterpart. Nonetheless, it is built up by an analogical extension of the latter's resources which results in the picture of a 'hidden' world underpinning the 'given' world of everyday. And some at least of its statements have to be given equivalents in primary-theoretical terms in order to make it applicable to the conduct of everyday life.[12]

Secondary-theoretical discourse is characteristically laced with paradox. So too is discourse about the relation between the world as described in secondary-theoretical terms and the world as described in primary-theoretical terms. As I argue most fully in 'Paradox and explanation', paradox in both these contexts arises from the fundamentally ironical character of the secondary-theoretical enterprise. Here, I hark back to the fact that, although the age-old task of secondary theory is that of transcending the cognitive limitations of its primary counterpart, the basic resources with which it has to work are those of primary-theoretical language. The principal implication of this fact is that, wherever secondary theory is deployed, primary-theoretical language is being put to uses for which it was not originally designed. Little wonder that, stretched to such unaccustomed usages, it groans and cracks under the strain.

Whereas there is a remarkable degree of cross-cultural uniformity about the way the world is portrayed by primary theory, there is an equally remarkable degree of cross-cultural variation in the way it is portrayed by secondary theory. Spectacular as it is, however, even this variation can be readily understood in terms of the single basic imaginative-cum-intellectual process whereby secondary theory is built up by the analogical extension of the resources of its primary counterpart. Briefly, since the aim of secondary theory is to display order and regularity underlying the residue of apparent disorder and irregularity left by primary theory, its founding analogies tend to be drawn from those areas of everyday experience maximally associated with order and regularity. Since those areas vary from culture to culture and even from individual to individual, so too do the kinds of analogies drawn and the kinds of theory that result. In both 'African traditional thought and Western science' and 'Tradition and modernity revisited', this thesis forms the basis of a contextual explanation of the fact that, whilst Africa tends toward personal, spiritualistic secondary theory, the West has tended more and more to impersonal, materialistic theory. Here, indeed, we have one promising component of a comprehensive theory of secularization.

So much for features of cognitive life shared by Africa and the West, and probably universal in their distribution. Let us turn now to contrasts. Here, I pursued the implications of the labels 'traditional' and 'modern' – the first commonly applied to African patterns of thought, and the second to modern Western patterns. I found that these labels did point to some quite deep contrasts, not only between African and modern Western thought, but also between earlier and later Western thought. Moreover, where earlier scholars had explored various particular aspects of the traditional, such as secondary elaboration, taboo, denial of the passage of time, and magical thinking,[13] I found that these various and apparently diverse traits were in fact so many manifestations of a more pervasive situation which underpinned them and held them together in a syndrome. I also found that the various traits of the modern were similarly underpinned and held together in a corresponding and strongly contrasted syndrome. In the later parts of 'African traditional thought and Western science' and 'Tradition and modernity revisited', I explore each of these two syndromes, point to the underlying situation of which its various traits are manifestations, and suggest the technological, economic and socio-political factors that sustain this situation.

In comparing these two essays, the reader will note considerable differences between their later parts. Thus in the first, I draw heavily upon Evans-Pritchard and Karl Popper, using a modified version of the latter's distinction between 'closed' and 'open' modes of thought, and making the absence or presence of a vision of alternative secondary-theoretical possibilities crucial to the contrast between the traditional and the modern.[14] In the second essay, for reasons which are fully explained therein, I abandon this formulation. Here, suffice it to say that I came to see the 'closed/open' distinction, on the one hand as conveying too static an image of traditional cognitive life, and on the other as conveying an oversimplified view of its modern counterpart.[15] In its place, I draw two distinctions: the first between a traditionalistic and a progressivistic concept of time; and the second between a consensual and a competitive mode of theorizing. I then point to a traditionalistic time-sense and a consensual mode of theorizing as the underlying features of the traditional; and to a progressivistic time-sense and a competitive mode of theorizing as the underlying features of the modern.

The reader may be interested to note that, implicit in all three essays in this section, there is a distinction between secularization and modernization. In view of a widespread tendency to see the two as aspects of a single process, he may find this unusual. For my part, I see the two processes as both analytically and historically distinct.

III

The perspective that emerges from the essays that make up this book has been described by many as 'Intellectualist'. In so far as I make the linked intentions of explanation, prediction and control central to my interpretative framework, I accept this label. True, given the importance I attach to the quest for practical control of the everyday world, 'intellectualist/ pragmatist' would have been more exact; but the portentous clumsiness of such a label rules it out. So let me stick with 'Intellectualist'.

Having accepted this label, I should nonetheless like to make the point that my approach is as much sociological, or better still contextualist, as it is Intellectualist. I make this point because, through the influence of Evans-Pritchard's writings on theories of religion,[16] there has grown up an association in many scholarly minds between Intellectualism and a non-sociological, non-contextualist approach to the comparative study of religions and world-views. By now, I hope, most readers of this introduction will have realised that, in my case, the association does not hold. For those who have still not got the message, however, let me conclude this exposition with a summary of the linkages I have tried to trace, at every stage of my explorations, between content and mode of thought and technological, economic and socio-political context.

Let me deal first with primary theory. Here, following the lead of the 'Ordinary Language' philosophers, I have treated this whole complex of thought as inextricably bound up with the emergence and persistence of that particular kind of socially-cooperative exploitation of the environment, mediated by language and manual technology, which is the distinguishing mark of the human. In addition, with one eye on the theory of gene-culture coevolution proposed by the sociobiologists, I have suggested that, because of its survival value in the context of this form of life, primary theory may even, through the operation of natural selection, have come to be supported by specific and distinctive cerebral structures. In making this suggestion, of course, I have broadened the relevant context to include, not just the technological, the economic and the socio-political, but also the biological.

In dealing with secondary theory, I portray the broader context as shaping it in three ways: first, through its influence on the type of analogy drawn during the building of theory; second, through the specific explanatory challenges which it poses; and third, through its influence on the mode of interaction (traditionalistic or modernistic) between theory and experience. I treat the first and third channels of influence most explicitly in 'African traditional thought and Western science' and 'Tradition and modernity revisited'. Though I say a bit about the second channel in these essays, I treat the topic more fully in a number of papers not published in this collection.[17]

I should like to emphasize that, in dealing with this whole question of the dependence of content and mode of thought on context, I have consistently followed a policy of even-handedness. That is, I have striven for contextual explanations, not only of those thought products and processes that the modern Westerner considers invalid and lacking in rational foundation, but also of those that he considers valid and rationally founded. In this, I like to think of myself as an early escapee from the hallowed tradition which sees contextual explanation as something appropriate to the irrational rather than the rational, to false beliefs rather than true ones.[18]

IV

Before leaving the reader to get his teeth into the papers themselves, let me explain briefly why I have divided my commentary on them into an introduction and a postscript.

My principal purpose in this introduction has been to say what I had in mind in writing the papers. In it, therefore, I have concentrated on summarizing and clarifying them, and on trying to show how they hang together in a coherent whole. Even where I have alluded to an earlier and a revised version of my thinking on a topic, I have outlined such criticism as the revised version makes of its predecessor, but have not in turn subjected *it* to criticism.

In the postscript, by contrast, I try to take a more distanced and more critical perspective. Thus on the one hand, I try to identify inadequacies and gaps left by my general approach to the field; and on the other, I try to suggest how such deficiencies might be rectified. Both of these exercises, I hope, are useful. For maximum effectiveness, however, I believe they should be kept separate.

Beginnings

1   A definition of religion, and its uses

In recent British anthropology three principal types of working definition
have been used in approaching the comparative study of religion. The first
treats the term 'religion' as lending itself with difficulty to further definition
and as covering an area of human activity which lacks sharply delineated
boundaries; where such a point of view prevails, the reader is simply asked
to accept as 'religious' any phenomena which the author happens to select
for treatment under this heading. The second type treats 'religion' as
referring to a class of metaphorical statements and actions obliquely denot-
ing social relationships and claims to social status. The third type treats the
term as referring to commerce with a specific class of objects, i.e. 'religion is
the belief in spirits' or 'religion is the belief in the supernatural'. As they
stand, I believe all of these approaches are unsatisfactory, and in this paper I
shall follow up their criticism with the proposal of an alternative definition.
Definitions being mere tools towards the discovery of empirical regularities,
I shall of course try to show that the alternative proposed is of value in terms
of the hypotheses and questions it suggests about the determinants of
religious forms.

The approach which would press on with the scope of the term 'religion'
left undefined has had some worthy advocates – among them, Professor
Nadel, author of one of the most comprehensive analyses of an African
religious system produced to date.

According to Nadel:

Whichever way we propose to circumscribe the province of things religious, we are
bound to encounter a border zone which defies precise *a priori* allocation on this or
that side of the boundary. To be sure, this residue of inaccuracy is entailed in the
broad view of religion which we made our starting point. But no other starting point
seems feasible. Bluntly stated, what we set out to do is to describe everything in a
particular culture that has a bearing on religion. And since 'religion' is precisely one
of those words which belong to the more intuitive portions of our vocabulary, and
hence cannot be given a sharp connotation, we have no choice but to feel our way
towards the meaning it should have in given circumstances. We must not risk
omitting anything that might be relevant; the risk we have to take is that of
including, besides 'religion proper', also that 'border' zone composed of mere

superstitions; of science misconstrued or all too crudely attempted; and of science aiming too high or incompletely severed from mystic thought.[1]

Now this is not enough. First of all, I believe that for non-anthropologists at least the term 'religion' has a much clearer connotation than is suggested here. Secondly, to go ahead with the comparative study of religion while leaving the scope of the term undefined is to behave in a self-stultifying way; for until some fairly precise criteria of inclusion of phenomena in the denotation of 'religion' have been given, it is impossible to specify those variables whose behaviour we have to try to explain in our study. Until such criteria have been given, it is also possible to carry on an endless and entirely barren argument about whether a given item of human behaviour is or is not religious.

The second type of approach makes up for the first in positiveness of attack; but, in defining religious activities as an oblique way of referring to relations between men, it grossly distorts fact. The point of view is certainly respectable in sociological studies; introduced by Durkheim[2] and adopted with variations by Radcliffe-Brown, it is maintained in essentials by many contemporary figures. E. R. Leach, one of the most forceful of these, has stated the position as follows:

Actions fall into place on a continuous scale. At one extreme, we have actions which are entirely profane, entirely functional, technique pure and simple; at the other, we have actions which are entirely sacred, strictly aesthetic, technically non-functional ... From this point of view, technique and rituals, profane and sacred, do not denote types of action but aspects of almost any kind of action.[3]

Leach looks upon activities which would commonly be called 'religious' as falling on to the sacred, aesthetic, technically non-functional end of his scale. He says:

It is these aspects which have meaning as symbols of social status and it is these which I describe as ritual whether or not they involve directly any conceptualization of the supernatural or the metaphysical ... In sum, then, my view here is that ritual action and belief are alike to be understood as forms of symbolic statement about the social order.[4]

Finally, Leach broadens the traditional Durkheimian view by admitting the symbolization in myth and ritual of social conflicts as well as social solidarities:

Since any social system, however stable and balanced it may be, contains opposing factions, there are bound to be different myths to validate the particular rights of different groups of people ... Myth and ritual is a language of signs in terms of which claims to rights and status are expressed, but it is a language of argument, not a chorus of harmony.[5]

It will be noticed that in these lines Leach lumps together performances of the sort commonly labelled religious with others generally described as non-religious ceremonials. Here, however, we shall be concerned solely with the applicability of his ideas to religious activity.

Now there is no doubt that in most cultures religious ritual and religious mythology do sometimes get used as symbols of social relationships and social alignments; but as to how far such use is integral or incidental to the nature of religious activity, it may be useful to answer by reference to a West African religious system with which I am familiar – that of the Kalabari of the Niger Delta.

In the Kalabari state, which consists of a congeries of primary segments or 'houses' controlled by chiefs, and a royal segment whose core is the lineage which provides the king, the cult of the chiefly and royal ancestors is one of the principal sanctions of authority at both 'house' and state level. This ancestral cult is particularly rich in activities interpreted by the congregations themselves as symbolic of social and political alignments. Thus, formerly, when a house chief conducted rites in honour of the dead chiefs of his line, the congregation of house members would be supplemented by a number of chiefs of other houses who would present rams for sacrifice to their host's ancestors, even though the latter were in no blood relationship to them. Asked why the house members attended such a rite, Kalabari informants say that it was because they wanted their dead masters to bring them wealth and free them from sickness. On the other hand, the presence of chiefs from other houses who presented rams is explained by saying 'it was a sign that they wished to remain friends of the feast-giving chief'. Again, when a new king succeeded to the headship of the state, he had to make the offering of a series of rams to the spirit of his predecessor. The first of these offerings was of a ram provided by himself: this was followed by the cutting of rams brought to him by each of the chiefs of Kalabari and, finally, by the cutting of rams brought by the heads of the various villages under Kalabari protection. Of this succession of sacrificial presentations, it is said, 'the bringing of a ram for cutting meant that the bringer accepted the new king'.

Here, then, we have examples of the act of sacrifice being used explicitly as a symbol of social alignment in the best Durkheimian manner. But what would Kalabari say about a man who indulged in the actions of ancestor-worship in this purely symbolic, gestural way, yet merely shrugged his shoulders and did nothing when told that his painful illness was due to ancestral anger and could be brought to an end only by sacrifice? Like us, I suspect they would say that the man no longer believed in his ancestors: indeed, I have sometimes heard hints to this effect in the case of educated men returned from abroad to take up a chieftainship, who have conducted ancestral rites for their house members without applying the cult to the vicissitudes of their own life. More common is the opposite situation, which often arises with modern Christian cult-practices in Kalabari. The various forms of Christian cult have become important symbols of high status in the community, probably through the association of Christian ideology with the Western education, which chiefs from an early date, using their riches, gave to their sons. Many chiefs, therefore, make a careful parade of their church adherence, especially on occasions of public Christian ritual. When some crisis of misfortune comes their way, they are apt to go surreptitiously to consult a diviner and, as a result of his advice, to make a sacrifice, either to the dead or to a water-spirit. In such circumstances, Kalabari say as readily as we should that the people concerned are not Christians, do not believe in the Christian God. In other contexts, Christian observances become symbols of factional allegiance; and here again, examples suggest that where they are seen as this and nothing else, the Kalabari reaction is to say that those concerned are not Christians. I am reminded in particular of the case of a Kalabari village whose headman and his descent-group were in chronic opposition to another descent-group which included a prominent water-spirit medium. When the time came round for the latter to give the periodic festival for his spirit, the headman, who had been invited to attend, refused to do so on the ground that, as a Christian, his God would not allow it. Although he was in fact a fairly regular church attender, many of the villagers on both sides of the cleavage interpreted his reply as a sign of his antagonism to the giver of the festival and his group. People felt this interpretation to have been vindicated when two days later his wife who had been ill for some weeks reached a crisis, and he actually came quietly to the medium to consult his spirit about what he should do. They all agreed that he was, in fact, no more a Christian than those who stayed away from church.

Where then a person is seen to be using a prayer, sacrifice, or profession of belief in a god merely to make a statement about social relations or about his own structural alignment, Kalabari say that the one concerned 'does not really believe'. To find out what he really believes, they watch to see which of the gods he goes to for help with the troubles of his life, which of the gods he communes with when he is off parade.

In the Near East and Europe, the history of Judaeo-Christianity is full of similar judgements. Christ himself condemns the Scribes and Pharisees for using religious ritual as a status-symbol and points to their attitude as the essence of irreligion. And Christian pastors up to our own day have con-tinually contrasted the true believer with one who uses the forms of church-going in a Pharisaic way. One might guess that comments from inside any religious congregation the world over would show much the same reaction to the definition of their activities in social-symbolic terms.

Such a reaction, of course, is a flat refutation of Durkheimian ideas. In this theoretical tradition, the statement 'I believe in God' implies 'I subscribe to the system of social-structural symbolism of which this belief-statement is part; and, in uttering this statement, I signify acceptance of certain social relationships and adoption of a certain social alignment'. Hence, a man's religious belief-statements should be verifiable solely by watching to see whether he does, in fact, accept the relationships or take up the alignments allegedly referred to by such statements. The instances we have raised above, drawn from an African culture and from one nearer home, suggest that the very reverse is the case.

All this must sound very trite and obvious to the average non-anthropologist of any culture who, if not religious himself, has been brought up in an environment which included one or two Christians or other cult-practitioners. But for those brought up academically in the Durkheimian tradition and possibly also living in a largely agnostic social environment, it seems that these things can still usefully be said. In effect, defining religion as structural symbolism comes to much the same thing as defining the substance 'linen' in terms of its occasional use as a flag: the symbolic function is as incidental to the nature of the first as it is to that of the second. The truth of the matter, surely, is this. One of the most important preconditions for one thing becoming the symbol of another is the regular association of the two in collective experience. Now, to the extent that certain religious activities and professions have become associated in the collective experience of a given culture with certain status-positions and social groupings, so these things may come to stand as symbolic for such positions and groupings; but this symbolic function is only a by-product of religious activity and is the result of prior structural associations whose formation has nothing to do with symbolism. This, I think, is a most important point: for it was just this co-ordination of gods and their cults with the enduring groups of a society that Durkheim and his successors seem to have felt inexplicable on any basis other than that of the assumption that religion was essentially structural symbolism. As I hope to show further on, however, the impressive systems of god-to-group co-ordination found in so many societies can be just as readily explained on the basis of a definition of religion which conforms perfectly well to more general usage.

Of the three approaches dealt with here, I have left till last the definition of religion as belief in a certain kind of object, whether this be 'spirits' or 'the supernatural'. The definition of religion as 'belief in spirits' has had currency as a working concept somewhere or other in anthropology ever since Tylor,[6] surviving the come-and-go procession of more exotic ideas with its robust closeness to common usage. In fact, the definition I shall put forward is so close to Tylor's that I hesitate to call it in any way new. 'Belief in spirits', however, is just a little too vague for our purposes; and before going any further, we shall do well to weed out the misleading implications of Tylor's formula from those that are of value. One way in which this formula can mislead is by making us think of 'spirits' as the label for a class of objects characterized by a specific mode of existence or in terms of specific conditions of knowledge relevant to the making of true statements about them. One is easily led into this mistake by conventional associations of the word 'spirit' with others such as 'immaterial'.

Now what happens if we follow up this error by trying to define the mode of existence and conditions of knowledge common to all those entities generally termed religious? We find, first of all, that we can point to no single ontological or epistemological category which accommodates all religious entities. Secondly, we find that every major ontological and epistemological category we can devise contains religious as well as secular entities.

Let us take a few illustrative examples from African cultures. First of all, from the Nuer as described by Evans-Pritchard:

Nuer philosophy is ... dominated by the idea of *kwoth*, Spirit. As Spirit cannot be directly experienced by the senses, what we are considering is a conception. *Kwoth* would indeed, be entirely indeterminate and could not be thought of by Nuer at all were it not that it contrasted with the idea of *cak*, creation, in terms of which it can be defined by reference to effects and relations and by the use of symbols and metaphors. But these definitions are only schemata, as Otto puts it, and if we seek for elucidation beyond these terms, a statement of what spirit is thought to be like in itself, we seek of course in vain. Nuer do not claim to know. They say that they are merely *doar*, simple people, and how can simple people know about such matters? What happens in the world is determined by Spirit, and Spirit can be influenced by prayer and sacrifice. This much they know, but no more.[7]

For religious objects of radically different epistemological status, we may turn to the Kalabari of the Niger Delta. In the Kalabari view of the world two main epistemological categories obtain – the first that of bodies, the second that of what we may call 'spirits' for want of a better word. Bodies are thought of by Kalabari in much the same terms as we think of material objects. Spirits are rather different. To the ordinary man, they are known only by their effects: he can neither see them, nor hear them, nor indeed have any direct experience of them. Such experience can be had only by experts who have undergone a series of herbal treatments known as 'clearing the eyes and ears', and can in consequence both see and hear spirits. These objects, nevertheless, are thought of as an order of existence entirely different from bodies. Thus, whereas a Kalabari would be as contemptuous as we should of someone who talked about a table as being in two places at one time, he would not be so of someone who said the same thing of a spirit: for instance, the dead, who are thought to exist 'in spirit' only, can be talked of without any sense of contradiction as both 'in the sky with God' and as 'in the burial ground' where experts may communicate with them. In this respect they, like Nuer Spirit, are compared with the wind: they are anywhere and everywhere at once. In Kalabari culture, however, the realm of practices which the eye of common sense would identify as religious is not directed to a range of objects co-extensive with that covered by the term 'spirits'. Of the three categories of religious objects which we may call Deads, Village Gods, and Water-People, the first two are seen as existing 'in spirit' only, while the last, like human beings, have both bodies and spirits: unlike Deads and Village Gods, they can be seen, heard, touched, and smelt by anyone who happens to cross their path in the rivers. They are not like the wind: they can be talked of as inhabiting definite localities as the Deads and the Village Gods cannot. Many other gods of primitive peoples could be cited as resembling the Kalabari Water-People in their thorough-going materiality.

A definition of the mode of existence and conditions of knowledge of religious objects which at once differentiated them from non-religious objects and included both Nuer Spirit and Kalabari Water-People must necessarily defeat the imagination: for it would have to include contradictory assertions. Further than this, it seems true to say that the epistemological characteristics of any religious object one can think of are shared with some class of non-religious objects. In the case of Kalabari Water-People this seems obvious enough, for existentially they are of the same order as human beings, tables, etc. Nuer Spirit and similar conceptions would seem at first sight to share their mode of existence with no secular objects; but as Gellner[8] has shown, even entities of this type fall into an epistemological category with others which are not religious, e.g. with certain of the theoretical entities of modern science such as atoms, molecules, and alpha particles. These entities are defined as incapable of direct observation, and statements about them can only be said to be verified by the behaviour of certain characteristics of observable phenomena which are assumed to be 'symptoms' of variations in the unobservables.[9] Thus the increasing pressure of a gas which is heated in a vessel of constant volume is indirect confirmation of the theory that molecules increase their velocity with increase in temperature, given the assumption that the observable pressure of a gas on the walls of its enclosure is the symptom of the impacts of countless unobservable molecules on this wall and that the increase in pressure is a symptom of increase in molecular velocity. Here, just as with the Nuer conception of Spirit, the behaviour of observable objects is held relevant to the truth of what is in principle unobservable, but only by virtue of an assumption that variations in the observable are symptoms of certain variations in the unobservable – an assumption which in both cases can have no further justification.

It appears, then, that even in the case of those entities whose mode of existence and conditions of knowledge remove them furthest from the sphere of ordinary, solid material things, we find the religious side by side with the secular.

So much for the misleading implication of Tylor's definition. The more valuable implication is that of analogy between human beings and religious objects generally. Extending this from the context of belief to the context of action, we can say that the value of Tylor's approach is that it leads us to compare interaction with religious objects and interaction with human beings.

This, of course, will encounter very strong objections. It will be said that so many crucial differences divide the two types of interaction as to make any comparison worthless. Anthropologists have long been drawn to regard the sentiments and actions evoked by religious objects as different in kind from those evoked by secular objects: this point of view came to the fore with Marett and received new strength from the work of the theologian Otto.[10] But it seems doubtful if the theory of specifically religious sentiments and modes of action will hold water. Thus, the sentiments of awe and reverence which we tend to regard as very closely associated with religious situations in our own culture are replaced by some very different sentiments in the religions of other parts of the world such as West Africa. A complex of sentiments and emotions common to all religions everywhere is as much of a chimera as an epistemological category which will contain all religious objects. Even within the bounds of the Christian tradition, evidence against the existence of a specifically religious sentiment seems patent in the fact that so many who have claimed close contact with God have not found it necessary to coin any special new terms in describing the feelings and emotions that such contact evoked.

All this was noted a long time ago by William James who, for some curious reason, is commonly misreported by anthropologists as having thought the essence of religion to consist in some peculiar kind of organic thrill. I can hardly do better than quote him:

Consider also the religious sentiment which we see referred to in many books as if it were a single sort of mental entity.... The moment we are willing to treat the term 'religious sentiment' as a collective name for the many sentiments which religious objects may arouse in alternation, we see that it probably contains nothing of a psychologically specific nature.

There is religious fear, religious love, religious joy and so forth. But religious love is only man's natural emotion of love directed to a religious object; religious fear is only the ordinary fear of commerce, so to speak, the common quaking of the human breast in so far as the notion of divine retribution may arouse it; religious awe is the same organic thrill which we feel in a forest at twilight or in a mountain gorge; only this time it comes over us at the thought of our supernatural relations; and similarly of all the various sentiments that may be called into play in the lives of religious persons ...

As there seems to be no one elementary religious emotion, but only a common store house of emotions on which religious objects may draw, so there might conceivably also prove to be no one specific and essential kind of religious object and no one specific and essential kind of religious act.[11]

Though the thinness of the case for a religious sentiment should encourage us to more exploration of the parallels between man-to-man and man-to-god relationships, we must first deal with some apparently widespread contrasts between ordinary human social activity and religious behaviour. Thus, it is undeniable that a great deal of religious behaviour is highly stereotyped, while activity oriented to other human beings contrasts with it in greater flexibility. Again, much religious behaviour is governed by the idea that its objects can be compelled by the actors involved; while behaviour oriented to other human beings usually contrasts with it in a much greater development of the idea that the objects have freedom of choice in their response.

On closer reflection, however, it should be clear that the stereotyping and ideas of compulsive efficacy of human action so markedly developed in very many religious situations are by no means entirely foreign to relations between human beings; nor are the flexibility and ideas of free choice which we tend to associate with inter-human relationships entirely unrepresented in certain religious contexts.

Let us look a little more carefully at the contrast between secular flexibility and religious stereotyping. In an interaction sequence involving two human beings taking up familiar roles in which they are co-operating towards definite ends, experience will have taught each participant the limited predictability of his partner's reactions to his own moves. Alter's reaction to ego on successive occasions will show a wide variation in response to a given move; and if ego is to achieve the ends he hopes to fulfil through the interaction with any degree of regularity, it is clear that he must be capable of a flexibility of action sufficient to compensate for the effects of alter's response variability and to secure consistent results despite it. This flexibility must be manifested as a capacity for moment-to-moment modification of action in the light of alter's observed reactions. To drive home the force of this, I suggest the example of a mother and her child. On each new day, the mother's response to a given move by the child is likely to vary as a function of such things as rows with her husband and late nights out; and if the child is consistently to secure various favours from its mother, it must be capable of modifying its own behaviour to compensate for her variability.

If now we substitute for the human alter a god, conditions for fulfilment of ego's aims become rather different. First of all, in the majority of contexts of religious behaviour there can be no question of modification of ego's action in the light of the god's reactions, since these are inaccessible to observation. In most cases, what happens is that the reaction is made known to ego by a sign after his part in the interaction is over: in the case of a curative ritual, the patient either gets better or he does not; in the case of a rain ritual, either it pours or it does not. Anyway, ego may get no 'feedback' as to the god's reactions to his behaviour until days, weeks, or months after he has completed it. Then, if the sign is negative, he may initiate another sequence of ritual actions and again wait for the results; and so on. In all this there is no equivalent to the need for moment-to-moment modification of ego's action in the light of alter's reaction; and in the absence of such pressures towards flexibility, stereotyping of action would seem inevitable. The resulting pattern contrasts strongly with most behaviour directed towards human partners; but is not entirely without parallel in this sphere. In quite a few contexts of man-to-man behaviour, for example, the uncertainties arising through the limited predictability of human partners are recognized as threatening to the business on hand; and steps are taken to obviate the danger by explicit definition of a limited number of permissible responses for any stage in the interaction. The result is the stereotyping so characteristic of 'official' correspondence and communication in our culture – a stereotyping whose resemblance to that of religious behaviour has given rise to much of the fun poked at civil servants. A contributory cause of this parallel may be the general tendency for large status differences between actors to be accompanied by stereotyping of their interactions. Since the gods are by definition the status superiors of men, we should expect action directed toward them to resemble in this respect action directed toward beings of markedly higher status than ego. By corollary, the flexibility associated with the majority of relationships between human beings does come to the fore in certain religious contexts – notably, as we should expect, in those where events which pass for moment-to-moment reaction by the gods replace the more usual situation where such 'feedback' is lacking. A typical case is where one or more human beings interact with a god who is 'possessing' a medium. Amongst the Kalabari of the Niger Delta, for example, a great deal of religious activity takes the form of highly stereotyped prayer and offering to the gods; and in these stereotyped situations there is no manifestation of the gods in moment-to-moment reaction to what the human congregation is doing: 'the gods are there but we do not see them.' On other occasions, however, one of the gods will be called by a human congregation to come to the community and possess a medium. What follows is sometimes a spectacular sequence of actions summing up the character of the god, sometimes a conversation between the god and men; but in both these conditions every action of the human congregation secures an observable reaction from the god, and in so far as such reactions have only limited predictability, we find just the same moment-to-moment modification of the congregation's behaviour in the light of the god's response as we should expect to see were the god replaced by a man. The other type of situation where the same thing should apply is where the man is confronted with his god in visual, auditory, or other types of hallucination. Here again, his every action has the same moment-to-moment reaction from the god as when the latter is possessing a medium; and once more the facts indicate a change from stereotyping to flexibility. Kalabari doctor-clairvoyants conversing with the dead in cemeteries behave little differently from Kalabari laymen passing the time of day with their fellow men in market places; and Christian mystics who have described their confrontations with God stress the conversational give-and-take of such experiences.

Stereotyping and flexibility, then, are opposite poles of behaviour dominant in religious and non-religious contexts respectively. But this contrast between the two contexts can now be seen as very far from absolute; and it is therefore of no use as a criterion for differentiating the religious from the non-religious.

Much the same conclusions present themselves when we investigate those ideas of compulsion of the object which seem to be much more strongly developed in the context of man's interaction with his gods than in that of his interaction with fellow men. In no culture is it thought very odd or unusual for one man to refuse another's request through sheer 'bloody-mindedness'; but there are relatively few cultures whose religious worldview admits of the possibility that a god may refuse human requests just because he chooses to. Nevertheless, ideas of compelling one's fellow-men do direct a good deal of secular action, and there are religious contexts in which the wide range of choice open to the gods when addressed by man is a prominent feature of doctrine.

All men, everywhere, are in some degree irked by the freedom of choice enjoyed by those with whom they pass the greater part of their lives; to have the ends that one hopes to see fulfilled with the help of other men constantly menaced by the latter's freedom is a source of anxiety the world over. The most obvious responses to this form of frustration, by statesmen who mobilize armies to batter neighbours who will not be reasonable, and police to truncheon recalcitrant subjects, have long been the sport of historians. But it is only more recently that students of human relations have drawn attention to the dreams and realities of more subtle methods of compulsion, which probably have as long a history as that of physical violence itself. And here again, the emphasis has been on rulers of men as the principal exponents of such methods – whereas, in truth, the ordinary man of no influence has, through the ages, been as deeply involved as his master in the attempt to compel and curtail the will of those around him.

Even in so-called 'primitive' societies, there exists a wealth of subtle techniques intended to 'change men's minds' – love magic designed to secure inevitable hopeless infatuation in place of the uncertainties of seduction; potions to compel approbation and spare the social climber from the exertions and hazards of having to win it. In modern Western culture, brain-washing and subliminal advertising are seized upon by power hounds as long-sought means of controlling human behaviour without risking the mediation of the victims' faculty of deliberate choice, means of sneaking round the backs of their rational, conscious minds to slug them mentally from behind;[12] while for the Little Man of no position there are the Occult Bookshops with their torrent of popular 'psychological' literature which offers him techniques of gaining control in a less ambitious way over the reactions of his acquaintances and employers. Some of the literature of the 'How to Make Friends and Influence People' genre looks, indeed, as if it might go a long way towards reinstilling a popular belief in the compulsive power of the spoken word.

The idea that a man can develop wide powers for restricting his fellow men's freedom of choice is thus a very live one in all societies we know. Nevertheless, in the context of social relationships among human beings, the obvious recalcitrance of one's fellows provides continuous empirical demonstration of the limits beyond which they cannot be compelled. On the other hand, the frequent unavailability of gods to continuous observation, which we found to be an important correlate of action stereotyping, also implies a lack of direct evidence of their uncoercibility. True, the benefit that fails to materialize when a god has been invoked to provide it might throw doubt on the compulsive efficacy of human actions in this sphere: but in a polytheistic world-view such doubt can be allayed by postulating interference from another god who, in his turn, is nonetheless susceptible to compulsion through prayer; and so on. Given that in many cases there is no further evidence which would differentiate between the two alternative explanations of failure, and given the anxiety-reducing value of beliefs which imply the elimination of free choice, it is likely that in such contexts explanations stressing interference by other gods and retaining ideas of the coercibility of gods in general will prevail over explanations which accept the failure as evidence that 'Man proposes, God disposes'. Out of this grows the common paradox of the god who greatly exceeds his worshippers in power, yet is under their close control.

Where there is monotheism, of course, such developments would seem to be ruled out by the absence of alternative agents to save the idea of compulsion in cases of prayer failure. From this assumption arises the hypothesis, which merits testing, that in a sample of world religions monotheism will be found highly correlated with the attribution of wide freedom of choice to the religious object, while polytheism will be associated with ideas of wide or total coercibility of the gods.

As we found with stereotyping of religious action, in the less common situation where the reactions of the gods to human beings are directly observed rather than merely inferred from eventual results, even polytheistic religions are forced to incorporate the possibility that the gods may not choose to accede to human requests. Thus, in Kalabari religion, one prays and makes offerings to a god in order to obtain a certain result. In most contexts, the god himself is not observably present; and the success of one's actions often becomes apparent only later when the result prayed for either materializes or does not. Normally, too, prayer in the correct terms and offering on the correct scale are thought of as sufficient conditions of success. If there is failure despite correct approach, this is not simply interpreted as due to the god's inscrutable freedom of choice: it is due either to interference by another god, or to a mistake on the part of the diviner who advised as to which of the gods was concerned in the situation. Sometimes, however, the god is visibly and audibly present when requests are made to him. This happens when he is addressed by human beings while possessing a medium; and, under these conditions, one quite frequently encounters a point-blank inscrutable refusal to accede to the request of a petitioner, which contrasts sharply with the prevailing view stressing the coercive power of human address to the gods.

Here again, we see that another common point of contrast between the religious and the non-religious is by no means absolute; hence it is no more useful as a differentiating criterion than stereotyping versus flexibility.

These findings justify us in making more explicit use of the implication of analogy between human beings and religious objects, which we pointed out earlier as the valuable aspect of Tylor's definition. For purposes of the definition put forward here, it will be assumed that in every situation commonly labelled religious we are dealing with action directed towards objects which are believed to respond in terms of certain categories – in our own culture those of purpose, intelligence and emotion – which are also the distinctive categories for the description of human action. The application of these categories leads us to say that such objects are 'personified'. The relationships between human beings and religious objects can be further defined as governed by certain ideas of patterning and obligation such as characterize relationships among human beings. In short, religion can be looked upon as an extension of the field of people's social relationships beyond the confines of purely human society. And for completeness' sake, we should perhaps add the rider that this extension must be one in which the human beings involved see themselves in a dependent position *vis-à-vis* their non-human alters – a qualification necessary to exclude pets from the pantheon of gods.

What are the criteria of a good definition in this sphere and how far does the approach outlined above measure up to them? First of all, we are concerned with a term which has a clear common usage in our own culture. To avoid confusion, therefore, any definition which we put forward as the basis of its use in anthropology should conform as closely as possible to the usage of common sense. At the same time, we must look for the universal aspect of the phenomena commonly denoted by the term: for a culture-bound label is of no use in cross-cultural comparisons. This universal aspect, fortunately, is not hard to discover; for laymen have freely used the word 'religion' to refer to happenings observed in a wide variety of cultures other than our own. Secondly, we should bear in mind that members of several other academic disciplines – notably Psychology and History – are also bent on the study of 'comparative religion'; and our definition should be sufficiently congruent with their assumptions for the results they achieve to be compared with our own findings.

Our approach seems to measure up fairly well to these requirements. It sticks close to common sense in preserving the connexion between 'religion' and other terms such as 'god' and 'spirit'; and it tallies closely with the assumptions of psycho-analysts and historians. Many anthropologists, of course, may continue to object that by laying all emphasis on the similarities between man-to-god and man-to-man relationships, we have missed the crucial 'something extra' which gives the real essence of religion. I have gone to considerable pains to show that in fact there is no 'something extra' which distinguishes all religious relationships from all secular relationships. In so far as the feeling of dissatisfaction persists despite such a demon-stration, I suggest that the mode of difference varies from society to society and has no universal features whatsoever. As far as I can see, the way in which religious relationships are seen to differ from secular relationships in any given society is much the same as the way in which any one category of secular relationships is seen to differ from all other categories of such relationships. If this is true, then to go on asking for the 'something extra' is to cry for the moon.

There still remains one very large question to be asked about our defi-nition. That is, is it scientifically useful? Does it point to a number of possible dimensions along which religious phenomena can be seen to vary? Does it suggest testable hypotheses about the way in which variation along these dimensions is connected with other social facts? As I said before, definitions are mere tools, standing or falling by their usefulness; so the last section of this paper will be taken up with a fairly lengthy discussion of some of the hypotheses which our approach suggests.

An obvious consequence of defining religion as an extension of social relationships beyond the confines of purely human society is the assumption that variables found useful in the analysis of man-to-man relationships will also be found useful in the analysis of man-to-god relationships; and in what follows, we shall select one of the most important of such variables to see how far it helps us in handling religious phenomena.

Two poles of relationship can be distinguished in the sphere of interpersonal behaviour among human beings. At the one pole, we have a situation well illustrated by the relationship between two unmarried lovers of equal financial and social standing in modern Western society. In such a relationship, ego's action is directed entirely towards obtaining certain responses from alter which he values intrinsically and towards giving certain responses to alter whose discharge is of similar intrinsic value to him. We may call this a pure communion relationship. At the other pole, let us take the example of a 'business' relationship between two unscrupulous financiers. Here, ego values intrinsically neither his own nor alter's responses, alter being treated as a mere means of arriving at a goal which can be defined without reference to the behaviour included in the relationship. We may call this a pure manipulation relationship. In between these two poles, of course, there is a continuum of relative importance of communion and manipulation aspects, on which every human relationship falls somewhere or other.[13]

As might be expected, granting the validity of our definition of religion, the same dimension of variability is important in the relationships of man with his gods. Its significance is brought out in Nadel's pioneering work on Nupe religion, in which he uses the sort of religious experiences and activities described by William James as comparisons for the African material.[14] The widespread differences both in content and in ends subserved by religious behaviour in the two cultures seem to have surprised him; but he is too good an ethnographer to have squeezed Nupe religion into a Jamesian mould and has left us instead with some stimulating, if unsystematic, comparisons. The point that emerges clearly is that James's American and European case material is mainly drawn from religious relationships of an extreme character in which sheer communion with God is stressed to the virtual exclusion of benefits accruing either in life or after death; while Nupe religion by contrast lays emphasis almost exclusively on the manipulation of God for this – worldly benefits of health, wealth, and increase. If, as I have a hunch, the communion aspect of religious relationships in all Christian denominations in our culture is becoming more and more important than manipulation, we need to remind ourselves very forcibly of the existence of the latter dimension of variation when we are observing alien religious systems where the position may be reversed. The sort of conditions that precipitate conversion, for instance, will be quite different in the case of a primarily communion relationship and in that of a primarily manipulative one concerned with various benefits of a material kind; and a member of the Church of England is unlikely to find insights derived from his own conversion experiences very helpful in a study of, say, the spread of fertility cults or even of Christianity in West Africa. (Although membership of a religious denomination may be valuable to the anthropological student of alien religions in so far as it gives him some modicum of sympathy with the psychological reality of religious relationships, it can clearly also be a drawback in so far as it may obscure insight into the sustaining conditions of such relationships, at least where these differ widely in character from those of the observer.)

So much for awareness of this dimension as a safeguard against the anthropologist's ethnocentricity in religious matters. In fact, the majority of religious relationships likely to be studied will have both communion and manipulation aspects and any comprehensive analysis and interpretation must reckon with both.

Several British anthropologists, prominent among them Forde and Worsley, have recently analysed systems of religious relationships in their manipulative aspect, i.e., as instrumental to the fulfilment of the various external goals pursued by the congregation members.[15] Pushed to its logical conclusion, such analysis may prove to have great explanatory value in such matters as the co-ordination of cult structure to social structure and the extinction and proliferation of religious relationships generally. A theory of god-to-group co-ordination capable of replacing those derived from Durkheim can perhaps be elaborated from it as follows:

Assumption I: The individual member of any society pursues a given goal with several different levels of social-structural reference. Such a goal will generally be pursued with different references on different occasions. To take an example, a member of a given social category in an African village community may actively pursue the goals of health, wealth, and increase for the village as a whole, for the descent group of which he is a member and for himself as an individual. Generally, his concern with one of these structural levels on a given occasion excludes for the moment his concern with the others.

Assumption II: The religious relationships in which the members of a society are involved function as instruments to the achievement of their various goals. Where there is any change in the structure of such goals, the religious relationships will always change and develop towards the point at which they can be seen by those involved as severally making a contribution to all of their goals at all of the latters' various levels of reference. Where the structure of goals becomes stabilized, this point is one at which the system of religious relationships also becomes stabilized.

Assumption III: In a society where the relations between segments of the total group are markedly competitive, the fact that a god and its cult are seen as contributing to the members' goals at the total group level of reference *ipso facto* implies that they cannot be seen as contributing to the same goals at the next lower level of reference, i.e. that of the segments. Thus, a cult which is defined as contributing to collective welfare of a group clearly cannot be seen as contributing to the welfare of any one of its segments in contexts where such welfare is defined as achieving benefits at the expense of the other segments. By converse, where relations between segments of a group are not markedly competitive, relevance of a god to members' goals at their total group level of reference does not debar it from relevance to the same goals at the segment level of reference.

From these assumptions there follow generalizations about the sort of cult structure which is likely to arise in connexion with a given social system. First of all, in the case of a system in which relations between the segments of a group at any level in the whole are markedly competitive, every level will have its own set of cults distinct from those of all other levels in the system. At each level, furthermore, there will be at least as many distinct, though mutually equivalent, cults as there are competing segments in it. At the lowest level – that of the individual – an alternative to the last condition may be the soliciting by many individuals of a single god whose culturally defined lack of concern with the welfare of any particular social group makes him a suitable instrument of individualistic aspirations through an implication of his readiness to sell to the highest bidder irrespective of provenance.

In a system where relations between segments at any level are predominantly non-competitive and harmonious, there may be one or more cults co-ordinated to the group at the top level and no additional cults co-ordinated to its segments or to the segments of the latter. The minimal intensity of competition which would give rise to this type of situation is, however, probably fairly rare.

To take a concrete illustration of the first type of system, let us consider a Kalabari village community. This consists of a congeries of apically unrelated descent-groups whose interrelations are normally characterized by strong competition. The component individuals of each such descent-group are also prone to compete vigorously among each other for headship and other positions of influence within the group. As we should predict on the basis of our assumptions, each of the three levels, village, descent-group and individual, has its distinctive set of cults: thus at village level, we find the cult of the Founding Heroes who are considered as instruments of collective village welfare, while at descent-group level we find the apical ancestors considered as instruments of collective descent-group welfare, each descent-group having its own one or more ancestors. At the level of the individual, though there is no co-ordination of a distinct god and its cult to each man, we find individualistic competitive aspirations catered for by the cults of the Water-People, who are defined as associated with none of the enduring social groups of the community and as conferring their benefits on all comers on a scale proportional to offerings made. The life of these various cults is maintained to an important extent by the decisions of individuals as to which they will make use of to meet a given contingency; and many Kalabari explain their choice in terms very similar to those of our assumptions. Thus, it is commonly believed that only the Water-People are capable of conferring on an individual a degree of wealth that is excessive in relation to that of fellow members of his community and descent-group. For such wealth, it is said, one would not go to the Founding Heroes of the village, or to the descent-group ancestors; for both of these are concerned alike with the welfare of all those under their surveillance and would hardly benefit one of their charges above the others. The Water-People, on the other hand, 'choose no one'. They 'look to see what one carries in one's palm for them' and give accordingly.

As I have said above, systems in which competition between segments at any level of grouping is virtually absent are probably rare; so I find it hard to provide examples. However, if Benedict was in any way correct in her analysis of Zuni culture and her thesis of Zuni non-competitiveness, this people provides the sort of contrast to Kalabari which our generalizations would lead us to predict.[16] Thus, descriptions of Zuni religious organization place very strong emphasis on cults whose effective congregation is the community as a whole and stress the lack of cults which could be seen as catering mainly for competitive aspirations at sectional or individual levels. Although many priestly offices and religious duties are vested in particular clan sections of the community, those concerned do what they have to do on behalf of Zuni as a whole and not on behalf of their own clans. Again, as Benedict points out, the Guardian Spirit cult which is so vital an instrument of individualistic aspirations over much of North America finds no equivalent in Zuni.

This attempt at explanation of the relations between cult-structure and social structure on non-Durkheimian lines also provides us with a broad answer to the general question, still sometimes asked, as to what is the social structural significance of religious activity. Given the assumption that religious systems tend to take such forms as are seen to make a contribution to all the goals of a society's members at all their levels of structural reference, it follows that where the constituent units of a wider group are in competition, cults will tend to be adopted by these units which contribute to achievement of the goals involved in this competition; and to the extent that the competition involves mutual hostility of the units involved, these cults can be seen as agents of disintegration acting in opposition to the cult concerned with the collective welfare of the inclusive group. Where, on the other hand, the constituent units are not markedly in competition, the god concerned with the welfare of the inclusive group will be adequate to their needs, and cults co-ordinated to these units and contributing to factional hostilities and disintegration are unlikely to appear. In other words, our approach leads us to look at religious relationships in their manipulative aspects as means toward accomplishing what those participating in them want to do: if what the participants want to do involves disintegrative competition, then the world of their gods is likely to include some who are defined as helping their human partners in such competition; or if what they want to do involves little competition, their world of gods is likely to be more concerned with the collective welfare and harmony of all. In a sense, then, religious activity tends to be as integrative or as disintegrative as the particular congregation or individual wants it to be.

An explanation of the co-ordination of religious system to social structure based on treatment of the gods as a set of instruments meeting human wants does of course imply a process occurring over time whereby the existing structure of wants acts to develop in cult certain religious ideas selected from a pool available to the society. The processes whereby this pool is kept filled have no necessary connection with the processes of selection; indeed, in many cases they may be quite random relative to these latter, as when trading contacts with neighbouring and alien cultures keep the members of a community acquainted with outline features of a number of cults which until the appropriate 'want situation' arises will not be utilized. The most illuminating analogy here appears to be that of Natural Selection operating on an animal population which has a certain fairly constant rate of spontaneous random mutation.

Given this assumption, the religious-social structural co-ordinations found in societies which are more or less static when observed by the anthropologist must be regarded as the outcome of a selection process which took place in an unobservable and often unrecorded past; and our theory will accordingly be strengthened by studies of ongoing religious change which demonstrate the universal operation of the selection of religious concepts in the light of wants and desires standard to the social group involved in the change. This sort of analysis of religious change has been commonly enough practised among historians such as Tawney and Weber;[17] but it is only recently that anthropologists in England have taken up the tune. One of the first to do so was Worsley, who recently made a vivid analysis of Melanesian Cargo Cults,[18] treating them as responses to new structural developments and hence to new (super-tribal) levels of structural reference for existing goals of action. Worsley shows that the pre-Cargo cult religious system of the peoples he deals with contained nothing which could be seen as contributing to their goals of action at the new level of reference and interprets the Cargo cults as being developed as fillers of this gap.

In my own fieldwork amongst the Kalabari of the Niger Delta, treatment of the traditional system of gods as a system of instruments, seen as contributing to the fulfilment of the standard action goals at their various levels of reference, has made the curiously selective effect of incoming Christian ideas readily understandable as the outcome of recent changes in village social structure. In Kalabari communities generally, there is a great emphasis on the incompatibility of the cults of the Village Founding Heroes with the new religious ideology; while at the same time there exists an elaborate series of rationalizations justifying continuing attention to descent-group ancestors and to the Water-People. The selectivity is all the more striking for the fact that these latter rationalizations are, from a logical point of view, no more and no less valid as justification for continuing the cult of the Village Heroes than as justification for continuing that of the ancestors and Water-People. All becomes clear, however, when we remember that the Village Heroes have special relevance to the collective welfare of the community as a whole, the ancestors special relevance to collective descent-group welfare, and the Water-People special relevance to individual aspirations. The last fifty years have seen the gradual withering away of solidarity at village level, the advent of the Pax Britannica having made otiose the crucial defensive functions of this level of organization. On the other hand, the descent-groups have lost no whit of their former importance, and individualistic status strivings remain as characteristic of the culture as ever. Given these structural changes and the respective instrumental relevances of the three categories of god, the selective elimination of the cult of the Village Heroes could readily have been predicted. In the Melanesian situation, the addition of another level of structural reference to the standard action goals of the population was followed by the adoption of a further series of cults. Here, we have a reversed situation, where dropping out of the top level of structural reference is being followed by dropping out of the corresponding series of cults.

A significant though more or less incidental contribution to the analysis of religious change was made by Nadel in his Nupe work, in which he mentions the current system of goals pursued by members of a society as an important determinant of cult importations. His particular contribution was to point out that recent importations into the Nupe cult system form only a limited selection from among the wide variety of models available to the population, who are acquainted with them through their contact with representatives of alien cultures but utilize only such as are seen to have relevance to current requirements. One hopes that future studies of religious change, by drawing attention to the unutilized as well as the utilized components of the pool of religious ideas available to a given population, will have similar relevance to testing the applicability of the Mutation-Selection model to this sphere.

If we assume that the gods of any population have become co-ordinated to individuals and the various levels of grouping that include them as a result of a process of selection based on perceived relevance to particular goals at particular levels of structural reference, we can expect to find 'written in' to the character of any god some implication of relevance in the particular social context where it has become fixed. In fact, so far as correlations between character and structural position are discoverable, it would seem that character may be either the independent or the dependent of the two variables. In the situation where it is the independent variable, the character of a god which forms part of the pool of unutilized models will determine its structural fate when changing conditions give it new relevance to human needs. Thus, in the West African coastal belt, extensive trade linkages give any community a large pool of unutilized religious models in the shape of the gods of its culturally alien neighbours; but whether or not the cult of a god spreads beyond the group with whom it originated depends partly, at least, on whether or not there is written in to the god's character an implication of exclusive relevance to the needs of that group. Contrast, for example, the fixed, static social co-ordinations of the Dahomean Clan-Founding Heroes (defined as exclusively concerned with the interests of their own descendants), with the continuous spread and congregational expansion of the cults of the *vodun*, the great gods in charge of the various natural elements who have no implication of restricted social relevance built in to their character. One might indeed say that the peculiar congregational structure of Dahomean religion, so much of it marked by recruitment virtually unconnected with social provenance and resulting in ritual groupings coincident with none of the enduring structural units of the kingdom, is a function of the character peculiarities of the *vodun*.[19]

Another context where character probably determines the type of social co-ordination reached is that of the Dead conceived as surviving in personal form. Whether a given population has or has not a developed cult of the Dead, in so far as the latter are seen as surviving on the other side of the grave, they are very generally considered to have passed over with the same values as they held during life. Where their cult is developed, this definition of their character implies a relevance restricted to the social context within which their various obligations lay during life. Thus, when the head of a Yoruba or Ibo patrilineage dies, his ghost will be seen as relevant to the needs of his descent-group more or less exclusively. Hence the cult of a given Dead tends to become co-ordinated to the group within which his principal obligation lay during life and is highly unlikely to be adopted by individuals and groups outside this social context. In so far as this inflexibility of co-ordination appears not to hold, the exceptions are likely to be the 'bad Dead', the ghosts of those who, during life, conducted themselves with ruthless disregard of the social obligations laid down for them by society. Among the Kalabari of the Niger Delta, for example, these, in so far as they carry over their amorality with them, can often be utilized for the purposes of anybody who approaches them with sufficient inducement, be his ends good or evil. Here again characterological definition would seem to determine the pattern of social co-ordination.

By contrast, character may be the dependent variable; as where implications of relevance to the particular interests of the worshipping group are the outcome of a steady process of moulding by members of this group, a process of wishful reinterpretation of the body of existing doctrine. An example of this moulding process is provided by Tawney's study of the modification of Christian doctrine under the pressure of a growing tendency for the individualistic pursuit of material wealth in sixteenth-century Europe[20]: such a pursuit of wealth was in fact a condition of damnation in earlier Christian doctrine; but with Christianity continuing as the religion of a class of people for whom this became irresistibly the primary value in life, it suffered gradual reinterpretation at their hands until financial individualism of a most ruthless sort became not a condition of damnation but, if successful, a sign of election for the enjoyment of bliss in the world hereafter.

The structure of the Bible, indeed, seems particularly fitted to make the character of the Judaeo-Christian god function as a dependent variable in relation to its social context: for different parts of the book provide widely differing models, and it is possible to select from amongst them a god congruent with almost any social setting. Thus where there is a readiness to identify with the Chosen People of the Old Testament, the latter's models can be easily utilized to cater for the aspirations of a group in conflict with others. New Testament models, on the other hand, are more easily connected with universalistic aspirations.

Our treatment of a human population's relationships with its gods as a system of social relationships viewed in its manipulative aspect does, I think it will be conceded, suggest a wide variety of hypotheses about the relations between religious forms and other socio-cultural variables. These hypotheses cover questions both of god-to-group co-ordination and of the character of the gods themselves. Equally, however, this type of treatment suggests very forcibly the limitations on our attempts to predict the type of religious organizations which will supervene in a given socio-cultural situation. In general, the gods as instruments are invited to intervene in human affairs in those situations where the apparatus of empirically-tried techniques currently available leaves a rather wide margin of uncertainty as to the accomplishment of a desired end. But in this position, the gods are functionally equivalent to a multitude of other non-empirical instruments which are of a secular nature, e.g. charms, medicines, and the host of techniques which utilize the principle that the symbolization of a desired end brings about its fulfilment. Thus, from the point of view of an instrumental analysis, whether a fighter pilot setting out on a hazardous mission prays to a god or packs a luck charm is a matter of chance.

This conclusion gives the lie to one of the strongest of anthropology's Durkheimian prejudices about religion; for, in asserting that either religious or secular means may be invoked to attain any end in any social context, it rejects the traditional association of religion with collective action and the attainment of socially approved goals, and of secular non-empirical techniques with individualistic action and anti-social goals. Such an association is generally supported by citing a selection of societies in which secular techniques satisfy individualistic aspirations and religious relationships the collective aspirations of wider social groupings. But the selection is a biassed one and can be countered without difficulty by citing a large number of societies (e.g. many in the West African and North American culture areas) in which religious relationships between a god and an individual are considered essential instruments of the latter's competitive and even anti-social aspirations.

In fact, whether any new situation demanding supplementation of empirical by non-empirical instruments is met by religious or secular means depends on which are more prominent in the stock of unutilized models available to the individual or group concerned at the time. And this is a question which will depend on such incidental factors as the cultural make-up of neighbouring communities and the particular idiom used by individual innovators.

As we pointed out earlier, every man-to-god relationship can be assigned a place on the communion/manipulation dimension of variability; and to the extent that the communion aspect is important in a given case, by so much interpretations based on the manipulative aspect are inadequate. This, of course, is true in man-to-man relations. To the extent that a relationship is purely 'business', so far is it capable of explanation in terms of the ends it is set up to serve; but as more and more of a 'personal' element enters in, so this sort of explanation becomes less and less applicable. It is fine for the choice of a partner in a marketing enterprise, disillusioningly applicable to the choice of a marriage partner, and quite inapplicable to the choice of a lover; and in so far as many religious relationships are as near the latter extreme as they are the former, the need for a complementary approach is acute.

Two types of question suggest themselves here. The first is, why do some societies like the Nupe have religious systems characterized by an extreme emphasis on manipulating the gods as tools for the achievement of health, wealth and issue, while other societies such as our own show a very high loading of emphasis on sheer communion divorced from the seeking of other benefits? The second is, how far can the particular characteristics of a society's various gods be explained in terms of the goals involved in the communion aspect of social relations?

We are hampered in answering these two questions by the rudimentary state of theorizing about the communion aspect. Some anthropologists still see social systems as made up of a myriad parts all grinding away madly to produce maximum cohesion, neglecting the goals and values actuating their members. Others cock a snook at cohesion and look at a system of social relationships as a set of tools serving the participants' material consumption goals. Few have acted upon the truism stressed by Linton that social relations are what they are partly because of the participants' continued seeking after a certain give and take of love, hate, approbation, contempt, dominance, submission and other kinds of action and reaction seen, not as instruments, but as valuable in themselves.[21] It is true that some workers have looked in this direction; but, in general, they have concentrated exclusively on the pursuit of approbation and dominance – a rather narrow part of the total range of these communion strivings.

In search of people who have been sensitive to the complexity of the communion aspect of social relationships, one turns naturally to the psycho-analysts. Unfortunately their theories on this subject multiply like rabbits; and their concern with problems of definition and empirical testing has lagged sadly behind their speculations. Nevertheless, they are the only people who have anything to say in this sphere; and certain persistent themes do emerge through the riot of their often conflicting ideas. One such is the tenet that the extent to which any particular type of give-and-take of response is fostered in one of a person's roles will affect the extent to which he actively seeks the same give-and-take of response in his other roles. Thus, the degree to which, say, discharge of anger is developed in one role will affect and be affected by the degree to which aggression is cultivated in other roles played by the same person. Such an interdependence will involve both roles taken at different periods of the person's life-history, and also roles taken up in different social contexts during a given phase of the life-history. In so far as one can summarize the general view, it seems to be that roles succeeding one another along the time dimension will tend each to reflect the various types of communion-striving – for love, hate, approbation, etc. – that have been fostered in earlier contexts. On the other hand, the several roles held by a person at a given phase of his life-history will tend to strike a balance in this respect: thus Parsons and Homans have both suggested that in any social system the field of impersonal relationships will always tend to be balanced somewhere else in the system by relationships that place heavy stress on personal affection, and that the more the field of impersonal relationships expands, the more the remaining relationships will stress such affection.[22] Homans treats the contrasting relationships with father and mother's brother in unilineal descent systems along these lines. Parsons gives a similar analysis of changes in marital relationships in the United States, treating what he regards as the greater and greater emotional loading of the attitude toward one's spouse as a counter-weight to the increasing depersonalization of 'business' relations.

At the present stage of anthropological theorizing, it is not at all easy to see how these concepts fit into the mainstream; but they do seem to provide some of the only clues available as to how we might set about studying those variables of religious relationships not covered by an analysis of their manipulative aspects. Given that we treat roles played *vis-à-vis* gods and roles played *vis-à-vis* men as parts of a unitary system, then it follows that variations in the communion content of relations with men must be interdependent with variations in the communion content of relations with the gods. If a balance of love, hate, and the rest of it is to be struck, this will be in the total field of people's relationships which includes both men and gods.

Work exploring this type of assumption has been done principally in America and, to date, is suggestive rather than scholarly. However, as it is suggestions rather than scholarship we are looking for in the present context, a couple of articles seem worth quoting by way of illustration.

In the first of these,[23] the author deals with a society in which a relationship of great intensity and affection exists between mother and child, but in which the mother withdraws herself abruptly when the child has reached about three years of age. For the female child in this society, growing up and marrying brings back the possibility of a further series of such warm, affectionate involvements in the role of mother. But for the male child, there is no equivalent in later life to the warmth, affection, and security received in this early period: both friendship and sexual relations later on are marked by insecurity, distrust, and little emotional depth. The author correlates with this situation the peculiar emotional intensity with which the cult of the Beneficent Virgin has become invested in this society; here, it would seem, the balance between types of relationships has been worked out, not in the field of purely human relations, but in the wider field which includes relations with the gods. In the second article, also by an American, more suggestions along these lines emerge during a discussion of cultural changes mediated by religious experts.[24] In speculating as to how an individual can suddenly take on a new social role whereby he frees himself to a great extent from involvement in certain crucial communion relationships, the author points out that exchange of these relationships with human beings for similar ones with gods may be one of the most important factors in enabling him to do this. As one example he quotes the acquisition of a personal Guardian Spirit in North American societies, an acquisition which enables the man concerned to satisfy his need for dependence and subordination with reference to a god and hence to act in a liberated, independent fashion *vis-à-vis* his parents and other close associates. Here again, we have a case where the majority of a population works out its balance of communion in the wider social field including both gods and man.

It will be noted that I use the word 'balance' here, in preference to terms such as 'compensation', 'substitution' and 'projection' more familiar in psycho-analytic literature. This use is an intentional rejection of the direction of causality implied in the usual psycho-analytic conceptual schemes. The tendency of such schemes is to suggest that religious relationships are always a sort of 'second best' for human ones; whereas it seems to me that to do justice to the facts such a simple view is quite inadequate. Love and other satisfying communion relationships in our society have been frequently given up for the more pressing demands of relations with a god: indeed, in an institution like the Catholic Church, someone who was applying for priestly office and appeared to be making no sacrifice of rich human relationships in order to be a servant of God would be an object of grave doubt.

One might suggest a number of very different reasons for the readiness of some people in all societies to throw up human for divine communion. At one extreme, some people's gods are like prostitutes: for those who can pay, they give more of a sort than ordinary human partners in return for a great deal less effort on the part of the clients. At the other extreme, they may demand far more effort and sacrifice than any human being, but may provide in return a perfection for those involved which quite eclipses the richest of their human involvements; they may, for example, combine in one person roles which are separated in the human social fields of their worshippers, e.g. those of mother, father, and spouse. For such reasons as these, our approach to studying the communion aspects of religion must be one that looks at a person's total social field of men and gods as one in which causal relations can have all possible directions: gods of unimaginable delight can seduce their worshippers away from men just as effectively as arid relation-ships with men can precipitate a turn towards the gods.

From all this, one answer to our question about the loadings of commu-nion and manipulation in religion seems to be that those religions with a highly manipulative emphasis are found in conjunction with human social systems whose communion aspects are 'balanced' in the sense sketched above; whilst those religions with a very strong element of communion occur where there is a similarly strong imbalance in the human social system. Whether the nature of the gods fostered the imbalance in the human sector, or whether the human imbalance nourished the gods must be a matter for historical research in each particular case.

Another possible answer to the same question seems of particular rele-vance to the history of Western culture. Variation of religious relationships along the communion/manipulation dimension could be connected with changes in the importance of scientific thinking. Science versus Religion has been a *cause célèbre* in much recent writing by well-known scientists, of whom Julian Huxley has been one of the more notable contributors.[25] Huxley and most other workers in the non-human sciences have tended to assume that as a wider and wider field of phenomena was covered by scientific explanation, so the field of relevance of the gods would shrink, eventually to nothing. Certainly, if we look at the purely manipulative aspect of religious relationships, this seems a likely outcome: for as empiri-cal science broadens its scope, room for belief in godly intervention as determining the results of various life crises becomes progressively reduced. This is so, at least for those who cannot tolerate the more blatant forms of contradiction in their belief systems. However, to infer from this the eventual demise of religion is to overlook the communion aspect of religious relationships, which is not directly affected by the advance of science. As this advance continues, it seems likely that the manipulative significance of our religious beliefs will be continuously eroded while communion remains.

Here of course, we touch on a very controversial point; for Huxley and others maintain that the scientific outlook has made logically absurd not only the idea of gods as interveners in the events of the physical world, but the very idea of gods at all. These are views which hold wide currency among Western intelligentsia at the present day; but the banner of 'Ration-alism' which they hold up to support their picture of a godless world is in one sense a banner of limited perspective which may well be abandoned by a future and no less scientific generation. For 'Rationalism' in the twentieth century implies the programme of holding testable beliefs only and of acting on the assumption that connexions between events in the future will continue to resemble connexions between events observed in the past. As philosophers now acknowledge, no further justification of such a programme can be found which does not appeal to the very principles involved. It is in other words a programme which has causes deep in the roots of our nature, but one which has no rationale; and as such its status is no different from a programme which accepts faith as sufficient ground for believing in a god or gods. Where a man is faced with certain statements that are empirically testable and others that are not, there is nothing logically absurd in his applying the rationalist programme to the testable statements and the programme of faith to the untestables. If the gods are so defined that no observations are relevant to the truth or falsehood of statements about them, such a scheme of action removes them from the rationalist purview and subjects them to the trials of faith. It may be simpler to live out one's life applying a single logical programme to all beliefs, but the man who applies a second programme to beliefs about which the first can say nothing is certainly no more or less logical than he who applies only one; and as we have seen, the pressures to behave in this way may be very powerful.

To sum up on this point, it looks as if the first flush of twentieth-century Logical Positivism led to a godless world-picture for an intellectual elite strongly valuing logical consistency in their beliefs; but the later elaborations of Positivism in which the implications of the position have been fully followed up leave the picture open for further religious developments. Having been thrown out with the bath-water, the baby bids fair to return through the window. For the reasons given above, it seems likely that future developments in our own culture will involve not the disappearance of religion, but a greater and greater emphasis on its communion aspect. Such a development, indeed, seems to have been going on for some time in sections of the Protestant Church, which has done a good deal of reinterpretation of dogma that formerly seemed to stress the functions of the Almighty as provider in the material world.

A final topic which seems usefully dealt with in terms of the manipulation/communion dimension of variation concerns the relations of those people known as prophets and shamans to the other members of their societies. In most groups where the relationships of the majority with their gods are primarily means of obtaining the prosaic benefits of health, wealth and issue, we still generally find a few individuals whose religious relationships contrast with this situation in a striking fashion. Their involvements with their gods are talked of with great stress on elements of love, dependence, and admiration; and in many cases they may well be people of unusual personality structure whose communion goals cannot be easily fulfilled in any of the various possible fields of human relationship laid down by their society as standard. For example, I think here of certain Kalabari possession priestesses whose gods are conceptualized as so persecuting and aggressive towards them that one is led to suspect a paranoiac personality for whose response requirements the purely human social fields of their communities cannot cater. Many such people play a markedly creative role in their cultures, introducing both religious innovation and wider social changes. Indeed, Wallace, in the article quoted above, suggests that for the introducer of any radical social innovation touching on the basic moral norms of the community, intense communion relations with a loving and approving god, who is seen as the ultimate sponsor of the changes, may be an essential condition for the maintenance of sufficient resolve to carry his programme through: this, because in challenging the basic moral norms of his society, he probably sacrifices the love and approval of most of his human nearest and dearest. This may be one very good reason why moral changes are generally hung on a religious peg.

The contrasting types of religious involvement shown by prophets and their congregations are well illustrated through the history of Judaeo-Christianity and of Islam.[26] Here, as elsewhere, such individuals as Moses and the Old Testament Prophets, Christ and Muhammad, are clearly people of exceptional personality; and it is likely that the conditions which led to their developing intense communion relationships outside the purely human context were seldom present in the general congregation who were influenced by their ideas. Often enough, it is an implication of manipulative relevance written into the prophet's definition or redefinition of his god which 'sells' the latter to his followers – in the case of Christianity and Islam the promise of present comforts and future bliss conditional on certain behaviour observances. Much of the phrasing of the character of a god in such circumstances is carried out by people involved with him in a way largely unparalleled in the congregation at large; and this wide difference of attitude can be a source of considerable tension between prophet and laymen, the prophet continually remonstrating against the 'worldly' manipulative approach of the rabble which he sees as an affront and an outrage to the god. This sort of prophetic exasperation has been well documented for Judaism in a recent comparative study.[27]

In the long run, of course, the rabble win; and there is an emotional 'desiccation' of the ritual resulting, as in present-day Christianity, in performances whose routinization and lack of emotional involvement seem strangely incongruous with the idea of the give-and-take of love recurring throughout the verbal part of the service. In many societies studied by anthropologists we get an even stronger impression of 'desiccation' in many of the religious relationships; though in this context we are generally not in a position to confirm the sort of interpretation outlined above. Nevertheless, contexts in which we have the historical depth we need do give us a useful warning about the limitations which we may expect to encounter in trying to interpret religious form where such depth is lacking. Let us take for example the religious forms of the Kalabari fishing-villages in the Niger Delta. In each community, we find the cult of a hero-god who, sometime in the distant past, lived as a human being, gave the community the code of norms it should live by and, finally, disappeared into the sky. Now, in one village, this god may be male, in the next female, and in the next male again. As regards the manipulative aspect of the situation, however, there is no parallel variation in the implications of benefit for the community written into the definitions of the various gods. Further, there seems no variation in the general socio-cultural make-up of the community concomitant with the variation in sex of its tutelary god. Though frustrating to any anthropologist not content with mere description, this is just the sort of situation that diachronic data on religious development would lead us to expect: the individuals responsible for the original formulations of the natures of the village gods may well have been actuated by needs for particular types of communion relationship duplicated neither in the majority of their contemporaries nor in the subsequent population, for whom the manipulative aspect is that which maintained the vitality of the cult. If this is a correct reconstruction, attempts to find socio-cultural variations concomitant with those in sex of the several village gods are clearly fruitless.

In an earlier paragraph, we noted that in certain situations the equivalence of gods to non-religious instruments made it difficult to say that in specified socio-cultural conditions gods would be introduced to meet new needs: in many cases there is an equal probability that non-religious means will be brought in instead. In this last section, another important restriction on our generalizing has emerged. The definition of a god's character, it seems probable, bears in large measure the imprint of the communion-strivings (for love, security, approval etc.) of the individual who introduced it to the community. But since it is generally some implication of manipulative relevance that is crucial for its survival in a particular society, a very wide range of possible imprints reflecting the communion strivings of the inventor will be compatible with such survival.

So much for some of the lines of thought on religious questions which are suggested by the common-sense definition of religion whose use was advocated in the first part of this paper. A major implication of this definition was that the comparative study of religion should go ahead through the systematic application of the variables of inter-human relationships to the relationships of men with their gods. In this paper, we have explored only one such variable, that of communion versus manipulation. The results, however, were encouraging in some of the possibilities of interpretation which they outlined; and if sympathetic readers of these paragraphs try to carry out the same sort of exploration with some of the many other variables of inter-human relationship, I feel that this sector of anthropology may at last escape from its imprisonment within the bonds of sheer description. Another value of the common-sense approach outlined above is that it enables us to see how the work done by members of disciplines such as History and Psychoanalysis fits in with the religious studies of anthropologists.

Besides these positive virtues, our approach has the negative one of highlighting the wide limitations which we may expect to encounter in trying to make a socio-cultural interpretation of a given religious system. Further, in so far as it emphasizes the close affinity of man-to-man and man-to-god relationships, it gives us a timely warning that a comprehensive theory of religious forms must wait on a comprehensive theory of human social relationships generally; and we all know how far we are from that.

Mainly Critical

2 Neo-Tylorianism: sound sense or sinister prejudice?

Over the last year or two a new pejorative, 'neo-Tylorian', has entered the vocabulary of British social anthropologists. What error is it supposed to castigate?

The short answer seems to be that when someone in a pre-literate society answers questions about the cause of an event by making a statement concerning the activities of invisible personal beings, the neo-Tylorian (following his ancestor Sir E. B. Tylor) takes the statement at its face value. He accepts it as an attempt at explanation, and goes on to ask why members of the culture in question should try to explain things in this unfamiliar way.

To the layman, this intellectualist approach is likely to seem self-evidently sensible. To the orthodox social anthropologist, however, it is misguided in the extreme. For the anthropologist, it is the height of error to take pre-literate religious belief-statements at their face value. Such statements may be many things; but they are not really attempts at explanation, and should not be analyzed as such.[1]

This is a very odd position. And its oddity stands out all the more clearly when one reflects that nothing of the kind has ever occurred to members of any other discipline concerned with the study of human beliefs. Thus historians of ideas have long been engaged in trying to answer questions as to why Europeans of earlier ages should have sought to explain worldly events in theoretical terms very different from those to which we are now accustomed. But however strange these theoretical terms have seemed, the historians have never stopped to doubt whether they should take the statements containing them at their face value. For the historians, such statements give every appearance of being attempts at explanation, and should therefore be analysed and interpreted as such.[2]

Why should the intellectualist approach, which is perfectly satisfactory to the historian of earlier European ideas, appear so unsatisfactory to the social anthropologist dealing with the ideas of pre-literate, non-European cultures? Certainly results can have very little to do with the matter. For the historian of ideas, operating on the premiss that 'things are what they seem', has been forging ahead most successfully with his interpretation of the

European thought-tradition; but the social anthropologist, operating on the premiss that 'things are *not* what they seem', has had little success in explaining why pre-literate peoples have the kind of ideas they do. If the anthropologist is so adamant in refusing to return to the more straight-forward and apparently more productive methods favoured by the historian of ideas, he must have some very powerful negative arguments to support him. In this article, I shall try to identify these arguments and examine their worth. There seem, in fact, to be five principal arguments involved; and in what follows, I shall review them one by one. For illustration, I shall draw principally on the African material with which I am most familiar.

1. *In the sort of pre-literate cultures that social anthropologists study, there has been little development of that ideal of objective understanding of the world which is so central to the modern Western ethos. Hence intellectualist interpre-tations of the ideas of such cultures are out of order.*[3]

Now I think it is fair to say that the emergence of the ideal of objectivity is something peculiar to modern Western culture. But anthropologists using this fact to rule out intellectualist interpretation in non-Western cultures seem to have misunderstood what is involved. Thus the emergence of an ideal of objectivity does not mean the growth of an interest in explanation where there was none before. Rather, it means the growth of a conviction that this interest, if it is to be pursued effectively, must be segregated from the influence of political manipulation, aesthetic values, wish-fulfilment, and so on. Pre-objective cultures, then, are not cultures where the desire to make sense of the world is absent. They are cultures where this desire is still intricately interwoven with many others. Hence what is required in study-ing them is not an abstention from intellectualist analysis, but a delicate balancing of intellectualist with political, aesthetic and other analyses.

Even with such a balanced, many-angled approach, there is good reason for thinking that, so far as beliefs and ideas are concerned, the intellectualist analysis must take precedence over others. The force of this contention is greatest in relation to the question of political manipulation. Modern social anthropologists have been fascinated by the political manipulation of ideas – perhaps because it is one of the most obvious bridges between the Senior Common Room and the Assembly Place Under the Iroko Tree. However, their analysis of such manipulation has a curious unreality; and I think it can be shown that this unreality is a direct outcome of the policy of rushing in with a political analysis before having made an intellectualist analysis.

An extreme illustration of this point is provided by Edmund Leach's *Political Systems of Highland Burma*.[4] Leach maintains that Kachin ideas about *nats* (spirits) are nothing but counters in the language of political argument; and it is precisely this contention which convinces one that his analysis is unreal. One cannot help protesting that if the *nats* are nothing more than counters in the power game, why do Kachins waste so much time talking about them? Why do they not couch their political arguments more directly? Less extreme but more instructive is John Middleton's *Lugbara Religion.*[5] Here is a book which starts with a vivid but rather conventional analysis of the way in which influential members of Lugbara communities manipulate ideas of ancestral power for political purposes, and ends with what is perhaps the most brilliant intellectualist analysis of an African system of religious ideas yet made. Reading this book in the order in which it was written, one gets the same feeling of unreality as one had from Leach. Why do these people not cut out the religion and get on with the politics? Rereading it with the intellectualist analysis put in before the political, one immediately regains a sense of reality. Now it becomes obvious why the old men spend such a lot of time talking about ancestral power and witchcraft when they are struggling for political position. It is because these ideas mean so much to Lugbara as intellectual tools for making sense of the world that they are such powerful instruments in the hands of the politicians. If they meant nothing in intellectual terms, they would be nothing in the hands of the politicians.

It is because he *has* got things in the right order that a novelist of traditional African life like Chinua Achebe gives us a sense of reality missing from the work of the anthropologists. His *Arrow of God* in particular, deals with the intricate relations between religious beliefs and power struggles.[6] Indeed, its two principal protagonists are priestly politicians. As backcloth to the struggle between the Eze Ulu and the Eze Idemili, Achebe gives us a compelling picture of the key place that their deities, Ulu and Idemili, occupy in the village world view. It is this backcloth that makes us see not only what powerful tools these deities are in the hands of would-be manipulators, but also what strict limits there must be to manipulation when those involved believe in and live by the ideas they are manipulating. Achebe's book, of course, is a novel and not a work of analysis; but a careful reading of it would do much to help anthropologists regain a sense of proportion in these matters.

To conclude, it is clear that social anthropologists have been seriously misled by the glib phrase 'manipulation of ideas'. What politicians manipulate is not ideas, but people's dependence on ideas as means of ordering, explaining, predicting and controlling their world. Only a prior analysis of the nature of this dependence can pave the way for an adequate grasp of the scope and limitations of manipulation.

2.   *Members of pre-literate cultures tend to be of a practical rather than of a theoretical bent. Hence analyses that treat the religious ideas of such cultures as explanatory theories are beside the point.*[7]

My first comment on this argument is that the truth of the premiss is dubious. West African experience certainly makes one very chary of asserting that pre-literate cultures lack people whose interest in theory outruns their practical concern. Nearly all of us who have worked in this area know the occasional old men who, having retired from the hurly-burly of everyday life, spend much of their time thinking it through and trying to make sense of it. And although there may be few such people in any particular community, they often play a disproportionate part in transmitting ideas to the next generation.

My second comment is that the argument appears to be based on the misleading colloquial opposition of 'theory' and 'practice'. As I have pointed out in a recent article, one of the principal intellectual functions of traditional African religious theory is that of placing everyday events in a wider causal context than common sense provides.[8] Traditional religious theory, indeed, complements common sense in its concern for the diagnosis, prediction and control of events. It is thus as intimately linked as is common sense with the practical concerns of its users. Conversely, it is reasonable to suppose that these practical concerns have played as great a part in stimulating the development of theory as they have in stimulating the development of common sense. So even if there were such a thing as a culture carried entirely by hard-headed pragmatists, one would still expect to find plenty of theory in it. Even in such a culture, then, there would be room for an intellectualist analysis.

3.   *The ideas of pre-literate cultures seldom form logically consistent systems. Hence in such cultures an intellectualist analysis, which assumes a search for logical consistency, is inappropriate.*[9]

A short answer to this argument is that the modern Western world-view is far from forming a logically consistent whole – especially where ideas about the nature of man are concerned! But this in no way stops us from interpreting the history of Western thought in terms of a striving for consistency. The achievement of consistency is one thing; the striving for it quite another.

Some social anthropologists go so far as to admit the reality of this striving in pre-literate cultures, but suggest that those involved are few in number and highly atypical.[10] Here, in fact, we are back with our old men whose interest in theory outruns their practical concern; and the answer is much the same as that given to argument two. These people may be few and atypical, but they characteristically play a crucial part in the transmission of ideas to the next generation. Hence the ideas of the general population bear the stamp of their interests.

In traditional Africa, the most significant index of the striving for consistency is the well-nigh ubiquitous presence of the idea of a supreme being who is the sustainer of all the lesser spiritual agencies, and so is indeed the ultimate prime mover of everything. If it is nothing else, this concept is surely an assertion that beneath the diversity and apparent haphazardness of the world of appearance, there is an ultimate unity and an ultimate consistency. The ways of the supreme being are often said to be somewhat inscrutable as compared with the ways of the lesser spirits – an admission that the details of this ultimate unity and consistency are perhaps beyond any power of men to work out. But the very existence of the concept is a profession of faith that it is there.

4. *The ideas which neo-Tylorians treat as explanatory are religious ideas, and we know from our experience in modern Western culture that religious ideas do not 'really' attempt to explain the events in the space-time world. They are concerned with other things.*[11]
Here we have the fallacy of regarding belief in spiritual beings as something which serves the same basic human aspiration wherever it occurs. A little thought should remind us that over the last fifteen hundred years of European history, religion has slowly abdicated a very considerable interest in the explanation, prediction and control of worldly events to the emerging sciences.[12] Hence modern Western Christianity's lack of interest in these things is a very poor index by which to judge traditional religions in pre-literate cultures.

All this was brought home to me very vividly by an aspect of my own fieldwork experience among the Kalabari people of the Niger delta. In Kalabari communities, traditional religious practitioners, orthodox Christian churches and breakaway spiritualist sects form a most interesting triangle. In this triangle, traditional practitioners and spiritualist sects are sworn enemies, whilst both compete for the friendship of the orthodox churches. Why should this be so? In the first place, the traditional practitioners and the spiritualists are direct competitors. Both diagnose and attempt to cure a variety of misfortunes and diseases, and their claims to significance are based on these activities. The diagnostic and curative techniques of the spiritualists are in fact so similar to those of the traditionalists that the latter often accuse them of stealing traditional stock-in-trade only to bring it out again under a Christian label. With the aid of some very convincing biblical exegesis, however, the spiritualists claim they are reverting, not to traditional Kalabari beliefs and practices, but to early Christian beliefs and practices. As a spectator on the sidelines, I am inclined to think that both claims are correct, and that in their overriding concern for the explanation, prediction and control of worldly events, the spiritualists draw inspiration both from Kalabari traditionalists and from elements in

the Bible that reflect early Christian ideas. Both traditionalists and spiritualists are able to adopt an amiable attitude toward the orthodox churches
precisely because the latter abstain from this-worldly predictive and
explanatory claims, and centre their work on the business of salvation. As
several attenders at spiritualist prayer houses have put it to me: 'The prayer
houses cure our sicknesses and the churches pilot [*sic*] our souls'.

Although this is only one example, it could be paralleled in many parts of
Africa. It does, I think, serve to bring home to us the fact that modern
Western Christianity, as a religion, is somewhat peculiar in its lack of
concern with the explanation of this-worldly events. This characteristic,
therefore, cannot be used to justify opposition to intellectualist analysis of
other religious systems.

5. *If we are wrong-headed enough to treat them as explanations, we have to
admit that traditional religious beliefs are mistaken. And the only possible
interpretation of such mistakes is that they are the product of childish ignorance.
Neo-Tylorians who take traditional beliefs at their face value therefore subscribe to the stereotype of the 'ignorant savage' and are illiberal racists. If on the
other hand we treat them as having intentions which, despite appearances, are
quite other than explanatory, we no longer have to evaluate traditional beliefs in
the light of the canons of adequacy current in the sciences. Anthropologists who
take this line are therefore not committed to the 'ignorant savage' stereotype.
They are good liberals.*

The germs of this argument, if argument it can be called, are to be found in
Lévy-Bruhl's early criticism of Tylor and Frazer.[13] Hints of it recur in
many expositions of the orthodox anti-intellectualist position over the last
two decades; and it has recently been given a highly explicit formulation by
Leach.[14] My own feeling is that it is this sort of attitude that underpins and
lends force to all the other arguments we have considered. In assessing its
appeal, we shall do well to note its affinities with that other powerful
offspring of Lévy-Bruhl's work, the militant ideology of Négritude.

There is a short and sharp answer to this whole line of thought. It is that,
by all normal criteria of assessment, many of the religious beliefs of pre-
literate cultures *are* primarily explanatory in intent; that by the criteria of
the sciences, many of them *are* mistaken; and that to wriggle out of
admitting this by the pretence that such beliefs are somehow not really what
they obviously are is simply to distort facts under the influence of extra-
neous values. In this respect liberal anthropology is no better than fascist
anthropology, racist anthropology, or what-have-you.

So much for the straight case against the liberals. It seems unlikely,
however, that a frontal attack of this kind will ever carry a position defended
by irrational obstacles of the strength we are facing here. What we have to

do is weaken the liberal position by persuading its adherents that the facts do not really come into conflict with their most cherished values.

Let us start by asking what is so very dreadful about holding theories which later turn out to be mistaken? The liberals, of course, are very put off by Tylor's contention that the mistaken theories of pre-literate peoples are the outcome of a childish mentality. But surely we do not have to follow Tylor in thinking that childishness is the only possible explanation for mistaken theories. On the contrary, it seems the least plausible of all conceivable explanations. In recent articles, I myself have explored what seems a fairly convincing interpretation of such mistakes, and one that casts no slur at all on the mental capacity or maturity of the peoples concerned.[15]

For those who will not easily see the point when it is made about pre-literate peoples, let us move over to the history of European ideas, and more specifically to the history of the sciences. Contrary to the view of many social anthropologists, science, though progressive, is not in any simple sense cumulative. It progresses through the overthrow of a goodish theory by one that gives wider coverage of the data; through the overthrow of this better theory by one that gives still wider coverage, and so on.[16] Under this system, today's intellectual hero is inevitably tomorrow's mistaken man. But the quality of his achievement will still stand tomorrow. Indeed, it is his achievement which has made possible the further advance that proclaims him mistaken. Newton is no less a hero for the overthrow of classical physics. Heisenberg will be no less a hero for the overthrow of quantum theory.

The trouble with the liberals, as I see it, is the belief that although their own theoretical framework may be elaborated by future generations, it will not be found radically mistaken. It is this belief which makes them feel there is something illiberal about imputing mistakes to pre-literate theorists. But if what I have said about the nature of scientific progress is correct, their view of their own conceptual framework is unduly optimistic. And if their own framework is inevitably going to be tomorrow's mistake, what is illiberal about imputing mistakes to pre-literates?

From here it is but a small step to my final piece of persuasion. I should like to suggest to the liberals that in certain fields the dichotomies 'wrong/right', 'mistaken/correct' are in fact far too strong to do justice to the relation between the beliefs of pre-literates and those of modern Westerners.

One of the things that makes the liberals see pre-literate explanatory theories as totally wrong-headed is the fact that they characteristically feature invisible personal beings. Here the positivist background of so many of them obtrudes itself. As positivists, they view themselves as revolutionaries in action against the old, pre-scientific order. And like most revolutionaries, their besetting error is that, in trying to liquidate the old order, they throw out the baby with the bathwater. Thus because many of the explanatory beliefs of pre-scientific Europe happen to have been couched in personal terms, they have declared any theory couched in such terms as *ipso facto* beyond the pale of the rational. In so doing, however, they have thrown out the basic canon of scientific method which lays it down that no type of theory can by judged right or wrong solely on the grounds of its content.

A very vivid exposition of this canon is to be found in the astronomer Fred Hoyle's science-fiction novel *The Black Cloud*.[17] Here we find an international committee of scientists trying to explain the nature and behaviour of a terrible opaque cloud which, coming between the earth and the sun, threatens to freeze up the planet. In what is clearly intended as a sermon on scientific method, Hoyle takes as his hero a gruff, monosyllabic Russian. All the others laugh at this man because, whenever they ask for his views, he simply repeats 'Bastard in cloud!' – thus showing himself to be either a joker in poor taste or a deluded animist. Later, however, it is the animist who has the laugh; for his theory and his alone covers the various puzzling aspects of the phenomenon, and provides a basis for the prediction of its behaviour.

Animistic explanations, then, have nothing *prima facie* unreasonable about them; and the liberal has no cause to blush when he meets them in pre-literate cultures.

The liberal can, of course, concede all that has been said so far, and still object that when it comes to accounting for the facts, the animistic beliefs of pre-literate cultures, considered as theories, make a very poor showing alongside the impersonal theories of the West. This is certainly true enough where we are dealing with inanimate matter, with plants, and with lower animals; but the nearer we come to the 'higher' activities of man, the more dubious it becomes. Traditional beliefs have very little of interest to say to the physicist, the chemist, and the biologist; but they have a surprising amount to say to the psychologist and the sociologist.

The truth of this contention is well illustrated by Evans-Pritchard's classic *Witchcraft, Oracles and Magic among the Azande*.[18] This monograph was the first to document in detail the way in which members of a traditional African culture used a corpus of explanatory 'mystical' theory to make sense of and cope with the vicissitudes of their everyday lives. In particular, it highlighted the connexion made by Zande theory between human misfortune and disturbance in the social fabric – a connexion which later research showed was typical of traditional thought. When this book came out thirty years ago, both the author and his readers talked on the assumption that, judged by the criteria of the sciences, Zande ideas on this subject were mistakes. Today, I think many commentators would be hesitant about making such an assumption. In an age where social disturbance, operating via psychological disturbance, is recognized as a probable contributor to a whole spectrum of human misfortunes ranging from high blood pressure to falling under a bus, it is no longer so easy to say that the Zande thinker is just mistaken. Now what brought about this change in Western beliefs? One factor at least seems to have been inspiration by just those pre-literate beliefs that once were considered so erroneous. It is not for nothing that Walter B. Cannon, commonly acknowledged as 'the father of psychosomatic medicine', called one of his early articles on the subject 'Voodoo Death',[19]

Another book which is likely to be seminal in this respect is Fortes's *Oedipus and Job in West African Religion*.[20] This book deals with what may be called Tallensi social psychology. It reveals a system of concepts in many ways uncannily similar to those of Western psychoanalysts, but with certain significant differences. Notably, Tallensi concepts postulate a somewhat different distribution of motives between conscious and unconscious sectors of the mind.[21] In a decade in which psychiatrists are becoming increasingly aware of the culture-bound nature of Western psychodynamic concepts, this and other West African social psychologies clearly merit a respectful hearing.

If the reader feels tempted to smile patronisingly at the last two paragraphs, he should ask himself the following question. After all the sound and the fury and the self-congratulation have been discounted, just how far have psychoanalysis, behaviourism, structural-functionalism, and other basic Western theories of higher human behaviour really advanced our understanding of ourselves? If he answers honestly, I think he will stop smiling.

Let me sum up on all of this. Behind the liberal's concern to play down the explanatory aspect of pre-literate religious beliefs lies a strong streak of the patronising. Basically he believes that, so far as explanatory value is concerned, his theories are in some absolute and final sense right, whilst pre-literate theories are in some equally absolute sense wrong. What I have tried to point out here is that the rightness of the current Western belief-system is in the nature of things transitory; and that in the sphere of 'higher' human behaviour, at least, pre-literate belief-systems may from time to time be the source of insights that seriously shake some Western foundations. In reminding the liberal of these things, I hope I have done something towards removing the sentimental obstacles which have hitherto prevented him from considering the intellectualist approach on its merits.

I should like to end this rather polemical article on a note of reconciliation. Social anthropologists often talk as though one had to choose between an intellectualist and a sociological analysis of pre-literate beliefs. In fact, however, such a choice is neither necessary nor desirable.

Tylor's intellectualism, it is true, was innocent of any sociological overtones. To the question of why some cultures had 'animistic' and others 'scientific' world-views, his ultimate answer was that members of the first lot of cultures had a childish mentality, whilst members of the second lot had an adult mentality. Whatever else this was, it was certainly not a sociological explanation. But, as I said earlier, we can be intellectualists without following Tylor in other respects.

As I see it, the only thing the intellectualist is entitled to ask is that we begin by analysing pre-literate belief statements in terms of the overt explanatory ends they serve. After this, he should welcome all comers – sociologists, psychoanalysts, the lot. In point of fact, it is almost impossible to make an intellectualist analysis of belief statements without doing some sociology in the process. This was borne in upon me most forcibly when I embarked on a generalised comparison of African and Western thought-traditions. I was driven to an intellectualist approach to this task by the singular failure of the anti-intellectualist establishment to make any headway with it. In trying to make intellectualist analyses of various traditional African religious theories, however, I came up against the fact that they were above all theories of society and of the individual's place in it. Hence it was impossible to gain understanding of them without taking detailed account of the social organizations whose workings they were concerned to make sense of. Much the same thing happened when I tried to understand why African traditional cultures favoured personalized models for their explanatory tasks, whilst Western culture favoured impersonal models. In tackling the question, I started out with the intellectualist assumption that both the gods and spirits of traditional Africa and the ultimate particles and forces of the Western world-view were alternative means to what was basically the same explanatory end. This assumption led to the further question of why the theoretical models of the two sets of cultures were founded on such very different analogies. And in trying to answer this second question, I found I had to take into account such unambiguously sociological variables as stability and complexity of social organization, and the relation between society and its non-human environment.[22]

On the basis of my own work, then, I regard the intellectualist approach as a healthy corrective to certain current fashions in social anthropology. I do not regard it as an alternative to sociological analysis.

3 Lévy-Bruhl, Durkheim and the Scientific Revolution

Over the last seventy years, Western intellectuals have shown an increasing interest in the thought-patterns of peoples who, though contemporary, have cultures which are at once pre-literate, pre-industrial and pre-scientific. One root of this interest is the belief that such thought-patterns provide us with a clue to the nature of our own lost heritage – a heritage supposedly destroyed by the advance of science. The other root is the belief that only through the study of pre-scientific thought-systems can we get a clear view of the nature of science. Only if we have some idea of what it is like to live in a world into which the scientific outlook has not yet intruded, can we be at all certain as to what are the distinctive features of this outlook and what are simply universals of human thought.

Anyone aiming to enter this momentous field of enquiry can do no better than start with a careful study of the two great French philosopher-sociologists Lucien Lévy-Bruhl and Emile Durkheim. Between them, these two have had an enormous influence on the comparative study of human thought; and even today many of the ideas that dominate the field derive from their work.

In the present paper, I shall begin by comparing the ideas of Lévy-Bruhl and Durkheim on the relation between 'primitive' and 'modern' thought.[1] I shall show that, between them, they have left posterity with two very different conceptions of this relation. I shall also show that, whilst anthropologists and sociologists have since come down very heavily in favour of one of these conceptions, the data point strongly to the other. I shall conclude by suggesting how this curious situation may have come to pass.

In much of what follows, I shall be concerned with the views of the two masters and their disciples on the nature of ideas about spiritual beings and other unobservable influences. The disappearance of such ideas from large areas of human thought has long been regarded as one of the principal indices of the transition from 'primitive' to 'modern'. And it should be clear from what follows that disagreement about the nature of such ideas is an important factor in disagreement about the nature of the Scientific Revolution.

Lucien Lévy-Bruhl

Born in France in 1857, Lévy-Bruhl came to the sociology of thought in middle age, after attaining a considerable reputation as a philosopher. Although grounded in the rich and subtle doctrines of Immanuel Kant, he later opted for the simpler and more clear-cut positivist approach.[2] The latter, as we shall see later, exerted a very strong influence over his sociology.

Lévy-Bruhl's entry into sociology seems to have been inspired by his fellow countryman Emile Durkheim. And though he did not go to work in Durkheim's immediate circle, he was influenced by some of its key ideas. But if Durkheim inspired Lévy-Bruhl, he was also his most perceptive and conclusive critic. So it is appropriate to deal with Lévy-Bruhl first and Durkheim second.

Lévy-Bruhl's work on the sociology of thought, falls into two parts: an early period from about 1900 to 1930, and a later period in which he modified his views in the light of the fieldwork reports of men such as Malinowski and Evans-Pritchard.

The main ideas of the early period are to be found in his *Fonctions Mentales dans les Societés Inférieures*, first published in 1910. Four other books belong to this early period; but, by and large, they do little more than produce additional documentation, together with restatements and clarifications.[3]

Les Fonctions opens with a typically Durkheimian statement on the subject matter of a sociology of thought. Lévy-Bruhl takes this subject matter to be 'collective representations'; and these he defines as ideas that are (a) common to all members of a social group, (b) transmitted from generation to generation, and (c) imposed on individuals from an external source, both pre-existing them and surviving them.[4]

This introductory statement is followed by a vigorous critique of the 'English School' of Tylor and Frazer. Lévy-Bruhl accuses members of this school of trying to explain the salient features of primitive thought patterns in terms of a rudimentary, infantile and erroneous use of processes of reasoning found fully developed only in highly educated Westerners. Not only does he take them to task for the obvious fallacy involved in comparing any adult thought with that of an infant. He also gives two reasons for rejecting a programme which starts off from the assumption that primitive thought is primarily concerned with explanation. First, in primitive societies various emotional needs override the need for explanation; and it is these emotional needs that largely determine the content of collective representations. Secondly, the simpler the society, the greater the importance of collective representations in the individual's world-view, and the less the importance of beliefs arrived at by his own exercise of reason.[5]

For a successful theory of primitive thought, then, we must discard all the preconceptions of the English School. We must abandon the idea that primitives are engaged in a fumbling, infantile use of our own canons of logic. And we must cease to think of them as having our own interest in pure, rational explanations. We must be prepared to find their thought obeying laws which are not even *logical* in the strict sense.[6]

According to Lévy-Bruhl, the key to the interpretation of primitive thought lies not with reason but with emotion.[7] It is the play of emotion which imparts to such thought the following salient characteristics:

1. *Mystical orientation.* Every time primitive man engages in an act of perception, the content of perception is strongly coloured by and invested with emotion. Feelings associated with objects are incorporated into his images, there to form the 'mystical' element. This mystical aspect of experience may be represented in the form of gods or spirits, as in Africa, or in an impersonal form, as in Polynesia. But, whatever the details, it is always represented as an invisible, intangible power.[8]

2. *Lack of objectivity.* As between the strictly perceived and the mystical element of an experience, the latter is the more important. Several consequences follow from this relatively low valuation of perceptual experience. Thus phenomena like dreams and visions, which modern Westerners consider subjective, are admitted to primitive reality on the same footing as ordinary, everyday perceptions. In general, too, the evidence of sight and touch is far from being the sovereign determinant of a belief's survival. A primitive belief is seldom shaken by the sort of observations that a Westerner would take as refuting it.[9]

3. *Participation.* In primitive life, the visual and tactual aspect of experience is represented by ideas that correspond to those of Western material-object discourse, whilst the emotional aspect is represented by ideas of mystical influence. But as the visual/tactual aspect is inextricably intertwined with the emotional, so objects are inextricably associated with mystical influences. The association, indeed, is so close as to amount to a virtual identity. The object is both itself and a spirit; the spirit both itself and an object. Further, when two objects share the same emotional and hence the same mystical associations, they themselves also become closely associated; so closely, once again, as to be virtually identified. Thus if a man and a parakeet arouse the same emotional association, a community of mystical essence is established between them, in virtue of which it becomes possible to say that men *are* parakeets and vice versa.

This kind of relation, either between a perceptual object and its mystical aura, or between two perceptual objects sharing the same mystical aura, is what Lévy-Bruhl calls a 'participation', Because the primitive is overwhelmingly mystical in his orientation, his principal way of linking things is in terms of such participation.[10]

4. *Pre-logical mentality.* An important consequence of the prevalence of ideas of participation is a degree of indifference to logical contradictions. Such ideas, as we have just seen, involve affirmations that objects are at once themselves and things other than themselves – at once themselves and not themselves. Hence mystical orientation and participation involve an overriding of the law of contradiction; and it is this that leads Lévy-Bruhl to term primitive thought 'pre-logical'.[11] In using such a term, however, he is at pains to defend himself against misunderstandings. He does not mean that primitive thought actually values contradictions, or that it is incapable of registering and avoiding them. What he does mean is that, where participations are involved, they take precedence over the elimination of contradictions.[12]

5. *Communion with the world.* This final characteristic of primitive thought is a consequence of several of the foregoing. In the first place, because primitive man's every perception is so heavily invested with emotion, he does not so much perceive the world around him as feel it. Secondly, because this emotion arises within him as well as investing what he perceives, he himself is involved in a continual participation in the world. Finally, because men, animals, plants and inert things are equally associated with mystical influence, there is a tendency to confront all categories of such objects as though they were in some sense personal – i.e. in some sense fellow subjects. Primitive man, then, is more accurately described as communing with the world about him than as perceiving it.[13]

So much for Lévy-Bruhl's view of primitive thought. What of his view of modern thought; of 'our' thought? Here we come to a rather puzzling feature of his exposition. For although his overriding concern is to establish a strong contrast between 'their' thought and 'ours', he is strangely reticent about the second term in the contrast.

I think there are two reasons for this reticence. First, he assumes that he is writing for a modern Western readership, and that this readership is both able to define modern thought for itself and able to agree on a definition.[14] Secondly, his own definition of modern thought is essentially a negative one. Modern thought is above all thought without the various encumbrances of primitive thought.[15] This said, we can go on to summarize what can be read between the lines about his view of the modern mind. Once again, five salient characteristics appear to be involved:

1. *Natural orientation.* The modern thinker is oriented to the natural aspect of his experience, i.e. to what reaches him through his organs of sight and touch. He discounts any emotional accompaniment there may be to input through these organs. In consequence, he perceives objects without any mystical aura, and lives in a world largely unencumbered by unobservable entities and influences.[16]

2. *Objectivity*. Since his perception is controlled almost exclusively by input through the organs of sight and touch, modern man sees things as they are in nature, and thus tends automatically toward objectivity.[17]

3. *Induction*. Discounting emotion, modern man is free to register naturally occurring conjunctions between events in the visible, tangible world. Objective experience replaces emotion in dictating the links man makes between things. Inductive generalizations are at the core both of common sense and of scientific thought, between which Lévy-Bruhl does not distinguish.[18]

4. *Logical attitude*. Once mystical orientation and participation are banished, man's natural sensitivity to contradiction is free to reassert itself. Modern man is therefore predominantly logical in his attitude.[19]

5. *Separation from and mastery of the world*. In modern life, perception has freed itself from emotional investment. Hence it is possible to talk of man seeing and touching things without feeling them or participating in them. Again, where the various categories of perceptual object are no longer overwhelmingly associated with personalized mystical influence, there is room for discrimination between human and non-human components of the world. So far as the non-human world is concerned, then, man perceives it as something separate and distinct from himself – something to be mastered and controlled rather than something to be communed with.[20]

Let us turn now to what Lévy-Bruhl has to say about the sociology of these two dramatically contrasted thought-syndromes. Here we are on controversial ground, for some reputable commentators complain that he shows little interest in the social factors that underpin this contrast.[21] It is true, in fact, that he does not provide a unified and coherent account. But by putting together what he says in passing at various places in *Les Fonctions*, we can arrive at the rudiments of a sociology of thought.

According to Lévy-Bruhl, the basic societal background to the primitive mentality is a situation in which the individual and his aims are thoroughly subordinated to the community and its aims. In such circumstances, the individual acquires the greater part of his idea-system via the accredited socializing agents of the community. What is more, he acquires it at ceremonies that provide an intense stimulus to the emotions. Hence the emotional aura that clothes his very perceptions of the world around him and gives them their mystical colouring. Again, in circumstances where the individual is thoroughly subordinated to the community, he is unable to think of himself without thinking simultaneously of the community; and this situation furnishes the prototype for all his other ideas of participation.

Now where social life develops in such a way that the individual becomes less and less subordinated to the community, and more and more a person in his own right, the situation becomes greatly changed. In the first place, the individual has less of his idea-system dictated to him by the accredited agents of the community, and thinks more of it out for himself. Hence emotion and mystical orientation give way to perceptual experience and natural orientation. Secondly, the individual becomes more and more able to think of himself as an entity distinct from his group. Hence the situation which formerly provided the prototype for his ideas of participation no longer obtains, and participation ceases to be a dominant feature of his thought.[22]

In summing up Lévy-Bruhl's early work, then, we can say that it not only provides a bold picture of radically contrasted primitive and modern thought patterns, but also gives some account of the social factors underlying the transition from one to the other.

From the publication of *Les Fonctions* onwards, Lévy-Bruhl's thesis attracted great interest in a number of disciplines concerned with the study of man. Among those interested were members of the new generation of anthropologists in Britain and America. Here were people stressing for the first time the importance of a lengthy period of participant observation in any attempt to understand non-Western modes of thought; and they took *Les Fonctions* into the field to test its assumptions against the results of such observation. The first of such fieldworkers was Malinowski, who criticized Lévy-Bruhl's views in the light of his experiences in the Trobriand Islands. A little later came Evans-Pritchard, several of whose early publications were examinations of Lévy-Bruhl's position in the light of his experiences amongst such East African peoples as the Azande, Nuer, Dinka and Anuak. His verdict, too, was critical in several respects. Lévy-Bruhl, for his part, lived up conscientiously to his scientific ideal and took account of the field reports of Malinowski, Evans-Pritchard and others. Thus there arose a dialogue between armchair theorist and fieldworkers which was a model of its kind.

Lévy-Bruhl's later books show something of the fruitfulness of this dialogue. Perhaps the main criticism levelled against him by fieldworkers like Malinowski and Evans-Pritchard was that he made primitive peoples much more mystical than they really were. He portrayed them as living continuously upon the mystical plane, whereas in fact they spent much of their time at the level of common sense, where the Western ethnographer could meet them without any difficulty.[23] Lévy-Bruhl's attention to this criticism emerges clearly in his final works. Thus, whereas in *Les Fonctions* he does indeed portray primitive man as dominated by the mystical, in *L'Expérience Mystique et les Symboles* and in his final *Carnets*[24] he concedes that even primitive man spends only some of his time in the world of mystical influences, and the rest of it in the workaday world of common sense. In these later books, indeed, he speaks of primitive thought as oscillating between the common-sense and the mystical orientation. At ordinary times, such thought is at the level of common sense. But a situation which is in any way unusual or anxiety-provoking triggers a flight to the mystical level. Then, when the situation is past, thought returns once again to the level of common sense. This alternation between one level and another leads Lévy-Bruhl to talk of primitive thought as 'less homogeneous than ours'. By contrast, fully modern thought is a vast expansion and systematization of common sense. It has no room for alternation between the common-sense and the mystical. Hence Lévy-Bruhl refers to it as 'homogeneous'.[25]

A second criticism made by a number of fieldworkers concerned Lévy-Bruhl's use of the term 'pre-logical'. In his *Carnets*, he also deals with this. He admits that the term is a misleading one, with its implication of mental deficiency. He also admits that, in many of the situations where he has applied it, what is at stake is the overriding of physical possibilities rather than of the law of contradiction. Thus a god who is half man, half leopard, or a man who is also a parakeet, is physically impossible yet not logically absurd. So he agrees to drop this most controversial of his characterizations of primitive thought.[26]

These two concessions have led modern commentators to say that Lévy-Bruhl's final works constitute a radical revision of his earlier position.[27] In fact, however, what he retains is more significant than what he withdraws. Thus, although his final picture of primitive thought allows a good deal of common sense in alongside the mystical, and although his final picture of modern thought allows a good deal of the mystical in alongside common sense, his characterization of the mystical remains unrepentantly the same. Again, in his final works we still find common sense lumped together with science, and both of them radically contrasted with the mystical.[28]

One of the enigmas of his later work, indeed, is that for all his positive response to the criticisms of Malinowski and Evans-Pritchard, he seems to have made no response at all to the lone but powerful voice which directed its criticism against these more enduring presuppositions of his thought. The voice in question was that of his colleague Emile Durkheim, to whose views we shall now turn.

Emile Durkheim

Durkheim was born a year later than Lévy-Bruhl, and died more than twenty years earlier. Nevertheless, he has left us a much richer and more complex body of thought. Indeed, whereas Lévy-Bruhl spent his sociological career working one compact, consistent and rather simple set of ideas to exhaustion, Durkheim played with and developed several sets of ideas, some of which were inconsistent or even in contradiction with others. This is true above all of his sociology of thought, and makes his views in this sphere a great deal more difficult to present.

As I read Durkheim, the core of his sociology of thought is the thesis that most aspects of human mental life have grown by differentiation and elaboration from a primitive religious basis. By 'most aspects', I mean not only religion as the moderns know it, but the arts, the theoretical constructions of the sciences, and indeed the very categories of logical thought. In the present essay, I shall concentrate my attention on Durkheim's sketch of the way in which primitive religious thought gives rise to the theoretical thought of the sciences.

A first hint of Durkheim's views in this sphere is to be found in his early essay *De Quelques Formes Primitives de Classification.*[29] Here, he notes (a) the continuity between primitive religious classifications and the theoretical classifications of the sciences, and (b) the difference between technical/practical and scientific classifications.[30] These remarks, which show an apprehension of the world of ideas startlingly different from Lévy-Bruhl's, provide a foretaste of the major theme of his *Formes Elémentaires de la Vie Religieuse.*[31]

The basic exposition of this theme is found in chapter 7, book 2 of *Formes Elémentaires.* In this chapter, Durkheim begins by giving an account of the origin of ideas about unobservable entities, then follows up with an account of the role of such ideas in human intellectual life. He shows how their role enables them to spread far beyond the context of their birth, and how it gives them a central place both in primitive religion and in modern science.

Durkheim's account of the genesis of these ideas will be familiar to most readers, so we shall not dwell long on it. Briefly, he says that religious ideas are born in the first instance at social gatherings. The impact of the group on the individual at such gatherings gives him the feeling of being transported, of being lifted into thoughts and actions that would be foreign to him were he on his own. Even in the intervals of such periodic gatherings, the presence of the group produces a less intense version of this effect. Now this feeling cannot be accounted for in terms of the particular human beings the individual sees around him: it is too profound to be ascribed to such inadequate causes. In the circumstances, then, the individual has no alternative but to invoke the idea of an all-powerful but unobservable force at work on him.[32]

Initially, says Durkheim, man helps himself to conceive this force by using material symbols or totems. Later, however, he comes to conceptualize it more literally, in ideas of force and influence such as the Polynesian *mana* and the Indian *orenda*, or in ideas of spirits or gods.[33]

Durkheim's account of what it is that gives these ideas of the unobservable a currency so much wider than their context of origin is as little publicized as his account of religious origins is well known. I therefore make no apology for considering it at some length.

For Durkheim, the moment at which religion is born is the moment at which the possibility of all higher forms of thought, including science, is also born. As we have already seen, the impact of society on the individual gives rise to the idea of an all-powerful yet unobservable collective force; and to help himself conceive this force, man adopts a material totem as its symbol. Now once this has happened, the invisible force comes to be seen as equally associated, on the one hand with the social group, and on the other with the totem. Group and totem are thenceforth seen as sharing a common essence and as mutually identifiable; and it is the invisible force that has made this identification possible. Again, the double association, with social group and material totem, gives this force a sort of intermediate nature, partly social and personal, partly physical and impersonal. Having acquired such an intermediate or neutral character, the force readily lends itself to association with any phenomenon, no matter what the latter's domain. Hence it becomes the agent of a host of identifications of the kind exemplified by that of the group with its totem – identifications of things which appear to the eye of common sense as drastically distinct.[34]

Now it is these curious identifications that Durkheim considers to be the point of departure for all higher forms of rational thought, the sciences included. Since what he says on this score is so seldom mentioned by his commentators, I shall quote him *in extenso*:

It is true that this logic [of identification] is disconcerting for us. Yet we must be careful not to depreciate it: howsoever crude it may appear to us, it has been an aid of the greatest importance in the intellectual evolution of humanity. In fact, it is through it that the first explanation of the world has been made possible. Of course the mental habits it implies prevented men from seeing reality as their senses show it to them; but as their senses show it, it has the grave inconvenience of allowing of no explanation. For to explain is to attach things to each other and to establish relations between them which make them appear as functions of each other and as vibrating sympathetically according to an internal law founded in their nature. But sensations, which see nothing except from the outside, could never make them disclose these relations and internal bonds; the intellect alone can create the notion of them. When I learn that A regularly precedes B, my knowledge is increased by a new fact; but my intelligence is not at all satisfied with a statement which does not show its reason. I commence to *understand* only if it is possible for me to conceive B in such a way that makes it appear to me as something that is not foreign to A, and united to A by some relation of kinship. The great service that religions have rendered to thought is that they have constructed a first representation of what these relations of kinship between things may be. In the circumstances under which it was attempted, the enterprise could obviously only attain precarious results. But then, does it ever attain any that are more definite, and is it not always necessary to reconsider them?

And also, it is less important to succeed than to try. The essential thing was not to leave the mind enslaved to visible appearances, but to teach it to dominate them and to connect what the senses separated; for from the moment when men have an idea that there are internal connections between things, science and philosophy become possible. Religion opened up the way for them. But if it has been able to play this part, it is only because it is a social affair. In order to make a law for the impressions of the senses and to substitute a new way of representing reality for them, thought of a new sort had to be founded: this is collective thought. If this alone has had this efficacy, it is because of the fact that to create a world of ideals through which the world of experienced realities would appear transfigured, a superexcitation of the intellectual forces was necessary, which is possible only in and through society.

So it is far from true that this mentality has no connection with ours. Our logic was born of this logic. The explanations of contemporary science are surer of being objective because they are more methodical and because they rest on more carefully controlled observations, but they do not differ in nature from those that satisfy primitive thought. Today as formerly, to explain is to show how one thing participates in one of several others. It has been said that the participations of this sort implied by the mythologies violate the principle of contradiction and that they are by that opposed to those implied by scientific explanations. [A footnote here referring to Lévy-Bruhl's *Les Fonctions* . . .] Is not the statement that a man is a kangaroo or the sun a bird, equal to identifying the two with each other? But our manner of thought is not different when we say of heat that it is a movement, or of light that it is a vibration of the ether, etc. Every time that we unite heterogenous terms by an internal bond, we forcibly identify contraries. Of course the terms we unite are not those which the Australian brings together; we choose them according to different criteria and for different reasons; but the processes by which the mind puts them in connection do not differ essentially . . .

Thus between the logic of religious thought and the logic of scientific thought there is no abyss. The two are made up of the same elements, though inequally and differently developed.[35]

In these paragraphs lies a treasury of profound reflection on the nature of theory and of its relation to common sense. In essence, Durkheim's case is that common sense is a very limited intellectual instrument, and that had we never gone beyond it we would never have started to develop the sciences. Yet we can only go beyond it by making use of ideas about an order of events which lies outside the direct grasp of the senses. By the use of such ideas about an unobservable order of things (what Durkheim calls 'a world of ideals'), we can grasp causal connections which common sense could never have dreamed of. We can grasp unities of process where common sense could have seen only diversity and unrelatedness. But such ideas, so crucial to the development of higher thought, could never have occurred to us had it not been for the primal religious situation in which man was driven to them as the only way of accounting for society's impact on him. So it is that we can find the vital germ of the most elaborate sciences in the first stirrings of the most primitive religions.

Some people, of course, will grant that Durkheim gives a fair account of the intellectual function of unobservable entities in the sciences, but will object that, in drawing a parallel with the spirits and occult influences of religion, he is seizing upon a superficial resemblance which conceals a very deep difference. Such critics will contend that, whilst ideas about atoms and forces refer to the context of the ordinary and the natural, ideas about gods and spirits refer to the context of the extraordinary, the mysterious, the supernatural. Durkheim, however, has already dealt with these objections. For in his first chapter he has given a very cogent dismissal of the attempt to define religion in terms of the mysterious and the supernatural. Several of the things he says there strongly reinforce the passages we have just considered. Thus:

the rites which he [primitive man] employs to assure the fertility of his soil or the fecundity of the animal species on which he is nourished do not appear more irrational to his eyes than the technical processes of which our agriculturalists make use, for the same object, do to ours. The powers which he puts into play by these diverse means do not seem to him to have anything especially mysterious about them. Undoubtedly these forces are different from those the modern scientist thinks of, and whose use he teaches us; they have a different way of acting, and do not allow themselves to be directed in the same manner; but for those who believe in them they are no more unintelligible than are gravitation and electricity for the physicist of today. Moreover, we shall see, in the course of this work, that the idea of physical forces is very probably derived from that of religious forces; then there cannot exist between the two the abyss that separates the rational from the irrational. Even the fact that religious forces are frequently conceived under the form of spiritual beings or conscious wills, is no proof of their irrationality. The reason has no repugnance *a priori* to admitting that the so-called inanimate bodies should be directed by intelligences, just as the human body is, though contemporary science accommodates itself with difficulty to this hypothesis. When Leibniz proposed to conceive the external world as an immense society of minds, between which there were, and could be, only spiritual relations, he thought he was working as a rationalist, and saw nothing in this universal animism which could be offensive to the intellect.[36]

Again:

In whatever manner men have represented the novelties and contingencies revealed by experience, there is nothing in these representations that could serve to characterise religion. For religious conceptions have as their object, before everything else, to express and explain, not that which is exceptional and abnormal in things, but, on the contrary, that which is normal and regular. Very frequently, the gods serve less to account for the monstrosities, fantasies and anomalies than for the regular march of the universe, for the movement of the stars, the rhythm of the seasons, the annual growth of vegetation, the perpetuation of species, etc. It is far from being true, then, that the notion of religions coincides with that of the extraordinary or the unforeseen.[37]

Having stressed the continuities which underlie the superficial differences between primitive religious and modern scientific thought, Durkheim does go on to say something about what makes science different from pre-scientific theoretical thinking. But although he makes it clear that the difference is one of profound importance for man's cognitive control of his environment, he nonetheless maintains that it is a difference in degree rather than in kind. In his own words:

contrary to all appearances, as we have pointed out, the realities to which religious speculation is then applied are the same which later serve as the subject of reflection for philosophers: they are nature, man, society. The mystery which appears to surround them is wholly superficial and disappears before a more painstaking observation: it is enough merely to set aside the veil with which mythological imagination has covered them for them to appear as they really are. Religion sets itself to translate these realities into an intelligible language which does not differ from that employed by science; the attempt is made by both to connect things with each other, to establish internal relations between them, to classify them and to systematize them. We have seen that the essential ideas of scientific logic are of religious origin. It is true that in order to utilize them, science gives them a new elaboration; it purges them of all accidental elements; in a general way, it brings a spirit of criticism into all its doing, which religion ignores; it surrounds itself with precautions to escape 'precipitation and bias', and to hold aside the passions, prejudices, and all subjective influences. But these perfectionings of method are not enough to differentiate it from religion. In this regard, both pursue the same end; scientific thought is only a more perfect form of religious thought.[38]

As a refined and hence more efficient instrument of explanation, science gradually but inexorably supersedes religion in area after area of human experience. Though it finds least resistance in the area of inert things, and most resistance in the area of 'higher' human behaviour, it seems destined to make inroads even into the latter. At the same time, however, there are certain residual functions of religion which science cannot fulfil. Hence whilst science seems destined to supersede religion in most contexts of life, it cannot do so in all:

Having left religion, science tends to substitute itself for this latter in all that which concerns the cognitive and intellectual functions. Christianity has already definitely consecrated this substitution in the order of material things. Seeing in matter that which is profane before all else, it readily left knowledge of this to another discipline, *tradidit mundum hominum disputationi*, 'He gave the world over to the disputes of men'; it is thus that the natural sciences have been able to establish themselves and make their authority recognized without very great difficulty. But it could not give up the world of souls so easily; for it is above all over souls that the god of the Christians aspires to reign. That is why the idea of submitting the psychic life to science produced the effect of a sort of profanation for a long time; even today it is repugnant to many minds. However, experimental and comparative psychology is founded and today we must reckon with it. But the world of the religious and the moral life is still forbidden. The great majority of men continue to believe that there is an order of things which the mind cannot penetrate except by very special ways. Hence comes the active resistance which is met with every time that someone tries to treat religious and moral phenomena scientifically. But in spite of these oppositions, these attempts are constantly repeated and this persistence even allows us to foresee that this final barrier will finally give way and that science will establish herself as mistress even in this reserved region ...

Since there is no proper subject for religious speculation outside that reality to which scientific reflection is applied, it is evident that this former cannot play the same role in the future that it has played in the past.

However, it seems destined to transform itself rather than to disappear ...

For faith is above all else an impetus to action, while science, no matter how far it may be pushed, always remains at a distance from this. Science is fragmentary and incomplete; it advances but slowly and is never finished; but life cannot wait. The theories which are destined to make men live and act are therefore obliged to pass science and complete it prematurely.[39]

In other words, in becoming more efficient, science becomes more cautious in its claims to explanatory competence and completeness. But, moving in this direction, it becomes less and less the complete guide to action which the average man requires to help him live his everyday life. Alongside it, therefore, we tend to find an all-embracing world-view which takes as its point of departure the agreed findings of the sciences, but which goes well beyond such findings to fill in the various gaps left by the scientists.

With all Durkheim's fanatical determination to provide social determinants for every nuance of human behaviour, it is a little surprising to find that *Les Formes Elémentaires* includes no clear suggestion as to the broad social determinants of the transition from the religious to the scientific consciousness. Probably, his untimely death anticipated a synthesis in which the scheme of social evolution outlined in *La Division du Travail Social* would have been co-ordinated with the scheme of ideational evolution outlined in *Les Formes Elémentaires*. From his brief remarks on the subject in *La Division du Travail Social*, one may surmise that he would have made the growth of individualism the crucial variable, but would have shown at the same time how the most individualist thought could operate only with the aid of devices inherited from collective thought.[40]

In this exposition of what I take to be Durkheim's central thesis, I have tried hard to convey the sustained argument, coherence and panache with which he presents it. However, I should be caricaturing his work if I did not admit that *Les Formes Elémentaires* contains a subsidiary train of thought which is not merely difficult to reconcile with the main thesis, but is actually in opposition to it.

I am thinking, here, of the contention that in all cultures there is to be found a division of the world into two radically contrasted categories of things sacred and things profane. The sacred, which includes not only gods and spirits but also holy objects and actions, is defined as the category of ideas, objects and actions which are associated with a peculiar attitude of awe and respect in virtue of their being symbols of society. The profane is defined as the category of ideas, objects and actions which have no such symbolic function and hence attract no such attitude of awe and respect.

Associated with this contention is the implication that, as social life becomes more complex, so the sacred declines in importance whilst the profane waxes stronger. Hence the transition from primitive to modern involves the decline of one mode of thought and the rise of another strongly contrasted with it.[41]

Quite clearly, this subsidiary train of thought has implications which are very hard to reconcile with Durkheim's main thesis. To have suppressed it in exposition, however, would have meant leaving out what to most modern social scientists is the more familiar aspect of his thought.

Most readers, indeed, are likely to be thoroughly puzzled by my exposition. For they have been brought up to believe that what I call Durkheim's subsidiary thesis is in fact his principal if not his only thesis. As for what I have taken as his principal thesis, this for many will be the first time they have heard of it. Some may even be wondering if it isn't just a figment of my imagination!

Since one of the central questions I shall be going on to tackle in this essay is that of why this very striking aspect of Durkheim's sociology of ideas has been so neglected by posterity, it may be as well at this point to try and whistle up some conclusive evidence that this *is* the central thesis and not just a marginal aberration.

Happily, the strongest possible piece of evidence does exist – nothing less than a review by Durkheim himself, in the *Année Sociologique*, which compares and contrasts Lévy-Bruhl's *Fonctions Mentales* with his own *Formes Elémentaires*.[42]

In this review, Durkheim notes that both Lévy-Bruhl and himself are concerned to explore the sense of the distinction that is commonly made between 'primitive' and 'modern' thought. Both are in agreement about the social determinants of all thought, and about the essentially religious nature of 'primitive' thought. Beyond this point, however, they part company. Thus Lévy-Bruhl sees 'primitive' and 'modern' thought as antithetical, and the movement from one to the other as the replacement of one pattern by its opposite. Durkheim, on the other hand, sees 'primitive' and 'modern' as two stages in a single evolutionary process, the latter developing out of the former. At many points where Lévy-Bruhl finds contrast and discontinuity, Durkheim claims that a closer look would reveal a fundamental continuity.

In this context, he singles out the so-called 'law of participation' for special mention. Lévy-Bruhl sees this 'law' as the exemplar of everything that is most opposed to the spirit of science. Durkheim suggests, to the contrary, that what Lévy-Bruhl calls 'participation' is at the core of all logical life. He ends his review, in fact, by referring the reader back on this matter to the passage in *Les Formes Elémentaires* which I quoted so extensively earlier on.[43]

Though I hesitate to argue from omission in a very compressed exposition of two substantial books, I think it is noteworthy that this review contains no mention of the sacred-profane dichotomy.

Whatever the significance of this last fact, the review in question leaves us in little doubt that Durkheim regarded the strand of his thinking which I have dwelt on at such length here as being the main burden of his message in the sociology of ideas.

Opposing views of the great transition

We are now in a position to compare the central views of Lévy-Bruhl and Durkheim on the characteristics of 'primitive' and 'modern' thought patterns, and on the nature of the transition from one type to the other.

Both masters define their field of operation in much the same way, taking sociology to be concerned with 'collective representations', rather than with individual thought-products. Both define collective representations as ideas that are not only shared by most members of the group, but also come to members from outside themselves, having been handed down by the accredited agents of tradition. This second criterion, incidentally, is almost impossibly restrictive of causal analysis; and, not surprisingly, both fall foul of it when offering causal interpretations of thought-patterns.[44]

Both masters make the impact of society on the individual responsible for the distinctive features of 'primitive' thinking. Both invoke the growth of individualism in society as the key to the transition from 'primitive' to 'modern' thinking.

For both Lévy-Bruhl and Durkheim, the impact of periods of intense group activity on the individual results in the formation of ideas about a world of unobservable forces lying behind the world of visible, tangible things. When it comes to the significance of this world of unobservables, however, the two masters take diametrically opposite views.

For Lévy-Bruhl, as we have seen, the essential point about the impact of intense social activity on the individual is the emotion which it provokes. Ideas about unobservables are essentially verbalizations of such emotion. Subjective rather than objective in origin, these ideas are the great obstacles to the emergence of rational thought; for they turn men's minds away from the world as it really is. True, they establish all sorts of links between events in the visible, tangible world. But these links, the notorious participations, do not correspond to anything in reality. Indeed, they distract men's attention from the links that do have an objective foundation. Until men's thoughts are turned away from the world of unobservables, then, science cannot be born.

For Durkheim, on the other hand, ideas about unobservables are an objective response to the impact of society upon the individual. Being objective rather than subjective in origin, they are the *sine qua non* of higher forms of reasoning. Indeed, the day on which they emerge is the birthday of such higher forms. This is so because one can only start to do justice to the patterning of the world when one has escaped from enslavement to common-sense appearances. Far from being a distraction from the world as it really is, the participations created by ideas of an unobservable order are man's most powerful tools for understanding this world.

Although both masters seem to agree that the key social factor in the transition from 'primitive' to 'modern' thinking is the growth of individualism, their diametrically opposed conceptions of the significance of unobservable entities lead them to very different notions as to the nature of this transition. Thus, for Lévy-Bruhl, it involves atrophy of all forms of thought featuring unobservables, and vast expansion of an undifferentiated common-sense/science which confines itself to induction from visible and tangible phenomena. One mode of thought gives way before its opposite. For Durkheim, the picture is very different. In the first place common sense, which is as distinct from science as it is from religion, remains on the sidelines, retaining much the same position in 'modern' thought as it enjoyed in 'primitive' thought. Secondly, the essence of the transition lies not in the scrapping of ideas about unobservables, but rather in their progressive specialization as tools of man's explanatory enterprise. To put it in a nutshell, Lévy-Bruhl sees the relation between 'primitive' and 'modern' in terms of contrast, and the transition between them as a process of inversion, whilst Durkheim sees the relation in terms of continuity, and the transition as a process of evolution. For purposes of shorthand, I shall talk in what follows of a contrast/inversion schema as opposed to a continuity/evolution schema.

This comparative summary is, of course, an oversimplification. For, as I said earlier, although there is recognizably one Lévy-Bruhl, there are at least two Durkheims. In choosing which Durkheim to use in the comparison, I have been guided by the master's own opinion. Nevertheless, we should not forget that, in some of Durkheim's remarks about the sacred and the profane, there is implicit a contrast/inversion schema which is difficult if not impossible to reconcile with the evolutionist main line in his thought, and which is reminiscent of Lévy-Bruhl. This conflict within Durkheim's sociology of ideas must be kept in mind if we are to understand fully the peculiar exegesis of the two masters in the work of subsequent generations of Western sociologists and social anthropologists.

The masters and the moderns

Before we review the influence of Lévy-Bruhl and Durkheim on the contemporary sociology of thought, we should first pause to note the enormous influence of Durkheim on the social sciences generally. In the context of Euro-American sociology and social anthropology, it is perhaps more than ever appropriate to accord Durkheim the accolade of 'The Master'; for despite new accumulations of data and new thereoreticians, people are mining the rich seams of his thought as energetically as ever, and yet these seams show little sign of exhaustion.

The most influential aspect of Durkheim's work is probably his boundary-drawing exercise, designed to establish the autonomy of sociology from psychology and other neighbouring disciplines. Since I have referred earlier to his definition of collective (sociological) facts as a species distinct from individual (psychological) facts, I will not dwell on it further here. Nor, for the same reasons, will I dwell on the difficulty of operating with this definition. I shall rest content with pointing out that the definition has had an enormous appeal to members of a young discipline struggling hard to establish a distinct identity and a distinct institutional existence, and that it is widely, indeed unreflectively, taught to most present-day students.

But Durkheim's general influence rests also on other more solid foundations. His attempt to find variables with which to characterize total organizations (e.g. mechanical versus organic solidarity) has rightly caught the imagination of posterity. So too has his feeling for the relationship between what to the untutored eye seem the most diverse aspects of social life (e.g. broad patterns of socio-economic cooperation, systems of legal procedure, suicide rates).

All these constitute grounds for influence which were established before either Lévy-Bruhl or Durkheim himself had published their main works on the sociology of thought. One reason for the approving reception given to Lévy-Bruhl by social scientists was that his work was sponsored by Durkheim (it was published in the *Année Sociologique* series), and that he proclaimed the Durkheimian goals of confining the study to the field of collective representations and of dealing with the relation of patterns of thought to types of society. Again, a major reason for the approving professional reception of Durkheim's own *Formes Elémentaires* was the nature of the general programme expounded in his earlier works.

So much for the factors that have made social scientists broadly receptive to what the two masters have had to say about the Great Transition. Let us now look at some details of their exegesis.

The most striking feature of this exegesis is its emphasis on a contrast/ inversion schema and its neglect of the continuity/evolution schema. Where the conceptual framework draws heavily on Lévy-Bruhl, the talk is of 'mystical' versus 'empirical' behaviour, or of 'mystical' versus 'rational' behaviour. Where the framework draws more heavily on Durkheim, the talk is of 'sacred' versus 'profane'. In both cases, religion and art tend to be bundled into one category; common sense, technology and science into the other. In both cases the two categories are seen as radically contrasted. Traditional societies[45] are thought to be strong in the first and weak, though not lacking, in the second. Hence the movement from traditional to modern is seen as a replacement of one category by its opposite.

The exact terms of the contrast between the categories are usually within the bounds of the possibilities laid down by the two masters; but they vary from scholar to scholar. Thus Radcliffe-Brown and Max Gluckman (who is perhaps his most direct heir) emphasize the contrast between the categories, but do not care to go into much detail about content. For them, the principal interest of the contrast is the indication it provides for different kinds of interpretation. Thus 'mystical' behaviour is to be accounted for in terms of its supposed contribution to social harmony – by 'sociological explanation'. 'Logico-empirical' behaviour, on the other hand, is to be accounted for in terms of ends in the minds of actors, together with objective observation of the conditions sufficient for the attainment of such ends. In Gluckman, especially, there is a strong implication that one of the main concerns of social anthropologists (if not of sociologists) is with 'mystical' behaviour and with 'sociological' explanation. He stresses the link between the two in his characterization of social anthropology as concerned with 'the logic of the irrational'.[46]

Malinowski, though he is one of the main critics of the early Lévy-Bruhl, sticks close to the latter's formulation of the contrast. Thus he talks of magico-religious behaviour as triggered by situations which arouse intense emotion, and as providing a channel for the expression of such emotion. He lumps together common sense, technology and science, and talks of them as concerned with a variety of ends for which the means are chosen by inductive observation.[47]

Roger Bastide, the eminent French Afro-Americanist, develops another facet of Lévy-Bruhl's contrast when he characterizes African traditional thought in terms of a communion between subject and object, and Western thought in terms of the mastery of subject over object. Like Lévy-Bruhl, he sees these two modes of relationship as opposed, and the transition from one to the other as an inversion rather than an evolution.[48] J. V. Taylor, the theologian, missionary sociologist and Africanist, works out a similar scheme in his *Primal Vision*.[49]

Among those who claim to derive their inspiration from Durkheim rather than from Lévy-Bruhl, most start out from his contrast between the sacred and the profane. They have tended, however, to pack into the first category not only behaviour symbolic of man's relation to society, but all other symbolic behaviour as well. The second category they reserve for behaviour directed to certain ends and guided by inductive observation of the means appropriate to those ends. For them, the sacred (or symbolic) includes ritual and art, the profane (or logico-empirical) common sense, technology and science. A further refinement on Durkheim is the thesis that the two categories refer, not to different spheres of behaviour, but to different aspects of every sequence of behaviour. But, whatever the particular reinterpretations they favour, these *soi-disant* followers of Durkheim tend to agree on seeing the sacred and the profane as radically contrasted, and on seeing the transition from 'primitive' to 'modern' as an inversion in which the sacred progressively gives way to the profane. Prominent among this school are Talcott Parsons the sociologist, and Firth, Leach and Beattie the social anthropologists.[50]

Even the great Claude Lévi-Strauss fits, albeit in his own inimitable way, into the contrast/inversion school.

Thus, although at several points in his work he inveighs against Lévy-Bruhl, he perpetuates the latter's radical opposition between religion, which he sees as the domain of confusion and emotion, and science, which he sees as the domain of distinction and reason.[51] And although he largely avoids reference to the religious component of traditional thought-patterns, apparently feeling it too distasteful to mention,[52] he seems to agree that one of the features of the move from tradition to modernity is a move from religious to scientific thinking.

Again, in his more positive characterization of the traditional and the modern, a neo-Durkheimian form of contrast/inversion schema is evident. Thus he distinguishes two forms of thought: 'wild thought' (*pensée sauvage*), dominant in traditional cultures, and 'domesticated thought' (*pensée domestiquée*), dominant in modern cultures. He stresses that the two forms are essentially incommensurable, and that they are devoted to different ends. Wild thought attempts to grasp the world through symbol and metaphor. It is non-practical in intent. Domesticated thought is concerned with fitting means to ends through the use of literal speech and discursive reason. It aims at achieving practical goals, and its development is controlled by success or failure in achieving these goals.[53]

In many respects, Lévi-Strauss's formulation resembles those of Parsons,

Firth and Beattie. But whereas these more sober souls tend to be concerned with the reference of particular symbols to particular phenomena, Lévi-Strauss is concerned with systems of symbols and with their reference, as wholes, to often complex relations between phenomena. To take a somewhat oversimplified example, the sober Anglo-Saxon symbolist may be interested in tracing the symbolic reference of a particular animal to some social group. Lévi-Strauss, in a comparable situation, will be interested in the symbolic reference of a number of different animal species, considered as a set, to the structural relations of a number of different sub-groups within a society. The concern with sets and relations gives his thought an elaborateness and intricacy which seem to distinguish it from the thought of most of his anthropological contemporaries. But this surface difference should not be allowed to obscure its affinities with other variants of the contrast/inversion schema.

A remarkable thing about so many adherents of this schema is the way in which they acknowledge Durkheimian inspiration, yet determinedly ignore the continuity/evolution schema which makes up an important part of their master's great work. This curious combination of attitudes is well exemplified by Talcott Parsons, whose *Structure of Social Action* is so often recommended to students as the classic exegesis of Durkheim, Pareto and Weber. Early on in this book, Parsons reluctantly notes Durkheim's ideas about the continuity between religion and the sciences, and dismisses these ideas with inadequate argument and an air of embarrassment. By the conclusion of the book, Parsons has managed to persuade himself that Durkheim never had any such ideas, and extols him as one of those who swept away Victorian ideas about religion as the precursor of science and about the transition from 'primitive' to 'modern' as an evolutionary process.[54]

To put it briefly, orthodox modern social scientists tend to proclaim themselves disciples of Durkheim in their approach to the study of religion. But, in their actual analyses, they ignore the main theme of their master's work in this sphere, and extol an inconsistent minor theme.

This is a very odd situation. Let us turn to a brief review of the relevant research data, to see whether these can help us to answer the questions it raises.

The data

Perhaps we should start by saying that, in the fifty years since the two masters first propounded their theses, no data have emerged that are in any way relevant to the question of ultimate origins. Indeed, it has become clear that such data are unobtainable. So we must conclude that, in providing elaborate accounts of the genesis of ideas about spiritual beings and similar entities, the masters have done no more than give us untestable 'just-so' stories.[55]

However, a great deal of what both Lévy-Bruhl and Durkheim have to say relates not to the ultimate origins of ideas about unobservables, but to the factors that sustain such ideas once they have been launched. Here we are dealing with testable theses. And in the last fifty years enough data have accumulated to allow us to decide between them. Such data are of three kinds. First, there are data on the thought-patterns of those pre-literate, pre-industrial societies known to the masters as 'primitive' and to ourselves as 'traditional' or 'underdeveloped'. Second, there are data on the thought-patterns of the sciences and of the modern industrial societies that support them. Third, there are data on certain features of human thinking which may well be common to all societies, whether traditional or modern.

In dealing with data of the first kind, I shall restrict myself to those thrown up by fieldwork in the traditional societies of Africa. One reason for this self-imposed limitation is that my own research and most intensive reading have been in the African field. The other is that African data have been the most frequently cited by recent theorists of the nature of traditional thought-patterns.

Five outstanding producers of data in this field are Evans-Pritchard, with his monographs on Zande and Nuer thought-systems; Fortes, with his brief but brilliant *Oedipus and Job* (a monograph on Tallensi religion); Lienhardt, with his *Divinity and Experience: the Religion of the Dinka*; Middleton, with his *Lugbara Religion*; and finally Turner, with his host of papers and books on Ndembu religion.[56]

In so far as they have been concerned with making theoretical points, all of these authors have relied on more or less explicit contrast schemes of the 'mystical/empirical', 'sacred/profane' type. But the message that the uncommitted outsider gets from reading these works is not really consistent with such schemata. For in all of them he sees ideas about 'mystical' entities as forming more or less coherent systems of postulates which serve to display the unity underlying the apparent diversity of everyday experience, the order underlying apparent irregularity, the causal enchainment underlying apparent randomness.[57] Again, in all of these works he sees a very subtle relationship between the observable world of people, animals, plants and things, and the unobservable world of the spirits. As Evans-Pritchard and Lienhardt have made particularly clear in their searching phenomenological examinations, the spiritual world is not an immediate datum of experience, but only a situationally invoked interpretation of it. For the African farmer as for the European townsman, the world immediately given and reacted to is the common-sensical world of living and talking men and women, living but uncommunicative animals and plants, and inert water, stone, soil and metal. Through much of life, this common-sensical framework is quite sufficient for the conduct of affairs. Only intermittently, when it fails to provide adequate guidance, is there a resort to ideas about the spiritual beings who are thought to underpin the common-sensical world and its events. From these works, then, the so-called animist no longer emerges as someone who sees and reacts to animals, plants and inert things as if they were persons, or as someone for whom the boundaries between the personal and impersonal are blurred.[58]

Reviewing the impressions he gets from this work, the uncommitted observer is likely to conclude that traditional ideas about unobservable entities are most appropriately described, neither as symbolic substitutes for literal discourse, nor as expressions of emotion, nor yet as manifestations of some mystic communion between man and nature, but simply as theoretical concepts couched in a slightly unfamiliar idiom. He may even go on, more specifically, to conclude that such ideas form the basis of often highly sophisticated social psychologies.

Since use of the phrases 'theoretical concepts' and 'social psychologies' inevitably implies comparison with thought-patterns in the modern West, this seems the appropriate point at which to turn to data of the second kind – i.e. data on the sciences. Here again, there has been a fairly spectacular accumulation since the days of the masters; either in the form of works by philosophers and historians of science on the nature of the scientific enterprise, or in the form of reports by eminent scientists on what they see as the essence of their calling. The main burden of such work has been to show the crucial importance of concepts relating to unobservable or theoretical entities, and the impossibility of giving an account of scientific activity that neglects such concepts. Indeed, a good deal of the debate among philosophers of science during the last two decades seems to have been inspired by Eddington's famous problem of the Two Tables – the hard, solid table of common-sense thought and action; and the largely empty space, peopled by minuscule planetary systems, of theoretical thought and action.[59] The key questions of the debate have been (a) which of the Two Tables is the real one? and (b) is there any sense at all in which both could be real? As the debate stands at the moment, a fair judgement would seem to be that, on the one hand, common-sense discourse and material-object concepts can never be eliminated from thought and life; whilst, on the other hand, the criteria used for deciding the validity of statements about theoretical entities do not differ in essentials from the criteria used for deciding the validity of statements about material objects. Hence we may have to settle for the reality of both tables, and for a mysterious unity-in-duality which holds between them.[60] The homology with 'mystical participation' could hardly be clearer.

Recent writings on the nature of the scientific enterprise have shown up all too clearly the inadequacy of the old inductivist account which ultimately made science out to be nothing more than a vast expansion and systematization of common sense. From now on, common sense and a good deal of technology must be viewed as distinct from science. As Stephen Toulmin pointed out in his study of Western chemistry, this distinction should have been obvious long ago to anyone who cared to consult the historical record. In the case of chemistry, for instance, chemical theory, for all its change and development down the ages, made little difference to the practical use of natural resources until after 1850.[61]

In view of these developments in the history, phenomenology and philosophy of the sciences, it is hardly surprising that their authors, looking across at the growing body of data on 'traditional' thought-systems, have been struck by continuities rather than by contrasts. Thus Polanyi has used Evans-Pritchard's portrayal of the way in which Azande relate their theory of misfortune to the vicissitudes of everyday existence as a means of throwing light on the way in which scientists relate theory to experimental data. And although some would say that Polanyi is describing science in an unfortunately conservative mood, the force of the parallel still remains.[62]

Again, Pierre Auger, himself an eminent theoretical physicist, has shown how Lévi-Strauss, in attempting to specify the distinctive features of *pensée sauvage*, has unwittingly succeeded in describing some of the key features of scientific thought. In particular, he points out that the use of analogy and of *bricolage* is central to the development of scientific theory.[63]

Karl Popper, too, has stressed the element of continuity between traditional and scientific theories. He has emphasized that they are to be distinguished, not in terms of content or even in terms of logical structure, but rather in terms of the presence or absence of the critical spirit. And this of course is a matter of degree rather than of kind.[64]

Much the same point has been made more obliquely by Fred Hoyle, who in a rather subtle science-fiction novel has shown that animism, in itself, has much the same status as any other kind of theory, and that, if the facts of the world were a little different, it could be used to provide a scientifically acceptable interpretation of them.[65]

Finally, let me turn to data of the third kind. Here, I am thinking in particular of the experiments performed by Michotte and his Louvain School of psychologists on the perception of causality. Although the subjects of these experiments are European men and women, there is good reason to believe that some of the findings on their behaviour may be universally applicable. The most interesting of these is that people tend to perceive causal connections between phenomena only under certain limited conditions, of which spatio-temporal contiguity and dimensional commensurability seem to be amongst the most important.[66] This finding has momentous implications for the understanding of human cognitive activity; for it enables us for the first time to understand why human beings in all cultures *have* to invoke theory in their attempt to gain cognitive control of their environment.   Briefly, what Michotte shows us is that the human being is not an inductive machine capable of automatic registration of all causal connections presented to him in his everyday experience. On the contrary, he has the most limited capacity for registering such connections. And so far in human history, theory, with its apparatus of unobservables underpinning the visible, tangible world, is the only means man has discovered of overcoming this limitation.

In summarizing the implications of these recent accumulations of data for our two opposed schemata, we can say for a start that they are unfavourable to all variants of the contrast/inversion schema.

So far as traditional thought-systems are concerned, variants of the contrast/inversion schema either misdescribe the data, or fail to account for them, or both. Misdescription is evident in the idea of traditional communion with nature. It is equally evident in the classification of statements about spiritual beings as symbolic rather than explanatory. Failure to account for the data is evident in all versions. Thus Lévy-Bruhl's version, in relating 'mystical influences' to an ill-defined and inchoate flow of emotion, is simply trying to dispose of a mystery by enfolding it in a far greater one. Gluckman's version, in seeking to explain ideas of spiritual beings in terms of their contribution to social equilibrium, fails to show why people should get addicted to this particular way of maintaining equilibrium, rather than to any one of a score of others. Why, for instance, should they not take to cathartic football matches rather than to religious rituals? Beattie's version, in seeking to explain ideas of spiritual beings as symbols, fails in a similar way. Beattie makes out quite a good case as to why people may feel the need for personal symbols of events and processes in their environment; but he makes out no case whatsoever as to why they feel the need for persons with the unobservability, omnipresence and other puzzling attributes of spirits. Beattie's version could account for the prevalence of priests in traditional societies. It cannot account for the prevalence of spirits.

So far as modern thought-patterns are concerned, variants of the contrast/inversion schema are equally fruitless. Thus their inductivist definition of science completely ignores the crucial role played by theoretical discourse and unobservable entities. It also blurs the distinction between common sense and technology on the one hand, and science on the other. None of the modern versions of this schema even attempts to explain the emergence of science.

When we turn to the continuity/evolution schema, however, we find that recent accumulations of data have given an almost prophetic quality to Durkheim's version of it. His emphasis on the limitations of common sense and on the universal need for theory as a means of extending man's grasp of causal relations not only foreshadows the work of Michotte, but draws out implications from this work which the author himself does not yet appear to have thought of. Durkheim's emphasis on the continuities between traditional religious theory and modern scientific theory foreshadows the work of such avant-garde historians and philosophers of science as Hesse, Popper and Polanyi.[67] In particular, his hint that traditional religious theory may be seen as a precursor of modern social psychology receives striking confirmation in Fortes's work on West African theories of the individual's relation to his society.[68] Again, in stressing that the mysterious relation of unity-in-duality which Lévy-Bruhl christened 'participation' is at the centre not only of religious but also of scientific thinking, he points forward to a topic that has been a prominent feature of the debates of the last decade in the philosophy of science.[69]

In Durkheim's specification of the differences between the traditional and the modern, we find an equally prophetic quality. His emphasis on the critical spirit, on the determination to exclude from the theory-building enterprise all notions other than those involved in the search for explanation, on the refusal to complete a theoretical picture when the data do not warrant it – all these are in line with attempts to define the distinctive character of science by such contemporary philosophers as Toulmin and Popper. His stress on the gradual evolution and differentiation of the scientific outlook from pre-scientific cognitive operations is also in line with the views of such thinkers.

Not only does Durkheim's schema provide the framework for adequate description of the relations between traditional and modern thought-patterns. It provides intellectually satisfying explanations of certain crucial features of such patterns, and also points to further possibilities of explanation. Thus, unlike any of the versions of the contrast/inversion schema, it accounts successfully for the universal presence of ideas about a world of unobservables in human cognitive operations. Again, by emphasizing that such ideas have the same function in traditional as in modern cultures, it leads us to look at the considerable amount of work done by Western philosophers on the relation between the forms of scientific theories and their functions, and on the relation between the idioms of these theories and the circumstances under which they are developed. By applying the results of this work to theories generally, we can start to ask and answer some crucial questions about differences of theoretical idiom. Thus we can ask, and answer, the question of why the theoretical idiom of traditional societies tends to be personal, whilst the idiom of modern societies tends to be impersonal.[70]

To sum up, we can say that a survey of recent accumulations of data in this area only deepens the mystery which surrounds the neglect of Durkheim's continuity/evolution schema. To dispel the fog, we shall have to approach the matter from another angle.

The contrast/inversion schema as a problem in the sociology of ideas

Three things have emerged clearly from our investigation so far. First, because of his boundary-staking activities on behalf of the subject, as well as because of other more constructive attitudes and insights, Durkheim is regarded down to this day as the founding father of Western sociology and social anthropology. Second, although most members of these disciplines tend to single out his *Formes Elémentaires* for special acclaim, the idea of radical contrast between religious and scientific thought, which they purport to derive from this book, is in fact entirely contradictory to his own published view of its main theme. Third, the recent accumulations of data, both on traditional and on modern thought-patterns, have made the contrast/inversion schema untenable whilst lending overwhelming support to Durkheim's continuity/evolution schema. Yet orthodox sociologists and social anthropologists continue to back contrast/inversion.

Since the outlook of contemporary orthodoxy owes so little either to its professed source of inspiration or to the recent accumulations of data, we can only treat this outlook as a problem in the sociology of ideas. That is, we have to ask ourselves what it owes to the broader ideological trends of the times, and to the social currents which underlie them. In what follows, I shall deal with two trends which seem to me to be highly relevant.

Liberal romanticism

The influence of late nineteenth-century ethos and social life on the founders of British social anthropology is impressed on most students of the subject early in their careers. Thus they are taught to look upon the works of Tylor and Frazer not as dispassionate reflections of the facts about traditional thought-patterns as these were then known, but rather as charters for the inflated Victorian self-image, and as typical products of a society engaged in the colonization and exploitation of non-Western peoples. Nor, I think, is this an unfair assessment.

Students, however, are often given the impression that with the advent of fieldwork and participant observation, in the early years of the present century, facts swept away ideology for good. And this is very far from being the case.[71]

It is true, of course, that no British anthropologist returning from two years of participant observation in an African or Polynesian village can ever again give serious consideration to Victorian theories that rest ultimately on a thesis of the childishness and stupidity of non-Western peoples. And thus far, facts *have* swept away ideology. As the present paper has shown, however, the body of theory which has come to replace these earlier doctrines bears very little more relation to the data than did its predecessors. And the reason is that, whilst facts have helped to sweep away the ideologically based theories of the nineteenth century, they have been overwhelmed again by ideology in the present century. For in Western ideology ethnocentrism and arrogance have given way to collective pessimism and self-questioning; and these are equally powerful and equally distorting in their influence on the study of man.

Some of the roots of this ideological revolution are two or three centuries old; for since their beginnings Western technology and science have generated not only a new confidence in man's power to control and improve his environment, but also an underlying doubt. The balance between confidence and doubt has tilted first to one side and then to the other; and the most one can say is that, through the greater part of the last three centuries, it has tended to come down on the side of confidence.

Here, we are more concerned with the doubt than with the confidence. Such doubt has focussed on two themes: the viability of social life, and the viability of reason. In what follows, we shall try to uncover the background to these preoccupations.

The rapid growth of industrial technology has in fact undermined the fabric of Western social life in four ways. First, through ever-changing organizational demands, it has introduced a more or less constant element of uncertainty into expectations about other people's behaviour. Second, through occupational specialization, it has given rise to a multiplicity of only partially overlapping world-views, and thence again to uncertainty in the sphere of role-expectations. Third, through depersonalization of the vast area of occupational relations in the name of efficiency, it has left one or two key relationships (e.g. marriage) with the enormous and all too frequently insupportable burden of fulfilling the entire range of human emotional needs. Fourth, through encouragement of addiction to an impersonal theoretical idiom, it has worked against religious belief and hence weakened an important emotional safety-net.[72] Here, clearly, we have the seeds of deep anxiety about the quality of social and emotional life.

Equally important has been the undermining of confidence in the discursive thought and the literal speech that we regard as the principal vehicles of human reason. Paradoxically, the loss of confidence in these areas has been largely due to the very factors that have promoted the growth of science.

There is little doubt that many features of the scientific outlook first developed as responses to the proliferation of competing idea-systems in seventeenth-century Europe. One effect of this proliferation was the growth of scepticism, of a readiness to challenge any and every idea regardless of its source. Another effect was the search for explicit criteria of choice in the realm of ideas. The most important outcome of this search was the gradual formulation of the ideal of objectivity: i.e. the rule that ideas which are to be used for purposes of explanation should not be allowed to become instruments of any other end, and that conversely any feature of such ideas which is not relevant to its explanatory purpose should be ruthlessly excised. Since the seventeenth century, scepticism and the search for objectivity have been the negative and positive mainprops of the scientific approach.

But the same proliferation of idea-systems generated another attitude which had very different implications. This was because it confronted men with two possible alternatives to ideas and words. First, they could continue to presume the old, unbreakable link between words and the situations they referred to – in which case they had to face the fact that there was no stable reality to which they could anchor themselves, but only an unpredictable flux. Second, they could accept the transience of the link between words and what they stood for – in which case they could console themselves with the belief in a reality that remained unchanged amidst the flux of ideas and words, a reality to which ideas and words might one day do justice. This second alternative was, of course, the one adopted; for whilst the first could only lead to despair, the second did provide some hope. With it, however, came a certain irreversible loss of confidence in the power of ordinary, literal language.

No one has drawn attention to this loss of confidence more vividly than Jean-Paul Sartre in his novel *La Nausée*. As Iris Murdoch puts it in her critical survey of Sartre's work:

The hero of *La Nausée* saw language and the world as hopelessly divided from each other. "The word remains on my lips: it refuses to go and rest on the thing." Language was an absurd structure of sounds and marks behind which lay an overflowing and undiscriminated chaos: the word which pretended to classify the infinitely and unclassifiably existent, the political slogan or social label or moral tag which concealed the formless heaving mass of human consciousness and human history.[73]

Here we have an attitude which, though it has been latent for long periods, has always constituted a potential denial of the very possibility of those faculties on which reason itself depends.

These two sources of pessimism have, as I have said, been counterbalanced over the last three hundred years by sources of optimism; and, through much of the nineteenth century, the latter certainly weighed more heavily in the scales.

With the advent of the twentieth century, however, two factors have intervened to push the balance heavily down on the side of pessimism. First, there have been numerous crude yet dramatic demonstrations of the potential horrors of science and technology – the very things on which Western superiority was allegedly based. Acceleration of the Industrial Revolution in the late nineteenth century produced a massive expansion of the urban proletariat and a spectacular deterioration in its living conditions.[74] Then came World War One, with its unprecedented revelation of the destructive power of technology. World War Two, Hiroshima, and the Pollution Era followed in quick succession. Second, there has been a profound and rapid change in the politico-economic relationship between the Western World and the non-West. From the seventeenth century down to the end of the nineteenth, there really was a sense in which European history was world history; for during this period events and policies in Europe had far more effect on events and policies in the rest of the inhabited world than vice versa. With the advent of the twentieth century, however, this has become increasingly untrue.

By the beginning of the century, European statesmen were already seeing many of their best-laid plans upset by events in Asia and America which were completely beyond their control. And in recent years the course of events in the Euro-American West has been increasingly influenced by events in the so-called Third World.[75] The resulting sense that the destiny of their civilization is at the mercy of pressures from outside the walls has led to a profound malaise amongst European intellectuals and leaders. The tail has begun to wag the dog; and the dog naturally feels alarmed.

The combination of these relatively recent disturbing factors with the long-established but latent forces enumerated earlier has been sufficient to evoke a full-blooded ideology of pessimism and self-doubt. Pervasive amongst non-scientific intellectuals, it has even established a partial hold over scientists themselves.

The key to this ideology is given by its attitude to the notion of progress. Of all the guiding notions of the nineteenth century, this is the one that has come in for the most ridicule. In its place have come notions of decline and decay, and of cyclical trends in human affairs. Though most professional historians have ridiculed Spengler and Toynbee for their inordinate explanatory ambitions, there are few who do not share their view of the downward trend in the fortunes of the West.[76]

There is a general despair about the quality of modern Western social life. Although Marxists have been most vociferous in deploring 'alienation', intellectuals at the other end of the political spectrum have been equally obsessed with such things as 'the essential loneliness of modern man'. An obverse of this despair is the cult of communion with nature as a means of 'getting away from it all', and the idea that such communion helps to repair the wounds inflicted on the soul by industrial society. Just as the forces making for dissatisfaction with the quality of Western social life have been gathering strength for several centuries, so too has the cult of communion with nature. In poetry, after all, it has been a prominent theme from Wordsworth onward.[77] Yet it is perhaps only during the last seventy years that this cult has played a major role in Western life, manifesting itself in a dozen ways that Westerners now take for granted but that non-Westerners find strange and distinctive: in the cult of the country hideaway, the lone walk through the woods, the lone scramble up the mountainside, or the lone voyage over the ocean – to name just a few.

Closely allied to the conviction that science and technology are destroying the fabric of society is the conviction that these things are choking the life of feeling. With this have come various movements assuming an antagonism between reason and feeling, and vociferously exalting the latter at the expense of the former. One of the most militant of these was Surrealism, a movement which was at its peak in the Paris of the twenties and thirties, but which created ripples in most Western capitals that have not yet died down. Its devotees displayed a contempt for reason, and for the outside world with which reason claimed to deal most effectively. They retreated into the inner world of emotion and feeling, and into modes of activity or inactivity which they saw as generating the most natural expressions of this world. Hence their interest in such things as automatic writing and dreaming.[78] Other movements in other Western countries had similar goals. In England, the exaltation of the 'dark, sensual side' of man was launched by D. H. Lawrence. In Germany, the same exaltation of feeling over reason was an important ingredient of Nazism. Though these and other movements have come and gone, the desire that feeling should conquer reason has remained close to the surface of Western life, ready to re-emerge at any time.

A final ingredient of the twentieth-century outlook is an obsession with the inadequacy of literal speech to reality, accompanied by a fascination with all forms of symbolism. Symbols are thought of as the means of 'saying' everything that is unsayable in terms of literal speech. They are thought to provide a superior means of grasping the particularity of events. Their non-conventional relation to their referents is seen as providing a more direct intuition of reality. Whereas ordinary literal speech gives a self-confessedly poor coverage of the inner world of emotion and feeling, symbolism claims a very extensive coverage of this world.

In their drive to eliminate everything irrelevant to the quest for explanation, scientists have tended to brand symbolism as a dangerous distraction. They have driven it into the licensed but somewhat second-rate enclave of the Arts. From this redoubt, however, its protagonists have waxed strong on those pervasive doubts about the adequacy of literal speech which even their opponents to some extent share with them.

The emergence of this new Western self-image has been closely accompanied by the emergence of a drastically new attitude towards the non-Western world. More specifically, the transition from nineteenth-century self-confidence to twentieth-century self-doubt has been accompanied by the transition from an attitude of contempt and aversion to one of respect and romantic fascination *vis-à-vis* non-Western cultures. Since the two transitions have occurred at the same times and places, often in the minds of the same people,[79] we may legitimately regard the link between them as non-accidental.

A more detailed portrayal of the various components of the new attitude will serve to elucidate the nature of this link.

Amongst Western intellectuals, the first two decades of the present century brought rebirth of respect for non-Western cultures; and this respect has been slowly but surely increasing ever since. It has been expressed in a determinedly sympathetic attitude towards non-Western cultures, in an avowal that each has its own peculiar merits, and above all in an avoidance of invidious comparisons. The resulting complex of attitudes can conveniently be summed up in the phrase 'liberal scruples'.

The influence of collective self-doubt on liberal scruples is not hard to understand. On the one hand, moral self-doubt leads to a heavy load of guilt about past arrogance *vis-à-vis* non-Western cultures, and to a very genuine desire to make amends for it. On the other hand, political self-doubt leads to a more circumspect attitude to powers over whom one would have ridden roughshod fifty years ago, and hence to a desire to maintain friendly relations with them for reasons of sheer expediency.

It is awareness of this dubious mixture of morality and expediency underpinning Western respect for non-Western cultures that evokes non-Westerners' bitter contempt for 'White Liberals'.

Like liberal scruples, the romantic fascination with non-Western cultures first made itself felt in the years just before World War One, and became even more noticeable in the years following the holocaust. Its noisiest propagandists were the Surrealists, who called for the abandonment of European values, and for wholesale importation of culture from Polynesia, China and other faraway places. Alongside them the Dadaists, led by Tristan Tzara, extolled the virtues of African culture.

To start with, the easiest way of getting oneself exposed to the regenerative influence of the traditional cultures was through contact with their material artefacts. Many of these were already lying about in European houses, museums and missionary headquarters, where they had been brought as trophies during the era of colonial expansion and conquest.

Given the right price, their possessors were perfectly willing to part with them to people fired with a more positive attitude toward them. Hence the quest for the traditional expressed itself first of all in a cult of 'primitive art'.[80]

Soon, however, other avenues of contact were discovered and utilized – for example, those representatives of traditional culture within the gates, the negro jazz musicians and blues singers. Later still, scores of holy men poured into Europe from India and points east. Some were real, some bogus, but all provided food for the insatiable appetites of the new West.

Since these early days, detailed tastes have varied with time and place. Sometimes China has been in vogue; sometimes India; sometimes Polynesia; sometimes Africa; sometimes Amerindia. But, whatever the variation in detail, the quest for contact with contemporary traditional cultures has been followed with unabated vigour down to the present day. Indeed, it is one of the stronger positive components of the enormously powerful Counter Culture of present-day America.[81]

Having noted this fascination with non-Western cultures, we must go on to ask which of their supposed characteristics provoke it. The following, perhaps, are the most important: the organic community, in which the individual never finds himself set over against his group; communion with nature; predominance of feeling over reason; predominance of symbolism over literary speech; predominance of art over science. One striking thing about this list of supposed salient features of non-Western cultures is its similarity to a list that might be drawn up of the supposed salient features of pre-industrial culture in the earlier West. Given the Western intellectual's awareness of the many parallels between contemporary traditional cultures and earlier phases of Western culture, the desire for contact with such cultures is revealed as being, in essence, a desire to be reunited with one's own lost heritage.[82]

If the reader casts his mind back to what was said earlier about recent accumulations of data relating to the traditional cultures, he will see that the influence of factual information on this image of the 'lost world' is tenuous. Once again, however, the influence of Western pessimism and self-doubt is clear. Thus if we make a list of the various unfulfilled yearnings and malaises of which the modern Western intellectual complains, we shall find that this image displays itself unmistakably as a compensatory fantasy in which every frustrated yearning of the West finds fulfilment and every malaise of the West is banished. Does Western man find himelf alienated from his society and lost in an abysmal loneliness? Then traditional culture is the seat of the Organic Community, in which the individual finds it impossible to think of himself as distinct from his group. Does Western man yearn to commune with nature, yet find himself frustrated by his awareness of the unbridgeable difference between people and things? Then traditional culture provides a world-view which minimizes this difference, and so makes communion fully satisfying. Does Western man suffer from the conviction that reason is killing the life of emotion and feeling? Then traditional culture provides a milieu in which feeling dominates reason. Does Western man despair of the adequacy of words, and attempt to use symbols to 'say' what is unsayable in literal speech? And is he frustrated, in this attempt, by the restricted role allotted to symbolism in the formal structure of Western institutions? Then traditional culture provides a world in which the symbol reigns supreme. Does Western man feel that science is killing art? Then traditional culture provides a world in which art dominates science.

In short, then, the romantic search for a 'lost world' has given rise to an image of traditional culture which can be understood entirely as a reaction to the stresses and strains of life in the modern West.

At this point, we have reached a position from which we can profitably return to deal with our main problem: the vogue of the contrast/inversion schema and the neglect of the continuity/evolution schema by social scientists. For once we have established our right to assume that the attitude to traditional cultures generally current among modern Western intellectuals is also powerfully entrenched amongst social scientists, we shall be in possession of a simple and elegant means of accounting for the situation.

Let us start with the question of 'liberal scruples'. Anthropologists who do fieldwork in the traditional cultures tend to be amongst those most strongly equipped with such scruples. Now that the victims of anthropological scrutiny nearly always include a few educated souls who are going to read the resulting report with the sensitive eyes of former colonial subjects, the anthropologist has to develop such scruples, if for no more honourable reason than as part of his basic survival equipment. For the Western anthropologist who not only does fieldwork in a non-Western nation, but who also lives and works in one of the universities of such a nation, the question 'will they be upset by my next paper?' often becomes an overriding obsession.

The main thing for the scrupulous liberal is, of course, to avoid invidious cross-cultural comparison. Now, in many spheres of traditional culture, the question of such comparison is hardly likely to arise. Take, for instance, the Arts. It would be a rash anthropologist indeed who could put his finger on the ends of Art, and who could swear that Western ballet achieved them more perfectly than African masquerade. Again, it would be a rash anthropologist who could bring himself to swear that Western family life was better attuned to the basic emotions of men and women than the family life of the Marquesas, or even that it was morally more elevated. Yet again, the student of traditional political systems is likely to conclude that most of them are as well adapted to the societies they serve as modern British parliamentary government is to the society it serves. When it comes to the sociology of thought, however, the question of invidious comparison becomes unpleasantly obtrusive. In all known traditional cultures, we find people producing explanations of events, using such explanations to make predictions about the likely consequences of various courses of action, and using the predictions in an attempt to extend their control of the world around them. In the modern West, we find people explaining, predicting and attempting to control the world in just the same sense of these words. However, if the West has done nothing else of indisputable worth it *has* succeeded in creating an institutional framework that has generated forms of explanation, prediction and control of a power hitherto unrivalled in any time or place. Such cognitive forms, moreover, are known to have developed from earlier and less efficient forms that have recognizable parallels in many contemporary traditional cultures.

Such a situation is deeply embarrassing to our scrupulous liberal. For either he sticks to the facts; and finds himself forced into a comparison strongly unfavourable to the traditional cultures. Or he dodges the comparison; but only at the price of denying the facts.

It is in terms of the latter course of action that we can at last understand the strange antics of the social anthropologist who refuses to take traditional explanations at their face value, and who maintains that at some deeper level of reality these are symbolic statements. For by such antics he converts the data into forms that stand in radical contrast with the explanatory statements of the sciences. Radical contrast means incommensurability, and incommensurability means impossibility of making invidious value judgements.[83]

That this really is one of the powerful ideological pressures behind the contrast/inversion schema is confirmed by the more or less moral overtones of disapproval expressed against those who, following the data, stick to continuity/evolution. Such disapproval finds its most explicit expression in a recent paper by Edmund Leach, entitled 'Virgin Birth', in which the author castigates all those who take 'primitive' explanations of the world at their face value.[84] Such people, he says, have an immoral wish to prove that 'primitives' are prone to stupid and childish mistakes. The good anthropologist realizes that, despite appearances, 'primitives' are not even trying to produce explanations, and he therefore avoids such imputations.

A clearer confession of the ideological basis of current anthropological theory could hardly be found!

Let us turn now to the second main component of the modern Western attitude – the romantic fascination with traditional cultures. The modern

Western anthropologist who elects to serve his fieldwork apprenticeship in a thoroughly traditional culture can hardly be other than a romantic. As far as intellectual stimulus or professional advancement is concerned, a modern or a transitional community would offer him an equal reward. This being so, his willingness to face two years of unpalliated heat, biting insects, bug-ridden water supply and non-existent sanitation can only spring from a strong expectation of the regenerative effect of encounter with a 'lost world'.

Given the fact that those who have fashioned the generally current romantic image of traditional culture have often scarcely pretended to acquaintance with the relevant data, it is remarkable just how much of this image has tended to reappear in sociological characterizations of traditional thought-patterns which *do* purport to be based on the data. Perhaps the most striking instance of this is provided by the Surrealists and Lévy-Bruhl. For the Surrealists, one suspects, would have admitted quite happily to dreaming up most of their ideas about the non-Western world. And Lévy-Bruhl, with equal justice, would have maintained that his ideas on the subject were based on a massive accumulation of data. Yet, although their writings show no explicit cross-references, the resemblance between their respective doctrines is uncanny. Thus, while the Surrealists divide the world of experience into the real and the sur-real, Lévy-Bruhl divides it into the natural and the supernatural. While the Surrealists associate real experience with reason and sur-real experience with feeling and desire, Lévy-Bruhl associates natural experience with reason and supernatural experience with feeling and desire. Both stress the role of feeling and desire in creating ideas and objects that are bizarre by the standards of common sense. Both stress the role of feeling and desire in breaking down the separation of man and nature. Both treat the domain of the sur-real/supernatural as something that is subordinate in Western culture, dominant in non-Western culture.[85]

In much the same way, the generally current romantic image of a 'lost world' in which symbolism and art reign supreme turns up again in characterizations of traditional thought-patterns favoured by anthropologists like Firth, Leach and Beattie.[86]

This general tendency for 'lost world' fantasies to find their way into anthropological orthodoxy accounts very nicely for the popularity of the contrast/inversion schema. For the 'lost world', being a world in which every frustrated yearning of the West is fulfilled and every malaise of the West banished, is inevitably defined as an inverted image of Western culture.

Positivism

In the conversation of social scientists, one frequently hears glib references to 'Durkheimian Positivism'. Durkheim may have been a positivist in some sense of that word and in some parts of his many-stranded career; but, as he makes clear in the introduction to *Formes Elémentaires*, one of his main concerns is to find a viable alternative to the positivist (or, as he calls it, empiricist) account of human intellectual activity.[87] I believe that it is his anti-positivist bias which has given his sociology of thought much of its prophetic quality *vis-à-vis* recent accumulations of data. Equally, I believe that widespread adherence to a positivist view of intellectual activity has contributed much to the errors of others in this field.

'Positivism', as a label, has been used in many ways by many people; so I had better preface further remarks with a definition. As I see it, positivism is a two-pronged ideology. First, it is a philosophical outlook which exalts the sciences as providing the only valid tools for acquiring knowledge of the world. Secondly, it is an outlook with a very peculiar conception of the sciences. That is, it holds them to be based largely on the process of induction from occurrences in the visible, tangible world. This process, it maintains, results in descriptive generalizations which show *how* things happen in the observable world. It does not yield explanations of *why* things happen. Such explanations, indeed, are no business of the sciences. For positivism, ideas about unobservable entities, which are so often associated with attempts to explain the workings of the world, are inessential to the process of scientific investigation. At best, they are crutches for thought; at worst, sources of dangerous confusion.[88]

As a product of the exuberance of scientists and their sympathizers, the first prong of the positivist ideology is not hard to understand. The second prong is more puzzling; for its conception of scientific activity is so far removed from what scientists actually do. Perhaps the best explanation is that this is a revolutionary ideology. As such, it has followed others of its kind in exaggerating the extent of change and in throwing out a valuable baby with the pre-revolutionary bath-water. Thus because the pre-revolutionary situation gave pride of place to spiritual beings, positivism condemns all ideas about unobservable entities as improper. Again, because the pre-revolutionary situation invoked the sanctions of tradition and authority to override experience, positivism condemns all forms of intellectual operation that are not directly tied to experience.

At this point, I can feel some of my readers getting restless. For I started by telling them that most of the errors of present-day sociology of thought were due to the infection of its practitioners with the ideology of liberal romanticism – an ideology based on a disillusion with science. And now, it seems, I am about to tell them that these errors are also due to infection with the ideology of positivism – an ideology based on excessive enthusiasm for science.

The paradox, though it looks severe, is in fact more apparent than real.

In the first place, members of the present sociological and anthropological establishment received their intellectual formation at a time when most of the generally available accounts of scientific method were positivist in tone. Other more sophisticated accounts were being evolved, but many of these were still confined to the pages of specialist professional journals. Social scientists who cling to positivist accounts of scientific method are therefore rather like historians, classicists and literary men who take Frazer as the last word on traditional cultures. It is all a question of a time-lag in the diffusion of new discoveries and new approaches from their discipline of origin into the general intellectual culture.[89]

But there is also a subtler reason for the amalgamation of liberal romanticism with certain aspects of positivism. Positivism, as I have stressed, is a two-pronged ideology; and it is perfectly possible to use one prong without the other. More specifically, it is perfectly possible to deny that science provides the only means of acquiring valid knowledge about the world, but to affirm that scientific method is largely a matter of induction from observables.

Not only is such a position possible. It fits in very well with an attitude of disillusion or hostility toward the sciences. For it gives the sciences such an extraordinary air of aridity, and assigns them such limited aims, that one can hardly help questioning their claim to a dominant position in Western culture, and wondering whether other ways of grasping reality are not perhaps more important.

Perhaps the first modern thinker to take up this limited form of positivism and use it as a weapon against the overweening claims of science was the great French Catholic physicist Pierre Duhem. The burden of his argument was that the sciences had the very limited function of showing *how* phenomena were correlated in space and time. They therefore presented no challenge to religion, whose function was that of explaining *why* things happened.[90]

If a devout Christian could thus show how one prong of the positivist ideology might be turned against its begetters, what was to stop liberal romantics from following suit? In fact, a positivistic definition of science has been prominent in the views of the social scientists who have supported the contrast/inversion schema. Lévy-Bruhl, Malinowski, Evans-Pritchard, Gluckman, Firth, Leach and Beattie – all of these in various ways have made it plain that they regard science as an extension of common sense; as based on induction from observables: and as limiting itself to questions of *how* these observables behave.[91]

Once such a position has been taken up with respect to science, it is inevitable that the magico-religious thinking of the traditional cultures should be seen as radically contrasted with it. For the mysteries of the world of unobservables and of unity-in-duality are then seen as peculiar to magico-religious thinking; and they are certainly poles apart from any simple process of induction from observables.

Again, the prominence of positivist indoctrination gives an alternative explanation of the modern social anthropologist's strange predilection for lumping all ideas that don't look like the results of inductive generalization into the catch-all category of 'symbolism'. For according to some of the better-known versions of positivism, propositions are either scientific (inductively based), or symbolic expressions of emotion.[92]

Not only, then, does a certain limited version of positivism articulate well with the twentieth-century Western ideology of pessimism and self-doubt. Thus articulated in the mind of the social scientist, it also strongly reinforces his support of the contrast/inversion schema.

Reconciling fancy and fact

The lesson of this paper is clear. In trying to define the relation between traditional and modern thought-patterns, twentieth-century social scientists can hardly be said to have made a notable advance on their nineteenth-century predecessors. Although Durkheim is the ancestral hero of their discipline, although he is one of the few twentieth-century figures who have had something illuminating to say on this topic, and although most of them have quoted him as their authority on it, they have in fact stood his actual teaching on its head. The result, which for brevity I have called the contrast/inversion schema, bears no worthwhile relation to the data.

This strange tale, I have suggested, can be understood only when one has realized that Western social scientists dealing with the non-Western world have escaped from the influence of one powerful ideology only to fall under the influence of another.

Is there any consoling feature to be extracted from this depressing tale? So far as interpretation of the data is concerned, the answer is definitely no. The modern contrast/inversion theorists have made no more sense of the data than did Tylor and Frazer. So far as sheer accumulation of data is concerned, the answer is yes. For whilst the Victorian idea of non-Western cultures as childish or half-baked forms of Western culture was surely a deterrent to fieldwork, the modern idea of such cultures as paradisiacal 'lost worlds' is equally surely an inducement to fieldwork. In the case of some of the more thoroughly tradition-oriented cultures, as I suggested earlier, it may even be the *sine qua non* of fieldwork. And although such fieldwork may be inspired by distorting preconceptions, it nevertheless makes for an influx of new and relevant data which may one day be used to overwhelm the preconceptions. Indeed, some of the data which I have used in this paper to show up the inadequacy of contrast/inversion theory have been amassed by exponents of the theory!

Liberal romanticism, clearly, is here to stay; for the factors which nourish it are likely, if anything, to increase in strength. The problem is, how do we harness it so that its interpretations come to run less grossly counter to the data which it helps to produce in such generous quantities?

What we have to try to do, clearly, is show that interpretations which are truer to the data do not necessarily conflict with its most cherished values.

As an example, let us take Durkheim's continuity/evolution schema, which fits the facts of the Great Transition admirably, but which is rejected by Leach and other contemporaries because it offends against their deepest liberal convictions. Let us see whether it really does run counter to these convictions.

The liberal objection to the schema, as we have seen, is that taking traditional explanations at their face value means admitting their inferior cognitive power *vis-à-vis* explanations produced by the sciences. In terms of liberal values, does this really matter?

In the first place, an erroneous explanation proves nothing about the intellectual capacity of those who put it forward. Indeed, it is in the nature of scientific 'progress by revolution' that today's acceptable explanations are tomorrow's errors. Hence pre-scientific non-Westerners hold no monopoly of erroneous explanations. They share the distinction of being prone to them with the most distinguished scientists.

Secondly, it is becoming more and more apparent that the sciences have made their mark very largely in those areas of human experience least associated with the deepest emotions – i.e. the spheres denoted by the labels 'physics' and 'chemistry'.[93] During the course of their tremendous advances in these spheres, they may well have sacrificed insights into the working of human social life that non-Western cultures still retain. If this is the case, then patient study of non-Western explanations may reveal, not a mere catalogue of errors, but a mixture of much error with a number of significant successes. That this is not fanciful is shown by the case of psychosomatic medicine, which was rediscovered, in the twentieth-century West, partly as a result of reflection on traditional ideas about the social causation of disease and death.[94]

A third consideration involves the past history and probable future development of the sciences. In many ways, the rise of the scientific outlook makes a strange tale. It starts in the Greek overseas colonies during the sixth century BC, continues first in Alexandria, then in Baghdad, then in southern Italy and Spain, then finally shifts to north-west Europe, the United States and the Soviet Union. One area after another has acted briefly as the home of science before yielding this pride of place to some other. In future, it is true, the tale is unlikely to continue just as before. The sciences have now started to feed the fruits of their activities into the wider culture in the form of benefits which all bearers of that culture can appreciate. So now there is less likelihood that a given area, having once acted as host to the sciences, will lose them again. It is hard to imagine Britain and the United States becoming scientific has-beens in quite the way that ancient Greece and Baghdad did. Nonetheless it is quite possible that, as the sciences spread throughout the world, some of the present centres will lose momentum and new centres overtake them. Already, American occupational psychologists have been asking themselves whether the type of personality thrown up by twentieth-century American culture is the type most likely to produce the creative scientist.[95] And at the other end of the world the Japanese, relative newcomers to the sciences, have been making extraordinarily vigorous progress in certain key subjects like elementary particle physics.

With ninety per cent of all the scientists who have ever lived still alive and working at the present day, we are clearly at the very beginning of the story. As the tale unfolds, the West may never again find itself without the sciences; but it may well find one day that the peak of creative momentum has passed on to one or more of the non-Western nations.

In this context, I think it is interesting to look at the situation in a country like Nigeria, where the less competent indigenous scientists tend to wax a little lyrical over such figures as native doctors and diviners, whilst the outstanding men tend to take a much more matter-of-fact view of them. I shall always remember one Yoruba medical scientist, an internationally respected leader in his field, who, on being asked at a conference to expatiate on the virtues of native doctors, replied: 'Don't let them give you anything to drink. Don't let them cut you. The rest of the performance is harmless'.

Coming as it does from an iconoclastic innovator, this comment goes to an extreme. But it does suggest that, once the non-Western scientist comes to feel that science really is 'his thing', he also feels free to make comparisons with the cognitive power of his fore-fathers' methods and generally to look at these methods with an objective eye.

Here, I think, we get close to the root of the liberal sentiment. For is not the inmost reason why the Western liberal feels compelled to allot the non-Westerner a special cognitive province a secret conviction that science can never really be the non-Westerner's 'thing'?

It would seem, then, that we need to convince the liberal of three things.

First, that from an erroneous belief, very little follows, one way or another, about the intellectual capacity of its holder. Second, that traditional theories, considered as *theories*, can in certain spheres of experience be a source of precious insight. Third, that non-Westerners are more than likely to take over the Western lead in some fields of science, and to make these fields 'their thing'. Once convinced of these points the liberal should be free to look at traditional thought-patterns with a more objective eye.

What about romanticism, that paradoxical source of bad interpretation and good data? This too, I believe, can be tamed and harnessed.

Personally, I must admit to sharing much of the romantic motivation which I have imputed to supporters of the contrast/inversion schema. I agree that we in the West have paid a heavy price for modernity in general and for the scientific outlook in particular. I share the belief that we in the West can discover something about the quality of our society before it paid this price by looking at contemporary traditional cultures. Finally, I share a conviction as to the regenerative effect of prolonged participation in the life of a culture that has not yet paid the price of modernity.

In these respects, I too am a romantic. But I think it is possible to be a romantic, with all this means in terms of motivation towards anthropological fieldwork, and yet avoid the distorting interpretations that so far have marred twentieth-century Western studies of the traditional. How to do this?

First of all, the romantic in search of his 'lost world' must come to see the impossibility of ever finding a place in which all the frustrated yearnings of the West are satisfied and all the malaises of the West absent. One reason for the impossibility is that many frustrated Western yearnings are the *products* of Western malaises, and do not even arise where such malaises are absent. Such, for instance, is the case with the Western yearning for communion with nature.[96] Another reason is that some Western yearnings are doomed to a degree of frustration in all cultures, human nature being what it is. This is the case with the yearning for the organic community in which the individual can never think of himself as at odds with the group.

However, there are many less simplistic senses in which traditional cultures can offer qualities of life lacking in the West. The romantic should have faith, and wait for the 'lost world' itself to show him what it has to offer.

Secondly, the romantic must come to see that all is not lost if he faces facts and admits that, in the sphere of explanation, prediction and control, modern cultures are pursuing the same goals as their traditional counterparts, but are pursuing them with greater efficiency. For the question of the price to be paid for such efficiency still remains to be asked.

Finally, what about positivism? The cure for this would seem to be more up-to-date reading in the history and philosophy of science. Social anthropologists concerned with the study of magico-religious thought in the traditional cultures should become aware of the extent to which their interpretations are coloured by an implicit vision of the nature of Western thought. They should accept the fact that they cannot be effective anthropologists of traditional magico-religious thought without at the same time being anthropologists of modern scientific thought.

Since social scientists still accept everything more easily when it comes to them via Durkheim, they might do well to start their reorientation by re-reading *Formes Elémentaires* and acquainting themselves with what the master *really* said.

4   Back to Frazer? (The Sir James Frazer Memorial Lecture, Cambridge, 1987)[1]

Opening remarks

Mr. Vice-Chancellor, Ladies and Gentlemen. Like others before me, I feel deeply honoured at having been invited to deliver this lecture. At the same time, for reasons which will shortly become apparent, I start my delivery with apprehensions which I suspect are greater than theirs were.

Although the Frazer lecture is officially defined as a commemoration of a great pioneer in the field of Comparative Religion, the actual practice on many if not most recent occasions has been to damn Frazer with a few faint praises, and then go on as quickly as possible to extol some trend in post-Frazerian thought which repudiates everything he stood for. Even amongst Frazer Lecturers, then, Frazer has been more than anything else a yardstick for showing just how far we have come in the social anthropology of magic and religion in the years since his death.

As one who has been referred to in the profession as a 'Back-to-Frazer Man', as a 'Neo-Frazerian', and recently, only half in jest, as 'Frazer Redivivus', I must confess that this background makes me very uneasy. Are my hosts sadistic post-Frazerians who have invited me with the intention of making cruel sport with a real live Frazerian? Or are they too a little tired of the established pattern, and looking for a break? I only wish I knew! Whatever their motives for inviting me, however, I feel I must do something to live up to my Frazerian reputation. Hence the title of this lecture. As to its content, whilst it may not come up to expectations in all respects, it will to some extent call in question the prevailing evaluation both of Frazer and of the dominant school of post-Frazerians.

Frazer: white mask, brown heart?

At the risk of disappointing those who came for a Roman Holiday, let me start by confessing that I too find much of Frazer's explicit general theorizing about magic, religion and science grossly misguided.

On magic, Frazer seems to have gone right off the rails. Thus he discards his predecessor Tylor's insights as to the key part played in this mode of thought and action, on the one hand by verbal incantations, and on the other by non-verbal symbols. In their place, he puts what I think we all must agree is a misleading comparison between magic and science, suggesting that both share the same concept of natural law.[2] Now if magicians ever make pronouncements on the laws governing the course of events in the world, these, surely, are pronouncements concerning the power of words and of non-verbal symbols to shape the portions of reality which they represent. Such pronouncements, of course, are sheer anathema to scientists, whose *credo* is that, however one manipulates words and symbols, the rest of reality remains unaffected by such manipulation.

On religion, Frazer is equally unsatisfactory. Thus he makes a striking contrast between a religious world-view, based on the idea of capricious gods and as such lacking any vision of order and regularity underlying the chaos of everyday experience, and a scientific world-view, based on impersonal entities and processes and as such incorporating a well-developed vision of underlying order and regularity.[3] Again, he makes a strong contrast between a religious world-view, which encourages constant human intervention aimed at diverting nature from its course, and a scientific world-view, which enjoins acceptance of the natural order of things.[4]

Both of these contrasts seem to me to be invalid. First, in most of the world's religious systems, the gods are thought of as having a modicum of order and regularity in their make-ups, and only exceptionally as being totally capricious. Here, it is perhaps salutary to remember that the concept of natural law so central to modern Western scientific thinking had its origin in the Christian idea of a God who bound Himself to abide by cosmological laws of His own making.[5] Second, *both* religious *and* scientific world-views encourage and provide guidelines for human intervention aimed at diverting events from the courses they would otherwise have followed. The scientific concept of causality, indeed, would seem to have been derived from that of intervention.[6]

Not only, then, does Frazer ignore important differences between magic and science. He also ignores important similarities between religion and science.

On science itself, Frazer sins by omission rather than by commission. Though he tells us that scientific theories are based on scrupulous observation, and that the scientific quest is guided by the idea of natural law, he tells us little else. Like many scholars of his time, he seems to think of himself as addressing a Western audience that knows what science is and does not have to be told. The assumption is fallacious and the result a serious gap in his interpretative framework.

The defects of Frazer's three-stage scheme of intellectual evolution are already well-known, and I only mention them for completeness' sake. First, there is no evidence for an initial phase of human thought dominated by magic and devoid of religion. Second, it is hard to divine the criterion by which he judges his three-stage sequence to be evolutionary. Thus magic, the initial stage, is oblivious to empirical data but gets one good mark for entertaining the concept of natural law. Religion, though supposedly one up in the sequence, gets no marks, since it neither takes any notice of empirical data nor entertains a concept of natural law. Finally, science, the culmination of the sequence, gets two good marks, one for controlling its generalizations in the light of empirical data and the other for entertaining the concept of natural law. So, instead of a steady process of intellectual development, we have first one step back then two steps forward. Frazer offers no justification of this odd feature of his evolutionary scheme.

Again, although Frazer makes it plain that he thinks different groups of people have travelled different distances through this sequence, he gives no satisfactory answer to the question of why this should be so. In view of his remarks about 'higher' and 'lower' intelligences, however, one can only assume that he has some sort of racial/biological determinism in mind. And in the light of our modern knowledge of these matters, the reality of such a determinism seems dubious, to say the least.

After listening to this critique, you may well ask what is left of Frazer to praise? The answer, I think, is: quite a lot!

Above all, if we turn from his general theoretical formulations to his interpretations of particular beliefs, practices and institutions, it is difficult to avoid being impressed by what I can only call his far-reaching intellectual imagination. By this, I mean his ability to grasp the first premiss of a particular magical or religious form, and to show the latter's various ramifications as deductive elaborations of this premiss. Perhaps the most spectacular example of this ability is his interpretation of the magico-religious ideas underpinning kingship: an interpretation which, in its broad outlines, has survived scholarly scrutiny down to the present day.[7]

As I see it, his singular ability to illuminate 'alien' thought-systems is linked to a remarkably open vision of the history of thought in his own Western culture. The vision is often merely implicit. Sometimes, however, it emerges clearly and explicitly – notably in the passage at the end of the *Golden Bough* where he refers to magic, religion and science as successive 'phantasmagoriae of thought', almost certainly destined to be superseded in their turn by other forms of thought as different from any of them as they are from one another.[8] I believe that this open vision, by preventing him from taking the current Western world-view as the last word on the nature of reality, provides the basis for his high degree of imaginative sympathy with non-modern and non-Western views of the world.

Modern social anthropologists have often presented Frazer to us as a rather simple man immersed in the ethnocentric prejudices of nineteenth-century Britain. My own feeling is that he was far from simple, and that his prejudices may not have run very deep. One cannot, of course, ignore the arrogance implicit in his evolutionary theorizing. Nor can one ignore his summary dismissal of the entire corpus of magical and religious thought as a 'melancholy record of human error and folly'.[9] These generalities, however, are belied by a thousand instances of sympathetic, imaginative identification with particular examples of such thought. To me, the generalities sound like the official noises Frazer felt he had to make to cover himself *vis-à-vis* the decidedly ethnocentric intellectual establishment of his time and place. After making them, however, he went on and did his own thing, which, far from being ethnocentric, was in fact culturally subversive. Giving a little twist to Franz Fanon's imagery, I suggest that we remember Frazer as a man who, though he wore a supercilious white mask, carried a brownish heart in his chest.

The Symbolists: a critical appraisal

Preliminaries

As I reminded you at the beginning of this lecture, Frazer's successors in Anglo-American anthropology have seldom tried to build upon his ideas. Rather, they have rejected them comprehensively. I use the word 'comprehensively' here, because their rejection has gone far beyond anything envisaged in my own critique. Thus whilst I take for granted the validity of Frazer's intellectualist framework, with its assumption that magic, religion and science all constitute bodies of theory about the working of the world, most post-Frazerian anthropologists in the Anglo-American tradition have repudiated this framework altogether, at least in so far as the interpretation of magical and religious phenomena is concerned. To give a preliminary idea of the scope of their revolution, let me highlight what seem to me to have been their three major moves. First, they have brought art into the forum of discussion alongside Frazer's magic, religion and science. Secondly, they have assimilated magic and religion to art, leaving science in lonely contrast to the other three. Third, in their interpretation of magic and religion, they have replaced Frazer's scientific concept of 'theory' with the aesthetician's concept of 'symbol'. It is in virtue of this third move that they refer to themselves as 'Symbolic Anthropologists'. Shortening this for convenience, I shall refer to them in the rest of this lecture as 'Symbolists'.

In what follows, I shall mount a critique of the Symbolists' approach, with the aim of trying to determine whether or not their claim to have advanced decisively beyond Frazer is justified. Before I start, however, let me say a word or two on procedure. First, I shall outline my understanding of the Symbolist interpretation of aesthetic, magical, religious and scientific thought, and follow it up with a preliminary critique. Second, I shall outline some Symbolist defences against the type of critique just offered, and follow up with a second round of critique directed against these defences. Third, I shall spotlight what I take to be the basic axiom on which Symbolists fall back when all other defences have failed them, and subject this, in turn, to a final round of critique. The exercise, then, will take the form of a dialogue in three rounds.

Let me admit that, in casting the exercise in this format, I have introduced a marked element of 'rational reconstruction'. I am not the only person to have engaged the Symbolists in criticism over the years.[10] Nor have exchanges with them conformed to the tidy sequence which will be unfolded in what follows. However, I do not think that my 'rational reconstruction' has distorted the content of Symbolist views and defences. And I do think that the format used here has some advantages. First, it helps make the critique more easily digestible. Secondly, it helps to display what I see as the various levels of Symbolist thinking. Proceeding in this way, indeed, will enable me to lead you from the superstructure of Symbolist thought to its sustaining foundation.

Round One

An outline of the Symbolist position. In presenting an outline of the Symbolist approach, I shall be presenting what is very much a generic image. Such images, I am well aware, have their dangers. Given the constraints of time, however, a generic image would seem more practicable than a catalogue of individual variants.[11]

In an exposition of the surface features of the Symbolist position, it seems appropriate to start with the thesis that, in all human cultures, there are two sharply contrasted modes of thought: the expressive and the instrumental. The principal manifestations of the expressive mode are aesthetic, magical and religious thinking. The principal manifestations of the instrumental mode are common-sense, technological and scientific thinking.[12]

The guiding intention of the expressive mode is the creation and mainte-nance of symbols or images which are satisfying in their own right, both to their producers and to their consumers.

One of the main tools for pursuing this intention is language. In this context, however, language is used, not literally, but symbolically or figu-ratively. Here, reference to a conventionally-established primary object is not an end in itself. Rather, the primary object is used as the means to a further end: that of referring to and 'saying' something about a secondary object. Unlike the relation between the linguistic sign and its primary object of reference, however, that between the primary object and the secondary object is not purely conventional. For there is a feature intrinsic to the primary object which 'calls to mind' the latter's secondary counterpart. This feature may be metaphoric: as where the primary object shares an attribute with its secondary counterpart. Or it may be metonymic: as where there is a relationship of present or past continuity between the two.[13] In the linguistic context, then, 'symbol' is the generic term; 'metaphor' and 'metonym' its specifics.

The other main tool of expressive thought is the non-verbal symbol. Like the primary referent of the symbolically-used verbal sign, the non-verbal symbol 'calls to mind' a notion or phenomenon by means of features of one or other of the kinds mentioned above. In the case of the non-verbal symbol, too, then, it would also seem appropriate to talk of 'symbol' as the generic term and of 'metaphor' and 'metonym' as its specifics.

In the Symbolist view, the symbols or images of expressive thought are typically created and maintained in order to represent notions or aspects of experience that cannot easily be conceptualized in terms of such literal, conventional language as is available in a given culture. In other words, the specific aim of expressive thought is not just that of representing, but that of representing the literally unsayable.[14]

Now it is easy enough to see how these general assertions about verbal and non-verbal symbols *might* apply to thought and action in the aesthetic and magical categories; for in both art and magic the symbolic character is usually more or less explicit. However, it is a little more difficult to see how such assertions might apply to religious thought and action. Nonetheless, Symbolists contend that they do so apply. Thus they hold that, although the gods and spirits are the primary objects of reference of religious discourse, they are in some sense imaginary objects even to the users of such discourse themselves, and serve first and foremost to 'call to mind', through their imputed features, a range of secondary objects of reference that are purely this-worldly in character. To put it crudely, when people purport to talk about their gods, they are really talking symbolically or figuratively about various goings-on in the everyday world. Again, they hold that, although religious ritural, on the face of it, appears to be an activity in which men address themselves to their gods, it too is really a series of symbolic performances, partly verbal and partly non-verbal, which refers to purely this-worldly phenomena.[15]

For those of you who are not Symbolists, two examples may help to clarify. When members of a community talk about their dependence on the favours of a local water-spirit in bringing them good fish-harvests, or engage in rituals addressed to the spirit that acknowledge and request such favours, what they are really doing, according to the Symbolists, is making symbolic statements about their dependence on the natural environment. Again, when the same people talk about the deified founder of their community or engage in rituals that acknowledge their dependence on him for survival in the face of disease, enemies and so on, what they are really doing, supposedly, is making symbolic statements about their dependence on the group of which they are members.

So much for the expressive mode. Let us turn now to the instrumental mode.

Here, the expositor finds himself in difficulty. For although instrumental thought certainly looms large in Symbolist minds, as something strongly contrasted with its expressive counterpart, Symbolists give us very little by way of a detailed characterization of it. Perhaps this is because, like Frazer, they see themselves as addressing an audience that knows all about this mode, and therefore doesn't need to be told much about it. Whatever the reason, precisely because instrumental thought *does* have a key place in their overall scheme, we must do our best to extract from Symbolist writings whatever slender clues we can as to their view of it.

Most Symbolists, it would seem, agree that the guiding intentions of instrumental thought are those of explanation, prediction and control of events in the space-time world. Most, it would seem, also agree that explanation is a means to prediction, and prediction a means to practical control of the world.

Most, I think, would further agree on a rather austerely positivistic view of instrumental thought; a view which sees its explanatory schemas as generalizations built up by induction from observables, and which regards ideas about unobservables as having no part to play in the formulation of such schemas. This view comes over most strongly in certain pronouncements by Leach, who proudly affirms his allegiance to positivism and inductivism as the basis both of the sciences generally and of social-scientific enquiry in particular.[16] But there are also hints of it in the writings of several other members of the movement. One symptom of a more generally current positivist/inductivist view is the tendency to deal with science, not as something distinct from everyday common-sense thinking, but rather as a mere extension of such thinking.[17]

Finally, most Symbolists would probably agree that the operations of instrumental thought are conducted above all via conventional linguistic signs, used literally. By 'conventional linguistic signs', they would mean signs whose reference and sense have been established over the years by community consensus; signs whose intrinsic features include nothing that 'calls to mind' their objects of reference. By 'literally', they would mean use of such signs *only* in relation to conventionally-established primary objects of reference, and *not* in relation to secondary objects. This literalist view of instrumental thinking comes over most vividly in James Fernandez' remarks about the 'imageless ideas' of scientific academia.[18] But it is also to be seen in the general Symbolist view of the proliferation of symbolic imagery in expressive thought as one of the things that places it in stark contrast with instrumental thought.[19]

Symbolist thinkers insist that the potential for both expressive and instrumental modes of thought is present in every human being, and that both modes have been present in all human cultures down the ages. At the same time, many of them concede that the balance between these two modes has varied greatly, not only as between different cultures at a particular point in time, but also within the same culture at different points in time. Indeed, one of the reasons they give for modern Westerners' inability to understand both non-Western cultures and earlier phases of their own Western culture is that modern Western culture is skewed so far in favour of the instrumental that its members have little familiarity with the expressive. Hence, where they deal either with other cultures or with earlier phases of their own, both of which have placed far greater emphasis on the expressive, they are correspondingly handicapped in their ability to interpret.[20]

Once cross-cultural differences of balance as between the expressive and the instrumental have been admitted, of course, questions inevitably arise as to the factors underpinning such differences. Here, the Symbolists, by and large, have been remarkably unforthcoming. Though in their broader approach to social life they have continued the drive initiated by Lévy-Bruhl, Durkheim and others to replace racial/biological explanation with sociological explanation, they tell us very little about the background social factors operating in this area.

Those that do deal at all with such questions tend to content themselves with the suggestion that instrumental thought and action has an inexorable tendency to squeeze out its expressive counterpart. And they cite modern Western history as evidence for this tendency. But they do not answer the question, raised by their own assertions, as to why this process has gone further in the West than elsewhere.[21]

A first critique. In presenting a preliminary critique of the Symbolists, I shall begin with their characterization of the various types of thought which they classify as expressive, turn next to their view of the various types which they classify as instrumental, and finally look at what they have to say about cross-cultural differences of balance as between the expressive and the instrumental.

In starting the exercise with a consideration of the Symbolists' view of the aesthetic, I shall be following their own inclinations. For it is this type of thought and activity that has provided much of the inspiration for their ideas about expressive thought generally.[22]

There is not in fact a great deal to be said by way of criticism in this area. That aesthetic activity is centred on the production and appreciation of symbolic images which are intrinsically satisfying both to producer and consumer; that these images 'call to mind' rather than just conventionally refer to various aspects of experience with which the apparatus of literal language is unable to cope: both these assertions are acceptable common-places of modern aesthetic theory. If there is anything to be said by way of criticism, it is that the Symbolist view of aesthetics is fine as far as it goes, but incomplete. For although Symbolists tell us much about the symbolic character of aesthetic activity, they tell us nothing about the place in such activity of the creation and appreciation of form. And this is a topic that any theory of art must cover if it is to be taken seriously.

This qualification notwithstanding, it seems fair to say that aesthetic thought and activity, at least, fit squarely into the Symbolists' expressive category. The question we must now tackle is that of the legitimacy of trying to drag magic and religion into this category alongside art.

We can have no quarrel with the Symbolist contention as to the overall importance of symbols in magical thought and action; for symbols of one kind or another are clearly central to most if not all operations we call magical. Nonetheless, there are two important reservations to be entered with respect to Symbolist views on magic.

First, although Symbolists stress that symbolic language and non-verbal symbols are typically brought into play in areas of experience where the resources of ordinary literal language are inadequate, what happens in the usual magical performance seems to refute this contention. For a key part of the performance is the verbal spell or incantation, in which, at some point or other, ordinary literal language is used to state the aim of the operation and to fix the meaning of any of the non-verbal symbols used in it as repre-senting the fulfilment of this aim. Thus where a magician is trying to bring about a man's death by sticking a small blade into a wooden doll, he may fix the reference of his non-verbal symbols by means of an incantation in which he verbally designates the blade as a sword, the doll as the victim, and the operation of one upon the other as a representation of the killing of the victim. He may say something like: 'You this blade are my sword. You this doll are X. As I plunge blade into doll, so may X die in agony'. In such a situation, clearly, non-verbal symbols are not being used to refer to aspects of experience for which there is no adequate literal verbal coverage. On the contrary, objects and actions are being given a symbolic, representational function by literal, verbal definition.

Secondly, although Symbolists stress that magical thought and action are brought into play solely or primarily because of the intrinsically satisfying character of the symbolic images they produce, this assertion seems to run counter to all the contextual evidence recorded by fieldworkers in magically-orientated cultures the world over, Symbolist fieldworkers included. On a myriad occasions, such fieldworkers have heard explanations given for a whole gamut of phenomena in terms of magical performances or omissions. Contextual evidence further suggests that such explanations have been offered and accepted in all seriousness. On a myriad occasions, again, such fieldworkers have witnessed the application of magical principles to the practical control of everyday life, and have seen the seriousness, even anxiety, with which the outcome of such application is awaited and assessed.[23]

In considering the symbolist view of magic, we at least found ourselves able to agree that the use of symbols was at the heart of the thought and activity in question. What stuck in our throats was the contention that such symbols were produced for their own sakes rather than for practical purposes. In considering the Symbolist view of religion, however, we are faced with an additional problem; for in this case even the contention that the use of symbols lies at the heart of the matter seems dubious.

To the mind that has not undergone Symbolist indoctrination, indeed, the idea that talk about the gods and actions directed to them are nothing but symbolic ways of referring to purely earthly things is little short of bizarre. Surely all the evidence from fieldwork in religious cultures is that, when men talk about the gods, they are talking about beings that are as real to them as men and women, sticks and stones, rivers and mountains. Surely all the evidence is that when people say their crops have been destroyed by the anger of the gods or prospered by their approval, they are talking literally. Surely all the evidence is that when people pray and sacrifice to the gods to ensure the survival and prosperity of their community, they, in their own minds, are doing just that.

I have deliberately hammered here on the phrase 'all the evidence'. For Symbolists make no attempt to back this their most implausible contention with any kind of evidence. Yet there *are* a number of common-sense rules of thumb which specify the sort of evidence relevant to deciding whether a piece of discourse is literal or symbolic/metaphorical/figurative in intent. And if we apply these rules of thumb in the religious field, we find that the evidence points overwhelmingly to the literal status of discourse about souls, spirits, gods and God.

Common-sense rules of thumb indicate at least three types of evidence relevant to deciding the status of religious discourse. The first of these is contextual evidence. The second is evidence derived from users' own metalinguistic categorizations. The third, closely allied to the second, is evidence derived from confrontation of users with the Symbolist interpretation of their discourse.

The key contextual evidence relevant to deciding the status of religious discourse is evidence as to whether or not the user takes the literal meaning of such discourse as a guide to action directed to achieving his salient aims. To put it more colloquially, the key to the matter is evidence as to whether or not the user 'puts his money where his mouth is'. Let us take a couple of examples to make the point clear.

For our first example, let us take the case of a middle-aged African villager who is always talking about the guardian deity of his community. He talks, amongst other things, of the anger aroused in the deity by actions which threaten to disrupt the harmony of the group, and of the way in which such anger can result in misfortune, sickness and even death for both the offender and his family. He also talks of the heavy sacrifices which are necessary to appease the deity in such cases.

Now although we know this man as someone who has the normal healthy concern for the welfare of himself and his family, we also know him as something of a trouble-maker in the community. We may therefore begin by doubting whether he really believes all he says about the deity, in the sense of taking its literal meaning as a guide to his everyday living. We may even hazard the opinion that all his talk about the deity is not literally intended, but is rather a wistful symbolic representation of the ideal harmony of the community on the part of somebody who finds himself unable to make much of a contribution to the realization of this ideal.

One day, however, a member of our friend's family falls seriously ill. After the usual first-line empirical remedies have failed, he consults a diviner. The latter tells him that, because of his disruptive behaviour in the community, the guardian deity is venting its wrath on him, and that, unless he makes a series of propitiatory offerings, it will kill off his family and himself one by one. Now we see real fear come upon him. Over the next few months, moreover, we see him engage in crippling expenditure on sacrifices designed to appease the deity, restore his sick child to health, and ensure the well-being of himself and his family. At the end of this period of trial, when he emerges materially impoverished, much chastened in conduct, but happy at the survival of his family, we find ourselves ready to accept that he did, after all, believe everything he had been saying about the deity. We now conclude that it had all been literally rather than figuratively intended.

For our second example, let us take a case of a rather different kind. This time, let us imagine ourselves in a Roman town in the early days of Christianity. We ourselves are good pagans; but we have a Christian friend who is always telling us that he doesn't worry too much about the trials and tribulations of this life, because his God has prepared for him a Life Everlasting beside which this one will seem a mere flash in eternity, and its troubles a nothingness. To us, our friend's talk is more or less incredible; and we find ourselves wondering whether he really intends it all literally, or whether he is speaking symbolically or figuratively about the emptiness and lack of meaning to this life.

Then one day the authorities march in and command everybody to make a gesture of reverence to the gods of the Roman state. Our friend refuses. He is put to torture, and still refuses. Then he is sent for trial, and from trial to the stake. As he goes to the stake, he shows no signs of fear, but rather appears to be in a state of bliss. As we wend our way sadly home from the place of his death, we find that all doubts in our minds about his talk of God and the Life Everlasting have been finally resolved. Quite clearly, the talk had been literally intended throughout.

In our studies of religious life world-wide and down the ages, cases like this, in which men and women are seen to be so obviously 'putting their money where their mouths are' in relation to statements about gods or about God, form the bulk of our records. It is a mass of contextual evidence of this kind that makes it difficult for those of us who have not undergone Symbolist indoctrination in the groves of academe to swallow Symbolist doctrines about the non-literal intention behind religious discourse.

Let us turn now to the second type of evidence: that derived from users' metalinguistic categorizations. Some Symbolists' contentions notwithstanding,[24] my own hunch is that, in many if not most of the world's cultures, people make distinctions that correspond more or less closely to the Western distinction between the literal use of discourse and its symbolic/metaphorical/figurative uses. In my work in Kalabari, for instance, I found a closely corresponding distinction; and my students tell me that similar distinctions are to be found in other Southern Nigerian cultures. Recently, moreover, Joanna Overing testified to a similarly corresponding distinction in the Piaroa culture of the Venezuelan rain-forest. In such cases, it seems, discourse about spiritual beings is put in the 'literal' rather than the 'symbolic' category.[25]

Finally, let us look at the third type of evidence: that derived from confrontations between religious people and Symbolist interpreters of their discourse. For obvious reasons, such encounters are not all that common. Where they do occur, however, the results are pretty unambiguous in their implications for our debate.

Perhaps the most impressive of these encounters to date is that which has taken place within the framework of the various Christian churches. Here, the more traditional Christians have been confronted, not by Symbolist anthropologists, but by *avant-garde* 'Christian' theologians peddling essentially Symbolist doctrines about the earthly reference of spiritual concepts. Within the Catholic fold, this confrontation took place earlier in the century between the 'traditionalists' and the 'modernists'.[26] Within the Protestant fold, it has been taking place more recently between 'traditionalists' and 'progressives' such as Paul van Buren, Thomas Altizer and Don Cupitt.[27] In both cases, the result has been a firm traditionalist rejection of Symbolist doctrines, which are seen as constituting a travesty of Christian religious discourse.[28]

Another example, smaller but no less impressive in its way, comes from my own experience as teacher of a course on Theories of Religion in a Nigerian university. Here, I deal with students for whom religious discourse, both Christian and pre-Christian, looms much larger than it does in the lives of their Western counterparts. How do they react when we get round to Symbolist interpretation of their various religious persuasions? By and large, I would say, they react with sheer puzzlement at such a weird, perverse interpretation of spiritual discourse. Away from the customary politeness of the classroom, I can imagine them asking each other: can Westerners really be *this* mad?

Such, then, are the sorts of evidence which convince many of us that much if not most talk about the gods is literally rather than symbolically intended.

So far, of course, I have been arguing against those theorists who have treated the symbolic import of religious discourse as a matter of more or less conscious intention. Some theorists, however, would say that, whilst the conscious intention of the user of religious discourse *is* literal, his unconscious intention is symbolic.[29] Against this second contention, the arguments offered above would not seem to have the same force. Other arguments, however, would seem to be more cogent.

In this modern age, anyone who attempts to propagate a doctrine of unconscious symbolism can be assumed to be indebted to and influenced by Freud. However, there are two key pillars of Freud's theory which our theorists, to their cost, have failed to incorporate into their own theses.

First of all, Freud sees the need to give an answer to the key question: 'Why should certain symbolic references be inaccessible to consciousness?' and the answer he gives is a very clear one. It is that such references provoke intense feelings of anxiety and guilt in the conscious mind. The latter is therefore constrained to exclude them.

Secondly, Freud gives equally clear answers to the questions: 'How does the psychoanalyst know that something is an unconscious symbol?' and 'How does he know what it is a symbol of?' In this regard, it is salutary to remember that even Freud, accused as he so often is of unsupported speculation, feels compelled to support his various assertions about unconscious symbolism with a definite specification of the process whereby such assertions may be verified. Here, of course, I refer to the importance he attaches to free association of ideas, under special conditions of relaxation of the conscious mind, as the principal source of evidence for unconscious symbolic references.

With respect to both sets of key questions, the exponents of the thesis that religious discourse is unconsciously symbolic show up badly by comparison with Freud.

First of all, on the question of why religious symbolism should be inaccessible to consciousness, they have nothing to offer. One may suspect them of trying to shelter under the umbrella of the Freudian explanation. However, if this is what they are trying to do, they are wasting their time. For the kinds of things they tell us religious discourse symbolizes – the relation between the individual and society, the relation between society and nature, and so on – are not the anxiety- and guilt-provoking things with which Freud peopled his unconscious. Hence his explanation of why certain things are excluded from consciousness and relegated to the unconscious can not apply to them. In so far as our theorists offer us no alternative explanation, they leave us with the first basic question unanswered.

Again, when it comes to providing evidence for their interpretations, our theorists make no mention, either of Freud's technique of free association under conditions of conscious relaxation, or of any other technique for eliciting unconscious references. Hence they leave us with the second set of questions equally unanswered.[30]

All in all, it seems to me that Symbolists of both types fail to make any sort of evidentially-based case for their thesis that religious discourse is a symbolic way of representing earthly things. In the absence of any worthwhile evidence to the contrary, then, we surely have every reason to follow Frazer in taking religious discourse as literally intended talk about spiritual beings or being.

This is not to deny that symbolism is of importance in religious contexts. It certainly is. The trouble, however, is that the Symbolists postulate a relationship between symbolism and religion which is the exact inverse of what obtains in reality. Thus for them, the gods are symbols of earthly things. In reality, however, as a great mass of historical and present-day cross-cultural evidence reminds us, it is earthly things that provide symbols of the gods.[31]

As I see it, there are in fact two types of symbol that are important in religious contexts. I shall call these types 'creative' and 'supportive'.

Creative symbols are those that make a first representation of the reality underlying observable phenomena, and from which the basic ideas about the character of that reality are abstracted to form a literally intended theory. In the religious context, human beings in their social relationships provide the symbols in terms of which the reality underlying phenomena gets its first representation; and from this set of symbols is abstracted a spiritualistic theory of the world and its working.

Supportive symbols are those that help to maintain commitment to a body of theory already built up. They serve their purpose, on the one hand by helping people visualize, tactualize and auralize the more abstract and difficult-to-grasp aspects of such a theory, and on the other by bringing to bear emotional associations which strengthen emotional commitment to the theory.[32] In the religious context, typical supportive symbols are to be found in the myriad painted and sculpted images of the gods, and in the vast corpora of religious poetry and religious music.

From the above, it should be clear that one major defect in the Symbolist view of religion is not so much that it exaggerates the importance of symbolism in religious life (though there is a sense in which it does so exaggerate), but rather that it totally mischaracterizes the latter's role in such life.

The Symbolist view of religion is also misleading in another way. By insisting that religious thought and action are centred on the production of symbolic images for their own sakes, it brushes aside what most students of comparative religion not committed to this approach would surely agree, on the basis of both direct and indirect observation, to be the *two* most important aspects of religious life the world over.

The first of these aspects is that which I have called 'communion'. Here, I refer to relationships with the gods or with God entered into and conceived as ends in themselves. This is an aspect of religion which has always been enormously important in the Christian tradition: so much so indeed that devout Christians often tend to exaggerate its importance in dealing with other religions. But it also has striking manifestations in Indian, Amerindian, African and other religious traditions. Such intrinsically satisfying relationships often drastically change the lives of those who enter into them. Sometimes, they gain such a grip as to transform or even undermine all of a person's relationships with his fellow human beings.[33]

As for the second aspect – explanation, prediction and control of this-worldly events – its importance has already been hinted at in our discussion of religion and symbolism. On the basis of massive evidence as to the contexts in which religious thought and action are evoked in everyday social life, we can confidently say that the vast majority of religions, both past and present, are above all else bodies of theory regarding the underlying character of the world, from which flow repertoires of action aimed at practical control of the vicissitudes of life. The religious life of the educated classes in the modern West seems, it is true, to be something of an exception to this generalization; but, as I shall argue later, it is an exception that proves the rule.[34]

Symbolists either ignore these aspects of religion altogether; or they deny that they have any deep significance for those involved in them; or they say they are mere secondary spin-offs from a primarily aesthetic activity. All such reactions seem to me to signify a truly amazing disregard for the phenomena.[35]

To round off my critique of the Symbolists on religion, let me ask how well this type of thought and action fits in to their expressive category. The answer seems to be that, like magic, it fits uneasily. Thus symbolism *is* important in religion; but far more important is literally intended language and action. Again, the communion aspect certainly involves activity entered into for its own sake; but it is activity very different from the production and consumption of aesthetically-satisfying images. And finally, the importance of the explanation/prediction/control aspect suggests most strongly the instrumental rather than the expressive.

So much, then, for the various types of thought and action classified by the Symbolists as expressive. Let us turn now to those classified by them as instrumental.

Here, of course, the first thing to be said by way of criticism concerns the sheer lack of elaboration on the contents of this category. Such a lack is particularly unfortunate given the part played in Symbolist thought by the idea of the expressive as something standing in stark contrast with the instrumental. For how on earth can someone establish contrast when he gives clear detail for only one of the two terms involved? Again, if it is really the case that the Symbolists tell us so little about the instrumental because they see themselves as addressing a largely Western-educated audience that knows all about such things and does not need to be told, then this, as I said in my critique of Frazer, is an omission based on a fallacy.

The second thing to be said is that, from the little the Symbolists do tell us about thought and action in this category, one is led to suspect that they themselves are somewhat ignorant of it and may indeed be the victims of serious mistakes about it. Thus consider the broadly positivist picture that emerges from the hints they do drop about it: the picture of a science essentially continuous with everyday practical thinking; of a science in which there is no room either for concepts of unobservable entities or for symbolic imagery used in the creation and support of such concepts. Surely this is a travesty of the realities.

First of all, the lack of a distinction between everyday practical thought and scientific thought blurs one of the most interesting lines of cleavage in human intellectual life.

Secondly, the failure to make a place for concepts of unobservable entities or for the idea of a reality underlying that of the visible, tangible everyday world excludes from our picture of science what is perhaps at the very heart of it. For scientific theorizing *is* the use of ideas about an unobservable underlying reality to make better sense of the world of everyday.

Thirdly, the failure to make a place for symbolic imagery obscures the fact that such imagery has always been indispensable for the creation and maintenance of theory.

As in religion, indeed, so in science there would seem to be two major types of symbolic imagery: the creative and the supportive.

As in the religious context, creative symbols are images, drawn from various aspects of everyday experience, from which the basic dimensions of theories of underlying reality are abstracted. They are what scientists call their 'theoretical models'. Examples include the clock model in early modern cosmology; and the current, wave and particle models in later physics and chemistry.

Again as in the religious context, supportive symbols are those that facilitate commitment to and use of already established theories. A striking example from the laboratory is provided by the ingenious, multicoloured ball-and-bar models of complex molecules, which play such an important part, not only in helping students learn chemical theory, but also in helping trained scholars manipulate it. Examples from outside the laboratory can be even more spectacular; for in the popularization of science by a media wizard like Carl Sagan, a stunning array of visual, plastic, poetic and even musical imagery may be brought into play.

As we did with art, magic and religion, let us round off here by asking how well everyday practical thought and scientific thought fit in to the broader category to which Symbolists have assigned them: this time the category of the instrumental.

Everyday practical thought, it seems to me, fits in well enough. Scientific thought, however, seems to fit less easily. True, scientific thought is enormously important as an instrument for the practical control of the world; and up to a point one may say that it is the general interest in such control that maintains the essential financial and institutional support for science. Nonetheless, the explanatory quest in science has never been merely a means to the end of practical control. There have always been scientists, often the greatest, who have sought explanations as ends in themselves. Again, the importance of symbolic imagery brings a definite whiff of the expressive into this alleged redoubt of the instrumental.

Finally in this preliminary critique, let us take a look at what Symbolists have to say about cross-cultural differences in balance between the expressive and the instrumental.

First of all, as we saw earlier, whilst admitting cross-cultural differences in this respect, particularly as between the West and the non-West, they have little or nothing to suggest about the technological, economic or socio-political determinants of such differences. This alone is a major gap in their approach.

Again, what they do have to say by way of an attempt to explain such differences is seriously question-begging. Thus, in trying to explain why, in the modern West, instrumental thinking has come to overshadow its expressive counterpart, they invoke the idea that the instrumental has an inexorable tendency to squeeze out the expressive. This, however, leaves quite unanswered the question of why it has done this so successfully in the West but not nearly so successfully in other parts of the world.

Lastly and most seriously, the Symbolists' thesis that the instrumental has a tendency to drive out the expressive seems inconsistent with their thesis of a stark contrast between these two categories.

Let me elaborate. If it were really true that the guiding intentions of art, magic and religion (creation of symbolic images for their own sake) were quite other than the guiding intentions of science (explanation, prediction and control), then there could be no direct competition between science and the first three. In such circumstances, we should expect to see art, magic and religion left uniformly untouched by science, rather than squeezed out by it as the Symbolists suggest they are.

In fact, what actually seems to have happened in the West is something that conforms to neither of these patterns. Thus the arts do indeed seem to have retained their vigour. By contrast, magic seems to have been almost totally vanquished. And religion, though forced to beat a retreat, has clung on to some semblance of life at the cost of a great restriction in scope.

Now if all three types of thought really did have the same guiding intention, this difference of response would be inexplicable. However, if we accept the characterizations of these three types that emerge from the earlier part of my critique, what has happened to them becomes more understandable. Thus, on the assumption that the arts *are* concerned above all with the production and appreciation of intrinsically satisfying symbolic images, it follows that the expansion of science, with its totally different guiding intentions, can pose no threat to their continued flourishing. Again, on the assumption that magic is concerned above all with explanation, prediction and control, it follows that it is in direct competition with science, and that, if science is perceived to be a more efficient way of fulfilling the same guiding intentions, it will dwindle away. Finally, on the assumption that religion is dedicated, on the one hand to the quest for explanation, prediction and control, and on the other to the quest for spiritual communion, it follows that, whilst one aspect of it is in competition with science, the other is not. So if science is perceived to be a more efficient way of fulfilling the quest for explanation, prediction and control, we shall expect to see the corresponding aspect of religion fade quietly away. At the same time, since science has nothing to say about the quest for spiritual communion, we shall expect to see *this* aspect of religion survive its advance. In fact, this is exactly what seems to have happened. For much of modern Western theological thought seems to have been engaged in showing that, whilst we must jettison the explanation/prediction/control aspect of Christianity as 'superstition', we must equally retain the communion aspect. And where the theologians have led, the more educated laymen seem to have followed.[36]

In short, the Symbolist approach does a poor job of accounting for alleged cross-cultural differences in balance between the expressive and the instrumental. It also does a poor job of charting and accounting for the impact of the expansion of science on artistic, magical and religious thought. Again, the fact that art, magic and religion have reacted very differently to the expansion of science suggests, once more, that these three modes of thought are not appropriately confined within the single category of the expressive.

Here, I come to the end of my preliminary critique of the Symbolist position. To me, the critique seems pretty devasting. The Symbolists emerge as being right about art so far as they go (though this is not far enough), but seriously wrong in their characterizations of magic, religion and science. Their attempt to draw a stark contrast between art, magic and religion as concerned with the production and appreciation of symbolic images for their own sakes, and everyday practical thought and science as concerned with explanation, prediction and control, via language and action devoid of symbolic imagery, fails miserably. Thus a critical scrutiny of the data reveals that art is set apart from the other types of thought and action by its lack of concern with explanation, prediction and control; whilst magic, religion and science, as Frazer saw, are united by their strong concern with these ends. Rather ironically, symbolic imagery, though playing different roles in different types, is important in all of them. A final Symbolist failure is their attempt to chart and account for cross-cultural differences in balance as between the expressive and the instrumental.

What overall lesson can be drawn from this critique? The obvious lesson might seem to be that we should simply move the line of demarcation between the expressive and the instrumental, whilst leaving the categories themselves to stand. Thus, instead of drawing the line between art, magic and religion on the one hand, and common sense and science on the other, we should draw it between art and the rest. Art would then be expressive, and the rest instrumental.

This move, however, would seem not to go far enough. For another implication of the critique is that the expressive/instrumental contrast is itself of doubtful value. Thus the contrast points to and draws its appeal from the alleged correlation between the two subsidiary contrasts: (1) thought and language engaged in for their own sakes versus thought and language engaged in for the ulterior end of practical control of the world; and (2) symbolic thought and language versus literal thought and language. Once the lack of correlation between these two subsidiary contrasts has been revealed, as it has been here, the major contrast itself loses its rationale.

Round Two

Some Symbolist defences. Symbolists have long been aware of resistance to their views along the broad lines followed here. Indeed, they have coined such phrases as 'neo-Tylorian' and 'neo-Frazerian', on the one hand to identify such resistance, and on the other to characterize it as reactionary. Some of them have been content to respond to it with little more than abuse and ridicule. Others, however, have developed painstaking counter-arguments aimed at defending the Symbolist position from neo-Frazerian assaults.

Now in attacking the Symbolist thesis that magical and religious pretensions to a deep concern with explanation, prediction and control are not to be taken at their face value, both I and others have appealed insistently to contextual evidence. Some Symbolists, however, maintain that, for all our protestations, we have not gone far enough in taking account of this type of evidence. They say that we have in fact neglected certain key contextual features which, once recognized, swing the balance of evidence right back in their favour.

One argument of this kind is almost as old as the Symbolist movement itself. Thus it appears in Langer's work of the 1940s, and is brought out thereafter by several different authors. The most recent appearance I am aware of is in a manifesto broadcast by Geertz in 1982.[37]

The argument runs as follows. In situations where people are striving to achieve specific worldly ends, they often opt for everyday, technological or scientific thought and action as sufficient in themselves for the achievement of these ends. By contrast, they do not take magical or religious thought and action as sufficient in themselves for the achievement of such ends. Rather, these kinds of thought and action are always brought in alongside empirically tried and tested facilitating conditions, whether natural or artificial. Thus the magico-religious 'rain-maker' does not perform his rituals at just any time of the year. He performs them under those seasonal conditions known to be the prelude to rain. Again, the practitioner of magico-religious crop-growth rites performs them, not by themselves, but in conjunction with empirically tried and tested operations of tilling, planting, weeding and harvesting. Now those involved in situations in which magico-religious rituals are performed in conjunction with such empirically warranted facilitating conditions are well aware that the latter are quite sufficient to bring about the desired results. Hence they must also be aware that, from a practical point of view, magic and/or religion are superfluous. If, despite this awareness, they still insist on bringing magic and religion in, this can only be because they see them as serving a different and complementary end: perhaps that of celebrating the results in advance by vividly symbolizing them.

Another more recent argument appealing in a similar manner to broader contextual considerations appears in the work of John Beattie.[38] Beattie contends that, when it comes to taking account of empirical evidence, there is a strong contrast between magical and religious thought on the one hand, and everyday, technological and scientific thought on the other. Thus, for all their professions of concern with explanation, prediction and control, magical and religious thinkers do not take serious account of empirical evidence bearing on their 'theories'. By contrast, everyday, technological and scientific thinkers continually test their theories against such evidence, and modify or replace them if they fail these tests. Now if constant testing against empirical evidence is the *sine qua non* of efficiency in achieving the goals of explanation, prediction and control, and if neither magic nor religion show any concern with such testing, then one can be forgiven for doubting whether they are seriously geared to the pursuit of these goals.

If these two arguments are accepted, then of course the Symbolist interpretation of magic and religion regains its plausibility.

A reply. As regards the first argument, there are two flaws in it.

In the first place, the alleged fact is untrue. Some magical and religious observances both have an evident practical intent and are performed by themselves. Amongst magical observances, sorcery designed to injure or kill an enemy provides an apt example. Amongst religious observances, invocation of a god in a curse against a wrongdoer provides a similar example.

Secondly, even in those cases where magical and religious observances are performed in conjunction with their more obviously warranted practical counterparts, the conclusion drawn by the Symbolists hardly follows. Indeed, if we compare the circumstances in which more obviously practical procedures are used by themselves with the circumstances in which they are supplemented by magical or religious observances, we may find ourselves tempted to draw the opposite conclusion. Thus it has often been pointed out that everyday, technological or scientifically-based operations are used by themselves in circumstances where those involved see the prospect of attaining success through these means alone as good; but that they tend to be supplemented by magical or religious observances where those involved see the prospect in question as less than good. If this observation is correct, then the most obvious interpretation is that, where people bring in the magical or the religious as supplements to other types of action, they do so because they see them as means of increasing a chance of success which otherwise would not be too bright.[39]

The second argument is equally flawed. On the one hand, the picture of magical and religious experts showing total disregard for evidence relevant to their theories carries a great deal less credibility than it did fifty years ago. At the very least, as many writers from Evans-Pritchard onward have pointed out, such experts, faced with adverse results of applications of their theories to the prediction and control of events, search anxiously for explanations of such results, and take whatever further action is suggested by the explanations they come up with as to how nonetheless to achieve their ends. Responses of this kind are hardly evidence of the sort of indifference to practical results that would make us suspect a lack of serious concern with explanation, prediction and control.[40] Furthermore, we now know that, outside the modern West, there is a great deal more empirically-based appraisal of particular pieces of magical and religious theory than we had previously suspected. Magical experts often discard recipes that show long runs of failure in practical application, and replace them with others that show more promise. Religious experts and their congregations often make running cost-benefit appraisals of relationships with particular gods, and show willingness to terminate contracts with old gods and enter into fresh contracts with new gods where these appraisals are consistently negative.[41] Once more, such attitudes are the reverse of those we should expect were magic and religion generally lacking in concern with explanation, prediction and control.

On the other hand, the picture of scientists as engaged in constant testing of their theories, and as ready to scrap and replace them should they fail any of their tests, also lacks the credibility it enjoyed some years ago. Testing in the sciences is now seen as a process more long-drawn-out and problematic than it was formerly thought to be. It is also increasingly seen as a process that involves, not absolute judgement on a single theory, but judgement of the relative merits of alternative theories. As such, with the best will in the world, it may be virtually impossible where only a single theory holds sway. Even where there are alternative theories, moreover, the proponents of each one tend to hang on to it as long as possible despite adverse evidence hurled at them by proponents of its rival. Again, testing is largely the business of the 'pure' scientist. The applied scientist or scientific technologist tends to take theories handed down to him by his 'pure' counterpart very much on trust. Taken together, these various observations suggest that, even in the area of thought which both neo-Frazerians and Symbolists agree to be shaped very largely by the concern for explanation, prediction and control, the picture of continuous testing against experience, accompanied by continuous scrapping and replacement of theories, is a considerable oversimplification of the realities. Rather, there are elements of dogmatic adherence to a theory come what may, as well as elements of a more critical and iconoclastic attitude. Just how these two sets of elements are combined is one of the questions historians and philosophers have been debating for the last twenty-five years.[42]

At the end of the day, we may well feel that we have to concede that the scientist has a greater preoccupation with testing his theories than has the magician or the religious expert. We may also feel that the scientist has introduced greater refinement into the testing process. In the light of what has been said here, however, we can no longer rest content with the stark, simple contrast between the magical or religious expert, indifferent to the practical outcome of his theoretical applications and averse to any kind of testing against empirical evidence, and the scientific expert, obsessed with the practical outcome and continuously preoccupied with testing. And with the contrast greatly blurred, the second argument loses whatever force it may once seem to have had.

With the demolition of both these arguments appealing to context, the neo-Frazerian may feel he has won the day. However, he has yet to breach the Symbolists' last and most fanatically held line of defence.

Round Three

The Symbolists: a last line of defence. If there is one thing above all others on which Symbolists pride themselves, it is on their successful struggle to free the discipline of social anthropology from the ethnocentric distortion of non-Western thought patterns which allegedly bedevilled the work of Frazer and other founding fathers. Hence it is not surprising to find that their last line of defence in this debate takes the form of an appeal to the taboo on ethnocentrism.

According to Symbolists, there are two principal ways in which a Western scholar, in attempting to portray a non-Western system of thought, may flout this taboo. The first is by attributing to bearers of that system a marked degree of shared irrationality. The second is by attributing to them a scientistic preoccupation with the explanation, prediction and control of the space-time world. These two ways of flouting the taboo evoke two distinct lines of critical argument.

In expounding the first line of argument, it is important to start by getting clear about what the terms 'rational' and 'irrational' mean to Symbolists. 'Rational', it seems, means a style of thought and action which is instrumental in the sense that it has an ulterior practical end, and in which the means chosen for the pursuit of that end are, *by the standards of the anthropologist*, adequate to the purpose. Conversely, 'irrational' means a style which again is instrumental in the sense that it has an ulterior practical end, but in which the means chosen for the pursuit of that end are, *by the standards of the anthropologist*, inadequate to the purpose.

Now since it is forbidden to attribute a marked degree of shared irrationality to the bearers of an alien thought-system, it follows that any shared pattern of alien thought and action, which appears to be instrumental, but whose means are, by current anthropological standards, inadequate to its professed end, *must* be reclassified as expressive and hence as concerned with the production and appreciation of symbols for their own sakes.[43] The reasoning involved here has been beautifully if disrespectfully summed up by Nigel Barley as 'It looks crazy. It must be symbolism.'[44]

Symbolists, following these guidelines, are able to congratulate themselves on avoiding ethnocentrism by abstaining from attributions of shared irrationality. For them, it is true, both magic and religion, *if* taken at face value, *are* irrational. Magic; because as every modern man knows, no amount of manipulation of words and symbols can bring about any changes in the portions of reality they refer to. Religion; because as every modern man knows, there are no gods, and the causal connexions postulated by god-based theories do not hold. Considered as bodies of theory-cum-practice, in other words, magic and religion employ cognitive and practical means thoroughly inadequate to achieving the ends they profess to pursue, and from this point of view are seriously defective. But Symbolists, of course, do not rest content with taking them at face value. Obeying their sacred injunction, they transfer them, *en bloc*, to the category of the expressive, where they lie beyond the reach of invidious judgements of rationality.

At this juncture, neo-Frazerians emerge as villainously ethnocentric. Just like the Symbolists, they judge magic and religion, taken at their face value, to be irrational; and for the same reasons. Unlike the Symbolists, however, they refuse to take the further step of transferring these two types of thought and action to the 'safe' category of the expressive. For them, then, the judgement of irrationality is not provisional but final.[45]

Let us now turn to the second line of argument.

Symbolists, as we saw earlier, are widely agreed that, in the modern West, the balance between the expressive and the instrumental has tipped massively in favour of the latter. In other cultures, by contrast, the balance tends to favour the expressive against the instrumental. The great danger for the Western anthropologist, therefore, is that he will misinterpret the thought of other cultures by seeing it exclusively or largely in instrumental terms.

Symbolists, by their steadfast determination to interpret magic and religion as types of thought dedicated to the production and appreciation of symbolic imagery for its own sake, avoid this over-scientistic approach and duly transcend the Western perspective in which they were brought up. By contrast, the neo-Frazerian, with his assertion that both magic and religion are to be taken as dedicated first and foremost to explanation, prediction and control, and with his obstinate determination to take everything literally, remains firmly trapped within his Western horizons.[46]

These two arguments appealing to the taboo on ethnocentrism are the most strongly held and deeply felt of all Symbolist doctrines. With them, I have taken you to the foundations of Symbolist thought.

A final reply. In my final critique, I shall try to dispose of the two lines of argument just reviewed.

In order to mount an effective critique of the first line of argument, I shall take it in two parts. First, I shall look at the procedure of using judgements of face-value rationality as the prelude to classifying alien thought and action. Then I shall look at the embargo on imputations of irrationality itself.

For many of us who are not Symbolists, there is something very odd about the Symbolist classification procedure. Just because a pattern of thought and action seems, by the standards of the anthropologist, to be inadequate to the achievement of its professed end, why should it be transferred from the category of theory-cum-practice to the category of the symbolic? Our sense of oddity, I believe, arises from a conviction that patterns of thought and action are ultimately classifiable in terms of their guiding intentions, and that evidence as to the character of such intentions can only come from the context in which these patterns are deployed. The Symbolist classification procedure strikes us as absurd because it allows other considerations to override those of context. Given the lip-service paid by Symbolists to contextual evidence, indeed, one may say that their classification procedure, in so far as it allows current Western appraisals of cognitive adequacy to override local contextual evidence, is grossly ethnocentric. In insisting on it, indeed, Symbolists seem to have tumbled back into the very bed of sin from which they boast they have escaped.[47]

Would a less ethnocentric concept of rationality make way for a classificatory procedure that avoided this overriding of context? Let us try one and see. Let us define a pattern of theory and practice as rational in relation to a particular end when, in the light of *the range of evidence available to the users and of certain elementary but universal criteria of verification and falsification shared by themselves and the anthropologist*, it strikes the latter as a plausible means to the achievement of that end. Conversely, let us define such a pattern as irrational in relation to a particular end when, in the light of *the range of evidence available to the users and of shared criteria of verification and falsification*, it strikes the anthropologist as an implausible means to the achievement of that end. This definition is by no means devoid of vagueness; but it does seem to eliminate at least some of the Symbolist definition's ethnocentric overtones. It also allows for two possibilities not envisaged by that definition.

The first possibility is that an alien theory may initially appear to the Western anthropologist as an inadequate, irrational guide to action, because he has command of a wider range of relevant evidence than is available to the theory's users, and because the theory fails in the light of this wider range. In the light of the more restricted evidence available to the users, however, the theory, even by the anthropologist's own canons of evidence, may appear as a plausible and rational guide to action. This possibility was recognized long ago by Frazer. In his own words: 'Their errors are not wilful extravagances or the ravings of insanity, but simply hypotheses, *justifiable at the time they were propounded, but which a fuller experience has proved inadequate*' [Italics mine].[48] It has also been long recognized by historians of science, one of whose major achievements has been to show that theories which seem ridiculous to the present-day eye are both comprehensible and plausible when viewed in the light of the limited evidence available to their propounders.[49]

The second possibility is the opposite of the first. It is that a particular alien theory may look to the anthropologist like an inadequate guide to action, because he either lacks or ignores evidence in its favour to which the users have access. Having grasped this evidence and its relevance, however, he will be less inclined to judge the theory as inadequate. An apt example here is provided by African religious theory. Many of the causal connexions between phenomena postulated by such theory continue, when judged by Western standards and in the light of the Western repertoire of evidence, to look invalid. Others, however, are beginning to appear in a more favourable light. In saying this, I am thinking particularly of those explanations, common throughout the continent, in which individual fortune and misfortune, sickness and health, are causally linked, via the gods, to a whole range of social conditions. A few decades ago, Western social and medical scientists would have considered such 'socio-somatic' ideas as ridiculous. Today, however, more and more of them, considering newly available or previously neglected evidence, are coming to believe that such ideas – albeit perhaps divested of their religious component – will have a vital part to play in future social and medical theory.[50]

To credit Frazer with awareness of this second possibility might require us to strain our reading of him unduly. Nonetheless, as I said at the beginning of this lecture, his remarks in the closing pages of the *Golden Bough*, in which he talks of the present-day hypotheses of science as almost certain to be superseded by others at once totally different and incomparably better, would seem to pave the way for an acceptance that non-Western theories may embody valid insights into causal connexions which present-day Western theory has not yet grasped. Once again, moreover, a very clear recognition of this possibility is found in the works of some historians and philosophers of science – especially in those of radicals such as Feyerabend.[51]

In this area, then, both Frazer and the historians/philosophers of science would seem to be a good deal less inflexibly bound to the here-and-now of modern Western thought than are the Symbolists.

Awareness and exploration of both the above possibilities would, I think, do much to restrain Symbolists from hasty judgements of face-value irrationality and from the consequent context-overriding reclassifications.

Even were Symbolists to agree with the rest of us on an amended definition of rationality, however, there might still be occasions on which we all felt the need to make judgements of deficient rationality in respect of some alien theories. For instance, contextual considerations might suggest that a certain pattern of thought was a theory deployed to help its users achieve some ulterior end. Nonetheless, we might all agree that the theory flew flagrantly in the face of adverse evidence that we knew to be abundantly available to the users themselves. In such circumstances, we might all want to make a judgement of face-value irrationality. However, whilst the rest of us might feel inclined to leave the matter there, Symbolists, still guided by the embargo on imputation of irrationality, would, I think, want to take the further step of transferring the thought-pattern in question from the category of theory to that of symbolism.

Here, finally, we come face to face with the embargo on imputations of irrationality itself. Is there something so compelling about this embargo that it *must* be allowed to override contextual evidence?

The trouble here is that the critic has little to get his teeth into. For Symbolists, taking the embargo as axiomatic, offer no argument in its support.

An argument one might put forward in its favour is that human communities have survived down the ages *only* on the basis of an exceptionally high degree of rationality. Imputation to the members of any community of a marked degree of shared irrationality is prima facie implausible, since, so burdened, the community could hardly have survived.

When subjected to closer scrutiny, however, this argument appears unconvincing. For common sense reminds us that, once armed with a strong core of rational beliefs about itself and its environment, any community can carry a considerable penumbra of irrational beliefs and still survive. After all, what about the vast amount of wishful thinking in our own Western society, in circles both low and high? Again, what about the vast amount of theory and practice which, though undeniably geared to the achievement of certain ends, is rendered quite inadequate to such ends by the distortions introduced by ideological and other motives? Or are we to say that such things prevail only in the West, and never outside it? Surely a piece of arrant nonsense, this last! The most the argument can support, therefore, is an embargo on imputations of total or near-total irrationality. Once an interpreter has conceded the existence of a strong rational core, nothing in principle stops him from imputing widespread irrationality in the penumbra.

We have already drawn attention to the ethnocentric consequences of the Symbolist embargo on imputations of widespread irrationality to non-Western peoples. In the absence of any other cogent argument in its favour, I suggest we reject the embargo as itself irrational. As I see it, indeed, the embargo draws its strength, not from the generally accepted canons of scholarly enquiry into human social life, but from preoccupations of an ideological rather than of a cognitive character. Of these preoccupations, I shall say more when I come to try and locate the Symbolist position in its Western cultural context.

Let us now turn to the second of the two arguments appealing to the taboo on ethnocentrism.

This one, you will recall, starts by noting the idiosyncratic character of Western scientism, and concludes that a necessary condition for avoiding ethnocentrism in dealing with the thought of non-Western peoples is the avoidance of scientistic perspectives and the maximum use of aesthetic perspectives; the avoidance of the concept of 'theory' and the maximum use of the concept of 'symbol'.

Here, it seems to me, Symbolists delude themselves rather seriously. For a little reflection will show that there is no such easy escape from Western cultural blinkers.

Now it is certainly wise to insist that, in using the concept of 'theory' in the translation and interpretation of alien thought, we exercise great care. For it surely is the case that aspects of its meaning are to some extent culture-bound. In our translation and interpretive work, therefore, we need to use it with a great deal of cautious qualification. However – and this is what the Symbolists have failed to notice – the same considerations apply to the concept of 'symbol'. In its modern sense, the concept owes much to the work of novelists, literary critics and philosophers working in the Romantic tradition. And here there is a considerable irony. For as historians of ideas have made clear to us, the Romantic movement in the West has been above all an impassioned and sustained reaction to the development of the sciences and to the kind of cold, clinical reasoning alleged to sustain them.[52] Romanticism, then, is in a sense the *product* of the Western scientific revolution, and as such is as quintessentially modern Western as is science itself. In rejecting the concept of 'theory' in favour of that of 'symbol', indeed, the Symbolists seem, once more, to be in danger of tumbling back into ethnocentrism in the very midst of their efforts to escape from it.

What I have just said, of course, applies to every area of modern Western discourse: scientific; aesthetic; religious; ethical; whatever. They are all equally modern Western; and the use of *any* of them for the translation and interpretation of non-Western thought and discourse is fraught with potential for ethnocentric distortion.

All this said, the fact remains that translation and interpretation in terms of a 'world' language are impossible to avoid in cross-cultural studies of thought. And, as things stand at the moment, 'world' language means Western language. But if all areas of Western discourse, considered as instruments for translation and interpretation, carry equal potential for distortion, what are we to do? Should we just give up?

No: I do not think we should give up. What we must do is start with an awareness that *no* area of Western discourse is ready for translational use as it stands, and that *no* area of Western meta-discourse is ready for interpretative use as it stands. At both levels, we should be ready to bend, stretch and otherwise modify. At both levels, too, we should be ready for the mindboggling task of trying to recombine areas of discourse, such as the scientific and the religious, that have become sundered in the highly compartmentalized world of modern Western culture.[53] Finally, in all these operations, we should be guided by the context of the thought and discourse we are studying. On no account should we allow other considerations to override the evidence of context.

As a recipe for avoiding ethnocentrism, of course, this one is a good deal more difficult and demanding than the simple aestheticist remedy offered by the Symbolists. However, I think the extra effort required in putting it into practice will prove well worth the trouble.

As I pointed out earlier on, the two arguments appealing to the taboo on ethnocentrism constitute the sustaining foundation of Symbolist thought; and with both shown to be threadbare, this critique is complete.

The Symbolists and their milieu: brown noses, white hearts?

Before bringing this lecture to a close, I should like to make a few further remarks on the subject of Symbolist ethnocentrism.

At the outset, let me affirm my belief that modern social anthropologists' constant preoccupation with the need to avoid ethnocentrism is, though sometimes boring, also admirable. For, amongst other things, it is our version of that ideal of objectivity in human enquiry which is currently so unfashionable both in the humanities and in the social sciences. As such, I believe we have a duty to cherish it, especially until our colleagues in allied disciplines return to their senses.

Now it is above all the Symbolists who claim to have liberated social anthropology from the ethnocentrism of its founding fathers, and who continue to be the most fervent in preaching against it. Yet, as we have seen in this Lecture, they themselves have shown ominous signs of sliding back into this mortal sin in the process of trying to escape from it. Before conceding their claim to a heroic role in the fight against sin, then, let me make a few suggestions as to how their theories, too, may have been shaped more by their specifically Western cultural background than by the world-wide phenomena for which they purport to account.

In pursuing this matter, let me deal first with what I call the Symbolists' 'mother-culture discourse skills', and then turn to their more general values and attitudes.

Reading between the lines of Symbolist writings, I pick up the following profile of mother-culture discourse skills. First, a relatively strong grounding in modern Western aesthetic-cum-literary discourse. Second, a relatively poor grounding in modern Western religious discourse. Third, a relatively poor grounding in modern Western scientific discourse. Now if I am right about this profile, what emerges is an endowment of discourse skills which is not only very skewed and partial, but also entirely characteristic of its time and place. Indeed, it corresponds closely to the kind of endowment described by C. P. Snow as going with his 'literary' culture.[54]

The assumption of such a skewed and partial endowment helps us to a better understanding of a number of otherwise puzzling features of the Symbolist position. For instance, there is the Symbolist determination, against the weight of contextual evidence, to assimilate magical and religious thought to the aesthetic-cum-literary. This now appears as a case of getting as much mileage as possible, in conducting one's translational and inter-pretative work, out of the limited mother-culture skills one does have. Again, there is the inversion of the actual relationship between the religious and the symbolic. This can be understood in terms of the want of any real grasp of Western religious discourse. Yet again, there is the failure to see the deep affinity between religious and scientific thought. This, as I have already hinted, seems to be the result of a defective vision of scientific discourse which leaves no place at all for the role of ideas about underlying reality, or for that of symbol and metaphor in creating and sustaining such ideas.

Ironically, the only valid point that Symbolists do seem to have grasped about religion and science in the modern West is that, in recent times, the two have been regarded as pursuing quite disparate aims. This, alas for them, is the one thing that does not help them in translating and interpreting the religious thought of other places and times. For, as I pointed out earlier, it represents a more or less unique development, and a very recent one even in the West. Once again, better acquaintance with the history of both religious and scientific discourse in the West would have made this point obvious.[55]

In short, then, many characteristic Symbolist ideas are more readily accounted for when viewed as manifestations of a particular partial configuration of Western discourse skills than they are when viewed as responses to a world-wide spectrum of magical and religious phenomena.

What of the more general values and attitudes of the Symbolists? To identify these, I think we have to start by reminding ourselves of the radical loss of cultural self-confidence that has affected so many reflective Westerners during the present century. Some of the principal factors behind this momentous change of heart have been: anxiety over social disorganization brought about by accelerated industrialization; doubts as to the benefits of technological and scientific thinking stemming above all from two world wars and from an increasingly vivid appreciation of the world-destroying power of chemical and nuclear pollution; and finally anxiety over challenges to the economic and political hegemony of the West. Together, these factors have done much to erode the collective arrogance and self-satisfaction rife amongst late nineteenth- and early twentieth-century intellectuals, and to replace these with a state of collective self-questioning and self-doubt. Together, too, they have triggered a dramatic resurgence of a counter-cultural tradition which has been present in the West in some measure ever since the eighteenth century. Here, of course, I refer once more to the Romanticism which repudiates the cold, analytic, scientific reason alleged to be the dominant emphasis of Western modernity, and longs to replace it with an utterly contrasted warm, intuitive, aesthetic and symbolic approach to the world.

I believe much of what seems inexplicable, even perverse in Symbolist thinking can be understood in terms of this background. The latter's effect seems to me to have been two-fold.

First, it has given the Symbolists a deep sense of guilt and anxiety about the arrogantly invidious comparisons made by their predecessors between the thought of the West and that of the non-West. As a result, they have been almost neurotically obsessed with avoiding any interpretation of non-Western thought that carries the smallest hint of arrogance and invidiousness. Only in these terms, I suggest, can we account for their otherwise perplexing taboo on imputing irrationality to the thought products of non-Western cultures, and for the various contortions which they perform in order to avoid what they see as infringements of this taboo.

Secondly, this background has led Symbolists to project on to non-Western cultures an image which satisfies their yearning for a counter-culture that replaces the major features of Western modernity with their opposites. Hence their vision of such cultures as dominated by a mode of thought whose guiding intention is totally different from that of the hated and feared technological-cum-scientific thought.

As I see it, then, Symbolist thinking is overwhelmingly shaped, not just by the endowment of specific discourse skills associated with the modern Western aesthetic-literary sub-culture, but also by the most general values and attitudes of that sub-culture.

So much for Symbolists' smugness about their liberation from ethnocentrism. For me, as will by now be obvious, their anxiety to avoid giving offence to the non-West, combined with their tendency to view non-Western thought through all-too-Western spectacles, points to an entirely different evaluation. Earlier, I suggested that we should picture Frazer as a man with a white mask and a brown heart. Adding a little dash of American scatology to my Fanonian imagery, I suggest we picture the Symbolists as people with brown noses and white hearts.

Concluding remarks

To conclude, let me return to the question; 'Back to Frazer?' What did I have in mind in putting it?

Some mischief, of course, as I admitted. But also a more serious intent. For the benefit of those who are still not sure of the message, let me offer a final clarification. First of all, as should be clear from my opening remarks, I am not advocating an uncritical return to Frazerian views. Rather, I am suggesting that the dominant post-Frazerian school of anthropological thought about magic and religion has made no real advance on those views. For one set of mistakes, it has merely substituted another set just as serious. For Victorian ethnocentrism (if indeed this label really fits the complexities of Frazer), it has merely substituted Elizabethan ethnocentrism.

In the circumstances, it seems to me that we should try to get back to the road-junction where we left Frazer; not with the idea of staying there with him, but rather with the idea of picking another and quite different road forward. On such a road, we should not be afraid, where the evidence warrants it, to make literal interpretations and generous use of the concept of theory. At the same time, we should give due recognition to the symbol: sometimes, as in the arts, as the queen of discourse; sometimes, as in religion and science, as the hand-maid of theory. Finally, on such a road, we should take as our guiding inspiration, not liberal scruples or romantic yearnings, but intellectual, imaginative and emotional curiosity. That way, we might come a little nearer to the escape from ethnocentrism for which we are all striving.

5   Professor Winch on safari

One of the most widely cited of recent writings on the borderland of philosophy and anthropology is Peter Winch's 'Understanding a Primitive Society' (referred to hereafter as UPS).[1] The main reason for the breadth of its appeal would seem to be a blend of general principle and particular application all too seldom found in the writings of philosophers of social science. Thus, on the one hand, Winch develops further some of the general principles of cross-cultural understanding which he first enunciated in his *Idea of a Social Science* (referred to hereafter as ISS).[2] And, on the other hand, he attempts to show us, in considerable detail, how these principles can be applied to the solution of a particularly vexing anthropological problem: that of interpreting 'primitive' mystical thought.

Now many reputable philosophers have produced critical articles on Winch's general principles of intra- and cross-cultural understanding.[3] And I have nothing very startling to add to what they have said about these principles. So, at this level, I shall simply make a few brief remarks to show where I stand. In the course of their critiques, several of these philosophers have also looked in passing at Winch's purported application of his principles to the particular problem of mystical thinking. It seems to me, however, that by and large they have not looked closely enough, either at the ethnographic sources from which he claims to derive his inspiration, or at the arguments by which he moves from his sources to his conclusions. It is at this level, then, that I wish to deliver the main thrust of my own criticism.

Winch's general principles

The basic thesis of UPS is a simple one. It is that, in order to understand the utterances of members of an alien culture, one must always seek, in the first instance, to discover the point which such utterances have *for them*. To discover this point, we must set these utterances as fully as possible in the context of social life within which they arise.[4] Only when we have done this shall we be in a position to say which utterances associated with our own conceptual system are the appropriate translation instruments. Further, in

138

the search for translation instruments, we must be as open-minded as possible. We must not exclude in advance *any* of the various universes of discourse available to us.[5] Nor must we exclude the possibility that *none* of them may be suitable.[6]

Given this view of the anthropological enterprise, the great pitfall, ever-present and ever-to-be-avoided, is the temptation to try and project on to an alien culture a point or purpose which looms very large in our minds, but which may feature peripherally or not at all in the minds of those whose life and thought we are trying to understand. For the twentieth-century Western anthropologist, the temptation, specifically, is to try and project a preoccupation with explanation, prediction and control which is central to the sciences and to technology, but which may have little or no importance in the life of many non-Western peoples.[7]

Most readers will find this argument persuasive. It does, however, create a problem as large as those it solves. Thus, on the one hand, it raises the possibility that members of different cultures may pursue totally disparate goals, and that their utterances may have totally disparate points. On the other hand, however, it stresses that the process of understanding is not complete until the anthropologist has specified the kind of utterance in his own culture that has the same point as the alien utterances he is trying to make sense of. To his credit, Winch sees the problem; and at the end of UPS he suggests a solution. He suggests that men in every culture confront the same 'limiting situations' of birth, sexual relations and death; and that from this confrontation arise certain universal attitudes, emotions and aims. These form a kind of inter-cultural bridge that permits translation and so makes possible the completion of the process of understanding.[8]

There is much shrewd sense in all of this. Winch conveys very vividly the delicate balance required for the successful pursuit of translational under-standing: a balance between, on the one hand, the need to avoid projecting one's own aims and purposes into a situation where they have little or no relevance; and, on the other hand, the need to find *some* area of discourse in one's own culture which has the same point as the area of alien discourse one is trying to make sense of. He also conveys the related and equally important message that there are two great prerequisites for this kind of understand-ing. One is the need for prolonged and sympathetic participant observation conducted through the language of those whose thought one is trying to understand. The other is the need for the scholar involved to have mastery of the greatest possible variety of kinds of discourse in his own culture. Now although the first prerequisite is emphasized by nearly all writers on this topic, the second is all too often neglected. And Winch's exposition has the virtue of reminding us that the two are equally vital.

These favourable comments must, however, be balanced by some criticisms. First of all, it seems clear that there is potentially much more to anthropological understanding than Winch would allow. For although the procedure he recommends seems indeed to constitute the vital first phase of comprehension, we have every reason to think that there are further possible phases. Here, let us look again at one of the problems which he raises in passing: the problem constituted by the fact that certain aims or purposes may provide the point of a vast corpus of utterances in one culture, yet be of purely peripheral importance in another. For Winch, such a situation is significant only as a potential pitfall for the anthropologist in quest of translational understanding. In itself, it does not call for a further and different act of understanding. For many of us, however, it is at precisely this point that the most intriguing questions arise. Of course, it may be possible to answer them within a Winchian framework: as when we discover that apparently disparate patterns of purpose are merely the products of differing environmental cicumstances that force people to pursue the same ultimate end by differing means. In other instances, however, we are likely to be confronted with patterns of purpose that are irreducibly different in their emphases. And if we wish to further our understanding in these cases, we shall be unable to avoid bringing in the kind of causal analysis for which Winch leaves no place.

One might be tempted to rest the critique at this point. But to do so would be a mistake. For the difficulty is not just that Winch's idea of translational understanding represents only the first phase of a multiphase interpretative process. The idea itself suffers from serious internal defects and incompletenesses.

To start with, Winch holds an unduly restricted view of the situational and motivational common ground which makes translational understanding possible. In taking birth, sexual relations and death as the locus of universal human strivings and purposes, he will be well received by those who prefer to think of man as poetic and religious rather than coldly pragmatic in his essence; for these are precisely the situations which, in Western culture at least, favour *homo poetico-religiosus* as against *homo scientifico-technologicus*. However, if we discount the warm glow which his writing on these matters produces, and think through the topic more coolly, we shall surely find his view of the range of universal human strivings inadequate. What, for instance, of the strivings to satisfy hunger and thirst? Of the strivings to avoid extremes of heat and cold? Of the striving for power? Geared as they are to biological needs, these and many other unromantic and remarkable strivings are common to all human beings in all ages and places. For all the persuasive warmth of Winch's writing on these things, scholars such as Malinowski, Piddington and Goldschmidt, with their dull sociological prose and their long shopping-lists of universal strivings, may well be better guides.[9] Once we accept one of these longer inventories, moreover, the translational bridge becomes much wider and more impressive than the one Winch offers.

However, whether we accept Winch's restricted list of situational and motivational universals, or whether we accept one of the longer lists, a major problem still remains. For though we can see, intuitively, that the broader the motivational common ground, the easier it will be to understand the thought and discourse of another culture, we still have to spell out just *how* we can move from what others share with us to what they do not share with us. And it is at the very point where we are led to hope that Winch will give some account of this process, that he signs off.

Here, perhaps, one can come to the rescue by spelling out the implications for this process of certain other things he says. Typically, a universal human striving derives its universality from the fact that it is geared to a biological need. But although this need may well be one which man shares with other, non-human species, the purposive striving to which it gives rise in the human case is something associated with a completely distinctive mode of behaviour. Notably, as Winch points out, man pursues his aims in a cooperation with his fellows which is mediated by language, and which involves planning, foresight and the following of rules.[10] Now, although he has laid considerable stress on this point, he has not followed through to its full implications. As several other philosophers have shown in recent years, cooperative endeavour of this kind would be impossible without something like our everyday Western conception of material objects which exist and persist independently of ourselves; without something like our everyday spatial and temporal concepts; without something like our everyday differentiation between persons and non-persons; without something like our everyday notion of causality; without something like our everyday idea of and attitude to contradiction; without something like our everyday concepts of truth, falsity and agreement with reality.[11]

Now in much of Winch's exposition, this whole apparatus of interlinked concepts and attitudes seems to be treated as a purely Western quirk. But if what these other philosophers have said is correct, it provides the crucial infrastructure for all the more specialized 'universes of discourse' and 'forms of life' in all cultures.

There is one very obvious sense in which this must be so. In so far as this conceptual apparatus is a prerequisite, not only for the very business of staying alive, but also for the sheer possibility of assembling at given times and places, it is clearly crucial to the viability of more specialized 'forms of life' such as the religious, the artistic and the scientific. But to say no more than this would be to say nothing further about the possibility of understanding these special forms. For even if one grants that the universal conceptual infrastructure is essential to a live human quorum, and that a live human quorum is essential to any 'form of life', however specialized, one still has to accept the possibility that this infra-structure may not help us to understand the special kind of discourse which goes with the 'form of life'. To give an example, it is certainly the universal infra-structure that ensures a live quorum for periodic church services. But it by no means follows that the infrastructure will help us to understand what people think and say once they are assembled in church.

In fact, however, I think there is a second and more relevant sense in which the universal conceptual apparatus provides an infra-structure for these more specialized 'forms of life'. It begins to look more and more as though this apparatus provides the raw material from which all the more specialized 'universes of discourse' are built up. Thus, as I suggested in a recent essay, a great deal of light can be thrown on the more esoteric features of both modern Western Christianity and modern Western Science (not to speak of traditional African religion), if we accept that the universes of discourse associated with both these special forms of life have been built up very largely by an extension (and in many places an over-extension) of the concepts of everyday material-object language.[12] Now this suggestion, if valid, is clearly relevant to the solution of our problem. For, if all the more specialized universes of discourse in all cultures are in large measure the products of secondary adaptation of the concepts of a universal material-object language, the problem of how to pass from what is shared to what is idiosyncratic largely evaporates.

So much for Winch's general principles of translational understanding. As I hope will be clear, the critique offered above is a limited one. I have accepted Winch's basic thesis, and have concentrated largely on the business of clarification and development.

Now, however, it is time to turn from qualified approval to unqualified disapproval.

The problem of mystical thinking

Winch's particular application of his general principles is to the under-standing of what anthropologists commonly call mystical thinking: i.e. thinking which involves unobservable entities of a spiritualistic kind, such as gods and witchcraft emanations. As his test case, he takes the thought and discourse of the Azande of the Southern Sudan. By implication, however, what he has to say about Zande mystical thinking is applicable to African and indeed to 'primitive' peoples generally.[13]

The main drift of his argument is that the interpretation of 'primitive' mystical thinking by Evans-Pritchard and other Western anthropologists provides a classic example of the projection, on to a vast body of alien utterances, of strivings and purposes which are centrally important in the culture of the interpreters but which have little or no importance in the minds of the utterers. Thus Evans-Pritchard and his colleagues, in interpreting mystical utterances as statements of hypotheses whose point lies in the area of explanation, prediction and control of everyday events, are simply projecting their own obsession with the goals of science and technology on to cultures where such goals are of peripheral importance. If they had made a serious effort to discover the point of such utterances for those concerned, they would have proceeded quite differently. In Winch's words:

But I do not want to say that we are quite powerless to find ways of thinking in our own society that will help us to see the Zande institution in a clearer light. I only think that the direction in which we should look is quite different from what MacIntyre [a follower of Evans-Pritchard in this] suggests. Clearly the nature of Zande life is such that it is of very great importance to them that their crops should thrive. Clearly too they take all kinds of practical 'technological' steps, within their capabilities, to ensure that they do thrive. But there is no reason to see their magical rites as a further, misguided such step. A man's sense of the importance of something to him shows itself in all sorts of ways: not merely in precautions to safeguard that thing. He may want to come to terms with its importance to him in a quite different way: to contemplate it, to gain some sense of his life in relation to it. He may wish thereby, in a certain sense, to *free* himself from dependence on it. I do not mean by making sure it does not let him down, because the point is that, *whatever* he does, he may still be let down. The important thing is that he should understand *that* and come to terms with it. Of course merely to understand that is not to come to terms with it, though perhaps it is a necessary condition for so doing, for a man may equally well be transfixed and terrorized by the contemplation of such a possibility. He must see that he can still go on even if he is let down by what is vitally important to him; and he must so order his life that he still *can* go on in such circumstances. I stress once again that I do not mean this in the sense of becoming 'technologically independent', because from the present point of view technological independence is yet another form of dependence. Technology destroys some dependencies but always creates new ones, which may be fiercer, because harder to understand, than the old. This should be particularly apparent to *us*.

In Judaeo-Christian cultures the conception of 'If it be Thy Will', as developed in the story of Job, is clearly central to the matter I am discussing. Because this conception is central to Christian prayers of supplication, they may be regarded from one point of view as freeing the believer from dependence on what he is supplicating for. Prayers cannot play this role if they are regarded as a means of influencing the outcome for in that case the one who prays is still dependent on the outcome. He frees himself from this by acknowledging his complete dependence on God; and this is totally unlike any dependence on the outcome precisely because God is eternal and the outcome contingent.

I do not say that Zande magical rites are at all like Christian prayers of supplication in the positive attitude to contingencies which they express. What I do suggest is that they are alike in that they do, or may, express an attitude to contingencies; one, that is, which involves recognition that one's life is subject to contingencies, rather than an attempt to control these.[14]

In short, Evans-Pritchard and his colleagues should have drawn their translation instruments, not from an area of Western discourse geared to explanation, prediction and control of events, but from an area geared to the development of an acceptance of events for better or for worse; not from the language of science and technology, but from a rather special kind of religious language.

Having pushed the line of interpretation of African mystical beliefs suggested by Evans-Pritchard's work a good deal further than Evans-Pritchard himself would have been prepared to go, I have, naturally, come to find myself in strong disagreement with Winch. And in a recent review of a collection of essays in honour of Evans-Pritchard, he in turn has castigated me for perpetuating the latter's mistake.[15]

In particular, Winch objects to the way in which I criticize 'orthodox' interpreters of African religious belief for refusing to take statements of such belief at their quasi-scientistic 'face value'. In a slick extension of my metaphor, he points out that a banknote has a 'face value' only in so far as it belongs to a definite system of currency. Hence my attempt to appeal to the 'face value' of African beliefs without answering the crucial questions about what currency these beliefs belong to simply pre-judges the issue. African mystical beliefs, he urges, can only be understood by someone who is willing to grant that they may belong to a currency quite other than that constituted by scientific-technological discourse.[16]

In point of fact, Winch twists my words. For in appealing to scholars to take African mystical beliefs at their 'face value', I was appealing to them precisely to look at such beliefs in their full context of use, and not make interpretations which run counter to all the evidence as to the nature of this context.[17] A very Winchian appeal, in fact! Be this as it may, the differences between Winch and myself on the interpretation of mystical belief are real enough. In what follows, I hope to show that it is Winch, and not Evans-Pritchard, MacIntyre or myself, who is the most appropriate target for the methodological *caveats* of 'Understanding a Primitive Society'.

To substantiate his critique of the 'scientistic' interpretation of African mystical beliefs, Winch makes extensive reference to Evans-Pritchard's classic monograph on Zande thought.[18] Since there is strong suspicion that many of those who have enrolled most enthusiastically under his banner have never in fact given Evans-Pritchard's long and demanding work a careful, cover-to-cover reading, let me start by saying something about its content.

As its title suggests, the book is an exploration of Zande concepts of the mystical influences involved in the operation of witchcraft, oracles and magic. Perhaps more than any other anthropological monograph before or since, it places mystical concepts in their full context of everyday usage. In this respect, it is a model of the kind of conceptual analysis that Winch and his disciples advocate. Yet what emerges from this exercise? Again and again, by means of anecdote and incident, Evans-Pritchard shows us mystical concepts mobilized in connection with the concern to account for and remedy present misfortune, and with the concern to predict and avoid future misfortune. He portrays the Azande as a people who struggle constantly, manfully and cheerfully to overcome their troubles in this world; a people who have little place in their thought for serene or resigned contemplation. The system of mystical belief, serving as a comprehensive apparatus for explanation, prediction and control, is the principal means whereby they are able to maintain this attitude.

In short, the great body of evidence which Evans-Pritchard presents on the social context of Zande mystical belief seems most unfavourable to Winch's interpretation. Indeed, it seems nothing less than perverse of him to have made this, of all books, the evidential base for his thesis.[19]

Someone holding Winch's general view of the nature of African mystical concepts could, of course, simply say that Evans-Pritchard, during his research and writing, was so overcome by his obsession with scientific-technical discourse that it distorted even his reports of individual instances of belief, behaviour and social context. If one took this position, however, one could hardly go on to use Evans-Pritchard's own material as the basis of a re-analysis – which is precisely what Winch tries to do. How in fact does he manage?

In the event, he accepts the descriptive material in Evans-Pritchard's monograph to the extent of admitting, albeit unwillingly, a strong *surface appearance* of similarity between Zande mystical beliefs and the beliefs associated with the sciences. This admission emerges at several points in his essay.

Thus, at one point, he cites the following key passage from Evans-Pritchard:

Azande observe the action of the poison oracle as we observe it, but their observations are always subordinated to their beliefs and are incorporated into their beliefs and made to explain and justify them. Let the reader consider any argument that would utterly demolish all Zande claims for the power of the oracle. If it were translated into Zande modes of thought it would serve to support their entire structure of belief. For their mystical notions are eminently coherent, being interrelated by a network of logical ties, and are so ordered that they never too crudely contradict sensory experience but, instead, experience seems to justify them. The Zande is immersed in a sea of mystical notions, and if he speaks about his poison oracle he must speak in a mystical idiom.[20]

Not only does Winch appear to approve the cogency of this particular comment. He suggests that, by transposing the terms 'Zande' and 'European', 'mystical' and 'scientific', it is possible to construct a parody which is also a cogent comment on the nature of scientific thinking:

Europeans observe the action of the poison oracle just as Azande observe it, but their observations are always subordinated to their beliefs and are incorporated into their beliefs and made to explain and justify them. Let a Zande consider any argument that would utterly refute all European scepticism about the power of the oracle. If it were translated into European modes of thought it would serve to support their entire structure of belief. For their scientific notions are eminently coherent, being interrelated by a network of logical ties, and are so ordered that they never too crudely contradict mystical experience but, instead, experience seems to justify them. The European is immersed in a sea of scientific notions, and if he speaks about the Zande poison oracle he must speak in a scientific idiom.[21]

Now although Winch uses this parody to criticize an aspect of Evans-Pritchard's position other than the one under discussion here,[22] his use of it constitutes a clear admission of apparent parallels between Zande mystical and European scientific thought.

Again, in trying to direct our minds to appropriate European parallels to the Zande poison oracle considered as a source of revelation about the mystical forces operating in any situation, he says:

A Zande would be utterly lost and bewildered without his oracle. The mainstay of his life would be lacking. It is rather as if an engineer, in our own society, were asked to build a bridge without mathematical calculation, or a military commander to mount an extensive coordinated attack without the use of clocks. These analogies are mine, *but a reader may well think they beg the question at issue* [italics mine].[23]

And a little further on, in discussing the appropriate logical placing of oracular revelations, he says:

We might say that the revelation has the logical status of an unfulfilled hypothetical *were it not that the context in which this logical term is generally used may again suggest a misleadingly close analogy with scientific hypotheses* [italics mine].[24]

In both these passages, we see him tempted by Evans-Pritchard's descriptions into drawing parallels between Zande mystical discourse and the area of European discourse geared to the ends of explanation, prediction and control. In the italicized portions of both passages, we also see him pulling himself up short, in embarrassed realization that his arguments are on the verge of providing ammunition for his opponents' fire!

Like Evans-Pritchard, MacIntyre and myself, then, Winch certainly thinks that Zande mystical notions *look* in many ways like Western scientific/technical notions. Unlike us, however, he thinks that the appearances are deceptive.

Now if two parties agree on appearances, but one of them maintains that the appearances are deceptive, the burden of argument falls upon the sceptic. In this instance, Winch is the sceptic; so let us see how he copes with the burden. In fact, he produces three arguments designed to show that 'things are not what they seem'.

One apparently plausible argument is to be found in the following passage:

The chief function of oracles is to reveal the presence of mystical forces – I use Evans-Pritchard's term without committing myself to his denial that such forces really exist. Now although there are indeed many ways of determining whether or not mystical forces are operating, these ways do not correspond to what we call 'empirical' confirmation or refutation. This indeed is a tautology, since such differences in confirmatory procedures are the main criteria for classifying something as a mystical force in the first place. Here we have one reason why the possibilities of 'refutation by experience' are much fewer than might at first sight be supposed. There is another closely connected reason. The spirit in which oracles are consulted is very unlike that in which a scientist makes experiments. Oracular revelations are not treated as hypotheses and, since their sense derives from the way they are treated in their context, they therefore *are not* hypotheses. They are not a matter of intellectual interest but the main way in which Azande decide how they should act. If the oracle reveals that a proposed course of action is fraught with the mystical dangers from witchcraft or sorcery, that action will not be carried out; and then the question of refutation or confirmation just does not arise.[25]

What Winch seems to be getting at here is that Zande beliefs do not take account of experience in anything like the way theoretical beliefs in the sciences do, and that they must therefore belong to an entirely different universe of discourse.

Now it would be silly to deny that, in this respect, there *are* differences between Zande mystical beliefs and Western scientific beliefs. But, as we shall see, the differences are more subtle than dramatic; more of degree than of kind. And, such as they are, they do nothing to help Winch prove his basic point.

Let us proceed by taking successively stronger senses of 'taking account of experience', and try to see at what point we can use this criterion to separate one set of beliefs from the other.

If we start with the broadest and weakest sense of the phrase, we find it impossible to separate the two. Thus, as Evans-Pritchard makes clear at so many points in his book, Azande do not waste time in disinterested speculation about what sort of thing witchcraft emanation is in itself. Rather, they are interested in the observable preconditions and the observable consequences of its coming into play. They are interested, not in what it is in itself, but in what it does in the observable world.[26] In this sense, their attitude to witchcraft influence, like that of scientists to their unobservable entities, is highly empirical, indeed highly 'operational'.[27]

Again, despite what Winch says, there are many occasions when, during the course of their everyday lives, Azande do put the predicted experiential consequences of their mystical beliefs to the test: as for instance when the oracle has told them that measures taken have cleared mystical obstacles from their path, and that they are therefore free to go ahead with projected plans. On such occasions, they are anything but indifferent to the relation between the predictions generated by their beliefs and subsequent experience. If such predictions are confirmed by experience, they point to this fact with satisfaction as evidence for the correctness of the original oracular revelation and for the efficacy of the oracle poison. If the predictions are refuted, they worriedly look for reasons: e.g. sorcerers interfering with the revelation or spoiled oracle poison.[28] Here again, we are still in a world not notably different from that of the scientist.

It may even be that Azande, in their mystical beliefs, have taken account of experience in a yet stronger sense. As I have pointed out elsewhere, some of the correlations suggested by these beliefs, especially those between social disturbance and disease, are by no means as fanciful as they may have seemed at the time when Evans-Pritchard was writing his monograph. Indeed, for a relatively non-mobile population faced with a fairly constant stock of diseases and thus having the fortune to acquire over time a moderate resistance to what might otherwise have been killer organisms, the Zande theory of disease may well have highlighted just those correlations which *were* crucial to death or recovery in a significant number of cases. Limited to a similar range of evidence, medical scientists might have come to strikingly similar conclusions.[29]

Winch, however, may well have in mind a stronger and more Popperian sense of 'taking account of experience' than any we have yet considered: a sense which carries connotations of thoroughgoing scepticism about established beliefs, and readiness for radical revolution in the face of adverse experience.

Now if we use the phrase in this sense, Azande certainly do not come up to scratch. For instance, where predictions generated by the central core of mystical beliefs are refuted by experience, they do not, under any circumstances, respond by rejection of this core. Rather, they produce *ad hoc* secondary elaborations, which account for the refutation of the predictions whilst leaving the core intact.[30] This lack of tentativeness or scepticism *vis-à-vis* core beliefs is, presumably, what Winch is thinking of when he says that, for Azande, such beliefs are not hypotheses.

Popper, of course, would say that a readiness to reject core beliefs in the face of adverse experience was precisely what distinguished scientists from other kinds of thinkers, Azande included. In recent years, however, this way of distinguishing scientists from others has been seriously called in question. Michael Polanyi, one of the first to challenge it, actually used Zande reactions to refutation of their predictions by experience as an illustration of the way in which scientists react to similar challenges.[31] Thomas Kuhn, a more recent and more widely-known challenger, has suggested that, during long periods of 'normal science', when people are primarily concerned to follow up the detailed implications of a core of established theory, particular failures of prediction evoke a response which differs little from that of Azande placed in similar circumstances. Only when failures begin to come thick and fast does some sense of unease arise, and a search for alternative theoretical cores begin. And only when a new core has been formulated and has begun to show promise do members of a discipline begin to react to the established core in the tentative, sceptical manner recommended by Popper.[32] Yet more recent commentators, notably Paul Feyerabend and the late Imre Lakatos, have repudiated Kuhn's 'one-at-a-time' picture as failing to do justice to the historical facts. In its place, they sketch a scene of institutionalized competition between different theoretical schools, each by its criticisms stimulating the others to greater feats of theoretical development and systematization. Even in this sort of characterization, however, the adherents of a particular school are portrayed as reacting to failures of prediction very much as Azande do.[33]

There are whole books to be written on this debate, of course; and here it is necessary to get on to other things. For the moment, suffice it to say that, in their eagerness to correct what they see as Popper's caricature of the scientific enterprise, these more recent commentators have tended to produce caricatures at the opposite extreme. My own feeling is that there will eventually be a synthesis; and that it will be one which keeps in mind the overriding requirement of the scientific enterprise, that one theory only be succeeded by another when the latter has provided overwhelming evidence of greater explanatory potential. If this is indeed the ultimate goal of scientific institutions, it means that they must provide places for two very different types of scholar. On the one hand, they must provide for the Kuhnian conservative who will make sure that an established theory is not abandoned until the last drop of explanatory potential is squeezed out of it. On the other hand, they must provide for the Popperian iconoclastic innovator who will make sure, not only that the established theory is subjected to constant destructive criticism, but also that there will always be an embryo new theory around ready for development in its place. As to how the balance is to be struck between these different intellectual types, perhaps there can be no single answer. But struck it surely must be.

One implication of this recent work in the philosophy, history and sociology of science is that it is much more difficult than Winch would have us believe to differentiate the Zande mystical thinker from the Western scientific thinker on the grounds that the former is not at all concerned with empirical confirmation and refutation, whilst the latter is centrally concerned with such things. Having said this, however, let us go some of the way with Winch. Let us grant that a certain overriding willingness to make radical revisions of core beliefs in the face of adverse experience is largely absent from the Zande scene but is a pervasive feature of the Western scientific scene, and that this does represent a very significant difference between the two types of thought we are trying to compare.

Having gone so far with him, however, one still has to ask; what does *this* finding do to help him prove his basic point? To which the answer, I fear, is: nothing! Remember that, in this essay, he is concerned above all to show that the whole complex of Zande mystical thinking is geared, not to the ends of explanation, prediction and control, but to the entirely different end of achieving resigned contemplation of the vicissitudes of life. But the essence of his first argument is nothing more than an inference, from the premiss that the Zande mystical thinker is unwilling to make radical revisions of his core beliefs in the face of adverse experience, to the conclusion that the point of such beliefs cannot be explanation, prediction and control. And this inference, of course, is a *non sequitur*.

This last remark brings me to my final objection to Winch's first argument. It is that, even if we accept his differentiation between the Zande mystical thinker and the Western scientific thinker on the grounds that the former is not 'open' to experience whilst the latter is, we can still only accept it as applicable to the Zande mystical thinker and the Western *research scientist*. For, as Winch himself would be the first to admit, the world of modern science comprises not only the research man who is concerned with the testing and development of theory, but also the scientific technologist who puts well-established theory into practice. And the latter is trained above all to accept established theory in an unquestioning spirit, the better to ensure that he will act decisively when he comes to make practical use of it. In consequence, all of Winch's remarks about the Zande mystical thinker's attitude to experience are equally applicable to the scientific technologist. He too treats his theory as an article of faith, not as a hypothesis. He too avoids trying out any course of action which his theory says would be practically disastrous. He too greets any disappointment of theory-based prediction with *ad hoc* excuses which account for the disappointment whilst leaving the core of the theory intact – excuses about probable carelessness of operators, faults in instruments, and impurities in materials. In short, the scientific technologist, 'closed' to adverse experience yet plainly dedicated to the linked ends of explanation, prediction and control, is a living pointer to the spuriousness of the inference on which the first argument of UPS depends.

Let us turn now to Winch's second argument. This one is based on the presence, at the heart of Zande mystical belief, of what looks to the Western observer like unresolved inconsistencies and even outright contradictions. In particular, Winch points to the fact that, whilst certain aspects of Zande doctrine about witchcraft influence stress its hereditary character, others deny any such character. Winch quotes with approval Evans-Pritchard's own comment on this situation: 'Azande do not perceive the contradiction as we perceive it because they have no theoretical interest in the subject, and those situations in which they express their belief in witchcraft do not force the problem upon them.'[34] And he concludes:

> This suggests strongly that the context from which the suggestion about the contra-diction is made, the context of our scientific culture, is not on the same level as the context in which the beliefs about witchcraft operate. Zande notions of witchcraft do not constitute a theoretical system in terms of which Azande try to gain a quasi-scientific understanding of the world. This in its turn suggests that it is the European, obsessed with pressing Zande thought where it would not naturally go – to a contradiction – who is guilty of misunderstanding, not the Zande. The European is in fact committing a category-mistake.[35]

There are several things seriously wrong with this argument.

To start with, it is not entirely clear from the text that Azande *are* completely indifferent to this apparent contradiction within their corpus of mystical belief. It is true that Evans-Pritchard implies this in some places. In others, however, he suggests that Azande *are* sometimes brought face-to-face with the contradiction, and that, when this happens, they use various intellectual devices to help themselves escape from it. For example, he says relatives of a proven witch may accept the thesis of the hereditary nature of witchcraft, yet vigorously deny that they themselves are witches. He also says that, in such situations, they attempt to escape from the contradiction by suggesting that the witch in question was a bastard rather than a true relative.[36]

Again, Winch makes a tendentious use of Evans-Pritchard's comment that Azande do not perceive the contradiction 'because they have no theo-retical interest in it'. For although *he* uses this comment in an attempt to persuade us that Zande mystical notions 'do not constitute a theoretical system in terms of which Azande try to gain a quasi-scientific understanding of the world' it is clear that Evans-Pritchard himself neither intends such a conclusion nor makes the comment in a sense that would justify it. Thus, earlier in his monograph, he says: 'The concept of witchcraft nevertheless provides them [the Azande] with a *natural philosophy* by which the relations between men and unfortunate events are *explained* and a ready and stereotyped means of reacting to such events [italics mine].'[37] And the immediate context of his comment on 'no theoretical interest' makes it clear that what he is trying to say at this juncture is simply that Azande have an 'applied' rather than a 'pure' interest in the subject of witchcraft.

In any case, whatever Evans-Pritchard says or does not say, just what is the inference involved here? It is an inference from the premiss that people are not bothered by apparent contradictions in their beliefs to the conclusion that these beliefs cannot be connected with the ends of explanation, prediction and control. And this seems as much of a *non sequitur* as the inference which was at the bottom of Winch's first argument.

Once again, this point gains additional weight when we turn to look at attitudes in the sciences. For we find that the body of theoretical propositions accepted by members of a particular scientific discipline at a given time is seldom free from patches of contradiction and inconsistency. However, even the research scientist tends to tolerate these patches, albeit uneasily, so long as current theory still seems to be generating interesting predictions and so long as no more promising theoretical alternative is in sight. One might even suggest that, the more the overall promise of a theory in the realm of explanation and prediction, the more tolerant the scientist is of apparent contradictions within it. Strong support for this thesis could be derived from the history of quantum physics.[38] Here again, then, the scientist provides a living pointer to the spuriousness of Winch's inference.

Winch's third argument is based on the alleged difference between the Zande mystical concept of influence and the Western scientific concept of causality. On this, he says:

There is no reason to suppose that the Zande magical concept of 'A affecting B' has anything like the same significance [as the Western scientific/technological concept]. On the contrary, since the Azande do, in the course of their practical affairs, apply something very like our technical concept – though perhaps in a more primitive form – and since their attitude to and thought about their magical rites are quite different from those concerning their technological measures, there is every reason to think that their concept of magical "influence" is quite different.[39]

This argument is as flimsy as its predecessors. In the first place, Evans-Pritchard makes it abundantly clear that there is nothing 'different' about Zande attitudes in situations where mystical forces are thought to be at work. Where a Zande discovers such an influence at work, he shows no special feeling of supernaturally-inspired awe. Indeed, where his aims are thwarted by such an influence, he reacts just as he would if thwarted by some ordinary, everyday occurrence: i.e. he gets very angry.[40]

Secondly, in trying to formulate their concept of mystical influence, Azande make great play with analogies drawn from the sphere of everyday causation. Thus they compare the projection of witchcraft with the shooting of guns and bows. And they refer to witchcraft emanation itself as 'the second spear'. Here, clearly, they are drawing attention to the similarities between mystical influence and everyday causation.[41]

Thirdly, although Azande do in some contexts draw attention to the peculiarities of mystical influence, they do so in a manner which can bring no comfort to Winch. For they do it by comparing witchcraft with hidden goings-on like adultery.[42] And this of course is strongly reminiscent of the scientist's attempt to elucidate the peculiarities of causation at the level of unobservable entities by using the image of a 'hidden mechanism'.[43]

Finally, in trying to characterize the kind of situation in which mystical influence is commonly thought by Azande to come into play, Evans-Pritchard makes another point which can only be an embarrassment to Winch. As he says, it is not only in the case of witchcraft that concepts of mystical force and influence are brought into use. Such concepts are also invoked when a man makes a herbal potion with the idea of influencing some faraway person or state of affairs. Yet again, they are invoked to explain the connection between the planting of a seed and its germination some time later. What is common to these apparently diverse situations? It is the fact that, in all of them, there is a spatial and/or temporal gap between an action and its result. The idea of a mystical force, it would seem, is used to bridge this gap.[44] Once more, here is an observation which brings to mind features of Western scientific/technological thought. Amongst Western adults, as the work of Michotte has shown, there is, built into everyday thought processes, a mechanism for direct perception of causality which is at once very sensitive and very limited. Thus it picks up causal connections almost infallibly when the events involved are contiguous in space and time, but loses efficacy rapidly with the emergence of a spatial and/or temporal gap.[45] Now, as I have suggested before, the most fruitful way of looking at the role of ideas about theoretical entities in the life of Western man is to look at them as intellectual devices which supplement his ordinary mechanism of causal perception and make up for its limitations. This they do in two ways. First, they help their users to transcend the limited causal sensitivity of everyday thought, and to spotlight causal connections which such thought could never otherwise have apprehended. Secondly, they help eliminate the sense of anomaly associated with those causal connections which have been registered by everyday perception *despite* a spatial and/or temporal gap between cause and effect. This they do by asserting that the gap is only apparent, and that, at the level of unobservables, there is contiguity.[46] Just like ideas about mystical forces in Zande thought, then, ideas about unobservable entities in Western thought seem important above all in relation to those causal connexions where there is a spatial and/or temporal gap. *Pace* Winch, both sets of ideas are, in a very real sense, 'stop-gaps'.[47]

So much for the three arguments by means of which Winch seeks to persuade us that superficial resemblances between Zande mystical thought and Western scientific/technological thought are merely a cloak for profound differences. We have found all three to be without substance. Since Winch's interpretation of Zande mystical thought rests on these arguments and these alone, it too is equally devoid of substance.

It is clear from Winch's essay that he sees his remarks as applicable, not only to the mystical thinking of Azande, but also to that of African peoples and of 'primitives' generally. It is possible, of course, that, in the Azande, Winch has accidentally stumbled upon a particularly bad case for treatment; and that mystical thinking amongst most African peoples, and indeed, amongst most 'primitives', lends itself rather better to his interpretation. This is a possibility we should at least consider before dismissing his essay altogether. Here, let me content myself with a few comments on the applicability of his thesis in other African cultures. Broadly, it would seem, in the light of the monographic material now available, that the same verdict is in order. For what comes out of this material is that mystical thinking is everywhere associated with the same dogged determination to gain control over the contingencies of life. True, there are in most African cultures sectors of life where Winch's beloved transcendence of contingency though contemplation comes to the fore: such for instance are the various arts, especially those of narrative and dance. But although there is often a good deal of overlap between those sectors of life ruled by mystical thinking and those sectors ruled by thought and purpose of a more Winchian kind, the overlap is never more than partial.[48]

In a series of articles written over the past few years, I think I have been able to show that, by accepting explanation, prediction and control as the principal end governing the development and persistence of African mystical thought, we are able to provide a coherent interpretation of a whole congeries of cultural phenomena which would otherwise have remained puzzlingly disparate.[49] Until Winch and those who think like him can produce coherent interpretations of greater explanatory power, rather than just throwing out dark hints about what might be done, they do not deserve to be taken very seriously.

I do not wish to bore readers by going over this well-worn ground again. Those unfamiliar with the literature can refer to it and judge for themselves. Instead, I shall turn now to a particular feature of African religious history which I believe constitutes a clear test case for the validity of our respective views.

The feature I refer to is the reaction of African peoples to Christian missionary activity. This reaction has been the subject of a mass of studies over the last few decades; and the authors of nearly all of these studies have come to the same broad conclusions. By and large, they have found a positive response to Christian teaching, and in particular to the Christian idea of the Supreme Being. At the same time, the most lively branches of the Christian Church are those in which certain decisive forms of 'Africanization' have taken place: forms so decisively different from anything countenanced by the older churches that their creators had to found new institutions in order to perpetuate them.

In defining this 'Africanization', our authors have shown a consensus which is remarkable given the variety of theoretical, religious, cultural and moral perspectives from which they write. By and large, they agree that the key feature of the situation is the central preoccupation of African Christians with the active control of sickness and health, fortune and misfortune. It is in this respect, they suggest, that African Christian ideas show maximum continuity with the pagan religious heritage and minimum continuity with the missionary world-view.[50]

All this is crucially relevant to the debate between Winch and myself. For what has happened here is simply that African peoples have been offered a Winchian conception of religion, and have rejected it. Let me elaborate. As I said earlier, Winch is in no doubt about the area of Western discourse that will provide the most appropriate tools for the translation of African mystical beliefs. He points firmly to that strand of Western religious discourse which features God, not as a being who might help one control the vicissitudes of everyday life, but rather as a being through whom one learns to transcend any care about such vicissitudes. Defined in such terms, religion is naturally seen as having ends quite different from those associated with science and technology, and as removed from any competition with the latter.

As Winch points out, there are traces of this kind of religious thinking as far back in the Western tradition as the Book of Job. And in more recent times, it has found highly articulate exponents in such figures as Kierkegaard, Simone Weil, Bonhoeffer, Wittgenstein, D. Z. Phillips and Winch himself. But it is a kind of thinking by no means confined to theologians and philosophers. Indeed, one might say that it is central to the life of many modern Western Protestants. I for one imbibed it, if not with my mother's milk, at least all through school and university chapel.

Now it was this strand of religious thinking that was brought to Africa at the turn of the century by Christian missionaries in general and by Protestant missionaries in particular. For reasons I have discussed elsewhere,[51] the newcomers' emphasis on an active, morally-concerned supreme being was in most places thoroughly acceptable; and it was this aspect of the Christian message that drew thousands of people to churches all over the continent. Once inside, however, they found they had been misled. For they were used to a cosmos of spiritual forces whose powers could be tapped to improve man's lot in the here and now; and it soon became clear that nothing of the kind was on offer in the churches. So, before long, many of the thousands who had poured into the churches began to pour out of them again, taking away the new message of an active, morally-concerned supreme being, but using it as the basis of a comprehensive scheme for the explanation, prediction and control of events in the space-time world. Hundreds of new 'spiritual' churches were founded to provide the institutional framework for the resulting world-view. Today, it is these churches rather than the missionary foundations that constitute a growing-point in African religious life.

The comments of those involved show beyond all doubt what the issues at stake have been. In the Eastern Niger Delta, where I have been doing fieldwork for a number of years, puzzled enquirers assailed the early evangelists with the question: 'Does your God wish us to climb up to the top of a tall palm tree, open our hands, and drop off?'[52] Many years later, when dozens of 'prayer-houses' (spiritual churches) were established alongside the three missionary-derived churches in the area, people summed up the differences between the two sets of institutions by saying: 'The prayer-houses heal our sicknesses; the churches give safe passage to our spirits'. Similar comments are reported from nearby Yorubaland. An early spiritualist, criticizing European Christians, said: 'They have no definite teaching as to how to meet the circumstances of life'; and 'The Englishman does not know much about the power working behind God's word'.[53] Present-day members comment on the new churches in such terms as: 'Since I joined Cherubim and Seraphim I have always seen good things; if there is any difficulty, once you pray, it will go away. Since I have joined, I have enjoyed life'; or 'If someone joins the Christ Apostolic Church, he will have rest of mind. There is no need to use medicine if you join; if you ask something from God immediately you will get the result'; or again (from a timber-dealer): 'Prayer relieves difficulties; whenever there is a glut in the market, I pray to relieve it; other people make medicine to help them; Christ Apostolic Church people just pray and receive God's grace'.[54] The same themes recur in comments from the Ghanaian spiritual churches. Defining the differences between his own church and the missionary foundations, the leader of the Musama Disco Christo Church says: 'Christ is not only a god of salvation of the soul but also a father that is prepared to meet all our needs'.[55] And a catechist in the same church was heard to begin his address with: 'We are all in the church because we have found healing here. But for this church the great majority of us here assembled would not be alive today'.[56] In South Africa, a prophet of one of the spiritual churches told his congregation: 'This is not a church, it is a hospital'.[57] And again in this area, the usual answer as to why someone has joined one of the new churches is: 'I was ill. They prayed for me. Now I am well'.[58]

These reactions to the Christian message are beautifully relevant to the present controversy. In the first place, they are the reactions of holders of mystical beliefs, not the interpretations of axe-grinding scholars. Secondly, they are reactions, not to questions about the nature of mystical beliefs posed in some unrealistic interview situation, but to options posed in the course of ongoing daily life. Thirdly and crucially, they are reactions to a concept of religious life which, though it was brought to African peoples by the missionaries, is more or less identical with the concept urged on us by Winch. Hence the rejection of this concept in Africa is a rejection not only of the views of the missionaries but also of the views of Winch. Since Winch makes so much of the need to accept other people's views of their own situation, this is one verdict he is bound to accept.

I think I have now shown clearly enough that Winch is wildly off course in his programme for the interpretation of African mystical concepts. It remains to try and discover what led him astray. One quick answer is that he never got out of his armchair to go and participate in the thought and life he was concerned to interpret. This, however, is unconvincing. For many scholars with years of African fieldwork to their credit have come up with interpretations just as wildly at variance with the facts – even when they themselves have helped to gather those facts.

A more penetrating answer would seem to be that Winch has fallen victim to the very error for which he castigates Evans-Pritchard and myself. Thus he insists that our attempts to understand 'primitive' thought-patterns are vitiated by an obsession with the dominant thought-patterns of our own time and place. The principal manifestation of this obsession is our determination to force African mystical thinking into the conceptual moulds associated with Western science and technology. Along the same lines, however, one can argue that it is he who has signally failed to escape from the tyranny of currently-dominant thought-patterns. Thus his conception of the religious life is nothing if not parochially modern Western. For whilst it is true that there have always been traces of the Jobian attitude to God in the Western Christian heritage, it is equally true that, up to four hundred years ago, a majority of Western Christians would have found this attitude as alien as most African Christians find it today. For them too, beliefs about God were first and foremost the constituents of a theory in terms of which they explained, predicted and attempted to control the events of the world around them.[59] Four hundred years ago, moreover, the theories of the scientists were still essentially works of religious thinking. In chemistry, a great deal of important research was still guided by notions of 'spirit' that bore clear marks of their animistic origin.[60] And in physics, God was an integral feature of the theoretical schemes of Newton himself. Indeed, it seems doubtful if his concepts of absolute space and time (which have been crucial for modern physics down to Einstein) could ever have emerged except as correlatives of his concept of God.[61]

In short, up till this late date in Western history, there was little or no sense of contrast between religious discourse and scientific discourse, religious activity and scientific activity. It was later, when post-Newtonian paradigms in the physical sciences began to dispense with the theistic component, and when the achievements of these sciences in the sphere of explanation, prediction and control became increasingly difficult to challenge, that religious leaders began to grope for definitions of their calling which emphasized its distinctiveness from the sciences. It was then that the theologians began to emphasize that the ends of religion were quite different from the ends of science, and to deny that they were in any sort of competition with the scientists. The sort of definition propounded by Wittgenstein, Phillips and Winch is simply the culmination of this trend.

Now one could say, with these modern theologians and philosophers, that such changes have been a movement toward religious truth; a progressive casting off of superstitious dross. But whether one regards these changes as progress or retrogress, one can hardly deny that the stimulus for them was the need to work out some means of coexisting with the sciences; the need to limit claims of competence to those which scientists were unlikely to contest. And if one grants that the success of the sciences with non-theistic paradigms was the stimulus for these changes in the definition of religious life, must one not also grant that the re-adoption of theistic paradigms in the sciences would in all probability trigger off a reversal of these changes? If this sounds like a piece of half-baked speculation, the reader should remember that the history of science to date is by no means a story of the irrevocable replacement of one paradigm by another. Rather, it is a story in which one paradigm comes into the ascendant whilst its predecessor goes dormant. The dormant paradigm, moreover, does not die. Instead, it is kept just alive, perhaps by a few people often labelled as cranks, only to re-emerge into the limelight decades or centuries later, totally refurbished but nonetheless recognizable as a reincarnation. Within the general category of impersonal paradigms, this has happened to the wave paradigm, the atomic paradigm and the field paradigm. Going outside this category, there is no reason to believe that the same thing could not happen to the theistic paradigm. Anyone muttering about such a paradigm not lending itself to mathematization, and therefore to exact treatment, should remember the Theory of Games!

Now I am not saying that anything like this is even in the wind. The efforts of Teilhard de Chardin[62] and Alister Hardy[63] to re-import a theistic paradigm into biology have so far failed to convince most serious scholars. And the claim that such a paradigm will have to be re-imported into psychology, in order to do justice to the increasingly accepted phenomena of ESP and pre-cognition, has so far fallen on equally deaf ears.[64] However, there is no reason to suppose that our present theoretical schemas represent anything like a close approach to some final set of truths. And there is no reason why, at some further stage in the struggle to attain such a set of truths, a theistic paradigm should not reappear.

If such a thing were to happen, what would be the attitude of the religious heirs of Kierkegaard, Wittgenstein and Winch? Would they still keep their noses in the air, and continue to maintain that questions of empirical confirmation and refutation were quite alien to religious discourse? Or would they jump on to the bandwagon, and declare themselves the guardians, in its time of adversity, of a paradigm now restored to respectability in the eyes of those supreme arbiters of reality, the scientists? I think there can be little doubt as to what would happen. As abandonment of theistic paradigms by scientists was the stimulus for renunciation of the ends of explanation/prediction/control by religious experts, so re-admission of theistic paradigms by scientists would be the signal for a renewed interest in explanation/prediction/control on the part of the divines.

The aim of this brief exercise in science-fiction is to bring home to the reader, as vividly as possible, the point that the definition of religious discourse which strongly contrasts it with scientific discourse is not just very recent in Western culture, but may also be downright ephemeral. In adopting such a definition, and in insisting on its value in the interpretation of African mystical beliefs, Winch is succumbing to the error of which he so loudly accuses his opponents. He is allowing himself to be blinded by a conceptual pattern peculiar to the culture of his own time and place.

Now to say this is to say that Winch is suffering from a lack of awareness. But a diagnosis in purely cognitive terms would be only half the truth. For what is also clear is that his writings on cultural matters are fired by powerful antipathies and passions. They are a crusade, against the allegedly overweening claims of science, and in favour of all those modes of thought whose aims are incommensurable with those of science. Winch does much to make us feel the unworthiness of the struggle for explanation, prediction and control, and the nobility of the struggle to achieve a resigned contemplation of life's contingencies. Seen in this light, his portrayal of 'primitive' societies as dominated by these non-scientistic modes of thought appears, above all, as the product of his desire for a fantasy haven where he can flee from the horrors of science.

Summary and conclusion

Winch's work on the general principles of anthropological/sociological enquiry is one of the major achievements in this field. Right or wrong, he has done more than any other recent writer to make us look again at the assumptions so many of us make about the continuity between the social and other sciences. Again, in the crucial field of understanding alien belief-systems, he has put his finger on what all thinking scholars must agree to be some of the key principles.

However, much of the popularity of the essay under consideration derives, not from the general principles Winch enunciates, but from the particular interpretation of 'primitive' mystical thinking which he would have us believe follows from the application of these principles. And it is precisely at this point that his work is weakest. For, in the course of his interpretation, he flouts his own principles so dramatically as to make one wonder if he is not giving us a tongue-in-cheek example of how not to set about 'understanding a primitive society'. Thus although one of his important general contributions is an analysis of the roots of ethnocentrism in anthropological enquiry, his interpretation of African mystical beliefs is vitiated by an outsize pair of ethnic blinkers. Again, whereas he repeatedly insists on a reverential readiness to learn *from* other peoples, his interpretation of mystical belief involves the projection *on* to these peoples of his own anti-scientistic fantasies.[65]

Our closing verdict on Winch must therefore be a mixed one. As a methodologist of the social sciences, he is clearly a figure who cannot be ignored. As a practitioner in the field of cross-cultural understanding, he seems to be just one more victim of the Leavis-Roszak Syndrome, one more mouthpiece for the siren song of the Counter Culture.

6   Judaeo-Christian spectacles: boon or bane to the study of African religions?

For much of the past fifty years, the study of the indigenous religious heritage of Africa has been dominated by social or cultural anthropologists of Western origin and agnostic or atheistic religious views. In recent years, however, the dominance of this set has been challenged by a new wave of scholars, some Western and others African, who repudiate the established approach to the field and advocate a radically different one. Some of these scholars, such as Evans-Pritchard and Victor Turner, have been anthropologists by formal professional affiliation. Others, like Idowu, Mbiti, Gaba and Harold Turner, have been affiliated to such disciplines as theology and comparative religion. Yet others, such as Winch, have been philosophers.[1] They are united, however, by a methodological and theological framework which has been strongly influenced, first and foremost by their own Christian faith, but also by a long tradition of comparative studies of religion carried out by Christian theologians.

The only outsider to have taken the challenge of the new wave of scholars at all seriously seems to have been the Ugandan poet/anthropologist Okot P'Bitek, who gave us a devastating exposé of some of the weaknesses of the new approach in his little book *African Religions in Western Scholarship*.[2] The book, however, was written in a furious, poetic, acid style rather than in cool, sober academic prose. And although some people, myself included, found this style both splendid and apt, it seems to have allowed many academics both old-style and new to convince themselves that P'Bitek's critique could be shrugged off. On top of the reaction produced by the style came the failure of the publishers to keep the book in print and the untimely death of the author. These various circumstances seem to have joined to prevent the book from having any great impact. Nonetheless, P'Bitek's critique was in many respects a penetrating one; and anybody embarking on a more sober and systematic critique will find himself compelled to reiterate its basic points. He may also find himself strongly tempted to reproduce some of the author's verbal acid-drops! Both basic points and acid-drops will be liberally used and acknowledged during the course of this essay.

Although they are the butt of the criticisms of the new wave of scholars, anthropologists in the established tradition have not taken the challenge very seriously. By and large, they have brushed it aside with short impromptu critiques which have not really penetrated their opponents' defences.

This cavalier attitude to the new wave is, I think, unwise. For its influence is growing apace. From the beginning, its members have been in control of the thinking and teaching of nearly all of the burgeoning religious studies departments in African universities; and they have continued to consolidate their hold on these departments. More recently, they have begun to gain influence in the universities of the United States and Europe, where the effective study of the indigenous religions of Africa had earlier been a monopoly of 'orthodox' anthropologists. Their growing self-confidence is epitomized by an uncompromising manifesto, issued recently by one of their leading spokesmen, whose message is that the *only* way forward in the study of African religions is one which follows their line.[3]

Being acutely aware of the growing influence of the new wave, and at the same time very doubtful as to the value of its basic approach, I believe that a serious and sustained critique is overdue. In what follows, I shall try to sketch the outline of such a critique. Since members of the new wave have not, so far, given their movement a name, the expositor/critic is faced with the problem of finding a convenient label. Some years ago, in an attempt to solve this problem, I coined the phrase 'Devout Opposition': 'Opposition' alluding to members' adversary attitude to the more established approach; and the qualifier 'Devout' alluding to the deep influence of personal Christian faith on their own approach.[4] Although this label is far from satisfactory, it seems to have caught on to some extent.[5] So for want of anything better, I shall continue to use it in this essay.

The common ground

Before embarking on an exposition and critique of the specifics of the 'Devout' approach, I should like to say a few words about certain very general features of this approach which the 'Devout' share with their 'orthodox' anthropological opponents. What I have to say may seem banal and abstract; but, as the reader will later see, it does serve to establish a framework within which the 'Devout' position and its relation to its 'orthodox' counterpart become more readily intelligible.

Both the 'Devout' and their 'orthodox' opponents are involved in the comparative, cross-cultural study of thought-systems. In this role, they utilize two distinct levels of interpretation, which I shall provisionally label 'translational understanding' and 'further explanation'.

By 'translational understanding', I mean the kind of understanding of a particular thought-system that results from the successful translation of the language and conceptual system that embody it into terms of a language and conceptual system that currently enjoy 'world' status. In talking of translation, of course, I am not just talking of the provision of dictionary equivalents for individual words or sentences. I am talking about finding a 'world-language' equivalent for a whole realm of discourse, and of showing, in 'world-language' terms, what the point of that realm of discourse is in the life of the people who use it. Translation, in this broader sense, can be very arduous. There may be no realm of discourse in the 'world' language that exactly fits the bill. We may have to bend and refashion existing realms, and even redefine their guiding intentions. We may have to recombine realms that have become separated during the evolution of the modern condition. Arduous though it may be, however, this operation is the vital preliminary to any further interpretative steps.[6]

There is nothing mysterious in all of this about the role of a 'world' language and its associated conceptual system. The 'world' status simply reflects present-day demographic and political realities. And these may of course change drastically in the future. Nonetheless, they are the realities of today, and they do provide the *raison d'être* of this kind of translation. In the first place, given these realities, such translation is the most economic means of bringing the characteristics of a particular thought-system to the attention of a world-wide audience. Secondly, without prior translation of all the various thought-systems of the world into terms of a common language and conceptual apparatus, there can be no comparison of such thought-systems with respect to their differences and similarities. And once again, given current realities, a 'world' language and conceptual apparatus would seem to be the best means of making this comparative exercise accessible to a world-wide audience.

It is the differences and similarities revealed by the comparative exercise that call forth interpretation at the second level: that of 'further explanation'.

Differences, perhaps, are the most provocative. Thus it may be that, in two thought-systems, we find comparable realms of discourse using different sets of conceptual means to achieve similar ends. For instance, we may find that, in two otherwise comparable bodies of theory, two totally different models are used to explain the same field of phenomena. Or we may find that, in two otherwise comparable bodies of poetry, two totally different sets of symbols are used to adumbrate the same area of human feeling. Again, it may be that, in two thought-systems, we are faced, not just with different means toward the same end, but with different balances between disparate ends. Thus one thought-system may emphasize poetic thinking and de-emphasize pragmatic thinking, whilst another may squeeze poetry into a corner and exalt pragmatism. Differences of this kind have fascinated curious students of humanity; and they have commonly given rise to 'further explanations' couched in terms of differences in the technological, economic, social and political backgrounds of the societies concerned.

Although differences have proved the most fascinating to the enquiring mind, similarities have not been without their allure. Thus some comparativists have claimed that there is a 'central core' of common-sense, everyday pragmatic thinking which has remained constant in all societies down the ages since the dawn of humanity. Others have claimed that certain symbolic themes have been similarly reiterated in all societies down the ages. And yet others, as we shall see in this essay, have claimed universality for the conception of God. Such similarities have also called forth gargantuan efforts at 'further explanation', this time in terms of universals of the human condition, either biological, psychological, social or spiritual.

A worthwhile comparative study can only be achieved by treating both of these levels of interpretation as equally important. Some comparativists are so keen to get on to 'further explanation' that they take inadequate pains with 'translational understanding'; and the result is grandiose nonsense. Others put all their effort into 'translational understanding' but abstain from any attempt at 'further explanation', feeling, it seems, that there is an element of *hubris* involved in pursuing the latter; but however admirable their modesty, the result is a failure to meet the demands of legitimate curiosity concerning the working of the human mind.

As we shall see in what follows, the 'Devout', in pursuing the comparative study of African religions, have engaged themselves with both these levels of interpretation. And any critique must examine their performance at both levels.

The 'Devout' opposition: an outline of the specifics of their approach

Translational understanding

If the above analysis is correct, it follows that, at the heart of every approach to the comparative study of thought-systems, there must be a particular set of translation recipes. It also follows that one of the roots of distinctiveness in any given approach is likely to be the distinctiveness of its set of translation recipes.

In fact, it does seem that the most fruitful way of comparing the various approaches to the study of African religions is in terms of their basic translation recipes. Thus many late nineteenth- and early twentieth-century approaches can be understood in terms of a recipe that relied on the half-formed language and conceptual apparatus of Western infants.[7] Similarly, the fashionable 'Symbolist' reaction to these approaches can be understood in terms of a recipe that advocates reliance on the symbolic discourse of Western adults as manifested in such verbal arts as poetry.[8] Again, a more recent and highly esoteric approach advocates reliance on that realm of Western discourse which the philosophers have labelled 'performative'.[9] Yet again, the 'Intellectualist' reaction to the 'Symbolists' and 'Performativists' advocates heavy reliance on the theoretical discourse of the modern West as manifested in the language and concepts of the sciences.[10] Finally, the 'Devout' reaction to all of these other approaches can be understood in terms of a rejection of all other translation recipes in favour of one which relies on modern Western religious discourse.

For the 'Devout', the main thing wrong with the translation recipes of other schools is that they classify religious discourse as a variety of some broader type of discourse. Since religious discourse is quite distinct from other types of discourse both in its rules and in its aims, such classification leads to travesty.[11]

The 'Devout' are quite clear as to the remedy. The scholar must turn to the religious discourse of his own culture as a translation instrument. Some members of the movement, indeed, would go so far as to maintain that a scholar lacking in personal religious experience is thereby deprived of the means of understanding the religious thought and life of another culture. In support of this view, they quote Pater Schmidt's famous rebuke to Renan: 'If religion is essentially of the inner life, it follows that it can be grasped only from within. But beyond a doubt, this can be better done by one in whose inward consciousness an experience of religion plays a part. There is but too much danger that the other (the non-believer) will talk of religion as a blind man might of colours, or one totally devoid of ear, of a beautiful musical composition.'[12] Since the 'Devout' are, by definition, Christians, it follows that, in their own work, their main translation instrument is Christian religious discourse.

So much for the general character of the 'Devout' translation recipe. Let us now turn to look at the picture of African religious thought that results from its application. For convenience, we may consider our findings under three headings: 'focal objects';[13] 'attitudes'; 'aims'.

(a) The focal objects of African religious thought. In the 'Devout' view, *all* systems of African religious thought, *without exception*, are focussed on the same ultimate object: the supreme being or God. He created the world and sustains it; is omnipresent, omnipotent and omniscient. He is the ultimate upholder of the good in human life, and the ultimate adversary of the bad. Though conceived of up to a point in human terms, he is

nonetheless so inscrutable and mysterious in his ways, so startlingly different from human beings in most of his attributes, that he can only be regarded as 'wholly other'.[14]

'Devout' scholars recognize African belief in and commerce with a multiplicity of lesser spiritual forces; but they tend to emphasize that the African worshipper regards such forces as mere intermediaries between himself and the supreme being, and as agencies whose powers and very existence depend, in any case, on the will of this being.[15] One of their most prominent spokesmen, Idowu, so discounts the independent reality of the lesser spiritual forces in the minds of worshippers that he feels justified in referring to African religious thought generally as 'Diffused Monotheism'.[16]

(b) The attitudes of African worshippers. 'Devout' scholars tend to follow Rudolf Otto in stressing a unique religious attitude or emotion in which awed fascination with the mysterious and uncanny bulks large. This attitude may not be very obvious in people's relations with lesser spirits. But it becomes more obvious in their relations with greater divinities and most obvious in their relations with the supreme being himself. This complex and unique attitude is a response to the immense and amazing powers of the supreme being, and to his mysteriousness and inscrutability.[17]

(c) The aims of African religious life. 'Devout' scholars may sometimes concede that African religious thought does have something to do with explanation, prediction and control of events in the everyday world; but they typically assert that these are not its central concerns. Rather, as their guiding definitions suggest, they assume that, for the African worshipper, the relation between man and God is something of intrinsic value, and the attainment of communion with God the overriding aim of life.[18]

A second major aim of African religious life is suggested by certain remarks in the writings of Idowu and H. W. Turner. Thus Idowu talks on the one hand about the Yoruba sense of a fallen, evil-ridden world, and on the other about the Yoruba (and African) yearning for paradise.[19] In similar vein, H. W. Turner talks about an African sense of 'distorted existence and lost destiny'.[20] With these phrases, our authors seem to be hinting at the presence, in African religious thought, of the idea of a flawed temporal world from which the individual yearns to escape into the perfection of eternity. At this juncture, it is perhaps worth remembering that, in Judaeo-Christian thought, this yearning for escape into eternity is closely linked to the yearning for communion; for in this tradition the eternal plane is the 'abode' of God.

Further explanation

'Devout' scholars are seldom totally hostile to 'further explanations' of African religious phenomena couched in terms of technological, economic, social and political factors.[21] Thus both Idowu and Mbiti admit that the numerous variant elaborations of African religious belief are the outcome of the operation of such factors.[22] More specifically, Idowu alludes to the process of anthropomorphism whereby a particular pattern of human social relations influences the spiritual conceptions of men living within that pattern. Similarly, in his monograph on Nuer religion, Evans-Pritchard talks of ideas concerning the lesser divinities as products of a process whereby the idea of God is 'broken up by the refracting surfaces of nature, of society, of culture, and of historical experience'.[23] H. W. Turner, at present perhaps the most prominent 'Devout' spokesman on methodology, once committed himself to the extreme view that the specifically religious factor always works *through* these more mundane factors.[24]

Nonetheless, with the exception of Evans-Pritchard and Victor Turner, 'Devout' scholars have not been noted for serious and sustained exploration of the influence of mundane factors on African religious thought. And even the two scholars just mentioned have always insisted on the limits of such influence. Indeed, all 'Devout' scholars would seem to share the conviction that explanations in terms of mundane factors can only take us a little way into the understanding of religious thought and action. For them, although the variable features of African religious thought can be ascribed to the influence of mundane factors, its invariant theistic core can only be accounted for in terms of a specifically religious factor.[25]

In defining this factor, the 'Devout' use such phrases as 'the universal response to the Divine',[26] 'the interplay between revelation of the transcendent and the response of the human', and 'the personal awareness of God on the part of man through God's own initiative'.[27] Common to these phrases are three basic assumptions. First, that there *is* a supreme being with approximately the attributes assigned to him by the modern Judaeo-Christian tradition of religious thought. Second, that he has endowed all human beings with awareness of his presence and desire for communion with him. Third, that he has endowed all human beings with some ability, albeit an inadequate one, to make veridical reports concerning his presence and his nature. For the 'Devout', it is these assumptions that provide the ultimate explanation of religious thought in Africa as indeed in other parts of the world.

The reader encountering 'Devout' explanatory ideas for the first time may well feel puzzled by them. Why, he may ask, should psychological and sociological explanations be considered appropriate to the variable features of religious belief but inappropriate to the invariant theistic core? And why should explanations in terms of the presence of the object and of human awareness of this presence be considered appropriate to the invariant theistic core but inappropriate to the variable features? Reading between the lines of much 'Devout' writing on this matter, we soon come to see that these ideas are connected with the belief that the variable features represent the veil of human error whilst the invariant theistic features represent the inner core of truth. This connection becomes explicit in the writings of Evans-Pritchard, who asserts that, where we are dealing with human error and illusion, as in the case of the variable 'refractions' of spiritual reality, the appropriate pattern of explanation is indeed one that invokes mundane psychological and sociological factors, but that, where we are dealing with true belief, as in the case of the invariant theistic element, the only appropriate explanation is one that refers to the presence of the object of such belief and to human awareness of this presence.[28]

Interestingly, this maxim has been shared to a remarkable degree down the years by both atheistic and theistic students of religions. However, because of their differing ideas as to which beliefs are erroneous and which true, they have drawn very different conclusions from it. The atheists have used it as a licence to provide psychological and sociological explanations for *all* aspects of religion, and have gone on to treat the possibility of producing plausible explanations of this kind as a sort of proof of the illusory character of the focal objects of religious belief.[29] The theists, as we have just seen, have used it as a licence to ban attempts at psychological and sociological explanation of the allegedly invariant theistic features of religion. They have also greeted the inadequacies of the psychological and sociological explanations offered so far with a sort of grimly gleeful 'We told you so'; as if these inadequacies in some way proved the truth of theistic beliefs.[30]

Since the study of religions has attracted and seems likely to continue to attract fair numbers of atheists as well as of theists, the dominance of this maxim seems to threaten us with a tragic impasse, in which people of opposed religious convictions are for ever destined to pursue irreconcilable programmes in their attempts to interpret the same area of data, and in which different interpretative programmes are for ever destined to be treated, not on their merits, but as symbols of mutually hostile metaphysical convictions. Some eminent scholars on both sides of the divide seem to have accepted this impasse with sad resignation.[31] So far as the study in which we are all engaged is concerned, however, this looks like a counsel of despair. As to whether or not we are forced to accept it, this is a question which I shall consider in the next section of the paper.

The 'Devout' approach: a critique

In the critical appraisal that follows, I shall use the same headings and sub-headings as those I used in outlining the 'Devout' position. The reader may refer back accordingly.

Translational understanding

(a) The focal objects of African religious thought. The 'Devout' translation recipe is most obviously misleading when used to convey information about the focal objects of indigenous African religious thought. True, it avoids the worst conceivable excess: that of finding translational work for the names of all three persons of the Trinity. Nonetheless, it does insist on finding such work for a fairly unamended Judaeo-Christian concept of God the Father; and given the realities of African religious thought, this is to say the least unfortunate.

It is true that, in many African cosmologies, we do find the concept of a supreme being who created the world and sustains it. But the other salient attributes of this being are often very different from those of its Judaeo-Christian counterpart. It may not, for instance, have the unambiguous association with the morally good that is always attributed to the Judaeo-Christian supreme being. Thus John Middleton, in his *Lugbara Religion*, shows us that the Lugbara supreme being is associated as much with evil as he is with good. And it seems to me that other ethnographic monographs suggest something similar.[32] Again, the supreme being may not have the same sex as its Judaeo-Christian counterpart. Among the Ijo-speaking peoples of the Niger Delta, for instance, this being is thought of as a woman and is referred to as 'Our Mother'.[33] One does not have to be a sexual chauvinist to see this as a fairly fundamental difference of concept! Yet again, the aura of mystery and inscrutability with which the 'Devout' tend to clothe the supreme being is remarkable for its absence from many of the more painstaking monographs on the religious thought of particular African cultures. In many such works, it is true, we find not only the concept of a supreme being, but also confessions of ignorance of many of his/her ways. What we don't seem to find is the sort of positive celebration of his/her mysteriousness and inscrutability that is so characteristic of modern Judaeo-Christian thought.[34]

A central feature of Judaeo-Christian religious discourse is, of course, that it celebrates the primacy and centrality of the supreme being as against all lesser spiritual agencies. And the 'Devout' translation recipe has tended to transfer this celebration to characterizations of indigenous African religious systems. Once again, we are faced with a powerful source of translational misunderstanding.

Where there is an indigenous concept of a being who created and sustains everything in the world, we might, on grounds of consistency, expect to find prominence given to a conception of the lesser spirits as mere manifestations of the supreme being, or as little more than intermediaries between man and this being. However, in many instances where there *is* a more or less clear idea of a being who created and sustains everything including the lesser spirits, thought about the relation between such a being and the lesser spirits is not, in everyday contexts, pressed this far. In such instances, the lesser spirits, to all intents and purposes, are thought of as realities in their own right, as independent sources of volition and action, and as the ultimate recipients of much everyday ritual attention. 'Devout' failure to recognize this has led to grave errors of interpretation.

A sobering example of what can happen in this respect is provided by the literature on indigenous Igbo religious thought. In this field, a line of 'Devout' scholars has established, over the years, the usual image of a world-view in which lesser spiritual agencies are considered as manifestations of and intermediaries with the supreme being, and in which the spiritual portion of man is thought to go and stay with this being in the after-life. Recently, however, S. N. Ubah, an Igbo historian brought up in a more open, sceptical tradition, decided to return to his own home community, to gather data on its religion by means of fieldwork more intimate and more prolonged than that conducted by his 'Devout' predecessors.[35] In the course of his fieldwork, Ubah took particular care to distinguish the views of those who, especially in their formative years, had had little or no exposure to Christian influence, from the views of those who, whilst not themselves Christians, had had much greater exposure to such influence. And in making his translations, he kept in mind the possible adverse consequences of over-reliance on a Judaeo-Christian translational apparatus. The results of his work must have come as a shock to his 'Devout' colleagues. In the first place, he found that, in the thought of those not overly exposed to Christianity, the lesser spirits were autonomous agencies who received human entreaties and offerings in their own right and in no way as intermediaries with the supreme being.[36] Secondly, he found that, in the thought of the same set, people were no more closely associated with the supreme being in the after-life than they had been in the everyday world. In his own words: 'The ancestors, who had had little to do with the supreme being here on earth, appear to have found him no less withdrawn in the other world'.[37] It was only in the thought of those with much greater exposure to Christianity that he found anything like the 'Devout' version of the Igbo world-view.

It is fascinating to find that, despite their formal pronouncements on the relation between God and the lesser spirits, several leading 'Devout' thinkers, in their less guarded moments, unwittingly concede that what

Ubah says about an Igbo world-view may be much more widely true. Thus there is a passage in Idowu's *African Traditional Religion* in which, having propounded his idea of 'Diffused Monotheism', he admits that it is more of an ideal than a reality, and that although African religious thinkers *should* treat the lesser spirits purely as manifestations of the supreme being, *in fact* they treat them all too often as forces in their own right.[38] Again, there is a passage in one of Ezeanya's articles in which the author, having stated that the supreme God is commonly believed to have created the lesser spirits as his agents, goes on soon afterwards to say that 'this is more so in theory than in practice'.[39] Yet again, there is a remarkable statement in Mbiti's *African Religions and Philosophy*, in which, having repeated the credo that the lesser spirits are thought of as intermediaries between man and God, he says this means that God is the ultimate recipient of sacrifices, 'whether or not the worshippers are aware of that'.[40] In the case of the statements by Idowu and Ezeanya, the alert reader will feel immediately moved to ask in whose head the 'ideal' and the 'theory' reside. And in the absence of any evidence offered to the contrary, he can only conclude that these things reside in the heads of the authors and not in those of the people whose beliefs they purport to describe. In the case of the statement by Mbiti, the same reader will want to know who is the holder of the belief that God is the ultimate recipient of all sacrifices in those cases where the worshipper 'is not aware of that'. And here again, the answer can only be that the holder is the author, not the worshipper. In these passages, it seems as if the sheer weight of recalcitrant reality has forced our authors into self-refuting slips of the tongue!

Over-pressing the 'Devout' translation recipe can also lead to a deceptive picture of the sheer amount of time, energy and thought allocated to the supreme being and lesser spirits respectively. Thus the 'Devout' all too often give the impression that such allocation overwhelmingly favours the former. In fact, however, even in cases where assertion of the ontological primacy of the supreme being is fairly unambiguous, allocation of time, energy and thought is often strongly in favour of the lesser agencies. In Yorubaland, for instance, the life of the *orisa* devotee centres, in these respects, upon the *orisa* rather than upon the supreme being.[41] And in Kalabari, the life of a medium of an *owu* or water-spirit centres, in the same respects, on the *owu* rather than upon the supreme being.[42] In both cases, assertions of the ontological priority of the supreme being are clear enough. At the same time, however, there is a very obvious sense in which this being is peripheral rather than central to religious life.

In the cases we have been discussing, there can be no dispute about the presence in people's thought of definite conceptions of a supreme being.

Also beyond dispute, however, is the variety of such conceptions, with respect, both to the attributes accorded to the being itself, and to ideas about his relationship with the lesser spirits. Equally beyond dispute is the fact that in these respects, many if not most indigenous conceptions of the supreme being are far removed from that peculiar to modern Judaeo-Christian thought. To ignore this fact can only lead to interpretative disaster.

One's apprehensions about the 'Devout' approach increase when one turns to consider a number of cases where it is clear that indigenous thought postulates, not one supreme creator and sustainer, but two coeval and coequal forces.

One long-attested case is that of the Fon of the pre-colonial kingdom of Dahomey. Here we find the creation and sustaining of the world attributed to the female deity Mawu, who is associated with the earth, the west, the moon, the night and the rising sun, and her male consort Lisa, who is associated with the sky, the east, the sun, the day and the setting sun. The two deities are thought to carry on their work through a third force, Dan, who is often described as their servant. This dualistic conception of the forces underpinning the world is considered by some historians to be relatively recent in the kingdom (perhaps only two or three hundred years old) and to have replaced an earlier conception of a single supreme being called Nana Buluku. However, although some versions of the cosmology preserve traces of the transition in the idea that Mawu and Lisa are the children of Nana Buluku, others accord supreme status to Mawu and Lisa, and omit any mention of a parent. So there can be no argument about the existence, among certain Fon thinkers and worshippers at least, of a genuinely dualistic tradition of cosmological thought.[43]

Again, despite Idowu's characterizations of Yoruba religious thought as 'Diffused Monotheism', a series of reports published over the last twenty years have made it clear that, in some parts of Yorubaland at least, a more dualistic conception of the forces underpinning the world prevails. Thus Morton-Williams's work strongly suggests that, in Oyo Yoruba cosmology, Heaven and Earth are regarded as coeval and coequal forces. Heaven is the source of individual destinies, and also presides over the sky-dwelling *orisa* spirits. Since the latter are associated not only with aspects of wild nature but also with individual fortunes, this gives Heaven a double link with human individuality. Earth presides not only over the spirits of the various settled territories, but also over ancestral spirits. Through both these categories, it is associated with community and morality. More recently, Babayemi, an Oyo son as well as a professional historian, has not only broadly confirmed Morton-Williams's picture, but has given it some further elaboration. Thus he shows us how the balanced but uneasy relationship between Heaven and Earth is thought to underlie and account for several areas of tension in everyday life. Notably, it is thought to be the root cause of the endemic struggle between the *alaafin* (backed by Heaven) and the Oyo *mesi* (backed by Earth).[44]

A similar dualism involving Heaven and Earth has been pointed out in Idoma, Igbira and Mosi religious thought.[45] There are even rumours of dualism among students of Igbo religious life. Thus one writer has suggested that the concept of the supreme being associated with the name Chukwu has spread relatively recently from Aro-Chukwu to other parts of Igboland, and that it was preceded by a dualistic outlook which saw the forces of Chi and Eke as controlling the world between them.[46] And only recently, I came across the record of a conversation between a Catholic priest and an old man from the north-western Igbo village of Ihembosi, in which the old man, with some hesitation, it seems, in the presence of the priest, appears to be expounding a dualism involving the heavenly force Chukwu and its earthly counterpart Ana.[47]

In the clearer of these instances of dualism, there can be no justification whatever for picking out one of each pair of forces postulated by indigenous thought and calling it 'God'. Yet in these instances, this would seem to be the only way of squaring the 'Devout' translation recipe with the facts.

If the 'Devout' recipe looks dubious in the face of dualistic conceptions, it looks worse still in the face of those cases in which apparently reliable reports indicate absence of any concept, either of a single overarching creator/sustainer, or of a pair of such creators/sustainers.

Two such cases stand out with particular clarity. One is Monica Wilson's report on the Nyakyusa, the other is Okot P'Bitek's work on the Acholi.[48] Both authors state quite unambiguously that, in the whole gamut of the indigenous concepts of the peoples thay are concerned with, they are unable to find one of a creator/sustainer of the world. In both cases, it seems, people's interest is concentrated on their local polity and its environment, and upon the heroes, ancestors and nature spirits whose actions determine the outcome of events in this local arena. There seems no good reason to doubt the competence and good faith of these two authors. Both had an excellent training in social anthropology. Wilson, although she was an outsider to Nyakyusa society, conducted intensive fieldwork through the indigenous language. P'Bitek was an Acholi son and a distinguished poet both in English and his own language.

Nor are these the only cases of their kind. I have given them prominence because of their clearcut character. But there are a number of others in which the data, though more ambiguous, seem to point to the same conclusion. Thus in a report on the religious ideas of the Gogo of East Africa,

Rigby mentions a being called Maduwo, referred to, sometimes as a world-creator, but more often as a vaguely defined malevolent force better known in strange far-away places than close to home.[49] Rigby, with good reason, wonders whether such a being can really be understood as the supreme being of the Gogo. Again, a number of scholars concerned with the religious history of the Shona-speaking peoples have pointed to a certain amount of evidence that Mwari, taken fairly unanimously by modern non-Christian Shona to be the creator and sustainer of the world as a whole, may in earlier ages have had a more restricted and local role. If this evidence is taken seriously, it then becomes an open question whether or not the Shona entertained the concept of a supreme being in earlier times.[50]

The last point leads us on to a more general consideration. For so far we have been discussing discrepancies between present-day patterns of focal objects in the indigenous cosmologies and 'Devout' stereotypes of them. And we have seen that these discrepancies are considerable, indeed sometimes huge. However, we have not yet taken into account the fact that much of our knowledge of these patterns is derived from areas long under the twin influences of Christian missionary enterprise and the accelerated social change of modern times. In what follows, I shall suggest that, had we been able to view the indigenous religions before the impact of these twin influences, we should, in all probability, have found the discrepancies even more dramatic.

Now, in many if not most cases, we lack the data that would have enabled us to delineate the patterns of focal objects as they were at the time when these influences first appeared and to chart changes in them from that time onward. Non-Christians all too often maintain stoutly that their present ideas as to the focal objects of their cosmologies are age-old, and deny that anyone could have developed these ideas in the recent past without their being aware of the fact. And there are no collateral data which would enable us to check the historical validity of this stance. Nonetheless, there are a number of cases where the views of non-Christians *can* be checked, either because the scholar who records them has himself made an earlier study of the religious system in question, or because he has access to other data which provide evidence as to the earlier situation. And a review of these cases gives us the basis at least for some tentative generalizations.[51] The broad picture that emerges is one of two mutually reinforcing processes.

On the one hand, missionaries busily engaged themselves in extracting from the peoples they were attempting to evangelize names for the supreme being. Sometimes, it seems, the peoples involved could only produce the names of lesser spiritual forces, and it was the missionaries who deceived themselves into thinking that they were in possession of indigenous names for the supreme being.[52] Sometimes, those concerned were able to produce appropriate names; but even then the missionaries reinterpreted them to give them a more Christian flavour.[53] Having extracted these names, missionaries then attempted to use them to persuade their audiences that their own religious outlooks were 'in-a-glass-darkly' adumbrations of the Christian message, and that, as such, they should be abandoned in favour of the latter.

On the other hand, the peoples on the receiving end of missionary activity found themselves in an era of rapidly expanding social horizons for whose comprehension their parochially oriented cosmologies were not fully satisfying. Some responded to this situation by entering the Christian fold and adopting in large measure what they could grasp of the Christian cosmology. Many others, however, were unwilling to go so far so fast. These preferred to remain outside the Christian fold, and to cope with the shortcomings of their cosmologies by re-working them so as to restore their adequacy. Faced with such a task, nonetheless, they also found certain elements of the missionary message concerning the supreme being particularly congenial to their purposes, and used them freely to create new though still unmistakably indigenous syntheses. In the course of such re-working, ironically, they often took back from the missionaries items of religious vocabulary that were subtle transformations of items which the missionaries themselves had earlier extracted from them.[54]

The result of these mutually reinforcing processes was that the patterns of focal objects in the indigenous cosmologies moved much closer to that characteristic of the Judaeo-Christian tradition than they had been to start with.

Inference from the small number of cases in which relevant evidence is available to sub-saharan Africa as a whole is of course not without its dangers. Nonetheless, it does seem probable that the changes we have sketched here were widespread. It follows that, great as are the discrepancies between present-day patterns of focal objects in the indigenous religions and 'Devout' stereotypes of them, they are probably as nothing compared with the discrepancies which we might have seen had we had wider access to the earlier indigenous traditions.

All in all, then, it seems that the 'Devout' translation recipe has given us a severely distorted picture of the focal objects of African religious thought. Here, perhaps, we ought to give the last word to Okot P'Bitek, who summed up the situation with the angry protest: 'The African deities of the books, clothed with the attributes of the Christian God, are, in the main, creations of the students of African religions. They are beyond all recognition to the ordinary Africans in the countryside.'[55]

(b) The attitudes of African worshippers. Since the 'Devout' have, by and large, not written in such detail about the attitudes of the African to his gods as they have about the characteristics of these gods, they have exposed

less of themselves in this respect to the probing critic. Nonetheless, they have made their salutations to Otto and to his idea of a uniquely religious attitude; and we must ask ourselves how useful or otherwise these salutations are.

In recent years, the debate about attitudes to spiritual agencies in the indigenous religions has centred on attitudes to the ancestors; and we may as well make a start by considering these.[56] Although the debate is far from closed, the upshot so far seems to be an emphasis on continuity between attitudes to the ancestors and those to living elders. There are, of course, qualifications to be made. Attitudes to ancestors often overemphasize one component of attitudes to living elders and underemphasize another. An example can be drawn from Fortes's painstaking work on Tallensi relations with the ancestors, in which he shows how the component of fear and respect is played up, and that of warm affection played down.[57] Again, attitudes to the ancestors are influenced by the fact that, under normal circumstances the latter are not directly seen or heard, but rather give indirect responses to human approaches at relatively long intervals. Nonetheless, it does seem that the central features of emotional and relational commitment to the ancestors are continuous with the central features of commitment to living elders. Furthermore, the monographic work reveals nothing in concept or behaviour that might be held comparable to the attitude of fearful fascination with the uncanny so central to Otto's 'Idea of the Holy'.

If we turn to the cults of non-ancestral spirits, much the same picture emerges. Here, the attentive student will very likely be struck by the sheer variety of attitudes: a variety which is clearly correlated with that of the spirits themselves. Sometimes, indeed, he will be struck by the sheer variety of attitudes to the gods, even within the confines of a single religious system. A good example here is provided by Yoruba religious life, in which a very broad spectrum of attitudes, ranging from amused tolerance to fearful respect, is a clear correlate of the equally broad spectrum of characterizations associated with the *orisa* spirits.[58] Despite the variety, however, careful scrutiny shows the same underlying continuity between attitudes to spiritual forces and those to living people as we saw in the ancestral cults. Thus a mischievous but benign spirit receives the same amused indulgence as would a mischievous but benign human being. And a powerful but touchy spirit receives the same fearful respect as would a powerful but touchy father. Once again, moreover, monographic work on the non-ancestral cults has failed so far to reveal anything parallel to the Ottovian fascination with the uncanny.

At this point, some 'Devout' scholars will object that what we have been considering are attitudes to the lesser spirits. They will insist that it is in relations, not with such lesser agencies, but rather with the supreme being, that we must look for the 'distinctively religious attitude'.[59] Even if we carry out this injunction, however, we are likely to find ourselves chasing a mirage. In the first place, in the numerous instances where the supreme being lies at the periphery rather than at the centre of the religious consciousness, we can only characterize attitudes to him as apathetic.[60] Secondly, where the supreme being lies nearer the centre of consciousness, much of what I have said about attitudes to the lesser spirits seems equally applicable. Once again there is some variety, which correlates with variety in the characterization of the supreme being. Once again, nonetheless, there are strong continuities between attitudes to the supreme being and attitudes to living people. Thus a female, maternal supreme being receives the same sort of attitudinal and emotional response as does a living mother; and a male, paternal supreme being receives the same sort of response as does a living father. Finally, even at this level, there is little evidence of anything that might be held parallel to or translatable into terms of fearful fascination with the uncanny.

These conclusions accord well with what I said earlier about the absence, in pre-Christian, pre-Islamic settings, of any great positive celebration of the mysteriousness and inscrutability of the supreme being. For it is only in relation to these qualities that the Ottovian religious attitude makes sense. Hence, where they are not celebrated, we should not expect to find it.

In short, then, there would seem to be considerable discrepancies between the realities of African religious attitudes to spiritual agencies and 'Devout' assumptions about such attitudes. Once again, it would seem that the 'Devout' translation recipe, if overenthusiastically pressed, will lead us into trouble.

(c) The aims of African religious life. The 'Devout', as we saw, are in broad agreement that the overriding aim of African religious life is communion with a spiritual being, such communion being felt and conceived as an end in itself. And it seems sensible to start by asking just how far this view of things corresponds with the prevailing realities as reported in the corpus of monographic work on the indigenous religions.

The monographic evidence on this point, it would seem, is overwhelmingly negative. In work after work, we find that explanation, prediction and control are the overriding aims of religious life. People want a coherent picture of the realities that underpin their everyday world. They want to know the causes of their fortunes and misfortunes in this world. They want to have some way of predicting the outcomes of their various worldly projects and enterprises. They want, above all, to have the means of controlling events in the space-time world around them.[61] These aims provide the measure of the efficacy of the gods; sometimes even the measure for decisions as to whether to retain their services or dismiss them.[62] In relation to these aims, the quest for communion takes a definite second place. In some cultures, such as Acholi, it seems virtually absent.[63] In others, such as Yoruba and Kalabari, it has overriding importance for a small number of rather special people, but means little to the majority. And even for this small number of special people, it should be remembered, the communion aspect of the man-spirit relationship is developed with one or other of the lesser spirits, and not with the supreme being.[64]

Perhaps the most impressive evidence for the overriding importance of explanation, prediction and control as goals of religious life in sub-Saharan Africa comes from continent-wide reactions to Christianity.

By world standards, the sub-Saharan reaction to late nineteenth- and early twentieth-century Christian missionary efforts was spectacularly positive. Hundreds of thousands of people up and down the continent poured into the mission churches with every sign of enthusiasm and sincerity. Indeed, as I pointed out earlier, although the message of an active, morally concerned supreme being was a new one in many areas, it was a message that people found particularly apt in the new circumstances they faced. Yet twenty to thirty years later, tens of thousands of these people were pouring out again into new foundations that called themselves Christian but differed in important respects from their 'orthodox' predecessors. And the trend has continued down to this day, to the point where even the leaders of the older Churches are forced to concede the greater vigour and appeal of the new institutions.

Why this spectacular reverse movement? From the observable differences between the old and new institutions, and from the abundant comments of leaders and followers in the latter, the root cause emerges with stark clarity. Once within the walls of the mission churches, 'converts' found themselves faced with a concept of the goals of the religious life just like that imputed to them by the 'Devout': a concept which made communion with God not just *an* end in itself, but *the overriding end* of the religious life. For people used to the idea that the powers of spiritual forces were there first and foremost to be tapped to improve man's lot in the here and now, this was a strange and comfortless concept. Hence an almost immediate drive to build up and enrol in institutions which repeated the new message of an active, morally concerned supreme being, but restored the old priority of explanation, prediction and control of the events of the everyday world.[65]

Even the 'Devout' have quailed in the face of these realities; which is why some of them have preferred to talk of appearances being deceptive rather than to deny them flatly. But when someone says that certain appearances are deceptive, the burden of proof is on him. And what we have had on this from the 'Devout' so far has smacked more of passionate assertion than of cogent argument backed by evidence.

So much for the alleged primacy of the quest for communion. What of that other element that features so prominently in the Judaeo-Christian heritage: the quest for release from this world to another and incomparably better one beyond the grave? Here, I think, we need to proceed carefully in order to avoid the accusation of setting up and attacking straw men. For some of the 'Devout', notably Mbiti, have asserted very clearly that this element of the heritage has no parallel in the African traditions.[66] Nonetheless, as we saw earlier, there are passages in Idowu and H. W. Turner which indicate that they are tempted to posit this aim as having a central place in African religious life. Some cautionary comment may thus be in order here.

In order to judge the validity of the claim that the quest for the 'other world' is an important feature of the indigenous traditions, it would seem sensible to turn for evidence to what we know of indigenous conceptions and evaluations of existence after death.

The first thing to be acknowledged is the variety of such conceptions.

Some are so negative and attenuated as to make the claim seem quite ridiculous. Such, for example, is the Tiv conception, in which, at death, the spiritual portion of the individual loses contact with the living only to linger on indefinitely in a joyless realm that no one would ever think of comparing favourably with the world on this side of the grave.[67] The strongest trans-Saharan echoes here are not of more recent Judaeo-Christian thought; but of the ancient Greek Hades and the ancient Judaic Sheol.

However, although such examples have to be taken into account in judging claims as to the importance of the quest for the 'other world', it must be admitted that they are in the minority. To give those who make these claims their due, we must look at some of the commoner conceptions of the after-life: conceptions which tend to be more positive.

The most widespread of these conceptions is that which provides the backing for all of those world-views in which ancestral forces are regarded as playing an important part in influencing the course of everyday life. In it, the ideal after-life is the one in which a man, having achieved high status as head of a large family or lineage, enjoys similar status in the after-life through the continued attention and deference of his living descendants. The most dreaded after-life, by corollary, is the one in which a man enters the world beyond the grave either with no surviving descendants, or with descendants who have repudiated their ties with him at burial as the result of witchcraft or other supreme wickedness on his part. Here, then, the ideal situation is one of maximum continued contact with the world of the living, and the abhorred situation one of minimum contact.[68]

A second common conception, incompatible with the first to the eye of the outsider but often in fact combined with it, is that usually summed up in the term 'reincarnation'. Where this conception reigns, we find that the ideal situation is one in which the spiritual portion of a good man returns to a worldly life even more satisfying and prestigious than the one he had previously lived. By corollary, a feared situation is one in which the spirit of a bad man comes back to a miserable human existence or even to an animal existence. Still more feared, in some communities, is the possibility of being prevented from any kind of return by ritual action taken at one's funeral ceremony: a possibility which may be actualized if funeral divination reveals one is a witch or a sorcerer. Here, the ideal situation involves return to the world of the living on good or improved terms; whilst the worst possible situation involves being debarred from return.[69]

Whatever difficulties the scholar may experience in seeing how these two pictures of the after-life fit together, he will have no difficulty in seeing that they resemble each other in one key respect. Both, that is, portray continued fruitful involvement with the world of the living as the ideal, and cessation of such involvement as the ultimate horror. Both, moreover, differ in this respect not only from mainstream Christianity either Catholic or Protestant, but also from major Eastern religions.

The difference from the Christian conception, with its stress on an escape from an inferior temporal life to a superior eternal life, is obvious. The difference from Eastern conceptions is initially less obvious, because of the prominence in them of ideas of reincarnation. However, African and Eastern conceptions of reincarnation are poles apart. As we have seen, the African ideal tends to be one of endless return. By contrast, the Eastern ideal is one of successive returns which nonetheless progress toward and culminate in escape from 'the wheel'. So, despite superficial differences from the Western conception of the after-life, the Eastern conception shares with it the ideal of ultimate escape from the temporal to the eternal.[70]

For the African religious thinker, then, it would seem to be true that the life in this world is the best there is. If anything is to come after it, this should, in one way or another, involve more of the same. Both the ideal of ancestorhood and the ideal of reincarnation presuppose this judgement. For Western Christian thinkers and their Hindu and Buddhist counterparts, however, there is something fundamentally flawed about the worldly life; something that forces one to regard it as a way-stage *en route* to a condition utterly different and incomparably better. In short, as between the African conceptions and those closer to the hearts of the 'Devout', there is once again a great gulf set.

We have now completed our critical consideration of the picture of indigenous religious thought that results from application of the 'Devout' translation recipe. With respect to focal objects, to attitudes to these objects, and to the aims of the religious life, we have found that the picture diverges markedly from the realities of the situation. We must conclude that the consequences of pressing the recipe are disastrous.

Further explanation

In criticizing the 'Devout' approach to further explanation, I shall start with the prescription which ordains that the variable features of religious belief should be explained in terms of physiological, psychological and socio-logical theory, whilst the invariant theistic features should be explained in terms of the presence of the supreme being and of human awareness of this presence. As we have seen, this prescription, rather puzzling in itself, is grounded in two other propositions which are somewhat easier to under-stand. The first is that the variable features of belief represent the veil of error whilst the invariant theistic features represent the core of truth. The second is that erroneous belief is appropriately explained in terms of physiological, psychological and sociological theory, whilst true belief is appropriately explained in terms of the presence of the object and of human awareness of this presence.

For the moment, at least, I should like to avoid quarrelling with the first proposition. Arguments about the truth-values of specific religious state-ments can be both endless and very tricky. And I have no intention of getting sucked down into a quagmire that has swallowed up many better men. As for the alleged invariance of the theistic element, I shall, as the reader will expect from my earlier comments, have something more to say on this later. Meanwhile, I believe that it is the critique of the second proposition that will most readily resolve the question of the validity of the 'Devout' explanatory prescription.

For all its popularity and its hold over laymen and over scholars in several disciplines, the second proposition is remarkably lacking in rational support. Those who use it tend, if challenged, to say that it is self-evident. And if they go further than this, it is to cite everyday usage.[71]

Now, on the face of things, it does seem that, in the everyday life at least of modern Western culture, this proposition is by and large accepted. What are commonly regarded as veridical beliefs are normally not thought of as calling for any special explanation. And if those who hold them are chal-lenged to provide such an explanation, they are liable to say something very minimal, such as: 'Well, the world is like that and we have the normal human faculties for observing it.' It is only when someone confesses to unusual beliefs which the community refuses to consider veridical that a more elaborate apparatus of physiological, psychological and sociological theory is brought in to provide an explanation. In this sense, everyday life does appear to provide the basis for a 'paradigm case' argument for the view that there is one pattern of explanation appropriate for valid beliefs and another appropriate for erroneous ones.

Like many other 'paradigm case' arguments, however, this one has little substance to it.

In the first place, even where physiological, psychological, sociological or combined theories are invoked to explain the genesis of erroneous beliefs or perceptual judgements, these are seldom purely and simply theories of error. They tend rather to be theories in which the mechanisms that produce veridical belief and perception are delineated in some detail, and in which erroneous belief and perception are explained in terms of factors interfering with these mechanisms.[72] Even in the context of everyday life, then, physiological, psychological, sociological or combined explanations of erroneous belief and perception tend to be parasitic on physiological, psychological, sociological or combined theories of veridical belief and perception.

Secondly, we must remember that the patterns of explanation current in everyday life are shaped by the special interests of everyday life, and that other patterns of explanation may be legitimately called forth by other interests.

Let me elaborate on this last assertion.

The smooth running of everyday life in the modern West is based on two main assumptions: first, that the world around us is furnished with objects of certain kinds that behave in certain predictable ways; and second, that we share normal perceptual faculties that enable us to be aware of this furniture and arrive at a consensus of veridical belief about it. So long as the beliefs of those around us call neither of these assumptions into question, everyday life rolls on smoothly and without problems. This is why we don't normally bother to produce explanations of beliefs commonly accepted as veridical, and why, if challenged to do so, we respond with very perfunctory ones. When someone comes up with odd beliefs about the world, however, the situation is radically changed. Such beliefs threaten the consensus on which the smooth running of everyday life is founded, and therefore evoke a much more careful and elaborate explanatory response.

Nonetheless, although everyday life is dominated by interests that require full-fledged explanations only of cognitive error, there are other situations where the interests in play demand full-fledged explanations of cognitive success. Nor are these situations confined to the ivory towers of the pure scientists. Some are governed by strongly practical interests. In the modern world, for example, there is an eminently practical interest in the possibility of constructing machines to take over some of man's work of veridical perception and theory-construction. And for those whose thinking is governed by such an interest, it is a matter of vital import that they should eventually be able to say, in the kind of terms that would provide useful clues for the machine-makers, just how veridical perception and belief are achieved.[73]

In short, the insistence that full-fledged explanations in terms of physiological, psychological, sociological factors are appropriate only to erroneous beliefs turns out, under closer scrutiny, to be a product of the peculiar circumstances of everyday life and to have no necessary applicability beyond the range of these circumstances. The powerful sense of 'rightness' that it carries with it merely exemplifies the age-old (and often far from fruitful) influence of everyday patterns of thinking on all others.[74]

In so far, then, as the 'Devout' embargo on physiological, psychological, sociological explanations of what they regard as the veridical core of religious belief is based on a 'paradigm case' argument from the context of everyday life, it is groundless. And in the absence of any other rational argument in its favour, we can dismiss it.

Should this line of argument be generally accepted, we shall have succeeded in extirpating the obnoxious conviction that scholars of different personal religious views are for ever destined to pursue irreconcilable explanatory programmes in the field of religious phenomena. For, in its light, the theist can feel as free as the atheist to explore the potential of physiological, psychological, and sociological theory in this field.

So much for the negative aspect of the 'Devout' approach to further explanation. What of the positive aspect? What of the special pattern of explanation that these scholars regard as uniquely theirs? What we have said so far may well have encouraged the reader to think of this 'special pattern' as little more than a poor relative of certain better-developed types of explanation. So far, however, we have not directly impugned its validity. Nonetheless, it too is more than ripe for our critical scrutiny.

Let me start by reminding the reader that this pattern of explanation depends on three premises: the first asserting the reality of a supreme being with certain basic attributes; the second asserting the gift by this being to all men at all times and places of an awareness of him and a desire to commune with him; and the third asserting the similar gift of a limited but crucial ability to make veridical statements about him.

Between them, these three premises offer rich temptations to metaphysical and methodological argument. Once again, however, I shall try to avoid getting sucked down into the quagmire of metaphysics. Millions of pages have been given over, down the years, to arguments both for and against the reality of a supreme being. And I have absolutely no pretension to being able to contribute anything new to this debate. I shall also try to avoid getting drawn into methodological discussions of the propriety of incorporating assumptions about the reality of the supreme being into explanations of religious phenomena. I see a danger here of coming up with just the sort of ultimately groundless *a priori* embargo that we found to be such a tiresome feature of the 'Devout' approach.

What I propose to do here is simply consider the 'Devout' explanatory scheme as constituting a theoretical hypothesis, featuring postulates about unobservables as well as observables, but none the worse for that. To appraise this hypothesis, I shall first set out what seems to be to be its most obvious deductive implication, and then go on to compare this implication with the realities of the situation.

The single most obvious and most important implication is, of course, that the world-views of all peoples at all times and places must feature as their focal object a supreme being with certain constant minimal attributes. Now unfortunately, as we began to see earlier in this paper, the realities of the situation in no way correspond with this implication.

In sub-Saharan Africa, many of the indigenous world-views have indeed focussed on a supreme being. But the sheer variety of attributes imputed to this being in itself casts doubt on the claim that we are dealing here with a set of veridical responses to a single unchanging entity. Many such world-views, moreover, do not focus on a single supreme being. Many focus on a pair of such things. And some have no place at all either for a single supreme being or for a pair of such beings.

If we go beyond Africa, the situation turns out to be no more encouraging. In the Far-Eastern homelands of Theravada Buddhism, we find a world pullulating with lesser spirits, but with no trace of a central supreme being. And in the modern West, we find whole sub-cultures which seem to be moving steadily toward a non-spiritual view of the world and of man's place in it.

The 'Devout' struggle desperately against these recalcitrant realities. As for the African data, they either ignore them stubbornly like so many anti-Galileans refusing to look down the telescope, or impugn the good faith of those who have gathered them or tried to draw attention to them.[75] As for the Far-Eastern Theravada data, they never mention them. And as for the horrendous Western data, some have even gone as far as to try turning them upside down. Thus they maintain that Western man is not in fact an atheist, but someone whose technological prowess has made him so arrogant that he cannot tolerate the presence of a being incomparably greater than himself. Resenting such a being, he tries to fight him by denying him.[76]

For the unbiassed onlooker, these efforts must do more to draw attention to 'Devout' discomfort than to secure sympathy for the 'Devout' case. The steadfast ignoring of data speaks for itself. The impugning of good faith carries no conviction in the light of our knowledge of the backgrounds, characters and capabilities of those concerned. And redefinition of the Western atheist as secret theist must seem ludicrous to anyone with more than a superficial knowledge of the contemporary West. To such a person, it will be all too clear that, even though there may be a few secret 'fighters against God' amongst the ranks of professed atheists, your average Western bearer of this metaphysical label is just what he says he is: a man for whom the idea of God has no place whatsoever in his view of the world, and in whom the idea excites no emotion either positive or negative.

Such antics in the face of the realities of the situation should in no way surprise us. For the head-on clash between these realities and the central deductive implication of the 'Devout' explanatory theory indicate that the latter is completely untenable.

With this conclusion, it has become clear that the 'Devout' have no more to offer us at the level of further explanation than they had at the level of translational understanding.

Diagnosis

Preliminaries

I should like to conclude this paper with some suggestions as to how the personal and social backgrounds of 'Devout' scholars may have contributed to the formation of their academic views.

Since the reader will by now be aware that I consider these views fundamentally misguided, he may feel inclined to complain that, in taking on this task, I am perpetuating the very idea of the special appropriateness of psycho-social explanations to erroneous belief which I criticized earlier on. I should like to make it very clear, therefore, that this is far from my intention. Let me repeat the credo that psycho-social explanation is appropriate both to true and to erroneous beliefs, and add that, even had we been dealing in this paper with a marvellously insightful approach to African religions, I should still have felt it interesting and fruitful to offer suggestions as to the psychological and sociological factors that prompted these insights.

This said, however, it is nonetheless true that the particular problem we face here is that of how an approach so palpably inadequate to the phenomena at the levels both of translational understanding and of further explanation can enjoy such rude health and such whole-hearted commitment from its advocates.

In what follows, I shall pay particular attention to two background factors that seem to me to have been powerful shapers of all of the various approaches made so far to the study of African religions. These are, first, the character and extent of the translational resources available to the scholar. And, second, the character and magnitude of the ideological pressures upon him.

Background factors

Translational resources. As I pointed out at the beginning of this essay, translation of the language and thought of a particular African religion into terms of a language and thought currently enjoying 'world' status is the key to the first level of understanding in this field. As I also pointed out, it follows that the character of the translation recipe adopted does much to determine the overall character of a given approach.

Now, ideally, the character of the language and thought to be translated should be the sole constraint on choice of translation recipe. But this ideal could only be realized given one of two conditions. Either all the scholars concerned would have to have infinite capacities for fashioning the appropriate translation recipes *ex nihilo*. Or all concerned would have to have an infinite diversity of ready-made translation instruments to draw upon.

In reality, of course, the character of the language and thought to be translated is far from being the sole constraint on choice of translation recipe: as witness the great variety of such recipes elicited by a particular area of 'alien' language and thought. And the main reason would seem to be that those involved in the translation enterprise *do not* have the ideal infinity of translational resources to draw upon. Rather, each one among them brings to the task such limited linguistic and conceptual resources as he has accumulated over the course of his education. For all that he bends, stretches, twists and recombines their elements, it is these limited resources that constitute his raw materials. Again, since each individual educational trajectory is different from every other, so the corresponding stock of raw materials differs from every other stock.

Clearly, the finitude and variability of translational resources rule out the very idea of a perfect translation. However, that does not mean that we should sit back and let anything go. For, with all the inevitability of imperfection, there is still the possibility of doing better or worse. And where this possibility exists, we have a duty to exploit it. This means, amongst other things, that we have a duty to try and isolate those variables that are the key to the quality of translation.

One of the most important of such variables is the richness/poverty of the scholar's translational resources. Given the character of the translation process as outlined in this paper, it follows that, the richer and more diverse the scholar's translational resources, the better his chances of hitting on at least an approximately appropriate translation recipe, and conversely that, the less diverse his resources, the worse his chances of hitting on a good approximation. In this field, then, it would seem that, other things being equal, the universal polymath is the type with the best chances of success; whilst the person with the narrowly specialized education is the type with the worst chances.

Unfortunately, the specializing tendency of education in the modern Western or Westernized societies that produce interpreters of African religions is such that its typical scholarly product is the narrowly educated man who has the least chances of success. Most of the 'Devout' alas, fall into the latter category; and this, as we shall soon see, is one root of their failure.

As I said earlier, the 'Devout' translation recipe fails in three respects: first, in its emphasis on the centrality of the supreme being; secondly, in its emphasis on an attitude to this being of which the central component is the kind of fearful fascination appropriate to the 'mysterious', the 'inscrutable', the 'uncanny' or the 'praeternatural'; and, thirdly and perhaps most seriously, in its emphasis on communion rather than explanation/prediction/control as the leading motive of the religious life. In what follows, I shall try to show how each of these failures stems from a limitation in translational resources.

The first failure is perhaps the most easily understood in these terms. For various reasons we haven't the space to go into here, leaders of Christian thinking down the ages have almost obsessively stressed the ontological subordination of all other spiritual forces to the one God. And they have treated any challenge to this line of thought as a severe threat to the survival of Christian religion. In the process, they have succeeded in imposing a type of religious discourse which renders its user incapable of thinking of lesser spiritual forces as having a reality and life of their own. In this respect alone, the 'Devout' are hampered from the start in their attempts to provide an adequate translational understanding of most African religions.

In order to understand the second and third failures, we have to turn to another aspect of the history of Christianity: to the fact that, over the centuries, the faith has been periodically embattled with other systems of thought and ways of life, and bears the marks of these battles.

One such mark is that left by Christianity's own most cherished defensive tactic. Faced with challenges to the rationality of their faith, Christian thinkers have tended, very characteristically, to take refuge in aggressive obscurantism rather than in rational counter-argument, proudly vaunting the unamenability of the object of their faith to rational comprehension. They became notorious for this tactic in their early battles with Mediterranean paganisms.[77] And they have dusted it down and brought it into action again in their more recent battles with science-inspired atheism.[78]

Someone looking at these battles from the sidelines may well be reminded of that elusive but hardy mollusc, the cuttlefish, who, when faced with superior muscle-power, retreats behind a formidable jet of opaque ink! Here, I suggest, we have the origin of that positive celebration of 'mystery' and 'inscrutability' which looms so large in the 'Devout' vision of the religious life. In African systems of religious thought, which have not been embattled in the same way and so have not been under the same pressure to evolve defences against rival systems, it is not surprising that such positive celebration is absent. In their determination to see it where it is not, the 'Devout' appear once again to be victims of the historically determined peculiarities of their translational resources.

To further our comprehension of the last two failures, let us look more closely at the mark left on Christianity by its confrontation with science-inspired atheism.

Four centuries ago, Western Christian discourse was shaped by the pursuit, both of explanation/prediction/control, and of communion. A good illustration of such dual shaping can be seen in the thought of those cosmologists who saw their theories, on the one hand as means of explaining the world, and on the other as means of giving praise to the Creator.[79] As time passed, however, the advent of a succession of ever-more-powerful theories couched in non-spiritual terms put the leaders of Christian religious thought on the defensive. Faced with the alternatives of continuing the unequal competition in the realm of explanation/prediction/control and of dropping out of the competition by a restrictive redefinition of the aims of the religious life, they tended increasingly to opt for the latter.

Some were reluctant to go the whole way in this. Whilst consigning the vast majority of worldly phenomena to the intellectual care of the scientists, they cherished the notion that there were certain kinds of phenomena that were impervious to scientific explanation and were direct manifestations of spiritual action. Others went the whole hog and consigned explanation/prediction/control of all worldly events to the scientists.

Those who took the first course came as a result to associate the spiritual with that which defied the 'natural' order of things. Hence the vogue of the terms 'supernatural' and 'praeternatural' as labels for the spiritual realm. This association further encouraged definitions of religion which emphasized the 'mysteriousness' and 'inscrutability' of the object of faith, and the attitude of fearful fascination appropriate to an object with such attributes.

Once again, this is a development with no parallel in African religious thought. In so far as the latter provides a framework of explanatory concepts that embraces *all* worldly phenomena, it has no place for a dichotomy corresponding to that between the 'natural' and the 'supernatural', and no place for special attitudes associated with that which defies the 'natural' order of things. Here, then, we see yet another way in which the historically determined peculiarities of 'Devout' translational resources constitute an obstacle to proper translational understanding.

Whether Western religious thinkers went most of the way or all of it in their concessions to the scientists, however, the result was in many respects the same. Gradually, a division of labour became established, whereby scientists pursued the ends of explanation, prediction and control, whilst religious thinkers pursued the end of communion with God. With the two sets of ends now by and large pursued by two different groups of specialists, two distinct types of discourse came to replace the original unity. And once these types were established, the specializing tendency of the educational apparatus ensured that, all too often, people well versed in one of them tended to be ill-versed in the other.

The present-day 'Devout' scholar merely exemplifies this general trend. Well versed in discourse shaped by the aim of communion with the spiritual, he is almost always correspondingly ill-versed in discourse shaped by the aims of explanation, prediction and control. In many other walks of life, this limitation would have been no great disadvantage. In his chosen walk, however, it is crippling. For it means that he has only one part of the total resources necessary for the development of a proper translational understanding of African religious thought, and the less important part at that.

Let us sum up our findings in this section. It has become clear that one root of all three 'Devout' failures at the level of translational understanding is inappropriateness or inadequacy of translational resources, Indeed, it would seem that a peculiar concatenation of historical and personal circumstances has landed the 'Devout' with translational equipment quite unequal to the enterprise to which they have committed themselves.

Ideological pressures. Ideology has been defined as ideas in the service of a wish or commitment. And, without prejudice to anything said above about translational resources, I submit that some of the worst distortions in the 'Devout' view can be further understood when we see this view as an ideology whose holders are above all else preoccupied with defending a strong egalitarian commitment against certain deeply inegalitarian implications of their own Christian faith.

Most modern Christians, of course, contend that their religion is egalitarian in its very essence. And they carry a great deal of conviction in so arguing. Certainly, 'All men are equal in the sight of God' is a very basic Christian tenet. Nonetheless, the same Christians tend to be uncomfortable when faced with questions about the standing of non-Christians in the sight of God. For despite sophisticated modern theological casuistry on the subject, the problem of how Christians should view those of their fellow men who live and die as non-Christians has yet to be resolved. In the minds of most Christian thinkers, the idea still persists that genuine Christians are 'redeemed' whilst non-Christians are 'unredeemed'. And to such thinkers, there is a sense in which 'redeemed' means 'first-class citizen of the universe' whilst 'unredeemed' means 'second-class citizen of the universe'. At the heart of Christianity, then, there is a conflict between its egalitarian aspects and some definitely non-egalitarian implications.

For the 'Devout' scholar engaged in the study of African religions, I see this conflict as creating an agonizing dilemma. Typically, such a scholar, be he African or Western, has a strong egalitarian commitment. More specifically, reacting to aspersions cast on the African by several generations of anthropologists in the nineteenth and early twentieth centuries, he is committed to demonstrating equality of mental and cultural capacity as between the African and his Western counterpart. In this commitment his Christian faith provides him with broad overall backing. In the matter of the adherents of African religions, however, Christianity threatens to let him down. For, insofar as these religions are non-Christian, their members are 'unredeemed' and so in a sense 'second-class citizens'. In short, the 'Devout' scholar's own faith threatens to push him back to just the sort of inegalitarian position that he is committed to resisting with every fibre of his being.

It is in terms of this predicament, I suggest, that we can make further sense of many 'Devout' errors.

Let us look first at its impact at the level of translational understanding. If the 'Devout' scholar provides a translation scheme which points to radical discontinuity between the African religion he is trying to understand and his own Christian faith, he thereby admits the 'unredeemed' character of the adherents of this religion, and reverts to a form of inegalitarianism. However, if he produces a scheme which points to a measure of continuity between the African religion and Christianity, he can assure himself that the adherents of this religion are in some sense 'redeemed', and so keep his feet out of the inegalitarian trap. Not surprisingly, our scholar takes the second option.

Let us turn now to the impact of the 'Devout' predicament at the level of further explanation. The important thing to notice here is the insistence, in the 'Devout' explanatory framework, not just on the existence of God, but also on his self-revelation to all peoples at all times and places. For although these explanatory premises do not amount to a profession of faith in a universal self-revelation of a specifically Christian kind, they *can* be taken as asserting a universal self-revelation of the God of the Christians. And the acceptance of such an assertion does surely allow all but the most narrow-minded Christians to regard their fellow men at all times and places as in some sense 'redeemed' and so as in some sense 'first-class citizens'. No wonder, then, that the two premisses play such a key part in 'Devout' explanatory activities.

Evidence for the aptness of this diagnosis emerges directly from the work of some of the leading 'Devout' authors.

One such author is Gaba, who ends one of his rather strained demonstrations of continuities between African and Christian concepts with the obviously relieved conclusion that the discovery of such continuities may absolve the Christian scholar or missionary from having to treat his non-Christian countrymen as 'eternally damned'.[80]

Another such author is Idowu, who spends much space reviling nineteenth-century Western belittlers of the African, and denounces more recent assertions of discontinuity between African and Christian concepts of a supreme being as extensions of the same tradition. For Idowu, such assertions imply that the one God has not revealed himself to Africans, and are therefore tantamount to the condemnation of Africans as 'scum'. Accordingly, it is only through their disproof that we can pave the way for a restoration of the dignity and worth of Africans in the eyes of the world.[81]

It is not surprising that the clearest indications of the ideological character of the 'Devout' position should come from African rather than Western scholars. After all, it is *their* non-Christian kith and kin whose status is at stake.[82] Nonetheless, similar overtones can also be heard in the works of their Western counterparts. From H. W. Turner's latest manifesto, for instance, it is clear that there is a strong link in the author's mind between establishing that African religions show the essential characteristics of True Religion and establishing the human worth and dignity of Africans.[83]

To those of us who share the 'Devout' egalitarian commitment but not the 'Devout' religious faith, all of this is apt to sound like a case of much ado about nothing. For we, mercifully, feel no need to dress our atheistic or polytheistic relatives and friends in Judaeo-Christian clothes before we can accept them as 'first-class citizens' of the universe. Indeed, asked to nominate a dozen people for such first-class status, some of us might be inclined to turn to those of our nearest and dearest who are atheists or polytheists before ever we turned to a monotheist or more specifically to a Christian! We find it difficult even to imagine, let alone to empathize with, the kind of heart-searching to which the 'Devout' are prone. For the 'Devout' scholar who is sincere in his Christianity, however, such heart-searching is all too real. And we must make an effort to empathize with it if we are to begin the sort of dialogue that might eventually lead him into more fruitful paths.[84]

The way forward

As I mentioned at the beginning of this essay, a leading spokesman for the 'Devout' approach recently maintained that the only way forward in our area of common concern was through the further cultivation of this approach.[85] From what has been said in this paper, however, it should be clear that this is disastrous counsel which can only lead to the compounding of already gross errors. Further advance will require a radically different approach.

In throwing out a few suggestions as to what direction we should be taking, let me follow once more the overall plan of this essay, and talk in terms of two stages of interpretation: translational understanding and further explanation.

With respect to the search for an appropriate translation recipe, I should like to make two suggestions. First of all, we should draw on a more 'demotic' strand of the Western heritage of religious discourse, one that allows reference to a wide diversity of spiritual forces without automatically reducing such forces to manifestations of a single supreme being. Second, whilst retaining elements of modern Western religious discourse in our tool-kit, we should bring in alongside them elements of the theoretical discourse that is now the monopoly of the sciences, elements which were once combined with their religious counterparts but which have now become separated. Only by use of elements from both areas of discourse can we do justice to the fact that, in the religious life of most African societies, the concern for communion with the spiritual is accompanied, indeed overshadowed, by the concern for explanation, prediction and control of worldly events. Initial efforts indicate that the task of re-amalgamating these separated elements in order to forge an effective translation instrument is likely to prove extremely difficult. And at this early stage of the enterprise, I don't think any general guidelines can be given. However, for a clue as to what the results of such a re-amalgamation might look like, perhaps we should turn to the conceptual apparatus of Freud, which a sympathetic commentator recently described as at once 'animistic' and 'scientific'.[86] And for attempts to use elements of the Freudian apparatus as a starting point for the creation of an effective instrument for the translational understanding of African religious systems, I would ask the reader to look at the essays by Fortes and myself in the recent re-issue of Fortes's *Oedipus and Job in West African Religion*.[87]

In our search for an appropriate scheme of further explanation, I suggest that we should again be guided by what we know of the primacy in African religious life of explanation/prediction/control over communion. Looking at African religions as systems of theory-in-practice, we may turn for inspiration to the spate of work on technological, economic, social and political determinants of theoretical beliefs that has appeared in recent years in the wake of the philosophical 'discovery' of the underdetermination of theory by evidence. At the same time, however, we should remember that, to those who believe in them, spiritual forces are people with whom one is involved in social relations. And in order to do justice to this aspect of our field of study, we may have to seek inspiration from the various psychologies of interpersonal relations.

If anyone should complain that these suggestions seem to be taking us far, far away from anything resembling the familiar programmatic nostrums of the 'Devout', I can only reply 'The further the better'!

Mainly Constructive

7 African traditional thought and Western science

1 From tradition to science

The first part of this paper seeks to develop an approach to traditional African thought already sketched in several previous contributions to this journal.[1] My approach to this topic is strongly influenced by the feeling that social anthropologists have often failed to understand traditional religious thought for two main reasons. First, many of them have been unfamiliar with the theoretical thinking of their own culture. This has deprived them of a vital key to understanding. For certain aspects of such thinking are the counterparts of those very features of traditional thought which they have tended to find most puzzling. Secondly, even those familiar with theoretical thinking in their own culture have failed to recognize its African equivalents, simply because they have been blinded by a difference of idiom. Like Consul Hutchinson wandering among the Bubis of Fernando Po, they have taken a language very remote from their own to be no language at all.

My approach is also guided by the conviction that an exhaustive exploration of features common to modern Western and traditional African thought should come before the enumeration of differences. By taking things in this order, we shall be less likely to mistake differences of idiom for differences of substance, and more likely to end up identifying those features which really do distinguish one kind of thought from the other.

Not surprisingly, perhaps, this approach has frequently been misunderstood. Several critics have objected that it tends to blur the undeniable distinction between traditional and scientific thinking; that indeed it presents traditional thinking as a species of science.[2] In order to clear up such misunderstandings, I propose to devote the second part of this paper to enumerating what I take to be the salient differences between traditional and scientific thinking, and to suggesting a tentative explanation of these differences. I shall also explore how far this explanation can help us to understand the emergence of science in Western culture.

In consonance with this programme, I shall start by setting out a number of general propositions on the nature and functions of theoretical thinking.

These propositions are derived, in the first instance, from my own training in biology, chemistry, and philosophy of science. But, as I shall show, they are highly relevant to traditional African religious thinking. Indeed, they make sense of just those features of such thinking that anthropologists have often found most incomprehensible.

1. *The quest for explanatory theory is basically the quest for unity underlying apparent diversity; for simplicity underlying apparent complexity; for order underlying apparent disorder; for regularity underlying apparent anomaly.*
Typically, this quest involves the elaboration of a scheme of entities or forces operating 'behind' or 'within' the world of common-sense observations. These entities must be of a limited number of kinds and their behaviour must be governed by a limited number of general principles. Such a theoretical scheme is linked to the world of everyday experience by statements identifying happenings within it with happenings in the everyday world. In the language of philosophy of science, such identification statements are known as correspondence rules. Explanations of observed happenings are generated from statements about the behaviour of entities in the theoretical scheme, plus correspondence-rule statements. In the sciences, well-known explanatory theories of this kind include the kinetic theory of gases, the planetary-atom theory of matter, the wave theory of light, and the cell theory of living organisms.

One of the perennial philosophical puzzles posed by explanations in terms of such theories derives from the correspondence-rule statements. In what sense can we really say that an increase of pressure in a gas 'is' an increase in the velocity of a myriad tiny particles moving in an otherwise empty space? How can we say that a thing is at once itself and something quite different? A great variety of solutions has been proposed to this puzzle. The modern positivists have taken the view that it is the things of common sense that are real, while the 'things' of theory are mere fictions useful in ordering the world of common sense. Locke, Planck and others have taken the line that it is the 'things' of theory that are real, while the things of the everyday world are mere appearances. Perhaps the most up-to-date line is that there are good reasons for conceding the reality both of common-sense things and of theoretical entities. Taking this line implies an admission that the 'is' of correspondence-rule statements is a unity-in-duality uniquely characteristic of the relation between the world of common-sense and the world of theory.

What has all this got to do with the gods and spirits of traditional African religious thinking? Not very much, it may appear at first glance. Indeed, some modern writers deny that traditional religious thinking is in any serious sense theoretical thinking. In support of their denial they contrast the simplicity, regularity and elegance of the theoretical schemas of the sciences with the unruly complexity and caprice of the world of gods and spirits.[3]

But this antithesis does not really accord with modern fieldwork data. It is true that, in a very superficial sense, African cosmologies tend towards proliferation. From the point of view of sheer number, the spirits of some cosmologies are virtually countless. But in this superficial sense we can point to the same tendency in Western cosmology, which for every common-sense unitary object gives us a myriad molecules. If, however, we recognize that the aim of theory is the demonstration of a limited number of *kinds* of entity or process underlying the diversity of experience, then the picture becomes very different. Indeed, one of the lessons of such recent studies of African cosmologies as Fortes's *Oedipus and Job*, Middleton's *Lugbara Religion*, Lienhardt's *Divinity and Experience*, and my own articles on Kalabari,[4] is precisely that the gods of a given culture do form a scheme which interprets the vast diversity of everyday experience in terms of the action of a relatively few *kinds* of forces. Thus in Middleton's book, we see how all the various oppositions and conflicts in Lugbara experience are interpreted as so many manifestations of the single underlying opposition between ancestors and *adro* spirits. Again, in my own work, I have shown how nearly everything that happens in Kalabari life can be interpreted in terms of a scheme which postulates three basic *kinds* of forces: ancestors, heroes and water-spirits.

The same body of modern work gives the lie to the old stereotype of the gods as capricious and irregular in their behaviour. For it shows that each category of beings has its appointed functions in relation to the world of observable happenings. The gods may sometimes appear capricious to the unreflective ordinary man. But for the religious expert charged with the diagnosis of spiritual agencies at work behind observed events, a basic modicum of regularity in their behaviour is the major premise on which his work depends. Like atoms, molecules and waves, then, the gods serve to introduce unity into diversity, simplicity into complexity, order into disorder, regularity into anomaly.

Once we have grasped that this is their intellectual function, many of the puzzles formerly posed by 'mystical thinking' disappear. Take the exasperated, wondering puzzlements of Lévy-Bruhl over his 'primitive mentality'. How could primitives believe that a visible, tangible object was at once its solid self and the manifestation of an immaterial being? How could a man literally see a spirit in a stone? These puzzles, raised so vividly by Lévy-Bruhl, have never been satisfactorily solved by anthropologists. 'Mystical thinking' has remained uncomfortably, indigestibly *sui generis*. And yet these questions of Lévy-Bruhl's have a very familiar ring in the context of

European philosophy. Indeed, if we substitute atoms and molecules for gods and spirits, these turn out to be the very questions cited a few paragraphs back – questions posed by modern scientific theory in the minds of Berkeley, Locke, Quine, and a whole host of European philosophers from Newton's time onwards.

Why is it that anthropologists have been unable to see this? One reason, as I suggested before, is that many of them move only in the common-sense world of Western culture, and are unfamiliar with its various theoretical worlds. But perhaps familiarity with Western theoretical thinking is not by itself enough. For a thoroughly unfamiliar idiom can still blind a man to a familiar form of thought. Because it prevents one from taking anything for granted, an unfamiliar idiom can help to show up all sorts of puzzles and problems inherent in an intellectual process which normally seems puzzle-free. But this very unfamiliarity can equally prevent us from seeing that the puzzles and problems are ones which crop up on our own doorstep. Thus it took a 'mystical' theorist like Bishop Berkeley to see the problems posed by the materialistic theories of Newton and his successors; but he was never able to see that the same problems were raised by his own theoretical framework. Again, it takes materialistically inclined modern social anthropologists to see the problems posed by the 'mystical' theories of traditional Africa; but, for the same reasons, such people can hardly be brought to see these very problems arising within their own theoretical framework.

2.   *Theory places things in a causal context wider than that provided by common sense.*

When we say that theory displays the order and regularity underlying apparent disorder and irregularity, one of the things we mean is that it provides a causal context for apparently 'wild' events. Putting things in a causal context is, of course, one of the jobs of common sense. But although it does this job well at a certain level, it seems to have limitations. Thus the principal tool of common sense is induction or 'putting two and two together', the process of inference so beloved of the positivist philosophers. But a man can only 'put two and two together' if he is looking in the right direction. And common sense furnishes him with a pair of horse-blinkers which severely limits the directions in which he can look. Thus common-sense thought looks for the antecedents of any happening amongst events adjacent in space and time: it abhors action at a distance. Again, common sense looks for the antecedents of a happening amongst events that are in some way commensurable with it. Common sense is at the root of the hard-dying dictum 'like cause, like effect'. Gross incommensurability defeats it.

Now one of the essential functions of theory is to help the mind transcend these limitations. And one of the most obvious achievements of modern scientific theory is its revelation of a whole array of causal connections which are quite staggering to the eye of common sense. Think for instance of the connexion between two lumps of a rather ordinary-looking metal, rushing towards each other with a certain acceleration, and a vast explosion capable of destroying thousands of people. Or think again of the connexion between small, innocuous water-snails and the disease of bilharziasis which can render whole populations lazy and inept.

Once again, we may ask what relevance all this has to traditional African religious thinking. And once again the stock answer may be 'precious little'. For a widely current view of such thinking still asserts that it is more interested in the supernatural causes of things than it is in their natural causes. This is a misinterpretation closely connected with the one we discussed in the previous section. Perhaps the best way to get rid of it is to consider the commonest case of the search for causes in traditional Africa – the diagnosis of disease. Through the length and breadth of the African continent, sick or afflicted people go to consult diviners as to the causes of their troubles. Usually, the answer they receive involves a god or other spiritual agency, and the remedy prescribed involves the propitiation or calling-off of this being. But this is very seldom the whole story. For the diviner who diagnoses the intervention of a spiritual agency is also expected to give some acceptable account of what moved the agency in question to intervene. And this account very commonly involves reference to some event in the world of visible, tangible happenings. Thus if a diviner diagnoses the action of witchcraft influence or lethal medicine spirits, it is usual for him to add something about the human hatreds, jealousies and misdeeds that have brought such agencies into play. Or, if he diagnoses the wrath of an ancestor, it is usual for him to point to the human breach of kinship morality which has called down this wrath.

Although I do not think he has realized its full significance for the study of traditional religious thought, Victor Turner has brought out this point beautifully in his analyses of divination and the diagnosis of disease amongst the Ndembu people of Central Africa. Turner shows how, in diagnosing the causes of some bodily affliction, the Ndembu diviner not only refers to unseen spiritual forces, but also relates the patient's condition to a whole series of disturbances in his social field. Turner refers to divination as 'social analysis', and says that Ndembu believe a patient 'will not get better until all the tensions and aggressions in the group's interrelations have been brought to light and exposed to ritual treatment'.[5] Although Turner himself does not refer to comparable material from other African societies, Max Gluckman, drawing on data from Tiv, Lugbara, Nyakyusa, Yao and several other traditional societies, has recently shown that the kind of analysis he has made of divination among the Ndembu is very widely applicable.[6] The point in all this is that the traditional diviner faced with a disease does not just refer to a spiritual agency, he uses ideas about this agency to link disease to causes in the world of visible, tangible events.

The situation here is not very different from that in which a puzzled American layman, seeing a large mushroom cloud on the horizon, consults a friend who happens to be a physicist. On the one hand, the physicist may refer him to theoretical entities. 'Why this cloud?' 'Well, a massive fusion of hydrogen nuclei has just taken place'. Pushed further, however, the physicist is likely to refer to the assemblage and dropping of a bomb containing certain special substances. Substitute 'disease' for 'mushroom cloud', 'spirit anger' for 'massive fusion of hydrogen nuclei', and 'breach of kinship morality' for 'assemblage and dropping of a bomb', and we are back again with the diviner. In both cases reference to theoretical entities is used to link events in the visible, tangible world (natural effects) to their antecedents in the same world (natural causes).

To say of the traditional African thinker that he is interested in supernatural rather than natural causes makes little more sense, therefore, than to say of the physicist that he is interested in nuclear rather than natural causes. In fact, both are making the same use of theory to transcend the limited vision of natural causes provided by common sense.

Granted this common preoccupation with natural causes, the fact remains that the causal link between disturbed social relations and disease or misfortune, so frequently postulated by traditional religious thought, is one which seems somewhat strange and alien to many Western medical scientists. Following the normal practice of historians of Western ideas, we can approach the problem of trying to understand this strange causal notion from two angles. First of all, we can enquire what influence a particular theoretical idiom has in moulding this and similar traditional notions. Secondly, we can enquire whether the range of experience available to members of traditional societies has influenced causal notions by throwing particular conjunctions of events into special prominence.

Theory, as I have said, places events in a wider causal context than that provided by common sense. But once a particular theoretical idiom has been adopted, it tends to direct people's attention towards certain kinds of causal linkage and away from others. Now most traditional African cultures have adopted a personal idiom as the basis of their attempt to understand the world. And once one has adopted such an idiom, it is a natural step to suppose that personal beings underpin, among other things, the life and strength of social groups. Now it is in the nature of a personal being who has his designs thwarted to visit retribution on those who thwart him. Where the designs involve maintaining the strength and unity of a social group, members of the group who disturb this unity are thwarters, and hence are ripe for punishment. Disease and misfortune are the punishment. Once a personal idiom has been adopted, then, those who use it become heavily predisposed towards seeing a nexus between social disturbance and individual affliction.

Are these traditional notions of cause merely artefacts of the prevailing theoretical idiom, fantasies with no basis in reality? Or are they responses to features of people's experience which in some sense are 'really there'? My own feeling is that, although these notions are ones to which people are predisposed by the prevailing theoretical idiom, they also register certain important features of the objective situation.

Let us remind ourselves at this point that modern medical men, though long blinded to such things by the fantastic success of the germ theory of disease, are once more beginning to toy with the idea that disturbances in a person's social life can in fact contribute to a whole series of sicknesses, ranging from those commonly thought of as mental to many more commonly thought of as bodily. In making this rediscovery, however, the medical men have tended to associate it with the so-called 'pressures of modern living'. They have tended to imagine traditional societies as psychological paradises in which disease-producing mental stresses are at a minimum. And although this view has never been put to adequate test, it is one held by many doctors practising in Africa.

In criticism of this view, I would suggest that the social life of the small, relatively self-contained and undifferentiated communities typical of much of traditional Africa contains its own peculiar and powerful sources of mental stress. Let me recall a few:

a) When tension arises between people engaged in a particular activity, it tends to colour a large sector of their total social life. For in societies of this kind a person performs a whole series of activities with the same set of partners.

b) Being caught up in hostilities or caught out in a serious breach of social norms is particularly crushing, since in societies of this kind it is often extremely hard to move out of the field in which the trouble arose.

c) There are a limited number of roles to be filled, and little scope for personal choice in the filling of them. Hence there is always a relatively large number of social misfits.

Apart from these sources of stress peculiar to such communities, there are others commonly thought to be absent from them, but which they in fact share with modern industrial societies. I am thinking here of fundamental inconsistencies in the values taught to members of traditional communities. Thus aggressive, thrusting ambition may be inculcated on one hand, and a cautious reluctance to rise above one's neighbour on the other. Ruthless individualism may be inculcated on one hand, and acceptance of one's ascribed place in a lineage-system on the other. Such inconsistencies are often as sharp as those so well known in modern industrial societies. As an anthropological fieldworker, one has come close enough to these sources of stress to suspect that the much advertised 'pressures of modern living' may at times be the milder affliction. One may even suspect that some of the young Africans currently rushing from the country to the towns are in fact escaping from a more oppressive to a less oppressive psychological environment.

The point I am trying to make here is that if life in modern industrial society contains sources of mental stress adequate to causing or exacerbating a wide range of sickness, so too does life in traditional village communities. Hence the need to approach traditional religious theories of the social causation of sickness with respect. Such respect and readiness to learn is, I suggest, particularly appropriate with regard to what is commonly known as mental disease. I say this because the grand theories of Western psychiatry have a notoriously insecure empirical base and are probably culture-bound to a high degree.

Then again, there are the traditional social-cause explanations of all those mysterious bodily ailments doctors try in vain to cure in their hospitals, and which finally get cleared up by traditional religious healers. Though we have no statistics on such cases, there is little doubt that they are always cropping up. Judging from a recent symposium on traditional medicine[7], even unromantic, hard-headed social anthropologists are now generally convinced of their reality. Accounts of cases of this kind suggest that they very often fall into the category which Western medical practitioners themselves have increasingly come to label 'psychosomatic' – i.e. marked by definite bodily changes but touched off or exacerbated by mental stress. This category includes gastric and duodenal ulcer, migraine, chronic limb pains, and certain kinds of paralysis, hypertension, diabetes and dermatitis. It includes many agonizing and several potentially lethal complaints. Forward-looking Western medical men now agree that effective treatment of this kind of illness will eventually have to include some sort of diagnosis of and attempt to combat stress-producing disturbances in the individual's social life. As for trying to find out what the main kinds of stress-producing disturbances are in a particular traditional society, the modern doctor can probably do no better than start by taking note of the diagnosis produced by a traditional religious healer working in such a society.

Finally, there are those diseases in which the key factor is definitely an infecting micro-organism. Even here, I suggest, traditional religious theory has something to say which is worth listening to.

Over much of traditional Africa, let me repeat, we are dealing with small scale, relatively self-contained communities. These are the sort of social units that, as my friend Dr Oruwariye puts it, 'have achieved equilibrium with their diseases'. A given population and a given set of diseases have been co-existing over many generations. Natural selection has played a considerable part in developing human resistance to diseases such as malaria, typhoid, smallpox, dysentery etc. In addition, those who survive the very high perinatal mortality have probably acquired an extra resistance by the very fact of having lived through one of these diseases just after birth. In such circumstances, an adult who catches one of these (for Europeans) killer diseases has good chances both of life and of death. In the absence of antimalarials or antibiotics, what happens to him will depend very largely on other factors that add to or subtract from his considerable natural resistance. In these circumstances the traditional healer's efforts to cope with the situation by ferreting out and attempting to remedy stress-producing disturbances in the patient's social field are probably very relevant. Such efforts may seem to have a ludicrously marginal importance to a hospital doctor wielding a nivaquine bottle and treating a non-resistant European malaria patient. But they may be crucial where there is no nivaquine bottle and a considerable natural resistance to malaria.

After reflecting on these things the modern doctor may well take some of these traditional causal notions seriously enough to put them to the test. If the difficulties of testing can be overcome, and if the notions pass the test, he will end up by taking them over into his own body of beliefs. At the same time, however, he will be likely to reject the theoretical framework that enabled the traditional mind to form these notions in the first place.

This is fair enough, for although, as I have shown, the gods and spirits do perform an important theoretical job in pointing to certain interesting forms of causal connection, they are probably not very useful as the basis of a wider view of the world. Nevertheless, there do seem to be a few cases in which the theoretical framework of which they are the basis may have something to contribute to the theoretical framework of modern medicine. To take an example, there are several points at which Western psychoanalytic theory, with its apparatus of personalized mental entities, resembles traditional West African religious theory. More specifically, as I have suggested elsewhere,[8] there are striking resemblances between psychoanalytic ideas about the individual mind as a congeries of warring entities, and West African ideas about the body as a meeting place of multiple souls. In both systems of belief, one personal entity is identified with the stream of consciousness, whilst the others operate as an 'unconscious', sometimes co-operating with consciousness and sometimes at war with it. Now the more flexible psychoanalysts have long suspected that Freud's allocation of particular desires and fears to particular agencies of the mind may well be appropriate to certain cultures only. Thus his allocation of a great load of sexual desires and fears to the unconscious may well have been appropriate to the Viennese subculture he so largely dealt with; but it may not be appropriate to many other cultures. A study of West African soul theories, and of their allocation of particular desires and emotions to particular agencies of the mind, may well help the psychoanalyst to reformulate his theories in terms more appropriate to the local scene.

Earlier, I said that modern Western medical scientists had long been distracted from noting the causal connexion between social disturbance and disease by the success of the germ theory. It would seem, indeed, that a conjunction of the germ theory, of the discovery of potent antibiotics and immunization techniques, and of conditions militating against the build-up of natural resistance to many killer infections, for long made it very difficult for scientists to see the importance of this connexion. Conversely, perhaps, a conjunction of no germ theory, no potent antibiotics, no immunization techniques, with conditions favouring the build-up of considerable natural resistance to killer infections, served to throw this same causal connexion into relief in the mind of the traditional healer. If one were asked to choose between germ theory innocent of psychosomatic insight and traditional psychosomatic theory innocent of ideas about infection, one would almost certainly choose the germ theory. For in terms of quantitative results it is clearly the more vital to human well-being. But it is salutary to remember that not all the profits are on one side.

From what has been said in this section, it should be clear that one commonly accepted way of contrasting traditional religious thought with scientific thought is misleading. I am thinking here of the contrast between traditional religious thought as 'non-empirical' with scientific thought as 'empirical'. In the first place, the contrast is misleading because traditional religious thought is no more nor less interested in the natural causes of things than is the theoretical thought of the sciences. Indeed, the intellectual function of its supernatural beings (as, too, that of atoms, waves, etc.) *is* the extension of people's vision of natural causes. In the second place, the contrast is misleading because traditional religious theory clearly does more than postulate causal connexions that bear no relation to experience. Some of the connexions it postulates are, by the standards of modern medical science, almost certainly real ones. To some extent, then, it successfully grasps empirical reality.

At this point, I must hasten to reassure the type of critic I referred to earlier that I am not claiming traditional thought as a variety of scientific thought. I grant that, in certain crucial respects, the two kinds of thought are related to experience in quite different ways, and I shall consider these differences in part 2 of this paper. Meanwhile, I want to point out that it is not only where scientific method is in use that we find theories which both aim at grasping causal connexions and to some extent succeed in this aim. Scientific method is undoubtedly the surest and most efficient tool for arriving at beliefs that are successful in this respect; but it is not the only way of arriving at such beliefs. Given the basic process of theory-making, and an environmental stability which gives theory plenty of time to adjust to experience, a people's belief system may come, even in the absence of scientific method, to grasp at least some significant causal connexions which lie beyond the range of common sense. It is because traditional African religious beliefs demonstrate the truth of this that it seems apt to extend to them the label 'empirical'.

All this does not mean that we can dispense with the term 'non-empirical'. The latter remains a very useful label for certain other kinds of religious thinking which contrast sharply with that of traditional Africa in their lack of interest in explaining the features of the space-time world. Here I am thinking in particular of the kind of modern Western Christianity which coexists, albeit a little uneasily, with scientific thought. I shall be saying more about this kind of religious thinking in part 2.

3. *Common sense and theory have complementary roles in everyday life.*
In the history of European thought there has often been opposition to a new theory on the ground that it threatens to break up and destroy the old, familiar world of common sense. Such was the eighteenth-century opposition to Newtonian corpuscular theory, which, so many people thought, was all set to 'reduce' the warm, colourful beautiful world to a lifeless, colourless, wilderness of rapidly-moving little balls. Not surprisingly, this eighteenth-century attack was led by people like Goethe and Blake – poets whose job was precisely to celebrate the glories of the world of common sense. Such, again, is the twentieth-century opposition to behaviour theory, which many people see as a threat to 'reduce' human beings to animals or even to machines. Much of the most recent Western philosophy is a monotonous and poorly reasoned attempt to bludgeon us into believing that behaviour theory cannot possibly work. But just as the common-sense world of things and people remained remarkably unscathed by the Newtonian revolution, so there is reason to think it will not be too seriously touched by the behaviour-theory revolution. Indeed, a lesson of the history of European thought is that, while theories come and theories go, the world of common sense remains very little changed.

One reason for this is perhaps that all theories take their departure from the world of things and people, and ultimately return us to it. In this context, to say that a good theory 'reduces' something to something else is misleading. Ideally, a process of deduction from the premisses of a theory should lead us back to statements which portray the common-sense world in its full richness. In so far as this richness is not restored, by so much does theory fail. Another reason for the persistence of the world of common sense is probably that, within the limits discussed in the last section, common-sense thinking is handier and more economical than theoretical thinking. It is only when one needs to transcend the limited causal vision of common sense that one resorts to theory.

Take the example of an industrial chemist and his relationships with common salt. When he uses it in the house, his relationships with it are governed entirely by common sense. Invoking chemical theory to guide him in its domestic use would be like bringing up a pile-driver to hammer in a nail. Such theory may well lend no more colour to the chemist's domestic view of salt than it lends to the chemically uneducated rustic's view of the substance. When he uses it in his chemical factory, however, common sense no longer suffices. The things he wants to do with it force him to place it in a wider causal context than common sense provides; and he can only do this by viewing it in the light of atomic theory. At this point, someone may ask: 'And which does he think is the real salt; the salt of common sense or the salt of theory?' The answer, perhaps, is that both are equally real to him. For whatever the philosophers say, people develop a sense of reality about something to the extent that they use and act on language which implies that this something exists.

This discussion of common sense and theory in Western thought is very relevant to the understanding of traditional African religions. Early accounts of such religions stressed the ever-presence of the spirit world in the minds of men. As Evans-Pritchard has noted, this stress was inevitable where the authors in question were concerned to titillate the imagination of the European reader with the bizarre.[9] Unfortunately, however, such accounts were seized upon by serious sociologists and philosophers like Lévy-Bruhl, who used them to build up a picture of primitive man continuously obsessed by things religious. Later on, fieldwork experience in African societies convinced most reporters that members of such societies attended to the spirit world rather intermittently.[10] And many modern criticisms of Lévy-Bruhl and other early theorists hinge on this observation. For the modern generation of social anthropologists, the big question has now become: 'On what kinds of occasion do people ignore the spirit world, and on what kinds of occasion do they attend to it?'

A variety of answers has been given to this question. One is that people think in terms of the spirit world when they are confronted with the unusual or uncanny. Another is that they think this way in the face of anxiety-provoking situations. Another is that they think this way in the face of *any* emotionally charged situation. Yet another is that they think this way in certain types of crisis which threaten the fabric of society. Of all of these answers, the most one can say is: 'sometimes yes, sometimes no'. All of them, furthermore, leave the 'jump' from common sense to religious thinking fundamentally mysterious. One wants to ask: 'Even if this jump does occur in a certain type of situation, why should the latter require specifically *religious* thinking?' A better answer, I think, is one that relates this jump to the essentially theoretical character of traditional religious thinking. And here is where our discussion of common sense and theory in European thought becomes relevant.

I suggest that in traditional Africa, relations between common sense and theory are essentially the same as they are in Europe. That is, common sense is the handier and more economic tool for coping with a wide range of circumstances in everyday life. Nevertheless, there are certain circumstances that can only be coped with in terms of a wider causal vision than common sense provides. And in these circumstances there is a jump to theoretical thinking.

Let me give an example drawn from my own fieldwork among the Kalabari people of the Niger Delta. Kalabari recognize many different kinds of diseases, and have an array of herbal specifics with which to treat them. Sometimes a sick person will be treated by ordinary members of his family who recognize the disease and know these specifics. Sometimes the treatment will be carried out on the instructions of a native doctor. When sickness and treatment follow these lines the atmosphere is basically commonsensical. Often, there is little or no reference to spiritual agencies.

Sometimes, however, the sickness does not respond to treatment, and it becomes evident that the herbal specific used does not provide the whole answer. The native doctor may re-diagnose and try another specific. But if this produces no result the suspicion will arise that 'there is something else in this sickness'. In other words, the perspective provided by common sense is too limited. It is at this stage that a diviner is likely to be called in (it may be the native doctor who started the treatment). Using ideas about various spiritual agencies, he will relate the sickness to a wider range of circumstances – often to disturbances in the sick man's general social life.

Again, a person may have a sickness which, though mild, occurs together with an obvious crisis in his field of social relations. This conjunction suggests at the outset that it may not be appropriate to look at the illness from the limited perspective of common sense. And in such circumstances, the expert called in is likely to refer at once to certain spiritual agencies in terms of which he links the sickness to a wider context of events.

What we are describing here is generally referred to as a jump from common sense to mystical thinking. But, as we have seen, it is also, more significantly, a jump from common sense to theory. And here, as in Europe, the jump occurs at the point where the limited causal vision of common sense curtails its usefulness in dealing with the situation on hand.

4. *Level of theory varies with context.*
A person seeking to place some event in a wider causal context often has a choice of theories. Like the initial choice between common sense and theory, this choice too will depend on just how wide a context he wishes to bring into consideration. Where he is content to place the event in a relatively modest context, he will be content to use what is generally called a low-level theory – i.e. one that covers a relatively limited area of experience. Where he is more ambitious about context, he will make use of a higher-level theory – i.e. one that covers a larger area of experience. As the area covered by the lower-level theory is part of the area covered by the higher-level scheme, so too the entities postulated by the lower-level theory are seen as special manifestations of those postulated at the higher level. Hence they pose all the old problems of things which are at once themselves and at the same time manifestations of other quite different things.

For an example of how this matter of levels works out in modern Western thought, let us go back to our manufacturing chemist and his salt. Suppose the chemist to be in the employ of a very under-developed country which has extensive deposits of salt and can supply a limited range of other simple chemicals, but which has no electricity. The government asks him to estimate what range of chemical products he can 'get out' of the salt, given the limited resources they can make available to him. Here the limited range of means implies a limited causal context and the appropriateness of a correspondingly low level of theory. In working out what he can do with his salt deposits under these straitened circumstances, the chemist may well be content to use the low-level, 'ball-and-bond' version of atomic theory, whose basic entities are homogeneous spheres linked by girder-like bonds. This level of theory will enable him to say that, with the aid of a few simple auxiliaries like chalk and ammonia, he can derive from his salt such important substances as washing soda and caustic soda.

Now suppose that after some time the chemist is told to assume that an electric power supply will be at his disposal. This additional element in the situation promises a wider range of possibilities. It also implies that salt is to be placed in a wider causal context. Hence a theory of wider coverage and higher level must be brought into play. Our chemist will now almost certainly make his calculations in terms of a more embracing version of the atomic theory – one which covers electrical as well as strictly chemical phenomena. In this theory the homogeneous atoms of the lower-level schema are replaced by planetary configurations of charged fundamental particles. The atoms of the lower-level theory now become mere manifestations of systems of particles postulated by the higher-level theory. For philosophical puzzle-makers, the old teaser of things that are at once themselves and manifestations of something else is with us again. But the puzzle becomes less acute when we see it as an inevitable by-product of the way theories are used in the process of explanation.

Once again, we find parallels to all this in many traditional African religious systems. It is typical of such systems that they include, on the one hand, ideas about a multiplicity of spirits, and on the other hand, ideas about a single supreme being. Though the spirits are thought of as independent beings, they are also considered as so many manifestations or dependants of the supreme being. This conjunction of the many and the one has given rise to much discussion among students of comparative religion, and has evoked many ingenious theories. Most of these have boggled at the idea that polytheism and monotheism could coexist stably in a single system of thought. They have therefore tried to resolve the problem by supposing that the belief-systems in question are in transition from one type to the other. It is only recently, with the Nilotic studies of Evans-Pritchard and Lienhardt,[11] that the discussion has got anywhere near the point – which is that the many spirits and the one God play complementary roles in people's thinking. As Evans-Pritchard says: 'A theistic religion need be neither monotheistic nor polytheistic. It may be both. It is the question of the level, or situation, of thought, rather than of exclusive types of thought'.[12]

On the basis of material from the Nilotic peoples, and on that of material from such West African societies as Kalabari, Ibo and Tallensi,[13] one can make a tentative suggestion about the respective roles of the many and the one in traditional African thought generally. In such thought, I suggest, the spirits provide the means of setting an event within a relatively limited causal context. They are the basis of a theoretical scheme which typically covers the thinker's own community and immediate environment. The supreme being, on the other hand, provides the means of setting an event within the widest possible context. For it is the basis of a theory of the origin and life course of the world seen as a whole.

In many (though by no means all) traditional African belief-systems, ideas about the spirits and actions based on such ideas are far more richly developed than ideas about the supreme being and actions based on them. In these cases, the idea of God seems more the pointer to a potential theory than the core of a seriously operative one. This perhaps is because social life in the communities involved is so parochial that their members seldom have to place events in the wider context that the idea of the supreme being purports to deal with. Nevertheless, the different levels of thinking are there in all these systems. And from what we have said, it seems clear that they are related to one another in much the same way as are the different levels of theoretical thinking in the sciences. At this point the relation between the many spirits and the one God loses much of its aura of mystery. Indeed, there turns out to be nothing peculiarly religious or 'mystical' about it. For it is essentially the same as the relation between homogeneous atoms and planetary systems of fundamental particles in the thinking of our chemist. Like the latter, it is a by-product of certain very general features of the way theories are used in explanation.

5.   *All theory breaks up the unitary objects of common sense into aspects, then places the resulting elements in a wider causal context. That is, it first abstracts and analyses, then reintegrates.*

Numerous commentators on scientific method have familiarized us with the way in which the theoretical schemas of the sciences break up the world of common-sense things in order to achieve a causal understanding which surpasses that of common sense. But it is only from the more recent studies of African cosmologies, where religious beliefs are shown in the context of the various everyday contingencies they are invoked to explain, that we have begun to see how traditional religious thought also operates by a similar process of abstraction, analysis and reintegration. A good example is provided by Fortes's recent work on West African theories of the individual and his relation to the society. Old-fashioned West African ethnographers like Talbot long ago showed the wide distribution of beliefs in what they called 'multiple souls'. They found that many West African belief-systems invested the individual with a multiplicity of spiritual agencies, and they baptized these agencies with fanciful names such as 'spirit double', 'bush soul', 'shadow soul' and 'over soul'. The general impression they gave was one of an unruly fantasy at work. In his recent book, however, Fortes takes the 'multiple soul' beliefs of a single West African people (the Tallensi) and places them in the context of everyday thought and behaviour. His exposition dispels much of the aura of fantasy.

Fortes describes three categories of spiritual agency especially concerned with the Tale individual. First comes the *segr*, which presides over the individual as a biological entity – over his sickness and health, his life and death. Then comes the *nuor yin*, a personification of the wishes expressed by the individual before his arrival on earth. The *nuor yin* appears specifically concerned with whether or not the individual has the personality traits necessary if he is to become an adequate member of Tale society. As Fortes puts it, evil *nuor yin* 'serves to identify the fact of irremediable failure in the development of the individual to full social capacity'. Good *nuor yin*, on the other hand, 'identifies the fact of successful individual development along the road to full incorporation in society'.[14] Finally, in this trio of spiritual agencies, we have what Fortes calles the '*yin* ancestors'. These are two or three out of the individual's total heritage of ancestors, who have been delegated to preside over his personal fortunes. *Yin* ancestors only attach themselves to an individual who has a good *nuor yin*. They are concerned with the fortunes of the person who has already proved himself to have the basic equipment for fitting into Tale society. Here we have a theoretical scheme which, in order to produce a deeper understanding of the varying fortunes of individuals in their society, breaks them down into three aspects by a simple but typical operation of abstraction and analysis.

Perhaps the most significant comment on Fortes's work in this field was pronounced, albeit involuntarily, by a reviewer of *Oedipus and Job*.[15] 'If any criticism of the presentation is to be made it is that Professor Fortes sometimes seems to achieve an almost mystical identification with the Tallensi world-view and leaves the unassimilated reader in some doubt about where to draw the line between Tallensi notions and Cambridge concepts!' Now the anthropologist has to find *some* concepts in his own language roughly appropriate to translating the 'notions' of the people he studies. And in the case in question, perhaps only the lofty analytic 'Cambridge' concepts did come anywhere near the congruence with Tallensi notions. This parallel between traditional religious 'notions' and Western sociological 'abstractions' is by no means an isolated phenomenon. Think for instance of individual guardian spirits and group spirits – two very general categories of traditional African religious thought. Then think of those hardy Parsonian abstractions – psychological imperatives and sociological imperatives. It takes no great brilliance to see the resemblance.[16]

One can of course argue that in comparing traditional African thought with modern Western sociological thought, one is comparing it with a branch of Western thought that has attained only a low degree of abstraction. One can go on to argue that traditional African thought does not approach the degree of abstraction shown, say, by modern nuclear physics. Such comparisons of degrees of abstraction are, I think, trickier than they seem at first glance. In any case, they cannot affect the validity of the point already made, which is that abstraction is as essential to the operation of traditional African religious theory as it is to that of modern Western theory, whether sociological or physical.

6. *In evolving a theoretical scheme, the human mind seems constrained to draw inspiration from analogy between the puzzling observations to be explained and certain already familiar phenomena.*

In the genesis of a typical theory, the drawing of an analogy between the unfamiliar and the familiar is followed by the making of a model in which something akin to the familiar is postulated as the reality underlying the unfamiliar. Both modern Western and traditional African thought-products amply demonstrate the truth of this. Whether we look amongst atoms, electrons and waves, or amongst gods, spirits and entelechies, we find that theoretical notions nearly always have their roots in relatively homely everyday experiences, in analogies with the familiar.

What do we mean here by 'familiar phenomena'? Above all, I suggest, we mean phenomena strongly associated in the mind of the observer with order and regularity. That theory should depend on analogy with things familiar in this sense follows from the very nature of explanation. Since the overriding aim of explanation is to disclose order and regularity underlying apparent chaos, the search for explanatory analogies must tend towards those areas of experience most closely associated with such qualities. Here, I think, we have a basis for indicating why explanations in modern Western culture tend to be couched in an impersonal idiom, while explanations in traditional African society tend to be couched in a personal idiom. The reader may see the point more readily if I introduce a little personal reminiscence. The idea that people can be much more difficult to cope with than things is one that has never been far from my own mind. I can recall long periods of my own boyhood when I felt at home and at ease, not with friends, relatives and parents round the fire, but shut up alone for hours with bunsen burners and racks of reagents in a chemistry laboratory. Potassium hydroxide and nitric acid were my friends; sodium phosphate and calcium chloride my brothers and sisters. In later life I have been fortunate enough to break through many times into a feeling of at-homeness with people. But such break-throughs have always been things to wonder at; never things to be taken for granted. My joy in people is all the more intense for being a joy in something precarious. And in the background there is always the world of things beckoning seductively towards the path of escape from people. English colleagues may shrug their shoulders and say I am a freak in this. But if they are honest with themselves, they will admit I am saying things which strike echoes in all their hearts. Nor do I have to depend on their honesty in this; for the image of the man happier with things than with people is common enough in modern Western literature to show that what I am talking about here is the sickness of the times.

Not long ago I was having a discussion with a class of Nigerian students, all of whom, I suppose, still had strong roots in traditional community life. We were discussing some of the characteristic ways in which life in Western industrial cities differed from life in traditional village communities. When I came to touch on some of the things I have just been saying, I felt that I had really 'gone away from them'. What I was saying about a life in which things might seem a welcome haven from people was just so totally foreign to their experience that they could not begin to take it in. They just stared. Rarely have I felt more of an alien than in that discussion.

Now the point I wish to make is this. In complex, rapidly-changing industrial societies the human scene is in flux. Order, regularity, predictability, simplicity, all these seem lamentably absent. It is in the world of inanimate things that such qualities are most readily seen. This is why many people can find themselves less at home with their fellow men than with things. And this too, I suggest, is why the mind in quest of explanatory analogies turns most readily to the inanimate. In the traditional societies of Africa, we find the situation reversed. The human scene is the locus *par excellence* of order, predictability, regularity. In the world of the inanimate, these qualities are far less evident. Here, being less at home with people than with things is unimaginable. And here, the mind in quest of explanatory analogies turns naturally to people and their relations.

7. *Where theory is founded on analogy between certain puzzling observations and other more familiar phenomena, it is generally only a limited aspect of such phenomena that is incorporated into the resulting model.*

When a thinker draws an analogy between certain puzzling observations and other more familiar phenomena, the analogy seldom involves more than a limited aspect of such phenomena. And it is only this limited aspect which is taken over and used to build up the theoretical schema. Other aspects are ignored; for, from the point of view of explanatory function, they are irrelevant.

Philosophers of science have often used the molecular (kinetic) theory of gases as an illustration of this feature of model-building. The molecular theory, of course, is based on an analogy with the behaviour of fast-moving, spherical balls in various kinds of space. And the philosophers have pointed out that although many important properties of such balls have been incorporated into the definition of a molecule, other important properties such as colour and temperature have been omitted. They have been omitted because they have no explanatory function in relation to the observations that originally evoked the theory. Here, of course, we have another sense in which physical theory is based upon abstraction and abstract ideas. For concepts such as 'molecule', 'atom', 'electron', 'wave' are the result of a process in which the relevant features of certain prototype phenomena have been abstracted from the irrelevant features.

Many writers have considered this sort of abstraction to be one of the distinctive features of scientific thinking. But this, like so many other such distinctions, is a false one; for just the same process is at work in traditional African thought. Thus when traditional thought draws upon people and their social relations as the raw material of its theoretical models, it makes use of many dimensions of human life and neglects others. The definition of a god may omit any reference to his physical appearance, his diet, his mode of lodging, his children, his relations with his wives, and so on. Asking questions about such attributes is as inappropriate as asking about the colour of a molecule or the temperature of an electron. It is this omission of many dimensions of human life from the definition of the gods which gives them that rarefied, attenuated aura which we call 'spiritual'. But there is nothing peculiarly religious, mystical or traditional about this 'spirituality'. It is the result of the same process of abstraction as the one we see at work in Western theoretical models: the process whereby features of the prototype phenomena which have explanatory relevance are incorporated into a theoretical schema, while features which lack such relevance are omitted.

8. *A theoretical model, once built, is developed in ways which sometimes obscure the analogy on which it was founded.*
In its raw, initial state, a model may come up quite quickly against data for which it cannot provide any explanatory coverage. Rather than scrap it out of hand, however, its users will tend to give it successive modifications in order to enlarge its coverage. Sometimes, such modifications will involve the drawing of further analogies with phenomena rather different from those which provided the initial inspiration for the model. Sometimes, they will merely involve 'tinkering' with the model until it comes to fit the new observations. By comparison with the phenomena which provided its original inspiration, such a developed model not unnaturally seems to have a bizarre, hybrid air about it.

Examples of the development of theoretical models abound in the history of science. One of the best documented of these is provided by the modern atomic theory of matter. The foundations of this theory were laid by Rutherford, who based his original model upon an analogy between the passage of ray-beams through metal foil and the passage of comets through our planetary system. Rutherford's planetary model of the basic constituents of matter proved extremely useful in explanation. When it came up against recalcitrant data, therefore, the consensus of scientists was in favour of developing it rather than scrapping it. First of the consequent modifications was the introduction of the possibility that the 'planets' might make sudden changes of orbit, and in so doing emit or absorb energy. Then came the substitution, at the centre of the planetary system, of a heterogeneous cluster of bodies for a single 'sun'. Later still came the idea that, at a particular moment, a given 'planet' had a somewhat ambiguous position. Finally, along with this last idea, came a modification inspired by the drawing of a fresh analogy. This was the introduction of the idea that, in some contexts, the 'planets' were to be considered as bundles of waves. Each of these modifications was a response to the demand for increased explanatory coverage. Each, however, removed the theoretical model one step further away from the familiar phenomena which had furnished its original inspiration.

In studying traditional African thought, alas, we scarcely ever have the historical depth available to the student of European thought. So we can make few direct observations on the development of its theoretical models. Nevertheless, these models often show just the same kinds of bizarre hybrid features as the models of the scientists. Since they resemble the latter in so many other ways, it seems reasonable to suppose that these features are the result of a similar process of development in response to demands for further explanatory coverage. The validity of such a supposition is strengthened when we consider detailed instances: for these show how the bizarre features of particular models are indeed closely related to the nature of the observations that demand explanation.

Let me draw one example from my own fieldwork on Kalabari religious thought which I have outlined in earlier publications. Basic Kalabari religious beliefs involve three main categories of spirits: Ancestors, Heroes and Water-People. On the one hand, all three categories of spirits show many familiar features: emotions of pleasure and anger, friendship, enmities, marriages. Such features betray the fact that, up to a point, the spirits are fashioned in the image of ordinary Kalabari people. Beyond this point, however, they are bizarre in many ways. The Ancestors, perhaps, remain closest to the image of ordinary people. But the Heroes are decidedly odd. They are defined as having left no descendants, as having disappeared rather than died, and as having come in the first instance from outside the community. The Water-spirits are still odder. They are said to be 'like men, and also like pythons'. To make sense of these oddities, let us start by sketching the relations of the various kinds of spirits to the world of everyday experience.

First, the Ancestors. These are postulated as the forces underpinning the life and strength of the lineages, bringing misfortune to those who betray lineage values and fortune to those who promote them. Second, the Heroes. These are the forces underpinning the life and strength of the community and its various institutions. They are also the forces underpinning human skill and maintaining its efficacy in the struggle against nature. Third, the Water-spirits. On the one hand, these are the 'owners' of the creeks and swamps, the guardians of the fish harvest, the forces of nature. On the other hand, they are the patrons of human individualism – in both its creative and its destructive forms. In short, they are the forces underpinning all that lies beyond the confines of the established social order.

We can look on Ancestors, Heroes and Water-spirits as members of a triangle of forces. In this triangle, the relation of each member to the other two contains elements of separation and opposition as well as of co-operation. Thus by supporting lineages in rivalry against one another, the Ancestors can work against the Heroes in sapping the strength of the community; but in other contexts, by strengthening their several lineages, they can work with the Heroes in contributing to village strength. Again, when they bring up storms, rough water, and sharks, the Water-spirits work against the Heroes by hampering the exercise of the village's productive skills; but when they produce calm water and an abundance of fish, they work just as powerfully with the Heroes. Yet again, by fostering anti-social activity, the Water-spirits can work against both Heroes and Ancestors; or, by supporting creativity and invention, they can enrich village life and so work with them.

In this triangle, then, we have a theoretical scheme in terms of which Kalabari can grasp and comprehend most of the many vicissitudes of their daily lives. Now it is at this point that the bizarre, paradoxical attributes of Heroes and Water-spirits begin to make sense: for a little inspection shows that such attributes serve to define each category of spirits in a way appropriate to its place in the total scheme. This is true, for example, of such attributes of the Heroes as having left no human descendants, having disappeared instead of undergoing death and burial, and having come from outside the community. All these serve effectively to define the Heroes as forces quite separate from the Ancestors with their kinship involvements. Lack of descendants does this in an obvious way. Disappearance rather than death and burial performs the same function, especially when, as in Kalabari, lack of burial is almost synonymous with lack of kin. And arrival from outside the community again makes it clear that they cannot be placed in any lineage or kinship context. These attributes, in short, are integral to the definition of the Heroes as forces contrasted with and potentially opposed to the Ancestors. Again, the Water-spirits are said to be 'like men, and also like pythons'; and here too the paradoxical characterization is essential to defining their place in the triangle. The python is regarded as the most powerful of all animals in the creeks, and is often said to be their father. But its power is seen as something very different from that of human beings – something 'fearful' and 'astonishing'. The combination of human and python elements in the characterization of the Water-People fits the latter perfectly for their own place in the triangle – as forces of the extra-social contrasted with and potentially opposed to both Heroes and Ancestors.

Another illuminating example of the theoretical significance of oddity is provided by Middleton's account of traditional Lugbara religious concepts.[17] According to Middleton, Lugbara belief features two main categories of spiritual agency – the Ancestors and the *adro* spirits. Like the

Kalabari Ancestors, those of the Lugbara remain close to the image of ordinary people. The *adro* however, are very odd indeed. They are cannibalistic and incestuous, and almost everything else that the Lugbara ordinarily consider repulsive. They are commonly said to walk upside down – a graphic expression of their general perversity. Once again, these oddities fall into place when we look at the relation of the two categories of spirits to the world of experience. The Ancestors, on the one hand, account for the settled world of human habitation and for the established social order organized on the basis of small lineages. The *adro*, on the other hand, are concerned with the uncultivated bush, and with all human activities which run counter to the established order of things. Like the Kalabari Water-spirits, they are forces of the extra-social, whether in its natural or its human form. The contrast and opposition between Ancestors and *adro* thus provides Lugbara with a theoretical schema in terms of which they can comprehend a whole series of oppositions and conflicts manifest in the world of their everyday experiences. Like the oddities of the Kalabari gods, those of the *adro* begin to make sense at this point. For it is the bizarre, perverse features of these spirits that serve to define their position in the theory – as forces contrasted with and opposed to the Ancestors.

In both of these cases the demands of explanation result in a model whose structure is hybrid between that of the human social phenomena which provided its original inspiration, and that of the field of experience to which it is applied. In both cases, oddity is essential to explanatory function. Even in the absence of more direct historical evidence, these examples suggest that the theoretical models of traditional African thought are the products of developmental processes comparable to those affecting the models of the sciences.

Some philosophers have objected to the statement that explanatory models are founded on analogy between the puzzling and the familiar, saying that the features of typical models in the sciences rather suggest that in them the relatively familiar is explained in terms of the relatively unfamiliar. They point to the abstract character of theoretical entities, contrasting this with the familiar concreteness of the world of everyday things. They point to the bizarre features of such entities, so far removed from anything found in the everyday world. These very objections, however, merely confirm the validity of the view they aim to criticize. For what makes theoretical entities seem abstract to us is precisely that they have taken over some key features from particular areas of everyday experience, while rejecting other features as irrelevant to their purposes. Again, what makes theoretical entities seem bizarre to us is precisely these features drawn from areas of familiar experience. The presence of some such features leads us to expect others. But the processes of abstraction and development produce results that defy these expectations: hence our sense of the odd.

In treating traditional African religious systems as theoretical models akin to those of the sciences, I have really done little more than take them at their face value. Although this approach may seem naive and platitudinous compared to the sophisticated 'things-are-never-what-they-seem' attitude more characteristic of the social anthropologist, it has certainly produced some surprising results. Above all, it has cast doubt on most of the well-worn dichotomies used to conceptualize the difference between scientific and traditional religious thought. Intellectual versus emotional; rational versus mystical; reality-orientated versus fantasy-orientated; causally oriented versus supernaturally oriented; empirical versus non-empirical; abstract versus concrete; analytical versus non-analytical: all of these are shown to be more or less inappropriate. If the reader is disturbed by this casting away of established distinctions, he will, I hope, accept it when he sees how far it can pave the way towards making sense of so much that previously appeared senseless.

One thing that may well continue to bother the reader is my playing down of the difference between non-personal and personal theory. For while I have provided what seems to me an adequate explanation of this difference, I have treated it as a surface difference concealing an underlying similarity of intellectual process. I must confess that I have used brevity of treatment here as a device to play down the gulf between the two kinds of theory. But I think this is amply justifiable in reaction to the more usual state of affairs, in which the difference is allowed to dominate all other features of the situation. Even familiarity with theoretical thinking in their own culture cannot help anthropologists who are dominated by this difference. For once so blinded, they can only see traditional religious thought as wholly other. With the bridge from their own thought-patterns to those of traditional Africa blocked, it is little wonder they can make no further headway.[18]

The aim of my exposition has been to reopen this bridge. The point I have sought to make is that the difference between non-personal and personalized theories is more than anything else a difference in the idiom of the explanatory quest. Grasping this point is an essential preliminary to realizing how far the various established dichotomies used in this field are simply obstacles to understanding. Once it is grasped, a whole series of seemingly bizarre and senseless features of traditional thinking becomes immediately comprehensible. Until it is grasped, they remain essentially mysterious. Making the business of personal versus impersonal entities the crux of the difference between tradition and science not only blocks the understanding of tradition. It also draws a red herring across the path to an understanding of science. This becomes obvious from a look at history. So far as we know, an extensive depersonalization of theory has happened spontaneously only twice in the history of human thought. Once in Europe and once in China. In Europe this depersonalization was accompanied by a growth of science, in China it was not.[19] Again, where depersonalization *has* been accompanied by the growth of science, the two have often parted company very readily. Thus in Western lay culture we have a largely depersonalized view of the world which is at the same time totally unscientific.[20] And in many of the developing countries, for which science appears as a panacea, it seems likely that the depersonalized world of the West may get through without the scientific spirit.[21] Yet again, in the recent history of Western psychology, we find both personalized (psycho-analytic) and non-personalized (behaviouristic) theories. And for each category there are those who handle the theories scientifically and those who do not.

All this is not to deny that science has progressed greatly through working in a non-personal theoretical idiom. Indeed, as one who has hankerings after behaviourism, I am inclined to believe that it is this idiom, and this idiom only, which will eventually lead to the triumph of science in the sphere of human affairs. What I am saying, however, is that this is more a reflection of the nature of reality than a clue to the essence of scientific method. For the progressive acquisition of knowledge, man needs both the right kind of theories *and* the right attitude to them. But it is only the latter which we call science. Indeed, as we shall see, any attempt to define science in terms of a particular kind of theory runs contrary to its very essence. Now, at last, I hope it will be evident why, in comparing African traditional thought with Western scientific thought, I have chosen to start with a review of continuities rather than with a statement of crucial differences. For although this order of procedure carries the risk of one's being understood to mean that traditional thought is a kind of science, it also carries the advantage of having the path clear of red herrings when one comes to tackle the question of differences.

2 The 'closed' and 'open' predicaments

In part 1 of this paper, I pushed as far as it would go the thesis that important continuities link the religious thinking of traditional Africa and the theoretical thinking of the modern West. I showed how this view helps us to make sense of many otherwise puzzling features of traditional religious thinking. I also showed how it helps us to avoid certain rather troublesome red herrings which lie across the path towards understanding the crucial differences between the traditional and the scientific outlook.

In part 2, I shall concentrate on these differences. I shall start by isolating one which strikes me as the key to all the others, and will then go on to suggest how the latter flow from it.

What I take to be the key difference is a very simple one. It is that in traditional cultures there is no developed awareness of alternatives to the established body of theoretical tenets; whereas in scientifically oriented cultures, such awareness is highly developed. It is this difference we refer to when we say that traditional cultures are 'closed' and scientifically oriented cultures 'open'.[22]

One important consequence of the lack of alternatives is very clearly spelled out by Evans-Pritchard in his pioneering work on Azande witchcraft beliefs. Thus he says:

> I have attempted to show how rhythm, mode of utterance, content of prophecies, and so forth, assist in creating faith in witch-doctors, but these are only some of the ways in which faith is supported, and do not entirely explain belief. Weight of tradition alone can do that ... There is no incentive to agnosticism. All their beliefs hang together, and were a Zande to give up faith in witch-doctorhood, he would have to surrender equally his faith in witchcraft and oracles ... In this web of belief every strand depends upon every other strand, *and a Zande cannot get out of its meshes because it is the only world he knows. The web is not an external structure in which he is enclosed. It is the texture of his thought and he cannot think that his thought is wrong* [italics mine].[23]

And again:

> And yet Azande do not see that their oracles tell them nothing! Their blindness is not due to stupidity, for they display great ingenuity in explaining away the failures and inequalities of the poison oracle and experimental keenness in testing it. It is due rather to the fact that their intellectual ingenuity and experimental keenness are conditioned by patterns of ritual behaviour and mystical belief. Within the limits set by these patterns, they show great intelligence, but it cannot operate beyond these limits. Or, to put it in another way; *they reason excellently in the idiom of their beliefs, but they cannot reason outside, or against their beliefs because they have no other idiom in which to express their thoughts* [italics mine].[24]

Yet again, writing more generally of 'closed' societies in a recent book, he says:

> Everyone has the same sort of religious beliefs and practices, and their generality, or collectivity, gives them an objectivity which places them over and above the psychological experience of any individual, or indeed of all individuals ... *Apart from positive and negative sanctions, the mere fact that religion is general means, again in a closed society, that it is obligatory, for even if there is no coercion, a man has no option but to accept what everybody gives assent to, because he has no choice, any more than of what language he speaks. Even were he to be a skeptic, he could express his doubts only in terms of the beliefs held by all around him* [italics mine].[25]

In other words, absence of any awareness of alternatives makes for an absolute acceptance of the established theoretical tenets, and removes any possibility of questioning them. In these circumstances the established tenets invest the believer with a compelling force. It is this force which we refer to when we talk of such tenets as sacred.

A second important consequence of lack of awareness of alternatives is vividly illustrated by the reaction of an Ijo man to a missionary who told him to throw away his old gods. He said: 'Does your God really want us to climb to the top of a tall palm tree, then take off our hands and let ourselves fall?' Where the established tenets have an absolute and exclusive validity for those who hold them, any challenge to them is a threat of chaos, of the cosmic abyss, and therefore evokes intense anxiety.

With developing awareness of alternatives, the established theoretical tenets come to seem less absolute in their validity, and lose something of their sacredness. At the same time, a challenge to these tenets is no longer a horrific threat of chaos. For just as the tenets themselves have lost some of their absolute validity, a challenge to them is no longer a threat of absolute calamity. It can now be seen as nothing more threatening than an intimation that new tenets might profitably be tried. Where these conditions begin to prevail, the stage is set for change from a traditional to a scientific outlook.

Here, then, we have two basic predicaments: the 'closed' – characterized by lack of awareness of alternatives, sacredness of beliefs, and anxiety about threats to them; and the 'open' – characterized by awareness of alternatives, diminished sacredness of beliefs, and diminished anxiety about threats to them.

Now, as I have said, I believe all the major differences between traditional and scientific outlooks can be understood in terms of these two predicaments. In substantiatiang this, I should like to divide the differences into two groups: A, those directly connected with the presence or absence of a vision of alternatives; and B, those directly connected with the presence or absence of anxiety about threats to established beliefs.

A.   *Differences connected with the presence or absence of a vision of alternatives*

Magical versus non-magical attitude to words. A central characteristic of nearly all the traditional African world views we know of is an assumption about the power of words, uttered under appropriate circumstances, to bring into being the events or states they stand for.

The most striking examples of this assumption are to be found in creation mythologies where the supreme being is said to have formed the world out of chaos by uttering the names of all things in it. Such mythologies occur most notably in ancient Egypt and among the peoples of the Western Sudan.

In the acts of creation which the supreme being has left to man, the mere uttering of words is seldom thought to have the same unconditional efficacy. Thus, so far as we know, there are no traditional cultures which credit man with the ability to create new things just by uttering new words. In most such cultures, nevertheless, the words of men are granted a certain measure of control over the situations they refer to. Often there is a technical process which has to be carried out in order to achieve a certain result; but for success, this has to be completed by a properly-framed spell or incantation foreshadowing the result. Such a situation is vividly described by the Guinean novelist Camara Laye. His father was a goldsmith, and in describing the old man at work, he says:

Although my father spoke no word aloud, I know very well that he was thinking them from within. I read it from his lips, which were moving while he bent over the vessel. He kept mixing gold and coal with a wooden stick which would blaze up every now and then and constantly had to be replaced. What sort of words were those that my father was silently forming? I don't know – at least I don't know exactly. Nothing was ever confided in me about that. But what could these words be but incantations?

Beside the old man worked a sorcerer:

Throughout the whole process his speech became more and more rapid, his rhythms more urgent, and as the ornament took shape, his panegyrics and flatteries increased in vehemence and raised my father's skill to the heavens. In a peculiar, I would almost say immediate and effective, way the sorcerer did in truth take part in the work. He too was drunk with the joy of creation, and loudly proclaimed his joy: enthusiastically he snatched the strings, became inflamed, as if he himself were the craftsman, as if he himself were my father, as if the ornament were coming from his own hands.[26]

In traditional African cultures, to know the name of a being or thing is to have some degree of control over it. In the invocation of spirits, it is essential to call their names correctly; and the control which such correct calling gives is one reason why the true or 'deep' names of the gods are often withheld from strangers, and their utterance forbidden to all but a few whose business it is to use them in ritual. Similar ideas lie behind the very widespread traditional practice of using euphemisms to refer to such things as dangerous diseases and wild animals: for it is thought that use of the real names might secure their presence. Yet again, it is widely believed that harm can be done to a man by various operations performed on his name – for instance, by writing his name on a piece of paper and burning it.

This last example carries me on to an observation that at first sight contradicts what we have said so far: the observation that in a great deal of African magic, it is non-verbal symbols rather than words that are thought to have a direct influence over the situations they represent. Bodily movements, bits of plants, organs of animals, stones, earth, water, spittle, domestic utensils, statuettes – a whole host of actions, objects and artefacts play a vital part in the performances of traditional magic. But as we look deeper the contradiction seems more apparent than real. For several studies of African magic suggest that its instruments become symbols through being verbally designated as such. In his study of Zande magic, for instance, Evans-Pritchard describes how magical medicines made from plants and other natural objects are given direction by the use of verbal spells. Thus:

The tall grass *bingba*, which grows profusely on cultivated ground and has feather-like branching stems, is known to all as medicine for the oil-bearing plant *kpagu*. A man throws the grass like a dart and transfixes the broad leaves of the plant. Before throwing it, he says something of this sort: "You are melons, you be very fruitful like *bingba*; may the melons flourish like *bingba*. My melons, you be very fruitful. May you not refuse".[27]

My own fieldwork in Kalabari constantly unearthed similar examples of non-verbal symbols being given direction and significance by verbal spells. My favourite example is taken from the preparation of a medicine designed to bring clients to an unsuccessful spirit medium. One of the important ingredients of this medicine was the beak of the voracious, mud-dredging muscovy duck – an item which the doctor put into the medicine with the succinct comment: 'Muscovy Duck; you who are always eating.'

Amongst the most important non-verbal magical symbols in Kalabari culture are the statuettes designed to 'fix' the various spirits at times of ritual. Of these, several Kalabari said: 'They are, as it were, the names of the spirits.' Explaining their use, one old man said: 'It is in their names that the spirits stay and come.' It is by being named that the sculpture comes to represent the spirit and to exert influence over it.[28]

In a recent essay on Malagasy magic,[29] Henri Lavondes discusses similar examples of the direction of magical objects by verbal spells. He shows how the various ingredients of a compound medicine are severally related by these spells to the various aspects of the end desired. And, following Mauss, he goes on to suggest that the function of the spell is to convert material objects into *mots réalisés* or concrete words. In being given verbal labels, the objects themselves become a form of language.

This interpretation, which reduces all forms of African magic to a verbal base, fits the facts rather well. One may still ask, however, why magicians spend so much time choosing objects and actions as surrogate words, when spoken words themselves are believed to have a magical potential. The answer, I would suggest, is that speech is an ephemeral form of words, and one which does not lend itself to a great variety of manipulations. Verbal designation of material objects converts them into a more permanent and more readily manipulable form of words. As Lavondes puts it:

Le message verbal est susceptible de davantage de précision que le message figuré. Mais le second a sur le premier l'avantage de sa permanence et da sa matérialité, qui font qu'il rest toujours disponible et qu'il est possible de s'en pénétrer et de la répandre par d'autres voies que celle du language articulé (par absorption, par onction, par aspersion).[30]

Considered in this light, magical objects are the pre-literate equivalents of the written incantations which are so commonly found as charms and talismans in literate but pre-scientific cultural milieux.

Through a very wide range of traditional African belief and activity, then, it is possible to see an implicit assumption as to the magical power of words.

Now if we take into account what I have called the basic predicament of the traditional thinker, we can begin to see why this assumption should be so deeply entrenched in his daily life and thought. Briefly, no man can make contact with reality save through a screen of words. Hence no man can escape the tendency to see a unique and intimate link between words and things. For the traditional thinker this tendency has an overwhelming power. Since he can imagine no alternatives to his established system of concepts and words, the latter appear bound to reality in an absolute fashion. There is no way at all in which they can be seen as varying independently of the segments of reality they stand for. Hence they appear so integrally involved with their referents that any manipulation of the one self-evidently affects the other.

The scientist's attitude to words is, of course, quite opposite. He dismisses contemptuously any suggestion that words could have an immediate, magical power over the things they stand for. Indeed, he finds magical notions amongst the most absurd and alien trappings of traditional thought. Though he grants an enormous power to words, it is the indirect one of bringing control over things through the functions of explanation and prediction. Words are tools in the service of these functions – tools which like all others are to be cared for as long as they are useful, but which are to be ruthlessly scrapped as soon as they outlive their usefulness.

Why does the scientist reject the magician's view of words? One easy answer is that he has come to know better: magical behaviour has been found not to produce the results it claims to. Perhaps. But what scientist has ever bothered to put magic to the test? The answer is, none; because there are deeper grounds for rejection – grounds which make the idea of testing beside the point.

To see what these grounds are, let us return to the scientist's basic predicament – to his awareness of alternative idea-systems whose ways of classifying and interpreting the world are very different from his own. Now this changed awareness gives him two intellectual possibilities. Both are eminently thinkable; but one is intolerable, the other hopeful.

The first possibility is simply a continuance of the magical world-view. If ideas and words are inextricably bound up with reality, and if indeed they shape it and control it, then a multiplicity of idea-systems means a multiplicity of realities, and a change of ideas means a change of things. But whereas there is nothing particularly absurd or inconsistent about this view, it is clearly intolerable in the extreme. For it means that the world is in the last analysis dependent on human whim, that the search for order is a folly, and that human beings can expect to find no sort of anchor in reality.

The second possibility takes hold as an escape from this horrific prospect. It is based on the faith that while ideas and words change, there must be some anchor, some constant reality. This faith leads to the modern view of words and reality as independent variables. With its advent, words come 'unstuck from' reality and are no longer seen as acting magically upon it. Intellectually, this second possibility is neither more nor less respectable than the first. But it has the great advantage of being tolerable whilst the first is horrific.

That the outlook behind magic still remains an intellectual possibility in the scientifically oriented cultures of the modern West can be seen from its survival as a nagging undercurrent in the last 300 years of Western philosophy. This undercurrent generally goes under the labels of 'Idealism' and 'Solipsism'; and under these labels it is not immediately recognizable. But a deeper scrutiny reveals that the old outlook is there all right – albeit in a strange guise. True, Idealism does not say that words create, sustain and have power over that which they represent. Rather, it says that material things are 'in the mind'. That is, the mind creates, sustains and has power over matter. But the second view is little more than a post-Cartesian transposition of the first. Let me elaborate. Both in traditional African cosmologies and in European cosmologies before Descartes, the modern distinction between 'mind' and 'matter' does not appear. Although everything in the universe is underpinned by spiritual forces, what moderns would call 'mental activities' and 'material things' are both part of a single reality, neither material nor immaterial. Thinking, conceiving, saying, etc. are described in terms of organs like heart and brain and actions like the uttering of words. Now when Descartes wrote his philosophical works, he crystallized a half-way phase in the transition from a personal to an impersonal cosmological idiom. While 'higher' human activities still remained under the aegis of a personalized theory, physical and biological events were brought under the aegis of impersonal theory. Hence thinking, conceiving, saying, etc. became manifestations of 'mind' whilst all other happenings became manifestations of 'matter'. Hence, whereas before Descartes we have 'words over things', after him we have 'mind over matter' – just a new disguise for the old view.

What I have said about this view being intellectually respectable but emotionally intolerable is borne out by the attitude to it of modern Western philosophers. Since they are duty bound to explore all the alternative possibilities of thought that lie within the grasp of their imaginations, these philosophers mention, nay even expound, the doctrines of Idealism and Solipsism. Invariably, too, they follow up their expositions with attempts at refutation. But such attempts are just as invariably, a farce. Their character is summed up in G. E. Moore's desperate gesture, when challenged to prove the existence of a world outside his mind, of banging his hand with his fist and exclaiming: 'It is there!' A gesture of faith rather than of reason, if ever there was one!

With the change from the 'closed' to the 'open' predicament, then, the outlook behind magic becomes intolerable; and to escape from it people espouse the view that words vary independently of reality. Smug rationalists who congratulate themselves on their freedom from magical thinking would do well to reflect on the nature of this freedom!

Ideas-bound-to-occasions versus ideas-bound-to-ideas. Many commentators on the idea-systems of traditional African cultures have stressed that, for members of these cultures, their thought does not appear as something distinct from and opposable to the realities that call it into action. Rather, particular passages of thought are bound to the particular occasions that evoke them.

Let us take an example. Someone becomes sick. The sickness proves intractable and the relatives call a diviner. The latter says the sickness is due to an ancestor who has been angered by the patient's bad behaviour towards his kinsman. The diviner prescribes placatory offerings to the spirit and reconciliation with the kinsmen, and the patient is eventually cured. Now while this emergency is on, both the diviner and the patient's relatives may justify what they are doing by reference to some general statements about the kinds of circumstance which arouse ancestors to cause sickness. And it is when he is lucky enough to be around on such occasions that the anthropologist picks up most of his hard-earned information about traditional theories of the world and its working. But theoretical statements of this kind are very much matters of occasion, not likely to be heard out of context or as part of a general discussion of 'what we believe'. Indeed, the anthropologist has learned by bitter experience that, in traditional Africa, the generalized, 'what do chaps believe?' approach gets one exactly nowhere.[31]

If ideas in traditional culture are seen as bound to occasions rather than to other ideas, the reason is one that we have already given in our discussion of magic. Since the member of such a culture can imagine no alternatives to his established system of ideas, the latter appear inexorably bound to the portions of reality they stand for. They cannot be seen as in any way opposable to reality.

In a scientifically orientated culture such as that of the Western anthropologist, things are very different. The very word 'idea' has the connotation of something opposed to reality. Nor is it entirely coincidental that in such a culture the historian of ideas is considered to be the most unrealistic kind of historian. Not only are ideas dissociated in people's minds from the reality that occasions them: they are bound to other ideas, to form wholes and systems perceived as such. Belief-systems take shape not only as abstractions in the minds of anthropologists, but also as totalities in the minds of believers.

Here again, this change can be readily understood in terms of a change from the 'closed' to the 'open' predicament. A vision of alternative possibilities forces men to the faith that ideas somehow vary whilst reality remains constant. Ideas thus become detached from reality – nay, even in a sense opposed to it. Furthermore, such a vision, by giving the thinker an opportunity to 'get outside' his own system, offers him a possibility of his coming to see it *as a system*.

Unreflective versus reflective thinking. At this stage of the analysis there is no need for me to insist further on the essential rationality of traditional thought. In part 1, indeed, I have already made it out as far too rational for the taste of most social anthropologists. And yet, there is a sense in which this thought includes among its accomplishments neither logic nor philosophy.

Let me explain this, at first sight, rather shocking statement. It is true that most African traditional world-views are logically elaborated to a high degree. It is also true that, because of their eminently rational character, they are appropriately called 'philosophies'. But here I am using 'logic' and 'philosophy' in a more exact sense. By logic, I mean thinking directed to answering the question: 'What are the general rules by which we can distinguish good arguments from bad ones?' And by philosophy, I mean thinking directed to answering the question: 'On what grounds can we ever claim to know anything about the world?' Now logic and philosophy, in these restricted senses, are poorly developed in traditional Africa. Despite its elaborate and often penetrating cosmological, sociological and psychological speculations, traditional thought has tended to get on with the work of explanation, without pausing for reflection upon the nature or rules of this work. Thinking once more of the 'closed' predicament, we can readily see why these second-order intellectual activities should be virtually absent from traditional cultures. Briefly, the traditional thinker, because he is unable to imagine possible alternatives to his established theories and classifications, can never start to formulate generalized norms of reasoning and knowing. For only where there are alternatives can there be choice, and only where there is choice can there be norms governing it. As they are characteristically absent in traditional cultures, so logic and philosophy are characteristically present in all scientifically orientated cultures. Just as the 'closed' predicament makes it impossible for them to appear, so the 'open' predicament makes it inevitable that they must appear. For where the thinker can see the possibility of alternatives to his established idea-system, the question of choice at once arises, and the development of norms governing such choice cannot be far behind.[32]

Mixed versus segregated motives. This contrast is very closely related to the preceding one. As I stressed in part 1 of this essay, the goals of explanation and prediction are as powerfully present in traditional African cultures as they are in cultures where science has become institutionalized. In the absence of explicit norms of thought, however, we find them vigorously pursued but not explicitly reflected upon and defined. In these circumstances, there is little thought about their consistency or inconsistency with other goals and motives. Hence, wherever we find a theoretical system with explanatory and predictive functions, we find other motives entering in and contributing to its development.

Despite their cognitive preoccupations, most African religious systems are powerfully influenced by what are commonly called 'emotional needs' – i.e. needs for certain kinds of personal relationship. In Africa, as elsewhere, all social systems stimulate in their members a considerable diversity of such needs; but, having stimulated them, they often prove unwilling or unable to allow them full opportunities for satisfaction. In such situations the spirits function not only as theoretical entities but as surrogate people providing opportunities for the formation of ties forbidden in the purely human social field. The latter function they discharge in two ways. First, by providing non-human partners with whom people can take up relationships forbidden with other human beings. Second, through the mechanism of possession, by allowing people to 'become' spirits and so to play roles *vis-à-vis* their fellow men which they are debarred from playing as ordinary human beings.

Examples of the first kind occur very commonly in association with the need for dependence created in children by the circumstances of their family upbringing. In some African societies male children are required to make an abrupt switch from dependence to independence as soon as they reach puberty. A prominent feature of the rites aimed at achieving this switch is the dramatic induction of the candidates into a relation of dependence with a powerful spiritual agency. The latter can be seen as a surrogate for the parents with whom the candidates are no longer allowed to continue their dependent relationships, and hence as a means of freeing the candidates for the exercise of adult independence and responsibility. This appears to be the basic significance of secret society initiations among the peoples of the Congo and the Western Guinea Coast. In other traditional societies, the early relation of dependence on parents is allowed to continue so long as the parents are still alive; and an abrupt switch to independence and responsibility has to be made on their death. Here, it is the dead parent, translated into ancestorhood, who provides for the continuance of a relationship which has had to be abruptly and traumatically discontinued in the purely human social field. This sequence, with its culmination in a highly devout worship of patrilineal ancestors, has been vividly described by Fortes in some of his writings on the Tallensi of Northern Ghana.[33]

Examples of the second kind occur more commonly in association with the need for dominance. Most societies stimulate this need more widely than they grant it satisfaction. In traditional African societies, women are the most common sufferers from this; and it is no accident that in the numerous spirit-possession cults that flourish up and down the continent women are generally rather more prominent than men. For in the male-authority roles which they tend to assume in possession, they gain access to a whole area of role-playing normally forbidden them.

Aesthetic motives, too, play an important part in moulding and sustaining traditional religious systems. This is especially true of West Africa, where narrative, poetry, song, dance, music, sculpture and even architecture use the spirits and their characters as a framework upon which to develop their various forms. These arts in turn influence the direction in which ideas about the spirits develop. In my own fieldwork on Kalabari religion, I have found a gradual shading of the cognitive into the aesthetic which can at times be most confusing. In oral tradition, for example, serious myths intended to throw light on the part played by the gods in founding social institutions shade into tales which, although their characters are also gods, are told for sheer entertainment. And although Kalabari do make a distinction between serious myth and light tale, there are many pieces which they themselves hesitate to place on one side or the other. Belief shades through half-belief into suspended belief. In ritual, again, dramatic representations of the gods carried out in order to dispose them favourably and secure the benefits which, as cosmic forces, they control, are usually found highly enjoyable in themselves. And they shade off into representations carried out almost solely for their aesthetic appeal. In the Kalabari Water-spirit masquerades, for instance, religion seems to have become the servant of art.[34]

There is little doubt that because the theoretical entities of traditional thought happen to be people, they give particular scope for the working of emotional and aesthetic motives. Here, perhaps, we do have something about the personal idiom in theory that does militate indirectly against the taking up of a scientific attitude; for where there are powerful emotional and aesthetic loadings on a particular theoretical scheme, these must add to the difficulties of abandoning this scheme when cognitive goals press towards doing so. Once again, I should like to stress that the mere fact of switching from a personal to an impersonal idiom does not make anyone a scientist, and that one can be unscientific or scientific in either idiom. In this respect, nevertheless, the personal idiom does seem to present certain difficulties for the scientific attitude which the impersonal idiom does not.

Where the possibility of choice has stimulated the development of logic, philosophy and norms of thought generally, the situation undergoes radical change. One theory is judged better than another with explicit reference to its efficacy in explanation and prediction. And as these ends become more clearly defined, it gets increasingly evident that no other ends are compatible with them. People come to see that if ideas are to be used as efficient tools of explanation and prediction, they must not be allowed to become tools of anything else. (This, of course, is the essence of the ideal of 'objectivity'). Hence there grows up a great watchfulness against seduction by the emotional or aesthetic appeal of a theory – a watchfulness which in twentieth-century Europe sometimes takes extreme forms such as the suspicion of any research publication not written out in a positively indigestible style. Also there appears an insistence on the importance of 'pure' as opposed to 'applied' science. This does not mean that scientists are against practical application of their findings. What it does mean is that they feel there should always be some disjunction between themselves and the people who apply their discoveries. The reasons for this are basically the same as those which lead the scientist to be on his guard against emotional or aesthetic appeals. For one thing, if a scientist is too closely identified with a given set of practical problems, he may become so committed to solving these as to take up any theory that offers solution without giving it adequate testing. Again, those lines of enquiry most closely related to the practical problems of the day are not necessarily those which lead to the most rapid advances in explanation and prediction. Finally, in so far as practical interests involve inter-business and inter-national competition, over-identification with them can lead to a fundamental denial of the scientific ideal by encouraging the observance of rules of secrecy. Since it is a primary canon of the scientific ideal that every new theory be subjected to the widest possible testing and criticism, free circulation of new findings is basic to the code of the scientific community. (See below.) Hence, in so far as commercial and international competition leads to the curtailment of such circulation, it is inimical to science. This is why brilliant and dedicated scientists tend to be among the most double-edged weapons in wars either hot or cold.

The traditional theoretical scheme, as we have noted, brings forth and nourishes a rich encrustation of cultural growths whose underlying motives have little to do with explanation and prediction. Notable among these are elaborate systems of personal relationships with beings beyond the purely human social order, and all manner of artistic embellishments.

As the insistence on segregation of theoretical activity from the influence of all motives but those defined as essential to it gains strength, these various growths are forcibly sloughed off and have to embark on an independent existence. To survive without getting involved in a losing battle with the now-prestigious 'science', they have to eschew loudly all explanatory pretensions, and to devote great energy to defining their 'true' ends. In doing this, they have often been accused of making a virtue out of sad necessity – of putting a brazen face on what is simply a headlong retreat before science. But their activities in this direction can, I think, also be seen in a more positive way. That is, they too can be seen as a direct outcome of the 'open' predicament, and thence of the general tendency to reflect on the nature of thought, to define its aims, and to formulate its norms. Now the conclusion such reflective activity arrives at for theory-making also holds for spiritual communion and for art: that is, there are several distinct modes of thought; and a particular mode, if it is to fulfil itself completely, must be protected from the influence of all motives except those defined as essential to it. Hence when we hear a Western theologian proclaim loudly the 'modern discovery' that the essence of religion has nothing to do with explanation and prediction of worldly events, but is simply communion with God for its own sake, we are only partly right when we sneer at him for trying to disguise retreat as advance. For in fact he can claim to be undertaking much the same kind of purifying and refining operation as the scientist. The force of this contention emerges when we come to consider the case of the artist. For when the latter proclaims that his activity is no longer the handmaid of religion, of science, or even of representation, we do in fact grant that this drastic circumscription of aims represents a form of progress akin to that of the scientist purging his subject in the pursuit of objectivity. The rationalist who says that the modern theologian is retreating while the modern artist is advancing is thus merely expressing an agnostic prejudice. Both, in fact, are in an important sense caught up in the same currents of thought as those that move the scientist.

It will now be clear that the scientist's quest for 'objectivity' is, among other things, a purifying movement. As has happened in many such movements, however, the purifying zeal tends to wander beyond its self-appointed bounds, and even to run to excess within these bounds. Such tendencies are well exemplified in the impact of the quest for objectivity on metaphor.

In traditional Africa, speech abounds with metaphor to a degree no longer familiar in the scientifically oriented cultures of the modern West. The function of such metaphor is partly, as anthropologists never tire of saying,[35] to allude obliquely to things which cannot be said directly. Much more importantly, perhaps, its function is to underline, emphasize and give greater impact to things which *can* be said literally. 'Proverbs are the palm-oil with which words are eaten', say the Ibo.[36] In this capacity, it is clearly a vital adjunct to rational thought. Often, however, metaphor subtly misleads. The analogy between the things which constitute its literal reference and the things which constitute its oblique reference usually involves only limited aspects of both. But there is always a temptation to extend the analogy unduly, and it can then run its users right off the rails. In sociology, for instance, this has happened with the use of organismic metaphors for thinking about societies and social relations. Organisms and societies do perhaps resemble each other in certain limited ways; but sociologists who have become addicted to organismic metaphor often go beyond these limited resemblances and end up by attributing to societies all sorts of properties possessed only by organisms.

These occasional dangers have led the purists to regard metaphor and analogy as one great snare and delusion. 'No palm-oil with our words', they have decreed with grim satisfaction. The resulting cult of plain, literal speaking, alas, has spread beyond the bounds of strictly scientific activity right through everyday life, taking much of the poetic quality out of ordinary, humdrum social relations. Not only this. The distrust of metaphor and analogy has in some places gone so far as to threaten intellectual processes which are crucial to the advance of science itself. Thus the positivist philosophers of science have often denigrated the activity of theoretical model-building. At best, some of them have contended, such model-building is a dubious help to serious scientific thought; and at worst, its reliance on the process of analogy may be extremely misleading. According to this purist school, induction and deduction are the only processes of thought permissible to the scientist. His job is not to elaborate models of a supposed reality lying 'behind' the data of experience. It is simply to observe; to make inductive generalizations summarizing the regularities found in observation; to deduce from these generalizations the probable course of further observation; and finally to test this deduction against experience. A then B, A then B, A then B; hence all A's are followed by B's; hence if there is an A in the future, it will be followed by a B; check. The trouble about this purist paradigm, of course, is that it condemns the scientist to an eternity of triteness and circularity. It can never account for any of the great leaps in explanatory power which we associate with the advance of science. Only in relation to some model of underlying reality, for instance, can we come to see that A and X, B and Y, so different in the eye of the observer, are actually outward manifestations of the same kinds of events. Only in relation to such a model are we suddenly moved to look for a conjunction between X and Y which we would never have noticed otherwise. And only thus can we come to see AB, XY as two instances of a single underlying process or regularity. Finally, so it seems, the only way yet discovered in which scientists can turn out the new models of underlying reality necessary to set such explanatory advance in motion is through the drawing of bold analogies.

To sum up on this point: one of the essential features of science is that it is a purifying movement. But like other purifying movements, alas, it provides fertile soil for obsessional personalities. If we can compare the traditional thinker to an easy-going housewife who feels she can get along quite nicely despite a considerable accumulation of dirt and dust on the furniture, we can compare the positivist who is so often a fellow traveller of science to an obsessional housewife who scrubs off the dirt, paintwork, and finally the handles that make the furniture of use!

B   *Differences connected with the presence or absence of anxiety about threats to the established body of theory*

Protective versus destructive attitude towards established theory. Both in traditional Africa and in the science-oriented West, theoretical thought is vitally concerned with the prediction of events. But there are marked differences in reaction to predictive failure.

In the theoretical thought of the traditional cultures, there is a notable reluctance to register repeated failures of prediction and to act by attacking the beliefs involved. Instead, other current beliefs are utilized in such a way as to 'excuse' each failure as it occurs, and hence to protect the major theoretical assumptions on which prediction is based. This use of *ad hoc* excuses is a phenomenon which social anthropologists have christened 'secondary elaboration'.[37]

The process of secondary elaboration is most readily seen in association with the work of diviners and oracle-operators, who are concerned with discovering the identity of the spiritual forces responsible for particular happenings in the visible, tangible world, and the reasons for their activation. Typically, a sick man goes to a diviner, and is told that a certain spiritual agency is 'worrying' him. The diviner points to certain of his past actions as having excited the spirit's anger, and indicates certain remedial actions which will appease this anger and restore health. Should the client take the recommended remedial action and yet see no improvement, he will be likely to conclude that the diviner was either fraudulent or just incompetent, and to seek out another expert. The new diviner will generally point to another spiritual agency and another set of arousing circumstances as responsible for the man's condition, and will recommend fresh remedial action. In addition, he will probably provide some explanation of why the previous diviner failed to get at the truth. He may corroborate the client's suspicions of fraud, or he may say that the spirit involved maliciously 'hid itself behind' another in such a way that only the most skilled of diviners would have been able to detect it. If after this the client should still see no improvement in his condition, he will move on to yet another diviner – and so on, perhaps, until his troubles culminate in death.

What is notable in all this is that the client never takes his repeated failures as evidence against the existence of the various spiritual beings named as responsible for his plight, or as evidence against the possibility of making contact with such beings as diviners claim to do. Nor do members of the wider community in which he lives ever try to keep track of the proportion of successes to failures in the remedial actions based on their beliefs, with the aim of questioning these beliefs. At most, they grumble about the dishonesty and wiles of many diviners, whilst maintaining their faith in the existence of some honest, competent practitioners.

In these traditional cultures, questioning of the beliefs on which divining is based and weighing up of successes against failures are just not among the paths that thought can take. They are blocked paths because the thinkers involved are victims of the 'closed' predicament. For them, established beliefs have an absolute validity, and any threat to such beliefs is a horrific threat to chaos. Who is going to jump from the cosmic palm-tree when there is no hope of another perch to swing to?

When the scientific outlook has become fairly entrenched, attitudes to established beliefs are very different. Much has been made of the scientist's essential scepticism towards established beliefs; and one must, I think, agree that this above all is what distinguishes him from the traditional thinker. But one must be careful here. The picture of the scientist in continuous readiness to scrap or denote established theory contains a dangerous exaggeration as well as an important truth. As an outstanding modern historian of the sciences has recently observed,[38] the typical scientist spends most of his time optimistically seeing how far he can push a new theory to cover an ever-widening horizon of experience. When he has difficulty in making the theory 'fit', he is more likely to develop it in the ways described in part 1 of this essay than to scrap it out of hand. And if it does palpably fail the occasional test, he may even put the failure down to dirty apparatus or mistaken meter-reading – rather like the oracle operator! And yet, the spirit behind the scientist's actions *is* very different. His pushing of a theory and his reluctance to scrap it are not due to any chilling intuition that if his theory fails him, chaos is at hand. Rather, they are due to the very knowledge that the theory is not something timeless and absolute. Precisely because he knows that the present theory came in at a certain epoch to replace a predecessor, and that its explanatory coverage is far better than that of the predecessor, he is reluctant to throw it away before giving it the benefit of every doubt. But this same knowledge makes for an acceptance of the theory which is far more qualified and far more watchful than that of the traditional thinker. The scientist is, as it were, always keeping account, balancing the successes of a theory against its failures. And when the failures start to come thick and fast, defence of the theory switches inexorably to attack on it.

If the record of a theory that has fallen under a cloud is poor in all circumstances, it is ruthlessly scrapped. The collective memory of the European scientific community is littered with the wreckage of the various unsatisfactory theories discarded over the last 500 years – the earth-centred theory of the universe, the circular theory of planetary motion, the phlogiston theory of chemical combination, the ether theory of wave propagation, and perhaps a hundred others. Often, however, it is found that a theoretical model once assumed to have universal validity in fact has a good predictive performance over a limited range of circumstances, but a poor performance outside this range. In such a case, the beliefs in question are still ruthlessly demoted; but instead of being thrown out altogether they are given a lesser status as limiting cases of more embracing generalities – still useful as lower-level models or as guides to experience within restricted areas. This sort of demotion has been the fate of theoretical schemes like Newton's Laws of Motion (still used as a guide in many mundane affairs, including much of the business of modern rocketry) and the 'ball-and-bond' theory of chemical combination.

This underlying readiness to scrap or demote established theories on the ground of poor predictive performance is perhaps the most important single feature of the scientific attitude. It is, I suggest, a direct outcome of the 'open' predicament. For only when the thinker is able to see his established idea-system as one among many alternatives can he see his established ideas as things of less than absolute value. And only when he sees them thus can he see the scrapping of them as anything other than a horrific, irretrievable jump into chaos.

Divination versus diagnosis. Earlier in this essay I drew certain parallels between the work of the traditional African diviner and the work of the Western diagnostician. In particular, I showed how both of them make much the same use of theoretical ideas: i.e. as means of linking observed effects to causes that lie beyond the powers of common sense to grasp. I now propose to discuss certain crucial differences between these two kinds of agent.

As I noted in the last section, in traditional cultures anxieties about threats to the established theories effectively block many of the paths thought might otherwise take. One path so blocked is the working out of any body of theory which assigns too distinctive an effect to any particular pattern of antecedents. Why this path should be blocked is not hard to see. Suppose that there is a theory X, which makes the following causal connections:

A ———————————————— E
B ———————————————— F
C ———————————————— G
D ———————————————— H

Now if situation E is disagreeable, and is unambiguously ascribable to cause A, action will be taken to get rid of E by manipulating A. If it fails, then the most obvious verdict is that A→E is invalid. A similar argument applies, of course, to B→F, C→G, D→H.

Suppose, on the other hand, that theory X makes the following connections:

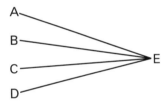

Now things are very different. If E is ascribed to A, action will still be taken to get rid of E by manipulating A. But if it fails, we are no longer compelled to admit that A→E is invalid. We can now say that perhaps B was present as a complicating factor, and that failure to take account of it was responsible for our disappointment. Or we can say that A was not present at all, but only D. So the theory remains protected.

Coming back to concrete terms, we find that traditional African theories of, say, disease approximate to the second of these patterns rather than to the first, and that this is their ultimate protection. In most traditional cultures, diseases are thought to be caused by the anger of several categories of spirits. Each of these categories is aroused by a different kind of situation. Thus in Kalabari thought Heroes, Ancestors, Water-spirits and Medicine-spirits are the main unseen bringers of disease. Heroes tend to be activated by offences against 'town laws', Ancestors by offences against kinsmen,

Water-spirits by failure to heed certain tangible signs that they wish to form personal attachments with human partners, Medicine-spirits by the machinations of enemies with whom one 'has case'. Hence there is a fairly clear correlation between the kind of activating situation and the kind of spirit brought into play. But although there are the beginnings of a second correlation, between the kind of spirit brought into play and the kind of misfortune inflicted, this has not gone very far. By and large, if a diviner attributes a disease to a certain spirit aroused by certain antecedent circumstances and if the remedy based on this attribution fails, another diviner can always say that the first attribution was a mistake, and that it was really another spirit, aroused by another set of circumstances, who caused the trouble. Studies like those of Evans-Pritchard on the Zande,[39] Nadel on the Nupe[40] and Forde on the Yako[41] suggest that this particular defensive pattern, based on converging causal sequences, is very widespread.

But a theory which postulates converging causal sequences, though self-protective to a high degree, faces serious problems in its application to everyday life. For the man who visits a diviner with misfortune E does not want to be told that it could be due to any one of four different kinds of spirits, activated by circumstances A, B, C or D. He wants a definite verdict and a definite remedial prescription.

Now given the nature of the theoretical model the diviner operates with, any amount of minute inspection and definition of E will not allow him to give a definite verdict as between A, B, C or D. Sometimes, he can and does find out from the client whether A, B, C or D have occurred in his life-history. But the client may well have forgotten the crucial activating circumstance. Indeed, as it is often a guilt-provoking circumstance, he is likely to have forgotten it. Or, the client may remember that happenings answering to both A, B, and C have occurred at various times in his life; and the diviner is still left with the problem of which of these happenings and which category of spirit is actually responsible for the present occurrence of E.

We have, then, an apparently insoluble conflict. For the diviner to give a causal verdict which transcends the limited vision of common sense, he must operate with a theory. But for the theory to survive, it must be of the converging sequence type which makes the giving of a definite causal verdict very difficult.

As I see it, the essence of divination is that it is a mechanism for resolving this conflict. Faced with a theory postulating several possible causes for a given event, and no means of inferring the actual cause from observable evidence, divination goes, as it were, 'over the head' of such evidence. It elicits a direct sign from the realm of those unobservable entities that govern the causal linkages it deals with – a sign that enables it to say which of the several sequences indicated by the theory is the one actually involved.

Just how it elicits this sign seems immaterial. Indeed, there is a fantastic variety of divination procedures on the African continent. The diviner may enter into a privileged contact with the realm of unobservable entities postulated by his theory, 'seeing' and 'hearing' them in a manner beyond the powers of his client. The diviner may force his client to choose from a collection of twigs, each representing one of the various spirits and causal linkages potentially involved in the situation. He may set spiders to chew leaves, and give his verdict on the basis of a series of correlations between patterns of chewing and kinds of causal sequence. He may cause a dead body to be carried by several men, suggest to the body the various possible causes of its death, and obtain from its consequent movements a reply as to which is the cause actually involved. He may administer poison to a series of fowls, put one of the several potential sequences as a question to each fowl, and infer from the life or death of the animal whether this particular sequence is the one actually involved. One might cite up to a hundred more ingenious procedures.

All of these divination techniques share two basic features. First, as I have said, they are means of selecting one actual causal sequence from several potential sequences. Secondly, they all carry a subtle aura of fallibility which makes it possible to 'explain everything away' when remedial prescriptions based on them turn out not to work. Thus many divination procedures require an esoteric knowledge or faculty which the client does not share with the operator. Hence the client has no direct check on the operator; and in retrospect there is always the possibility of the latter's dishonesty or sheer incompetence. Again, nearly all of these procedures are thought to be very delicate and easily thrown out of kilter. Among other things, they may be affected by pollution, or by the machinations of those who have a grudge against the client.

So, whereas the positive features of the divining process make it possible to arrive at a definite causal verdict despite a converging-sequence theory, the aura of fallibility provides for the self-protecting action of such a theory by making it possible, in the event of a failure, to switch from one potential sequence to another in such a way as to leave the theory as a whole unimpugned. In the last section, we noted that the context of divination provided some of the clearest illustrations of the defence-mechanism known as 'secondary elaboration'. Now I think, we can go further: that is, we can say that divination owes its very existence to the exigencies of this mechanism.

Where the 'open' predicament prevails, anxieties about threats to the established theories decline, and previously blocked thought-paths become clear. We now witness the development of theories that assign distinctive effects to different causes; and in the face of this development the type of theory that assumes converging sequences tends to disappear. Nowadays, of course, it is more fashionable to talk of covariation than to talk of cause and effect. But the continuous-covariation formula of the type $\underline{ds = f.dt}$, so prominent in modern scientific theory, is in fact an instance of the tendency I am referring to. For, spelled out, the implication of such a formula is that, to an infinite number of values of a cause-variable, there correspond an infinite number of values of an effect-variable.

Where this type of theory comes into the ascendant the diviner gives place to the diagnostician. The latter, whether he is concerned with bodily upsets or with aeroplane disasters, goes to work in a way which differs in important respects from that of his traditional counterpart. Dealing as he does with theories that postulate non-converging causal sequences, he has a task altogether more prosaic than that of the diviner. For, given non-convergence, a complete and accurate observation of effect, plus knowledge of the relevant theory, makes it possible for him to give an unambiguous causal verdict. Once these conditions have been fulfilled, there is no need for the additional operations of the diviner. No need for special mechanisms to elicit signs from the realm of unobservable entities. No need for a way of going 'over the head of' observable evidence in order to find out which of several potential causes is the actual one.

Modern Western diagnosis, it is true, has not lost all of the aura of fallibility that surrounds traditional divining. Incomplete and inaccurate observation of effect may sometimes provide a plausible defence for failures of diagnosis based on outmoded theory. But such a defence is a poor thing compared with that provided by converging-sequence theory and a divining mechanism characterized as inherently delicate and subject to breakdown. In the modern West, of course, the diagnosticians and remedialists are usually not the same as the people who are actively concerned with the developing and testing of theory. (Hence the division between 'pure' and 'applied' scientists.) Nevertheless, it is often through reports of failure from these men that the developers and testers get their stimulus for the replacement of an old theory with a new one. Thus in medicine, reports from general practitioners about widespread breakdown of well-tried diagnostic and healing procedures have often provided the stimulus for medical researchers to make drastic revisions in the theory of disease.

Far from being an integral part of any mechanism for defending theory, then, the diagnostician often contributes his share to the circumstances that lead to the abandonment of old ideas and the adoption of new ones.

Absence versus presence of experimental method. Anyone who has read part 1 of this paper should be in little doubt as to how closely adjusted traditional African theoretical systems often are to the prevailing facts of personality, social organization, and ecology. Indeed, although many of the causal connections they posit turn out to be red herrings when subjected to scientific scrutiny, others turn out to be very real and vital. Thus an important part of traditional religious theory posits and attempts to explain the connection between disturbed social relationships and disease – a connection whose reality and importance Western medical scientists are only just beginning to see. Nevertheless, the adjustments of the systems to changing experience are essentially slow, piecemeal and reluctant. Nothing must happen to arouse public suspicion that basic theoretical models are being challenged. If changes are to take place, they must take place like movements in the game of Grandmother's Footsteps: i.e. when grandmother is not looking, and in such a way that whenever she turns round, she sees somebody standing stock-still and in a position not too obviously different from the one he was in when she last looked. The consequence of all this, if the reader will excuse me for mixing my metaphors, is that traditional idea-systems are usually catching up on experience from a position 'one jump behind'.

Scientific thought, by contrast, is characteristically 'one jump ahead' of experience. It is able to be so because of that distinctive feature of the scientist's calling: the experimental method. This method is nothing more nor less than the positive expression of the 'open' attitude to established beliefs and categories which we referred to in section 5. For the essence of experiment is that the holder of a pet theory does not just wait for events to come along and show whether or not it has a good predictive performance. He bombards it with artificially produced events in such a way that its merits or defects will show up as immediately and as clearly as possible.

Often, the artificially produced events involved in an experiment are ones that would take a long time to observe if left to occur of their own accord. Thus a medical research worker who has a theory about the destructive effect of a certain chemical upon pneumonia germs does not wait for the next severe English winter to bring its heavy toil of pneumonia victims. He gets a large batch of monkeys (or, in America sometimes, condemned human volunteers), deliberately infects them with pneumonia, gives some the chemical and others an inert substance, and observes the results. In many cases the artificially produced events are of a kind which would almost certainly never occur were nature left to take her own course; but the experimentalist sets great store by them because they are expressly designed to provide a more unequivocal test of theory than any naturally occurring conditions. Most laboratory experiments in biology, chemistry and especially physics are of this kind.

We can say, then, that whereas in traditional thought there is continual if reluctant adjustment of theories to new experience, in science men spend much of their time deliberately creating new experience in order to evaluate their theories. Whilst in traditional thought it is mostly experience that determines theory, in the world of the experimental scientist there is a sense in which theory usually determines experience.

The confession of ignorance. The European anthropologist working in a traditional African community often has the experience of soliciting people's theories on a number of (to him) interesting topics, and of getting the reply 'we don't know anything about that' with the implication 'we don't really care'. Thus the anthropologist usually comes to Africa with ideas about the wonderful 'creation myths' to be found there. Very often, however, he finds that the people he has come to live with are not at all curious about the creation of the world; and apart from acknowledging that it was the work of a supreme being, they are apt to say with a shrug of their shoulders 'the old people did not tell us anything about it'. (Often, of course, an equal lack of curiosity on the anthropologist's part leads him to miss an elaborate body of indigenous explanatory theory covering some area of experience his own lack of interest prevented him from enquiring about.)

What the anthropologist almost never finds is a confession of ignorance about the answer to some question which the people themselves consider important. Scarcely ever, for instance, does he come across a common disease or crop failure whose cause and cure people say they just do not know.

Given the basic predicament of the traditional thinker, such an admission would indeed be intolerable. For where there are no conceivable alternatives to the established theoretical system, any hint that this system is failing to cope must be a hint of irreparable chaos, and so must rouse extreme anxiety.

In the case of the scientist, his readiness to test every theory to destruction makes it inevitable that he will have to confess ignorance whenever a theory crumbles under testing and he has no better one immediately available. Indeed, it is only in a culture where the scientific attitude is firmly institutionalized that one can hope to hear the answer 'we don't know' given by an expert questioned on the causes of such a terrible human scourge as cancer. Such willingness to confess ignorance means that the world-view provided by scientists for wider consumption is apt to seem far less comprehensive and embracing than many of the world-views of pre-scientific cultures. In fact, it tends to give the impression of a great expanse of darkness illuminated only at irregular intervals. This impression, of course, is tolerable to scientists precisely because the beliefs they hold at a given time are not things of absolute value to which they can imagine no possible alternatives. If current beliefs let in the dark, this does not rule out the possibility of other beliefs which may eventually shut it out.

Coincidence, chance, probability. Closely related to the development of a capacity to tolerate ignorance is the development of concepts which formally recognize the existence of various kinds of limitation upon the possible completeness of explanation and prediction. Important among such concepts are those of coincidence, chance and probability.

Let us start with the idea of coincidence. In the traditional cultures of Africa, such a concept is poorly developed. The tendency is to give any untoward happening a definite cause. When a rotten branch falls off a tree and kills a man walking underneath it, there has to be a definite explanation of the calamity. Perhaps the man quarrelled with a half brother over some matter of inheritance, and the latter worked the fall of the branch through a sorcerer. Or perhaps he misappropriated lineage property, and the lineage ancestors brought the branch down on his head. The idea that the whole thing could have come about through the accidental convergence of two independent chains of events is inconceivable because it is psychologically intolerable. To entertain it would be to admit that the episode was inexplicable and unpredictable: a glaring confession of ignorance.

It is characteristic of the scientist that he is willing to face up to the inexplicability and unpredictability of this type of situation, and that he does not shrink from diagnosing an accidental convergence of different chains of events. This is a consequence of his ability to tolerate ignorance.

As with the idea of coincidence, so with that of probability. Where traditional thought is apt to demand definite forecasts of whether something will or will not happen, the scientist is often content to know the probability of its happening – that is, the number of times it will happen in a hypothetical series of, say, a hundred trials.

When it was first developed, the probability forecast was seen as a makeshift tool for use in situations where one's knowledge of the factors operating was incomplete, and where it was assumed that possession of all the relevant data would have made a definite forecast possible. This is still an important context of probability forecasting, and will continue to be so. An example of its use is in prediction of the incidence of the mental disease schizophrenia. Psychiatrists have now come to believe that heredity plays a large part in causing the disease; and given a knowledge of the distribution of previous cases in a person's family history, they are able to calculate the probability of his contracting it. Their forecasts only run to probabilities, because they are not yet sure that they know all the other factors which reinforce or inhibit the effect of heredity, and also because they are seldom in a position to observe all those factors they do know to be relevant. Nevertheless, the assumption remains that if all the relevant factors could be known and observed, the probability forecasts could be replaced by unequivocal predictions.

In the twentieth century, a yet more drastic step has been taken in acknowledging the limits of explanation and prediction. For physicists now admit that the entities they postulate as the ultimate constituents of all matter – the so-called elementary particles – have properties such that, even given all obtainable data about their condition at any instant, it is still impossible to give more than a probability forecast of their condition at any instance in the future. Here, the probability forecast is no longer a makeshift for an unequivocal prediction: it is ultimate and irreducible.

From one angle, then, the development of the scientific outlook appears more than anything else as a growth of intellectual humility. Where the pre-scientific thinker is unable to confess ignorance on any question of vital practical import, the good scientist is always ready to do so. Again, where the pre-scientific thinker is reluctant to acknowledge any limitation on his power to explain and predict, the scientist not only faces such limitations with equanimity, but devotes a good deal of energy to exploring and charting their extent.

This humility, I suggest, is the product of an underlying confidence – the confidence which comes from seeing that one's currently held beliefs are not the be-all and end-all of the human search for order. Once one has seen this, the difficulty of facing up to their limitations largely dissolves.[42]

Protective versus destructive attitude to the category-system. If someone is asked to list typical features of traditional thinking, he is almost certain to mention the phenomenon known as 'taboo'. 'Taboo' is the anthropological jargon for a reaction of horror and aversion to certain actions or happenings which are seen as monstrous and polluting. It is characteristic of the taboo reaction that people are unable to justify it in terms of ulterior reasons: tabooed events are simply bad in themselves. People take every possible step to prevent tabooed events from happening, and to isolate or expel them when they do occur.

Taboo has long been a mystery to anthropologists. Of the many explanations proposed, few have fitted more than a small selection of the instances observed. It is only recently that an anthropologist has placed the phenomenon in a more satisfactory perspective by the observation that in nearly every case of taboo reaction, the events and actions involved are ones which seriously defy the established lines of classification in the culture where they occur.[43]

Perhaps the most important occasion of taboo reaction in traditional African cultures is the commission of incest. Incest is one of the most flagrant defiances of the established category-system: for he who commits it treats a mother, daughter or sister like a wife. Another common occasion for taboo reaction is the birth of twins. Here, the category distinction involved is that of human beings versus animals – multiple births being taken as characteristic of animals as opposed to men. Yet another very generally tabooed object is the human corpse, which occupies, as it were, a classificatory no-man's-land between the living and the inanimate. Equally widely tabooed are such human bodily excreta as faeces and menstrual blood, which occupy the same no-man's-land between the living and the inanimate.

Taboo reactions are often given to occurrences that are radically strange or new; for these too (almost by definition) fail to fit in to the established category system. A good example is furnished by a Kalabari story of the coming of the Europeans. The first white man, it is said, was seen by a fisherman who had gone down to the mouth of the estuary in his canoe. Panic-stricken, he raced home and told his people what he had seen: whereupon he and the rest of the town set out to purify themselves – that is, to rid themselves of the influence of the strange and monstrous thing that had intruded into their world.

A sort of global taboo reaction is often evoked by foreign lands. As the domains of so much that is strange and unassimilable to one's own categories, such lands are the abode *par excellence* of the monstrous and the abominable. The most vivid description we have of this attitude is that given for the Lugbara by John Middleton.[44] For this East African people, the foreigner is the inverted perpetrator of all imaginable abominations from incest downwards. The more alien he is, the more abominable. Though the Lugbara attitude is extreme, many traditional African cultures would seem to echo it in some degree.[45]

Just as the central tenets of the traditional theoretical system are defended against adverse experience by an elaborate array of excuses for predictive failure, so too the main classificatory distinctions of the system are defended by taboo avoidance reactions against any event that defies them. Since every system of belief implies a system of categories, and vice versa, secondary elaboration and taboo reaction are really opposite sides of the same coin.

From all this it follows that, like secondary elaboration, taboo reaction has no place among the reflexes of the scientist. For him, whatever defies or fails to fit in to the established category-system is not something horrifying, to be isolated or expelled. On the contrary, it is an intriguing 'phenomenon' – a starting point and a challenge for the invention of new classifications and new theories. It is something every young research worker would like to have crop up in his field of observation – perhaps the first rung on the ladder of fame. If a biologist ever came across a child born with the head of a goat, he would be hard put to it to make his compassion cover his elation. And as for the social anthropologists, one may guess that their secret dreams are of finding a whole community of men who sleep for preference with their mothers!

The passage of time: bad or good? In traditional Africa, methods of time-reckoning vary greatly from culture to culture. Within each culture, again, we find a plurality of time-scales used in different contexts. Thus there may be a major scale which locates events either before, during or after the time of founding of the major institutions of the community: another scale which locates events by correlating them with the lifetimes of deceased ancestors: yet another which locates events by correlating them with the phases of the seasonal cycle: and yet another which uses phases of the daily cycle.

Although these scales are seldom interrelated in any systematic way, they all serve to order events in before-after series. Further, they have the very general characteristic that *vis-à-vis* 'after', 'before' is usually valued positively, sometimes neutrally, and never negatively. Whatever the particular scale involved, then, the passage of time is seen as something deleterious or at best neutral.

Perhaps the most widespread, everyday instance of this attitude is the standard justification of so much thought and action: 'That is what the old-time people told us.' (It is usually this standard justification which is in the forefront of the anthropologist's mind when he applies the label 'traditional culture'.)

On the major time-scale of the typical traditional culture, things are thought of as having been better in the golden age of the founding heroes than they are today. On an important minor time-scale, the annual one, the end of the year is a time when everything in the cosmos is run-down and sluggish, overcome by an accumulation of defilement and pollution.

A corollary of this attitude to time is a rich development of activities designed to negate its passage by a 'return to the beginning'. Such activities characteristically depend on the magical premiss that a symbolic statement of some archetypal event can in a sense recreate that event and temporarily obliterate the passage of time which has elapsed since its original occurrence.[46]

These rites of recreation are to be seen at their most luxuriant in the ancient cultures of the Western Sudan – notably in those of the Bambara and Dogon. In such cultures, indeed, a great part of everyday activity is said to have the ulterior significance of recreating archetypal events and acts. Thus the Dogon labouring in the fields recreates in his pattern of cultivation the emergence of the world from the cosmic egg. The builder of a homestead lays it out in a pattern that symbolically recreates the body of the culture-hero Nommo. Even relations between kin symbolize and recreate relations between the primal beings.[47]

One might well describe the Western Sudanic cultures as obsessed with the annulment of time to a degree unparalleled in Africa as a whole. Yet other, less spectacular, manifestations of the attempt to 'get back to the beginning' are widely distributed over the continent. In the West African forest belt, for instance, the richly developed ritual dramas enacted in honour of departed heroes and ancestors have a strong recreative aspect. For by inducing these beings to possess specially selected media and thus, during festivals, to return temporarily to the company of men, such rituals are restoring things as they were in olden times.[48]

On the minor time-scale provided by the seasonal cycle, we find a similar widespread concern for recreation and renewal. Hence the important rites which mark the end of an old year and the beginning of a new one – rites which attempt to make the year new by a thoroughgoing process of purification of accumulated pollutions and defilements.

This widespread attempt to annul the passage of time seems closely linked to features of traditional thought which I have already reviewed. As I pointed out earlier, the new and the strange, in so far as they fail to fit into the established system of classification and theory, are intimations of chaos to be avoided as far as possible. Advancing time, with its inevitable element of non-repetitive change, is the vehicle *par excellence* of the new and the strange. Hence its effects must be annulled at all costs. Rites of renewal and recreation, then, have much in common with the processes of secondary elaboration and taboo behaviour. Indeed, their kinship with the latter can be seen in the idea that the passage of the year is essentially an accumulation of pollutions, which it is the function of the renewal rites to remove. In short, these rites are the third great defensive reflex of traditional thought.[49]

When we turn from the traditional thinker to the scientist, we find this whole valuation of temporal process turned upside down. Not for the scientist the idea of a golden age at the beginning of time – an age from which things have been steadily falling away. For him, the past is a bad old past, and the best things lie ahead. The passage of time brings inexorable progress. As C. P. Snow has put it aptly, all scientists have 'the future in their bones'.[50] Where the traditional thinker is busily trying to annul the passage of time, the scientist may almost be said to be trying frantically to hurry time up. For in his impassioned pursuit of the experimental method, he is striving after the creation of new situations which nature, if left to herself, would bring about slowly if ever at all.

Once again, the scientist's attitude can be understood in terms of the 'open' predicament. For him, currently held ideas on a given subject are one possibility amongst many. Hence occurrences which threaten them are not the total, horrific threat that they would be for the traditional thinker. Hence time's burden of things new and strange does not hold the terrors that it holds for the traditionalist. Furthermore, the scientist's experience of the way in which successive theories, overthrown after exposure to adverse data, are replaced by ideas of ever greater predictive and explanatory power, leads almost inevitably to a very positive evaluation of time. Finally, we must remember that the 'open' predicament, though it has made people able to tolerate threats to their beliefs, has not been able to supply them with anything comparable to the cosiness of the traditional thinker ensconced amidst his established theories. As an English medical student, newly exposed to the scientific attitude, put it: 'You seem to be as if when learning to skate, trying to find a nice hard piece of ice which you can stand upright on instead of learning how to move on it. You continue trying to find something, some foundation piece which will not move, whereas everything will move and you've got to learn to skate on it.'[51]

The person who enjoys the moving world of the sciences, then, enjoys the exhilaration of the skater. But for many, this is a nervous, insecure sensation, which they would fain exchange for the womb-like warmth of the traditional theories and their defences. This lingering sense of insecurity gives a powerful attraction to the idea of progress. For by enabling people to cling to some hoped-for future state of perfect knowledge, it helps them live with a realization of the imperfection and transience of present theories.

Once formed, indeed, the idea of progress becomes in itself one of the most powerful supports of the scientific attitude generally. For the faith that, come what may, new experience must lead to better theories, and that better theories must eventually give place to still better ones, provides the strongest possible incentive for a constant readiness to expose oneself to the strange and the disturbing, to scrap current frameworks of ideas, and to cast about for replacements.

Like the quest for purity of motive, however, the faith in progress is a double-edged weapon. For the lingering insecurity which is one of the roots of this faith leads all too often to an excessive fixation of hopes and desires on an imagined utopian future. People cling to such a faith in the same way that men in pre-scientific cultures cling to the past. And in doing so, they inevitably lose much of the traditionalist's ability to enjoy and glorify the moment he lives in. Even within the sciences, an excessive faith in progress can be dangerous. In sociology, for instance, it has led to a number of unfruitful theories of social evolution.

At this point, I should like to draw attention to a paradox inherent in the presentation of my subject. As a scientist, it is perhaps inevitable that I should at certain points give the impression that traditional African thought is a poor, shackled thing when compared with the thought of the sciences; yet as a man, here I am living by choice in a still-heavily-traditional Africa rather than in the scientifically oriented Western subculture I was brought up in. Why? Well, there may be lots of queer, sinister, unacknowledged reasons. But one certain reason is the discovery of things lost at home. An intensely poetic quality in everyday life and thought, and a vivid enjoyment of the passing moment – both driven out of sophisticated Western life by the quest for purity of motive and the faith in progress. How necessary these are for the advance of science; but what a disaster they are when they run wild beyond their appropriate bounds! Though I largely disagree with the way the 'Négritude' theorists have characterized the differences between traditional African and modern Western thought, when it gets to this point I see very clearly what they are after.

So much, then, for the salient differences between traditional and scientific thought. There is nothing particularly original about the terms in which I have described the contrast between the two. Indeed, all of my eleven points of difference are to be found mentioned somewhere or other in previous anthropological literature. This literature, however, leaves much to be desired when it comes to interpretation. Thus one author deals with secondary elaboration, another with magic, another with taboo, and so on. A particular explanation covers a particular trait of traditional thought, but seems to have very little relevance to the others. Most social anthropologists would acknowledge that the eleven characteristic traits of traditional thought listed in this essay tend to occur together and vanish together; but so far they have offered no overall interpretation that does justice to this concomitance.

In so far as my paper makes a fresh contribution, I think this lies precisely in its provision of just such an overall interpretation. For the concept of the 'closed' predicament not only provides a key to the understanding of each one of the eleven salient traits of traditional thought; it also helps us to see why these eleven traits flourish and perish as a set. Where formerly we saw them as an assemblage of miscellaneous exotica, we can now see them as the components of a well-defined and comprehensible syndrome.

So far, however, the interpretation, though it breaks new ground, remains largely intellectualist. At this stage, it does not allow us to relate ideational differences to broader socio-cultural differences. It does not as yet allow us to suggest answers to such questions as 'Why did the scientific attitude emerge spontaneously in Europe but not in Africa?' or, 'Why, in Europe, did it emerge at particular times and places'. None the less, I think it does give a valuable clue as to the sort of circumstances we should be looking for: i.e. circumstances tending to promote awareness of alternatives to established theoretical models. Three relevant factors of this kind suggest themselves at once:

Development of written transmission of beliefs.[52] Earlier in this essay, I talked of the paradox of idea-systems whose users see them as static, but which are in fact constantly, albeit slowly, changing. This paradox, as I said, seems to imply something like a game of Grandmother's Footsteps, with

Grandson moving a little at a time when Grandma's back is turned, but always taking care to be still when Grandma rounds on him.

Now it is, above all, the oral transmission of beliefs which makes this intellectual Grandmother's Footsteps possible. For in each generation, small innovations, together with the processes of selective recall, make for considerable adjustments of belief to current situation. But where they cannot refer back to the ideas of a former generation 'frozen' in writing, both those responsible for the adjustments and those who accept them remain virtually unaware that innovation has taken place. In a similar manner, a small and seemingly marginal innovation in belief can occur without anyone realizing that it is part of a cumulative trend which, over several generations, will amount to a very striking change.

In these circumstances, everything tends to give the main tenets of theory an absolute and timeless validity. In so doing, it prevents the development of any awareness of alternatives. Oral transmission, then, is clearly one of the basic supports of the 'closed' predicament.

Where literacy begins to spread widely through a community, the situation changes radically. The beliefs of a particular period became 'frozen' in writing. Meanwhile, oral transmission of beliefs goes on, and with it the continuous small adjustments to changing circumstances typical of pre-literate society. As time passes these adjustments produce an idea-system markedly different from that originally set down in writing. Now in an entirely oral culture, as we have seen, no one has the means of becoming aware of this change. But in a literature culture, the possibility of checking current beliefs against the 'frozen' ideas of an earlier era throws the fact of change into sharp relief.

In these circumstances, the main tenets of theory can no longer be seen as having an absolute and timeless validity. In the consciousness that one's own people believed other things at other times, we have the germ of a sense of alternatives. The stage is set for the emergence of the 'open' predicament.

Not only does attention to the question of literacy help us to understand why the 'open' predicament developed in Europe but not in Africa. It also helps us to understand why, in Europe, this predicament developed just when and where it did. Thus in their sketch of the history of writing,[53] Goody and Watt point out that pictographic writing developed in the Middle and Far East from the end of the fourth millenium B.C. But the various pictographic systems were so unwieldy and their assimilation so time-consuming that they tended to be the exclusive possessions of specially trained, conservative ruling elites. The interests of such elites in preserving the *status quo* would naturally counteract the 'opening' tendencies of written transmission. It was in sixth-century B.C. Greece that a convenient, easily learnable phonetic alphabet became in some communities a majority possession; and it was in this same sixth-century B.C. Greece that the 'open' predicament made its first notable appearance. The subsequent fortunes of literacy in the Mediterranean world seem to correspond rather well with the subsequent fortunes of the 'open' predicament. Thus what we term the 'Dark Ages' was at once a period which saw the restriction of literacy to small, conservative ruling elites, and at the same time a period in which the 'closed' predicament reasserted itself in full force. And in the reawakening of the twelfth to the seventeenth centuries, a great expansion and democratization of literacy was the precursor of the final, enduring reappearance of the 'open' predicament and the scientific outlook. Notable during the early part of this period was the rediscovery, via Arab sources, of the 'lost' writings of the great Greek philosopher-scientists. Since in early medieval times current theoretical tenets were taught very much in the 'this is what the ancients handed down to us' spirit of the closed society, the sudden forced confrontation with the very different reality of what these ancestral heroes actually did believe must have had an effect which powerfully supplemented that due to the growth of literacy generally.

Development of culturally heterogeneous communities. There is one obvious, almost platitudinous answer to the question: what gives members of a community an awareness of alternative possibilities of interpreting their world? The answer, of course, is: meeting other people who do in fact interpret the world differently. But there are meetings and meetings: and it is clear that whilst some make very little difference to the outlooks of those involved, others are crucial for the rise of the 'open' predicament.

Now neither traditional Africa nor early Europe lacked encounters between bearers of radically different cultures. So our aim must be to show why, in Africa, such encounters did little to promote the 'open' predicament, when in Europe they did so much.

My own very tentative answer goes something like this. Traditional African communities were as a rule fairly homogeneous as regards their internal culture, and their relations with culturally alien neighbours tended to be restricted to the context of trade. Now such restricted relations did not make for mutual encounter of a very searching kind. In extreme cases, indeed, they were carried on without actual face-to-face contact: take, for instance, the notorious 'silent trade' between North African merchants and certain peoples of the Western Sudan – an exercise in which the partners neither met nor spoke. Much trade between bearers of radically different cultures was, of course, carried out under conditions far less extreme than these; and it was even common for members of a given community to speak the languages of the culturally alien peoples they traded with. Yet culturally contrasted trading partners remained basically rooted in different communities, from which they set out before trade, and to which they returned after it. Under these limitations, confrontations with alien world-views remained very partial. The trader encountered the thought of his alien partners at the level of common sense but not usually at the level of theory. Since common-sense worlds, in general, differ very little in comparison with theoretical worlds, such encounters did not suffice to stimulate a strong sense of alternatives.[54]

Even where the member of a traditional community did make contact with his alien neighbours at the level of theory, the content of theory was such that it still presented an obstacle to the development of a real sense of alternatives. As I pointed out in part 1 of this paper, the bulk of traditional theory was concerned with its users' own particular community. There was an implicit premiss that the world worked one way within one's own community, and another way outside it. Hence if one's neighbours believed some very strange and different things, this was in no way surprising or disturbing in terms of one's own beliefs. In such circumstances, radically contrasting belief-systems could seldom be seen as genuine alternatives.

When we turn from Africa to Europe, it is important to note just when and where the 'open' predicament came to prevail. Its first home, historians seem to agree, was in certain parts of sixth-century-B.C. Greece. Not in such centrally placed, culturally homogeneous states as Sparta, whose self-contained agricultural society remained rigidly 'closed'; but in the small, cosmopolitan trading communities on the frontiers of the Greek world – old-established Ionian cities like Miletus and Ephesus, and more recently established colonies like Abdera and Syracuse.[55]

After declining in this area the fortunes of the 'open' predicament flourished for several centuries in Alexandria. Later, they waxed briefly in the cities of the Arab world. Thence, in late medieval times, the current passed to the cities of the Iberian peninsula and coastal Italy. Finally, it passed to the cities of north-western Europe.

What was it about the communities that lay along this devious path that made them such excellent centres for the development of the 'open' predicament? First and foremost, it was the conditions of contact between the bearers of different cultures. Whereas in Africa intercultural boundaries tended to coincide with inter-community boundaries, in these Mediterranean and European cities they cut right through the middle of the community. In these centres, people of diverse origins and cultures were packed together within single urban communities. And although the 'sons of the soil' were frequently the only people who had full citizenship rights, most of the inhabitants had feelings of common community membership and common interests vis-à-vis such outsiders as territorial rulers, the lords of the local countryside, other cities, and so on.

Under these conditions, relations between bearers of different cultures were much broader in scope than the purely commercial relations which typically linked such people over much of traditional Africa. And a broader context of social relationship made for a deeper and more searching intellectual encounter. Here, the encounter was not merely at the level of common sense where differences were negligible. It was also at the level of basic theory where differences were striking. Much of the 'open' temper of late and medieval and Renaissance times, for instance, can probably be traced to the confrontation of the basic tenets of the Christian, Islamic and Jewish thought-traditions in the twelfth-century cities of Spain and coastal Italy.[56]

Another factor making for more searching encounter was the actual content of the theories involved. The various traditions of thought making up the intellectual inheritance of these Mediterranean and European cities were the products of peoples who had been living in communities far more integrally linked to the wider world than was usual in traditional Africa. As such, they were more universalistic in their content. So here, when a confrontation took place, it was no longer possible to rest content with saying: 'My theory works for my little world, and his works for his.' My theory and his theory were now patently about the same world, and awareness of them as alternatives became inescapable.

Development of the trade-travel-exploration complex. So much for encounter between bearers of different cultures within a single community. A second important kind of encounter arises from voyages of travel and exploration in which members of one community go to live temporarily amongst members of a culturally alien community, with the express aim of intellectual and emotional contact at all levels from the most superficial to the deepest.

Now although individual members of many traditional African cultures must have made such voyages from time to time, these, so far as we know, have never become a dominant theme of life in any of the traditional cultures. But in sixth-to-third-century-B.C. Greece, in the medieval Arab world, and finally in fifteenth-to-seventeenth-century western Europe – all crucial centres for the development of the 'open' predicament – these voyages were such important features of social life that they coloured everyone's outlook on the world.

The evidence we have from ancient Greece indicates that many of the great independent thinkers such as Thales, Anaximander, Democritus, Herodotus and Xenophanes probably made extensive exploratory voyages themselves. And in some of their writings, the connexion between first-hand experience of a variety of alien ways of looking at the world and an 'open' sceptical tenor of thought becomes explicit.[57] Again, in fifteenth-to-eighteenth-century western Europe, exotic world-views personified in figures like the Noble Savage, the Wise Egyptian and the Chinese Sage haunt the pages of many of the sceptical writings of the times; and here too the link between confrontation with alien world-views and 'open' thinking is often explicit.[58]

It is, of course, possible to argue that these voyages and these confrontations were a consequence and not a cause of the 'open' predicament; that 'open-minded' people embarked on them with the idea of putting parochial views to the deliberate test of wider horizons of experience. This may have been true once the voyages had become a dominant feature of the life of the times. But I believe the beginnings of the eras of exploration can still be best understood in terms of the aims and interests of essentially 'closed-minded' societies.

One's suspicions on this score are aroused in the first instance by the fact that in both of the great eras of exploration, many of the voyages were encouraged if not directed by the pillars of tradition: in early Greece by the Delphic Oracle, and in western Europe by the Popes.

Again, it is clear that the motive forces behind the voyages included the aim of reducing population pressure by overseas settlement and that of extending commerce to include new items to be found only in faraway lands. The detailed probings of alien world-views can thus be understood as intelligence operations directed towards solving the problems of human coexistence involved in overseas settlement and commerce. There was probably little 'open-mindedness' in the intentions which originally lay behind them.

Perhaps the most interesting example of the essentially 'closed' motivations behind activities which were to make a great contribution to the development of the 'open' predicament is provided by the operations of Christian missionaries in the fifteenth-to-eighteenth centuries. The fanaticism with which the missionaries worked to convert distant peoples of alien faith can, I think, be understood as a product of the 'closed' society's determination to protect itself from the possibility of being disturbed by confrontation with alien world-views – a possibility which loomed large in this era of exploration. But the more intelligent missionaries saw that effective evangelization required a prior understanding of the faiths of those to be converted; and they set themselves, however reluctantly, to acquire such an understanding. The result was a body of records of alien world-views that came to colour much of the thought of the times, and that was undoubtedly one of the most important contributions to the genesis of the open thinking of the seventeenth century.

The eras of exploration encouraged the growth of the 'open' predicament in a second way. This was through the rich material fruits of the voyages. In traditional culture, as we have seen, distant lands tend to epitomize all that is new and strange, all that fails to fit into the established system of categories, all that is tabooed, fearful and abominable. Hence, whether among the Lugbara of East Africa or among Dark Age Europeans, we find them peopled with abominations and monsters. In the eras of exploration, however, reports came back not of monsters but of delights and riches. Slowly, these pleasant associations of the Great Beyond extended themselves to new and strange experience generally. The quest for such experience came to be seen not as something dangerous and foolhardy, but as something richly rewarding and pleasantly exciting. This relation between the fruits of exploration and the new attitudes to the strange and category-defying is portrayed very clearly in some of the metaphors of these eras. Take, for instance, Joseph Glanvill's notion of 'An America of Secrets and an Unknown Peru of Nature', waiting to overthrow old scholastic ideas and force men to replace them with something better.[59]

Not only, then, did the events of these eras undermine the feeling that one's established beliefs were the only defence against chaos and the void. They gave a less horrifying, nay benign, face to chaos itself.

In naming these three factors as crucial for the development of the 'open' predicament, I am not implying that wherever they occur, there is a sort of painless, automatic and complete transition from 'closed' to 'open' thinking. On the contrary, the transition seems inevitably to be painful, violent and partial.

Even in ancient Greece, the independent thinking of the great pre-Socratic philosophers evoked strong and anxious reactions.[60] In late medieval times, a few decades of confrontation with alien world-views and 'open' sceptical thinking tended to be succeeded by decades of persecution of those responsible for disturbing established orthodoxy and by a general 'closing-up' of thought.[61] In present-day Nigeria, we seem to be seeing yet another example of the atrocious birth-pangs of the 'open' society.

Why should the transition be so painful? Well, a theme of this paper has been the way in which a developing awareness of alternative world-views erodes attitudes which attach an absolute validity to the established outlook. But this is a process that works over time – indeed over generations. Throughout the process there are bound to be many people on whom the confrontation has not yet worked its magic. These people still retain the old sense of the absolute validity of their belief-systems, with all the attendant anxieties about threats to them. For these people, the confrontation is still a threat of chaos of the most horrific kind – a threat which demands the most dramatic measures. They respond in one of two ways: either by trying to blot out those responsible for the confrontation, often down to the last unborn child; or by trying to convert them to their own beliefs through fanatical missionary activity.

Again, as I said earlier, the moving, shifting thought-world produced by the 'open' predicament creates its own sense of insecurity. Many people find this shifting world intolerable. Some adjust to their fears by developing an inordinate faith in progress towards a future in which 'the Truth' will be finally known. But others long nostalgically for the fixed, unquestionable beliefs of the 'closed' culture. They call for authoritarian establishment and control of dogma, and for persecution of those who have managed to be at ease in a world of ever-shifting ideas. Clearly, the 'open' predicament is a precarious, fragile thing.

In modern western Europe and America, it is true, the 'open' predicament seems to have escaped from this precariousness through public acknowledgement of the practical utility of the sciences. It has achieved a secure foothold in the culture because its results maximize values shared by 'closed'- and 'open'-minded alike. Even here, however, the 'open' predicament has nothing like a universal sway. On the contrary, it is almost a minority phenomenon. Outside the various academic disciplines in which it has been institutionalized, its hold is pitifully less than those who describe Western culture as 'science-orientated' often like to think.

It is true that in modern Western culture, the theoretical models propounded by the professional scientist do, to some extent, become the intellectual furnishings of a very large sector of the population. The moderately educated layman typically shares with the scientist a general predilection for impersonal 'it'-theory and a proper contempt for 'thou'-theory. Garbled and watered-down though it may be, the atomic theory of matter is one of his standard possessions. But the layman's ground for accepting the models propounded by the scientist is often no different from the young African villager's ground for accepting the models propounded by one of his elders. In both cases the propounders are deferred to as the accredited agents of tradition. As for the rules which guide scientists themselves in the acceptance or rejection of models, these seldom become part of the intellectual equipment of members of the wider population. For all the apparent up-to-dateness of the content of his world-view, the modern Western layman is rarely more 'open' or scientific in his outlook than is the traditional African villager.

This takes me back to a general point about the layout of this paper. If I spent the whole of part 1 labouring the thesis that differences in the content of theories do more to hide continuities than reveal genuine contrasts, this was not, as some readers may have imagined, through a determination to ignore the contrasts. Rather, it was precisely to warn them away from the trap which the Western layman characteristically falls into – the trap which makes him feel he is keeping up with the scientists when in fact he is no nearer to them than the African peasant.

8 Paradox and explanation: a reply to Mr Skorupski

The starting point of Mr Skorupski's searching critique[1] is my contention that, in seeking out adequate instruments for the translation of African religious discourse, we should give serious consideration to the potentialities of modern Western scientific discourse. He suggests that my preoccupation with scientific discourse in this context stems from my failure to consider other candidates for the translational job. His own view is that if we consider the candidacy, not only of scientific discourse, but also of modern Western religious discourse, we may find that the latter is more suited to our purposes.

In arguing his case, Skorupski focusses attention on the question of paradox. He maintains that, contrary to what I have claimed, the process of explanation in the sciences is *not* inherently paradoxical. Indeed, he says that such paradoxes as do arise during the course of theory-building are deliberately and speedily eliminated. On the other hand, he maintains that Western religious discourse *is* inherently paradoxical; and he produces some compelling evidence to show that, far from trying to eliminate paradox, the users of such discourse cultivate and even flaunt it. Finally, turning to a consideration of African religious discourse, he suggests that, unlike scientific discourse and like modern Western religious discourse, it too is inherently paradoxical. He further suggests that, although African religions are concerned, amongst other things, with the provision of explanations of the world and its working, neither their paradoxicality nor most of their other distinctive features can be related to this concern. These are his reasons for maintaining that, in trying to understand African religions, we shall find comparisons with modern Western religion more fruitful than comparisons with modern Western science.

As a prelude to his critique, Skorupski gives a very fair summary of my arguments and views; so unlike many repliers to objections, I shall not waste a lot of space on indignation about having been misinterpreted. My only protest on this score is that, in an article earlier than the ones he cites,[2] I do in fact make a brief comparative evaluation of the potential usefulness, in this context, of both modern Western religious discourse and modern

Western scientific discourse. However, the arguments in favour of scientific discourse given in that article do not really meet the points which he makes. So in what follows, I shall try to develop fresh lines of argument rather than refer the reader back.

I shall start by elaborating my original suggestion, made in a somewhat throwaway manner, that the sciences are full of Lévy-Bruhlian assertions of unity-in-duality and identity of discernibles. These assertions occur whenever observable entities are identified with theoretical entities. Against Skorupski, I shall argue not only that they are irreducibly paradoxical, but also that their paradoxicality is integral to their role in the process of explanation. I shall then go on to show that ideas about theoretical entities themselves are often elaborated in ways that result in combinations of properties which are not merely bizarre but downright paradoxical. I shall show that, although many (but by no means all) scientists are concerned to eliminate such paradoxical combinations wherever they occur, fresh ones keep popping up no sooner than the old ones have been weeded out. And I shall suggest that, as in the case of 'theoretical identity', this recurrence of paradox within the realm of theoretical discourse is integral to the process of explanation.

After dealing with the sciences, I shall turn to African religion. I shall try to show that, in their nature and location, the paradoxes of African religious discourse are very similar to those of scientific discourse. I shall also try to show that, as in the latter, the occurrence of paradox can only be understood in terms of the quest for explanation.

Unlike Skorupski, I shall leave consideration of modern Western religious discourse till last. I shall do this (a) because, for reasons which will become apparent, I think that the study of African religions throws more light on modern Western religions than vice versa; and (b) because I think that, in many ways, modern Western religion is the odd one out in the trio. As I shall show, whilst many of its paradoxes are reminiscent of those found in the sciences and in African religions, at least one is quite distinctive. Again, whilst explanation is the central concern both of the sciences and of African religions, it is not even a peripheral concern of the most modern variants of Western religion. Hence, initially at least, it seems doubtful whether the interpretation of paradox offered in connection with the first two areas of discourse can be made to stick in this third area. Yet again, although I agree with Skorupski that, in elevating paradox to the status of 'mystery', Western Christians are behaving quite differently from Western scientists, I suggest that, in this respect, they are behaving quite differently from *both* Western scientists *and* African religious thinkers. Even in this third case, though, I hope to show that the assumption of an earlier if now outmoded concern with explanation takes us a good way toward understanding at least some of the salient paradoxes of Christian belief.

Paradox and explanation in the sciences

In dealing with the question of 'theoretical identity', let me start by enumerating what would seem to be points of agreement between Skorupski and myself.

First of all, we agree that the operation of 'theoretical identification' plays a crucial part in the process of scientific explanation.

We agree that, in a theoretical identity, one term *apparently* refers to an observable entity or property – i.e. one which is accessible to direct, naked-eye observation, whilst the other term *apparently* refers to a theoretical entity or property – i.e. one which is either unobservable in principle or observable only indirectly, and which stands in an explanatory relation to what is observable. Alternatively, one term refers to a lower-level theoretical entity or property – i.e. one which seems to invite further explanation, whilst the other term refers to a higher-level theoretical entity or property – i.e. one which satisfies this need for further explanation.[3] Examples acceptable to both of us would, I think, include: 'this table is a complex system of molecules'; 'the temperature of a gas is the mean kinetic energy of its molecules'; 'a lightning flash is a stream of electrons'; 'a salt crystal is a lattice of sodium and chlorine atoms'; 'carbon atoms are planetary systems of elementary particles'; 'neutrons are energy'.

We agree on the intellectual functions of theoretical identities. One such function is that of displaying the incredibly diverse phenomena of the world of direct observation as so many manifestations of a more unified underlying order of things. Another such function is that of explaining known causal connections linking directly observable events, and of suggesting hitherto unsuspected connections and regularities. Theoretical identities fulfil this latter function by spotlighting the implications, for the realm of observables, of the various regularities which govern the behaviour of the theoretical entities to which they refer.

We agree in taking a 'realist' stand with respect to the terms involved in theoretical identities. We agree, that is, in believing it is as appropriate to talk about the reality of electrons, protons, atoms and molecules as it is to talk about the reality of tables, chairs, crystals, buckets of water and volumes of gas.[4]

We agree that theoretical identities, like other alleged identities, are to be assessed in the light of (a) the Principle of Symmetry, (b) the Principle of Transitivity, and (c) the Principle of the Indiscernibility of Identicals. By (a), if x is identical with y, y is identical with x. By (b), if x is identical with y and y is identical with z, then x is identical with z. By (c), if x is to be identified with y, then x must have all and only the properties which y has.[5]

As just stated, these criteria refer to particular entities. Many theoretical identities, however, take a general form: e.g. 'all volumes of water are systems of molecules' or 'all crystals are lattices of atoms'. Now I think Skorupski would agree with me that, to facilitate assessment of such statements, we can, by a process of extension, supply reasonable criteria for what we may call 'general identity'. Thus, by extension of (a), we can say that, if 'all xs are ys' is to be taken as an identity-statement, it must be true that every x is a y and every y an x. By extension of (b), we can say that, if 'all xs are ys' and 'all ys are zs' are both to be taken as identity-statements, then it must be true that every x is a z and every z an x. By extension of (c), we can say that, if 'all xs are ys' is to be taken as an identity-statement, then it must be true that every x has all and only the properties of the y with which it is identified, and that every y has all and only the properties of the x with which it is identified.

Finally, we agree that, crucial though they may be to an enterprise regarded as the quintessence of rationality, theoretical identities have struck many thinkers, both philosophical and scientific, as more than a little puzzling.

At this point, however, agreement gives place to difference. For whilst Skorupski believes all of the puzzles posed by these statements to be soluble, I believe that, of the four main puzzles, three are soluble and the fourth insoluble. In what follows, I shall dispose fairly speedily of the first three puzzles, then go on to consider the fourth at some length.

The first two puzzles arise when we try to assess theoretical identities in the light of the Principles of Symmetry and Transitivity. By the first, if 'all xs are ys' is to be taken as an identity-statement, then it must be true that all xs are ys and all ys are xs. Again, if 'all xs are ys' and 'all zs are ys' are both to be taken as identity-statements, it must be true that all xs are zs and all zs are xs. This follows from the two Principles taken in conjunction. By the first, if all zs are ys, all ys are zs. By the second, if all xs are ys and all ys are zs, then all xs must be zs. By the first again, if all xs are zs, all zs are xs. Now at first glance, many theoretical identities fail dismally to meet these conditions. Take, for instance, the example of tables, volumes of water and systems of molecules. 'All tables are systems of molecules' is true; 'all systems of molecules are tables' is false. 'All volumes of water are systems of molecules' is true; 'all systems of molecules are volumes of water' is false. Again, though 'all tables are systems of molecules' and 'all volumes of water are systems of molecules' are both true, 'all tables are volumes of water' and 'all volumes of water are tables' are both false. Or, take a speculation of Heisenberg about the relation between the penultimate and the ultimate level of reality.[6] Here, we shall have to say: 'neutrons are energy, but energy is not neutrons; protons are energy, but energy is not protons; electrons are energy, but energy is not electrons'. We shall also have to say: 'although neutrons, protons and electrons are energy, neutrons are not protons or electrons, protons are not neutrons or electrons, and electrons are not neutrons or protons'.

Such asymmetries and intransitivities in statements purporting to be identities cannot but be alarming to the tidy-minded philosopher. Placed in their proper context, however, they soon lose their aura of paradox. Just what is this proper context? The question, I think, is answered with great clarity in the following passage from the work of a well-known historian/philosopher of science:

The diversity of materials is explained by the theory that each is composed of molecules which are different combinations of atoms of a smaller number of basic materials. Thus methane gas is a material whose molecules or least parts are formed by combination of four hydrogen atoms with one carbon atom, while octane is a material the molecules of which are formed by the combination of eighteen hydrogen atoms with eight carbon atoms. There are thousands of different hydro-carbons whose diversity can be explained as due both to the different proportions of hydrogen and carbon atoms that are combined in their molecules, and so different arrangements in space of the constituent atoms. Thus a thousandfold multiplicity of materials is transformed into a thousandfold multiplicity of combinations of a mere duality of materials. Similarly, physicists have offered an account of the hundredfold diversity of the chemical elements as due, not to a hundredfold diversity of materials but to there being one hundred different arrangements of a mere threefold diversity of more basic materials, protons, neutrons and electrons. Encouraged perhaps by the philosophical arguments for unity of material, and now almost by instinct, scientists seek to transfer diversity of materials into diversity of structure of a lesser diversity of materials. Perhaps they hope in the end to reduce all diversity to structural diversity of combinations of only one kind of ultimate stuff.[7]

Now the point about the statements we are considering here is that, although they too aim at explaining the apparently irreducible diversity of phenomena in terms of the diversity of states, structures or combinations of a small number of underlying kinds of things, they do so in a highly elliptical manner. More specifically, they stress underlying unities, but omit to mention the diversity of states, structures or combinations of these unities. Thus (to put it still somewhat elliptically) 'tables and volumes of water are systems of molecules' is an ellipsis for 'tables are systems of molecules of type A and volumes of water are systems of molecules of type B'. Again, 'neutrons, protons and electrons are energy' is an ellipsis for 'neutrons are energy in state A; protons are energy in state B; electrons are energy in state C'.

There are a number of reasons for the prevalence of these elliptical explanations in scientific discourse both popular and technical. As caricatures, they serve to bring out in a particularly dramatic way the unifying function of scientific explanation. Again, amongst colleagues in the same discipline, they form a convenient short-hand for fully spelled-out explanatory statements. Yet again, where fully spelled-out explanations can not yet be given, they nonetheless provide helpful indications of the general form such explanations may one day take. A good example of this last situation is Heisenberg's suggestion about elementary particles and energy. At present, physicists simply do not know by what differentiae they should qualify the concept of energy in order to generate a satisfying explanation of the differences between neutrons, protons and electrons. Nonetheless, Heisenberg's suggestion may turn out to be a valuable clue as to the direction in which such an explanation is to be found.[8]

Having established the elliptical nature of many statements of theoretical identity, we can now go on to dispose of the puzzles of apparent asymmetry and intransitivity which they pose.

As Skorupski points out, one important implication of saying that x is identical with y is that x is y and nothing else.[9] Now it is this implication that is at the root of asymmetry in the statements under consideration. Take for instance 'tables are systems of molecules' and 'systems of molecules are tables'. Clearly, it is true to say that tables are systems of molecules and nothing else. Equally clearly, it is false to say that systems of molecules are tables and nothing else. (False, because they are also volumes of water, volumes of chlorine gas, lumps of steel, blocks of ice, and so on.) Hence, whilst we can identify tables with systems of molecules, we cannot identify systems of molecules with tables. Again, take 'neutrons are energy' and 'energy is neutrons'. Once more, whilst it is true to say that neutrons are energy and nothing else, it is false to say that energy is neutrons and nothing else. (False, because it is also protons and electrons.) Hence, whilst we can identify neutrons with energy, we cannot identify energy with neutrons.

Not only does Skorupski's point show why our elliptical identity statements are bound to be asymmetrical; it also shows why the spelled-out versions of such statements are free from this puzzling characteristic. Let us consider our two examples in their spelled-out forms: 'tables are molecular systems of type A' and 'molecular systems of type A are tables'; 'neutrons are energy in state A' and 'energy in state A is neutrons'. The situation is now clearly changed. For it is perfectly reasonable to assert, both that tables are molecular systems of type A and nothing else, and that molecular systems of type A are tables and nothing else. Again, it is perfectly reasonable to assert, both that neutrons are energy in state A and nothing else, and that energy in state A is neutrons and nothing else. Hence in each pair of spelled-out identity statements, both members of the pair are true and the element of asymmetry disappears.

The spelling-out of our elliptical statements also resolves the problem posed by apparent intransitivity of identity. Thus, where tables are molecular systems of type A (and vice versa) and volumes of water molecular systems of type B (and vice versa), and where systems of type A are non-identical with systems of type B (and vice versa), it follows, by the converse of the very Principle of Transitivity which seemed to have been contravened, that tables cannot be volumes of water nor volumes of water tables. Again, where neutrons are energy in state A, protons energy in state B, and electrons energy in state C (and vice versa), and where states A, B, C are mutually non-identical, it follows that neutrons cannot be protons or electrons, that protons cannot be neutrons or electrons, and that electrons cannot be neutrons or protons.

This way of resolving the problems of asymmetry and intransitivity is also applicable to the hoary problems of how what is many can also be said to be one. This is a problem which vexed the pre-Socratics, and which has raised its head from time to time down to the present day.[10]

Let us take a selection of statements of the kind that exemplify the 'many/one' problem. One such statement is: 'Rusting and burning are two different processes; but both are also oxidation, which is a single process.' Another is: 'Wood, water and chlorine gas are different kinds of substance; but all are molecules, and hence are one.' Yet another is Heisenberg's suggestion: 'Electrons, protons and neutrons are all energy.' In all these cases, the 'many/one' problem arises because the statements involved are ellipses, referring to an underlying unity but omitting mention of the diversity of its states. If the statements were fully spelled-out, they would mention as many distinct states of the underlying unity as there were different entities or processes underpinned by this unity. If this were done, the problem would, of course, evaporate.

From the point of view of the professional philosopher of science, everything I have said so far will seem trivial and obvious. However, I have said it at some length because I think it sheds light on the nature of the asymmetrical, intransitive, many/one identities which will confront us when we come to consider religious discourse both African and Western.

The various puzzles I have dealt with so far are, so to speak, mere surface symptoms; tractable in themselves, but masking a deep-seated and far less tractable problem. The essence of this problem is vividly indicated in the following passage from A. J. Ayer:

But if we insist on posing the ontological question, then the scientific and common-sense descriptions of the world do come into conflict, if only because they compete for the same regions of space. We can consistently accept the commonsense statement that there is a table here, together with the scientific statement that there is a set of particles here, because there are independent ways of testing both statements, and these different groups of tests can be satisfied. But if we are constructing a picture of the world, then I do not see how we can consistently think of this area as being exclusively occupied by a solid, continuous, coloured object and as being exclusively occupied by a set of discontinuous, volatile, colourless, shapeless, particles.[11]

The trouble is that the view which Ayer says we cannot consistently adopt is precisely the view which our ordinary ideas as to the nature of explanation would seem to demand that we *do* adopt. Thus on the one hand, when we say we have explained something, we imply that the explanans is something different from the explanandum.[12] Yet on the other hand, in order to use the laws governing the behaviour of the explanans as a basis for explanation and prediction of the behaviour of the explanandum, we have to identify the latter with the former. In other words, if we are explaining the behaviour of Ayer's table in terms of the behaviour of a system of molecules, we have to admit (a) that the system of molecules is something different from the table, and (b) that it is nonetheless identical with the table. In short, we are committed to admitting that discernibles are identical.

Now it is at this point that Skorupski enters the fray. The main theme of his critique is that, by making a few reasonably simple logical distinctions and by avoiding one or two fairly elementary fallacies, we can show that all this is a lot of fuss about nothing. More specifically, we can show that the fuss is the result (a) of failure to distinguish between meaning and reference, with consequent failure to distinguish between non-contingent and contingent identity; and (b) of fallacious arguments from the properties of parts to the properties of wholes and vice versa.[13]

Before criticizing Skorupski's assertion that theoretical identity is a straight-forward form of contingent identity, let me make a brief summary of the argument leading up to it.

First of all, the logical ignorami, who fail to distinguish between meaning and reference, naturally take as their paradigmatic identity-statement one of the non-contingent kind in which both meanings and references actually happen to be identical – e.g. 'All bachelors are unmarried men'. Since 'bachelors' and 'unmarried men' are identical in meaning as well as in reference, the denial of this statement results in a contradiction.

With this paradigm in mind, our ignorami turn their attention to statements like 'all tables are systems of molecules'. They note that 'table' differs in meaning from 'system of molecules'. They note, too, that 'this is a table' and 'this is a system of molecules' are independently verifiable statements. Quite correctly, they infer from these observations, first, that 'all tables are not systems of molecules' is not a contradiction, and second, that 'all tables are not systems of molecules' is a potentially verifiable statement. Confusing meaning and reference as they do, however, our ignorami go on to draw the conclusion that tables and systems of molecules *cannot* be identical. And this conclusion is totally unwarranted.

Once our eyes have been opened, and we have learned to distinguish between meaning and reference, it becomes easy to conceive of contingent identities: i.e. identities in which meanings differ but references coincide. Examples are legion. The following few, however, will serve as adequate illustrations: 'Scott is the author of *Waverley*'; 'the man driving the Mercedes is the man who won the pools last week'; 'the Morning Star is the Evening Star'; and (Skorupski's own example) 'the Presidential is the hotel where you can get a room for the night for less than the price of a pizza'.

If we approach any of these statements without the requisite distinction between meaning and reference, we are liable to end up tearing our hair over apparent assertion of the discernibility of identicals. Once we approach them with this distinction in mind, however, we no longer find them in any way puzzling. The same thing applies to statements like 'all volumes of water are systems of molecules' and 'all lightning flashes are streams of electrons'.

As Skorupski points out, statements of non-contingent identity are in fact uttered very rarely in everyday discourse. Since they merely assert what everyone knows already, they are just not very useful. On the other hand, statements of contingent identity are extremely common. The terms involved in them, not being synonymous, leave open the question of the identity of their referents. Hence such statements convey information which is not *prima facie* obvious, and can often be very useful. This point, too, helps to clear up perplexities about theoretical identity. Thus the logical ignorami feel that, once one has admitted that a statement like 'all tables are systems of molecules' is a straightforward identity, one has reduced its status to that of an empty tautology and has thereby annulled its explanatory force. On the other hand, those who have grasped the possibility of contingent identity are thereby enabled to see how such a statement can be at once a straightforward identity, and at the same time a vehicle of valuable insight.

All in all, Skorupski has made out a good case for thinking that confusion of meaning and reference has been at the root of much of the widespread puzzlement over theoretical identities. (When our discussions on this topic started it was certainly one reason for my own puzzlement, and I am grateful to him for eliminating it!) Nonetheless, I think we should not give up our puzzlement too readily; for there may be other, more solidly-based reasons for it. In particular, I think we must beware of being lulled into non-puzzlement by the apparently straightforward nature of so many of the contingent identity-statements that crop up during the course of everyday conversation. For although 'all tables are systems of molecules' is also a contingent identity-statement, it may well prove to pose problems very different from any we encounter in its more common-or-garden kin. In this context, I think it is relevant to look more closely at two examples on our list: 'the man driving the Mercedes is the man who won the pools last week', and 'the Morning Star is the Evening Star'. The first of these is a simple case of two complementary descriptions of the same entity. Here, there is no question of the compatibility of the descriptions involved, whereas (as the passage I quoted from Ayer makes very clear) compatibility of descriptions is a central question where theoretical identities are concerned. The second example is a little more complicated. 'The Morning Star is the Evening Star' is an ellipsis for 'the Morning Star and the Evening Star are the morning and evening appearances of the planet Venus'. The elliptical nature of this example gives rise to various interesting possibilities: amongst them, the possibility of apparently incompatible descriptions. Thus one can say: 'the Morning Star is the Evening Star, yet the Morning Star is orange and the Evening Star is not orange'. Such a statement is perfectly puzzle-free, since all one is saying is that Venus undergoes regular colour changes, such that it is orange every morning and not orange every evening. However, if a similar statement were to arise in connection with the tables and systems of molecules, it would by no means be puzzle-free. For whilst 'Morning Star' and 'Evening Star' refer to different time-slices of the same persisting entity, 'table' and 'system of molecules', whatever else they do or do not refer to, quite clearly refer to a single space-time region.

The results of our scrutiny are instructive. First, they suggest that some familiar contingent identities are free from certain puzzles which bedevil theoretical identity. Second, since they show that even between the more familiar contingent identities there can be significant differences of logical structure, they suggest that theoretical identity, though a member of the larger class of contingent identities, may yet turn out to have a logic all its own.

Let us now proceed to assess theoretical identity in the light of the Principle of the Indiscernibility of Identicals; and let us take as our paradigmatic example the statement: 'a volume of chlorine gas is a system of Cl_2 molecules'.[14]

Now the volume of chlorine gas has certain characteristic properties: e.g. temperature, colour and smell. The system of molecules, too, has certain characteristic properties: e.g. mean kinetic energy, tendency to absorb radiation of some wavelengths and to scatter radiation of others, tendency to emit molecules which trigger particular reactions in the human olfactory receptors. Both are thought of as occupying the same region of space-time, and as occupying the same position in a wider cause-effect nexus.[15] It is in virtue of these last two, indisputably shared properties that (a) the volume of chlorine gas is identified with the system of molecules, and (b) each property of the volume of gas is correlated with a property of the system of molecules which stands in an explanatory relationship to it. Thus temperature is correlated with mean kinetic energy of molecules, colour with absorption/scattering tendencies *vis-à-vis* radiation, and so on.

Let x be the volume of chlorine gas and A, B, C its temperature, colour and smell. Let y be the system of molecules and D, E, F the corresponding explanatory properties. Finally, let G and H be the indisputably shared properties: occupancy of a given space-time region and occupancy of a given position in the wider cause-effect nexus. Then we can say that, if x is identical with y, the entire set of properties A, B, C, D, E, F, G, H, must be attributable both to x and to y. In other words, if the volume of gas is really identical with the system of molecules, we must be able to assert of either that, in addition to the obviously shared properties, it has a certain temperature, a certain colour, a certain smell, a certain mean molecular kinetic energy, a certain absorption/scattering tendency *vis-à-vis* radiation, and a certain tendency to emit free molecules which trigger off particular reactions in the human olfactory receptors.

In some ways, this assertion seems innocuous; yet in other ways it is disturbing. One reason why it disturbs us is that it leaves us wondering whether we have really done any more than substitute, for two different entities in a puzzling relationship to one another, a single entity with two different clusters of properties in a puzzling relationship to one another. For the volume of chlorine and the system of molecules, have we done more than substitute a single entity which nonetheless has both 'gaseous' and 'molecular-systemic' properties?[16]

Now one way of banishing this source of disquiet would be to establish that each 'gaseous' property was identical with the 'molecular-systemic' property which stood in an explanatory relationship to it. How do we set about doing this? The obvious answer would seem to be that we once again assess each alleged identity in the light of the Principle of Indiscernibility of Identicals. Here, however, we are getting into deep and tricky waters. In the first place, the assessment would seem to require the notion of 'properties of properties' or 'second-order properties'; and it seems doubtful whether we can attach any clear meaning to such a notion. Secondly, if, having overcome this obstacle, we find ourselves ready to make the assessment, we are still not much further forward. For even if it produces a positive verdict, the latter may well do no more than postpone our disquiet. Thus, for two properties in a puzzling relationship to one another, we may find that we have merely substituted a single property which has two different clusters of second-order properties standing in a puzzling relation to one another. And here, quite clearly, we have the beginning of an infinite regress.[17]

Perhaps, however, this is not the only move open to us. Perhaps we can say instead that the Principle of Indiscernibility of Identicals is applicable to entities rather than to their properties, and that, once two entities have passed the test of assessment in the light of it, any two properties, one of which stands in an explanatory relationship to the other, can also be regarded as identical. If this is accepted, then the temperature of our chlorine gas can be regarded, without further ado, as identical with the mean kinetic energy of the system of molecules; and so on. This seems to be the essence of Skorupski's position.[18]

With this move, we have avoided infinite regress and obvious circularity. By means of a fiat which falls just short of a fiddle, we seem to have freed ourselves from perplexity. Alas, however, there is a further difficulty which we have not yet considered. It is that, in every theoretical identity, there are some properties which it seems appropriate to ascribe to the explanandum but inappropriate to ascribe to the explanans. Thus it seems appropriate to ascribe temperature, colour and smell to a volume of chlorine, but inappropriate to ascribe such properties to the system of molecules with which it is identified. If there is any sound basis for these feelings of appropriateness and inappropriateness, then theoretical identities must fail to meet the requirements of Indiscernibility of Identicals. Skorupski seems to think that here we are simply dealing with eradicable linguistic fads. I, on the other hand, am convinced that there are fundamental issues at stake.

More specifically, I think our feelings of appropriateness and inappropriateness derive from a fundamental axiom of scientific thought which I shall take the liberty of christening 'Democritus' Principle'. I give it this name because Democritus seems to have been one of the first thinkers to draw attention to its importance, and because it has been a guiding principle of scientific explanation ever since. To refresh the reader's memory, let me re-quote Heisenberg's succinct statement of the Principle:

Democritus' atomic theory ... realizes that it is impossible to explain rationally the perceptible qualities of matter except by tracing these back to the behaviour of entities who themselves no longer possess these qualities. If atoms are really to explain the origin of colour and smell of visible material bodies, then they cannot possess properties like colour and smell.[19]

The implications of Democritus' Principle for theoretical identity seem all too clear. Let us assume that what is to be explained is the fact that a certain entity x has properties A, B, C. Then if y is an entity specifically invoked to explain x's possession of the properties in question it cannot itself have these properties. But if x is y (and the assumption that it is forms an integral part of the process of explanation), it *must* have them. Hence theoretical identity appears to require both the assumption that x is not y and the assumption that x is y.[20]

One way of trying to avoid this horrific paradox would be to say that, although a given set of properties can only be explained in terms of other kinds of properties, the entities that possess these other kinds of properties do also possess the properties to be explained. To take a specific example, one might try to say that, although the temperature of a volume of chlorine gas can only be explained in terms of a property of the system of Cl_2 molecules other than temperature, the system nonetheless does have a temperature. However, anyone who has the wit to side-step Democritus in this way inevitably finds himself confronted by the principle of economy, equally fundamental to scientific explanation, whereby one is forbidden to attribute to a theoretical entity or system of such entities any property which has no relevance to the explanatory task. Hence, if temperature is explanatorily irrelevant, it cannot be attributed to a system of molecules; and our paradox remains unresolved.

It is at this point in the debate that Skorupski unleashes his second line of attack, with the claim that any residual puzzlement over theoretical identity is the result of fallacious arguments from properties of parts to properties of wholes and vice versa.

Skorupski claims that, even if it is true to say of individual atoms and molecules that they cannot have the properties they are invoked to explain, it does not follow that the systems composed of such entities cannot have these properties. Because individual atoms and molecules lack temperature, colour and smell, it does not follow that systems of atoms and systems of molecules must lack them.

Now I agree that Skorupski makes a valid point when he claims that many properties, which are not appropriately attributed to individual entities, are nonetheless attributable to the wholes composed of such entities. But I do not agree that this point is relevant to the problem posed by theoretical identities.

The mistake lies in failing to see that Democritus' Principle is concerned, not with the relationship of part to whole, but solely with the relationship of explanans (be it part or whole) to explanandum. In this context, it is significant that each of us has quoted Heisenberg's formulation of the Principle – Skorupski in support of his point of view and I in support of mine. For although Heisenberg's formulation is vivid, it is misleading on just this issue. By its reference to individual atoms, it lumps the relationship of part to whole with the relationship of explanans to explanandum. In so doing, it obscures the fact that the two relationships seldom coincide.

It is perfectly true that individual atoms and molecules (parts) lack many of the most important properties of systems of atoms and molecules (wholes). Thus the individual atom of silicon or oxygen cannot be described as a three-dimensional space lattice; but a system of silicon and oxygen atoms can be and is so described. Again, an individual chlorine molecule cannot be described as having a mean kinetic energy; but a system of chlorine molecules can be and is so described. All this, however, has very little bearing on the central problem of theoretical identity. For, so far as I can see, the explanans in a great many explanations in physics and chemistry is not an individual atom or molecule, but a system of atoms or a system of molecules. Thus the hardness of a quartz crystal is explained in terms of the pattern of bonds involved in the three-dimensional lattice of silicon and oxygen atoms with which it is identified. Again, the difference in colour between a piece of graphite and a piece of diamond is explained in terms of the different arrangements in the systems of carbon atoms with which they are respectively identified. Yet again, to take Skorupski's own example, the temperature of a volume of gas is explained in terms of the mean kinetic energy of all the molecules in the system with which it is identified. In each of these cases, the properties of an observable whole are explained in terms of the properties of a theoretical whole with which it is identified.

Hence, true as it is that there are many properties, ascribable to wholes, that cannot be ascribed to the parts of which they are composed, this fact in no way helps us to resolve our paradox. For in so far as theoretical identities involve identification of chairs, tables, quartz crystals, pieces of diamond, volumes of water, volumes of chlorine, etc. with *systems* of atoms or molecules, and in so far as explanation of many of the properties of these directly observable objects is in terms of the properties of the *systems*, then, if we follow Democritus and Occam, these *systems* cannot have the properties they are being invoked to explain.

Against this position, Skorupski launches a final attack. It depends heavily on the parallel between, on the one hand, individual atoms, systems of atoms and material objects, and, on the other hand, individual people, sets of interacting people and social groups. The essence of the argument is that, if we extend to the latter case the reasoning put forward in connexion with the former, we reach absurd conclusions.

In detail, the argument runs as follows. Systems of atoms have certain properties (e.g. lattice structure) which cannot be ascribed to their individual constituents; and in the same way, sets of interacting people have certain properties (e.g. cohesiveness) which cannot be ascribed to individual people. Again, it is very often the properties of *systems* of atoms rather than of individual atoms that are invoked to explain the properties of material objects; and in the same way, it is very often the properties of *sets* of interacting people rather than of individual people that are invoked to explain the properties of social groups. Now on my premises, use of the properties of systems of atoms to explain the properties of material objects debars us from making a straightforward identification between the one and the other. Further, if my premisses are extended to cover the social sphere, use of the properties of sets of interacting people to explain the properties of social groups must similarly debar us from identifying the former with the latter. But to say that a set of interacting individuals is not straightforwardly identifiable with a social group is absurd. Hence there must be something wrong with my premisses.

To the foregoing I would reply that, although the conclusion is indeed absurd, the fault lies not with my premisses but with Skorupski's parallel. For whilst I accept that the relation between an individual atom and a system of atoms is comparable to the relation between an individual person and a set of interacting people, I do not accept that the relation between, say, a system of atoms and a quartz crystal is comparable to the relation between a set of interacting people and a social group.

Let us consider the relevant identity-statements; 'a quartz crystal is a system of interacting atoms' and 'a social group is a system of interacting human individuals'. The differing logic of these two statements becomes apparent as soon as we consider their denials: 'a quartz crystal is not a system of interacting atoms' and 'a social group is not a system of interacting human individuals'. In the first case, 'this is a quartz crystal' and 'this is a system of interacting atoms' are independently verifiable statements; hence 'a quartz crystal is not a system of interacting atoms' is not only meaningful but potentially verifiable. In the second case, 'this is a social group' and 'this is a system of interacting human individuals' are identical in meaning; hence 'a social group is not a system of interacting human individuals' is a self-contradictory statement. In other words, whilst the first identity is contingent, the second is non-contingent.

Along with this difference goes another. Whereas the first identity-statement has an explanatory significance, the second has a purely definitional significance. Let me illustrate. Suppose we require an explanation of the fact that quartz crystals are amongst the hardest of all mineral substances. At some stage in his reply, the physical chemist will tell us: 'Well, the arrangements in this lattice are of a particularly stable kind.' Hearing something along these lines, we shall certainly feel we are getting what we asked for. Suppose now we require an explanation of the fact that a certain social group is stable and well-integrated. A sociologist may tell us: 'Well, this social group is a system of interacting individuals, and the majority of the interactions in the system are friendly and unaggressive'. Though this sort of thing has been known to pass for explanation in the sociological fraternity, those of us who are uninitiated will, on hearing this, be likely to reply: 'But you still haven't *explained* the stability and integration. You have simply told us that the situation in the system is such that it passes assessment in the light of those criteria which define stability and integration'.

This brief comparison shows up very clearly the invalidity of Skorupski's parallel. If the comparison points to any positive moral, it is that there is an inverse correlation between the straightforwardness of an identity-statement and its explanatory value. Although such a conclusion is not necessarily inconsistent with Skorupski's position, neither is it inconsistent with mine.

When all has been said and done, then, our paradox remains unresolved. The notion of theoretical identity carries with it the inescapable implication that x is both non-identical and identical with y.

So far in our discussion, both Skorupski and I have maintained a thoroughgoing realism with respect both to theoretical and to observable entities. Now can it be that this very realism is the root of all our troubles, and that if we dropped it we should escape from them? Instead of supposing that systems of Cl_2 molecules and volumes of chlorine gas are equally real, can we not suppose, either that systems of Cl_2 molecules are real and volumes of chlorine gas mere appearance, or that systems of Cl_2 molecules are merely useful fictions and volumes of chlorine gas the only realities? If either of these positions were to prove tenable, our paradox would automatically dissolve; for either x or y would vanish from the scene. Let us therefore have a closer look at them.

The first position, currently known as 'super-realism', has been popular with scientists since the time of the pre-Socratics.[21] They have been greatly attracted by the aura of almost mystical cognitive superiority with which it invests their role. 'Super-realist' propaganda has frequently struck fear into the poets, who, with their heavy commitment to the world of directly observable phenomena, seem to be genuinely afraid of the scientist's power to conjure this world away. (Goethe, Blake and Keats were all greatly troubled by Newtonian physics.) In recent years, 'super-realism' has been espoused by scientists and philosophers of science who have found the paradoxes of thoroughgoing realism hard to swallow, and who have seen it as a potential escape route. Prominent amongst such scholars have been the physicist Eddington (formulator of the 'two tables' paradox), and the American philosophers Feyerabend, Maxwell and Sellars.[22]

The immediate objection to 'super-realism' is of course the common-sense one that explanation means answering questions as to why things are as they are and not denying their reality. Closely allied to this is the objection that it confuses explaining things with explaining them away.

Behind this common-sense gut reaction there is in fact a serious philo-sophical objection – one which was made many years ago by Susan Stebbing in her all-too-often neglected critique of Eddington's ideas.[23] The objection is based on the fact that terms like 'real' and 'merely apparent' derive their meaning from the content of everyday discourse at the material-object level

– i.e. from the context of discourse about people, animals, plants, tables, buckets of water, and so on. If a certain sequence of sensory input inclines us to say 'this is a table', and if the expectations as to further input which we set up in ourselves in making this utterance are in fact fulfilled, we conclude: 'that is a real table'. On the other hand, if we have the same initial sequence of sensory input and make the same initial statement, but then find that our expectations are not fulfilled, we say: 'that was the mere appearance of a table'. Now it seems very doubtful if a pair of terms which derive their meaning from contrasting patterns of relationship between expectations and results at a particular ontological level can be used, without absurdity, to characterize the nexus between two different ontological levels. Indeed, if the contrast between 'reality' and 'appearance' is applied at all in this unaccustomed context, it can be little more than a somewhat obscurantist restatement of the puzzling relation which it was invoked to elucidate. 'Super-realism', then, offers us no escape from the paradoxes of thoroughgoing realism.

Let us turn, then, to the second position, which formerly went under the label 'positivism', but which nowadays is more usually referred to as 'instrumentalism'. This position first became popular in the nineteenth century, but has attracted numerous scientists and philosophers of science right down to the present day. It is remarkable for the diversity of interest-groups to which it has appealed. Thus, on the one hand, it has always had a special appeal to those involved in the battle against religion; for, with its refusal to accord the status of reality to any entities other than those accessible to direct, naked-eye observation, it can be seen as allowing little room for spiritualistic explanations. On the other hand, it has had a strong appeal to those heirs of Cardinal Bellarmine who would defend religion from science by conceding to the latter only the very restricted intellectual function of 'saving the appearances'. In more recent years, it has also appealed to scholars in flight from the difficulties of thoroughgoing realism.[24]

The immediate common-sense reaction to 'instrumentalism' is that it debars us from asking or getting answers to the question 'why?' The second reaction is that, in so far as scientists do try to explain things, they try to do so in terms of entities *other* than the explananda.

A more serious philosophical objection is based on an extension of Stebbing's argument. Very briefly, the objection is as follows. In everyday life, it is patterns of relationship between expectation and result that form the basis of those criteria by means of which we decide whether to accept or reject statements about material objects, and whether to use 'real' or 'apparent' in connection with such objects. In the sciences, similar patterns of relationship form the basis of criteria for deciding whether to accept or reject theoretical objects. Hence it seems inconsistent to refuse to take them as the basis of criteria for use of the terms 'real' and 'apparent' in connection with such objects.

In dealing with the 'super-realists', Stebbing argued that they erred in using terms associated with a single ontological level to characterize relations between levels. In dealing with the 'instrumentalists', we can argue that, although these terms derive their primary meaning from their use in the context of the world of material objects, the patterns that govern this use are repeated at every level. Hence, though we should eschew the *inter-level* use of 'real' and 'apparent', we should be prepared to use these terms *at* every level. In short, a consistent extension of the use of the terms 'real' and 'apparent' forces us back to just that thoroughgoing realism from which we were attempting to escape!

There remains one position which seems, on the face of it, to offer a chance of slipping round this impasse. Evidence of its importance in the thinking of chemists and physicists is to be found in their frequent use of phrases like 'hidden mechanism', 'underlying process', and 'inner structure'. These are phrases which imply causal relationships – either between what is hidden and what is visible, or between what is underlying and what is overlying, or again between what is inside and what is outside. When pressed about this sort of talk, some scientists would probably say they were using metaphor. Others, however, would almost certainly admit that they did think of the relationship of the events described in theoretical language to those described in observational language as one of cause to effect.

In a later section of this paper, I shall suggest that such causal terminology may well have played a crucial role in the historical genesis of theoretical language. However, more of this later on. For the moment, let us content ourselves with enquiring how far it makes sense to say that the relation between a system of Cl_2 molecules and a volume of chlorine gas is a causal one.

Though at first sight such a formulation avoids some of the difficulties implicit in the other three positions, it raises quite as many difficulties of its own. In the first place, though causality is commonly held to require the spatio-temporal contiguity of the events involved, it is not held to require their spatio-temporal identity. Indeed, such spatio-temporal identity, though crucial to the relation between explanans and explanandum, actually rules out a causal relationship. Secondly, if the relationship between explanans and explanandum were causal, one would be able to ask the question 'why?' in connexion with all the pairs of variables related by correspondence-rule statements. Thus one would be able to ask 'why does the temperature of a volume of chlorine gas vary with the mean kinetic energy of the system of Cl_2 molecules?' But in this context, the question would be nonsensical. Indeed, the only proper answer to it would be 'but variation in the temperature of the volume of chlorine is not the effect of variation in the mean kinetic energy of the Cl_2 molecules; it *is* the variation in their mean kinetic energy'. In short, the causal formulation seems to lead us into as much trouble as any of the others.

Between them, the four positions I have outlined would seem to exhaust our present resources for characterization of the relationship between explanans and explanandum. Yet, although each of these four seems to have some prima facie plausibility in relation to the explanatory enterprise, each turns out, on closer inspection, to be fraught with paradox. Perhaps it is an intuitive realization of this which leads many intelligent scientists, in characterizing the explanatory relationship, to oscillate between the notions of identity, appearance/reality, and causality.

But why should we keep coming up against paradox in this area? I suggest that it is because, as things stand at present, it is only by means of ideas whose normal, primary use is *at* the material-object level that we can attempt to characterize the relationship *between* this level and others that are ontologically 'higher' in the sense that they provide explanations of its events and processes. This extension of use from the intra-level to the inter-level context may well be at the root of most of the troubles I have enumerated in this section.

Spectacular as are the problems they pose, statements about inter-level relations are by no means the only locus of paradox in scientific discourse. Statements about events *at* the theoretical level also furnish many examples of paradox.

This is particularly apparent in the case of statements associated with now-discredited theoretical entities such as phlogiston and ether. Phlogiston, for example, ended its career with an inventory of mutually inconsistent attributes so astonishing that Lavoisier was moved to say of it:

Chemists have made a vague principle of phlogiston which is not strictly defined, and which in consequence accommodates itself to every explanation into which it is pressed. Sometimes this principle is heavy and sometimes it is not; sometimes it is free fire, and sometimes it is fire combined with the earthy element; sometimes it passes through the pores of vessels and sometimes they are impenetrable to it. It explains at once causticity and non-causticity, transparency and opacity, colours and absence of colours. It is a veritable Proteus which changes its form every minute.[25]

The ether, too, ended its career with a similar inventory, in which solidity was combined with low density and extreme elasticity – a combination showing almost as high a degree of inconsistency as that associated with phlogiston.[26]

There is a temptation to dismiss theoretical concepts of this sort on the ground that they are the product of a pre-modern phase of scientific endeavour, and are therefore irrelevant to the characterization of modern science. Such a temptation should be resisted. In the first place, it is doubtful whether the spirit of enquiry which moved the creators of these concepts was radically different from that which moves their present-day successors. Secondly, a number of thoroughly modern theoretical concepts are as deeply imbued with paradox as are the earlier concepts we have just dealt with. Good examples of such concepts are provided by the notions of quantum jumps, waves-in-nothing, and particles that are also wave-packets.

The notion of quantum jumps was built into the Rutherford–Bohr atomic schema in order to explain the discontinuous character of the emission spectra of the various chemical elements. Very briefly, it asserted that electrons moved around the nucleus in a limited number of 'permitted' orbits. When an electron absorbed a quantum of energy, it jumped from a smaller to a larger orbit; and when it emitted a quantum, it jumped in the opposite direction. Now in order to account for spectral discontinuity, it was necessary to postulate that the jumps were instantaneous; that each electron moved from one orbit to another without ever occupying a position intermediate between the two. Such a notion was, of course, highly paradoxical: for, by definition, a single particle moving from point A to point B *must* traverse all points in between. Yet physicists, though they were aware of the paradox, continued to use the notion of quantum jumps until it was replaced by another notion of greater explanatory fertility.[27]

This later notion was that of 'packets' of waves. The postulate of instantaneous re-arrangements of wave-pattern was free from the particular paradox presented by quantum leaps; and it provided a basis for explaining spectral discontinuities and many other phenomena besides. At the same time, the whole wave idea introduced a fresh paradox. For waves, by definition, are waves *of* something or waves *in* something. But in the case of the matter-wave concept, physicists were asked to believe in waves that were neither waves of something nor waves in any specifiable medium. A pure-wave theory of matter, still carrying this paradox with it, has survived down to the present day in some not disreputable quarters.[28]

Thirdly, let us consider the problem posed by 'wavicles' in modern physical thought. Though it looked at one time as if the pure-wave theorists might seize the initiative from the particle theorists in the field of atomic physics, the latter have in fact continued to dominate the field. Contemporary particle theory, however, has come a long way from Rutherford's original planetary atom. Not only have there been numerous amendments to the basic planetary schema: e.g. postulation of electrical in addition to gravitational forces between particles in the system; postulation of reversible changes of orbit; postulation of a multiplicity of nuclear 'suns'. Successive challenges to the explanatory capacity of the schema have led its protagonists to build in to their characterization of the elementary particles of the system a series of attributes which seem incompatible with a rigorously minimum definition of the concept of a particle. Some of the more new-fangled quasi-and-pseudoparticles, for instance, have such decidedly non-particulate negative attributes as lack of mass, lack of sharp localization, and lack of independent existence. All of them are now supposed to partake of the nature, not only of particles, but also of 'wave packets'. This involves further inconsistencies. Thus a particle, by definition, occupies a limited region of space at a given time; occupies this region to the exclusion of other particles; collides with and rebounds from other particles. A wave disturbance, on the other hand, occupies the whole of space; does not occupy it to the exclusion of other wave disturbances; does not collide with and rebound from other wave disturbances. These elements of paradox notwithstanding, physicists seem determined to hang on to the 'wavicle' concept until something of greater explanatory power turns up.[29]

Further developments of 'wavicle' theory seem likely to bring even worse surprises for the logically fastidious. Thus some physicists feel that the data derived from recent cloud-chamber experiments can only be accounted for by assuming that certain types of elementary particle can travel backwards in time. Now not only is there more than a suggestion of self-contradictoriness about the very notion of 'travelling backwards in time', there is also the objection that, once one introduces the possibility of temporary time-reversals in connection with the path of a particle, one introduces with it another possibility which involves the most flagrant self-contradiction – the possibility that the *same* particle can be in two *different* places at the *same* time![30]

This continuing strand of paradox at the heart of modern physical and chemical theory may well irritate the philosophers; but for historians and sociologists of ideas, it need not be particularly mysterious. Indeed, a little familiarity with the ways in which analogical models are used in the creation and elaboration of scientific theory makes it readily intelligible.

I have discussed the whole question of models at some length in the papers to which Skorupski refers; and there is, of course, a mountain of more specialized literature in the philosophy-of-science journals. Suffice it to say here that the typical theoretical schema is built up on the basis of an analogy, drawn at the material-object level, between a puzzling field of experience and some better-explored field. A pattern of events similar to that characteristic of the better-explored field is assumed to underpin the phenomena of the puzzling field, and statements about this pattern provide the basis for subsequent explanation. In the course of its extension to further fields of experience, the resulting theoretical schema receives a series of challenges to its explanatory adequacy. In order to meet these challenges, its protagonists elaborate it in two ways, which have been christened 'deployment' and 'development'.[31] In deployment, they build in further features associated with the field of experience which formed the basis of the original analogy. Thus they elaborate the planetary model of the atom by adding the concept of electronic spin to that of electronic orbit. In development, by contrast, they add further features which have little or no connection with the original analogy. Sometimes, development involves piecemeal, *ad hoc* responses to particular explanatory challenges. Instances of these are the addition of extra 'suns' to the atomic nucleus to account for the existence of isotopes of the various chemical elements, and the postulation of instantaneous jumps between electronic orbits to account for spectral discontinuities. In other cases, development involves the building in to the original schema of a whole series of features inspired by the drawing of a fresh analogy. The best example of this is provided by modern quantum physics, in which protagonists of the particulate model of matter have found themselves compelled to build into this model a whole series of wave-like attributes.

It is, I think, fair to say that, the longer the life of a theoretical model, the more explanatory challenges it has to face, and the greater the amount of both deployment and development it undergoes by way of response. Now deployment, controlled as it is by the original analogy, does not give rise to paradoxical combinations of attributes. But development, not being so controlled, is a fertile source of such combinations. Hence we can say that the longer the life of a model, the greater the likelihood of its becoming associated with paradox. Scientists, of course, do feel considerable discomfort when the model they operate with enters into the paradox-ridden phase of its existence. However, so long as they feel that the original analogy has not lost its fertility, and that further deployment of attributes associated with this analogy is fruitful, they tend to stick to their guns. So although they do not cultivate paradox, they frequently learn to live with it.[32]

From what has been said so far, it will be clear that paradox is a characteristic feature, both of statements about relations between directly observable entities and their theoretical counterparts, and of statements which refer to theoretical entities alone. It will also be clear that, in statements of both kinds, the occurrence of paradox is clearly related to what may be called a 'stretched' use of concepts whose primary meaning derives from the content of discourse about directly observable material objects.

Modern expositions of the nature of scientific thinking tend to lay a great deal of stress on its esoteric character, and to emphasize the dangers of trying to understand it in terms of common-sense attitudes and patterns of thought. Up to a point, such expositions are salutary. Thus, to take one example, the warnings of N. R. Hanson against the demand that theoretical entities be picturable were responses to a misunderstanding that is genuinely widespread amongst members of the intelligent lay public.[33] At the same time, there is a danger that they may obscure the extent to which the scientist is still both guided and limited by conceptual patterns primarily associated with the world of material objects. If it does nothing else, what has been said here certainly does something to restore the balance.

From all this, the scientist emerges as more *bricoleur* than *ingenieur*.[34] Whether this is a transient status, or one to which he is condemned in perpetuity, I do not think we are yet in a position to say. Meanwhile, just as the materials of the *bricoleur*, having been designed primarily for other purposes, tend to crack under the strain when used for some quite different end, so too the material-object concepts of the scientist tend to crack when pushed too far in the building of theory. Paradox is the principal symptom of this tendency.

Paradox and explanation in African religions

In dealing with African religious thought, Skorupski uses a rather small number of examples. Much of his exposition, indeed, draws exclusively from the classic monographs on Nuer and Dinka religions.[35] At first glance, this looks like laziness or sheer perversity. In fact, however, his selectivity is scarcely avoidable; for, as things stand at present, these two monographs are virtually the only works on African religious life in which data relevant to the questions raised in the present debate are available for our consideration. In this section, therefore, I shall follow him in confining discussion to the Nuer and Dinka material.

Skorupski talks of three main 'areas of obscurity' in Nuer and Dinka religious discourse. He gives these areas the labels 'unity-in-multiplicity', 'multi-presence', and 'manifestations and materializations'.[36] Under the first heading comes the puzzle posed by a multiplicity of lesser spirits who in some sense *are* a single supreme being. Under the second comes the puzzle posed by spirits that are thought of, either as existing beyond the confines of space and time, or as being in many different places at the same time, or as being *both* omnipresent *and* present at particular places. Under the third heading come three puzzles. One is posed by the notion of an event or entity that *is* God, even though God *is not* that event or entity. Another is posed by the notion that although two entities may be identified with God, they are not identifiable with each other. Yet another is posed by the notion of God as at once a being who is clearly distinct from observable events or entities, and at the same time a being with whom such events or entities are to be identified.

For purposes of demonstrating the comparability of 'areas of obscurity' in African religious discourse with 'areas of obscurity' in scientific discourse, I shall re-classify the five puzzles just enumerated into two kinds: first, puzzles which arise out of attempts to characterize the relationships between different levels of being; second, puzzles which arise out of attempts to characterize the entities, events and processes which belong to levels of being higher than that associated with material-object discourse.

Under the first heading, I shall place the puzzles associated with the asymmetrical identification of observable phenomena and of lesser spirits with the supreme being, with the non-identifiability of different phenomena all of which are nonetheless identifiable with the supreme being, with assertions that the many lesser spirits are one supreme being, and with assertions that the supreme being is at once an entity with which observable phenomena and lesser spirits are to be identified, and at the same time an entity which is quite distinct from these things. Under the second heading, I shall place the puzzle associated with the curious spatial attributes of spiritual beings.

By now, I hope, something will have 'clicked' in the minds of my more attentive readers. Skorupski's exposition may well have left them convinced that the paradoxes of African religious discourse are worlds apart from anything to be found in the sciences. My re-classification should, in itself, do much to recall attention to underlying similarities. However, for the benefit of those who remain unconverted, let us look a little more closely, first at the 'inter-level' puzzles, then at the 'intra-level' puzzles.

Let us start with the asymmetry and intransitivity which, as Skorupski has noted, are such prominent features of 'inter-level' identities in both Nuer and Dinka religious discourse. For Nuer, rain *is* Spirit, but Spirit *is not* rain. Thunder *is* Spirit, but Spirit *is not* thunder. And, though both rain and thunder *are* Spirit, rain is not thunder nor thunder rain. For Dinka, Macardit *is* Divinity, but Divinity *is not* Macardit. Garang *is* Divinity, but Divinity *is not* Garang. Again, though both Macardit and Garang *are* Divinity, Macardit is not Garang nor Garang Macardit.[37]

To grasp the point of such statements, we must start by noting that Spirit and Divinity stand in an explanatory relationship to the phenomena and entities which are asymmetrically identified with them. Why does rain fall under certain circumstances but not under others? Rain is Spirit. Why does Macardit afflict some people but not others? Macardit is Divinity. Once we have seen this, the direction which our interpretation should take becomes clear. What we are confronted with is a series of explanation-sketches; elliptical statements which emphasize the unity underlying the diversity of the phenomena and entities to be explained, but which omit to mention particular states of this unity. Fully spelled out, such statements would go as follows: 'Rain is Spirit-state A', 'Thunder is Spirit-state B'; 'Macardit is Divinity-state A', 'Garang is Divinity-state B'. If this analysis is correct, we can argue, from the same premises as we used in connection with explanation-sketches in the sciences, that these spelled-out versions must be reversible. That is, if it is true that rain is Spirit-state A, then it must be true that Spirit-state A is rain. And so on. Once the ellipsis is spelled out, then, the asymmetry is exposed as being more apparent than real. At this point, it also becomes clear why our puzzling identity-statements are intransitive. For if rain and thunder are different Spirit-states, they obviously cannot be identified with one another. And if Macardit and Garang are different Divinity-states, the same considerations apply to them.

The analysis given above is equally applicable to the problem of 'the many and the one' – the problem that is, of the many lesser spirits which *are* a single supreme being.[38] Once again, we have a puzzle arising out of the fact that the statements involved are explanation-sketches; ellipses which refer to an underlying unity but not to the diversity of its states. If such ellipses were spelled out, there would be a state of the supreme being corresponding to each lesser spirit; and the problem of the many and the one would simply dissolve.

At this point, the reader may well object that the Nuer and the Dinka are not in fact capable of expanding their alleged explanation-sketches. Thus they cannot tell us anything about the differentiae between Spirit-state A and Spirit-state B, or between Divinity-state A and Divinity-state B. Hence the interpretation offered here must be regarded as dubious, to say the least.

To this objection, I would reply by recalling a typical explanation-sketch in the sciences: that offered by Heisenberg in his suggestion that electrons, protons and neutrons *are* energy. Like Nuer and Dinka statements about lesser spirits and the supreme being, it involves asymmetrical, intransitive identities. Again like such statements, it involves the assertion that what is many is also one. Finally, although it is indisputably an explanation-sketch, neither its author nor anyone else is currently capable of expanding it into a complete explanation. What I suggest is that the Nuer and Dinka statements we have been considering acquire their meaning in just the same way as Heisenberg's statement acquires its own: that is, through intuitively perceived kinship with numerous other explanation-sketches which *do* permit of expansion.

Let us now turn to the last of our 'inter-level' puzzles: the one posed by the fact that, although observable phenomena are thought of as quite distinct in their attributes from the supreme being which created and sustains them, they are also identified with this being. Thus rain has attributes such as wetness and heaviness which Spirit lacks; and Spirit has attributes such as personality which rain lacks; yet rain *is* Spirit.[39] Here, clearly, is an assertion of the discernibility of identicals.

Like the puzzles we have already dealt with, this one is also a by-product of the quest for explanation. Unlike them, however, it refuses to disappear when we have placed it in its explanatory context. In this case, as with that of theoretical identities in the sciences, we seem to be confronted with an irreducible element of obscurity at the very heart of the explanatory enterprise. Thus on the one hand, for an explanation to be a satisfying one, the explanans must be seen as something other than the explanandum. Yet on the other hand, application of what is known about the behaviour of the explanans to the explanation and prediction of observable phenomena would seem to require identification of the latter with the former. In other words, the puzzles associated with 'rain is Spirit' are particular examples of the puzzles associated with explanatory statements generally.

In his exposition of *Nuer Religion*, Skorupski points out that Evans-Pritchard mentions how Nuer, when pressed to comment on statements of the kind exemplified by 'rain is Spirit', tend to say things like 'rain is sent by Spirit'.[40] But neither Skorupski nor Ernest Gellner, another shrewd commentator on *Nuer Religion*, are entirely happy with the weight which Evans-Pritchard puts on this exegesis.[41] In the first place, the exegetes do not seem to be very forthcoming about *how* Spirit sends rain. In the second place, their statements implying identity are very firm and unambiguous. In the third place, such statements are supplemented by others, which, if they do not unambiguously imply identity, certainly imply a relation very different from that of 'sender' to 'sent'. Here, I am reminded in particular of the following passages quoted by Skorupski: 'In storms they pray to God to come to earth gently and not in fury – to come gently, it will be noted, not make the rain come gently'[42] and 'Nuer sometimes speak of him (God) as falling in the rain and of being in the lightning and thunder'.[43]

To me, the most plausible interpretation of all this is one which accepts that Nuer in fact oscillate between several different ways of characterizing the relationship between explanans and explanandum. Each particular way involves a concept, associated primarily with material-object discourse, which is not entirely adequate to its secondary usage. The nearest anyone can get to overcoming this (in fact insuperable) inadequacy is to use each concept in alternation with several others. Here again, of course, Nuer are behaving rather like their scientist counterparts.

So much for 'inter-level' puzzles. Now for the 'intra-level' puzzles: those which arise out of attempts to characterize the spiritual beings themselves.

In both Nuer and Dinka religious discourse, the most dramatic puzzles of this kind are connected with questions of space and time. Both Nuer and Dinka make statements and perform actions which have some intriguing implications with regard to the spatial location of spiritual beings. Many of their statements and actions, as Lienhardt remarks, lead one to conclude that they do not think of their spiritual beings as having spatial location or extension.[44] Many other statements or actions, whilst not forcing such an extreme conclusion, nevertheless lead one to accept that they think of spirits as beings that can be present in a great many different places at any given time.[45] And finally, alongside these notions implying omnipresence or multipresence, there are, in certain special contexts, notions which seem to imply the unambiguous presence of a spirit in one particular place at one particular time.[46]

I do not want to be drawn more than a little way into a discussion of how far notions of non-extended omnipresent or multipresent personal beings are paradoxical in the sense of concealing internal contradictions. These are matters for lengthy debate between professional philosophers possessing technical equipment that I lack. The following few remarks will have to suffice. Let me start with the notion of a non-extended personal being. Here, I suggest that the statement 'there is an X' automatically licenses the question 'where?'. Hence a notion of existence which rules out this question may possibly be self-contradictory. Next, let me deal with the notion of an omni- or multi-present personal being. Here, the situation seems clearer; for such a notion implies that the *same* entity is in *different* places at the *same* time, and therefore contravenes the principle of Indiscernibility of Identicals. Finally, there is the case where spiritual beings are thought of as *both* multipresent, *and* present in particular places at particular times. Here, the paradox is flagrant.

Now what reason can we find for this plethora of puzzling if not downright paradoxical notions relating to the spatial extension of spiritual beings? I think Skorupski himself gives us the essence of the answer when he suggests that 'God is everywhere' has the sense that God can act everywhere at the same time.[47] Nuer and Dinka ideas about the supreme being and the spirits are, as the authors themselves point out, developed primarily in the context of explanation of events in the world of directly observable phenomena.[48] In this context they serve, amongst other things, to link a great array of events to causal antecedents which would not be evident to the unaided eye of common sense. Now in order to function in this way, they must be conceived of as present both wherever the events they are invoked to account for take place, and wherever the causal antecedents of these events take place. If such events occur at many places simultaneously, then it follows that the supreme being and the spirits must be thought of, either as having a mode of existence which transcends the limitations of space and time, or as being omni- or multi-present.

The same general line of thought can be extended to cover those concurrent statements which seem to imply that God and the spirits have particular spatial locations. Let us take, for example, the idea that God 'is in the sky' – an idea propounded in all seriousness by Nuer and Dinka alongside assertions implying omni- or multi-presence.[49] The idea is quite clearly connected with the fact that the most impressive and significant natural phenomena known to these peoples – i.e. rain, thunder and lightning – either come from the sky or take place in it. Again, let us take those ideas of definite and restricted spatial location associated with spirit possession and with the appearance of spirits to men in visions and dreams.[50] Here it seems likely that people feel constrained to talk of a spiritual being having a definite location (with the implication that it has, at that time, no other location) by the very nature of the phenomena which confront them. In these phenomena, people are faced with entities very closely comparable to human beings. Hence, in so far as they interpret them in spiritual terms, it is tempting for them to say that here, at least temporarily, the spirits are present in much the same way as human beings might be.

The paradoxes of spiritual location in Nuer and Dinka religious discourse inevitably call to mind the paradoxes of particle location in the discourse of modern Western physicists. The resemblance could, of course, be entirely coincidental. And, because it is just the sort of thing that the cruder religious apologists so often pounce on, one is tempted to dismiss it. On close inspection, however, it turns out to be deep-rooted. For what emerges clearly from the material is the link between paradox and explanation. If ideas about spirits involve paradoxical notions of spatial location, this is because Nuer/Dinka religious discourse cannot achieve its explanatory aims without such notions. Here, as in the sciences, it is an aspect of the everyday world – in this case people and their relationships – which provides the basic inspiration for the explanatory schema. But this schema cannot give the required interpretative coverage unless it is subjected to the processes of deployment and development; and the latter involves stretching to breaking point the everyday concepts upon which the schema is based.

Before concluding this discussion of African religious discourse, let us look briefly at what Skorupski has to say about Nuer and Dinka general attitudes to paradox. In actual fact, he makes no direct pronouncements on this topic. By implication, however, he says a good deal. Thus for him, all systems of religious discourse are distinguishable from scientific discourse in that they welcome paradox rather than shun it; and since his Nuer and Dinka cases are examples of such systems, one must assume that he sees them as

associated with this attitude.[51] Now a thorough reading of the Nuer and
Dinka monographs does little to substantiate such a view. In the first place,
it is clear from the monographs that neither Nuer nor Dinka have a
tradition of reflective, second-order thinking. Under normal circumstances, therefore, the occasion for taking up a generalized attitude to the
paradoxes associated with religious thought simply does not arise. Where
the pesterings of the anthropologist create such an occasion, the evidence
seems to indicate that Nuer and Dinka are embarrassed rather than
gratified by paradox. One suspects that their attitude is probably much like
that of the scientist: 'What does it matter so long as we get the results?'[52]

This survey of Nuer and Dinka religious discourse has made it abundantly
clear that, in nature, location and source, such paradoxes as occur bear
strong resemblance to those associated with scientific discourse. Thus we
have come up once more against the puzzles of asymmetrical, intransitive
identities, and of the assertion that what is many is also one. And we have
seen how, as in the sciences, such puzzles are the by-products of the quest
for unities underlying the diversity of what is directly observed. We have
come up against the puzzling assertion of the discernibility of identicals.
And we have seen how, as in the sciences, this puzzle is a by-product of the
basic requirement of theoretical explanation, which is that the explanans
should on the one hand be something different from the explanandum, and
should on the other hand be something with which the explanandum can
be identified. Finally, we have come up against paradox in the definitions of
the spirits themselves. And we have seen how, as in the sciences, such
paradox is related to the nature of the situations which ideas about spirits
are invoked to explain and of the causal links which such ideas are invoked
to establish.

   In looking for the underlying causes of this association between paradox
and explanation, we are driven once again to take note of the extent to
which the African religious thinker, like his scientist counterpart, is both
guided and limited by conceptual patterns primarily associated with the
everyday world of material objects. Thus in his attempt to formulate the
relationship between explanans and explanandum, he veers uneasily
between concepts of identity and concepts of causality, both of which are
derived from everyday discourse. Again, in his attempts to define the
explanans itself, he is constrained by everyday ideas about breeze, breath
and people. Here too, then, it would seem that the explanatory quest
becomes invested with all manner of paradoxes because it is dependent on
humble tools and materials which it uses for purposes quite different from
those they were originally designed to serve, and which not unnaturally
tend to crack under the strain.

Paradox and explanation in the Christian religion

Like the paradoxes we have enumerated in previous sections, most of those typical of Christian discourse can be classified into two kinds: paradoxes arising out of attempts to characterize relations between different levels of being, and paradoxes arising out of attempts to characterize a level of being higher than that associated with material-object discourse.

Falling under the first heading are a number of familiar puzzles. First of all, there is the paradox of asymmetry. Particular things can be said to be God; but God cannot be said to be any of these particular things. Then there is the paradox of intransitivity. Several things may be said to be God; but they cannot be identified with one another. Again, there is the paradox of the many and the one: Father, Son, and Holy Ghost are one God. Finally, there is the paradox implicit in the idea that God is at once a being quite other than the totality of worldly phenomena (transcendent), and at the same time a being with whom all phenomena are to be identified (immanent). All four of these puzzles bear striking resemblances to the 'interlevel' puzzles we dealt with in the last section. And in what follows, I shall show that, once we are prepared to assume the centrality of the quest for explanation, prediction and control of worldly events in Christian religious life, we can make sense of these puzzles in much the same way as we made sense of their African counterparts. I know that the assumption involved here is a very dubious one. However, for reasons whose validity will I hope become apparent later, I shall start by pushing it as far as it will go, then stop to ask questions afterwards.

Let us start by taking this approach to the puzzles of asymmetrical, intransitive, many/one identities. As we did with comparable statements dealt with in previous sections, we shall treat these Christian identity statements as explanation-sketches; elliptical statements in which the basic explanatory entity is mentioned, but the diversity of its states ignored. Although in this case, as in others already dealt with, people are not in fact able to cite the relevant diversity of states of the explanans, it seems reasonable to assume that the statements in question are potentially expandable into complete explanations, and that they draw their meaningfulness from their intuited kinship with other ellipses which *can* be so expanded. If these statements *were* expanded, they would postulate a distinct God-state corresponding to every entity or state of affairs to be explained. In such circumstances, our first three puzzles would dissolve. With the reversibility of the expanded statements, asymmetry would disappear. With the identification of different phenomena with different God-states, the appearance of intransitivity would disappear. With as many distinct God-states as there were entities, processes or states of affairs to be explained, even that version of the problem of the many and the one which we call the Mystery of the Trinity would surely lose something of its awesome incomprehensibility. In short, these classic Christian theological puzzles are readily understandable once we see them as illustrations of that very general feature of explanatory systems – the reduction of a diversity of entities or processes to a diversity of states of one or a few more basic entities or processes.

The same approach can, I think, be profitably applied to the paradox of transcendence and immanence. That is, we can see the statements embodying it as satisfying the universal requirement that a theoretical explanans should be, at once an entity or set of entities distinct from the explanandum, and at the same time an entity or set of entities with which the explanandum can be identified. This indeed seems to me to be the only way in which we can make sense of it. Notice that, whereas in the first three puzzles we dealt with, the element of paradox disappeared once we saw the point of the statements involved, in this case the intractability of the paradox becomes the more obvious when we see the point. But this, it will be recalled, is also true of the counterparts of such statements both in African religious and in Western scientific discourse.

So much for the paradoxes arising out of attempts to characterize relations *between* different levels of being. Let us turn now to those Christian paradoxes whose referents lie *at* levels higher than that associated with material-object discourse.

The salient paradox of this kind is associated with notions of omnipresence or multipresence, or with notions that combine assertions of these with assertions of presence in particular places. Such notions are of great importance in Christian thought, since they provide the essential base for those other characteristic attributes of God – omnipotence and omniscience. These notions would seem to have exact counterparts in the complex and paradoxical notions of spiritual location which loom so large in Nuer and Dinka religious thought. Here again, it seems reasonable to treat them as we treated their African counterparts – that is, as adaptations of the idea of presence to the explanatory task which ideas about spiritual beings are called upon to perform. Once more, then, we have nothing which need disturb our contention that, with respect to the nature, location and sources of paradox, there is a strong element of continuity, not only between Christian and African religious discourse, but also between Christian and scientific discourse.

At this point, we may well feel tempted to relax. However, some of the most prominent items on Skorupski's list of Christian paradoxes remain to be dealt with. They are a mixed bag. The paradox of the Eucharist does not seem to fit into any scheme of parallels with scientific discourse, and must be dealt with separately. The other items seem to qualify only doubtfully as paradoxical.

Let us deal first of all with the Eucharist. The problems raised by the doctrine of trans-substantiation are clearly very special ones. If it were said simply that 'Jesus Christ' was to be taken as referring to a spiritual being, the doctrine could probably be accounted for, without too much distortion, as a species of theoretical identity. Again, if the same thing were said, with the gloss that the identity was a symbolic one, there would be no problem at all. But, as Skorupski points out, the official position of the Catholic Church has long been, and still is, that the consecrated bread and wine *are literally* the body and blood of Christ.[53] And here, of course, we have flagrant paradox, since the presence of the body and blood of Christ and the absence of bread and wine is asserted together with an admission that the observations made by participants are in every respect such as to warrant a judgement that there is no body and blood but only bread and wine. Clearly, this is paradox of a kind we have not come across so far in our review. At the risk of rushing in where angels (or Catholic theologians) fear to tread, let me offer one or two tentative and possibly unverifiable suggestions. One is that Christ's original statement that, 'this is my body and my blood', was part of a symbolic act of communion familiar enough both in relationships between men and men and in relationships between men and spiritual beings. Later, there grew up in the Christian Church a very strong 'bookish' tradition of adhering to the *ipsissima verba* of the founder, and of regarding any attempt at re-interpretation as a dangerous threat to the accurate transmission of the true faith. In the light of such a tradition, the determination to stick to a rigidly literal interpretation of Christ's words, even at the cost of flagrant paradox, becomes understandable.[54]

The second suggestion is that, given a choice of interpretations, a long succession of church leaders have chosen the most improbable one out of a desire to emphasize the paradoxical, mysterious nature of the Christian faith. Here we touch on a general attitude about which I shall have more to say shortly.

So much for the Eucharist. As for the other items on Skorupski's list, they seem to represent not so much paradoxes as inadequacies in the explanatory coverage of Christian theory. Thus the problems raised by the existence of evil and human free-will would seem not to differ in kind from the problems raised for any theory by recalcitrant data. Many theologians, indeed, have reacted to these problems in ways not unlike those which one might expect of scientists faced with similar situations – i.e. by trying to show that the conflict between theory and data is more apparent than real, that the data themselves are not what they are commonly reported to be, and so on. In saying this, of course, one must also admit that there has always been a powerful body of theologians who prefer simply to say that the conflict between theory and data is one more example of the 'mysteries' of the faith. But of this, more anon.

So far, then, we have reached the position of being able to say that, although at least one major paradox of the Christian faith is a product of special factors not encountered either in the background of African religions or in that of the sciences, most such paradoxes can be adequately accounted for when we view them as by-products of the same quest for explanation as lies at the heart of both these other areas of discourse.

At this point, I think I should redeem my promise to question the basic assumption on which my interpretation of Christian paradox has been based – the assumption that the quest for explanation, prediction and control of the vicissitudes of everyday life is central to Christian thought. On the face of it, this assumption is dubious in the extreme. For in very many branches of the Christian Church today, the concern with explanation, prediction and control of observables is virtually non-existent. In such circles, indeed, this concern is apt to be considered superstitious and even irreligious.[55] Christians who take this view are bound to object that, however much the paradoxes of their faith may look like the paradoxes typical of both African religious and Western scientific discourse, they do in fact spring from quite different roots.

Serious as it looks at first glance, this objection can be answered without too much difficulty. For as soon as we take a more historical view of Christianity, it becomes apparent that this lack of concern with explanation, prediction and control is the outcome of an abdication of these functions to the sciences which started only some four hundred years ago. If we go back to the earlier days of the faith, we find the concern with explanation, prediction and control quite central.[56] (Here, indeed, lies the reason why I said, at the beginning of this paper, that the traditional African religions throw more light on modern Christianity than vice versa, and why I chose to discuss these religions before turning to Christianity. For with their still-living emphasis on the explanatory quest, they can help us to reach a more sympathetic understanding of what Christianity meant to the mass of its adherents for the first millennium-and-a-half of its history.) Now most of the paradoxes we are considering are of great antiquity. Some are almost certainly part of the pre-Christian Greek and Judaic heritage of Christian thought. Hence the objection to our treatment of them as by-products of the explanatory quest has no real force. The only additional assumption we have to make is that cultural inertia has ensured the survival of these paradoxes after the disappearance of the conditions that gave rise to them. And there seems nothing particularly implausible about this.

Before closing this discussion of paradox in the Christian faith, let me comment briefly on Skorupski's view of 'mystery'. Skorupski's contention is that, whilst the scientist feels discomfort in the presence of paradox and tries to eliminate it, the religious thinker glories in and does his best to preserve the paradoxes inherent in his faith. It is this attitude which is summed up in the concept of 'mystery'.[57]

As I said in the last section, Skorupski's thesis seems to me to be false if asserted of African religions. So far as Christianity is concerned, however, there is no doubt about the importance of the concept of mystery and of the tendency to glorify the central paradoxes of the faith for which it stands. Nor is there any doubt about the antiquity or the persistence of these features: as Skorupski quite rightly points out, they made their appearance shortly after the founding of the faith, and have remained a prominent feature of it down to the present day.

In approaching this problem, it is useful to keep two things in mind. The first is that spiritual beings, even where they are primarily theoretical entities, are also people. The second is that Christianity, unlike most of the African religions, has from its birth onwards been in more or less constant competition with other world-views.

It is useful to remember that spiritual beings are people; for one of the attributes most commonly associated with powerful people is that of inscrutability. Hence there is nothing particularly surprising about a powerful god who is defined as inscrutable and mysterious in these ways. Hence, too, there is no cause for surprise if the paradoxes of religious belief come to be celebrated as manifestations of a god's inscrutability and thus of his power.

But if all this is valid, why is the glorification of paradox characteristic of Christianity but not of the African religions? Here, I think, we should remember the factor of intense competition. Constant questioning, by representatives of other world-views, both of the logical consistency and of the empirical adequacy of Christian beliefs, has inevitably stimulated defensive reactions. One such reaction, all along, has been an attempt to systematize and to iron out logical inconsistencies and empirical inadequacies. The other has been to refuse the challenge and to extol the inconsistencies and inadequacies as evidences of the inscrutability and hence of the power of the Christian God.

What is important to note here is that the doctrine of mystery has never in Christian history been more than one of two alternative attitudes to paradox.[58] Indeed, as Skorupski himself makes clear, the most explicit and aggressive statements of the doctrine have been triggered by the excesses of systematizers and rationalizers within the church.[59] Far from counting against my position (as Skorupski seems to think it does), this fact would seem to indicate that the celebration of paradox is an optional rather than an essential feature of Christian religious discourse.

The balance of influence between rationalizers and mystifiers seems to have swung back and forth over the centuries. In the present context, earlier phases of this process are not particularly relevant. Here, I want to concentrate on the latest phase: the heavy swing in favour of the mystifiers that has taken place over the last century. As I said earlier, Christianity, over some four hundred years, has been steadily abandoning its claim to explanatory competence in the face of overwhelming competition from the sciences. It has survived because it has continued to offer certain profound personal relationships which cannot be achieved in the purely human social field. For some, indeed, it has provided *the* personal relationship; one which illuminates and gives deeper meaning to all others.

At the beginning of this process, Christianity responded to the challenge of the sciences by a rather grudging kind of retreat; it renounced explanatory competence in fields where the sciences had already achieved spectacular results, but continued to assert competence in fields where they had not yet achieved anything impressive. Thus it quickly renounced competence in the sphere of the natural sciences, but continued, long and vociferously, to claim competence in the sphere of 'higher' human behaviour. In the nineteenth century, however, many leaders of Christian thought came to see such rearguard action as doomed, and urged believers to abandon altogether the strategy of trying to take on the scientists at their own game.[60] Having taken this decision, they inevitably came to rely more and more on the remaining alternative – i.e. that of taking refuge in the doctrine of Mystery. In turn, the connotation of the concept of Mystery became enlarged; for now it included not only the various paradoxes, both apparent and real, but also the fact that the existence of God was no longer a testable hypothesis in any ordinary sense of the words. Recent events, then, have given the doctrine of Mystery a predominance and breadth of meaning greater than it has ever previously attained.

However, it is by no means certain that we have heard the end of the story, or even seen the last swing of the pendulum. God, as I have already pointed out, has survived in the minds of modern men because, although no longer treated as the keystone of an immense explanatory edifice, he remains for many the focus of the most profound personal relationship they have. Now in an era in which science offers so much in the spheres of medicine and general welfare, the Christian believer in a position to benefit from its fruits finds it is easy enough to accept that he must no longer try to use God as a means for avoiding sickness or securing health, for avoiding misfortune and securing good fortune. But just as the lover of a woman, however steadfast, non-utilitarian and generally pure his love, demands signs that this love is reciprocated, so the lover of God, despite all injunctions to faith, yearns for signs that the supposed reciprocator of his love is not just a wishful fantasy, but is in some sense 'there'.

So long as this yearning persists, the defiant celebration, both of paradox and of the lack of any explanatory competence, is going to remain less than completely satisfying to many believers. Such people are going to grasp at any new discoveries about the world which seem to require the re-instatement of a spiritualistic explanatory framework; for only such re-instatement can provide the requisite signs of 'thereness'. Hence the continuing undercurrent of interest in works such as those of Teilhard de Chardin and Alister Hardy; biologists whose thinking about evolution has led them to postulate a Directing Power.[61] Hence, too, the growing interest in the work of the parapsychologists, whose findings in the sphere of extra-sensory perception seem to be leading them toward the repostulation of a spiritual domain.[62] In short, the very factor which ensured that Christianity would survive its renunciation of explanatory competence has also ensured that there will always be at least a residual dissatisfaction with the retreat into an all-enveloping doctrine of Mystery, and at least a residual yearning for the re-instatement of some explanatory competence.

Let me sum up briefly this somewhat tortuous discussion of Christianity. With the exception of the paradox of trans-substantiation, which is almost certainly the product of special circumstances, the other paradoxes of Christianity are best understood as hang-overs from an era when this religion was centrally concerned with the explanatory quest. In nature, location and source, they are strikingly similar, not only to the paradoxes of African religious thought, but also to those of scientific thought.

Alongside these similarities there are, it must be admitted, some contrasts. Thus Christianity, throughout its history, has had to face competition from rival world-views. And one reaction has been a positive celebration of paradox and explanatory inadequacy which is very different from anything to be found in the other areas of thought I have reviewed here. But this reaction has always coexisted with a willingness to play the opposition at its own game.

Again, in more recent times, Christianity has begun to diverge from both African religions and Western sciences in its progressive abandonment of the explanatory quest, covering its retreat with a powerful smokescreen of Mystery. But even though lack of interest in explanation and dedication to the doctrine of Mystery are the dominant traits of modern Christianity, they are traits with which many contemporary believers feel uneasy.

In so far as modern Christianity is the odd one out in our trio, then, it is not so far out as first appearances would suggest.

Theoretical explanation: the grass roots

In the foregoing sections, I have established that nearly all of the major paradoxes in the three areas of discourse we have reviewed are by-products of the quest for explanation. I have also established that the constant recurrence of paradox in the explanatory context is the result of our being compelled, in the course of applying and elaborating theory, to stretch to breaking point the limited resources of everyday, material-object language.

Having made these points, however, I realize that I have left the reader with a question which is possibly more interesting than any I have tried to answer so far. The question is: why, in the course of our more ambitious intellectual operations, do we find ourselves so effectively constrained by the resources of material-object language?

One clue, I think, comes from the work of child psychologists like Piaget, who have shown us, amongst other things, just how much of the infrastructure of our thought is laid down during spontaneous infantile explorations of our immediate environment.[63] Much as it may discomfit the heirs of Durkheim, we may have to admit that the fundaments of our intellectual activity are laid down before the agents of society have much chance to get a grip on us.[64] Thus it seems that the complex co-ordinations of visual, tactual and kinaesthetic stimuli, which are prerequisite to the individual's location of himself as an enduring body amongst other enduring bodies, are very largely established during the period of autonomous 'messing about' which precedes effective linguistic socialization. Similarly, a great corpus of expectations as to what events follow what is established by the extensive exploration and manual manipulation of surrounding people and objects which takes place during the same period. According to the child psychologists, linguistic socialization, when it comes, can only succeed if it latches on to this great mass of pre-verbal schemata. Hence the basic material-object and causal concepts of adults rest fairly and squarely on a pre-verbal, pre-social foundation.[65] Furthermore, so long as human beings continue to spend much of their adult life walking, sitting, lying down and indulging in the manual manipulation of 'moderate-sized specimens of dry goods',[66] they are engaging in a type of interaction with their environment which, in so far as it is in some degree continuous with the type of interaction that characterized their infancy, can only serve to reinforce their pre-verbal schemata.

In the light of all this, we should no longer be surprised at the existence of a relatively autonomous 'material-object' or 'observation' language, which differs little from culture to culture, survives successive changes of theoretical framework, and indeed constitutes the 'given' with which any such framework must ultimately articulate.[67] Nor should we be surprised to find a set of thought-patterns, derived from this language, which are so deep-seated and so pervasive that they influence and restrict even those theory-building operations most strongly concerned to transcend its limitations.[68]

A second clue is more specific. It is a clue as to why, even in our attempts to characterize the relationship between explanans and explanandum, we find ourselves imprisoned within the inadequate confines of material-object terminology. It is to be found in certain of those precious Western historical documents which give us insight into the minds of inaugurators of new world-views.

Some of the earliest such documents record the origins of those ancient Greek cosmologies whose basic theoretical entity is *pneuma* – 'breath-soul'. Perhaps the first name of note in this context is that of the pre-Socratic Anaximenes, who is said to have based his cosmology on the suggestion that 'As our soul being air holds us together and controls us, so does wind (or breath) and air enclose the whole world'.[69] This suggestion he elaborated by saying that

Infinite air was the principle, from which the things that are becoming, and that are, and that shall be, and gods and things divine, all come into being, and the rest from its products ... Through becoming denser or finer it has different appearances; for when it is dissolved into what is finer it becomes fire, while winds, again, are air that is becoming condensed, and cloud is produced from air by felting. When it is condensed still more, water is produced; with a further degree of condensation earth is produced, and when condensed as far as possible, stones.[70]

Similar ideas were propounded by a later pre-Socratic, Diogenes of Apollonia. Diogenes started from much the same initial inspiration: 'Men and other creatures live by means of air, through breathing it. And this is for them both soul (i.e. life-principle) and intelligence, as will clearly be shown in this work; and if this is removed, then they die and intelligence fails.'[71] And from this inspiration, there followed, once more, the same general thesis: 'The substance of the universe is infinite and eternal air, from which, when it is condensed and rarefied and changed in its dispositions, the form of other things comes into being.'[72]

Fragmentary as these sayings are, they shed valuable light on the genesis of one of the Western world's most significant explanatory schemata.[73] In both cases we find that the original inspiration is provided by the relationship between human breath and human body. The breath pervades the body, holds it together, and causes death and disintegration when it departs. This is a straightforward causal relationship, between two sets of phenomena at the material-object level. But in the cosmological schemes which result from this inspiration, we find that a subtle change has taken place. For in these schemes, all things are no longer *caused* to behave in certain ways by the action of breath or air. They *are* breath or air in various states. Statements of causal relationship have given way to statements of theoretical identification.

Turning to more recent times, we find something very similar in the work of Descartes, one of the founders of seventeenth-century mechanism. Consider for example the following passage:

My assigning definite shapes, sizes and motions to insensible particles of bodies, just as if I had seen them, and this in spite of admitting that they are insensible, may make some people ask how I can tell what they are like. My answer is this. Starting from the simplest and most familiar principles which our minds know by their innate constitution, I have considered in general the chief possible differences in size, shape and position between bodies whose mere minuteness makes them insensible, and the sensible effects of their various interactions. When I have observed similar effects among sensible objects, I have assumed that they arose from similar interactions of insensible bodies; especially as this seemed the only way of explaining them. And I have been greatly helped by considering machines. The only difference I can see between machines and natural objects is that the workings of machines are mostly carried out by apparatus large enough to be readily perceptible to the senses (as is required to make their manufacture humanly possible), whereas natural processes almost always depend on parts so small that they utterly elude our senses. But mechanics, which is a part or species of physics, uses no concepts but belong also to physics; and it is just as 'natural' for a clock composed of such-and-such wheels to tell the time, as it is for a tree grown from such-and-such seed to produce a certain fruit. So, just as men with experience of machinery, when they know what a machine is for, and can see part of it, can readily form a conjecture about the way its unseen parts are fashioned, in the same way, starting from sensible effects and sensible parts of bodies, I have tried to investigate the insensible causes and particles underlying them.[74]

Here, once again, we see a causal relationship between two entities at the material-object level (unseen parts and seen parts of a machine) furnishing the prototype for the basic theoretical identification of an entire cosmology.

A third example comes, not from the work of the originator of a particular world-view, but from that of a well-known modern philosopher of science:

There is a continuity between explanations of the elementary kind illustrated in my example of the toy engine and the explanatory use of the advanced theories of modern science in that the technique of explanation is the same. The demand for explanation of the toy engine was stimulated by the fact that some part of the mechanism was hidden and it was satisfied by an account of that mechanism. However more complex and mathematical the sciences have become, they rely constantly on hidden mechanisms. One of the things that makes for greater complexity is that the mechanisms are more securely hidden; another is that the mechanisms may not always be 'mechanistic' in the sense of classical mechanics. But the principle is the same.[75]

Here, yet again, we see a highly sophisticated mind slipping readily from a causal assertion to a theoretical identification.

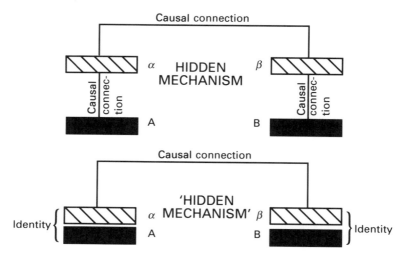

Figure 1

In the light of these examples, it does not seem too fanciful to suppose that observations of causal links *at* the material-object level have, quite generally, provided the starting points for the development of ideas about the relation *between* the material-object level of being and another level which is 'higher' in the sense of standing in an explanatory relationship to it. The transition from the idea of a hidden but nonetheless material-object explanans to that of a theoretical explanans is not in fact a very drastic one. All it requires is that, instead of taking statements correlating observables with 'hidden' variables as causal assertions, we take them as identities. The overall form of the explanation remains the same, as the diagram in figure 1 makes clear.

In this context, it is significant that ideas about breath and/or wind are so widely associated with pre-scientific explanatory systems, both in contemporary Africa and in earlier Europe. Breath and wind, being visually unobservable, yet able to penetrate the interstices of and thus pervade many bodies, form particularly apt prototypes for theoretical entities, which are inaccessible to the same acts of observation as we use to verify statements about events at the material-object level, and are at the same time coextensive with such events. Ideas concerning these phenomena may well have formed the original bridge between ideas about hidden goings-on and theoretical ideas *sensu stricto*.

All this sounds like some hare-brained Victorian excursion into unverifiable origins. However, although it is inconceivable that we shall ever have any direct evidence about the earliest origins of theoretical explanation, the suggestion made here is not without some cash value. Apart from anything else, it does give an answer to our question as to why the theorist finds himself trapped by the inadequacies of material-object language whenever he tries to characterize the relationship between explanans and explanandum. For it is only natural that theoretical explanation, like other human activities, should be in some respects constrained and limited by the nature of its origins.

Summary and conclusion

The essence of Skorupski's argument is three-fold. First of all, paradox is not characteristic of scientific discourse, but is the staple of all religious discourse – whether traditional African or modern Western. Secondly, in so far as paradoxes do sometimes arise in scientific discourse, they are quite different, both in nature and location, from the paradoxes of religious thought. Thirdly, whilst the scientist is upset by paradox and tries to eliminate it, the religious thinker is delighted by paradox and celebrates it as Mystery. Skorupski concludes that, with respect to paradox, scientific discourse is poles apart from any kind of religious discourse – be this traditional African or modern Western.

In this paper, I have shown that he is mistaken on all three counts. First of all, I have shown that paradox is as endemic to scientific discourse as it is to religious. Secondly, I have shown that the kinds of paradox characteristic of scientific discourse are also of central importance both in African and in Western religion. In all three cases, they arise as by-products of the quest for theoretical explanation. (Though widespread lack of interest in such explanation on the part of modern Christians might seem to invalidate this last conclusion, the difficulty disappears when we remember that the basic paradoxes of Christianity emerged in an era when believers were centrally preoccupied with explanation.) Thirdly, I have shown that, although Skorupski is on to something interesting with his distinction between paradox-rejecting and paradox-accepting thought-systems, he is in error when he aligns the African religious thinker with the Christian as one who rejoices in paradox. It would seem truer to say that the African religious thinker, like the scientist, tends to tolerate paradox in so far as it is part of the explanatory enterprise, but does not actively glory in it. Even in Christianity, positive acceptance of paradox has been only one of two alternative defences against the intellectual assaults of non-Christians.

So much for criticism. On the more constructive side, the underlying theme of this paper has been that the link between theoretical explanation and paradox is inevitable. The reason is that human intellectual life is limited and constrained by the resources of the material-object language, and overstretches these resources whenever it applies them in contexts radically different from those to which they are primarily adapted. Paradox is the product of such overstretching. Going a step further, I have suggested two reasons for the virtual immutability of material-object language and its immense influence on other areas of discourse. One is that this language is an adaptation to pre-verbal, pre-social schemata which the accredited agents of socialization can do little to modify. The other is that, historically, theoretical explanations involving ideas about relations between different levels of being have developed from explanations involving ideas of causal links at the material-object level.

In conclusion, I should like to point to a methodological moral which seems to me to be implicit in this paper. Social scientists have often criticized the intellectualist approach to the study of ideas on the ground that it ignores the inconsistencies and contradictions which bedevil most human belief-systems, and is therefore fundamentally unrealistic. Now in so far as its central interpretive concept is that of a universal human quest for explanation, this paper is a perfect example of the intellectualist approach. Yet not only does it draw attention to inconsistencies and contradictions, it also shows how their prevalence and persistence may be accounted for. On present evidence, then, intellectualism is by no means synonymous with an unrealistic interpretative charity.

9   Tradition and modernity revisited

In an article published in 1967,[1] I compared and contrasted patterns of thought in Africa and the West, taking Africa as a living exemplar of 'traditionality' and the West as a pioneer of 'modernity'. I began the article by elaborating on Durkheim's neglected insight concerning the continuities between, on the one hand the spiritualistic thought of traditional cultures in Africa and elsewhere, and on the other the mechanistic thought of Western cultures. I showed how the former, no less than the latter, gave rise to theoretical systems whose basic *raison d'être* was the extension of the magnificent but nonetheless limited causal vision of everyday common-sense thinking. I also proposed a technological/economic/sociological explanation for the divergence in theoretical idiom as between Africa and the West. Having made much of continuities between the two streams of thought, I went on to redress the balance by setting out a scheme of contrasts. Here I proposed an amended and developed version of Popper's celebrated 'closed'/'open' dichotomy, with Africa exemplifying the 'closed' and the West exemplifying the 'open'. Finally, invoking once again a technological/economic/sociological determinism, I alluded to a number of factors that seemed to me to have underpinned the transition from 'closed' to 'open' ways of thinking in earlier Europe.

Down through the years, this article has enjoyed a certain notoriety. Some few scholars have agreed enthusiastically with part or all of it. Others, more numerous, have been affronted by its assault on certain hoary orthodoxies in the comparative sociology of ideas, and have given strong critical responses. Yet others have used it as a stick with which to chastise the orthodox, but have then gone on to point to the defects of the stick and to discard it in favour of their own allegedly superior interpretative instruments. Others again have seen it variously as vacuous, naive, hubristic, Afrocentric and Eurocentric. All in all, the responses to the article have been predominantly unfavourable. But they have continued in surprising profusion down to the present day. So, on the approach of the old thing's fifteenth anniversary, it seems opportune to take an author's second look at it, and to ask what amendments, if any, are necessary.

301

In what follows, I shall start by reviewing the main lines of criticism, and by trying to sort out the cogent from the misdirected. This done, I shall also review the two bodies of recent scholarly work which, though not themselves concerned with my 1967 article, none the less have a bearing on the views expressed in it. One such body deals with change in African world-views, the other with change in Western world-views. Once again, I shall try to extract those aspects of the two bodies of work which suggest a need for reformulation of my 1967 views.

Having thus cleared the ground, I shall propose an amended scheme of continuities and contrasts between African 'traditionality' and Western 'modernity'. This scheme will, I hope, improve on my 1967 effort in two respects. First, in its greater adequacy to the facts. Second, in the greater adequacy of its answers to the two linked major questions which confront all philosophers and historians of science: i.e. 'Just how far can scientific theorizing claim greater cognitive efficiency than its pre-scientific counterparts?' and 'In so far as the claim of cognitive superiority is justified, what is the source of this superiority?'. After presenting my revised scheme, I shall follow up by suggesting how we might account, in technological/economic/sociological terms, for the transition which it implies.

Finally, I shall consider the relevance of the analysis and interpretation presented to some of the broader themes of this symposium. In particular, I shall consider its relevance to the confrontation which I take to be central to the collection – the confrontation between Universalist and Relativist programmes for cross-cultural understanding.

Review of criticism

For many scholarly critics of the 1967 article, the entire project is invalidated at the outset by the arbitrariness and/or Eurocentricity of the comparison between African and Western thought-systems.[2] This reaction, I believe, demonstrates above all else the failure of the scholars concerned to think the matter through. None the less, it is clear that lack of an explicit rationale for the comparison has contributed much to the various misunderstandings of the article. So it seems eminently sensible to start this section by providing such a rationale.

At the outset, we have to face the fact that the scholar working on 'traditional' African thought-systems in a contemporary African setting cannot but become involved in broad African/Western comparisons.

In the first place, consider the implications of monographic work on the thought-patterns of a particular African community. Typically, the scholar doing this kind of work is concerned to convey an understanding of such thought-patterns to the world at large. He is therefore compelled to translate these patterns into terms of one or other of the two or three languages that currently enjoy 'world' status. Now there is nothing in any way fixed about such 'world' status. In a few decades, political or demographic upheavals may confer it on languages quite other than those that currently enjoy it. For the moment, however, it is the Western languages of English and French that enjoy this status. Hence their use as translation instruments is unavoidable.

In saying that translation is at the forefront of the intellectual processes involved in the monographic enterprise, moreover, I am talking about something more than a mere rough-and-ready search for dictionary equivalents. I am talking about a search for the appropriate Western conceptual pigeon-holes for African concepts and thought-patterns; about a search in the course of which Western concepts may themselves have to be stretched and bent in order to provide such pigeon-holes.

If this is a correct analysis of the problem, it follows that, in the process of producing an adequate translation, our scholar must inevitably build up for himself a schema of similarities and differences between the African thought-patterns he wishes to expound to the world and the Western thought-patterns in terms of which he is translating. So, given the current prerequisites of expounding the thought-patterns of a particular African community to the world at large, it turns out that the kind of African/ Western comparison I attempted in 1967, far from being arbitrary, is quite simply inescapable.

Again, consider the predicament of the scholar doing this kind of monographic work in a present-day African academic setting.

Whether he likes it or not, such a scholar is apt to find himself facing a constant challenge as to the contemporary relevance of his work. Behind this challenge lies a faith in what, for want of a better phrase, we may call 'intellectual modernization'. Now although it is seldom explicitly defined by the academic community, intellectual modernization is seen, above all else, as involving a move *away* from certain aspects of traditional patterns of thought, and *toward* certain aspects of contemporary Western patterns. Such a transition, it is claimed, is justifiable on the grounds of the spectacular increase in efficiency in the explanation, prediction and control of events that it will bring. In the light of this definition and this call, the scholarly student of traditional thought-systems is characteristically branded as someone who wants to hold back the hands of the clock.

This negative image, however, is the product of shallow thinking. Deeper consideration shows that, far from being an obstacle to progress, the scholarly 'traditionalist' has a vital part to play in paving the way for it. How so? Well, to start with, it is clear that the call to intellectual modernization can only be wholeheartedly accepted after thorough critical appraisal. Even if all thinking people involved agree to give priority to the linked ends of explanation, prediction and control (and such consensus is in any case problematic), they must still scrutinize carefully the claim that intellectual modernization can enable African peoples to achieve these ends with greatly improved efficiency. And before they can adjudicate this claim, the character of the transition advocated must be much more carefully charted. But any such charting requires a comparison of the point of departure ('traditionality') with the point of arrival ('modernity'): a comparison for which our 'traditionalist' holds one of the two keys. Once again, then, given an African academic setting, a comparison of the type I attempted in 1967 appears not arbitrary but inescapable. It should now be clear that between myself and my critics, it is they who have been wearing the Euro-tinted spectacles!

So much for the peculiar relevance of a comparison with modern Western thought-patterns to the scholar whose starting-point is that of traditional African thought-patterns. There is almost as strong a case to be made for the peculiar relevance of a study of traditional African thought-patterns to the scholar whose primary interest is in the genesis of Western intellectual modernity.

All responsible scholars working in sub-Saharan Africa acknowledge the enormous and fascinating diversity of world-views and thought-patterns nourished by the myriad communities of the continent. One would indeed be lacking in normal human sensitivity if one were not more than a little daunted by this diversity. Nonetheless, scholars through the years *have* searched for the unities underlying this diversity. And I think we now have some idea of what they might be. (As a partial inventory of them, I think my 1967 article still remains useful.) One notable thing about these unities, however, is that, by and large, they do not seem specific to sub-Saharan Africa. Rather, most of the features involved are features which reappear in the earlier cultures of the Mediterranean, the Near East, and Europe. In other words, it begins to look as if the universals of 'African traditional' are in fact universals of 'Old World traditional'. Further, it begins to look as if a study of 'African traditional' can suggest to us quite a lot about the living flesh that once clothed the bare bones presented to us in records, inscriptions and remains of earlier phases of Mediterranean, Near Eastern and European thought.

All this has not been lost on the historians of these neighbouring 'Old World' areas. In varying degrees of co-operation with social anthropologists, they have been looking enthusiastically to Africa to provide them with inspiration as to how the thought-patterns all too often incompletely glimpsed through their records were actually set in a context of ongoing social life. In earlier days, some of the scholars concerned were more than a little incautious, assuming without further question that if a certain thought-pattern is found in Africa in a certain social context, and that if the existence of an apparently equivalent thought-pattern in earlier Europe is indicated by the relevant record, then the European equivalent *must* have been set in a similar context. Such rashness threatened at one time to bring the pursuit of African inspiration into total disrepute. Nowadays, as a result, both historians and anthropologists tend to be more cautious. If they find a thought-pattern in Africa set in a certain social context, and an apparently equivalent thought-pattern in earlier Europe, they use the African data on pattern and context as the basis of a hypothesis which, before it can be accepted in the European domain, must be subjected to testing against data related to that domain. Present-day caution notwithstanding, however, it seems that an impressive number of such hunches based on African data are turning up trumps for the historians of these neighbouring non-African areas.[3]

The study of traditional African thought-systems, then, is of peculiar relevance to the historian concerned with the emergence of modern Western thought because it is a fertile source of inspiration for his attempts to build up a picture of that once living traditionalism from which Western intellectual modernity arose.[4]

Finally in this statement of rationale, let me draw the reader's attention to something every good anthropologist knows: namely, that comparison of the world-view in which we ourselves have been reared with *any* world-view less familiar to us has an enormous potential for increasing our grasp of both. First, if we have been brought up within one world-view and later look across to another strongly contrasted with it, we are likely, in our survey of the latter, to be forcibly struck by a number of patterns of thought and belief which have never been remarked upon by their users. This, of course, is because the patterns are strange to us but totally humdrum to the users. Second, if we immerse ourselves long enough and deep enough in this 'alien' world-view, and then look back from it to the world-view in which we were reared, the same thing will apply in reverse. Thought-patterns which we would never have remarked on before our 'excursus' now stand out as strange, remarkable, and demanding of explanation.[5]

In this particular case, where the terms of the comparison are the modernizing world-view of the West and the traditional world-views of Africa, we should therefore feel entitled to an increase in our understanding of both. Now if any valid criticism can be made of my earlier shot at this comparison, it is that the increase in understanding was one-sided. Looking across at the world-views of Africa from a Western vantage-point, I believe I was able to highlight certain key patterns that had not been previously remarked upon. However, when it came to looking back at Western intellectual modernity from an African vantage point, I failed to exploit the reverse opportunity. Nothing I said about science would have caused even mild surprise to the professional philosopher or historian of science. Most of it, indeed, must have struck those of that ilk who read it as somewhat out-of-date. This time round, I hope to avoid the one-sidedness. As well as advancing our understanding of the African traditional by looking at it from the vantage-point of Western modernity, I hope to do a little to advance our understanding of modernity by looking at it from the vantage-point of the traditional.

So much for those who have doubted the legitimacy of the comparative exercise itself. Amongst those who concede its legitimacy, however, are a great many who complain of my mistakes in the execution of it. And it is to their criticisms that I now turn.

Much hot ink has been directed against my thesis of a basic *continuity* of structure and intention as between traditional religious and modern scientific thought. This thesis, indeed, has provoked reactions close to horror from members of two well-established schools. First, from the 'Symbolists', who like to think of all religious life, whether traditional or modern, African or Western, as a species of poetic jollification rather than as a system of theory and practice guided by the aims of explanation, prediction and control.[6] Second, from the Wittgensteinian 'Fideists', who like to think of all religious life as the expression of an autonomous commitment to communion with Spiritual Being, and again as something totally different from thought and action directed by the ends of explanation, prediction and control.[7]

Both 'Symbolist' and 'Fideist' approaches to traditional religious life have already been subject to massive and cogent criticism.[8] And since I have already made my own contribution (certainly massive and I hope cogent) to such criticism,[9] I will not spend long on it here. Two points, I think, should suffice. First, in denying the paramount importance of explanation, prediction and control as guiding aims of traditional African religious life, both 'Symbolists' and 'Fideists' are committing the cardinal interpretative sin of flouting the actor's point of view. Second, both 'Symbolists' and 'Fideists' have failed to face up to the implications for their position of the historic confrontation between African peoples and twentieth-century missionary Christianity. Now over much of sub-Saharan Africa, large numbers of people have entered the missionary churches. However, very considerable numbers have subsequently come out again, to found and/or support institutions which, though propagating certain key features of the Christian message about God, are in other respects very different in outlook. Fortunately for us, the people concerned in this exodus and regrouping have been most articulate in giving their reasons for it. All over the continent, moreover, they have given much the same reasons. Above all, they have objected to the underplaying of explanation, prediction and control in the missionary credo, and have set up their new institutions with the express purpose of restoring these aims to a central position in religious life. Here, African populations are giving their own unsolicited but beautifully clear answer to 'Symbolists' and 'Fideists' alike.[10]

If relevant evidence and well-aimed argument could have killed, indeed, both 'Symbolism' and 'Fideism' would have fallen in the fields of Africa a decade ago. They survive, not because they have any genuine interpretative value, but because they serve an ideological need: i.e. the need to place traditional religious thought beyond the range of invidious comparison with Western scientific thought in respect of efficiency in the realms of explanation, prediction and control.[11]

'Symbolist'/'Fideist' outrage notwithstanding, I have continued to develop the continuity thesis in post-1967 articles. Thus I have shown that it accounts quite neatly for the apparently paradoxical character of much traditional religious discourse.[12] Again, I have shown that it accounts for stereotypy and other puzzling characteristics of ritual action.[13] Yet again, I am developing a limited comparison to show how it can account for different elaborations of religious ideas in different economic and social settings.[14] By and large, I am optimistic about the future of this approach, if for no better reason than that it is the only one in the field which takes off from the actor's perspective rather than flouting it. I am not saying that one must begin *and* end with the actor's perspective. (I myself go beyond it by asking and trying to answer the question as to why African thinkers have continued to elaborate essentially spiritualistic world-views whilst Western thinkers have been increasingly attracted to mechanistic world-views.) But one must certainly begin with it.

For all the criticism directed at the *continuity* thesis, an equal volume has been directed at my attempt to outline what seemed to me to be the principal *contrasts* between 'tradition' and 'modernity'. Unlike the former the latter appears to contain much that is well-directed. Since I have made little serious attempt to come to terms with it in previous writings, I make no apology for considering it at length in what follows.

Most readers of the 1967 article have found fault with my use of the Popperian 'closed' versus 'open' contrast as a way of characterizing the difference between traditionalist and modern thinking. Above all, they have found fault with the contrast between static and dynamic thinking allegedly implicit in my use of the Popperian terms. Thus, so far as the individual member of society is concerned, they insist that the tradition-bound thinker is *more* critical and reflective, and *less* conservative, than I make him, and that the modern, scientifically-trained thinker is *less* critical and reflective, and *more* conservative than I make him. So far as the world-view associated with a society is concerned, they insist that the typical traditionalist world-view is far more open to change and external influence than I allow, and that the typical modern world-view is rather less open to change than I would like to think.[15]

This general line of criticism has been well spiced with examples drawn both from traditionalistic African contexts and from modern Western scientific contexts. Although I could claim that the critics have ignored some of my cautionary qualifications, I think that by and large they have proved their point. The Popperian contrast between 'closed' and 'open', as I applied it in 1967, *did* carry implications of a contrast between static and dynamic thinking, static and dynamic world-views; and, as I now acknowledge, such a contrast *does not* do justice either to the African or to the Western subject-matter.

Most critics have also fastened upon two more particular contrasts from which I tried to derive a multiplicity of others. One of these was the contrast between presence and absence of anxiety about threats to the established body of theory. The other was the contrast between absence and presence of an awareness, on the part of individual thinkers, of alternative theoretical frameworks.

No-one has been much impressed by the 'anxiety thesis'. Some critics have suggested that there is little evidence, either direct or indirect, for the presence of a special anxiety of the kind I postulated for traditional settings.[16] Others have suggested that anxiety about threats to one's own preferred theoretical framework is by no means peculiar to traditional settings, but is equally present at the heart of modernity.[17]

My own inclination is to disagree with the first lot, but agree with the second. I still believe that the taboo reaction and the rites for annulling the passage of time can be understood, at least in part, as defences against the anxiety-provoking threat of novel experience to an established theoretical framework. This interpretation accords well with actor's perceptions of both types of rite as responses to dangerous (i.e. anxiety-provoking) situations. It relates both types of rite to more general features of the 'traditional' predicament. And to date, it has no serious rival. At the same time it seems evident from a great mass of historical writing that anxiety about threats to one's preferred theoretical framework is *equally* a motive factor at the heart of modern intellectual life. If we find taboo and time-annulment rites missing in the modern setting, this is because here the threats have a rather different source, and hence require a different type of defence. What I mean by this last remark will become clearer in the constructive section of the paper. Meanwhile, let us transfer anxiety about threats to one's own theoretical framework from the inventory of things peculiar to traditional settings to that of things common to both traditional and modern settings.

Many scholars have also lambasted the 'awareness of alternatives' thesis.

A typical line of argument here has been that since, in most of the traditionalistic societies of Africa, witchcraft, sorcery, gods, ghosts, etc., provide potential alternative explanations of untoward events, it can make no sense to say that individual members of these societies lack an awareness of alternative theoretical possibilities.[18] Another related line has pointed to the long coexistence, in many of these societies, of indigenous religion and Islam or Christianity, and has cited this too as evidence that individuals therein cannot be lacking in awareness of theoretical alternatives.[19] Some critics have gone even further than this. Not only have they used arguments of the type just cited to show that individuals in traditionalistic societies have a well-developed awareness of alternatives. They have used a Kuhnian presentation of science to show that it is precisely individuals at the heart of intellectual modernity who lack a developed awareness of alternatives.[20]

Like the more general criticism of the 'closed' versus 'open' contrast, this line has been well spiced with text and verse drawn from both traditionalistic and modern contexts. Nonetheless, it seems to me far less convincing.

In the first place, the arguments drawing on evidence from traditionalistic contexts do not seem to me to prove what they set out to prove. Take for instance the argument from the fact that most traditionalistic cosmologies allow for the possibility that any one of a number of different types of spiritual agency may be involved in the causation of a given untoward event. Now surely what we have here is not a multiplicity of alternative theoretical frameworks, but a multiplicity of agencies postulated *within* a single theoretical framework. To cite this as a counter-example therefore makes no more sense than would citing a Western medical man's awareness of the potential involvement of any one of a number of different types of bacterial agent in a given illness as evidence that he is poised between alternative theoretical frameworks. Again, take the argument based on the coexistence of indigenous religion with Islam or Christianity. As I have shown elsewhere, both Islam and Christianity allow for a multiplicity of lesser spiritual agencies operating under the aegis of the supreme being, whilst most if not all indigenous cosmologies allow for the same combination. Hence the conflict between the traditional religions and the so-called 'world religions' is not so much a conflict between radically different world-views as a conflict over what to worship and what to eschew within a single pantheon.[21] Indeed, I would say that it is not the missionaries of the 'world religions' who threaten to bring a vivid awareness of alternative theoretical frameworks into the minds of erstwhile traditionalistic thinkers, but rather the bearers of modern Western mechanistic materialism. It is when the latter becomes more influential in Africa than it is at the present that we shall see the sparks fly! In short, it would seem that, on the basis of evidence so far cited, the critics have failed to prove their case as regards awareness of

alternative theoretical frameworks amongst thinkers in the more traditionalistic sectors of African society.

So much for the argument drawing on evidence from traditionalistic
contexts. The arguments drawing on evidence from modern science seem
little better founded. Since I shall be going into more detail about this later
on, let me not waste too much space at this point. Suffice it here to say that
more recent scholarship, playing Kuhn at his own game of backing characterization of scientific thought and activity with detailed historical evidence, has shown that his insistence on one-at-a-time dominance of a
succession of uncontested theoretical schemes is a gross distortion of the
record.[22] If anything, the latter endorses my own contention that individual
awareness of alternative theoretical frameworks is a typical feature of
scientific milieux.

Perhaps a more cogent criticism of the 'awareness of alternatives' thesis
than any of the foregoing is one put forward by Ernest Gellner.[23] Gellner
suggests that there is a 'valuable intuition' behind my contrast, but that its
value is obscured by an excessively individualist perspective. Though he
himself does not elaborate much on this comment, he has said enough to
point to the real trouble. It is not that the contrast is invalid. Rather, in
concentrating on the individual rather than on individuals-in-a-community,
it is incomplete. What we are faced with is not just absence versus presence
of individual awareness of alternatives, but also, as its corollary, absence
versus presence of a multiplicity of competing theoretical frameworks sponsored by rival 'schools'. Of this, much more anon.

A final line of criticism concerns the alleged lack of a technological,
economic or sociological explanatory framework as underpinning for my
analysis of continuities and contrasts in thought-patterns.[24]

This line I find rather disheartening. In the first place, my 1967 article
contained a technological/economic/sociological explanation for the prevalence of a spiritualistic theoretical idiom in Africa as against that of a
mechanistic idiom in the West.[25] Secondly, it suggested a number of
technological, economic and social factors behind the transition from a
'closed' to an 'open' style of theoretical thought.[26] However naive or inept
these explanation-sketches may appear to subsequent scholars, they are
incontrovertible evidence of my guiding intellectual passion at that time,
which was precisely the quest for an explanatory framework which would
deal 'symmetrically' (to use the now fashionable term) with the 'traditional'
and the 'modern', the 'pre-scientific' and the 'scientific'.

If the above be granted, then why this aspect of the critical reaction?
Well, part of it seems simply enough explained. Thus most of the critics,
judging by their citations, read, not the original article, but the abridged

version of it reprinted in 1970.[27] During the production of this version, foolishly as it seems in retrospect, I agreed to the excision of that very section in which suggestions about the technological, economic and social factors underpinning the transition from 'closed' to 'open' thinking were contained. Now it seems to me that the reader of an abridged version prepared with the author's co-operation can reasonably assume that the abridgements were guided by the author's assessment of what was important and what unimportant in the original. So the failure to go back to the original and to register its contents is perfectly understandable. Nonetheless, it seems worthwhile drawing the critics' attention to what those contents actually were. More puzzling is the failure to spot the technological/economic/sociological explanation for the contrast between the spiritualistic and the mechanistic idioms in theory, an explanation which *was* included in the 1970 abridged version.[28] The one suggestion I can make here is that, having been identified by the 'Symbolists' as a 'Neo-Tylorian Intellectualist' (an identification which must seem incongruous to anyone who has ever read Tylor!) I have become the victim of a well-entrenched dogma to the effect that 'Intellectualist' and 'Sociological' explanations are mutually incompatible, coupled with a failure to recognize anything on the printed page that does not square with the dogma. I hope those who carry on to read the latter part of this article will see what a load of nonsense this alleged incompatibility is.

All in all, quite a lot of the 1967 article seems to have survived the critical assault. The basic comparative exercise itself stands vindicated. The continuity thesis is virtually undamaged. The scheme of contrasts is shown as standing in need of extensive amendment rather than of complete replacement. And the explanatory suggestions, having had their existence denied, still await the critics' jaws.

Some recent research results and their implications for the project

Some of the most fruitful inspiration for improvement on my 1967 effort has come, not only from the numerous critical ripostes, but from recent work in a number of fields which either makes no allusion to my ideas or is at most peripherally concerned with them. A brief review of such work would seem a sensible prelude to the more constructive part of this essay.

The first item I want to consider under this heading bears on the thesis of a basic continuity between traditional religious and modern scientific thinking. This thesis, as I pointed out in the last section, has stood up well enough to the barrage of criticisms directed at it. Nonetheless, certain recent work in the philosophy of science has brought home to me the need to amend one aspect of it.

Here, I refer to the challenge to the distinction between 'observation' or 'everyday' language on the one hand, and 'theoretical' language on the other. Mary Hesse, for one,[29] has argued convincingly that 'everyday' concepts like 'earth', 'sky', 'man', 'tree', 'fish' are as indissolubly linked to causal laws as are 'theoretical' concepts like 'proton', 'atom', 'wave' and 'electric current', and that in this respect they are neither more nor less 'theoretical' than the latter. Hence, insofar as established usage implies that the 'observational' or 'everyday' level is 'non-theoretical', it sets up a false antithesis.

Now both in my 1967 article and in subsequent writing I have taken the complementary coexistence of 'everyday' and 'theoretical' languages as one of the most important continuities between African traditionalism and Western modernity. In particular, I have tried to show in detail how the more puzzling features both of African spiritualistic theory and of Western mechanistic theory arise from the peculiar relationship between these two types of language.[30] If Hesse and others are correct, however, this aspect of my exposition of continuities is built on a false antithesis. In the circumstances, either rejection or reformulation seems called for.

Of the two my preference is for reformulation. Timely and apt as Hesse's challenge may be, it could lead the over-enthusiastic to throw out the baby with the bathwater. True, the established usage leads us to misconstrue the character of the difference between the two levels of language. But there is a danger that the rebels against it, chanting the slogan 'everything is theory', may blind us to the fact that there *is* a difference, albeit one that has not yet been properly characterized. The need, then, is for a fresh characterization of the two-levels distinction that avoids the false implications of established usage but nonetheless does justice to the difference that undoubtedly is there. I shall attempt such a characterization in the later and more constructive part of this essay.

The second item for consideration bears on the question of change in the thought-patterns of 'traditionalistic' African communities. As we saw earlier, the critics have rightly rejected the implication of changelessness which attends the application of the Popperian term 'closed' to such thought-patterns. However, it is to a body of monographic studies of change in African religious thought conducted over the last thirty years that we must turn in order to form a judgement, not only as to the *extent* of change in such contexts, but also as to its *mode*.

The studies in question can be divided for convenience into two sets: first, those concerned with the indigenous (i.e. pre-Islamic, pre-Christian) religious traditions; second, those concerned with so-called 'conversion' to Islam and Christianity.

Social anthropologists, who have long held a virtual monopoly of intensive studies of indigenous African religions, have often been castigated by members of other disciplines, first for presenting entirely synchronic pictures of African religions, and worse for implying that such pictures have a sort of timeless validity. It is true that some anthropologists (notably members of the Griaule School in France) have fallen so deeply in love with the systems of thought they have encountered that they have been well content simply to map them as they stood at the time of encounter. On the other hand, many more (particularly members or followers of Evans-Pritchard's Oxford School) have genuinely strained to put historical depth into their accounts. If the results are scanty and the historical depth seldom exceeds fifty to a hundred years, this is above all due to the intractability of the sources, of which oral tradition is the most prominent. As we shall have cause to recall several times before this essay is through, oral tradition, over three or four generations, preserves a fair recollection of religious innovations and their authorship; but, as more and more generations slip by, it tends to relegate such innovations and their authors to a timeless, eponymously-peopled 'time of the beginnings'.[31] Even so, more recent monographic work carried out within the limits set by this constraint has given us a picture of the traditional world-views different from anything available fifty years ago.[32]

None of these studies, it is true, has seriously called in question the importance to the peoples they deal with of a 'traditionalistic' mode of legitimation of belief – a mode, that is, which treats a belief as valid when it can be shown to be part of the legacy of the ancients. Nor, I think, would their authors deny that this type of legitimation is a powerful factor favouring cognitive conservatism. At the same time, however, none of these studies allows us to see 'traditionalistic' legitimation as the overwhelming brake on cognitive change that earlier observers judged it to be. On the contrary, despite the short time-spans within which their authors have been forced to work, they have painted a striking picture of adaptability and responsiveness to novel experience.

For those who want to get an index of the degree of ideational change over longer periods, indirect but none the less illuminating clues can be obtained through co-operation with the linguists. Thus linguistic evidence indicates pretty clearly that whole clusters of present-day sub-Saharan societies have come into being through the expansion, fission and dispersal of single ancestral groups. This is almost certainly true, for instance, of the Bantu- and Mande-speaking peoples. In each of such clusters at the present day, we find a spectacular variety of religious belief-systems. In each member of a given cluster, moreover, we find two things. On the one hand, a conviction that the main pillars of the belief-system have been handed down from the ancients. On the other, a belief-system *in fact* elaborated in such a way as to give a subtle and sophisticated explanatory account of the particular social and environmental situation in which it flourishes at the present day. Given the evidence as to origins, it would seem that, convictions as to the antiquity of belief notwithstanding, the spectacular religious variety shown by each cluster can only be interpreted as the result of equally spectacular divergences from an original unity – divergences arising from adaptive change over the centuries to widely diverging social and environmental circumstances. Once again, then, the picture is of a conservatism which nonetheless permits a high degree of adaptability and responsiveness to change.

So much for the general picture of a balance between conservatism and adaptability as it emerges from these newer monographs. Before moving on, let me draw attention to two particular sets of observations that seem to point to a way in which we may shortly fill out the picture yet further. One such set is the fruit of work in Yorubaland, the other that of work in Kalabari.

The Yoruba study I have in mind is one recently reported by Chappel, on ideas about twin-birth in Yorubaland.[33] Chappel shows fairly conclusively that, before the mid-eighteenth century, Yoruba, like many African peoples, regarded twins as a challenge to the established distinction between men and animals, and hence as an abomination to be countered with an eliminative taboo reaction. Later, however, various pressures, including, one may suspect, an abnormally high twinning rate followed by a concern for population maintenance during the internecine wars of the nineteenth century, triggered off a series of attempts to devise an explanation of the phenomenon within the general framework of existing religious theory. As a result, twins came to be seen as a means whereby Eshu, the traditionally revered trickster god, gave the sign of his interest to families whom he wished to serve him. And as the explanation became established, so the taboo reaction weakened and finally disappeared.

A parallel example, so far unpublished, comes from my own experience among Kalabari of the Eastern Niger Delta. Kalabari say that, when a fisherman first reported the appearance of white men at the mouth of the estuary, the initial response was one of horror, and was followed by massive purification of the community. Their account, in short, describes a typical taboo reaction. At the same time, they have a perfectly good explanation for the symbiotic relationship between themselves and white people which developed during the centuries after the latter's initial appearance; an explanation which postulates that the national goddesses of Kalabari and of the whites are in fact sisters. Furthermore, whatever may have been the initial reaction to the appearance of white people, they have not, it seems, been taboo objects during the past century or two. If (as I think we reasonably may) we take the story of the first appearance as having a core of historical truth, then we may take this as another instance where the initial response to novel experience took the thoroughly conservative form of a taboo reaction, but where this initial response was followed by explanatory innovation and disappearance of the taboo reaction.

Though we can hardly draw firm conclusions on the basis of these two instances, they do provoke a tentative suggestion. This is that the taboo reaction, that classic 'traditionalistic' defence against the threat of novel experience, is not so much an absolute support of the *status quo*, as a holding device that allows the theoretical system to adjust in its own good time. So the very reaction that once seemed to be purely and simply a bulwark of cognitive conservatism now looks as though it might have an additional function as part of the mechanism of adaptive innovation!

Let us turn now from studies of the indigenous religious traditions to studies of so-called 'conversion'. On first reflection, the reader may find it strange that studies of 'conversion' should be considered relevant to gaining a further understanding of the traditional religious systems. But I think he will get the point soon enough.

Earlier writing on 'conversion' to Islam and Christianity in Africa tended to treat it as an all-or-nothing jump from error to enlightenment, and as a more or less inevitable consequence of exposure to the 'true message' carried by God's appointed bearers. Such writing, however, failed dismally to make sense of the most prominent features of the sub-Saharan response to the so-called 'world religions'. Notably, it failed to provide any kind of explanation as to why, despite its enthusiastic acceptance in some areas, the 'message' was flatly rejected in others. Again, it had nothing illuminating to say about the constantly recurring situation in which what looked like simple acceptance contained in reality such a large element of selection and remoulding that the results were no longer identifiable as 'Islam' or 'Christianity'.

In recent years, scholars drawn from a variety of disciplines have come to see that the earlier approach has created an impasse. And in their attempts to find a way out of this impasse, they have shown a degree of intellectual convergence which is remarkable given the diversity of their disciplinary origins and personal religious commitments. Above all, there is now a very general agreement that the phenomena of 'conversion' can only be understood if we put the initial emphasis, not on the incoming religious messages, but rather on the indigenous religious frameworks and on the challenges they face from massive flows of novel experience.[34] Advocates of the new approach accept, of course, that the ideational changes subsumed under the label 'conversion' have involved extensive borrowing, from Islam, from Christianity, and, sometimes, from both at once. At the same time, they see such borrowing as largely directed, (a) by the structure and content of the existing cosmology, and (b) by the challenge to the explanatory capacity of this cosmology offered by novel events in the local social and natural environment.

This newer approach accounts for just those aspects of 'conversion' that the earlier writers found so puzzling. Thus it accounts for the way in which the messages of the world religions are accepted in some circumstances and rejected in others. Again, it accounts for the high degree of selection and remoulding which so often brings despair to the hearts of the proselytes of these religions. At the same time, this approach reveals 'conversion' as a further actualization of the traditional cosmologies' vast potential for creative elaboration in response to the challenge of new experience.

All in all, then, the picture emerging from the work just reviewed is one of a balance between opposing tendencies. On the one hand, there is the 'traditionalistic' view of belief, pressing toward cognitive conservatism. On the other, there is the desire for an adequate response to new experiential challenges, pressing toward cognitive innovation. Such innovation involves both purely endogenous creativity, and development of the existing belief-system through borrowing, reworking and integration of originally alien ideas. 'Traditionalistic', then, the thinking of these societies may be, but 'closed' it obviously is not.

So much for the reality of ideational change in these cultures. What can we say about the *mode* of change?

In general, the mode of change would seem to be one in which a single theoretical framework is subject to a more or less continuous series of innovations in response to the flow of novel experience. However loosely articulated and whatever its inconsistencies, this framework nonetheless retains an enduring unity through change. In talking like this, of course, we must avoid the extreme which Paulin Hountondji so scornfully labels 'the myth of primitive unanimity'.[35] Every thinking individual in a 'traditionalistic' community does his own little bit of reworking of the world-view handed down to him, in the course of applying it to everyday life in the light of his own interests. So every thinking individual has his own idiosyncratic version of such a world-view. Again, particular categories and sections within the community engage in similar reworking, and develop similar categorial and sectional versions. However, although the different interests and viewpoints of different individuals, categories and sections within the community do give rise to markedly different versions of the overall world-view, the disparity between these versions seldom becomes so great as to lead to the formation of a plurality of competing theoretical frameworks.

Thus it is true that, within a given community, we often find differences of opinion between interested parties as to the relative power and importance of the various categories of spiritual agency postulated by its cosmology. In Kalabari, for example, the 'wives' (possession priestesses) of the Water-spirits tend to extol the powers of the water-beings relative to those of other types of spirit; whilst specialists in clairvoyance tend to extol the powers of Ancestral and Medicine-spirits relative to those of Water-spirits. Again, in eastern Yorubaland, priests of the *orisa* (nature spirits) tend to extol their spiritual masters and mistresses *vis-à-vis* those of medicine spirits; whilst herbal healers tend to extol the powers of medicine spirits *vis-à-vis* those of the *orisa*.[36] Such differences, however, are differences between parties accepting the same inventory of categories of spiritual force, and the same ideas about how forces in the various categories work. They are not differences between parties adhering to rival and competing frameworks.

Not only do the bearers and developers of a particular framework successfully keep their differences within its confines. They actively resist attempts to create a confrontation between that framework and any other. Thus one of the more remarkable findings of recent monographic studies is that, even where the agents of trans-Saharan world-views, and in particular the agents of Christianity, have tried to confront the bearers of the indigenous world-views with what *they* see as competing alternatives, the local thinkers have nearly always succeeded in taking over some of the key concepts of these supposed alternatives, reworking them for their own purpose, integrating them into their own frameworks, and blissfully ignoring the attempts at confrontation.[37]

To sum up on 'traditionalistic' thinking as it emerges from recent monographic studies in Africa, let me reiterate two points. First, despite its conservatism, such thinking has an essentially 'open' character. Second, it tends to produce and sustain a single over-arching theoretical framework rather than a multiplicity of such frameworks.

Finally in this review of relevant findings from recent research, let me turn to work that bears on the characterization of intellectual 'modernity' generally and of scientific thinking in particular.

The last fifteen years have produced a spate of work both in historically-informed philosophy of science and in philosophically-informed history of science. And for an outsider to these disciplines, the problem has been one of selection. None the less, I have found two bodies of work particularly stimulating in relation to the pre-occupations of this essay.

The first of these consists of works concerned with the development and vicissitudes of the idea of progress in both early and later modern Europe.

Here I think of Toulmin's *Discovery of Time*; Plumb's *Death of the Past*; Medawar's essay 'On the Effecting of All Things Possible'; Sklair's *Sociology of Progress*; and above all Webster's *The Great Instauration*[38]. If these works convey any one message relevant to the present project, it is that the idea of cognitive progress, far from being something derived by simple induction from the actual course of early scientific achievement, was something in the air *before* modern science took off; something which was in fact a powerful motive force in this take-off.

The second body of work is concerned with the central role of inter-theoretic competition in the growth of knowledge. Here, let me start by reminding readers of Mill's *Essay on Liberty*, which is the precursor and inspirer of much of the more recent writing on this topic.[39] As regards the latter itself, I think particularly of Feyerabend's *Against Method*; of Lakatos's *Methodology of Scientific Research Programmes*; and of Laudan's *Progress and its Problems*.[40] These are some of the authors I mentioned earlier as playing Kuhn at his own game of backing characterization of science with detailed historical case-studies, and as demonstrating that his insistence on the one-at-a-time dominance of a succession of uncontested theoretical frameworks or 'paradigms' was not supported by the historical data.

In place of Kuhn's vision, these writers have proposed one in which the growth of knowledge depends precisely on healthy competition between supporters of rival theoretical frameworks. They back up their own vision, moreover, with a series of compelling examples. Thus they show how, from its beginnings, Copernican-Galilean astronomy developed in competition with a Ptolemaic rival. Again, they show how, both during the lifetime of its founder and for long after his death, Newtonian dynamics grew and flourished in intense competition with Hobbesian, Cartesian and other bodies of theory. Yet again, they show how the Huygenian wave theory of light appeared and developed in competition with Newtonian particle theory. Perhaps the most telling point in this context is made by Lakatos,[41] who reminds us that the posthumous development of Newtonian dynamics was at its most sluggish in England, which was precisely where it enjoyed unchallenged dominance, and at its most vigorous on the Continent, where it faced intense Cartesian competition.

We can, I think, carry the story nearer to our own times with two further examples. The first is that of Darwinian evolutionary theory. Darwin originally developed his theory in the face of intense resistance from the supporters of a variety of rival doctrines. And the development of neo-Darwinian orthodoxy owes much more than it cares to admit to the way in which respected supporters of these rival doctrines have continued, through their hostile criticism and competition, to keep its leading thinkers 'on their toes'.[42] The second example is that of Quantum Theory in physics. Once

again, the originators of this theory developed it in the teeth of resistance
from supporters of competing doctrines. And their successors have been
kept on their toes by similar resistance down to the present day.[43]

So much for inter-theoretic competition as a necessary if not sufficient
condition for the flourishing of science. But just how, according to our
authors, does it work its creative magic?

The post-Kuhnian scholars I have mentioned are not always as clear as
they might be on this question. Two crucial points, however, emerge from
their writing. The first, which is implicit in Feyerabend and Lakatos, and
more or less explicit in Laudan, is that some if not all judgements of
theoretical merit depend on criteria, such as economy, coverage, and predictive power, which are relative rather than absolute in character. Hence, a
context of inter-theoretic competition is necessary if they are to be brought
to bear effectively. The second, which emerges most clearly in Feyerabend
and Lakatos, is that supporters of a body of theory in competition with a
rival constantly search out and/or devise new configurations of experience,
in the hope that the rival will be unable to cope with them whilst their own
theory will digest them with ease. Hence competition generates new experience, and new experience provides stimulus to new theorizing.

In summing up the broad implications of this recent work in the history
and philosophy of science, let me emphasize two things. First, the fundamental importance of a faith in cognitive progress as a motive force in the
scientific enterprise. Second, the equal importance of inter-theoretic competition.

The critical response reviewed earlier and the work in various fields just
considered can be seen as complementary in relation to my 1967 essay.
From the critical response, one learns more about what was wrong with it,
and less about what, if anything, would put it right. From the recent work
considered, one learns again a certain amount about what was wrong with it,
but more about what would put it right. Taken together, however, the two
would seem to provide a fairly consistent set of indications for revision. Let
me end this section by trying to summarize these indications.

First, the basic enterprise, of African-Western comparison, is potentially
fruitful in a number of ways.

Second, subject to a little reformulation, the thesis of important continuities between traditional religious and modern scientific thinking is fundamentally sound.

Third, the 'closed'/'open' dichotomy is ripe for the scrap heap.

Fourth, more prominence must be given to the contrast between faith in
tradition and faith in progress. This now seems to me to be basic and not
merely subsidiary.

Fifth, the contrast between presence and absence of anxiety about threats to one's established theoretical framework must go. Such anxiety should be seen, not as peculiar to traditional settings, but rather as a human universal manifesting itself in different ways in traditional and in modern settings.

Sixth, the contrast between absence and presence of an awareness of theoretical alternatives should be replaced by a contrast which emphasizes lack of inter-theoretical competition in the traditional setting as against prominence of such competition in the modern setting. Here, I am not so much abandoning my earlier position as following Gellner's advice to reformulate the basic intuition behind it in a less solipsistic and more sociological manner. Thus in talking now of absence versus presence of inter-theoretic competition, I am not denying the significance for the individual thinker of the factor of awareness of theoretical alternatives. Rather, I am drawing attention to the fact that, where they are present, these alternatives are not just passively floating in the thinker's mind, but are being aggressively projected into it by other thinkers who wish to obliterate his own preferred theory.

Seventh, elements of a technological/economic/sociological interpretation should be spelt out in letters large enough for the most myopic 'anti-intellectualist' to read.

Tradition and modernity: a reformulation

Continuities

Since my original continuity thesis has been further elaborated in a number of articles since 1967,[44] and since it seems to need relatively little amendment, I shall try here to keep discussion of it short. I cannot avoid it altogether, however, because it is in terms of the cognitive 'common core' shared by African traditionalism and Western modernity that I hope to elucidate the contrasts between them.

The most important element of continuity between African traditionalism and Western modernity is the presence of two distinct yet intimately complementary levels of thought and discourse: the two levels which, up till recently, I have been content to refer to, on the one hand as 'common-sense' or 'everyday' and on the other hand as 'theoretical'. For the reasons given earlier, I now accept that this orthodox formulation of the relation between the two levels implies an antithesis which is in fact false. At the same time, I insist there *are* two distinct levels of thought and discourse, and that we need a terminology which does justice to their existence and their relationship. With these considerations in mind, I propose that, for 'everyday discourse' and 'theoretical discourse', we substitute 'primary theory' and 'secondary theory'. I hope that the aptness of this terminology will become apparent in what follows.

Primary theory really does not differ very much from community to community or from culture to culture. A particular version of it may be greatly developed in its coverage of one area of experience, and rather underdeveloped in its coverage of another. The next version may be undeveloped in its coverage of the first area, but greatly developed in its coverage of the second. These differences notwithstanding, however, the overall framework remains the same. In this respect, it provides the cross-cultural voyager with his intellectual bridgehead.

Primary theory gives the world a foreground filled with middle-sized (say between a hundred times as large and a hundred times as small as human beings), enduring, solid objects. These objects are inter-related, indeed inter-defined, in terms of a 'push-pull' conception of causality, in which spatial and temporal contiguity are seen as crucial to the transmission of change. They are related spatially in terms of five dichotomies: 'left/right'; 'above/below'; 'in-front-of/behind'; 'inside/outside'; 'contiguous/separate'. And temporally in terms of one trichotomy: 'before/at the same time/after'. Finally, primary theory makes two major distinctions amongst its objects: first, that between human beings and other objects; and second, among human beings, that between self and others.

In the case of secondary theory, differences of emphasis and degree give place to startling differences in kind as between community and community, culture and culture. For example, the Western anthropologist brought up with a purely mechanistic view of the world may find the spiritualistic world-view of an African community alien in the extreme. And Nigerian university students frequently find the modern Western mechanistic world-view equally alarming.[45] The diversity of world-pictures presented by secondary-theoretical discourse, indeed, is such that it almost defies any general characterization.

Amongst the few general remarks one can make about the content of secondary theory are the following. For a start, whilst the entities and processes of primary theory are thought of as directly 'given' to the human observer, those of secondary theory are thought of as somehow 'hidden'. This idea of the 'hiddenness' of the entities and processes of secondary theory is as central to African thought about gods and spirits as it is to Western thought about particles, currents and waves. Again, when contemplated against the background furnished by primary theory, the entities and processes postulated by secondary theory present a peculiar mixture of familiarity and strangeness. Characteristically, they share some properties with their primary-theory counterparts, lack some which the latter possess, and have many others which the latter do not possess. Once more, this blend of the familiar and the strange is as characteristic of the gods and spiritual forces of African world-views as it is of the impersonal entities of Western world-views.

From the above remarks, it should be clear that it is difficult to talk generally about the content of secondary theory except by making comparisons with that of primary theory. And this suggests the need for a general characterization of the relationship between the two levels of theory. Here, I think, two main points stand out.

The first point relates to causal vision. As the 'Ordinary Language' philosophers have never ceased to stress, primary theory is a marvellous instrument for coping with the world. But it is an instrument associated with a limited, 'push-pull' causal vision, and as such leaves man with a wide range of events and contingencies for which he cannot account and which he therefore has no prospect of predicting or bringing under control. Now if there is any single characteristic which enables us to make a clear functional distinction between primary theory and its secondary counterpart, it is the latter's vastly enlarged causal vision. Hence it seems plausible to suggest that it is the desire to transcend the limited causal vision of primary theory that has sustained secondary theory down the ages in societies both African and Western.

How does secondary theory help its users to achieve this aim? Principally by the postulation of a 'hidden' or 'underlying' realm of entities and processes of which the events of everyday experience, as described in primary-theory terms, are seen as surface manifestations. Once the causal regularities governing this hidden realm have been stated, their implications for the world as described in primary-theoretical terms are spelled out by a process akin to translation, guided by a 'dictionary' which correlates aspects of the 'hidden' world with aspects of the 'given'. As a result, many types of event which were previously inexplicable, unpredictable and uncontrollable lose this disturbing status.[46]

The second point is that, successful as it has been in transcending the limitations of primary theory, secondary theory remains, in at least four major ways, indebted to and/or dependent upon its primary counterpart.

To begin with, development of ideas as to the character of the 'hidden' realm is based on the drawing of analogies with familiar everyday experiences as described in primary-theory terms. Thus in the building of secondary theory in traditionalistic African contexts, ideas of gods and spirits are developed on the basis of analogies drawn from experiences of human action and interaction. And in modern Western theory-building, ideas concerning atoms, molecules, elementary particles, electric currents, waves and rays are developed on the basis of analogies drawn from experiences of moving and colliding balls, water-currents, water-waves, and so on. Subsequently, of course, the ideas about entities and processes so built up are subjected to further development by way of response to fresh explanatory challenges. This kind of development may involve: either the modification of features drawn from the original analogy; or the building in of features drawn from new analogies unrelated to the first one; or a mixture of both. The results, not surprisingly, include such 'bizarre' entities as gods who combine human and animal attributes, and particles that are also wave-packets. Hence the characteristic impression which secondary theory creates, of an amalgam of the familiar and the strange. In some cases, the process goes to extremes in which some of the newly built-in-attributes are to all intents and purposes incompatible with some of those derived from the original analogy. Thus we have gods who are thought of as enjoying both definite location and omnipresence; particles that move from point A to point B without traversing any intermediate positions, or can be located in two places at a given time. Here, clearly, the resources of primary-theoretical discourse are being strained almost to breaking point.[47]

Again, ideas of causality in secondary theory, both African and Western, have retained to a remarkable extent the age-old primary-theory emphasis on 'push-pull' or contact action. Thus in African religious theory, the emphasis on the omnipresence of spiritual force is nothing more or less than a way whereby, whilst respecting the principle of contact action, a spirit can be thought of as acting at any place.[48] And in Western secular theory, many of the modern developments of physical ideas can be seen as attempts to escape from the unwelcome hints of action-at-distance implicit in the Newtonian world-picture.[49]

Yet again, ideas about the relationship between the-world-as-described-by-primary-theory and the-world-as-described-by-secondary-theory have consistently been framed in terms which are primary-theoretical in origin. Thus the two 'worlds' have been variously characterized: as identical; as standing in a causal relationship to one another; as standing in the relationship of illusion to reality, and, lastly but perhaps most commonly, as standing in the relationship of the manifest to the hidden. Each of these characterizations proves inadequate when pursued to any length, leading its users into a bog of contradiction and paradox. In the attempt to overcome the inadequacies of the various individual characterizations, thinkers often oscillate between two or more of them. But since the individual characterizations are themselves mutually incompatible, such oscillation creates a further round of contradictions. Once again, then, it seems that we have a stretching of the resources of primary-theoretical discourse almost to breaking-point.[50]

Lastly, it would seem that explanations couched in terms of secondary theory are only complete when their implications for the world *as described by primary theory* have been set out.

Even from these highly condensed remarks, it should be obvious that we are faced here with a most curious situation. For whilst on the one hand the whole *raison d'être* of secondary theory is its success in transcending the limited causal vision of its primary counterpart, it seems on the other hand shackled to, dependent upon, and sometimes even hamstrung by, the resources of this counterpart. If what we have here is merely two bodies of theory, one with a more restricted causal vision and one with a wider, why does the latter, far from replacing the former, remain enslaved to it?

A search for the solution to this puzzle takes us into some of the mistier realms of prehistory, biology and psycho-linguistics, and involves a collation of findings which are as yet only tentative. Nonetheless, the outlines of a possible answer can, I think, be discerned.

Let us start by taking another look at primary theory. Now, there is a sense in which such theory must 'correspond' to at least certain aspects of the reality which it purports to represent. If it did not so 'correspond', its users down the ages could scarcely have survived. At the same time, its structure has a fairly obvious functional relationship to specific human aims and to the specific human equipment available for achieving them. In particular, it is well tailored to the specific kind of hand-eye co-ordination characteristic of the human species and to the associated manual technology which has formed the main support of everyday life from the birth of the species down to the present day. Think here of the 'manageable' dimensions and the enduring character of the foreground objects; also of the causal attributes in terms of which they are defined, so many of which are functional in the context of manual technology. Further, it is well tailored to the fact that this manual technology depends to an important extent on a type of social co-operation mediated by verbal communication. Here, think again of the dimensions of the objects, of their enduring character, and of the system of concepts for locating them in space; all of these in relation to the prerequisites of conveying reference to aspects of reality between human speaker and human listener.[51]

This striking 'fit' between primary theory and a co-operative manual technology suggests a great antiquity for the former. Thus, if we are to believe the prehistorians, co-operative manual technology is something which can be traced back to the birth of the human species. Moreover, primary theory seems to be, not just a happy adjunct to an economic and social set-up which could have been in operation for hundreds of thousands of years before its invention, but a *sine qua non* of anything more than the most rudimentary development of such a set-up.[52] Primary theory, then, must date back at least to the very early days of a co-operative manual technology.

Having thus dated primary theory back to the dawn of human history, we find ourselves face-to-face with a further interesting possibility: the possibility that an element of innate predisposition lies behind its obstinate entrenchment at the base of human intellectual life. Thus, if we are to believe the prehistorians once more, we are talking about an era in which active evolution of the human brain under the pressures of natural selection was still in progress. Now for early human groups, the survival value of the cultural complex comprising co-operative manual technology and a language structured in terms of primary theory must have been immense. And the survival value of all those genetic traits making for the type of cerebral organization capable of supporting such a complex must have been correspondingly great. So, given the working of natural selection on such traits over hundreds of thousands of years, the human species may well have come to have a central nervous system innately fitted, not just for co-operative manual technology, but for the primary-theoretical thought and discourse which is essential to it.[53]

If this version of human emergence is correct, there should be tell-tale present-day clues, both in the realm of cerebral structure and function, and in that of behavioural development. In fact, such clues do seem to have been coming to light in recent years. Thus, after a long period of flirtation with a *tabula rasa* model of higher brain centres, human biologists seem inclined by more recent evidence to think that the brain has elements of genetically-programmed structure and physiology particularly fitted to seeing, thinking and talking in primary-theoretical terms.[54] Again, the psycho-linguists, contemplating the extraordinary facility with which children learn primary-theoretical discourse under a minimum of deliberate instruction, have felt compelled to invoke an element of genetic programming to account for this phenomenon.[55]

All this, of course, does not mean that we can ignore any other factor in intellectual and linguistic development. Thus we have to face the fact that a child does not come to produce primary-theoretical discourse unless he is exposed to his elders' use of such discourse; and the fact that, when he does come to produce primary-theoretical discourse, it is couched in the language of the community in which he has been brought up. And these facts, it would seem, can only be accounted for in terms of a large element of learning. However, the recent findings in human biology and psycho-linguistics would seem to rule out for good the old empiricist emphasis on a *tabula rasa* brain and a development of intellectual and linguistic skills that depends entirely on learning. Present-day debate, indeed, centres, not on innate disposition versus learning, but on the question of just how these two factors are combined.[56]

Whatever the exact manner in which innate predisposition and learning are combined, it seems clear that, in each new generation, the foundations of primary-theoretical thinking are laid afresh in the pre-verbal phase of infancy, and that non-verbal schemata prefiguring the principal primary-theory concepts arise during the infant's active exploration of his surroundings. If this is indeed so, it follows that, by the time he is ready to start trying to talk, the infant has already begun to see and think about the world in a manner which is consistent with the emphases of primary-theoretical discourse. Again, if the infant's world is already so structured by the time he starts making his first efforts to talk, it seems likely that his linguistic socialization can get under way only through his exposure to that aspect of discourse that latches onto the existing structures: i.e. primary-theoretical discourse.[57]

And what of secondary theory? Well, although we shall never have even the roughest idea of the *time* of its first emergence, it seems likely that the *cause* of such emergence was the sheer efficiency of primary theory in explaining, predicting and controlling the course of events in so many areas of human experience. The efficiency in so many areas would have served to highlight its incompetence in a few. And since these few included some of great significance to human welfare, the highlighting would have brought in its train anxiety and further intellectual effort aimed at rectifying the situation. Such effort, however, would have had to use the resources already available: i.e. those of primary theory. Existing ideas of 'hidden' agency (e.g. enemy throwing spear from cover) would have provided the prototypes for ideas concerning the more radical 'hiddenness' of the entities and processes postulated by nascent secondary theory. Other existing concepts, subjected to analogical extension, would have been used to fill in the details of such theory.

So much for conjectural history. In each new generation, the secondary status of secondary theory is reinforced by the processes of pre-verbal exploration and early linguistic socialization which I have already outlined. These leave secondary-theoretical discourse in the position of a Johnny-Come-Lately in every individual life. The very learning of it by the individual can only be through analogical elucidation in terms of primary-theoretical ideas.

In short, then, if the picture I have presented is anywhere near correct, the two types of theory are respectively primary and secondary not only in an historical but also in a developmental sense. Hence the inevitable dependence of the latter on the former in all ongoing intellectual activity.

At this point, we can truly appreciate both the aptness and the irony of Russell's famous characterization of 'Ordinary Language' as 'Stone Age Metaphysics'. With this striking phrase, he was one of the first to draw attention to the fact that 'Ordinary Language', far from being a 'Neutral Observation Language', embodied a theory like any other, and an ancient and in many respects outmoded one at that, tailored as it was to age-old and rather limited human capabilities and interests. Russell, however, used the characterization as a means of denigrating 'Ordinary Language' and of pouring ridicule on those philosophers who devoted their lives to studying it. What he failed to consider was the possibility that, through the operation of evolutionary processes at the dawn of human history, 'Stone Age Metaphysics' had left an indelible imprint on the human brain. If indeed it has left such an imprint, then, like it or not, we are stuck with it.[58]

So far in this survey of continuities between African and Western thought, I have made little of the fact that impresses most people, whether laymen or anthropologists, more than any other. Here I refer to the fact that the 'hidden world' presented by secondary theory in the typical African community is, and probably has been since very early times, a world of personal forces; whereas the 'hidden world' presented by Western secondary theory has, in recent centuries, become more and more a world of impersonal entities and processes. For a person who lives with one type of 'hidden' world, it is sometimes difficult even to imagine what it would be like to live with the other type.[59] Clearly, then, unless the approach in terms of continuities can also do justice to this momentous difference, it is not going to impress anyone. Fortunately the approach can cope quite adequately, as I shall now show.

Here, let me start from the observation that the builder of secondary theory is concerned above all to show order, regularity and predictability where primary theory has failed to show them. In search of his key analogies, therefore, he tends to look to those areas of everyday experience maximally associated with these qualities.

Now in the African setting, we are faced with societies possessed of fairly clear-cut patterns of social organization; societies changing, it is true, but changing for the most part at an easy pace which allows those who are members at any given time a good deal of certainty in their expectations as to the responses of those around them. At the same time, these societies have a fairly simple manual technology and a relatively low degree of control over the vicissitudes of non-human nature. In the consciousness of the member of such a society, it is human action and interaction that is maximally associated with order, regularity and predictability: hence it is from this area of experience that the key analogies are mostly drawn, with largely personalized theoretical schemes as a result.

The remarks made above about African societies are also applicable to Western societies up till about AD 1200. From that time on, however, there was a steady acceleration of social change coupled with a steady increase in technological development and environmental control. Many historians, indeed, would probably agree that the technological advances were a major factor in the destabilization of society. Be this as it may, the result was that order, regularity and predictability came to be associated less and less with the realm of human action and interaction, more and more with that of non-living phenomena, both artificial and natural. Hence the search for key analogies, though it started with the former, shifted gradually but inexorably to the latter. As a result, secondary theory became more and more impersonal and mechanistic in its content.[60]

To sum up, it would seem that even those differences in the content of secondary theory, which make most people feel that the religious world-views of Africa and the impersonal world-views of the modern West are poles apart, turn out to be readily explicable in terms of the continuity thesis. In the light of this thesis, indeed, such differences come to seem relatively superficial. The really deep differences between traditionalism and modernity lie elsewhere. It is to them that we must now turn.

Contrasts

Let me start this section by blocking out two contrasts which I take to be basic. First, that between a 'traditionalistic' and a 'progressivist' concept of knowledge. Second, that between a 'consensual' and a 'competitive' mode of elaborating secondary theory.

By a 'traditionalistic' concept of knowledge, I mean one which sees the main lineaments of the community's accepted body of theory as having been handed down from the ancients. By a 'progressivistic' concept of knowledge, I mean one which sees the body of theory as something in the process of gradual but steady improvement; one which sees the ancients as having had a minimum of acceptable theory, the thinkers of today as having a rather better theoretical achievement, and the thinkers of tomorrow as likely to have an achievement much greater than anything we can conceive of today.[61]

By a 'consensual' mode of theorizing, I mean a situation in which all members of a community, differences over matters of detail notwithstanding, share a single over-arching framework of secondary-theoretical assumptions, and carry out intellectual innovation within that framework. By a competitive mode of theorizing, I mean a situation involving competition between rival 'schools' of thinkers promoting mutually-incompatible frameworks of secondary-theoretical assumptions.[62]

Having sketched these contrasts, I define cognitive 'traditionalism' in terms of a 'traditionalistic' concept of knowledge closely coupled with a 'consensual' mode of theorizing, and cognitive 'modernism' in terms of a 'progressivistic' concept of knowledge closely coupled with a 'competitive' mode of theorizing.

Why emphasize these particular contrasts? Quite simply because they are pivotal. Thus on the one hand, they underpin most if not all of the other cognitive contrasts which we normally associate with the labels 'traditionalism' and 'modernism'. And on the other hand, they themselves are more or less directly underpinned by contrasts in the realms of technology, economy and social organization.

In what follows, I shall start by presenting, first 'traditionalism', then 'modernism', as syndromes underpinned by the two pairs of key factors mentioned above. I shall then try to place the two syndromes in their broader technological, economic and social contexts.

If we are to gain a proper understanding of cognitive 'traditionalism', a little more needs to be said at the outset about the 'traditionalistic' concept of knowledge.

Considered superficially, the concept is a descriptive one. Thus it tells us the source of our main pillars of knowledge (the ancients), and the means whereby they reached us (person-to-person transmission down the ages). However, it also contains within itself a criterion for legitimating any item of belief. (The item has been passed down from the ancients, therefore it must be valid.)

This manner of legitimating belief, moreover, presumes rather than excludes legitimation in terms of efficacy in relation to the aims of explanation, prediction and control. Thus an item of belief is legitimated, *not just* because it is certified as having come down to us from the ancients; but *ultimately* because the beliefs of the ancients, in general, are thought to have proved their worth down the ages as instruments of explanation, prediction and control. To put it in a nutshell, beliefs are accepted, not just because they are seen as age-old, but because they are seen as time-tested.

Thus defined, the 'traditionalistic' concept of knowledge does have some braking effect on intellectual innovation. For a start, the idea that the main lines of worthwhile knowledge were revealed once and for all to the ancients is in itself a profound discouragement, both to anyone carrying the rudiments of a new vision of the world, and to any wider audience to whom he may expose these rudiments. Again, the idea that these main lines of knowledge have served the community well from the time of the ancients down to the present day does much to take the edge off a current run of predictive failures. For where a body of theory is seen as having such a long run of predictive success behind it, any current run of failures must seem of relatively minor consequence. In these circumstances, certainly, such a run can hardly encourage ideas of replacing current theory with something totally new.

Having acknowledged the undoubted conservative influence of the 'traditionalistic' concept of knowledge, we must also note that this influence is far from putting a complete stop to change. As we have seen, 'traditionalistic' legitimation of belief itself implicitly acknowledges efficacy in relation to explanation, prediction, and control as the ultimate criterion of cognitive validity. And where this criterion reigns supreme, it must exercise a residual pressure for change. Thus whenever new events occur which cannot be explained, predicted or controlled by means of the existing body of theory, the latter is shown up as wanting, and pressure created toward whatever innovation is necessary to remedy the defect. Nor do the results necessarily offend against 'traditionalistic' sentiments; for those main lines of the body of theory which are thought to have been passed down from the ancients are broad enough to permit quite a lot of detailed change. Successive doses of such detailed change down the centuries can, and do, of course, eventually amount to a change in the main outlines of the body of theory. But this is a process of which, for reasons which we shall enlarge on later, members of the community at a particular time remain unaware.

So much for the 'traditionalistic' concept of knowledge. The 'consensual' mode of theorizing makes an equally important contribution to the general character of the 'traditional' syndrome.

In the first place, where this mode of theorizing predominates, anxiety-provoking challenge to the theoretical *status quo* comes not from rival theory (which is by definition absent) but from the flow of experience. Hence the prominence in such settings of the taboo reaction, which is an attempt to hold at arm's length and where possible eliminate recalcitrant experience; and of the time-annulment rite, which is an attempt to set at nought the very process which brings about the accumulation of such experience. Striking though these defensive reactions are, however, we should remember that they are only one side of the response to novel experience, and that another more positive side is provided by theoretical innovation. Perhaps, as I suggested earlier, we should view them, not as attempts to ward off novelty in any absolute and final way, but as attempts to buy time for the intellectual innovators.

Secondly, where the consensual mode prevails, there is little to promote the sort of continuous critical monitoring of the theoretical framework which we associate with cognitive 'modernism'.

For a start, the Old Adam, observed either at the heart of African traditionalism or at the spearhead of Western modernity, is anything but spontaneously self-critical. So far as possible, he hangs on to his established framework come what may. If he starts to criticize it himself, this is usually only by way of anticipating the critical assaults of other thinkers committed to rival frameworks. In the consensual setting, such others are by definition absent.

Again, most of the criteria so far devised for the critical assessment of efficacy in relation to the goals of explanation, prediction and control – e.g. simplicity, scope, degree of dependence on *ad hoc* assumptions, predictive power – are essentially relative rather than absolute in character. They are designed to tell us which of a pair of theoretical frameworks is, cognitively speaking, the 'better'. They are not designed to tell us whether a single framework, considered in isolation, is 'good' or 'bad'. In a setting where a single over-arching framework is what we have, there is nothing to stimulate their formulation, and nothing to apply them to, even were they by some miracle to be formulated.

Thirdly, there is nothing in the 'consensual' setting to break the 'natural' link between secondary theory and practical life. I use the word 'natural' here because, as I suggested earlier, secondary theory very probably originated as a response to the demands of practical life; and because, in more recent times, the *ultimate* sustainer of secondary theorizing in cultures both African and Western does seem to have been the belief of the community at large in the actual or potential relevance of such theorizing to practical life. If the link is a natural one, it follows that it requires rather special circumstances to break it; and in this setting such circumstances do not arise. As a result, secondary theory is closely geared to such concerns as war and peace, social harmony, health, adequate food supplies and so on. And the specialist custodians, elaborators and innovators of this theory are the very men who are engaged in applying it to such concerns. This is not to say that their thought does not sometimes soar above everyday matters. Nonetheless, it returns to them again and again as does a ground-feeding bird to earth.

One consequence of this link between theory and practice would seem to be a concern with systematization and consistency somewhat slighter than that which prevails among 'modernized' intellectuals. Now I don't want to put as much emphasis on this business of consistency as do some scholars obsessed with their own idiosyncratic reading of Evans-Pritchard on the Azande. On the one hand, 'traditionalistic' thinkers find inconsistency as repugnant as do 'modernists' when it is thrust under their noses.[63] On the other hand, as I pointed out earlier, all thinkers engaged in elaborating secondary theory stretch the resources of primary theory in a way which leads them constantly toward inconsistency and contradiction. And the results of this show up, not just in African religious theory, but also at the heart of such Western theoretical enterprises as Quantum Theory. However, where secondary theory is also predominantly applied theory, it tends to be developed and mobilized piecemeal, as particular kinds of practical exigency arise. In the absence of any pressure for constant cross-reference between one piece and another, there is a tendency toward loose articulation and what seems to the unsympathetic 'modernist' an undue tolerance of contradictions.

Another consequence of the theory-practice link is a limitation in the sheer scope of secondary theory. For whilst the link remains unbroken, the theorist's attention remains centred on the somewhat restricted circle of experience that has current practical significance to himself and to his community.[64] Though he may sometimes venture briefly beyond the perimeter of the circle, there is nothing in his setting to force him into sustained exploration of the vast territories outside.

Let me now try to sum up the characteristics of the 'traditionalist' syndrome. To start with, there is an overall conservatism which nonetheless allows for gradual adaptive change. Then there is a well-developed set of defences against new and/or recalcitrant experience, which however seems designed less to block off such experience for good than to give breathing space for its assimilation. Again, although there is a determined pursuit of the goals of explanation, prediction and control, there is little if any explicit critical monitoring of secondary theory in terms of general criteria of empirical adequacy or consistency. Finally, there is a limitation of scope which stems from the fact that the coverage of secondary theory is centred on experience that is of current practical significance.

If this seems a rather negative characterization of cognitive 'traditionalism', let me not give the reader the impression that I ignore or despise its fruits. On the contrary, I maintain that, although these fruits may be limited in the domain of non-human phenomena, they are much more impressive than most Western scholars have so far acknowledged in the domain of human affairs.[65] But of this, more anon.

Let us now turn to a brief sketch of cognitive 'modernism'. Here, we are on more difficult ground; for the two underlying factors, a 'progressivistic' concept of knowledge and 'competitive' mode of theorizing, generate, not one set of consequences, but a whole spectrum of sets. Given limitations of space, perhaps the only solution is to convey the range of the spectrum by brief descriptions of its two poles. In order not to run ahead of the argument, let me give these poles the characterless labels A and B.

Pole A

The 'progressivist' concept of knowledge has some profound consequences for human intellectual activity. The idea that very little of enduring worth has been handed down to us by the ancients, that even the theoretical contributions of today's older generation are likely to turn out flawed, and that the future will bring a much larger revelation of theoretical truth than any available to us at the present day, is clearly a liberating one so far as individual intellectual innovation is concerned. For a start, whilst the 'traditionalist' concept enjoined a broad adherence to the theoretical *status quo*, the 'progressivist' concept enjoins attempts either to modify it drastically or to overthrow it. Again, where the 'traditionalist' concept encouraged the thinker to make light of a run of predictive failure in accepted secondary theory, the 'progressivist' concept encourages a less forgiving attitude.

Profound though its effect may be, however, the 'progressivist' concept of knowledge is not the sole key to the understanding of intellectual modernity. Just as important, if not more so, is the 'competitive' mode of theorizing. Indeed, one can say without exaggeration that, once consensus gives way to competition, an entirely new situation arises.

To start with, the principal challenge to existing secondary theory comes, no longer primarily from novel experience, but from rival theory; and the principal source of anxiety is no longer recalcitrant fact but aggressive intellectual competitor.

As in the 'consensual' setting, such anxiety evokes a defensive response designed to eliminate the threat that triggered it. But as the character of the threat is now different, so too is that of the defensive response. In place of taboo reaction and time-annulment rite, we now have the campaign of denigration against the rival school of theorists, and the attempt to suggest a degree of silliness that renders their product unworthy of serious consideration.[66]

Again, as in the 'consensual' setting, the purely negative response is combined with a more constructive one. But again, as the challenge is now different, so too is the response. This time round, each school of theorists attempts to show the superiority of its product by invoking criteria of cognitive adequacy common to all parties.

One criterion which features prominently in these inter-school disputes is that of consistency or freedom from contradiction. Each party devotes a great deal of time and energy, not just to pointing out the inconsistencies of the theory promoted by its rivals, but also to scanning for and eliminating inconsistencies in its own theory in anticipation of counter-attacks by those rivals. The result is a considerable increase, on all sides, in the systematization of theory.

Other criteria prominent in these battles include simplicity, scope, explanatory power and predictive power. As we saw earlier, such criteria are essentially relative. In the 'consensual' setting, therefore, they can hardly be formulated, let alone brought into operation. Once inter-theoretic competition is established, however, they can be developed and used to make invidious comparisons between bodies of theory. Here again, each party uses such criteria, not just to expose the inadequacies of the theory promoted by its rivals, but also to spotlight and stimulate development work on those aspects of its own favoured theory which require strengthening if counter-attacks are to be successfully repelled.

Most if not all of the criteria in this second group are concerned, not so much with the internal characteristics of theory, as with its ability to cope with experience. Not surprisingly, then, the offensive use of such criteria often involves the searching out or devising of new configurations of experience with the aim of showing up the explanatory-cum-predictive incompetence of rival theory whilst highlighting the corresponding competence of one's own product. Hence a tremendous emphasis on observation and experiment. From one point of view, this could be seen simply as an expansion of something that was there already in the consensual setting. The situation, however, is not quite so simple as that. For whereas in the 'consensual' setting it is practically significant experience which serves as the challenge and stimulus to theoretical innovation, in the 'competitive' setting it is inter-theoretic competition that stimulates the quest for new experience through observation and experiment. In a sense, then, the relation between theory and experience is reversed as we pass from the 'consensual' to the 'competitive' setting.[67]

We can, of course, qualify the contrasts made above by pointing out that, whatever the *ultimate* stimulus to theoretical innovation in the 'competitive' setting, the *proximate* stimulus still remains experience. But if we look at the matter in this way, we are forced to attend to yet another striking contrast. Thus in the 'competitive' setting, the leading part in stimulating theoretical innovation is played, not by practically-significant experiences and problems, but by configurations of experience selected or devised specifically for purposes of inter-school warfare. As a result, we get a progressive divorce of secondary theory from practical life. Such a divorce has been a major feature of the development of Western 'modernism'. From the beginning of the seventeenth century to the middle of the nineteenth, the great flowering of secondary theory owed little to practically significant experience and had virtually no impact on practical life.[68] As for the spectacular increase in such impact from the middle of the nineteenth century to the present day, this has been due almost entirely to the growth of an army of specialist intermediaries between unrepentantly unpractical theorists and unrepentantly non-theoretical practical men.

Perhaps the most striking thing about all this is the relation which it creates between expansion of the range of experience and expansion of the empirical coverage of theory. Thus inter-theoretic competition generates a constantly expanding range of experience. In turn, the constantly expanding range of experience faces each school of theorists involved in the competition with a standing ultimatum: 'Either match each new access of experience with an appropriate extension of theoretical coverage; or see your theory drop out of the competition.' The result is a kind of dynamic and direction which is absent from cognitive 'traditionalism'.

As to the actual area of human intellectual enterprise to which this description is meant to apply, it is broadly that of secondary-theoretical thinking about non-human nature in Europe and North America over the last three hundred years.

Pole B

Like its Pole A counterpart, the Pole B outcome is one in which the 'progressivist' concept of knowledge encourages theoretical innovation and proliferation. In this respect, indeed, the latter concedes nothing to the former.

Again like its Pole A counterpart, the Pole B outcome is one in which the 'competitive' setting ensures that rival theory rather than practically significant experience provides the ultimate source of anxiety for the theorist. Here, however, there are some significant differences in the manner of response to the challenge and to the anxiety.

In the first place, the negative aspect of the response is far more pronounced. Participants in inter-school rivalry sometimes give one the impression that, if they could get away with it, they would stick at nothing to eliminate members of other schools from the arena.

Secondly, whilst there are elements of the more positive response described for the Pole A outcome, they are overshadowed by other, very different phenomena. Thus it is true that criteria of cognitive adequacy such as consistency, simplicity, scope, explanatory power, predictive power and so on are brandished in inter-school battles. Again, lip-service at least is paid to the strategy of searching for experience which will show up the incompetence of rival theory and the competence of one's own theory in the light of these criteria. Such elements, however, are above all a facade for polemical exchanges of another kind, governed by considerations quite distinct from those of strictly cognitive adequacy. At stake here are the moral, aesthetic or emotional acceptability of particular theoretical schemes. This is an area in which there is very little in the way of agreed criteria of 'better' and 'worse'; and as a result, inter-school argument tends to take on a no-holds-barred 'smear and sneer' quality.

Here, then, for all the innovation, the proliferation and the competition, there is none of the steady expansion of the circle of experience and of the empirical coverage of theory which we found to be the hallmark of the Pole A outcome.

Very few people except some of the more humourless of those involved will be in any doubt as to the area of human activity which this description is intended to apply to. It is of course that of the so-called social sciences as pursued in Europe and North America over the last hundred years.

The two outcomes just sketched are, as I pointed out earlier, the poles of a spectrum; hence there is a virtual continuum between them. The nearer we are to the domain of non-living phenomena, the more the course of inter-school warfare is dominated by shared criteria of efficacy in relation to explanation, prediction and control, and by aggressive use of newly-discovered or devised configurations of experience to criticize rival theory and boost one's own in the light of such criteria. The nearer we get to the domain of human social life, the more such warfare is dominated by rival visions of what is morally, aesthetically, or emotionally acceptable, with little in the way of shared criteria of 'better' or 'worse' to encourage any element of genuine reasoning.

The key factor here seems to be the strength of all parties' commitment to the goals of explanation, prediction and control relative to that of their commitment to other values. The greater the relative strength of this commitment, the more the outcome approximates to that described for Pole A. The smaller its relative strength, the more the outcome approximates to that described for Pole B.

I think we have now arrived at the point at which we can appraise the claims of intellectual 'modernism' to some sort of cognitive superiority over 'traditionalism'.

As long as we stay near Pole A, such claims seem very plausible. First, the 'progressivist' concept of knowledge encourages a willingness to try radically new theoretical ideas which has no counterpart in traditional settings. Secondly, inter-theoretic competition brings with it a continuous critical monitoring of theory, in respect both of consistency and of empirical adequacy. Such monitoring, which is surely important in eliminating cognitive defects, also has no real counterpart in traditional settings. Thirdly and most significantly, inter-theoretic competition leads to a more or less continuous expansion in the range of experience; and this in turn leads to a more or less continuous expansion in the empirical coverage of theory. The practical orientation of theory in traditional settings encourages no comparable expansion in the range of experience, and therefore provides no comparable stimulus to expansion of empirical coverage.[69]

The nearer we stray to Pole B, the less plausible the claim to cognitive superiority. The willingness to try radically new theoretical ideas is still there. But competition, however fierce, now produces little or no serious critical monitoring in respect of consistency or empirical adequacy. Nor does it produce that steady expansion in range of experience and degree of empirical coverage which is perhaps the strongest ground for any 'modernist' claims to cognitive superiority.[70]

On the question of cognitive superiority, then, our answer must be: it depends on the domain in which the theorizing is being carried out. 'Yes' in the domain of non-living things. 'No' in the domain of human social life. 'Perhaps' in the middle.

This, of course, is an answer proposed by a 'modernist'. In principle, however, it is one which the 'traditionalist' himself might be brought to accept; for it appeals to criteria of efficacy in relation to goals which have a high priority in his own approach to the world: explanation, prediction and control.

Having given descriptive sketches of the two syndromes, let me complete my task with some brief suggestions as to their broader human and environmental contexts.

Here, I am going to make two assumptions. First, that much of what I have said about the 'traditionalistic' syndrome in Africa is applicable to the thought of earlier Europe. Second, that much of what I am about to say as to the technological, economic and social background of this syndrome is also applicable in the case of earlier Europe. The reader will have to judge the validity of these assumptions for himself.[71] Meanwhile, it follows that the explanatory suggestions I am about to make concern, not only the differences between African 'traditionalism' and Western 'modernism', but also the transition from Western 'traditionalism' to Western 'modernism'.

At the outset, note that, in both of our two pairs of key underlying factors, each member of the pair supports the other.

Consider the two factors underlying the 'traditionalistic' syndrome. On the one hand, the 'traditionalistic' concept of knowledge receives crucial support from the 'consensual' mode of theorizing. Since 'tradition' can be taken as a guide to present-day affairs only when it speaks with a reasonably unanimous voice, the 'traditionalist' concept of knowledge will wax strong only where there is a broad theoretical consensus available for handing down. As soon as 'tradition' starts to transmit two or more clearly competing bodies of secondary theory, it must lose its influence as a guide to the present. On the other hand, the 'consensual' mode of theorizing also gets support from the 'traditionalistic' concept of knowledge. The latter, as we have seen, discourages the elaboration of radically new theoretical schemes which would convert the 'consensual' setting into a 'competitive' one.

Consider also the two factors underlying the 'modernistic' syndrome. On the one hand, the 'progressivist' concept of knowledge receives support from a well-established 'competitive' situation. For at least in the domain of non-living things, the steady increase in empirical coverage of theory which results from such a situation has a clearly progressive character. On the other hand, the 'competitive' situation is supported by the progressivist concept. For by encouraging the elaboration of radically new theoretical schemes, the latter ensures the theoretical proliferation which sustains competition.

From the above, it follows that any external influence which tends to strengthen or weaken one member of a pair of underlying factors will, albeit indirectly, have a corresponding effect on the other member.

With this preliminary clarification, let us get down to some specific suggestions as to what the relevant external influences may be.

Two variables would seem to be particularly relevant to the strengthening or weakening of the 'traditionalistic' concept of knowledge: mode of transmission of ideas and pace of social and environmental change.

As regards mode of transmission, it would seem that the oral mode favours the 'traditionalistic' concept of knowledge, whilst the written mode tends to weaken its hold.[72]

In considering oral transmission, we must stress that its most distinctive effects depend on the use of the human memory as a storage device. On the one hand, memory tends to remould the past in the image of the present, and hence to minimize the amount of change that has taken place down the ages. On the other hand, memory tends, over the generations, to ascribe all innovations, whether socio-cultural or intellectual, to an initial 'time of the beginnings'. Oral transmission, therefore, encourages a view of the past which sees the main outlines of one's society as having been shaped long ago and as having undergone little essential change since then. Again, it tends to produce a conviction that the main outlines of the body of theory which guides present-day life were laid down equally long ago and have served well ever since. Here, clearly, we have one foundation of the 'traditionalistic' concept of knowledge and the 'traditionalistic' legitimation of belief. For, as Ernest Gellner remarked some years ago in a passage which deserves more recognition than it has had, if all available information leads one to believe that present-day society and its environment are not essentially different from earlier society and its environment, then it is good inductive policy to use a supposedly age-old, time-tested body of secondary theory to cope with present-day exigencies.[73]

When written transmission comes in alongside oral, it profoundly shakes the view of the past encouraged by the latter. Thus, on the one hand it highlights the difference between the present state of society and various earlier states. And on the other hand, it reveals that a body of secondary theory taught by the accredited socializing agents as age-old and time-tested is nothing of the sort. Now once the difference between the present and earlier states of society and environment is thus emphasized, use of allegedly age-old theory no longer looks like good inductive policy. And in any case, no body of theory with such claims to antiquity is now in sight. In this way, then, written transmission weakens the hold of the 'traditionalistic' legitimation of belief.

Pace of change would seem to have much the same relation to the 'traditionalistic' concept of knowledge as does mode of transmission ideas. All societies, of course, are involved in more or less continuous change. Nonetheless, change is sometimes slow and gentle; sometimes rapid and all-disturbing. And whether it is one or the other would seem to have appreciable effects on the concept of knowledge.

In periods of slow and gentle change, the idea of a fundamental continuity between social present and social past is easily sustained, particularly where oral tradition prevails. Such periods, accordingly, favour the use of allegedly age-old and time-tested secondary theory, and hence the 'traditionalistic' concept of knowledge.

In periods of prolonged and drastic social upheaval, however, the conviction of fundamental continuity between past and present is shattered, oral transmission or no oral transmission. During such a period, the thinking man is painfully aware that he faces a totally new situation. Confronted with allegedly age-old and time-tested theory, he can only see it as a gigantic irrelevance. In such circumstances the hold of the 'traditionalistic' concept of knowledge is greatly weakened.[74]

So much for the ways in which a switch from oral to written transmission of theory and an acceleration in the pace of social change may, singly or jointly, weaken the 'traditionalistic' concept of knowledge. How far, if at all, do these factors contribute to the emergence of its 'progressivistic' counterpart?

This is a difficult question to answer. To start with, it is clear that deprivation of the guidance of 'tradition' leaves the thinking man in a terrifying vacuum. What is not clear is whether or not there is any inevitability about the filling of this vacuum with a 'progressivistic' concept of knowledge. After all, a community and its thinkers, faced with such a vacuum, may just fall into despair and cognitive inaction. There is some evidence that this is what happened to some of the Greek centres of thought in the century or two before the birth of Christ. And it seems to have been the reaction of some thinkers in sixteenth-century Europe.[75] Nonetheless, historical and comparative studies would seem to teach us that despair generates amongst those it afflicts a fairly desperate search for means of escape. Such studies would also seem to teach us that one very characteristic means of escape from current despair is the development of a faith in 'jam tomorrow'. Perhaps, then, we may see the 'progressivist' concept of knowledge as a means of escape through faith in cognitive 'jam tomorrow'!

If this sounds a little crude, I think it has to be admitted that it fits the historical evidence for Europe rather well. True, as I have pointed out, the 'progressivist' concept gets inductive support from the fruits of well-established competitive theorizing in the 'hard sciences'. However, in the actual course of European history, this concept was first developed at the start of that great flowering of competitive theorizing which we call the Scientific Revolution, and not at its heyday. As one of the first prophets of cognitive progress, Bacon was an inspirer of the revolution, not a summarizer of its achievements.[76] One could perhaps argue that the 'progressivistic' concept was an inductive extrapolation from progress in technology, which had been considerable since about AD 1000, and which had borne practical fruit in a number of fields.[77] This achievement, however, was the result of applying, either genuinely age-old secondary theory (e.g. Ptolemaic astronomy), or even older primary theory. And it had coexisted for some time with an essentially 'traditionalistic' concept of knowledge. Considered purely as a piece of induction, then, the 'progressivist' concept would have been an over-extrapolation, and a belated one at that. So even if we do take this possibility into account, we still need some additional factor to complete our explanation. One factor which has been mooted frequently in recent historical writings is the Judaeo-Christian religious heritage; the suggestion being that the millennial overtones of this heritage provided the seeds from which a full-blown 'progressivist' faith developed.[78] Whilst accepting the probable importance of this factor, however, we should also note that the millennial aspect of Judaeo-Christian ideas has tended to lie dormant for long periods, and to emerge to prominence only when and where widespread anxiety and despair are the order of the day. Once again, then, we are back with the idea of the 'progressivist' concept as drawing its strength from the solace it provides to thinkers deprived of the comforting support of 'tradition'.

Let us turn now to variables more particularly relevant to the prevalence of a 'consensual' or 'competitive' mode of theorizing.

Here too, mode of transmission of ideas seems important. By minimizing differences between past and present secondary theory, and by pushing back credit for theoretical innovation into a remote 'time of the beginnings', oral transmission lessens the possibility of contention arising between supporters of an earlier body of secondary theory and supporters of the present-day body of theory. In this way, it helps to support a 'consensual' mode of theorizing. On the other hand, by highlighting differences between present and past secondary theory, written transmission encourages a theoretical pluralism which could become the basis for inter-theoretic competition.

This of course is one of the things that happened at the beginning of the European Scientific Revolution – as witness the battle between 'Ancients' and 'Moderns'.[79]

Another variable which would seem to be of key importance in this context is degree of homogeneity in cultural background and in range of everyday experience. Since the drawing of analogies based on culturally-conditioned perceptions of everyday experience is the key to the building of secondary theory, it follows that a high degree of cultural and experiential homogeneity is likely to encourage a high degree of homogeneity in the realm of secondary theory, and so to promote the 'consensual' mode of theorizing, whilst a low degree of cultural and experiential homogeneity is likely to make for a correspondingly low degree of homogeneity in the realm of secondary theory, and so to facilitate 'competitive' theorizing.

What further factors affect the degree of cultural and experiential homogeneity? This, obviously, is a question one could spend a lifetime trying to answer. Here, I can offer only a few tentative thoughts.

On the one hand, if all sections of a community have lived and moved together over a long period, and have faced common challenges over that period, this will have encouraged homogeneity. Again, where the economy is such as to encourage a rather low degree of occupational specialization, occupationally-specific sub-cultures and occupationally-specific ranges of experience will have little chance to develop, and the tendency once more will be to homogeneity. The agriculturally-based societies of pre-colonial Africa and early medieval Europe probably came nearer to exemplifying these conditions. And this, I would suggest, is one reason for the prevalence in them of a 'consensual' mode of theorizing.

On the other hand, consider the case of the kind of 'melting pot' or 'frontier' community where, usually through the exigencies of commerce, groups having very different historical and cultural origins find themselves bound together into a single social unit. Here, the plurality of disparate world-views gives strong encouragement to the 'competitive' mode of theorizing. This is a situation that seems to have played a recurrent part in the development of Western cognitive 'modernism'. Think of the 'frontier' communities of sixth-century BC Greece; of the Judaic/Christian/Islamic communities of southern Spain toward the end of the Middle Ages; and of the commercial cities of the Netherlands at the beginning of the era of Scientific Revolution.[80] Again, where the economy is such as to encourage a high degree of occupational specialization, occupationally-specific sub-cultures and ranges of experience will develop, and thus provide another source of heterogeneity. Such occupational specialization is typical of a commercial-cum-industrial economy, and has often developed most precociously in the type of community alluded to above, thus giving additional encouragement to the development of theoretical pluralism and competition.

Finally in this consideration of influences relevant to the mode of theoretical activity, let me focus on one highly specific change which seems to me to have played a key part in the development of 'competitive' theorizing in the modern West. Here I refer once more to the growth of the commercial and industrial sectors of the economy, and to the way in which this growth produced, on the one hand, a period of prolonged change which meant a marked decline in the stability and predictability of all social relationships, and on the other hand a tremendous development in control of the non-human environment through technology. Earlier on, I suggested that it was this set of changes that led to a gradual but steady shift from a spiritualistic to a mechanistic idiom in secondary theory. And it is this shift to which I wish to draw attention here. Now as I said earlier, I do not follow the various neo-Marxist and neo-Weberian scholars in taking 'disenchantment' as the key to intellectual modernization. The exchange of a personal for an impersonal idiom in theory seems to me a relatively superficial transformation, and one which, in itself, cannot account for the profound changes involved in such modernization. What I do want to stress is the fact of a long period of transition during which, although some thinkers had gone over to the impersonal idiom, others remained attached to the personal idiom. The resulting coexistence of two dramatically contrasted types of secondary theory, both supported with equal fanaticism, gave what was perhaps the biggest boost of all to the 'competitive' mode of theorizing.

What I have done in this section obviously does not begin to amount to a proper sociological or historical analysis. Nonetheless, it does provide a number of specific suggestions as to how the principal contrasts between cognitive 'traditionalism' and cognitive 'modernism' can be set in a broader framework of technological, economic and social variables. In this way, it provides at least a starting-point for the sociologists and the historians.

Concluding remarks

In this essay, I have tried to present a programme for the cross-cultural study of human thought-systems. Although I have applied it here to the thought-systems associated respectively with the peoples of sub-Saharan Africa and with those of Western Europe, I should like to think that, with some modifications and elaborations, it might turn out to be universally applicable.

Basic to this programme is the assumption of a strong core of human cognitive rationality common to the cultures of all places on earth and all times since the dawn of properly human social life. Central to this 'common core' of rationality is the use of theory in the explanation, prediction and control of events. Central too is the use of analogical, deductive and inductive inference in the development and application of theory.

I distinguish two types of theory: primary and secondary. Secondary theory strives endlessly, and often with considerable success, to transcend the limitations of its primary counterpart; but it is brought back to earth, just as endlessly, by its dependence on the latter's resources. This curious relationship is the source of most if not all of the apparently paradoxical features of secondary theory. I have argued that it can be understood on the supposition that primary theory, though neither more nor less theoretical than secondary theory, is nonetheless historically and developmentally prior to it.

How do we get from the 'common core' of rationality to the dramatic differences which we observe between, for example, the styles and patterns of thought in sub-Saharan Africa and the styles and patterns in the recent West? Or indeed, from the 'common core' to the almost equally dramatic differences between twelfth-century and twentieth-century Western styles and patterns? Very briefly, the answer is that, in different technological, economic and social settings, the 'logic of the situation' dictates the use of different intellectual means to achieve the same ends. In this programme, then, the typical explanation of differences involves specification (a) of the 'common core', and (b) of the different settings within which it operates.

The programme outlined in this essay exposes a number of hoary misconceptions in the field of cross-cultural studies.

First, it gives the lie to the idea of a deep-seated antithesis between an 'intellectualist' and a 'sociological' scheme of explanation. For in its own scheme, the 'intellectualist' and 'sociological' elements are both complementary and mutually indispensable.

Second, it gives the lie to the idea that if one asserts that the goals of explanation, prediction and control are of more or less equal importance in all cultures, but also asserts that the yield from pursuing these goals is greater in modern Western scientific culture than in others, one is asserting the superior rationality of Westerners. It does this by showing that what has led to the high cognitive yields of modern Western science is nothing more than *the universal rationality* operating in a particular technological, economic and social setting. This conclusion, I venture to think, could have momentous implications for cross-cultural studies generally.

For most people seriously involved in cross-cultural studies, the evident success of the 'hard' sciences in the modern West is an embarrassment. Because on their assumptions such success suggests a superior rationality in the pioneers of these sciences, if not also in their most prominent followers, it offends against a strong egalitarian commitment. As I said earlier, most of the more recent programmes for cross-cultural understanding have been attempts to evade this offensive implication by insisting that much of what looks like theoretical thought in non-Western cultures is in reality thought of an entirely different genre, with goals quite distinct from those of explanation, prediction and control. As such, it cannot be subjected to invidious comparison with Western scientific thought in respect of cognitive yield. Because they flout the actor's point of view, all of these programmes run aground sooner or later on the hard facts. But because of the horror inspired by what seems to be the anti-egalitarian alternative, otherwise reputable scholars cling on to them.

I believe that the explanatory scheme outlined in this essay is one that can bring an end to this unwholesome state of affairs. For, by accounting for the cognitive success of the 'hard' sciences in terms, not of a superior rationality, but of the universal rationality operating in a particular setting, it enables the egalitarian scholar to cast away his fear of invidious comparisons and look at non-Western theory with the eye of its user.

Third, my scheme (here following Gellner) undermines the still fashionable Weberian antithesis between 'traditional' and 'rational' legitimation of belief. Thus on the one hand, it shows that 'traditional' legitimation, given the settings in which it flourishes, is impeccably 'rational'. And on the other hand, it shows that Weber's beloved culture of 'rational' legitimation, in so far as it is sustained by a 'progressivist' concept of knowledge, is grounded in an idea whose origins, at least, emit a strong whiff of 'irrationality'. Clearly the relations between rationality and cognitive yield are more complex than we had thought!

To close this essay, let me try to place the explanatory scheme outlined in it in the context of the confrontation which the present symposium is designed to highlight: the confrontation between Universalist and Relativist programmes for cross-cultural understanding. If we follow the implicit definitions shared by editors and fellow-contributors, my scheme falls fairly and squarely into the Universalist category, and is opposed to all efforts that fall into the Relativist category. In the last few paragraphs, let me have a quick shot at demonstrating the superiority of this particular form of Universalism to Relativist alternatives.

To start with, note that Relativist enthusiasm flourishes on the alleged deficiencies of the sort of Universalism propounded in this essay. In particular, it flourishes on the alleged inability of this sort of scheme to account for the dramatic differences in thought-patterns that confront the cross-cultural enquirer at every turn; and on its allegedly invidious comparisons in respect of rationality.

Both of these alleged deficiencies, it seems to me, exist only in the minds of Relativists. Thus it should be clear from the present essay that the kind of Universalism I have been pursuing in it has a large and exciting potential for the explanation of all manner of cross-cultural differences in thought-patterns. Again, it should be clear that this kind of Universalism makes no invidious comparisons in respect of rationality. In short, Relativist enthusiasm flourishes on the basis of purely imaginary deficiencies in Universalism. On this ground alone, it is suspect.

Again, for all the talk about the desirability of their kind of programme, Relativists have not yet presented even the outline of a descriptive and explanatory scheme of their own. Nor is this a coincidence; for the basic premises of Relativism make the attempt to pursue it self-defeating.

In the first place, any programme of cross-cultural understanding must start by translating all of the idea-sets under consideration into terms of a single 'world' language.[81] It is only when this has been done that a schema of similarities and differences can emerge to constitute an explanandum. But without the kind of area of comparable concepts, intentions, rules of inference and so on which primary theory *ex hypothesi* provides, there can be no 'bridge' for the crossing from one language to another, and translation cannot get under way. In so far as thoroughgoing Relativism denies such an area of comparability, it precludes the possibility of translation and is therefore, literally, a non-starter.[82]

Secondly, even if a Relativist programme managed by some logical miracle to circumvent this obstacle, and to produce a schema of irreducible differences between thought-systems, there would still be something profoundly unsatisfactory about any explanation of these differences which it proffered. For any such explanation would be (a) acceptable in the light of canons of inference peculiar to the scholar's own culture, and (b) couched in the language of that culture. Hence, on Relativist assumptions, it would be in principle both unacceptable and unintelligible to members of any other culture. For a programme whose specific object is cross-cultural understanding, this would seem to be rather a large defect.

By comparison with the prospect for Relativism sketched above, the prospect for the kind of Universalist programme outlined in the body of this essay seems bright indeed.

First of all, there is no obviously self-defeating element in the programme. The assumption of a 'common core' of rationality, based on the universality of primary theory and of the goals of explanation, prediction and control, gives the go-ahead to the would-be translator. The same assumption ensures that, once a schema of similarities and differences has been unearthed by the translator, any explanation of its contents will be at least potentially acceptable, not to say intelligible, to members of a culture other than that of the scholar propounding it.

Again, and this is just as important, the programme is not just emptily self-fulfiling.[83] True, the idea of a 'common core' of rationality is a presupposition of anyone embarking on the translation phase of a programme of cross-cultural understanding. Nonetheless, so long as we can conceive of the possibility of defeat for the translation enterprise (and surely we *can* do this), the presupposition remains one that experience could prove misguided.

Not only, then, has Relativism so far failed to deliver whilst the kind of Universalism sketched in this essay has already shown at least promise. Relativism is bound to fail whilst Universalism may, one day, succeed.

Postscript

Most of the papers in this collection were written more than five years ago; and some were written more than ten years ago. It seems appropriate, therefore, to round off with an author's view of how they appear in the light of more recent developments in the comparative study of religions and world-views.

Unfortunately, there is neither the time nor the space for a systematic updating of the approach embodied in these essays. Nor perhaps would such a massive enterprise even be desirable, in a collection designed primarily to bring together the author's past efforts, warts and all. Here, then, I shall restrict myself to brief reviews of and replies to some of the main lines of criticism that have emerged during the last decade.

During the sixties and seventies, when most of these articles were written, the would-be propounder of a new theoretical framework had to contend with just two rival movements: that of the Symbolists and that of the Theologians. And this refreshingly simple situation is reflected in the critical pieces here assembled. The 1980s, however, have produced a veritable cornucopia of theories of religion and world-view. Indeed, it has almost been a period of 'one man, one theory'. The resulting diversity has been somewhat daunting for anyone trying to take a critical overview of what has been going on. Given the task of this postscript, however, the situation is made easier by the fact that, despite the diversity of their own positive views, many of the newer theorists have not only been united in their hostility to my approach, but have produced a manageably limited number of lines of objection to it. It is with these lines of objection that I shall deal in what follows.

Religion and science: similarity or contrast?

If there is one thesis that unites the essays assembled in this volume, it is that of the deep-seated similarity between much of the world's religious thought, past and present, and the theoretical thought of the modern sciences. The thesis can be summed up in three simple propositions. (1) Both types of thought enter into human social life to make up for the explanatory, predictive and practical deficiencies of everyday, common-sense reasoning. (2) Both perform this function by portraying the phenomena of the everyday world as manifestations of a hidden, underlying reality. (3) Both build up their schemas of this hidden reality by drawing analogies with various aspects of everyday experience. I have of course drawn attention to numerous other less immediately obvious similarities between the two types of thought; but I have derived all of these from the three basic similarities just mentioned. Again, I have duly noted the striking differences between the personal idiom of religious thought and the impersonal idiom of the modern sciences. But I have shown how even this can be understood as a case of similar basic intellectual and imaginative processes working themselves out in different ways in different social and environmental contexts.

It seems to me that the Similarity Thesis, as expounded in these essays and as summed up above, may turn out to be my most enduring contribution to this area of study. That is why, in this postscript, I shall deal with it first.

At this point, I can hear someone exclaiming 'Wow!'. And well he may so exclaim. For if anything has continued to unite most scholars engaged in the comparative study of religions, it is their opposition to the Similarity Thesis.

Recent opponents of the thesis appear to rely on one or more of four main lines of argument, all of which seem flawed.

The first line is based on the 'like should be compared only with like' maxim first introduced into this area of discussion by Evans-Pritchard.[1] This maxim would have us compare the religion of any given culture only with the religions of other cultures, and the science of any given culture only with the sciences (or *faute de mieux* the technologies) of other cultures. Goody repeated Evans-Pritchard on this,[2] and Tambiah and Lloyd seem to have taken it over from Goody, appealing strongly to entrenched orthodox intuitions as to what is similar to what and what dissimilar to what.[3] This line of argument can be quickly dismissed. For it is really no more than an appeal to the self-evidence of the established consensus: an appeal which blissfully ignores the fact that most major advances in our understanding are based precisely on a willingness to scrap established intuitions about similarity and dissimilarity.

The second line of argument is that the Similarity Thesis is based on a positivist or logical empiricist outlook, and that it is as inadequate and as outdated as are positivism or logical empiricism themselves.[4] This line I find hard to understand. As I said in 'Lévy-Bruhl, Durkheim and the Scientific Revolution' (paper 3) and 'Back to Frazer?' (paper 4), it has been the positivist background of many of my anthropological colleagues which has prevented them from seeing the basic similarities between the religious and the scientific. Thus positivism, with its rather strictly inductive concept of scientific explanation, and with its refusal to grant ideas about unobservable entities any serious role in such explanation, has always made the scientific seem far removed from the religious. It needed a post-positivist outlook, with its emphasis on the importance of ideas about a realm of unobservables in scientific explanation, and on the role of analogy in building up schemas of such a realm, to bring out the basic similarities between religious and scientific thought. I was amongst those who tried to supply such an outlook at a time when most of our anthropological colleagues were still benighted by positivism. Though some of the same colleagues now make great play with the names of Kuhn, Feyerabend and other post-positivist figures in the philosophy of science, it seems to me that in fact they are still way back where they always were in their basic conception of science: i.e. way back with the positivists.[5]

A third line of argument is based on the alleged failure of the Similarity Thesis to account for the continuing role of religion in the modern West, and for the fact that modern Western religion, unlike science, seems to have little or no concern with explanation, prediction and control of the everyday world.[6] I do not want to go too far with this one at the moment, since I shall be dealing with the vicissitudes of religion in the West in more detail a little later in this postscript. In the meantime, let me refer the reader back to 'African traditional thought and Western science' (paper 7) and 'Tradition and modernity revisited' (paper 9) for an account of how Western religion lost its authority in the sphere of explanation, prediction and control; and to 'Back to Frazer?' (paper 4) and 'Judaeo-Christian spectacles' (paper 6) for an account of why it survived nonetheless. Turning to the critics' own perspective on modern Western religion, I see them (even those of them who are atheists) as being too ready to take it as the paradigm of religions generally, and as failing to see how exceptional it is. My own approach, as I shall shortly show, gives a coherent account of its genesis, whilst doing full justice to its exceptional character.

The fourth and still perhaps most commonly reiterated line of argument against the Similarity Thesis is in a sense an extension of the third line. For it extends to religions generally the point made about religion in the modern West, asserting flatly and without qualification that explanation, prediction and control are *not* the essential, guiding intentions of religious thought and action. As to which *are* the essential, guiding intentions, there are now almost as many different answers as there are individual theorists; and it would take several fat volumes to do justice to them. Here, let me mention just a few in passing; metaphorical adumbration of earthly matters which defeat the resources of literal language (Fernandez);[7] achievement and maintenance of communicative success (Habermas);[8] promotion of awareness of the transcendent (Tambiah);[9] communion with the world (Grinevald, Tambiah);[10] the building up of elaborate self-referential structures, apparently as ends in themselves (Lawson and McCauley);[11] solving semeiological and semantic puzzles (Devisch).[12] Having given an idea of the variety of positive suggestions on offer, let me get back to the aspect of all this recent theorizing which is more immediately relevant from the point of view of the postscript: i.e. its unanimous opposition to the Similarity Thesis in the matter of explanation, prediction and control.

Recent theorists seem to rely on two specific arguments against the primacy in this area of explanation, prediction and control. One is that since, by the standards of modern Western science, the alleged referents of religious statements are non-existent, such statements are not to be taken as serious attempts to refer to some kind of underlying reality external to themselves. Further, since explanation involves reference to an external underlying reality, and since religious statements do not make such reference, then they are not to be taken as having serious explanatory intent.[13] The other is that since, by the same standards, religious statements do not appear to take serious account of challenging experience derived from the world, they cannot be interpreted as serious attempts to explain, predict and control the world.[14]

I have already dealt with similar contentions by earlier theorists in my 'Back to Frazer?'. Let me add a few words addressed specifically to these more recent contentions.

The first thing to be said here is that, in categorizing and interpreting other people's discourse, we must in the first instance respect and be guided by their own intentions. And evidence for these intentions can only come from the verbal and non-verbal context of such discourse. If we accept this maxim, then both of the above objections will appear misdirected. Thus, in so far as the contextual evidence we have suggests that speakers alluding to spiritual beings *intend* to refer to entities 'out there' in the world external to their discourse, then their pronouncements must be categorized and interpreted as referring to a reality other than themselves – and not for instance as non-referring or self-referring. Again, in so far as the contextual evidence we have suggests that most speakers outside the modern West who allude to spiritual beings *intend* statements about these beings to provide explanations of present phenomena, predictions of future phenomena, and recipes for control of the future course of events, then their pronouncements must be categorized and interpreted as explanatory.

This said, all that remains is for me to repeat in summary form what I said on this matter in 'Back to Frazer?'. Very briefly, when it comes to taking serious account of challenging new experience, the difference between the personal schemas of non-modern, non-Western religion and the impersonal schemas of modern Western science appears a good deal less stark than it used to. Thus in both instances, we have conservative responses which try to adjust to challenging new experiences with a minimum of conceptual change. And in both, we have more radical responses which involve either major developments of existing theory or the proposal of a more or less new theory. It is true that, in the case of religion, the balance between the two kinds of change seems to favour the first, while in the case of science it seems to favour the second. In my 'Tradition and modernity revisited' (paper 9), moreover, I have offered what still seems to me a broadly acceptable explanation of this difference. Nonetheless, what we are dealing with is a difference of degree rather than of kind. We are not dealing with the sort of difference which would warrant the conclusion that explanation, prediction and control are of negligible importance in one case and of central import- ance in the other.

The reader looking at all of this from outside the disciplines of social anthropology and comparative religion may wonder why the critics persist in defying such weighty arguments and evidence in favour of the Similarity Thesis. The answer, I think, is twofold.

First of all, as I said earlier, even those of my colleagues who are atheists continue to take modern Western religion as the paradigm of religions generally. And modern Western religion is defined as something starkly contrasted with science. Invincibly ethnocentric, they still fail to realize how exceptional this contrast is.

Secondly, most of my colleagues are still haunted by the idea that accepting the Similarity Thesis means labelling non-Western religions as 'failed science', and that such labelling leads in its turn to invidious com- parisons between Western and non-Western thought. For them, this is still the compelling bottom line of all cases against the Thesis.[15]

I have already exposed the spurious character of earlier versions of this kind of argument in 'Neo-Tylorianism' (paper 2), 'Lévy-Bruhl, Durkheim and the Scientific Revolution' (paper 3), and 'Back to Frazer?' (paper 4). And there seems to be nothing new in more recent versions that would exempt them from similar treatment. Suffice it then to remind the reader of the highlights of the diagnosis which I offered in the last of these papers. I started by emphasizing that what we were dealing with were not cognitively compelling arguments, but rather a massive intrusion of non-cognitive interests into the interpretative enterprise – interests that were a major obstacle to intellectual progress in the area. I then went on to be more specific about this intrusion, pointing to a combination of three elements: (1) a eurocentric lack of imaginative sympathy for the explanatory possi- bilities of spiritual theorizing and for the evidential contexts in which such theorizing takes place; (2) a strong liberal injunction not to be nasty about non-Western cultures; and (3) an equally strong romantic determination to treat such cultures as reserves for the preservation of the non-scientistic modes of thought allegedly endangered by the sciences. Or, to put it once more in words of one or two syllables: White Hearts, Brown Noses!

Nuisance as it is, this cloud of eurocentric liberal-romantic ideology seems likely to be with us for some time to come; and, other things remaining equal, its continuing presence augurs ill for the worldly prospects of the Similarity Thesis. Nonetheless, there are some hopeful signs that other things may not remain equal.

One factor that may well make things easier for the Similarity Thesis is, ironically, the very cognitive relativism with which some of its critics have begun to flirt.

A popular version of cognitive relativism suggests that, although theories and world-views throughout historical space and time have been shaped by an interest in explanation, prediction and control, there are no universally-agreed criteria for showing that one world-view is any more efficient than others in relation to this interest. From this, it follows that claims to superior cognitive efficacy made on behalf of the modern Western science-based world-view are nothing less than fraudulent.[16]

Later in this postscript I shall have some critical things to say about this and other versions of cognitive relativism. In the present context, however, the important thing to notice is its burgeoning popularity and its likely future influence on the reception of the Similarity Thesis. Here, let us return to the ideological climate of liberal romanticism. What I want to argue is that cognitive relativism enables the liberal romantic to espouse the Similarity Thesis without breaking faith with either his liberalism or his romanticism. Thus on the one hand, it allows the scrupulous liberal to consider non-Western religious world-views in their own terms, as systems shaped by the interest in explanation, prediction and control, *without* thereby exposing himself to the risks of invidious comparison. And on the other, it allows the romantic to extol such non-cognitive qualities as the 'warmth' of the religious world-views of the non-West as against the 'cold impersonality' of the science-generated world-views of the West. A lead here has already been given by Paul Feyerabend, one of the most notorious of the cognitive relativists and a great hero of some of the anthropological avant-garde. Feyerabend, incidentally, has not only enthusiastically endorsed the Similarity Thesis, but has castigated its opponents in terms very similar to my own – as hampered by a liberalism which barely conceals a eurocentric and patronizing attitude to the non-West.[17] In this last, he has been taken up by at least one influential member of the avant-garde, namely Joanna Overing, who has some thought-provoking comments on the need to take non-Western world-views and their explanatory pretensions literally.[18]

Two cheers, then, for the cognitive relativists: dubious allies for Similarity Theorists, but allies nonetheless.

Other factors are also working to erode the power of liberal-romantic ideology to block reception of the Similarity Thesis.

First of all, as Western scholars draw away from the colonial era, the weight of liberal scruples presses less crushingly upon them. The sense of guilt for the sins of the fathers lessens, and, little by little, they become freer to see the non-Westerner in his own terms. One result of this is that we are beginning to get a trickle of monographic work on non-Western religions, the authors of which have been willing to let themselves see the importance of the quest for explanation, prediction and control in the shaping of religious ideas and practices. In the African field, for instance, there are the works of Igor Kopytoff, Michael Buckley, Rosalind Hackett and John Peel; and those of several of the contributors to Phillip Peek's recently-published collection of essays on African divination.[19] In the Indian field, again, there is the work of Jonathan Parry.[20]

Another source of changing perceptions in this area is a body of modern work on the history of Western ideas produced by such scholars as Peter Brown, Karen Jolly, Jerry Ravetz, Keith Thomas, Charles Webster, Robert Westfall, Lynn White and Frances Yates.[21] Because of their area of interest, these scholars have been mercifully untroubled by the liberal scruples about invidious comparisons afflicting their anthropological colleagues, and have found it correspondingly easier to see their forebears in the latter's own terms.[22] One of the fruits of their work has been the finding that, before the eighteenth century, the Western quest for explanation, prediction and control of the world was pursued *through* religion and was indeed the most vital shaper of religious ideas; and that, before this time, the idea of religion and science as distinct and contrasting fields of thought and action simply did not exist. Scholars like Webster, Westfall and White have further shown how the impersonal theories of modern Western science did not grow up *alongside* the personal schemas of religion, but rather grew slowly and steadily *out of them*.[23] Yates and Ravetz have gone even further, to contend with some plausibility that the scientific spirit of critical appraisal of theory in the light of experiment was developed in the first instance by people who held essentially spiritual theories of the world and its working.[24]

Together, these newer bodies of monographic work, on the one hand on non-Western cultures and on the other on their earlier Western counterparts, seem to be exerting a new pressure for recognition of the Similarity Thesis.

A final important factor in this context is a small but growing new trend in contemporary Western theology. As I hinted earlier, the present century has witnessed a long period during which the dominant characterization of the relationship between religion and science by Western theologians has been a strongly contrastive one. However, for reasons which I shall discuss at greater length later in this postscript, the dominance of this contrastive characterization shows signs of slipping. Significant numbers of theologians, theologically-inclined scientists and philosophers of religion have started to edge back to a less starkly contrastive position, and in certain cases to something very near a denial of the religion-science dichotomy.[25] Now just as present-day anthropologists and other scholars of comparative religion, taking at least some of their cues as to the character of religious thought and language from their Western theological contemporaries, have been encouraged thereby to adopt a contrastive view of the relation between religion and science, so future generations of scholars, taking their cues from the same source, may be expected to edge toward the Similarity Thesis.

Let me now sum up on the validity and prospects of the Similarity Thesis. As regards validity, it seems to me that, in its essentials, the Thesis remains unimpugned. All of its more recent critics have fallen on their faces at one point or another in their critiques. As regards prospects, I would say that, although the Thesis is currently regarded by most scholars in the comparative study of religion as little short of eccentric, a variety of factors now in play seem likely, in the not-too-distant future, to work in its favour. My own hunch (heavily wishful, of course!) is that, in twenty years time, scholars will be wondering however their predecessors could have rejected it.

'Theories of' and 'theories for'

Several recent critics, among them Peel, van Binsbergen and Stirrat,[26] whilst giving qualified approval to the Intellectualist approach to religious life, also castigate it on the ground that it makes religious ideas out to be entirely dependent variables with respect to the social order, and indeed to be mere passive mirrors of that order. This, they say, does grave injustice to the phenomena of religious life, by leaving out of account the extent to which religious ideas also function as independent variables with respect to the social order, and as forces in their own right for social change and innovation. To use terminology which has enjoyed a considerable vogue since Clifford Geertz introduced it in his much-quoted programmatic essay on the study of religion, they see the Intellectualist approach as distorting the reality of religion by treating it exclusively as a source of 'models of' the social order, and by neglecting the extent to which it also constitutes a source of 'models for' that order.[27]

My first reply to this objection is that it is based on a rather serious mis-characterization of my approach. Thus I most definitely do not hold that the religious world-view stands in an explanatory relationship to the social order alone. Rather, I assert that it stands in such a relationship to a world that includes, not just the social order, but also its individual members and its natural environment. I add that the religious world-view may very well consider these three aspects of the world as mutually independent variables which may even be at odds with one another. In a recent comparative essay,[28] for instance, I suggest that many African religious world-views explore the possibility that the social *status quo* may be undermined or drastically changed by individual striving and innovation. In this sense alone, then, my approach is a far cry from one that sees religion as a passive reflection of the social order.

I think the critics would have been on firmer ground had they talked in terms, not of the social order but of the world as a whole, and had they attacked me for treating religion solely as a source of 'models of' the world and neglecting to stress that it was also a source of 'models for' the world. Here, it seems to me, I have indeed given quite a few hostages to the opposition. To explain how this came about, let me say something concerning the climate of opinion in British social anthropology when I started to develop my version of the Intellectualist approach. At that time, members of the discipline took their cue from Evans-Pritchard's insistence that there was a stark antithesis between an Intellectualist and a Contextualist approach to religious life.[29] Critics, accordingly, took me to task for going down a road which led inexorably away from the basic insights of anthropology regarding the contextual influences on religious ideas.[30] In fact, from the start, I had been greatly drawn to the project of developing an Intellectualist approach which gave due weight to contextual influences; and this ill-directed but influential line of criticism merely reinforced my determination to show that one could have an Intellectualist approach that nonetheless took full account of the social and environmental context of ideas. It would be fair enough to say that, as a result, I did greatly overemphasize one of the two possible kinds of relation between the world and ideas: i.e. the influence *of* the world *on* ideas.

Having conceded this much, however, I should like to argue that there is nothing intrinsic to the Intellectualist approach which rules out the possibility of taking religion as a force for change in its own right. On the contrary indeed, I would claim that, precisely in so far as it does take religious ideas seriously as constituting bodies of theory about the underlying forces at work in the world, this approach greatly *helps* us to envisage some of the ways in which religion may act as an independent variable *vis-à-vis* the world.

To set the stage for my argument, let me draw attention to two very general features which are common to both personal/spiritual and impersonal/mechanistic theories of the world and its working.

In the first place, theory does not passively 'mirror' the world as the latter is described and comprehended by everyday discourse. Rather, as a little reflection on both the personal, spiritual theories of sub-saharan Africa and the impersonal, mechanistic theories of the modern West will quickly bring home to the reader, theory always denies the absolute validity of the characterizations of reality embodied in everyday discourse. In this respect, what Karl Marx said about religion giving an 'inverted' picture of the world could be said with equal validity about the impersonal theories of modern Western science.[31] Very generally, indeed, terms such as 'denial' and 'inversion' would seem as appropriate to the characterization of the explanatory enterprise as terms like 'mirroring'.

Secondly, although the formulation of a theory may be triggered by a desire to explain certain familiar but nonetheless puzzling features of the world as envisaged in everyday discourse, the theory nonetheless places these features in a perspective both deeper and broader than that of everyday. In so doing, it not only makes sense of the pre-existing situation that evoked it, but also actively shapes its users' responses to new situations. Every good 'theory of', then, sooner or later becomes a 'theory for'.

By way of illustration of this second point, let me give two West African examples.

My first example relates to the idea of the Earth-spirit, considered as a principal spiritual guardian of the community, and the assiduous cult of this spirit as the basis for the continued flourishing of the community. This is an age-old feature of religious life in West Africa, and one invoked to account for and support age-old socio-political structures.[32] It seems to have been inspired by the recurrent observation that particular communities had, during the course of their histories, become enlarged through the gradual and peaceful influx of groups unrelated in lineage or clan terms to their original founders, and by the further observation that such communities, despite their resulting heterogeneity, had preserved high degrees of cohesion. This recurring situation was neatly accounted for in terms of the idea that, whilst the continued cohesion of individual lineage groups was due to their several sets of protecting ancestral forces, the continued cohesion of the community as a whole was due to an earth-spirit under whose aegis these forces worked. However, whilst the Earth-spirit accorded equal protection to the various constituent lineages inhabiting its territory, it did of course have a particularly close relationship with the lineage whose members had first settled this territory. Hence responsibility for the communal earth-cult, and often overall community headship as well, was characteristically vested in this founding lineage. Here, then, we have a good instance of a religious 'theory of', and of its practical employment to ensure the persistence of the social *status quo*.

Let us now shift our attention, from situations characterized by gradual and peaceful immigration, to later situations in which some groups embarked on the conquest of others and tried to build up stable state structures on the basis of such conquest. These groups, of course, operated with the 'theory of' outlined above; but it now became a 'theory for', which shaped and guided their responses to the new challenge of state-building. According to the theory, the conquering group was backed by its ancestral spiritual protectors; but the conquered territory remained under the aegis of its Earth-spirit or Earth-spirits. The conquerors, then, had to work with the idea of a delicate balance between intrusive ancestral forces and indigenous earth forces. And this idea seems to have done much to guide the subsequent development of administrative patterns. Thus the conquerors tended to leave local administration as far as possible in the hands of sons of the soil, who in turn were intermediaries with the Earth-spirit or spirits.[33] Again, though during an interregnum they produced a short-list of candidates for the kingship, they left final selection from this list to a council of king-makers who, once more, were sons of the soil.[34] Yet again, though the king was at the head of the central administration, he ran it with the assistance and advice of the same council of indigenous king-makers. As sons of the soil, of course, the latter were vital intermediaries with the earth forces. Where conquerors were facing an area with special terrestrial resources which they wished to control, they tended to be even more careful to respect the position of the sons of the soil. Thus in a campaign designed to gain control of the gold trade through a neighbouring area, they might subdue and subsequently administer the evacuation routes, whilst leaving the producing area itself as an autonomous enclave.[35] Once more, this cautious approach to the indigenes seems to have been the product of a lively consciousness of the need to respect the balance between ancestral and earth forces.

Another example of a 'theory of' becoming a 'theory for' is provided by the West African state of Asante. Asante in the early eighteenth century was a federation of previously autonomous chiefdoms, each made up of a bundle of unrelated matrilineages in which the founding lineage provided the chief. Early Asante political theory featured the usual balance of ancestral and earth forces underpinning each of the constituent chiefdoms, and in addition an overruling 'spirit of the nation' underpinning the federation as a whole.[36] In this instance, however, we are concerned less with broader political theory and more with the theory of the individual and his relationship to society. Here, the age-old matrilineal organization of the area had evoked a theory which postulated a threefold spiritual control of the individual's life. The *saman*, coming from the matrilineage pool, underpinned the individual's identity as a member of the lineage into which he was born. The *sunsum*, coming to him via his father, underpinned his individual character and skills. The *kra*, which somehow overruled the first two agencies, underpinned his total life-course.[37]

So much for the 'theory of' which guided everyday life in the Asante federation of the early eighteenth century. Let us now turn our gaze to developments in the state during the latter part of the century. Through this period, successive Asante kings embarked on a programme of centralization and rationalization designed to replace the older federal structures with others at once more monolithic and more efficient. One important aspect of their programme was the creation of a large number of specialist offices, succession to which was, *de facto* if not *de jure*, from father to son.[38] Now there is nothing exceptional about the effort to create an occupationally specialized central bureaucracy in a state not previously endowed with one. Indeed, such efforts were made at various times and with varying degrees of success in kingdoms the length and breadth of West Africa. What *is* more remarkable is the use, in a matrilineally-biassed society, of the device of father-son succession to office. One can of course view this in purely secular political terms, as a way of avoiding accumulation of office-derived wealth in the matrilineages. To view it thus, however, would be to engage in eurocentric secularization. To be faithful to the Asante point of view, we have to bring in the pre-existing religious theory, which saw individual character and skills as attributes transferred via the *sunsum* from father to son, and which further insisted that the *sunsum* could only be effective in this transfer where there was a close relationship between father and son. In the light of this theory, the obvious move for the would-be creator of a cadre of skilled and specialized bureaucrats was to select people of suitable skills to fill the new offices, and then insist on their sons succeeding them. Here once more, then, we seem to see the transformation of a pre-existing 'theory of' into a 'theory for' which gives a distinctive shape to people's responses to a new challenge.

In these examples, I have pointed to two fairly undramatic ways in which a theory whose elaboration is initially inspired by a recurrent everyday situation can actively shape people's responses to new situations. In what follows, I should like to consider a very general feature of 'theories of' which gives them a much more dramatic potential as 'theories for'. Here, I refer to the way in which all theory deepens and broadens our view of the world by postulating causal connexions not recognized in everyday discourse. Causal generalizations, as we know, characteristically take the form: 'If and only if A, then B.' Such generalizations, however, always have implied converses of the form: 'If and only if not-A, then not-B.' These converses accompany the positive generalizations like shadows. As a result, every theory contains, not only an explanation of the *status quo* which inspired its formulation, and a recipe for supporting that *status quo*, but also a 'shadow recipe' for destroying it. Every theory, then, has both conservative and revolutionary implications.

Some simple but apt African illustrations of how 'shadow recipes' work can be drawn from my papers on conversion to the so-called 'world' religions.[39] Since they are not included here, let me briefly recapitulate some of their highlights.

In many parts of pre-colonial Africa, there was a relatively fragmented pattern of political organization, whereby hundreds of small, mutually-autonomous communities lived somewhat inward-looking collective lives. Nonetheless, alongside the resulting parochial outlook, there was also an awareness of belonging to a wider world and to a wider humanity. Now in such areas, there was in the typical community a two-tiered body of religious theory. On the one hand, this body of theory postulated a set of spiritual guardians of the community and a set of spiritual owners of the surrounding wilds. Together, these underpinned the life of the local polity. On the other hand, it postulated a supreme being which underpinned the life of humanity as a whole and the existence of the world at large. As the local polity and its environs were part of the wider world, so the lesser spirits were seen as being somehow under the aegis of the supreme being. From these postulates, it followed that an assiduous cult of the lesser spirits would keep the life of the local community on course, whilst attention to the supreme being would deal with the needs of the individual and of his community *vis-à-vis* the wider world. However, since the life of the local community had priority in this somewhat parochial set-up, it is not surprising to find that the balance of emphasis in religious practice was typically on the cults of the lesser and locally-based spiritual forces.

Here, then, was a body of theory which, whilst it by no means 'mirrored' the *status quo*, both accounted for it and showed people how to perpetuate it. However, although the key causal generalizations in the theory in this sense favoured the *status quo*, their negative 'shadows' provided recipes for its destruction. Thus the generalization that assiduous cult strengthened a community's spiritual guardians, and that the strength of the guardians in turn promoted the strength of the community, clearly favoured the persistence of the latter. However, the 'shadow' generalization, to the effect that withdrawal or repudiation of cult fatally weakened the spiritual guardians, and that the weakening of the guardians led to the weakening or disintegration of the local polity, just as clearly offered a recipe for the destruction of the existing order.

Now religio-political leaders in pre-colonial Africa were very much alive to the subversive and revolutionary possibilities of this particular 'shadow' generalization.

One way in which they used it was in situations where they intended to change the local balance of power by destroying one of their neighbours. Thus before embarking on physical warfare, they sent saboteurs to the shrines of the rival community's spiritual guardians, to desecrate them by pouring substances repugnant to their owners over the latter's altars.[40] The resultant weakening of the enemy's spiritual guardians was thought to bring about a decisive weakening of his resolve. The desecration, indeed, seems to have been carried out in much the same spirit as that of a preliminary bombardment in modern Western-style warfare.

Another more spectacular way in which they used it was in launching movements intended to break down the boundaries of the numerous local polities, and thereby pave the way for a wider socio-political order. Some of these movements seem to have relied on purely indigenous ideas. In others, the indigenous ideas received a boost from Islam. In both cases, however, the initial inspiration was the same. It was the 'shadow' generalization we have already referred to, or more accurately its specific implication that anyone wishing to destroy the boundaries of the numerous local polities and thereby make way for a wider socio-political order should radically terminate the cults of the local community guardians whilst continuing or intensifying the cult of the supreme being. Without such theoretical inspiration, indeed, it seems possible that revolutionary movements aimed at creating a wider socio-political order would never have gotten off the ground.[41]

The foregoing examples, I hope, will have served to show the reader how theories which started as 'theories of' (i.e. dependent variables with respect to the existing social-cum-natural order) may later become 'theories for' (i.e. independent variables with respect to that order).

Using the same examples, we could easily extend the argument by pointing out that, once a new situation and people's response to it has resulted in a new *status quo*, the 'theory for' which guided the change may once more become a 'theory of'.

To sum it all up, let me say that it is in the nature of theory that 'theories of' are constantly being transformed into 'theories for', and vice versa. There is a complex reciprocal relationship between theory and the social-cum-natural order.

Peel and his fellow critics see the intellectualist approach to African religion, and indeed to religions generally, as one of many approaches which fall into the dilemma: 'Do religious values determine or are they a reflection of social relations?'[42] In the foregoing discussion, I think I have managed to show that intellectualism, in so far as it makes the concept of theory central to its analyses, does not have to cope with any such dilemma.

Theory and ritual

Many critics, through John Beattie down to Maurice Bloch, have suggested that an intellectualist approach to religion may go some way to account for beliefs, but can do nothing to account for ritual.[43]

I believe I have a good deal to answer for here. For in my work so far, I have in fact said much about religion as a corpus of secondary-theoretical postulates and beliefs, and relatively little about the practical application of this corpus in ritual. This neglect is not in any way the result of a feeling that ritual is unimportant. Rather, it is the result of a feeling that religious theory is *the* great shaper of ritual. With this in mind, I have tended to take it for granted that, once one has understood the role of religious theory in human social life, one is *ipso facto* in a position to understand its application in ritual.

From the critical reaction to my work, it is now clear that leaving the reader to himself to draw the obvious implications of intellectualism for the understanding of ritual has not been a good idea. By and large, he has either failed or refused to draw these implications, and has gone on to deny that they exist. Nonetheless, I contend that, once these implications *are* drawn, the assertion that the Intellectualist approach can do nothing to account for ritual loses its credibility.

To substantiate this contention, let me return to the critics. One of the principal complaints of people like Beattie and Bloch is that Intellectualism completely fails to account for the deep emotional impact that ritual has on those who participate in it. This is an objection that has long puzzled me. However, I think I now see one compelling reason for it. The reason, I suggest, is that those involved cannot accept that other people could possibly take religious beliefs literally or seriously. Their imagination simply does not stretch that far. To me, it is *because* they cannot accept a literal meaning for the beliefs that they cannot see how the latter account for the power of ritual. However, once one adopts an Intellectualist stance, and accepts that other people do take such beliefs literally and seriously as means of explanation, prediction and control of the world, the power that ritual has over its practitioners loses much of its aura of mystery.

Let me illustrate what I am getting at here by means of a very crude and simple example. Consider a small village that pays reverence to a supposedly powerful male deity, to whom it attributes the ability to maintain communal prosperity and harmony, and whom it casts in the role of a benevolent super-father. Villagers engage in occasional ritual communication with this deity in response to crises. Over and above such occasional communication, however, there is a spectacular annual festival, at which sacrifices are first made to the deity, and the latter then signals his acceptance and continued protection by mounting his priest and performing a celebratory dance with his people. During the festival, the villagers appear deeply moved; and after it, they appear deeply transformed and renewed. Clearly, the annual festival has a profound effect on their emotional lives.[44]

Now for the typical twentieth-century social anthropologist who simply cannot accept that the villagers take the background beliefs either literally or seriously, the deep impact of the annual festival is a puzzle which requires explanation in terms of some factor quite other than those beliefs. However, for the anthropological maverick whose imagination, at least, encompasses the possibility of a communally-benevolent, communally-sustaining super-father, there is no great mystery and no great problem. People anxious about the continued prosperity and harmony of their community have received an assurance that these vital things are guaranteed for another year. Is it any wonder that they are elated? Adults in need of continued paternal support have had an immensely reassuring encounter with a father-figure who is as real to them as a Winston Churchill, a Fidel Castro or a Saddam Hussein is to his followers. Is it any wonder that they seem deeply renewed?

In short, far from it being the case that an Intellectualist approach debars one from understanding the grip which ritual has on man, it is precisely this approach, with its implications properly spelled out, that gives us the key to understanding ritual's grip.

So much for one very general feature of ritual. Despite my relative neglect of this topic, however, I have, within the overall Intellectualist framework, thrown out one or two hints about more specific features. These hints add further strength to my contention that the Intellectualist approach *can* account for ritual.

One such hint is the suggestion, made in 'A definition of religion' (paper 1), that the characteristic stereotyping of ritual can be accounted for in terms, (a) of the status differences between the performers and the recipients, and (b) of the fact that the recipients are not perceptually accessible to the performers. Quite why status differences make for stereotyping is still a matter of debate. But that they do so is clear from a study of purely inter-human relations. As to why unobservability of the recipients makes for stereotyping, the answer seems ready to hand. Human interaction with other human beings is usually flexible because it has to be continuously modified in the light of responses from these others. By contrast, human interaction with spiritual beings tends to run in long set sequences because what count as observable responses from the others occur only at long intervals.

Another such hint, dropped in a more recent paper not included in this volume,[45] concerns the aura of 'otherness' which characteristically surrounds the activities and artefacts associated with ritual. Here, the suggestion is simply that, since these activities and artefacts cannot be given a rationale in primary-theoretical terms, they are, in such terms, mysteriously alien.

To conclude here, let me make two points. First, that *so far* the Intellectualist approach has not done enough to substantiate its claim to be able to handle ritual as well as belief. Secondly, that *if* certain implications are properly drawn out and certain suggestions properly elaborated, it *will* be able to substantiate this claim.

Theory and power

One frequent criticism of the approach expounded in this volume is that it pays insufficient attention to religion as an instrument in the quest for power.[46]

The view of religion as first and foremost an instrument of the power quest may be said to have come into vogue with the decline in the credibility of structural-functionalism. A pioneering landmark here was Edmund Leach's *Political Systems of Highland Burma*. This was followed by: John Middleton's *Lugbara Religion*; Victor Turner's *Drums of Affliction*; Ioan Lewis's *Ecstatic* Religion; and Eugene Mendonsa's *Politics of Divination*.[47] As these works on religion *sensu stricto* were appearing, a similar stream of power-oriented studies of beliefs in witchcraft and sorcery appeared alongside them.[48] In more recent years, the trend has received a new boost: first from an injection of Marxist influence into social anthropology; second from the high fashion enjoyed by the works of Michel Foucault;[49] and third from the feminist preoccupation with theory as an instrument of male domination. Amongst the results of this new boost are the works of Maurice Bloch, culminating in his *From Blessing to Violence*; and edited works such as Richard Fardon's *Knowledge and Power* and Phillip Peek's *Ways of Knowing*.[50]

Clearly, the idea of religion as an instrument in the quest for power has been a guiding notion in social anthropology for at least the last thirty years. In the earliest part of this period, it was often combined with the Symbolist approach. However, after its recent life-prolonging transfusions from beyond the boundaries of the discipline, it seems destined to outlive even this hardy working partner. In such an intellectual climate, my own rather austerely Intellectualist approach to the comparative study of religion must seem to a high degree naive.

Here once again, however, I remain unrepentant. My reason is one which

I gave long ago in my 'Neo-Tylorianism' (paper 2), and which I still find compelling. The basic point was made in an otherwise laudatory appraisal of Middleton's *Lugbara Religion*, where I said that the book was marred by an order of presentation in which an analysis of the politics of belief came before a comprehensive outline of belief and an analysis of its cognitive functions. Why was the order wrong? Quite simply because the politics was parasitic on the belief and on its cognitive functions. Without the importance people attached to these functions, beliefs would hardly attract the manipulative activities of the politicians.

A more recent statement of the point is to be found in Barry Barnes's *Interests and the Growth of Knowledge*. In this book, Barnes stresses that ideological distortion, to be effective, must remain, both for its promoter and for its recipient, within the bounds of what is cognitively plausible; for its effectiveness *depends upon* this cognitive plausibility.[51] The point receives vivid support from David Lan's *Guns and Rain*. In this study of the Shona guerrilla movement in colonial Rhodesia, Lan shows how the guerrilla leaders' initial attempt at ideological mobilization of the rural masses through a Marxist-Leninist message fell completely flat because, given the background of the recipients, the message lacked any kind of cognitive appeal. It was only when the leaders later switched to manipulation of age-old beliefs in the power of the chiefly ancestors that they got an immediate massive response.[52]

Let me sum up by saying that I do not see the Intellectualist approach to the comparative study of religions and world-views as in any way antithetical to the study of such systems as ideologies shaped by the quest for power. However, I do see it as undertaking the essential groundwork without which the ideological analyst, like the Shona guerrilla leaders and for the same reason, is likely to find himself with egg on his face.

I cannot help wondering if the various fashionable attempts to emphasize the political aspect of religion at the expense of its cognitive aspect are not just one more manifestation of the 'White Hearts, Brown Noses' syndrome. Thus for the agnostic Western anthropologist, the attempt to explain the world in spiritual terms is a ridiculous enterprise which the good liberal should not seriously impute to the non-Westerner. The quest for power, on the other hand, is a perfectly reputable enterprise which can be imputed without any suggestion of illiberal slur. After all, it is meat and drink to the typical LSE don!

Theory and narrative

To my mind, the most cogent objection to the Intellectualist approach so far is one which has been troubling me for some years, but which even the most zealous of my many critics seem to have overlooked. Here I refer to the fact that, of the two principal modes of religious thought and discourse – the generalizing/theoretical and the particularistic/narrative – the approach deals only with the former. To put it more succinctly though perhaps less accurately, it deals with doctrine and not with myth.

This objection is by no means devasting to the Intellectualist approach. For it implies, not that the characterization of religious discourse as theoretical is wrong, but rather that it is one-sided and incomplete. Nonetheless, easy as I have found most other objections to answer, I have found this one more or less intractable so far.

The initial difficulty here is that scarcely anyone has raised the problem of the relationship between the two kinds of religious thought and discourse before, let alone tried to tackle it. Thus other Intellectualists have tended, like me, to concentrate on the generalizing, theoretical strand of religious thought and discourse, whilst neglecting the particularistic, narrative strand.[53] And on the other hand, the mythologists who have concentrated on the particularistic, narrative strand have tended to neglect its generalizing, theoretical counterpart.[54] As a result, there is rather little by way of previous relevant thinking on the matter which one could use as a point of departure.

One exception to this general tendency would seem to be the theologian Rudolph Bultmann. As I understand him, Bultmann is saying that religious thought and discourse consists of: (a) a core of theoretical insights into the character of underlying reality and its relation to the visible, tangible world; and (b) a periphery of narrative which, although not to be taken as literally true, nonetheless provides an important symbolic adjunct to the understanding of the theoretical core.[55] In other words, mythical narrative stands in the same relation to the theoretical or doctrinal core of religion as do more obviously symbolic elements such as sculpture, dance and music.

This is certainly a tempting view for the Intellectualist. For it preserves the centrality of the theoretical and makes sense of the narrative as an adjunct to its understanding and acceptance. I have also found it a tempting view in relation to my own study of the religious life oʃ the Kalabari people of the eastern Niger Delta. For in Kalabari religious discourse, there is not only a balance between the theoretical and the narrative aspects but also a fairly obvious consistency between them. And one way in which to characterize this consistency would seem to be by saying that Kalabari myths about the gods are concrete symbolic illustrations of the more abstract theoretical generalizations about their attributes and ways of working in the world.

Having said this much about the Bultmannian view, I must confess myself uneasy about it. As I made plain in 'Back to Frazer?' (paper 4), one of my objections to the Symbolist approach to religious discourse has always been that it takes no account of the evidential criteria that we normally require to be satisfied before we categorize something as symbolic or metaphorical rather than literal. I have always maintained that, if we apply such criteria to the theoretical strand of religious discourse, the results compel us to opt for a literal interpretation. Having come this far, however, we must surely accept that what is sauce for the theoretical goose must also be sauce for the mythical gander. And if we do accept this, the results are embarrassing for the Bultmannian approach. For in most cases, it would seem that here too they compel us to accept a literal interpretation. It is true, of course, that Bultmann is by no means an isolated figure; and that his view is a particularly explicit form of one held more implicitly by hundreds of thousands of modern Western Christians. Nonetheless, as indignant reactions to some of the more Bultmannian pronouncements of the present Bishop of Durham about the Virgin Birth, the Empty Tomb and other episodes in the narrative of Christ's life make clear, hundreds of thousands of other modern Western Christians take the narrative strand of their religious discourse as literally as they take the theoretical strand. What is true for them, moreover, seems to be true of the adherents of most religions at most times and places in human history. The long and short of it all, then, is that the combination of a Literalist interpretation of religious theory and a Symbolist interpretation of religious narrative, however attractive it may seem at first glance, can only be carried through at the price of an inconsistent application of evidential criteria. Here, then, we seem to be back to square one.

But if the Bultmannian approach will not do, what will? At the moment, I fear, I have little to offer. Perhaps we might start by broadening the discussion. Thus we might reflect on the fact that, just as religious theory is a species of theory-in-general, so religious myth is a species of myth-in-general, and myth-in-general a species of narrative.[56] From here, we might go on to tackle the question of the relation between theoretical and narrative explanations generally, and the question of why it is that men in all societies appear to have a deep need for both. Whether or not the results of our enquiry would leave us wiser about the question from which we started remains, of course, uncertain. But it just might!

If this seems something of a lame conclusion, I believe our discussion has nonetheless been of value in raising issues which have too long been ignored by comparative students of religion. Here, I refer not just to the issue of the relation between religious theory and religious narrative. For once we face this one, our attention is inevitably drawn to the equally neglected issue of cross-cultural differences in balance between the theoretical and the narrative aspects. In sub-saharan Africa alone, such differences are quite striking. Thus in culture areas such as those of Tallensi and Igbo, the balance seems to fall heavily in favour of the theoretical. In others, such as those of Kalabari and Yoruba, the balance seems more even. And in yet others, such as those of Dogon and Bambara, the balance is tipped heavily in favour of the narrative.

The two strands of religious discourse, moreover, are linked to two different modes of ritual action. Thus theoretical discourse is linked to a type of action which consists essentially in putting the causal prescriptions of theory into practice; whilst narrative discourse is linked to a type of action whose essence is the re-creation or re-enactment of the events described in the narrative. And as we should expect, differences in balance between the two types of discourse give rise to differences in balance between the two types of ritual. Thus in high-theory-low-narrative cultures like those of Tallensi and Igbo, we see a predominance of 'applied-theory' rites. Again, where the balance between the two kinds of discourse is more even, we see a mixture of 'applied-theory' and 're-enactment' rites. And finally, where the balance is tipped in favour of the narrative mode, we see a predominance of 're-enactment' rites.

Let me sum up. Intellectualists' coverage of religious phenomena is strong where the mythologists' coverage is weak, and vice versa. As a result, neither side has yet managed to produce an interpretative framework which can even pretend to do justice to the two kinds of religious discourse or to the two modes of ritual which flow from them. If this section has performed a useful function, it has been that of alerting both sides to the problem, and so of stirring up further thought on the matter.

The cold and the hot in religious life

One of the criticisms of the Intellectualist approach that has come from otherwise well-disposed colleagues is that it is all very well as far as it goes, but that it leaves the reader with the feeling that it is somehow too 'cold' or too 'thin' to do full justice to the facts.[57]

Up to a point, I think this defect can be put down to a mere failure to spell out all the various implications of the approach. Thus when I have talked of religious life as being shaped above all by the linked aims of explanation, prediction and control, I have always assumed that a word was enough for the wise, and that readers would spell out for themselves the concrete details of all the divers aspirations that fall under the heading of 'control'. Evidently, however, I have been too sanguine in this. So let me remind the critic that when he reads 'control', he should be thinking of such diverse abhorred human states as sickness in all its ramifications, mental anguish, poverty in all its guises, powerlessness, and social conflict; and of such desired states as health in all its ramifications, peace of mind, wealth in all its guises, power, and social harmony. He should be thinking of religion as shaped by the aim of converting each of the abhorred states to its desired opposite. Once he gets himself down to this more concrete level of thinking, he will realize how ridiculous it is to say, for instance with Droogers, that: 'for suffering, so much stressed by the preceding models, there is no place in Horton's model'.[58] On the contrary, once he gets down to this level, he will see that my model, albeit implicitly, allows a central place for suffering and anguish, joy and relief.

Perhaps the underlying problem here is posed by the term 'theory'. I continue to see this term as providing the key to our understanding of religious life. But I now see more clearly the need, in using it, to issue constant *caveats* to the reader. Here, let me return to a point I made years ago in my 'Neo-Tylorianism' (paper 2). The point is that the Western or Westernized scholar, when he reads the word 'theory', automatically registers an antithesis with 'practice'. Hence, when he reads that religious thought is a species of theoretical thought, he automatically takes the writer to be saying that religion is something removed from the hurly-burly of everyday life; and, understandably enough, he jibs. In so reacting, however, he is being misled by a feature of theoretical activity in the modern West – i.e. the hiatus between such activity and its practical counterpart. What he has to be made to realize is that this hiatus is *peculiar* to the modern West (or at least to the modern West and to ancient Greece before it), and that, at most if not all other times and places in human history, theory has been indissolubly linked with practice, and with all the trials, tribulations and emotional accompaniments of practice. If this *caveat* is kept constantly in mind, one important source of objection to the Intellectualist approach will have been removed.

All this said, I believe the critics will still have a point if they continue to maintain that, even now, something vital is being left out. The better to pin down this elusive something, let me return once more to an early paper: this time to my 'Definition of religion' (paper 1), in which I emphasize the importance of the communion aspect of religious life – of the quest for social partners other than those provided within the purely human social field. In most subsequent publications, I have continued to allude to communion as a very frequent if not constant counterpart to explanation/prediction/ control. However, as I admitted in the introduction, I have not seen my way as clearly with communion as I have with explanation/prediction/control. As a result, these allusions have mostly been in the small print; and it seems in retrospect that the print has been too small for most people to take notice.

Now once we take the communion aspect seriously as a frequent if not constant accompaniment to explanation/prediction/control, any residual feeling that an intellectualist approach debars us from consideration of the warm, emotionally-rich side of religious life must surely evaporate. For as soon as we accept the proposition that religious people participate in a social field containing non-human fathers, mothers, husbands, wives, friends and enemies, all of whom are as real to them as are fellow human beings, we place ourselves in an ambience dominated by warmth and emotion. Clearly, then, any future development of my approach must include elaboration of a framework adequate to the analysis and explanation of the communion aspect.

In search of inspiration for the elaboration of such a framework, we may turn in the first instance to two rather different groups of theorists: the Theological Theorists and the Freudian Psychoanalysts.

The Theological Theorists have provided us with a treasury of insights into the deep importance of this aspect of religious life. They have also provided us with valuable hints as to how this aspect may dominate and shape even that part of the individual's field of social relations which involves purely human partners.[59] Nevertheless, as I pointed out in my 'Judaeo-Christian spectacles' (paper 6), the work of this group of theorists is misleading in a number of ways.

First, they tend toward gross overemphasis on the communion aspect; often going as far as to relegate concern with explanation/prediction/control to the marginal status of 'superstition'.

Second, they tend to overemphasize the uniqueness and spookiness of the emotions which arise in man-god communion, and to neglect the important emotional elements which man-god relations share with their human counterparts.

Third, they tend to associate communion exclusively with the supreme being; whereas, as any comparative student of religions who pays close enough attention to the phenomena can confirm, this aspect of religious life is very often most marked in human relations with various lesser spiritual agencies.

Finally, their explanation of religious communion, as the product of the universal self-revelation of God to man, is, for a number of reasons detailed in 'Judaeo-Christian spectacles', fundamentally unsatisfactory.

So much for what the Theological Theorists can and cannot give us in this area of concern. Let us turn now to the Freudian Psychoanalysts.

Many theorists of religion have been put off Freud by the improbable and in many cases unverifiable 'just-so' stories of origin which are central to his *Totem and Taboo*.[60] I believe they would have been less alienated had they started with his more sober and less obviously unverifiable *The Future of an Illusion*.[61] In this little book, for all its antipathy to religious belief and practice, we find an emphasis on the deep importance of the communion aspect which parallels that of the Theological Theorists.[62] In addition, however, we have an attempt to anchor the quest for spiritual communion to mundane antecedents which is strikingly (though understandably) absent from the work of the Theologians.

The essence of Freud's thesis is that early life in the bosom of the family creates certain enduring communion needs; notably the need for a male parental figure. As the individual grows to adulthood, however, he finds that society progressively denies him satisfaction of these needs in a purely human context. Hence the deep appeal of the idea of a spiritual father to whom one can turn till death and beyond.

This simple central thesis, I suggest, provides a valuable starting-point for the elaboration of a cross-cultural theory of religious communion. Note, however, my use of the phrase 'starting-point'. For there is much refining and modification to be done before the thesis can be used as a tool for cross-cultural understanding.

First of all, the thesis as it stands is strongly androcentric. That is, it deals specifically with the impact of family life on the young *male*, and on the way in which this gives rise to a specific type of spiritual communion. Though implying that the impact of the family on the young female is very different, it does nothing to spell out the consequences of this implied difference for women's religious belief. This one-sidedness, indeed, leaves us with an uncomfortable paradox. Thus on the one hand, Freud treats religious beliefs and practices as things shared by the two sexes. Yet on the other, he implies that the specific factors which he has postulated as the *sine qua non* of adult religious communion are absent from the early life of the female of the species!

Secondly, the thesis is strongly ethnocentric. Thus it deals specifically with the impact on the individual of early twentieth-century European Judaic family life, and with the consequent appeal of a Judaic type of religious communion. It has nothing to say about *other* patterns of family life, and about the consequences *they* might have for later religious activity. Nor does it have anything to say about patterns of religious life radically different from those characteristic of Judaism.

Thirdly, the thesis concentrates on features of *very early* life as the determinants of later religious belief and practice. It has nothing to say about the contribution of the human social context of *adult* life to the flourishing of religious communion.

Fourth and finally, the thesis stresses that it is the pattern of man-man communion which determines that of man-god communion. It does not consider the possibility of determination in the opposite direction.

Having identified all these defects, let us turn to the process of reconstruction.

Here, I think we can take as our foundation Freud's idea of the importance of early experience in the purely human context as a crucial shaping
influence on later religious communion. Even if we refuse to accept such
experience as the sole determinant of adult religious life, it nonetheless
seems a promising candidate for consideration as one important factor.

Building on this foundation, our first step must be one designed to
eliminate the androcentric bias. Thus, within the bounds of each particular
culture, we must look more closely at the differential impact of a specific
pattern of family life on infants and children of the two sexes, and ask
whether there is any evidence that this differential impact produces systematic differences between the sexes with respect to the later pattern of
spiritual communion. Despite the current vogue for Women's and Gender
Studies, I am not aware of any work done so far along these lines. Feminist
scholars of religion tend to take the view that, up till now, women have
endured, resentfully but more or less uncomplainingly, definitions of religion imposed on them by men; and they concentrate their energies on urging
that their sisters should combine to evolve definitions which owe more to
their distinctive urges and aspirations. They seem not to have considered
the possibility that women, because of different patterns of childhood
experience, may already have evolved their own distinctive patterns of
spiritual communion. Here is something well worth looking into.

The second step in our reconstruction must be one designed specifically
to avoid the ethnocentric bias. We shall have to switch from an intra-
cultural to a cross-cultural perspective, and look for correlations between
different patterns of family life and different patterns of religious communion. Here, it would seem, quite a bit of work has already been done. Thus
Whiting and Levine have suggested some global cross-cultural correlations
in this area, whilst Spiro has focussed more specifically on the question of
family pattern and its influence on the sex of the principal spiritual partner
in religious communion.[63]

The third step must be one which balances Freud's emphasis on early-life
factors with one on later-life factors. Here, we may extend his basic insight,
that man-god communion relationships arise where society generates
certain communion needs which it then refuses to satisfy, by suggesting that
this can happen not only in childhood but also in adulthood. Not much
systematic work has been done in this direction so far. But interesting hints
can be found in the work of Meyer Fortes, who suggests that in societies
where a son's dependence on his father is prolonged into adulthood, and is
then suddenly brought to an end by the father's death, communion relations
with the dead father and with other ancestral figures are apt to have a
peculiar intensity.[64] Another such hint is to be found in the work of Peter
Brown, who, at several points in his history of early Christianity, suggests

that it was certain specific conditions of adult life in parts of the Roman Empire that drove people into the intense communion relationships with a father-figure so characteristic of that religion.[65]

The fourth and final step must be to eliminate the one-way character of Freudian ideas about the causal link between society and religion, by exploring the way in which man-god relationships can have a shaping effect on man-man relationships. Here, we may want to call in the Theological Theorists as an inspirational counterweight to Freud. For their reluctance to ground patterns of religious communion in any kind of social causation is matched by their readiness to spell out how at least one pattern of religious communion may shape relationships between man and man. Their principal limitation in this context is one already mentioned: that is, their virtually exclusive preoccupation with communion relationships with the supreme being. Some ways in which communion relationships with lesser spiritual forces can have equally powerful effects on people's relationships with their fellow human beings are discussed in my 'Definition of religion'. One notable example there given is the way in which a dependent relationship with a lesser spiritual agent can free the individual for a more decisive leadership role *vis-à-vis* his fellow human beings.

This, I think, is as far as I want to go for the moment in suggesting how we might elaborate a framework that would do justice to the communion aspect of religious life.

At this point, it should be clear that what I am advocating (and what I have been advocating all along, though perhaps with less clarity) is a two-factor approach, in which religion is seen as growing, persisting and declining under the influence of two completely independent strivings: on the one hand, the striving to achieve an adequate level of explanation, prediction and control of the world; and on the other, the striving to achieve certain communion relationships not permitted in the purely human context.

The reader may well feel a certain intellectual discomfort at this proposal, which appears to be advocating a juxtaposition of two entirely disparate analytical and explanatory frameworks. One answer to his uneasiness may have to be that the duality is an irreducible one with which we just have to live; and that much of the religious life of the world has indeed unfolded at the intersection of the spheres of influence of these two disparate strivings. Having said this, however, I also think that we can go a little further, and assign an order of causal priority to the two factors postulated by the theory.

Let us start by looking at certain facts about the disjunctions and combinations of our two principal aspects of religion. The first thing to note here is that all *vigorously flourishing* religious traditions include a strong emphasis on explanation, prediction and control of worldly events. The second thing to note is that quite a few such traditions seem to get along very well without any accompanying emphasis on the communion aspect. In Africa, for example, Tiv religion as described by the Bohannans[66] and Southern Luo religion as described by Okot P'Bitek[67] seem very coolly pragmatic in their general tone. Again, the religions of such peoples as the Ifugao of the Philippines and the Garia of Melanesia, picked out for mention by Mary Douglas,[68] seem to be marked by a similar cool pragmatism. The third thing to note is that the opposite does not seem to be true: that is, we do not come across *flourishing* religious systems in which there is a strong communion emphasis with no accompanying emphasis on explanation, prediction and control.

At this point, I can imagine an indignant shout from some Christian scholars, to the effect that modern Western Christianity is in fact a religion in which the communion aspect remains supreme, and from which the 'superstitious' element of explanation, prediction and control has been successfully jettisoned. My answer to such scholars is that, whilst their characterization is perfectly apt to certain strands of contemporary Western Christianity, these strands, precisely as a result of their one-sidedness, have never *flourished*. Rather, their cutting off of the explanation/prediction/control aspect can be compared in its effects to the cutting off of air supply to an underwater diver. After it, a lot of noisy, desperate gasping goes on, but the long-term prospects are not good. Because we are in the midst of the gasping, and because it is very noisy, we are apt to be impressed by its vigour. But it does not take much perspicacity to see that this is the vigour of desperation, and that it is accompanied by a steady slide, either into atheism, or back into religious traditions that have not made the mistake of jettisoning the concern with explanation/prediction/control.

I shall have a good deal more to say about this in the next section. Meanwhile, it seems from what has been said that the pursuit of explanation, prediction and control is both necessary and sufficient for the flourishing of religious life, whilst the quest for communion is neither necessary nor sufficient. Of the two strivings, the first would seem to be the basic sustainer of religious life, whilst the second would seem to be more of an optional extra.

Why should this be? To put it simply, it is above all the constant use of certain theories of underlying reality in the context of explanation, prediction and control of this-worldly events that gives a sense of the 'thereness' of the entities postulated by the theories. And it is this sense of the 'thereness' of spiritual beings which is vital for sustaining communion relations with them. Where spiritual beings no longer feature in the theories used in the explanation, prediction and control of the world, the sense of 'thereness' evaporates, and communion becomes difficult if not impossible to sustain.

The upshot of all this, of course, is that although for the purposes of a comparative study of the world's religions the Intellectualist emphasis on explanation/prediction/control needs to be supplemented by an emphasis on communion, in the final analysis it is the Intellectualist approach which provides us with the key to answering the question: 'Why Religion?'

The cold, the hot, and the West

Critics of the Intellectualist approach often make the comment that it may be all very well for Africa, but that it completely fails to do justice to religion in the West and more especially to religion in the modern West.[69]

I have always been puzzled by such comments. Over the years, I have left an accumulation of scattered remarks on the development of religion in Western society; and although these remarks need bringing together, they do I think show that an Intellectualist approach, particularly one suitably balanced by an emphasis on the communion aspect, can throw a good deal of light on this area.[70] In recent years, moreover, I have had to face the challenge of a series of lectures entitled 'Religion and science in Western history'. And though I will admit to the sleepless nights occasioned by the challenge, I have certainly found that my approach provides a useful framework with which to face it.

Though this vast topic deserves a book rather than a section in a post-script, let me offer here at least a rough sketch of a possible approach to it.

In trying to make sense of the early spread of Christianity in the eastern Mediterranean, let me start with some hints thrown out in Peter Brown's majestic *World of Late Antiquity*.[71] In this book, Brown emphasizes two aspects of the early Christian message: first, the way in which the Christian God pulls the individual out of the local group and local environment, and places him in the wider world of mankind at large; and second, the way in which the same God provides an intense parental relationship which becomes a backdrop to all of the individual's relationships with his fellow men. He sees these two aspects of the Christian message as answering to two salient aspects of the predicament of those migrants from the countryside to the great urban trading centres who made up such a large proportion of the early Christian converts. First, here were people uprooted from cosy local communities and environments and thrown into a much larger world. As such, they were ready recipients of a message which enjoined them to abandon as irrelevant the old gods of family, lineage and locality, and offered them instead a broader, more universalistic framework in terms of which to define, interpret and guide their new lives.[72] Second, here were people for whom the human social field of the urban centres did not provide the cosy emotional security of their old family, lineage, clan and local matrices. As such, they were very ready to accept a peculiarly intense parental relationship with a spiritual being – a relationship whose intensity had no real parallel in the locally-based cults in their earlier lives.[73]

Though Brown does not use the terminology of 'explanation/prediction/ control' and 'communion', and would probably reject it as insufficiently mellifluous even were he confronted with it, it is surely clear from his own writing that, in early Christianity, we are confronted with a message whose appeal owed much to its powerful blend of these two aspects of the religious life. Thus on the one hand, it answered to the migrants' needs for a system of explanation, prediction and control which would do justice to their new experience of life in a wider world. (Note here the parallel with my own Intellectualist interpretation of conversion to Islam and Christianity in Africa.) And on the other hand, it answered to communion needs which were no longer satisfied within the purely human social field.

In these early days, large sections of the elite of the urban centres remained rooted in a rival body of theory, also strongly concerned with the explanation, prediction and control of the world, whose origins were largely Greek, and which was known to the Christians as 'pagan science'. To gather in members of this elite, some of the most prominent of the early Christian leaders of thought embarked on a systematic assimilation into their own theoretical framework of those elements of 'pagan science' which they deemed compatible with it, in the process re-designating as forerunners of Christianity such ancient Greek philosopher-scientists as Plato and Aristotle.[74] The resulting body of thought survived without major modification for over a thousand years. To understand it, we have to cast aside the modern Western distinction between religion and science, and take as our guiding category John Peel's simple but poignant 'religion-science'.[75]

It was not until the eighteenth century that the modern Western distinction emerged. For it was only then that Western thinkers started to elaborate systems of explanation, prediction and control from which the spiritual element had been totally banished.[76] Historians of the West have continued to agonize over this momentous development without coming up with anything very convincing. Here, I think my own attempt at explanation does as well as anything else offered so far.

Briefly, as the reader will recall, my attempt is based on the postulate that the type of analogy used to guide theoretical elaboration is determined, amongst other things, by the perceived locus of order, regularity and predictability in everyday experience. Where, as in most societies down through the course of history, the locus is the realm of inter-human relations, the guiding analogies are likely to be personal, and hence to give rise to a personal or spiritual theoretical framework. But where, as in the West from the seventeenth century on, the human realm is increasingly perceived to be in flux whilst the non-human realm emerges more and more clearly as the locus of order, regularity and predictability, there is likely to be a turn from the personal to the impersonal in the choice of guiding analogies, and hence a turn from a spiritual to a mechanistic system of explanation, prediction and control. This, I suggest, was the key factor in initiating the eighteenth-century secularization of theoretical thinking.[77]

As historians now agree, the resulting surge of interest in impersonal theoretical schemas antedated any systematic evidence that these schemas 'worked' better than their older spiritual counterparts. Indeed, this had to be so. For the impersonal schemas had to have gained enough prominence to present a challenge to their spiritual counterparts before any serious comparisons of cognitive value could get under way. Nonetheless, once such comparisons did get under way, the impersonal schemas registered consistent and often spectacular superiority, particularly in the realm of non-human phenomena; and this of course further increased their prestige.

The upshot of this combination of factors was that, by the end of the nineteenth century, all serious theorizing about the visible, tangible world was being carried out in a more or less strictly impersonal idiom, and that prophecies of the imminent end of religion were rife.

Prophecies notwithstanding, however, religion in the West has been a long time a-dying. True, with the continued inexorable elaboration of impersonal theoretical systems, more and more Westerners have come to see it as otiose, and have become out-and-out atheists. At the same time, for all that, various new forms of religious life have been developed to face and survive the challenge of these systems. Perhaps the most characteristic of these forms, particularly amongst the educationally more sophisticated, is one in which all attempts to compete with the sciences in the explanation, prediction and control of this-worldly events have been renounced, and in which there has been more and more emphasis on communion with God as something to be sought for and sustained as an end in itself.[78]

It is easy to see how engagement in such a form of religious life can appear quite compatible with the acceptance of an impersonal system of explanation, prediction and control of this-worldly events. The question that remains is: 'What gives such a form its undoubted continuing appeal?'

Here, we have to take note of the double-edged impact on religion of the increasing flux, instability and unpredictability of Western social life. On the one hand, for the reasons already given, this trend *weakens* the appeal of a spiritually-based system of explanation, prediction and control. On the other hand, in creating a pervasive sense of insecurity in the context of purely human social relations, it *enhances* the appeal of an intense and over-riding communion relationship with a spiritual parent. The upshot of all this is a religious life which virtually excludes any concern with explanation, prediction and control, and is based more or less wholly on communion.

Prominent as it has been in the West over the last hundred years, however, this form of religious life lacks secure foundations; and the prognosis for it is poor. As I said in the last section, it is through constant use of spiritual concepts in systems of explanation, prediction and control that people acquire a sense of the 'thereness' of spiritual beings. And the attempt to build and sustain communion relationships with these beings in the absence of such constant use must therefore be correspondingly precarious. After increasingly desperate efforts by an older generation of theologians to justify a 'communion-only' form of religious life, there are signs that a new generation is coming to realize this. Notable here is a renewed vogue for a type of natural theology that went out of fashion at the end of the nineteenth century. One way of interpreting this new trend is to see it as engaged in the age-old enterprise of assimilating into the body of Christian thought whatever elements of non-Christian scientific theory appear compatible with it. A more penetrating scrutiny reveals that its basic impulse is that of restoring the sense of 'thereness' of the spiritual realm – a sense so vital to stable communion relationships with spiritual beings – by bringing a spiritual element back into contemporary systems of explanation, prediction and control.[79]

As to what the future holds for this new trend, it would be rash to venture a prediction. Certainly, the environmental and social conditions in which it operates still strongly favour the use of impersonal analogies in the building of scientific theories. Nor has anyone yet come up with specific theories, couched in a personal idiom, that account for whole areas of human experience more convincingly than do their prevailing impersonal counterparts. As one who sees nothing essentially irrational or even essentially anti-scientific about a personal, spiritual idiom of theoretical elaboration, I keep an open mind as to what the latter's future may be. What I *do* believe, however, is that the longer-term prospects of religion are bound up with its ability to re-assert itself in the sphere of explanation, prediction and control of this-worldly events.

This has been a shamelessly rapid *tour d'horizon*. However, I believe it has made the point that an Intellectualist approach, suitably enriched and balanced by an emphasis on communion, offers insights into several aspects of the development of religion in the West which have been troubling and taxing historians. To date, I have not seen anything of comparable scope coming from the pens of those anthropological colleagues who suggest that such an approach cannot cope with this shared area of interest!

Tradition and modernity

Looking back at what I have written over the years on the topic of intellectual modernization (see especially papers 7 and 9), I am more than ever afflicted with the sense of having been the fool who rushed in where the angels feared to tread. Nonetheless, it may be useful to point to what appear to be some insights of enduring worth in this area, as well as to ideas that call for amendment.

As I said in the introduction, my strategy in this area has been twofold. On the one hand, I have tried to identify the key *cognitive* factors in intellectual modernization: i.e. those cognitive factors upon which all other more specific features of intellectual modernity would appear to depend. On the other hand, I have tried to identify the key *contextual* factors: i.e. those features of technological, economic and socio-political context upon which the key cognitive factors appear to depend.

Let me deal first of all with ideas concerning the key cognitive factors.

Here, one point on which I and others appear to have been vindicated by recent scholarship is in our emphasis on the *mode of use* as opposed to the *content* of theory. I have always seen intellectual modernization in terms of the former rather than of the latter. One consequence has been that I have tended to see the transition from a pre-scientific to a scientific mode of thinking as a process distinct from that of the transition from a personal to an impersonal idiom of theoretical elaboration. To put it more succinctly, I have tended to separate the question of intellectual modernization from that of intellectual secularization. Here, I have taken sides in a protracted and important debate. On one side of this debate, Marxists and positivists have asserted a close link between modernization and secularization. They have seen the rejection of a personal, spiritual idiom of theorizing as the necessary if not sufficient condition for the development of a scientific approach to the world. Although this appears to be an older position, it nonetheless has some influential contemporary advocates: for instance, Charles Gillispie, Ernest Gellner and Maurice Bloch.[80] On the other side, post-positivists have tended to set aside the question of secularization in their analyses of modernization; as witness the work of Popper, Kuhn and Lakatos.[81] Despite my disagreements with scholars in the latter group on specific points, my position agrees with theirs on this broader issue.

Although the debate is still far from closed, some of the more recent work by historians of Western thought has given considerable support to the 'separationist' view. Here, I am thinking particularly of those recent studies which indicate that some of the most important pioneers of intellectual modernization in the West were bearers of essentially spiritual world-views, and that intellectual modernization got under way before radical secularization.[82]

Let us now turn to more specific ideas about the key cognitive factors.

Here, I think my position as stated in 'Tradition and modernity revisited' (paper 9) has stood up rather well in the light of recent work. In this piece, I tried to account for the entire process of intellectual modernization in terms of just two key factors: inter-theoretic competition and faith in cognitive progress. Despite the somewhat breathtaking rashness of this attempt, I am encouraged to see that scholars as diverse as Geoffrey Lloyd, Peter Munz, Roger Brown, and the Evolutionary Epistemologists, all of them considerably more versed in the history of Western thought than myself, have been stressing the importance of the competition factor with growing enthusiasm.[83]

Nonetheless, I am beginning to think that trying to generate the whole of cognitive modernity from the interaction of just two key factors may be pushing the principle of parsimony a little too far. As I now see it, we need to incorporate at least two more factors into the model to make its account of intellectual modernization anywhere near adequate.

One such factor is that of world-view universalism. World-view parochialism, which sees each local community and its environment as governed by a distinct set of underlying forces, renders confrontation with a neighbour's alien world-view unproblematic. Given the postulate of different sets of forces underpinning different local enclaves, such alienness of world-view is just what one would expect from a neighbour, and so poses no challenge to one's own view. In this way, world-view parochialism virtually *rules out* inter-theoretic competition. By contrast, world-view universalism, which insists that the entire world is governed by a single set of underlying forces, makes every confrontation with an alien world-view a challenge to one's own view. It therefore greatly *encourages* inter-theoretic competition.

A second factor which needs to be accorded key status is the presence of an explicit and specific ideal of objectivity. Such an ideal is based on the perception that the quest for explanation, prediction and control is incompatible with the simultaneous pursuit of other quests, and that ideas used in the service of explanation, prediction and control must therefore not be allowed to come under the influence of other aims and aspirations. In my two earlier papers dealing with intellectual modernization, I suggested that the ideal of objectivity, together with other explicit rules governing the cognitive quest, was a dependent variable with respect to inter-theoretic competition; my reasoning being that it was such competition which raised the possibility of theoretical choice, and that it was the possibility of choice which led to the formulation of explicit rules to govern it. My feeling now is that, although the emergence of the ideal of objectivity and of other explicit rules governing the cognitive quest may be partly dependent on the growth of inter-theoretic competition, it is also, at least partly, an independent cognitive factor, linked directly to features of context.

So much for key cognitive factors. Let us turn now to their contextual counterparts. Here, I must confess once more to uneasiness about my previous attempts to link key cognitive factors with features of the technological, economic and socio-political context. Not that the enterprise is illegitimate. Far from it. Rather, my own and other attempts so far have almost certainly been too simple-minded. Clearly a lot remains to be done in this area; and here I can do no more than make one or two crude additional suggestions.

One contextual factor which featured fairly prominently on my old list, but which may now have to be struck off or at least suspended pending further enquiries, is written transmission of ideas. We are now faced with some embarrassing cases, such as that of India, in which the development and wide diffusion of written transmission does not seem to have been followed by intellectual modernization. As a result, a consensus seems to be developing amongst historians and social anthropologists that the relation of written transmission to intellectual modernization is both more complex and less direct than had previously been believed.[84]

If one contextual factor has to be struck off the list, however, others may have to be added. Thus the addition of further key cognitive factors to our model may make it necessary to bring in additional contextual factors to account for them.

One such factor is the emergence of a pattern of social life in which the local community is very much open to the wider world: the pattern characteristic, for instance, of a network of urban centres with strong involvements in long-distance trade. This sort of background would appear to be an important factor in the development of world-view universalism.[85]

Another such factor is the emergence of occupational and institutional specialization. Such specialization brings in its wake the concern to define more or less precisely the goals of a given occupational role or institution, and to formulate rules designed to promote efficient pursuit of these goals. It seems possible that the development of specialized roles and institutions for the pursuit of explanation, prediction and control may be part of this larger movement toward occupational and institutional specialization; and that the emergence of the ideal of objectivity and of other explicit norms governing the cognitive quest may be part of the resulting larger preoccupation with the definition of goals and of what constitutes efficiency in achieving them.[86]

This somewhat disjointed collection of remarks on intellectual modernization reflects, I fear, a currently untidy state of mind. I only hope that the historians of Western thought who claim to be the masters of this field of study will not take the quality of these remarks as one more excuse for banning social anthropologists from attempting to make their own contribution to it. I say this because I continue to see the social anthropologist, the man who has ventured beyond the realm of modernity and who looks back into it from outside, as having a distinctive contribution to make in this field. He scarcely ever has the background of specialized scholarship from which the historian of Western thought routinely operates. At his best, however, he has two priceless outsider's gifts. First, the gift of taking nothing about modernity for granted. Second, that of an overall view which sees the wood of modernity as well as the trees.

Premises and preoccupations

To conclude this postscript, I should like, first to clarify and defend certain basic features of my approach that have not been discussed so far, and second to say something about the personal circumstances and preoccupations that may have shaped and coloured it.

Perhaps the most pervasive feature of my approach is what may be described as its *cognitive foundationalism*. Thus I base my study of human society and culture on certain techniques of inference (e.g. induction, deduction, analogy), certain procedures for judging empirical validity (verification, falsification), and a certain level of thought and discourse (the primary-theoretical) which functions as a court of final appeal for the application of these procedures. These I take to be foundational to the human cognitive enterprise at all times and places. Again, I base my translational efforts on the premiss that the same foundational universals provide us with the crucial 'bridgehead' through which to gain understanding of the thought of other peoples and other cultures. Finally, I believe that most if not all of the fascinating diversity of human world-views can be explained in terms of the supposition that the same set of foundational processes produces different results when operating in different technological, economic and socio-political circumstances.

All of this no doubt sounds terribly old-fashioned, particularly in view of the Cognitive Relativism which is now so much in vogue amongst my anthropological colleagues. In fact, however, it seems to me that the Relativist quarrel with the Foundationalists is largely specious, and that Relativist rant covers a strong element of Foundationalist practice. Thus Relativists use the same procedures of inference and of empirical validation as do Foundationalists; and, for all their protestations, they use them as though they intended them to be compelling to people of all times and places. Again, for all their talk about 'communicating the incommensurable',[87] they use the same assumptions about a primary-theoretical 'bridgehead' as do the Foundationalists. Their translations are full of primary-theoretical English and its metaphorical extensions; and everything indicates that they intend us to take this strand of English as providing semantic equivalents to the contents of the alien languages they are translating from. In short, it seems to me that Relativists ignore their own precepts whenever they actually get down to business.

Conversely, it seems to me that the only point at which Cognitive Relativists manage to square practice with precept is the point at which they refuse to get down to what many would regard as the most important part of their rightful business. Here, I refer to the fact that, for all their celebration of the diversity of human world-views, they are conspicuously reluctant to attempt any explanation of this diversity. Now since explanation of diversity, almost by definition, involves the postulation of some underlying unity, any attempt in this direction would embroil them with foundationalism. So in this reluctance, if nowhere else, one can at least applaud them for consistency. Nonetheless, the diversity of world-views is one of the most fascinating challenges both to lay curiosity and to the alleged expertise of the professional anthropologist; and an anthropology that refuses to accept the challenge of trying to account for it is a poor thing indeed.

It seems, then, as if the Cognitive Relativists are caught on the horns of a dilemma. Either they try to say something significant about human world-views, and fall foul of their own precepts in doing so. Or they try for consistency, and find themselves unable to say anything of significance. Until my Relativist colleagues can show me a way round this impasse, I shall remain a foundationalist.

All this said, let me concede that foundationalism itself is a troubling doctrine. Thus after centuries of intellectual struggle, foundationalist philosophers have come to acknowledge that neither the basic forms of human inference nor the basic procedures of empirical validation are further justifiable. They have also come to realize, moreover, that primary theory is not a flawless mirror of reality but a construction shaped by certain human interests and, more fundamentally, by the human struggle to survive in the world. As such, it tells us as much about human interests and about the social framework within which they are pursued as it does about the reality to which it supposedly refers. Our foundation, then, is not firmly anchored to a rock. Rather, it is one of those 'raft' devices which people use nowadays when they want to build their houses on shifting sands.

Perhaps the best that can be said about foundationalism is that its premisses, albeit implicitly held, are the *sine qua non* of trying to communicate with other people about the world we all live in. As such, it does appear more promising than relativism, which if consistently pursued would surely rule out any communication at all.

A second feature of my approach, and one which is closely related to its cognitive foundationalism, is its concern with *cognitive efficacy*. Now it is an article of relativist faith that each world-view has its own totally idiosyncratic criteria of cognitive efficacy, which are really little more than its instruments of propaganda. For Relativists, therefore, cross-cultural comparisons of cognitive efficacy by anthropologists and others amount to little more than prejudiced rantings on behalf of their own world-view. As such, they are to be avoided. The Foundationalist, by contrast, holds that there are certain elementary criteria of cognitive efficacy which are universally acknowledged, and which can be appealed to in discussions of world-view both intra-cultural and cross-cultural. For him, then, there is nothing illegitimate or meaningless about cross-cultural comparisons of cognitive efficacy. On the contrary, indeed, there is much that makes such comparisons seem very important.

Social anthropologists, sociologists and historians who have studied beliefs and world-views have always been concerned, not only with the causes of these phenomena, but also with their effects. And one of the reasons why the Foundationalist, at least, considers cross-cultural comparisons of cognitive efficacy so important is that differences between world-views in respect of such efficacy lead directly to differences in their holders' ability to impose themselves on their environment and on their fellow men. Perhaps the most striking illustration of this is provided by the modern hegemony of the West over the Rest. For one undeniable factor in this hegemony has been the cognitive superiority, at least in the physical, chemical and biological realms, of the modern Western world-view. It is this and other such dramatic consequences that make it imperative for the student of intellectual modernization to identify and account for the emergence of those aspects of the process that have given rise to superior cognitive efficacy.

This, of course, is not to say that cross-cultural comparisons of cognitive efficacy always work out in favour of the intellectually modernized West. As I have said several times in the pieces that make up this volume, the nearer we get to the realm of 'higher' human behaviour, the less obvious the cognitive superiority of the modern Western world-view, and the more obvious the cognitive contributions of its non-Western counterparts. This decline in extra cognitive yield as we go from the physical to the psychological/sociological is another feature of intellectual modernization which has momentous consequences both for the West and for the Rest, and which also merits close scholarly attention.

A third salient feature of my approach is its prohibition on moving from premises concerning the *causal antecedents* of beliefs and world-views to conclusions as to the *cognitive efficacy* or *truth-value* of such items. Like the advocates of the 'Strong Programme' in the sociology of science, I am committed to a search for technological, economic and socio-political causes that deals 'symmetrically', both with those items that the searcher believes to be cognitively efficacious or true, and with those that he believes to be cognitively inefficacious or false. At the same time, I reject the idea that, having established such a causal background for a particular item, one is then entitled to draw conclusions as to its cognitive efficacy or falsity. This idea, which lacks any kind of rational warrant, seems to owe its sway to the superstitious notion that to attribute a mundane cause to a theoretical conception is somehow to demean or downgrade it. Unwarranted as it is, however, the idea is both pervasive in the comparative study of human thought-systems and pernicious in its effects. Thus on the one hand, it encourages people who wish to discredit certain theoretical conceptions to embark on rash and improbable causal attributions. And on the other, it encourages people who are intensely committed to avowing the truth of certain conceptions to rule out any causal attribution whatsoever. In the study of religion, for instance, the idea comes into play in connexion with the belief in a supreme being. Here, atheists recklessly fasten on any old causal explanation that comes to mind as a means of discrediting belief in such a being, whilst theists all too often reply to them in kind, by ruling out any attempts at such explanation as inappropriate. The idea also seems to be at work in the historiography of science. Here, some writers seem to pursue causal explanations of the emergence of major scientific theories as a way of showing that there is nothing very marvellous about such theories, whilst others seem equally concerned to ban such explanations as a way of defending the uniquely truthful status of their pet theories.[88]

In these and other related fields, I believe that a firm embargo on this habit of trying to link mundane causation with cognitive inefficacy is of the greatest methodological importance. For it both liberates scholars to undertake systematic exploration of the causal determinants of all beliefs and world-views including their own, and encourages them to do so in a spirit of scholarly calm rather than of missionary rage.

The fourth and last feature of my approach to which I want to draw attention in this postscript is what I call its *multi-intentionalism*. I use this label, first of all to point to the key place, in all my attempts at explanation, of the concept of intention working itself out in a social context. This may sound trivial, but it does serve to distinguish my approach from that of the Structuralists, whose key concept appears to be that of an inexorable structuring tendency which operates quite independently of human intentions. For me, by contrast, it is intentions that create and sustain structures. Secondly, and more crucially in this context, I use the label to signal my awareness of the multiplicity of human intentions, and of the multiplicity of forms of life linked to and shaped by these intentions. Quite apart from the theoretical-pragmatic intention and form of life, so emphasized in the essays that make up this volume, there are the communion-oriented, the political, the ethical, the aesthetic, and ludic, and probably quite a few others which have escaped me for the time being. In real life, of course, several intentions are often in play simultaneously, and there is considerable overlap between the corresponding forms of life; but the categories just referred to are nonetheless very useful for purposes of analysis and explanation.

The point of stressing these commonplaces is to try and remove what seems to be the commonest source of misunderstanding of my work. Critics tend to label me a 'rationalist',[89] referring to my apparent assumption of an overriding role in human social life of the linked ends of explanation, prediction and control. This is an impression for which one cannot blame the reader of the papers assembled in this volume. However, I believe these papers need to be placed in a broader perspective before they can be properly understood and fairly assessed. I further believe that when they are so placed, the 'rationalist' label will no longer seem quite as appropriate.

I myself have always felt that anthropologists and sociologists appeal to a very narrow range of human intentions in their interpretations of social life. I clearly remember early complaints to longer-established colleagues that they seemed to be reducing everything to the struggle for power and the craving for social acceptance. I also remember dreams of building a systematic theory that would do justice to the full range of human intentions and to their associated forms of life. Somewhere along the line, however, I got immersed in the study of African religions and in the problem of interpreting them. In grappling with this problem, I became convinced that the root of it was that social anthropologists and others were mistakenly placing religion in the category of the aesthetic when they should have been placing it in the category of the theoretical-pragmatic; and this conviction led in turn to thirty years spent trying to do justice to the theoretical-pragmatic element in religious life generally. In short, when I started to grapple with a particular problem, the problem took charge and demanded more and more of my time and energy. That, however, in no way led to my forgetting all other human intentions or all other aspects of human social life. Even when delving deeper and deeper into the theoretical-pragmatic aspect of religion, I did not lose sight of the very different communion aspect. And I have certainly always intended, time permitting, to return to the consideration of other aspects of life such as the moral and the aesthetic.[90]

The point I am trying to make is this. Although I once dreamed of building a systematic and comprehensive 'grand theory' of human social life à la Parsons or Habermas, what I ended up doing was trying to solve a particular problem posed by a particular aspect of social life. My emphasis on 'reason' (i.e. the quest for explanation, prediction and control) should be judged, not in the context of the first, grand project, which I never undertook, but in the context of the second, more limited one, which I did undertake. In relation to the first, my emphasis on 'reason' would certainly have been an exaggeration; for it would have neglected so many other aspects of human social life. In relation to the second, it seems to be in order.

All this said, perhaps I should put in a final word for 'reason'. 'Reason', as critics like to remind me, 'is the slave of the passions'. Yes indeed. But the passions are many, and 'reason' not only serves all of them, but also adjudicates between them. It is like one of those slaves who becomes so indispensable to the lives of so many masters that he ends up in control of all of them. Apart from this, 'reason', too, is a passion in itself.

Having spent so much time ruthlessly diagnosing the theories of others as products of their own personal and social preoccupations rather than responses to the phenomena for which they are supposed to account, it seems only fair that I should end this postscript with some kind of psycho-social diagnosis of my own approach. I do not of course propose to strip naked. There are a lot of unflattering things about myself which, however relevant they might be to a diagnosis, I have not the faintest intention of revealing. But let me at least make an attempt to admit the admissible and indicate its possible part in the formation of my views.

First of all, I believe that anyone trying to understand how I came to hold such views should take account of the fact that, over the last thirty years, I have been based in universities in the region whose religious life I have been writing about, and even on campus have never been altogether away from the realities of that religious life. One consequence, I believe, is that my line of interpretation remains more faithful than some of its rivals to indigenous ways of seeing things – or to what American anthropologists like to call the '-emic' aspect. Especially where Western colleagues based in Western universities are concerned, it seems to me that although the -emic aspect may be very vivid to them when they are in the field, it tends to lose its hold over them on their return to the groves of Western academe, to be replaced by pseudo-emic visions more congruent with the latter's world-view. The reality of the spirits is apt to fade, to be replaced by visions of people engaging in elaborately veiled power-plays, composing secular poetry, or participating in complicated semeiological parlour games.

Having said this, let me not be seen as claiming to be more 'indigenized' than my fellow Western scholars. I had a thoroughly English upbringing, which I have never shaken off, and am subject to enduring hang-ups and preoccupations which are wholly English. Looking back with the wisdom of hindsight, I see one of these preoccupations as having been particularly relevant to the shaping of my theoretical framework.

Earlier in this postscript, I spoke of the predicament of the modern

Westerner who has a yearning for spiritual communion, but suffers from a painful feeling of the 'not-thereness' of the spiritual. I further suggested that this situation was beginning to lead to disillusion with the dominant contrastive characterization of the relation between religion and science, and to a renewed quest for spiritual systems of explanation, prediction and control which would restore the sense of spiritual 'thereness'. At this juncture, I think I should say that I am one of those who has long faced this predicament. Way back in my teens, when I was a starry-eyed member of the Science Sixth, it was already drawing me toward the possibility of a theistic evolutionary biology. I remember long, solemn monologues which must have bored some of my schoolmates almost to tears, and notebooks filled with what, although I knew nothing of Teilhard de Chardin at the time, seems in retrospect to have been very much a Teilhardian evolutionary scheme. These efforts also got a certain encouragement from a brilliant left-wing biology master. (I now think he was probably a Lysenkoist, for whom it was a case of 'my enemy's enemy is my friend'.) Then came a period of National Service in Nigeria, and a tantalizing glimpse of a spiritual world-view applied to the explanation, prediction and control of everyday life by Igbo villagers. Then Oxford, where I plunged once more into Teilhardian speculations during a prelim-year biology course. This time round, however, there was no genial teleologist to encourage me, but instead a hard-nosed Darwinian who threatened me with academic outer darkness if I failed to bow to orthodoxy. I am ashamed to say that this scared me off my Teilhardian adventures; though in mitigation I would also say that I came in time to see why this particular line of natural theology would not work. As a result of this set-back, I was content, when I returned to Africa, to take an interest in other people's natural theologizing rather than pursue my own. But the predicament and the need for a solution to it have still haunted me; and they have given me an openness to the possibility of a spiritual system of explanation, prediction and control which I believe many of my Western anthropological colleagues lack.

My approach, then, has been as strongly influenced by personal (and Western) preoccupations as have those of other Western colleagues. The difference, I would claim, is that, in my case, by happy coincidence, the personal preoccupations have led me towards rather than away from the -emic realities.

Notes

INTRODUCTION

1 On the Nike fieldwork, see R. Horton, 'The Ohu System of Slavery in a Northern Ibo Village-group', *Africa*, 24, 4, 1954, and 'God, Man and the Land in a Northern Ibo Village-Group', *Africa*, 26, 1, 1956. For an overview of the evolution and character of pre-colonial Kalabari society, see R. Horton, 'From Fishing Village to City State', in M. Douglas and P. Kaberry, eds., *Man in Africa*, London: Tavistock Publications, 1969. For various aspects of Kalabari religious life, see R. Horton, *The Gods as Guests*, Lagos: Nigeria Magazine Special Publications, 1960, 'The Kalabari World-View: an Outline and an Interpretation', *Africa*, 32, 1, 1962, 'The Kalabari Ekine Society: a Borderland of Religion and Art', *Africa*, 33, 2, 1963, 'Kalabari Diviners and Oracles', *Odu*, New Series, 1, 1, 1964, *Kalabari Sculpture*, Lagos: Department of Antiquities, Federal Republic of Nigeria, 1965, 'Duminea: a Festival for the Water Spirits', *Nigeria Magazine*, 86, 1965, 'Igbo: an Ordeal for Aristocrats', *Nigeria Magazine*, 90, 1966, 'Ikaki: the Tortoise Masquerade', *Nigeria Magazine*, 94, 1967, 'Types of Spirit Possession in Kalabari Religion', in J. Beattie and J. Middleton, eds., *Spirit Mediumship and Society in Africa*, London: Routledge & Kegan Paul, 1969, 'Ikpataka Dogi: a Kalabari Funeral Rite', *African Notes*, 5, 3, 1969, and 'A Hundred Years of Change in Kalabari Religion', in J. Middleton, ed., *Black Africa*, New York: Macmillan, 1970.

2 For some philosophical sources which I found helpful in thinking about the importance of translation in cross-cultural studies of world-view, see P. Winch, *The Idea of a Social Science, and its Relation to Philosophy*, London: Routledge & Kegan Paul, 1958; W. V. Quine, *Word and Object*, Cambridge, Mass.: MIT Press, 1960 (see especially chapter 2); E. Gellner, 'Concepts and Society', *Transactions of the Fifth World Congress of Sociology*, 1962; P. Winch, 'Understanding a Primitive Society', *American Philosophical Quarterly*, 1, 1964; M. Hollis, 'Reason and Ritual', *Philosophy*, 43, 165, 1967; M. Hollis, 'The Limits of Irrationality', *European Journal of Sociology*, 7, 1967; S. Lukes, 'Some Problems about Rationality', *European Journal of Sociology*, 8, 1967. (All of the last five are reprinted in B. Wilson, ed., *Rationality*, Oxford: Basil Blackwell, 1970.) For some anthropological sources which I found similarly helpful, see L. Bohannan and P. Bohannan, *The Tiv of Central Nigeria*, London: International African Institute, 1953 (see pp. 84–5 on problems of translating the word *tsav*); G. Lienhardt, 'Modes of Thought', in E. Evans-Pritchard *et al.*, eds., *The Institutions of Primitive Society*, Oxford: Basil Blackwell, 1954;

E. Evans-Pritchard, 'Zande Theology', in *Essays in Social Anthropology*, London: Faber & Faber, 1962 (on problems of translating the word *mbori*); E. Evans-Pritchard, *Theories of Primitive Religion*, Oxford: Clarendon Press, 1965 (see especially the Introduction); In addition to acknowledging the inspiration gained from these written sources, I must also acknowledge that gained from Paul Bohannan during a long conversation I had with him on problems of translation when I was still an undergraduate in the Philosophy Programme at Oxford.

3 John Peel has recently given us a salutary reminder on this. See his 'History, Culture and the Comparative Method: a West African Puzzle', in L. Holy, ed., *Comparative Anthropology*, Oxford: Basil Blackwell, 1987.

4 Quine, *Word and Object*, 1960.

5 R. Horton, 'A Definition of Religion, and its Uses', *Journal of the Royal Anthropological Institute*, 90, 2, 1960.

6 Prominent representatives of this approach are Firth, Lienhardt, Beattie, Cohen, Fernandez and van Binsbergen. For publication details of their works, see notes to 'Back to Frazer?'.

7 R. Horton, 'Neo-Tylorianism: Sound Sense or Sinister Prejudice?', *Man*, New Series, 3, 4, 1968, 'Lévy-Bruhl, Durkheim and the Scientific Revolution', in R. Horton and R. Finnegan, eds., *Modes of Thought*, London: Faber & Faber, 1973. A shorter version of 'Back to Frazer?' was delivered as a Frazer Lecture in Cambridge in November 1987. The amended version appears in print for the first time in this book.

8 Prominent representatives of this school include Evans-Pritchard, Harold Turner, Victor Turner, Parrinder, Idowu and Mbiti. For publication details of their works, see notes to 'Judaeo-Christian spectacles'.

9 R. Horton, 'Professor Winch on Safari', *European Journal of Sociology*, 17, 1976, 'Judaeo-Christian Spectacles: Boon or Bane to the Study of African Religions?', *Cahiers d'Etudes Africaines*, 96, 24–4, 1984.

10 R. Horton, 'African Traditional Thought and Western Science', *Africa*, 37, 1–2, 1967, 'Paradox and Explanation: a reply to Mr Skorupski', *Philosophy of the Social Sciences*, 3, 3–4, 1973, 'Tradition and Modernity Revisited', in M. Hollis and S. Lukes, eds., *Rationality and Relativism*, Oxford: Basil Blackwell, 1982.

11 Works by philosophers to which I am heavily indebted for my ideas on primary theory include: S. Hampshire, *Thought and Action*, London: Chatto & Windus, 1959; P. Strawson, *Individuals*, London: Methuen, 1960; P. Zinkernagel, *Conditions for Description*, London: Routledge & Kegan Paul, 1962; W. D. Joske, *Material Objects*, London: Macmillan, 1967. On gene-culture coevolution, see E. O. Wilson, *Sociobiology*, Cambridge, Mass.: Harvard University Press, 1974; C. J. Lumsden and E. O. Wilson, *Genes, Mind and Culture*, Cambridge Mass.: Harvard University Press, 1981. There is a considerable inter-disciplinary debate on the extent of the innate cerebral basis for primary-theoretical thinking. For a strong anti-innatist statement, see P. Strawson, 'Grammar and Philosophy', 'Intention and Convention in Speech Acts' and 'Meaning and Truth', in his *Logico-Linguistic Papers*, London: Methuen, 1971. See also J. Ziman, *Reliable Knowledge*, Cambridge: Cambridge University Press, 1978. For a more 'innatist' approach, see N. Chomsky, *Reflections on Language*, London: Collins Fontana, 1976; G. Stent, *Paradoxes of Progress*, San Francisco: W. H. Freeman, 1978.

12 For illuminating introductions to the importance of analogy in secondary-theory building in the sciences, see R. Harré, *An Introduction to the Logic of the Sciences*, London: Macmillan, 1965; M. Hesse, *Models and Anaologies in Science*, London: Sheed & Ward, 1963.

13 On secondary elaboration, see E. Evans-Pritchard, *Witchcraft, Oracles and Magic among the Azande*, Oxford: Clarendon Press, 1937. On taboo see M. Douglas, *Purity and Danger*, London: Routledge & Kegan Paul, 1966. On denial of the passage of time, see M. Eliade, *The Myth of the Eternal Return*, Princeton: Princeton University Press, 1954. It is difficult to pick out any single corresponding modern classic on magical thinking.

14 For this distinction, see K. Popper, *The Open Society and Its Enemies*, London: Routledge & Kegan Paul, 1945. I also draw heavily upon Evans-Pritchard, *Witchcraft, Oracles and Magic*, whose thought on this matter may be seen as having anticipated Popper.

15 For work on change in Kalabari religious life, which did much to erode the credibility of the static image of traditional thought, see Horton, 'Types of Spirit Possession', and 'A Hundred Years of Change'. For a more general survey which reinforced this effect, see T. Ranger and I. Kimambo, *The Historical Study of African Religion*, London: Heinemann, 1972. I grew doubtful about my Popperian image of science on a more careful re-reading of M. Polanyi, *Personal Knowledge*, Chicago: University of Chicago Press, 1958; T. S. Kuhn, *The Structure of Scientific Revolutions*, Chicago: University of Chicago Press, 1962; I. Lakatos, 'Falsification and the Methodology of Research Programmes', in I. Lakatos and A. Musgrave, eds., *Criticism and the Growth of Knowledge*, Cambridge: Cambridge University Press, 1970.

16 E. Evans-Pritchard, 'The Intellectualist (English) Interpretation of Magic', *Bulletin of the Faculty of Arts*, Egyptian University, Cairo, 1, 1933. See also his *Theories of Primitive Religion*.

17 See especially R. Horton, 'African Conversion', *Africa*, 41, 2, 1971, 'On the Rationality of Conversion', *Africa*, 45, 3–4, 1975, 'Social Psychologies: African and Western', in M. Fortes and R. Horton, *Oedipus and Job in West African Religion*, Cambridge: Cambridge University Press, 1983.

18 In this matter, I think I can claim to have anticipated, in my own quiet way, the breast-beating machos of the 'Strong Programme'. The latter is the title used by a group of scholars based in the Science Studies Unit, University of Edinburgh, to characterize their work on the history of Western science. Their key tenet is a thoroughgoing contextualism which they apply 'symmetrically' to the allegedly true and the allegedly false alike. For the 'Strong Programme' manifesto, see S. B. Barnes, *Scientific Knowledge and Sociological Theory*, London: Routledge & Kegan Paul, 1974; D. Bloor, *Knowledge and Social Imagery*, London: Routledge & Kegan Paul, 1976.

1   A DEFINITION OF RELIGION, AND ITS USES

1 S. F. Nadel, *Nupe Religion*, London: Routledge & Kegan Paul, 1954, pp. 7–8.

2 E. Durkheim, *The Elementary forms of the Religious Life*, London: Allen & Unwin, 1915.

3 E. R. Leach, *Political Systems of Highland Burma*, London: Bell, 1954, pp. 12–13.
4 *Ibid.*, p. 14.
5 *Ibid.*, p. 278.
6 E. B. Tylor, *Primitive Culture*, Vol. I, London: John Murray, 1871, p. 383.
7 E. E. Evans-Pritchard, *Nuer Religion*, Oxford: Clarendon Press, 1956, pp. 315–16.
8 In a paper read to the London University joint post-graduate anthropological seminar in 1956.
9 W. C. Kneale, *Probability and Induction*, Oxford: Clarendon Press, 1952, pp. 89–113.
10 R. R. Marett, *The Threshold of Religion*, London: Methuen, 1914; R. Otto, *The Idea of the Holy*, London: Oxford University Press, 1928.
11 W. James, *Varieties of Religious Experience*, London: Longmans Green, 1902, pp. 28–9.
12 A. Huxley, *Brave New World*, London 1930; *Brave New World Revisited*. London, 1930; V. Packard, *The Hidden Persuaders*, Harmondsworth: Penguin, 1957; W. Sargant, *Battle for the Mind*, London: Pan Books, 1958.
13 This formulation owes a great deal to Talcott Parsons's distinction between 'Instrumental' and 'Expressive' poles in human relations. Nevertheless, I have not used his terminology, partly because I am not sure whether the distinctions made here are quite the same as his own, partly because I found the word 'Instrumental' had all sorts of irrelevant associations for British readers.
14 Nadel, *Nupe Religion*; James, *Religious Experience*.
15 D. Forde, *The Context of Belief*, The Frazer Lecture, 1957, Liverpool: Liverpool University Press, 1958, and 'Spirits, Witches and Sorcerers in the Supernatural Economy of the Yako', *Journal of the Royal Anthropological Institute*, 88, 1958, pp. 165–78; P. Worsley, *The Trumpet Shall Sound*, London: McGibbon & Kee, 1956.
16 R. Benedict, *Patterns of Culture*, London: Routledge & Kegan Paul, 1935.
17 R. H. Tawney, *Religion and the Rise of Capitalism*, Harmondsworth: Penguin, 1938; M. Weber, 'The Social Psychology of World Religions', in H. H. Gerth and C. Wright Mills, eds. and trans., *From Max Weber: Essays in Sociology*, London: Routledge & Kegan Paul, 1948, pp. 267–307.
18 Worsley, *The Trumpet Shall Sound*.
19 M. Herskovitz, *Dahomey*, New York: J. J. Agustin, 1938.
20 Tawney, *Rise of Capitalism*.
21 R. Linton, *The Cultural Background of Personality*, New York: Appleton-Century, 1945.
22 T. Parsons, *The Social System*, London: Tavistock Publications, 1952; G. Homans, *The Human Group*, London, 1951.
23 J. Bushnell, 'La Virgen de Guadelupe as Surrogate Mother in San Juan Atingo', *American Anthropologist*, 60, 2, 1958, pp. 261–5.
24 A. F. C. Wallace, 'Revitalization Movements', *American Anthropologist*, 58, 2, 1956, pp. 264–81.
25 J. Huxley, *Religion without Revelation*, London, 1957.
26 See for example E. E. Evans-Pritchard, *The Sanusi of Cyrenaica*, Oxford: Clarendon Press, 1949.
27 H. H. Rowley, *Prophecy and Religion in Ancient China and Israel*, London, 1956, pp. 111–20.

2 NEO-TYLORIANISM: SOUND SENSE OR SINISTER PREJUDICE?

1 Complaints about a 'neo-Tylorian' or 'back to Frazer' movement seem to have been touched off by a number of recent challenges to the anti-intellectualist establishment in British social anthropology. For one of the first of these in a colourful plea for intellectualism roughly as practised by Frazer, see I. C. Jarvie, *The Revolution in Anthropology*, London: Routledge and Kegan Paul, 1964. For later provocative articles in a volume resulting from a confrontation of British and American anthropologists, see C. Geertz, 'Religion as a Cultural System' and M. E. Spiro, 'Religion: Problems of Definition and Explanation'; both in M. Banton, ed., *Anthropological Approaches to the Study of Religion*, London: Tavistock Publications, 1966. For two of my own papers which have taken much the same intellectualist line see R. Horton, 'Ritual Man in Africa', *Africa*, 34, 1964, pp. 85–104; 'African Traditional Thought and Western Science', *Africa*, 37, 1967, pp. 50–71, 155–87.

    The response to these intellectualist views has been a grumbling one. Jarvie's book got a generally ill-tempered reception, typical of which was E. Ardener, 'Review of *The Revolution in Anthropology*', *Man*, 95, 1965, pp. 57–8. For a more concerted and constructive statement of opposition, which puts very strongly the thesis that pre-literate magico-religious beliefs are 'not what they seem', see J. Beattie, 'Ritual and Social Change', *Man*, New Series, 1, 1966, pp. 60–74. For some anti-intellectualist injunctions which come a little surprisingly in the wake of a revolutionary intellectualist interpretation of pollution behaviour, see M. Douglas, *Purity and Danger*, London: Routledge and Kegan Paul, 1966, ch. 5. Finally, for a strongly worded condemnation which contends that the intellectualist approach to pre-literate beliefs is not only wrong, but symptomatic of vicious prejudice, see E. R. Leach, 'Virgin Birth', *Proceedings of the Royal Anthropological Institute 1966*, 1967, pp. 39–49.

2 For a good account of the intellectualist assumptions of modern historians of science, see T. S. Kuhn, *The Structure of Scientific Revolutions*, Chicago: Chicago University Press 1962, Introduction.

3 For a warning against intellectualist approaches to those cultures which have not developed a 'conscious reaching for objectivity', see Douglas, *Purity and Danger*, ch. 5.

4 E. R. Leach, *Political Systems of Highland Burma*, London: Bell, 1954.

5 J. Middleton, *Lugbara Religion*, London: Oxford University Press, 1960.

6 C. Achebe, *Arrow of God*, London: Heinemann, 1964.

7 This again is implied in Douglas, *Purity and Danger*. See for instance p. 89: 'it is a practical interest in living and not an academic interest in metaphysics which has produced these beliefs'. For an earlier warning, see M. Gluckman, *Order and Rebellion in Tribal Africa*, London: Cohen and West, 1963. For instance p. 141: 'They had elaborate theologies, but these were developed in social relations, rather than in intellectual speculations'.

8 Horton, 'African Traditional Thought', pp. 53–8.

9 For remarks on the general reluctance of British social anthropologists to make the striving for consistency the starting-point of their analyses, see A. I. Richards, 'African Systems of Thought: an Anglo-French Dialogue', *Man*, New

Series, 2, 1967, p. 291. For an example of this reluctance, see Douglas, *Purity and Danger*.

10 Richards ('African Systems of Thought') comments: 'Sceptical British anthropologists have also suggested from time to time that such consistent and logical systems as those described in the case of the Dogon must be the product of a single mind and a philosophical one at that – an Ogotemmeli in fact'.

11 This is one of the arguments in Leach. See for instance: Leach, 'Virgin Birth', p. 45: 'An alternative way of explaining a belief which is factually untrue is to say that it is a species of religious dogma; the truth which it expresses does not relate to the ordinary matter-of-fact world of everyday things but to metaphysics'.

12 R. Firth, 'Religious Belief and Personal Adjustment', *Journal of the Royal Anthropological Institute*, 78, 1950, pp. 25–43.

13 See the critique of 'L'Ecole Anglaise' in the Introduction to L. Lévy-Bruhl, *Les Fonctions Mentales dans les Societés Inférieures*. Paris: Presses Universitaires de France, 1910.

14 The whole tone of Leach's 'Virgin Birth' is one of strong moral disapproval of the intellectualist approach. Thus (p. 41) he accuses Spiro of being 'positively eager to believe that the aborigines were ignorant' and says that intellectualists 'seem to gain assurance from supposing that the people they study have the simple-minded ignorance of small children'.

Since submitting this article, I have read Spiro's rejoinder to Leach. (M. E. Spiro, 'Virgin Birth, Parthenogenesis and Physiological Paternity: an Essay in Cultural Interpretation', *Man*, New Series, 3, 1968, pp. 242–61.) Although Spiro's argument is very similar to my own, I have left the text of this article unamended, as I think it carries the argument somewhat further than he himself has taken it.

15 Horton, 'African Traditional Thought'.

16 For a very clear picture of this process see the closing chapter on 'Progress through Revolutions' in Kuhn, *Scientific Revolutions*.

17 F. Hoyle, *The Black Cloud*, Harmondsworth: Penguin, 1960.

18 E. E. Evans-Pritchard, *Witchcraft, Oracles and Magic Among the Azande*, Oxford: Clarendon Press, 1937.

19 W. B. Cannon, 'Voodoo Death', in W. A. Lessa, and E. Z. Vogt, eds., *A Reader in Comparative Religion*, New York: Harper & Row, 1965.

20 M. Fortes, *Oedipus and Job in West African Religion*, Cambridge: Cambridge University Press, 1959.

21 R. Horton, 'Destiny and the Unconscious in West Africa', *Africa*, 34, 1964.

22 Horton, 'African Traditional Thought', pp. 54–5.

3 LÉVY-BRUHL, DURKHEIM AND THE SCIENTIFIC REVOLUTION

1 I have put the terms 'primitive' and 'modern' between quotation marks to express a degree of doubt about their usefulness. Since these are the terms used by our authors, they will recur frequently in the exposition that follows. The reader will be best advised to take it that by 'primitive' our authors mean 'pre-literate, pre-industrial, pre-scientific'; and that by 'modern' they mean 'literate, industrial, science-oriented'. For more on this see note 45.

2 L. Lévy-Bruhl, *Les Carnets de Lucien Lévy-Bruhl*, Paris: Presses Universitaires de France, 1949. See preface by Maurice Leenhardt, pp. vi–vii.

3 L. Lévy-Bruhl, *Les Fonctions Mentales dans les Sociétés Inferiéures*, Paris: Alcan, 1910, *La Mentalité Primitive*, Paris: Alcan, 1922, *L'Ame Primitive*, Paris: Alcan, 1927, *Le Surnaturel et la Nature dans la Mentalité Primitive*, Paris: Alcan, 1931, *La Mythologie Primitive*, Paris: Alcan, 1935.

4 L. Lévy-Bruhl, *Fonctions*, p. 1.

5 Ibid., pp. 7–24, 27–31.

6 Ibid., pp. 70, 76–93.

7 Ibid., pp. 28–9; Lévy-Bruhl, *Surnaturel*, Introduction, pp. xx, xxvii–xxxv.

8 Lévy-Bruhl, *Fonctions*, pp. 28–31, 33, 40, *Surnaturel*, Introduction, pp. xv–xix.

9 Lévy-Bruhl, *Fonctions*, pp. 56–7, 61–7.

10 Ibid., pp. 74–80.

11 Ibid., pp. 76–8.

12 Ibid., pp. 79–80; Lévy-Bruhl, *Mentalité Primitive*, p. 12.

13 Lévy-Bruhl, *Fonctions*, pp. 33, 426, 452–4.

14 Ibid., p. 21.

15 Ibid., pp. 39, 116.

16 Ibid., p. 39.

17 Ibid., pp. 40, 56.

18 Ibid., p. 40, *Surnaturel*, Introduction, p. xvi.

19 Lévy-Bruhl, *Fonctions*, p. 116.

20 Ibid., pp. 33, 426, 452–4.

21 See for instance E. Evans-Pritchard, 'Lévy-Bruhl's Theory of Primitive Mentality', *Bulletin of the Faculty of Arts*, Egyptian University, Cairo, 2, 1934; M. Douglas, *Purity and Danger*, London: Routledge & Kegan Paul, 1966. In chapter 5, Douglas criticizes Lévy-Bruhl for being interested in ideas rather than in institutions.

22 Lévy-Bruhl, *Fonctions*, pp. 29–30, 426–32.

23 See B. Malinowski, 'Magic, Science and Religion', in J. Needham, ed., *Science, Religion and Reality*, London: Sheldon Press 1928, pp. 27–36. Evans-Pritchard, *Lévy-Bruhl's Theory*.

24 L. Lévy-Bruhl, *L'Expérience Mystique et les Symboles Chez les Primitifs*, Paris: Alcan, 1938 and *Les Carnets*.

25 Lévy-Bruhl, *L'Expérience Mystique*, pp. 10, 12–15, 38–49, 47–55, 68, 78–9, 127–8, 169–70; *Les Carnets*, pp. 20–2, 33–8, 49–50, 54–6, 69–70, 120–1, 193–8, 223–32, 238–40.

26 Lévy-Bruhl, *Les Carnets*, pp. 8–14, 47–51, 60–4, 177–82, 228–32.

27 See for instance, R. Firth, 'Problem and Assumption in an Anthropological Study of Religion', *Journal of the Royal Anthropological Institute*, 89, 1959, p. 147, note 4; E. Evans-Pritchard, *Theories of Primitive Religion*, Oxford: Clarendon Press, 1965, p. 79; G. Lloyd, *Polarity and Analogy: Two Types of Argumentation in Early Greek Thought*, Cambridge: Cambridge University Press, 1966, pp. 3–6.

28 In actual fact, the greater part of *Les Carnets* is taken up, not with recantation, but with clarification and development of the two key concepts of *Les Fonctions Mentales*: 'mystical orientation' and 'participation'.

29 E. Durkheim, and M. Mauss, 'De Quelques Formes Primitives de Classification: Contribution a l'Etude des Représentations Collectives', *Année Sociologique*

1901–1902, 6, 1903. (Translated by R. Needham as *Primitive Classification*, London: Cohen and West, 1963.)

30 Durkheim and Mauss, *Primitive Classification*, pp. 81–2.

31 E. Durkheim, *Les Formes Elémentaires de la Vie Religieuse*, Paris: Alcan, 1912. (Translated by J. Swain as *The Elementary Forms of the Religious Life*, London: Allen & Unwin, 1915.) References that follow are to the fourth impression of the English translation.

32 Ibid., pp. 205–19.

33 Ibid., pp. 219–23.

34 Ibid., pp. 236–7.

35 Ibid., pp. 237–9.

36 Ibid., p. 26.

37 Ibid., pp. 28–9.

38 Ibid., p. 429.

39 Ibid., p. 431.

40 E. Durkheim, *De la Division du Travail Social*, Paris: Alcan, 1893. (Translated by G. Simpson as *The Division of Labour in Society*, New York: Macmillan, 1933.) See book 2, ch. 3.

41 Durkheim, *Elementary Forms*, pp. 37–47.

42 E. Durkheim, Review of *Les Fonctions Mentales* ... and *Les Formes Elémentaires* ... *Année Sociologique 1909–1912*, 12, 1912, pp. 33–7.

For this reference, and for both moral support and intellectual stimulus in pursuing the somewhat unusual view of Durkheim's message set out here, I am greatly indebted to Steven Lukes. In a more intensive study of Durkheim's entire work, he has, quite independently, reached conclusions very similar to the ones advanced here.

43 Durkheim, *Elementary Forms*, pp. 236–7.

44 For more on the way in which the idea of 'collective representation' inhibits both causal and logic-of-the-situation analyses, see my 'Boundaries of Explanation in Social Anthropology', *Man*, 63, 6, 1963.

Briefly, Durkheim's definition of 'collective' and 'individual' is such that, once one gives an analysis of either kind, one automatically transfers the ideas interpreted from the category of the 'collective' to the category of the 'individual'. Nonetheless, the notion of 'collective representation', though it is misleading as to the way in which ideas are *actually* transmitted in pre-literate, pre-industrial societies, does point to the way in which members of such societies *think* they are transmitted. Thus, as J. Goody and I. Watt, ('The Consequences of Literacy', *Comparative Studies in Society and History*, 5, 3, 1963) have remarked, every individual does his own little bit of reworking of what is handed down to him as 'collective representations'; and it is this reworked material which he hands on to the next generation. Yet while this process of reworking goes on inexorably for generation after generation, all those involved see the process as the handing down of timeless 'tradition'.

45 Faced with the need to find a short, snappy label for societies which are pre-industrial, pre-literate, pre-scientific, and which are characterized by a relatively low degree of role and institutional specialization, I prefer the term 'traditional' to the term 'primitive' as used by Lévy-Bruhl, Durkheim, and quite a few more recent scholars. Not only has 'primitive' acquired strong overtones of contempt

and opprobrium; it has very few factual connotations to compensate for these overtones. 'Traditional', by contrast, seems to have retained a slight overtone of approval; and, in addition, it does point to an attitude of fundamental importance for the sociology of ideas – the attitude which sees what is handed down to the current generation as an immutable, timeless heritage.

Bringing this topic into relation with that of 'collective representations', one may say first of all that no society really has collective representations of the Durkheimian kind. One may further define 'traditional' societies as those whose members believe that they are living in the light of such representations, and 'modern' societies as those whose members no longer have any such illusion.

46 A. Radcliffe-Brown, *Structure and Function in Primitive Society*, London: Cohen and West, 1952 (see essays on 'Taboo' and 'Religion and society'); M. Gluckman and E. Devons, eds., *Closed Systems and Open Minds*, Edinburgh and London: Oliver & Boyd, 1964 (see Conclusion, pp. 254–9); M. Gluckman, *Politics, Law and Ritual in Tribal Society*, Oxford: Blackwell, 1965, pp. 216–67.

47 Malinowski, 'Magic, Science and Religion'. The general pattern which emerges from Malinowski's essay is in fact very similar to that which emerges from Lévy-Bruhl's final works.

48 R. Bastide, 'Religions Africaines et Structures de Civilization', *Présence Africaine*, 66, 1968.

49 J. Taylor, *The Primal Vision*, London: SCM Press, 1963 (see ch. 6, 'The Unbroken Circle').

50 T. Parsons, *The Structure of Social Action*, 2 vols., New York: Free Press, 1949, pp. 5, 420–5, 431, 721; Firth, 'Problem and Assumption', p. 136; E. Leach, *Political Systems of Highland Burma*, London: Bell, 1954, Introduction; E. Leach, 'Virgin Birth', *Proceedings of the Royal Anthropological Institute for 1966*, 1967; J. Beattie, *Other Cultures*, London: Cohen & West, 1964, pp. 202–40; J. Beattie, 'Ritual and Social Change', *Man*, New Series, 1, 1966.

51 C. Lévi-Strauss. *La Pensée Sauvage*, Paris: Plon, 1962. See pp. 295–302 for a subtly invidious comparison between totemic and religious thought.

52 It is remarkable that, in a book entitled *La Pensée Sauvage*, religion is mentioned in a passage of a dozen pages, and then only grudgingly.

53 Lévi-Strauss, *La Pensée Sauvage*, passim.

54 For Parsons' attempt to dismiss Durkheim's continuity/evolution thesis, see his *Structure of Social Action*, pp. 419–25. For his concluding classification of Durkheim with those concerned to sweep away the idea of linear evolution and the idea of religion and magic as pre-science, see p. 721.

55 For this apt expression, I am indebted to Evans-Pritchard, *Theories of Primitive Religion*, p. 25.

56 E. Evans-Pritchard, *Witchcraft, Oracles and Magic among the Azande*, Oxford: Clarendon Press, 1937; and *Nuer Religion*, Oxford: Clarendon Press, 1956; M. Fortes, *Oedipus and Job in West African Religion*, Cambridge: Cambridge University Press, 1959; G. Lienhardt, *Divinity and Experience: the Religion of the Dinka*, Oxford: Clarendon Press, 1961; J. Middleton, *Lugbara Religion*, London: Oxford University Press, 1960; V. Turner, – see for example *The Forest of Symbols*. Ithaca: Cornell University Press, 1967; and *The Drums of Affliction*, Oxford: Clarendon Press, 1968.

57 Evans-Pritchard's *Witchcraft, Oracles and Magic* is perhaps the most striking

example of a monograph which starts with the orthodox antithesis between the 'mystical' and the 'empirical', but which goes on to display the 'mystical' in a way which shows its continuity with the 'empirical'.

58 See Evans-Pritchard, 'Lévy-Bruhl's Theory', and *Theories of Primitive Religion*, pp. 88–9. See also Lienhardt, *Divinity and Experience*, pp. 32–3, 147–8.

59 A. Eddington, *The Nature of the Physical World*, Cambridge: Cambridge University Press, 1928. Although Eddington's views are now considered outmoded, his formulation of the 'Two Tables' problem was certainly fruitful as a stimulus to debate.

60 For defence of the Common-sense Table, see S. Stebbing, *Philosophy and the Physicists*, London: Methuen, 1937, chs. 3–4; W. Watson, *On Understanding Physics*, Cambridge: Cambridge University Press, 1938. For defence of the Theoretical Table, see N. R. Hanson, *Patterns of Discovery*, Cambridge: Cambridge University Press, 1958; P. Feyerabend, 'Explanation, Reduction and Empiricism', in H. Fiegl and G. Maxwell, eds., *Minnesota Studies in the Philosophy of Science*, 3, Minneapolis: University of Minnesota Press, 1962; W. Sellars, *Science, Perception and Reality*, London: Routledge & Kegan Paul, 1963, ch. 4. For a defence of both Tables, see W. Quine, *From a Logical Point of View*, Cambridge, Mass.: Harvard University Press, 1953, ch. 1; M. Born, *Physics in My Generation*, London: Pergamon Press, 1956, pp. 49–54, 105–6, 150–63; R. Harré, *Theories and Things*, London: Sheed & Ward, 1961; A. Ayer, *The Origins of Pragmatism*, London: Macmillan, 1968, pp. 298–336; D. Mellor, 'Physics and Furniture' in N. Rescher, ed., *Studies in the Philosophy of Science*, *American Philosophical Society Monograph No. 3*, Oxford, 1969.

61 S. Toulmin, and J. Goodfield, *The Architecture of Matter*, London: Hutchinson, 1962, pp. 25, 38, 39, 262; L. White, 'Medieval Uses of Air', *Scientific American*, 223, 2, 1970.

62 M. Polanyi, *Personal Knowledge*, Chicago: University of Chicago Press, 1958, pp. 112–13, 150–9, 286–94.

63 P. Auger, 'The Regime of Castes in Populations of Ideas', *Diogenes*, 22, 1958.

64 K. Popper, *Conjectures and Refutations*, London: Routledge & Kegan Paul, 1963, pp. 38, 50, 102, 126–31, 187, 190, 257, 319.

65 F. Hoyle, *The Black Cloud*, Harmondsworth: Penguin, 1960.

66 A. Michotte, *The Perception of Causality*, (Eng. trans.) London: Methuen, 1963.

67 M. Hesse, *Science and the Human Imagination*, London: SCM Press 1954; Polanyi, *Personal Knowledge*, pp. 112–13, 150–9, 286–94; Popper, *Conjectures and Refutations*, pp. 38, 50, 102, 126–31, 187, 190, 257, 379.
    Turning from positive to negative evidence, it is interesting to note that references to the personality or impersonality of the content of theory are very rarely found in the current debate about the nature of the scientific outlook. This seems to indicate that most people consider the question of content irrelevant.

68 Fortes, *Oedipus and Job*.

69 See note 60.

70 See my 'African Traditional Thought and Western Science', *Africa*, 37, 1967.

71 My attention was first drawn to this aspect of anthropological indoctrination by Ernest Gellner's characteristically astringent 'Concepts and Society' (*Transactions of the Fifth World Congress of Sociology*, 1, Washington D.C., 1962). Though our diagnoses of what followed upon Victorian ethnocentricity differ

considerably, I think we both agree that its demise was *not* followed by a new era of objectivity.

72 Though this statement may seem to contradict the intellectualist approach of the present essay, the contradiction is only apparent. As I have always stressed, we can understand the spirits only if we accept that they are *both* theoretical entities *and* additional members of the human social field.

73 I. Murdoch, *Sartre*, New Haven: Yale University Press, 1963, p. 51.

74 G. Barraclough, *An Introduction to Contemporary History*, Harmondsworth: Penguin, 1967, pp. 50–2, 235–7.

75 Ibid., chs. 3–4.

76 On the unfashionableness of the idea of progress amongst contemporary historians, see: J. Plumb, 'The Historian's Dilemma', in J. Plumb, ed., *Crisis in the Humanities*, Harmondsworth: Penguin, 1964; E. H. Carr, *What is History?*, Harmondsworth: Penguin, 1964, chs. 2 and 5.

77 For an interesting treatment of Wordsworth's communion with nature, see B. Willey, *Seventeenth Century Background*, Harmondsworth: Penguin, 1962 (ch. 12, 'Wordsworth and the Locke tradition') and *Eighteenth Century Background*, Harmondsworth: Penguin, 1967 (ch. 12, '"Nature" in Wordsworth'). For a stimulating exposition of a parallel theme in the visual arts, see K. Clark, *Landscape into Art*, Harmondsworth: Penguin, 1956 (ch. 5, 'The natural vision'), and *Civilization*, London: J. Murray, 1969 (ch. 11, 'The worship of nature').

78 For a very clear statement of both the origins and the doctrines of the Surrealist Movement, see M. Nadeau, *History of Surrealism*, (Eng. trans.) London: Cape, 1968. For a sympathetic, but for an Anglo-Saxon mind less clear, outline of Surrealist philosophy, see Alquié. F. *The Philosophy of Surrealism*, (Eng. trans.) Ann Arbor: University of Michigan Press, 1965.

79 Dramatic examples are provided by the Surrealists and the Dadaists, both of whom preached that the regeneration of an exhausted Western culture could come only from an injection of non-Western values.

80 For the origins of the European cult of 'primitive art', see M. Leiris and J. Delange, *African Art*, London: Braziller, 1968, pp. 1–33.

81 See T. Roszak, *The Making of a Counter-Culture*, London: Faber & Faber, 1979 (ch. 8, 'Eyes of Flesh, Eyes of Fire').

82 See Roszak, *Making of a Counter-Culture* and also F. Perls, R. Hefferline and P. Goodman, *Gestalt therapy*, New York: Julian Press, 1951. On p. 307, the authors contend that the task of anthropology is 'to show what of human nature has been "lost", and, practically, to devise experiments for its recovery'.

83 On this, see also I. Jarvie and J. Agassi, 'The Problem of the Rationality of Magic', *British Journal of Sociology*, 18, 1967, pp. 62–3.

84 Leach, 'Virgin Birth'.

85 At various points in his anthropological works, Lévy-Bruhl stressed that standard Western concepts and categories were virtually useless for the translation of 'primitive ideas', and that anyone who wished to embark on such translation would have to fashion a new set of concepts for this express purpose. The form taken by such concepts would, of course, be determined solely by the nature of the data under investigation.

Although he clearly saw his own key interpretative concepts as conforming to this requirement, a recent glance at his bibliography, and a re-reading of Leenhardt's introduction to *Les Carnets* as well as of certain passages of *Les Fonctions Mentales*, have strengthened my suspicion that the sources of his inspiration may not have been quite what he liked to think they were.

First of all, bibliographic references on the fly-sheet of *Les Fonctions*, together with certain remarks by Leenhardt, suggest that Lévy-Bruhl started with a deep interest in German Romantic 'philosophies de sentiment', and turned to his later rather ascetic positivism by way of reaction.

This view of his personal intellectual development receives some corroboration from his general attitude to the supposed emotional 'mystical' orientation of the traditional cultures with which he deals – an attitude in which fascination vies with impatience. It receives further corroboration from an apparently little-read passage at the end of *Les Fonctions* (pp. 451–51), in which he speaks of the continuing survival of 'pre-logical thought' in the anti-intellectualist doctrines that still wax strong in the modern West, and in which he gets somewhat carried away whilst describing the delights of the 'participation' between subject and object that is so often the central ideal of such doctrines. All this suggests a love-hate relationship with anti-intellectualist creeds which we should expect from a recent convert to rationalism.

Further, the corollary of Lévy-Bruhl's treatment of modern anti-intellectualist doctrines as survivals of a full-blown 'primitive mentality' is the assumption that the categories and concepts of such doctrines can be used as instruments for translating the thought of contemporary 'primitives'.

All in all, the implication is that, like the Surrealists and others of his contemporaries whose romanticism was unaccompanied by any great ethnographic learning, Lévy-Bruhl projected a body of essentially Western ideas and values (with which he still had a lingering identification) on to the traditional cultures.

At present this interpretation of Lévy-Bruhl is of course something of a hunch. However, in the hands of a scholar who is willing to read his early works on the history of Western philosophy with an eye to possible connections with his later anthropological work, I think it might bear fruit.

86 Firth, 'Problem and Assumption', p. 136; Leach, *Political Systems*, Introduction, and 'Virgin Birth'; Beattie, *Other Cultures*, pp. 202–40, and 'Ritual and Social Change'.

87 Durkheim, *Elementary Forms*, pp. 9–20.

88 Some of the principal sources of this view are E. Mach, *The Analysis of Sensations*, Chicago: Open Court Publishing Company, 1914; P. Duhem, *The Aim and Structure of Physical Theory*, Princeton: Princeton University Press, 1954; P. Bridgeman, *The Logic of Modern Physics*, New York: Macmillan, 1927; K. Pearson, *The Grammar of Science*, A. & C. Black, London, 1911; R. Carnap, *The Unity of Science*, London: Kegan Paul, 1934; A. J. Ayer, *Language, Truth and Logic*, London: Gollancz, 1936.

89 The only recent work on the history/philosophy of science to have caught the imagination of the wider intellectual public is Thomas Kuhn's *The Structure of Scientific Revolutions*, Chicago: University of Chicago Press, 1962. From the point of view of the thesis put forward here, it is perhaps significant that the main reason for the popular success of the book would appear to be the (mistaken) belief that Kuhn demonstrates the essential irrationality of science.

90 Duhem, *Aim and Structure of Physical Theory*, ch. 1.

91 See works of these authors referred to in previous footnotes. In particular, see the definitions of 'empirical' and 'mystical' in Evans-Pritchard, *Witchcraft, Oracles and Magic* and *Theories of Primitive Religion*, pp. 11–12; Gluckman, *Politics, Law and Ritual*, p. 216. Also Leach, 'Virgin Birth', p. 39, for a proud acceptance of the label 'vulgar positivist'. For a criticism of the effect of a positivist (or, as he calls it, 'inductivist') stance on the work of social anthropologists generally, see I. Jarvie, *The Revolution in Anthropology*, London: Routledge & Kegan Paul, 1964.

92 See R. Carnap, *Philosophy and Logical Syntax*, London: Kegan Paul, 1935, p. 18; Ayer, *Language, Truth and Logic*.

93 On this, see Barry Barnes's paper 'The Comparison of Belief-Systems: Anomaly versus Falsehood', in R. Horton and R. Finnegan, eds., *Modes of Thought*, London: Faber & Faber, 1973.

94 See, for instance, W. Cannon, 'Voodoo death', *American Anthropologist*, 44, 1942.

95 R. Cattell, 'The Personality and Motivation of the Researcher from Measurements of Contemporaries and from Biography', in C. Taylor and F. Barron, eds., *Scientific Creativity*, New York: Wiley, 1963 (see pp. 129–31).

96 For more on the idea that the urge towards communion with nature may be the product of certain forms of 'alienation' from modern Western society, see my 'The Romantic Illusion: Roger Bastide on Africa and the West', *Odu*, New Series, 3, 1970.

4   BACK TO FRAZER?

1 This text preserves the broad outline and most of the detail of the lecture as originally delivered. There are, however, a few amendments and additions.

First, in order to guide the reader through a long and somewhat complex argument, I have put in headings and sub-headings.

Secondly, whereas in the original lecture I presented my critique of the Symbolists in the form of a dialogue in two rounds, in this version I present it in the form of a dialogue in three rounds. However, the various Symbolist contentions reviewed, and my objections to them, remain essentially the same. The point of the new format is simply to make the various arguments and counter-arguments easier to follow.

Finally, I have added some pages (114–18) on evidence against the Symbolist contention that religious discourse is intended to refer, not literally to spiritual beings, but symbolically or metaphorically to earthly things. In the original delivery, time constraints led me to skate somewhat lightly over this matter. Later, however, I realized that this cavalier treatment had greatly weakened the critique. The addition is designed to remedy this weakness.

2 J. G. Frazer, *The Golden Bough*, Abridged Edition, London: Macmillan, 1967, pp. 14–16, 25–36, 64–5.

3 Ibid., p. 67.

4 Ibid., p. 67.

5 On this, see for example: F. Oakley, 'Christian Theology and the Newtonian Science: the Rise of the Concept of the Laws of Nature', *Church History*, 30, 1961.

6 On this, see: M. Black, 'Making Something Happen' in *Models and Metaphors*, Ithaca: Cornell University Press, 1962.

7 For modern appreciations of Frazer's contributions in this sphere, see: M. Young, 'The Divine Kingship of the Jukun: a Re-evaluation of Some Theories', *Africa*, 36, 2, 1966; M. Sahlins, *Islands of History*, Chicago: University of Chicago Press, 1985.

8 Frazer, *The Golden Bough*, p. 932.

9 Ibid., p. 930.

10 For my own previous critical efforts, see: R. Horton, 'Neo-Tylorianism: Sound Sense or Sinister Prejudice?', *Man*, New Series, 3, 1968; 'The Romantic Illusion: Roger Bastide on Africa and the West', *Odu*, New Series, 3, 1970; 'Spiritual Beings and Elementary Particles: a Reply to Mr Pratt', *Second Order*, 1, 1, 1972; 'Lévy-Bruhl, Durkheim and the Scientific Revolution' in R. Horton and R. Finnegan, eds., *Modes of Thought*, London: Faber & Faber, 1973; 'Understanding African Traditional Thought: a Reply to Professor Beattie', *Second Order*, 5, 1, 1976. Other authors and works to have made cogent criticisms of the Symbolists include: J. Goody, 'Religion and Ritual: the Definitional Problem', *British Journal of Sociology*, 12, 1961; M. Spiro, 'Religion: Problems of Definition and Explanation', in M. Banton, ed., *Anthropological Approaches to the Study of Religion*, London: Tavistock Publications, 1966, 'Virgin Birth, Parthenogenesis and Physiological Paternity', *Man*, New Series, 3, 2, 1968; I. Jarvie, and J. Agassi, 'The Problem of the Rationality of Magic', *British Journal of Sociology*, 18, 1967; J. Peel, 'Understanding Alien Thought-Systems', *British Journal of Sociology*, 20, 1968; J. Skorupski, *Symbol and Theory*, Cambridge: Cambridge University Press, 1976. The criticisms set out in this lecture are my own. In some cases, however, they have been independently formulated or even anticipated by other authors mentioned. Wherever I am aware of such anticipation, I acknowledge it. Any failure in this respect is inadvertent.

11 In building up my generic image, I have taken account of the following authors and works. L. Lévy-Bruhl, *Les Fonctions Mentales dans les Societés Inférieures*, Paris: Presses Universitaires de France, 1910; E. Durkheim, *Les Formes Elémentaires de la Vie Religieuse*, Paris: Alcan, 1912 (Trans. J. W. Swain, *The Elementary Forms of the Religious Life*, London: Allen and Unwin, 1915); S. Langer, *Philosophy in a New Key*, Cambridge, Mass.: Harvard University Press, 1942 (Reprinted 1951); A. R. Radcliffe-Brown, Essays on 'Religion and Society' and 'Taboo' in his *Structure and Function in Primitive Society*, London: Cohen & West, 1952; E. R. Leach, *Political Systems of Highland Burma*, London: G. Bell and Sons, 1954, *Rethinking Anthropology*, London: The Athlone Press, 1961, 'Ritualization in Man in Relation to Conceptual and Social Development', in J. Huxley, ed., *Ritualization of Behaviour in Man and Animals*, *Philosophical Transactions of the Royal Society*, Series B, No. 251, 1966, 'Virgin Birth', *Proceedings of the Royal Anthropological Institute 1966*, London, 1967, 'Ritual', in *International Encyclopedia of the Social Sciences*, 13, New York, 1968; R. Firth, 'Problem and Assumption in an Anthropological Study of Religion', *Journal of the Royal Anthropological Institute*, 89, Part 2, 1959 and *Symbols: Public and Private*, London: Allen & Unwin, 1973; G. Lienhardt, *Divinity and Experience: the Religion of the Dinka*, Oxford: Clarendon Press, 1961; J. Beattie, *Other Cultures*, London: Cohen & West, 1964, 'Ritual and Social Change', *Man*, New Series, 1, 1966, 'On Understanding Ritual', in B. Wilson, ed., *Rationality*, Oxford: Basil Blackwell, 1970, 'Understanding African Traditional Religion: A

Comment on Horton', *Second Order*, 2, 2, 1973; A. Cohen, *Two-Dimensional Man*, London: Routledge & Kegan Paul, 1974; D. Sperber, *Rethinking Symbolism*, Cambridge: Cambridge University Press, 1975; M. Crick, *Explorations in Language and Meaning*, London: Malaby Press, 1976; J. Fernandez, 'African Religious Movements', *Annual Review of Anthropology*, 1978; W. Van Binsbergen, *Religious Change in Zambia*, London: Kegan Paul International 1981; C. Geertz and J. Miller, 'Dialogue with Clifford Geertz', in J. Miller, ed., *States of Mind*, London: British Broadcasting Corporation Publications, 1983.

Of the various authors mentioned here, Lévy-Bruhl and Durkheim, the pioneers of the Symbolist movement, propound what one may describe as 'restricted' Symbolist theories. Thus for Lévy-Bruhl, religious discourse refers symbolically to the inner world of the emotions; whilst for Durkheim, such discourse symbolizes the individual's sense of dependence on his social group. Subsequent authors, by and large, propound what one may describe as 'generalized' Symbolist theories. Thus they tend to see religious and other expressive discourse as referring symbolically to the whole gamut of human experience.

12 On this, see: Beattie, *Other Cultures*, chs. 5, 12, 13, 'Ritual and Social Change', passim, 'Understanding African Traditional Religion', passim; Leach, *Political Systems*, pp. 11–16, 86, 172–4, 182, 278, 'Virgin Birth', passim, 'Ritual', passim.

13 Beattie, *Other Cultures*, pp. 69–70.

14 On this, see: Beattie, *Other Cultures*, pp. 70–1; Langer, *Philosophy in a New Key*, p. 149; Firth, 'Problem and Assumption', p. 135.

15 Durkheim, *Elementary Forms*, pp. 188–296; Radcliffe-Brown, *Structure and Function*, pp. 157–77; Leach, *Political Systems*, pp. 11–16, 86, 172–4, 182, 278; Firth, 'Problem and Assumption', pp. 134–6, *Symbols*, pp. 28, 53, 163, 409–11, 427–8; Beattie, *Other Cultures*, pp. 219–39, 'Ritual and Social Change', pp. 68–72, 'Understanding African Traditional Religion', passim.

16 Leach, *Rethinking Anthropology*, p. 5, 'Virgin Birth', pp. 39, 43.

17 Beattie, 'Ritual and Social Change', p. 63; 'Understanding Ritual', pp. 253–4, 257; 'Understanding African Traditional Religion', p. 4.

18 Fernandez, 'African Religious Movements', pp. 220–1.

19 Beattie, 'Ritual and Social Change', p. 65.

20 Beattie, 'Ritual and Social Change', p. 68; Fernandez, 'African Religious Movements', pp. 220–1, 228; Crick, *Language and Meaning*.

21 On this squeezing out, see Beattie, 'Ritual and Social Change', p. 68.

22 On this, see: Firth, 'Problem and Assumption', p. 136; Beattie, 'Ritual and Social Change', pp. 60, 65, 68, 72.

23 Of all the Symbolists, John Beattie seems to be the only one to admit frankly the obvious concerns of both magic and religion with the explanation, prediction and control of the everyday world. Thus he not only concedes the importance of this concern. (Beattie: *Other Cultures*, pp. 204, 207, 212, 238, 'Ritual and Social Change', p. 69, 'Understanding Ritual', p. 246, 'Understanding African Traditional Religion', p. 3.) He even goes so far as to say that the flourishing of magic and religion is conditional upon the poor development of scientifically-based theories and techniques of control and that both tend to disappear once this development is under way. (Beattie, *Other Cultures*, pp. 205, 207, 212, 227–8, 'Understanding Ritual', pp. 249, 251, 253, 260, 'Understanding African Traditional Religion', pp. 4, 6.) Nonetheless, he *still* wants to say that it is the making

of symbolic images for their own sakes (the expressive), rather than explanation/ prediction/control (the instrumental), that is the 'essential' aspect of both magic and religion. (Beattie, *Other Cultures*, pp. 71, 72, 203, 212, 215, 238, 'Ritual and Social Change', pp. 63, 65, 68, 'Understanding Ritual', p. 243.) And it is here that he falls into difficulties of the kind that bedevil all those who try to have their cake and eat it.

Now Beattie would surely agree that the 'essential' aspect of a human phenomenon is that aspect which gives it its continuing human appeal and thereby keeps it in being as part of a culture. At the same time, he would agree that, in this sense, the 'essential' aspect of both technology and science is the instrumental. But if magic and religion flourish where these 'essentially' instrumental phenomena are poorly developed, and languish where they are well developed, this can only be because: (a) their appeal is largely if not entirely due to their supposed instrumental efficacy; and (b) they are nevertheless perceived as instrumentally less efficacious than technology and science. In short, it follows from Beattie's own premisses that the 'essential' aspect of magic and religion is the instrumental and not the expressive!

24 See for instance Langer, *Philosophy in a New Key*, p. 149.

25 In Kalabari, there are two sets of distinctions that correspond closely to the literal/figurative distinction: *papa ekwen/egberi ekwen* (= 'ordinary speech'/'*egberi* speech'); and *Kalabarinaye/tominaye* (= 'Kalabari language'/'the language of the people'). Talk about the gods is normally put in the first or 'literal' category. (R. Horton, Unpublished field notes.) In Piaroa, too, there is a similarly corresponding distinction; and again, talk about the gods is put in the 'literal' category. (J. Overing, 'Today I shall Call Him Mummy', in J. Overing, ed., *Reason and Morality*, London: Tavistock Publications, 1985, pp. 158–61.)

26 On Catholic modernism, see: J. Macquarrie, *The Scope of Demythologizing*, London: SCM Press, 1960, pp. 113–19.

27 P. Van Buren, *The Secular Meaning of the Gospel*, London: Macmillan, 1963; T. J. Altizer and J. Hamilton, *Radical Theology and the Death of God*, New York: Bobbs-Merrill, 1966; D. Cupitt, *Taking Leave of God*, London: SCM Press, 1980, *The Sea of Faith*, London: BBC Publications, 1984, *The Long-Legged Fly*, London: SCM Press, 1987.

28 For a sympathetic but firmly negative response from a traditional Christian theologian, see: J. Macquarrie, *God and Secularity*, London: Lutterworth Press, 1968.

29 This is said most clearly by Cohen (*Two-Dimensional Man*, p. 8), but Firth (*Symbols*, pp. 163, 411, 427) also flirts with the idea.

30 For a somewhat different but nonetheless complementary line of criticism, see Skorupski, *Symbol and Theory*, pp. 37–41.

31 Skorupski (*Symbol and Theory*, p. 35) makes this point in passing, but does not seem to feel any need to develop it. My own feeling is that it must be central to any critique of Symbolist ideas about religion.

Since scholars of religion outside social anthropology and sociology take for granted that it is earthly things which provide symbols of the spiritual realm rather than vice versa, there is an *embarras de richesses* in the literature in this area. However, for some of the more important modern statements, see: E. Bevan, *Symbolism and Belief*, London: Allen & Unwin, 1938. R. Bultmann

'New Testament and Mythology', in H. W. Bartsch, ed., *Kerygma and Myth*, London: S.P.C.K., 1960. (See especially his definition of mythology on p. 10.) F. W. Dillistone, *The Power of Symbols*, London: SCM Press (1986). For important statements by a social anthropologist, see: V. Turner, *Chihamba: the White Spirit*, Rhodes-Livingstone Papers No. 38, Manchester: Manchester University Press, 1962, *The Forest of Symbols*, Ithaca: Cornell University Press, 1967. Some readers, who think of Turner as the 'Symbolic Anthropologist' *par excellence*, may be surprised to find him omitted from my list of Symbolists. I omit him precisely because he sees earthly things as symbols of the gods, and not the gods as symbols of earthly things.

32 On this latter function of religious symbols, see: Turner, *Chihamba*, and *Forest of Symbols*.

33 For more on the communion aspect of religion, see: R. Horton, 'A Definition of Religion, and its Uses', *Journal of the Royal Anthropological Institute*, 90, Part 2, 1960, pp. 201–226. (Re-printed as paper 1 of this volume.)

34 See p. 123 and note 36 of this essay.

35 See note 23 for Beattie's unsuccessful attempt to evade this criticism by admitting the importance of the explanation/prediction/control aspect of religion whilst maintaining its 'essentially expressive and symbolic' character.

36 Although the author does not use my terminology, this aspect of change in Protestant theology emerges very clearly from D. Jenkins, *The Bishop of Durham's Guide to the Debate about God*, Cambridge: Lutterworth Press, 1985. For the same changes going on in society at large, see: K. Thomas, *Religion and the Decline of Magic*, London: Wiedenfield & Nicholson, 1971. (See especially p. 640.)

37 See: Langer, *Philosophy in a New Key*, pp. 158–9; Lienhardt, *Divinity and Experience*, p. 283; Geertz and Miller, 'Dialogue', pp. 200–5.

38 Beattie, *Other Cultures*, pp. 207, 215, 'Ritual and Social Change', pp. 63, 65, 72, 'Understanding Ritual', pp. 241, 258, 261, 'Understanding African Traditional Religion', pp. 3, 5, 8, 10.

39 This seems to have been Malinowski's interpretation. See: B. Malinowksi, 'Magic, Science and Religion', in J. Needham, ed., *Science, Religion and Reality*, London: The Sheldon Press, 1928. (See pp. 29–34.)

40 For a classic monographic exposition, see: E. E. Evans-Pritchard, *Witchcraft, Oracles and Magic among the Azande*, Oxford: The Clarendon Press, 1937. On the compatibility of the Zande Data with an interpretation based on the primacy of the concern for explanation, prediction and control, see: W. O. Mounce, 'Understanding a Primitive Society', *Philosophy*, 48, 186, 1973.

41 On critical appraisal and amendment of a body of magico-religious theory in direct response to failure of prediction and control, see: J. Buxton, *Religion and Healing in Mandari*, Oxford: The Clarendon Press, 1973, pp. 358–62. A. D. Buckley, *Yoruba Medicine*, Oxford: The Clarendon Press, 1985, pp. 139–65. K. Nwokamma, 'The Rise of the Cassava Goddess in Western Ikwerre', Unpublished final year research essay, Department of Philosophy and Religious Studies, University of Port Harcourt, 1989.

42 Two classic works that threw doubt on previous over-simplistic ideas about testing in the sciences are: M. Polanyi, *Personal Knowledge*, London: Routledge & Kegan Paul, 1958; T. Kuhn, *The Structure of Scientific Revolutions*, Chicago: Chicago University Press, 1962. Landmarks in further discussion of Kuhn's ideas

are: I. Lakatos and A. Musgrave, eds., *Criticism and the Growth of Knowledge*, Cambridge: Cambridge University Press, 1970; G. Gutting, ed., *Paradigms and Revolutions*, Notre Dame, Indiana: University of Notre Dame Press, 1980.

43 For examples of this line of argument, see: Firth, 'Problem and Assumption', p. 135; Leach, 'Ritualization in Man' and 'Virgin Birth'; Sperber, *Rethinking Symbolism*, p. 4.

44 N. Barley, *Symbolic Structures*, Cambridge: Cambridge University Press, 1983, p. 10.

45 For angry condemnation of neo-Frazerians on these grounds, see Leach, 'Virgin Birth', pp. 39–42.

46 For versions of this argument, see: Beattie, *Other Cultures*, pp. 68, 202–3, 'Ritual and Social Change', p. 68; Crick, *Language and Meaning*; Fernandez, 'African Religious Movements', pp. 220–1, 223, 225, 228–9.

47 The thesis that Symbolist reclassification of apparently instrumental magico-religious thought and action as expressive stems from nothing more solid than the desire to avoid invidious imputations of irrationality is first adumbrated by Goody ('Religion and Ritual') and then stated more clearly by Jarvie and Agassi ('Rationality of Magic'). Beattie ('Understanding Ritual', p. 248) indignantly denies the applicability of such a diagnosis to his own work. Even if we take him at his word on this, however, the explicit avowals of other members of the movement such as Firth, Leach and Sperber certainly suggest that the diagnosis *is* applicable to them. (Here, see once again: Firth, 'Problem and Assumption', p. 135; Leach, 'Virgin Birth', pp. 39–42; Sperber, *Rethinking Symbolism*, p. 4.)

48 Frazer, *The Golden Bough*, pp. 347–8.

49 J. Agassi, 'Towards an Historiography of Science', *History and Theory*, Supplement 2, 1963.

50 For the term 'socio-somatic', I am indebted to: V. Skultans, *Intimacy and Ritual*, London: Routledge & Kegan Paul, 1974. The term more commonly used to refer to phenomena of this type is, of course, 'psycho-somatic'. However, since the 'psychic' conditions which are thought to precipitate illness are characteristically the result of 'social' pressures, I believe that Skultans's term is more appropriate and more fruitful in drawing attention to what may be the key variables. For the development of Western ideas in this area, see: W. B. Cannon, 'Voodoo Death', *American Anthropologist*, 44, 1942, pp. 169–81. J. L. Halliday, *Psychosocial medicine: a Study of the Sick Society*, New York: W. W. Norton, 1948. F. Alexander, *Psychosomatic Medicine*, London: Allen & Unwin, 1952. S. Black, *Mind and Body*, London: William Kimber, 1969. In relation to what I have said here, it is interesting to note that Cannon, who is sometimes referred to as 'The Father of Psychosomatic Medicine', seems to have drawn his inspiration, at least in part, from reports of ideas and practices bearing on sickness, death and healing in a number of non-Western cultures.

51 P. Feyerabend, *Against Method*, London: New Left Books, 1975, pp. 45–53, 296–307, *Science in a Free Society*, London: New Left Books, 1978, pp. 100–5, 118–19, 135.

52 On Romanticism, see: M. H. Abrams, *The Mirror and the Lamp*, Oxford: Oxford University Press, 1953, *Natural Supernaturalism*, New York: W. W. Norton, 1971; F. Kermode, *The Romantic Image*, London: Collins Fontana, 1971; I. Berlin, *Against the Current*, Oxford: Oxford University Press, 1981. (See

especially the essays entitled 'The Counter-Enlightenment', 'The Divorce between the Sciences and the Humanities' and 'Hume and the Sources of German Anti-Rationalism'.)

53 For some early remarks on this problem, with respect to the study of African religious thought, see: R. Horton, 'Conference: the High God in Africa', *Odu*, 2, 2, 1966. For a poignant encapsulation of the problem in a single phrase, see John Peel's designation of his field of study as 'Yoruba Religion-Science' (J. D. Y. Peel, *Aladura*, London: Oxford University Press, 1968). For a more extended discussion, see Buxton, *Religion and Healing*, pp. 358–60. For some later remarks of my own, see: R. Horton, 'Judaeo-Christian Spectacles: Boon or Bane to the Study of African Religions?', *Cahiers d'Etudes Africaines*, 24, 4, 1984. (See pp. 424–5.) For some comments on this problem by a philosopher, see: C. Taylor, 'Rationality' in M. Hollis and S. Lukes eds., *Rationality and Relativism*, Oxford: Basil Blackwell, 1982.

54 C. P. Snow, *The Two Cultures and the Scientific Revolution*, Cambridge: Cambridge University Press, 1960.

55 There is a sense in which scholars like Tylor and Frazer were closer to the reality of most of the world's religious life than are the Symbolists. For in their times the unique development whereby Western Christianity set about handing over the task of explanation, prediction and control of this-worldly events to the scientists had not yet gone so far as it has in the last seventy or so years. Looking at the relation between religion and science in their own culture, then, they were able to see the two as pursuing the same aims and hence as competing. And this made it easier for them to grasp the dominant aims which shaped and guided much of the religious life of non-Western peoples.

5   PROFESSOR WINCH ON SAFARI

1 P. Winch, 'Understanding a Primitive Society', *American Philosophical Quarterly*, 1, 1964. Reprinted in B. Wilson ed., *Rationality*, Oxford, 1970. (Page references are to the reprinted version).

2 P. Winch, *The Idea of a Social Science and its Relation to Philosophy*, London: Routledge & Kegan Paul, 1958.

3 Amongst the more interesting of these are: E. Gellner, 'The New Idealism: Cause and Meaning in the Social Sciences', in I. Lakatos and A. Musgrave, eds, *Problems in the Philosophy of Science*, Amsterdam: North Holland, 1968; I. Jarvie, *Concepts and Society*, London: Routledge & Kegan Paul, 1972 (see especially ch. 2, 'Understanding and Explaining in the Social Sciences'); J. Kekes, 'Towards a Theory of Rationality', *Philosophy of Social Sciences*, 3, 1973; S. Lukes, 'Some Problems about Rationality', *European Journal of Sociology*, 8, 1967; H. Mounce, 'Understanding a Primitive Society', *Philosophy*, 48, 1973; A. MacIntyre, 'A Mistake about Causality in the Social Sciences', in P. Laslett and W. Runciman, eds., *Philosophy, Politics and Society*, Vol. II. Oxford: Basil Blackwell, 1963; A. MacIntyre, 'The Idea of a Social Science', *Aristotelian Society Supplement*, 41, 1967.

4 Winch, 'Understanding a Primitive Society', pp. 78–95.

5 Ibid., p. 102.

6 Although Winch does not explicitly state this extreme possibility, some of his

more gnomic remarks, like 'our idea of what belongs to the realm of reality is given for us in the language we use' and 'logical relations between propositions depend on social relations between men', have led more than one commentator to read him in this sense. See for instance Lukes, 'Problems about Rationality'.

7 Winch, 'Understanding a Primitive Society', pp. 93, 102, 106.

8 Ibid., pp. 107–11.

9 B. Malinowski, *A Scientific Theory of Culture*, Chapel Hill: University of North Carolina Press, 1944; R. Piddington, 'Malinowski's Theory of Needs', in R. Firth, ed., *Man and Culture*, London: Routledge & Kegan Paul, 1957; W. Goldschmidt, *Comparative Functionalism*, Berkeley: University of California Press, 1966.

10 Winch, *The Idea of a Social Science*, pp. 40–65.

11 On this, see: S. Hampshire, *Thought and Action*, London: Chatto & Windus, 1959; W. Joske, *Material Objects*, London: Macmillan, 1967; Lukes, 'Problems about Rationality'; S. Lukes, 'On the Social Determination of Truth', in R. Horton and R. Finnegan, eds., *Modes of Thought*, London: Faber & Faber, 1973; P. Strawson, *Individuals*, London: Methuen, 1960; P. Strawson, *The Bounds of Sense*, London: Methuen, 1966; P. Zinkernagel, *Conditions for Description*, London: Routledge & Kegan Paul, 1962.

12 R. Horton, 'Paradox and Explanation: a Reply to Mr Skorupski', parts 1 and 2, *Philosophy of the Social Sciences*, 3, 1973.

13 Winch does not make it very clear what he understands by 'primitive'. Here, I assume he means pre-literate, pre-industrial, pre-scientific.

14 Winch, 'Understanding a Primitive Society', pp. 103–5.

15 P. Winch, 'Savage and Modern Minds', *Times Higher Education Supplement*, 7 September, 1973, p. 13.

16 These remarks are part of a critique of my essay 'Lévy-Bruhl, Durkheim and the Scientific Revolution' which was published in Horton and Finnegan, *Modes of Thought*.

17 For my use of the phrase 'face value', see Horton, 'Lévy-Bruhl, Durkheim and the Scientific Revolution', pp. 294–5. It should be placed in the context of my remarks on pp. 276–83.

18 E. Evans-Pritchard, *Witchcraft, Oracles and Magic among the Azande*, Oxford: Clarendon Press, 1937.

19 Relevant passages are found virtually throughout the book. I suggest, however, that the reader in a hurry look particularly at the following: top of p. 88 to top of p. 89; top of p. 90 to halfway down p. 91; halfway down p. 148 to top of p. 149; pp. 261–6; p. 341. In using the word perverse to characterize Winch's interpretation of these and other passages, I have unwittingly followed John Skorupski. See J. Skorupski, 'What is Magic?' *Cambridge Review*, January, 1975.

20 Evans-Pritchard, *Witchcraft, Oracles and Magic*, p. 319.

21 Winch, 'Understanding a Primitive Society', p. 89.

22 Winch uses this parody in the course of criticizing Evans-Pritchard for evaluating Zande mystical beliefs in terms of their truth or falsity as judged by the criteria of contemporary Western science. Since my particular interest in the present paper has been in other issues, I have by-passed this one. Suffice it to say here that my own view is (a) that, for obvious reasons, it is unfruitful, as an initial move, for the sociologist of thought to classify particular beliefs in terms of their truth or

falsity; but (b) that having classified such beliefs in terms of other criteria, it is perfectly legitimate to go on and ask whether, as a matter of fact, they are true or false.

23 Winch, 'Understanding a Primitive Society', p. 87.
24 Ibid., p. 88.
25 Ibid., p. 88.
26 Evans-Pritchard, *Witchcraft, Oracles and Magic*, pp. 21–49, 63–84.
27 'Operationalism' in the sciences is the doctrine that an entity must be defined solely in terms of the human operations associated with assertions about it.
28 This point is well made by Mounce, 'Understanding a Primitive Society'.
29 On this, see R. Horton, 'African Traditional Thought and Western Science', part 1, *Africa*, 37, 1967, pp. 54–8.
30 Evans-Pritchard, *Witchcraft, Oracles and Magic*, passim.
31 M. Polanyi, *Personal Knowledge*, Chicago: University of Chicago Press, 1958, pp. 286–94.
32 T. Kuhn, *The Structure of Scientific Revolutions*, Chicago: University of Chicago Press, 1962.
33 On this, see I. Lakatos, 'Falsification and the Methodology of Scientific Research Programmes', and P. Feyerabend, 'Consolations for the Specialist'; both in I. Lakatos and A. Musgrave, eds., *Criticism and the Growth of Knowledge*, Cambridge: Cambridge University Press, 1970.
34 Evans-Pritchard, *Witchcraft, Oracles and Magic*, p. 25.
35 Winch, 'Understanding a Primitive Society', p. 93.
36 Evans-Pritchard, *Witchcraft, Oracles and Magic*, p. 25.
37 Ibid., p. 63.
38 On this, see the essays and discussions in S. Toulmin, ed., *Quanta and Reality*, London: Hutchinson, 1962. See especially the postscript by N. R. Hanson, pp. 85–93. See also Lakatos, 'Methodology of Scientific Research Programmes', especially pp. 142–54, where he characterizes Bohr's development of early quantum theory as 'progress on inconsistent foundations'.
39 Winch, 'Understanding a Primitive Society', p. 103.
40 Evans-Pritchard, *Witchcraft, Oracles and Magic*, p. 64.
41 Ibid., pp. 37, 74.
42 Ibid., p. 269.
43 For the importance of this image, not only in the elucidation of theoretical activity, but perhaps even in its genesis, see my 'Paradox and Explanation', especially pp. 248–50, 303–8.
44 Evans-Pritchard, *Witchcraft, Oracles and Magic*, pp. 33, 464.
45 A. Michotte, *The Perception of Causality*, London: Methuen, 1963.
46 On this, see S. Toulmin and J. Goodfield, *The Architecture of Matter*, London: Hutchinson, 1962, pp. 194–7; M. Born, *Natural Philosophy of Cause and Chance*, Oxford: Clarendon Press, 1951, pp. 8–9, 16–17, 25–30, and *Physics in My Generation*, London: Pergamon Press, 1965, pp. 21–2, 96–8.
47 Winch, 'Savage and Modern Minds': 'But one of the points which Evans-Pritchard was at pains to emphasize in his work on the Zande was precisely that the appeal to the notion of witchcraft was not used as a stop-gap or underpinning of commonsense explanations, but occurred in the context of answering *different kinds of questions*'.

48 Both Evans-Pritchard and I have emphasized the need to treat various African arts *as Art*. See for instance E. Evans-Pritchard, *The Zande Trickster*, Oxford: Clarendon Press, 1967; R. Horton, 'The Kalabari Ekine Society: a Borderland of Religion and Art', *Africa*, 33, 1963. I think Winch would find some of the methodological attitudes in the latter very close to his own.

49 See for instance R. Horton, 'African Traditional Thought', 'Paradox and Explanation', 'African Conversion', *Africa*, 41, 1971, 'On the Rationality of Conversion', *Africa*, 45, 1975.

50 Amongst the more relevant studies of this phenomenon are B. Sundkler, *Bantu Prophets in South Africa*, London: Oxford University Press, 1961; B. Pauw, *Religion in a Tswana Chiefdom*, London: Oxford University Press, 1960; C. Baëta, *Prophetism in Ghana*, London: SCM Press, 1962; H. Turner, *African Independent Church*, 2 vols., Oxford: Clarendon Press, 1967; J. Peel, *Aladura*, London: Oxford University Press, 1968.

51 Horton, 'African Conversion'.

52 Rev. Wariboko Amakiri, a pioneer Kalabari evangelist, recalled this reaction vividly in a conversation I had with him not long before his death.

53 Peel, *Aladura*, p. 110.

54 Ibid., p. 212.

55 Baeta, *Prophetism in Ghana*, pp. 4, 137.

56 Ibid., p. 54.

57 Sundkler, *Bantu Prophets*, p. 220.

58 Ibid., p. 220.

59 The transition from a religious life of this kind to a religious life of the kind expounded by Winch is one of the themes of K. Thomas, *Religion and the Decline of Magic*, London: Weidenfeld & Nicholson, 1971.

60 On this, see Toulmin and Goodfield, *Architecture of Matter*, pp. 51–2, 61, 101–5, 148–56, 194–5.

61 On this, see E. Burtt, *The Metaphysical Foundations of Modern Science*, London: Routledge & Kegan Paul, 1967, pp. 202–99.

62 P. Teilhard de Chardin, *The Future of Man*, New York: Harper & Row, 1964.

63 A. Hardy, *The Living Stream*, London: Collins, 1965.

64 Arthur Koestler is a typical figure in this context. See his *The Roots of Coincidence*, London: Hutchinson, 1972.

65 It was this aspect of his interpretation which suggested to me the somewhat waspish title of this paper: safari being notoriously the type of expedition on which one learns nothing *from* either the locals or the locale!

6 JUDAEO-CHRISTIAN SPECTACLES: BOON OR BANE TO THE STUDY OF AFRICAN RELIGIONS?

1 For representative works by social anthropologists, see: E. E. Evans-Pritchard, *Nuer Religion*, Oxford: Clarendon Press, 1956, 'Religion and the Anthropologists', in *Essays in Social Anthropology*, London: Faber & Faber, 1962, *Theories of Primitive Religion*, Oxford: Clarendon Press, 1965; V. W. Turner, *Chihamba: The White Spirit. A Ritual Drama of the Ndembu*, Rhodes-Livingstone Papers 33, Manchester: Manchester University Press, 1962. For representative works by scholars trained in theology and/or comparative religion, see E. B. Idowu,

Olodumare: God in Yoruba Belief, London: Longman, 1962, 'The Study of Religion, with Special Reference to African Traditional Religion', *Orita: Ibadan Journal of Religious Studies*, 1, 1, 1967, pp. 3–12, *African Traditional Religion: a Definition*, London: SCM Press, 1973; J. S. Mbiti, *African Religions and Philosophy*, London: Heinemann, 1969, *Concepts of God in Africa*, London: S.P.C.K., 1970; C. R. Gaba, *Scriptures of an African People*, New York: Nok, 1973, 'Man's Salvation: Its Nature and Meaning in African Traditional Religion', in E. Fashole-Luke, R. Gray, A. Hastings and G. Tasie, eds., *Christianity in Independent Africa*, London: Rex Collings, 1978; S. N. Ezeanya, 'The Place of the Supreme God in the Traditional Religion of the Igbo', *West African Religion*, 1, 1963, pp. 1–4, and 'God, Spirits and the Spirit World (With Special Reference to the Igbo-Speaking People of Southern Nigeria)' in K. Dickson and P. Ellingworth, eds., *Biblical Revelation and African Beliefs*, London: Lutterworth Press 1969, pp. 30–46; H. W. Turner, 'A Methodology for Modern African Religious Movements', *Comparative Studies in Society and History*, 7, 3, 1966, pp. 281–94, *African Independent Church* Vol. I, *The Church of the Lord (Aladura)*, Vol. II, *The Life and Faith of the Church of the Lord (Aladura)*, Oxford: Clarendon Press, 1967, 'A Model for the Structure of Religion in Relation to the Secular', *Cahiers des Religions Africaines*, 3, 6, 1969, pp. 173–97, 'The Primal Religions of the World and their Study', in V. C. Hayes, ed., *Australian Essays in World Religions*, Adelaide: Australian Association for the Study of Religions 1977, pp. 27–37, 'The Way Forward in the Religious Study of African Primal Religions', *Journal of Religion in Africa*, 12, 1, 1981, pp. 1–5. For a fascinating contribution from a scholar who has tried to synthesize the approaches of social anthropology and comparative religion, see E. M. Zuesse, *Ritual Cosmos: the Sanctification of Life in African Religions*, Athens: Ohio University Press, 1979. For a highly influential intervention by a philosopher who, though more concerned with fundamental methodological issues than the writers listed above, nonetheless puts forward a viewpoint in some respects remarkably similar to theirs, see P. Winch, 'Understanding a Primitive Society', in B. Wilson, ed., *Rationality*, Oxford: Basil Blackwell, 1970, pp. 78–111.

2 O. P'Bitek, *African Religions in Western Scholarship*, Nairobi: East African Literature Bureau, 1971.

3 Turner, 'The Way Forward'.

4 R. Horton, 'On the Rationality of Conversion', *Africa*, 45, 3–4, 1975.

5 R. W. Wyllie, 'On the Rationality of the Devout Opposition', *Journal of Religion in Africa*, 11, 2, 1980.

6 Credit for making social scientists engaged in cross-cultural studies aware of the central importance of translational understanding must go in the first instance to Evans-Pritchard and his colleagues in the Oxford Institute of Social Anthropology of the 1950s and 1960s. See especially E. E. Evans-Pritchard, 'Zande Theology', in *Essays in Social Anthropology*, London: Faber & Faber, 1962, and *Theories of Primitive Religion*. For a short but important contribution by Evans-Pritchard's close associate, see G. Lienhardt, 'Modes of Thought', in E. E. Evans-Pritchard et al., eds., *The Institutions of Primitive Society*, Oxford: Basil Blackwell, 1954. Inspired at least in part by the Oxford school, a number of philosophers also made useful contributions to the discussion of this topic during the same period. For representative contributions, see: P. Winch, *The Idea of a*

Social Science and its Relation to Philosophy, London: Routledge & Kegan Paul, 1958, 'Understanding a Primitive Society'; W. V. Quine, *Word and Object*, Cambridge Mass.: Technology Press of the Massachusetts Institute of Technology, 1960, especially chs. 1–3; E. Gellner, 'Concepts and Society', *Transactions of the Fifth World Congress of Sociology*, 1, Louvain: International Sociological Association 1962, pp. 153–83; S. Lukes, 'Some Problems about Rationality', *European Journal of Sociology*, 8, 2, 1967, pp. 247–64; M. Hollis, 'The Limits of Irrationality', *European Journal of Sociology*, 7, 2, 1967, pp. 265–71; 'Reason and Ritual', *Philosophy*, 63, 165, 1968, pp. 231–47. For two more recent discussions by social scientists, see M. Crick, *Explorations in Language and Meaning: Towards a Semantic Anthropology*, London: Malaby Press, 1976; S. P. Turner, *Sociological Explanation as Translation*, Cambridge: Cambridge University Press, 1980.

7 For the classic exposition of this recipe, see E. B. Tylor, *Primitive Culture*, London: John Murray, 1871.

8 For the clearest and most systematic exposition of this recipe by a scholar with a special interest in African religions, see J. H. M. Beattie, *Other Cultures*, London: Cohen & West, 1964; 'On Understanding Ritual', in B. Wilson, ed., *Rationality*, Oxford: Basil Blackwell, 1970, pp. 240–68; 'Understanding Traditional African Religion: A Comment on Horton', *Second Order*, 2, 2, 1973, pp. 3–11.

9 The foremost proponent of this recipe is S. J. Tambiah, 'The Form and Meaning of Magical Acts', in R. Horton and R. Finnegan, eds., *Modes of Thought*, London: Faber & Faber, 1981; 'A Performative Approach to Ritual', *Proceedings of the British Academy*, 45, 1981, pp. 113–69.

10 For the latest version of a thoroughgoing intellectualist approach, see R. Horton, 'Tradition and Modernity Revisited', in M. Hollis and S. Lukes, eds., *Rationality and Relativism*, Oxford: Basil Blackwell, 1982, pp. 201–60.

11 For strong statements along these lines, see Evans-Pritchard, *Nuer Religion* (especially the preface and ch. 13), *Essays in Social Anthropology*, and *Theories of Primitive Religion* (especially the concluding chapter); V. W. Turner, *Chihamba*, ch. 3; H. W. Turner, 'Modern African Religious Movements', 'Structure of Religion', 'Primal Religions', 'The Way Forward'; Winch, 'Understanding a Primitive Society'.

12 W. Schmidt, *The Origin and Growth of Religion: Facts and Theories*, London: Methuen, 1931, p. 6. For approving citations of this passage, see Evans-Pritchard, *Theories of Primitive Religion*, p. 121; Idowu, *African Traditional Religion*, p. 19.

13 For the useful terminology of 'focus' and 'focal object', I am indebted to N. Smart, *The Phenomenon of Religion*, London: Macmillan, 1973.

14 For emphasis on the mysterious and inscrutable aspect of the supreme being, see Evans-Pritchard, *Nuer Religion*, ch. 13; V. W. Turner, *Chihamba*, ch. 3; Idowu, *African Traditional Religion*, p. 75; Mbiti, *Concepts of God*, pp. xiv–xv.

15 Evans-Pritchard, *Nuer Religion*; Mbiti, *African Religions and Philosophy*, and *Concepts of God*; Idowu, *African Traditional Religion*; F. A. Arinze, *Sacrifice in Ibo Religion*, Ibadan: Ibadan University Press, 1970, pp. 8–31; E. I. Metuh, *God and Man in African Religion*, London: Geoffrey Chapman, 1981, pp. 48–104.

16 Idowu, *African Traditional Religion*, pp. 135–6.

17 Evans-Pritchard, *Nuer Religion*, pp. 311–22; Idowu, *Olodumare*, pp. 129–30, *African Traditional Religion*, pp. 52–4.

18 For a very clear assertion, by one of the founders of modern comparative religion, of the importance of communion as the real end of all religions, see J. Wach, *Sociology of Religion*, London: Kegan Paul, Trench, Trubner, 1947, pp. 383, 386, 391:

> The ultimate source and the meaning of an expression or form valid in the realm of religion is its origin from and testimony to a significant religious experience. Wherever such expressions are genuine, they are meant not to serve external – that is social, political, economic or personal – aims and purposes, but to formulate and perpetuate man's deepest experience, his communion with God ... Because a wide range of ostensibly or allegedly religious acts and rites can be shown to be of a pragmatic character, all religious acts and rites have been suspected by some older and modern critics, who are inclined to draw from these instances conclusions as to the pragmatic character of religion in general. Such a generalisation is entirely unjustified ... Religion is sound and true in its nature only as long as it has no aim or purpose except the worship of God.

Though Wach himself never did any research in the African field and seems to have known little about African religions, his work is widely cited by those of the 'Devout' who have come up via the discipline of comparative religion, and has clearly been a formative influence on their views. For typical 'Devout' statements on the primacy of communion, see V. W. Turner, *Chihamba*, ch. 3; Idowu, *African Traditional Religion*, pp. 55, 56–7, 75, 133.

Three authors who are uncomfortably aware of the *apparent* prominence of the linked goals of explanation, prediction and control, yet go to great lengths in arguing that the *real* goal of African religious life is communion are: Gaba, *Scriptures*, and 'Man's Salvation'; Zuesse, *Ritual Cosmos*; and Winch, 'Understanding a Primitive Society'.

The splendid ingenuity with which Gaba transmutes an apparent overriding concern with this-worldly welfare into a fundamental concern with communion can be seen in the following passage:

> Through the performance of rituals Anlo man hoped to achieve one definite goal: the fulfilment of his material needs. Ostensibly this may indicate a complete absorption with this-worldly concerns. However, as I have tried to indicate before, in Anlo thought existence is always a personal involvement in transcendence. And so the visible, the physical, the profane is an indispensable vehicle for or true reflection of, the invisible, the metaphorical and the sacred. In effect, the traditional Anlo man's preoccupation with worldly concerns is a preoccupation with the realisation of a positive I-Thou relationship. Indeed it is not a fundamentally different attitude from that which makes him objectify his concept of man's religiousness in the entire ritual of worship.
>
> Salvation then is equivalent to deliverance from material want in all its manifestations, and peace can be equated with material contentment. This concept of salvation does not negate the view of man in Anloland as *homo religiosus*, of salvation as the totality of involvement of being in Being. (Gaba, *Scriptures*, pp. 2–3)

In Zuesse again, we find great rhetorical ingenuity deployed in the attempt to demonstrate that what appears to be a predominantly this-worldly emphasis is in reality something very different. Zuesse starts off by assigning African religions to the category 'religions of structure' and Western Christianity to the category 'religions of salvation'. Religions of structure accept and rejoice in the things of this world. Religions of salvation promise the adherent escape from the things of this world. From this initial distinction, it looks as though Zuesse means to suggest that African religions and other religions of structure are oriented to this-worldly goals such as fecundity, prosperity, health and social harmony, whilst Western Christianity and other religions of salvation are oriented primarily to attaining communion with God. (Indeed, this is what the publisher's blurb promises.) Soon, however, we find that this is far from his intention. What he wants to say is that, for all the value they set on this-worldly things, African religions value such things, not in themselves, but as symbols of and avenues of approach to 'transcendental otherness'. By contrast, Western Christianity tries to attain communion with the transcendental with the minimum use of this-worldly symbolism. In other words, although the means are very different in the two cases, the end is the same.

The following passages sum up Zuesse's view. The first relates to the goal of religions generally: 'The core of religion is the experience of and aspiration after the Holy; this is the real point of all cults.' (*Ritual Cosmos*, p. 4.) The second relates to African religions in particular: 'African spirituality, above and beyond the specific focus of particular ritual actions, is always a piety directed toward the sanctity of the universe as a whole. Every action on its deepest level seeks to sustain the divine order and its continual self-regeneration; in this sense, every ritual enactment, however superficially oriented to utilitarian goals, is utterly selfless.' (Ibid., p. 242.)

Like the other two authors, Winch ('Understanding a Primitive Society') admits that African religions appear to be directed to this-worldly goals. The appearance, however, is deceptive, and the reality quite other. As to what the reality is, the following gives us the key.

In Judaeo-Christian cultures the conception of "If it be thy will", as developed in the story of Job, is clearly central to the matter I am discussing. Because this conception is central to Christian prayers of supplication, they may be regarded from one point of view as freeing the believer from dependence on what he is supplicating for. Prayers cannot play this role if they are regarded as a means of influencing the outcome for in that case the one who prays is still dependent on the outcome. He frees himself from this by acknowledging his complete dependence on God; and this is totally unlike any dependence on the outcome precisely because God is eternal and the outcome contingent.

I do not say that Zande magical rites are at all like Christian prayers of supplication in the positive attitude to contingencies which they express. What I do suggest is that they do, or may, express an attitude to contingencies; one, that is, which involves recognition that one's life is subject to contingencies, rather than an attempt to control these. (Ibid., p. 104.)

Despite broad 'Devout' agreement on this matter, it should nonetheless be noted that there is at least one prominent dissenting voice. Here I refer to J. S. Mbiti. For all his uncompromising insistence on the centrality of the supreme being in African religious thought, Mbiti breaks ranks quite definitely in the matter of the overriding goal of African religious life, as comes out very clearly in the following passage:

And this faith [in God] is utilitarian, not purely spiritual, it is practical and not mystical. The people respond to God in and because of particular circumstances, especially in times of need. Then they seek to obtain what he gives, be that material or spiritual; they do not search for him as the final reward or satisfaction of the human soul or spirit. Augustine's description of man's soul being restless until it finds its rest in God, is something unknown in African traditional religious life. (Mbiti, *African Religions and Philosophy*, p. 67.)

19 Idowu, *African Traditional Religion*, pp. 176, 188.

20 H. W. Turner, 'The Way Forward', p. 14.

21 I am grateful to Wyllie, 'Rationality of the Devout Opposition', for reminding me of this.

22 Idowu, *African Traditional Religion*, pp. 59–61, 132, 137, 148; Mbiti, *African Religions and Philosophy*, p. 30, *Concepts of God*, p. xiii.

23 Evans-Pritchard, *Nuer Religion*, p. 121.

24 H. W. Turner, *Modern African Religious Movements*, p. 293. Turner's argument here comes very close to giving the game to his opponents. For they could with some justice use it to claim that the theological factor should be omitted on grounds of intellectual economy. Such a conclusion, of course, he would find unthinkable.

25 Evans-Pritchard, 'Religion and the Anthropologists', and *Theories of Primitive Religion*; V. W. Turner, *Chihamba*, ch. 3; H. W. Turner, *Modern African Religious Movements*, 'Structure of Religion', and 'The Way Forward'.

26 From the publisher's blurb for J. O. Awolalu, *Yoruba Beliefs and Sacrificial Rites*, London: Longman, 1979.

27 H. W. Turner, 'The Way Forward', p. 13; Idowu, *African Traditional Religion*, p. 56.

28 Evans-Pritchard, *Nuer Religion*, pp. 121–322, and *Theories of Primitive Religion*, p. 121.

29 A reading of the major atheistic theorists of religion from Tylor down through Marx and Freud to Durkheim makes it clear that they did see their explanations as helping to establish the falsity of religious belief generally. In this respect, Evans-Pritchard, ('Religion and the Anthropologists', and *Theories of Primitive Religion*) seems nearer the mark than Wyllie, 'Rationality of the Devout Opposition'.

30 This attitude comes through in Evans-Pritchard, 'Religion and the Anthropologists', *Theories of Primitive Religion*, pp. 1–19, 100–22. It also comes through in V. W. Turner, *Chihamba*, p. 92.

31 On the atheistic side, this resignation is evident in M. Fortes, 'Preface. Anthropologists and Theologians: Common Interests and Divergent Approaches', in M. F. C. Bourdillon and M. Fortes, eds., *Sacrifice*, London: Academic Press, 1980. On the theistic side, it is evident in Evans-Pritchard, *Theories of Primitive Religion*, p. 121.

32 On the evil aspect of God in Lugbara thought, see J. Middleton, *Lugbara Religion*, London: Oxford University Press, 1960, pp. 250–62. In many other ethnographic descriptions, the supreme being seems to be morally neutral, and certain lesser spiritual agencies such as the spirit of the local community earth and the ancestors to be the guardians of morality.

33 R. Horton, 'The Kalabari World-View: An Outline and an Interpretation', *Africa*, 32, 3, 1962, pp. 197–220, and *Kalabari Sculpture*, Lagos: Department of Antiquities, Federal Republic of Nigeria, 1965.

34 One of the things for which P'Bitek takes the 'Devout' to task is the imputation to African peoples of a celebration of the unknowability of God. Thus he says:
    Mbiti wrote, "May God forgive me for attempting to describe him, and for doing it so poorly. Even if I am presenting here the wisdom and reflections of many African peoples, it is only at its best an expression of a creature about the creator. As such it is limited, inadequate and ridiculously anthropocentric. God is still beyond our human imagination,

understanding, and expression." Most African peoples know the names, abodes and characteristics of their deities. They know them by the diseases they cause. The task of the diviner is, precisely, to determine which deity is responsible for a particular misfortune, and how to deal with it. In northern Uganda certain chiefdom deities were carried from place to place. The knowledge of Africans about their deities are not limited, inadequate or ridiculous in any way. (P'Bitek, *African Religions*, p. 19.)

35 C. N. Ubah, 'The Supreme Being, Divinities and Ancestors in Igbo Traditional Religion: Evidence from Otanchara and Otanzu', *Africa*, 52, 2, 1982. For 'Devout' accounts of the Igbo world-view, see: Ezeanya, 'The Place of the Supreme God', and 'Spirit World'; Arinze, *Sacrifice in Ibo Religion*; Metuh, *God and Man*.

36 Ubah, 'Igbo Traditional Religion', pp. 91–4.

37 Ibid., p. 103.

38 Idowu, *African Traditional Religion*, p. 173.

39 Ezeanya, 'Spirit World', pp. 41–2.

40 Mbiti, *African Religions and Philosophy*, p. 58.

41 On the lives of *orisa* devotees, see: U. Beier, *A Year of Sacred Festivals in One Yoruba Town*, Lagos: Nigeria Magazine Publications, 1959; J. Wescott and P. Morton-Williams, 'The Symbolism and Ritual Context of the Yoruba *Laba Shango*', *Journal of the Royal Anthropological Institute*, 92, 1, 1962, pp. 23–37; K. Barber, 'How Man Makes God in West Africa: Yoruba Attitudes Towards the *Orisa*', *Africa*, 51, 3, 1981, pp. 724–45.

42 On the lives of water-spirit media, see R. Horton, 'Types of Spirit Possession in Kalabari Religion' in J. Beattie and J. Middleton, eds., *Spirit Mediumship and Society in Africa*, London: Routledge & Kegan Paul, 1969, pp. 14–49.

43 For a relatively recent summary of our knowledge of Fon cosmology, see W. J. Argyle, *The Fon of Dahomey: A History and Ethnography of the Old Kingdom*, Oxford: Clarendon Press, 1966, pp. 174–200.

44 For strong suggestions of a basic dualism in the Oyo Yoruba cosmology, see P. Morton-Williams, 'The Yoruba Ogboni Cult in Oyo', *Africa*, 30, 4, 1960, pp. 362–74, and 'An Outline of the Cosmology and Cult Organization of the Oyo Yoruba', *Africa*, 34, 3, 1964, pp. 243–61. For a more recent and more explicit statement, see S. O. Babayemi, 'The Ideological Base of Power of the Alaafin of Oyo and of his Chiefs', *Kiabara, Journal of the Humanities*, 4, 2, 1981, pp. 56–62.

45 For Idoma, see R. G. Armstrong, 'Is Earth Senior to God? An Old West African Theological Controversy', *African Notes*, 9, 1, 1982, pp. 7–14. For Igbira, see J. Picton, 'Concerning God and Man in Igbira', *African Notes*, 5, 1, 1968. For Mosi, see D. Zahan, 'Towards a History of the Yatenga Mossi', in P. Alexandre, ed., *French Perspectives in African Studies*, London: Oxford University Press, 1973, pp. 110–13.

46 I. Chukwukere, '*Chi* in Igbo Religion and Thought: The God in Every Man', *Anthropos*, 77, 3–4, 1983, pp. 519–34.

47 Conversation between Father R. G. Arazu and Ezenwadeyi of Ihembosi (September–October, 1966), in E. Isichei, *Igbo Worlds: an Anthology of Oral Histories and Historical Descriptions*, London: Macmillan, 1977, pp. 172–177.

48 M. Wilson, *Communal Rituals of the Nyakyusa*, London: Oxford University Press, 1959; O. P'Bitek, *Religion of the Central Luo*, Nairobi: East African Literature Bureau, 1971.

49 P. J. A. Rigby, 'Sociological Factors in the Contact of the Gogo of Central Tanzania with Islam', in I. M. Lewis, ed., *Islam in Tropical Africa*, London: Oxford University Press, 1966, pp. 268–95.

50 For doubts as to the earlier status of Mwari, see H. Bucher, *Spirits and Power: An Analysis of Shona Cosmology*, Cape Town: Oxford University Press, 1980, chs. 2 and 6.

51 The works by Wilson, P'Bitek, Ubah and Bucher cited above all give some picture of changes in the patterns of focal objects, in particular indigenous religious traditions, consequent on the advent of Christian missionary influences. For additional case studies, see: R. Horton, 'A Hundred Years of Change in Kalabari Religion', in J. Middleton, ed., *Black Africa: its People and their Cultures Today*, London: Macmillan, 1970; G. Lienhardt, 'The Dinka and Catholicism', in J. Davis, ed., *Religious Organization and Religious Experience*, London: Academic Press 1982, pp. 81–95.

52 Wilson (*Communal Rituals*, pp. 154–6), shows how the missionaries who came to Nyakyusa took up in this way the name of Kyala, one of several local hero-deities whose cults were important in the indigenous tradition. P'Bitek (*African Religions*, pp. 61–2, and *Religion of the Central Luo*, pp. 41–58) retells the horrific story of how, after persistent missionary attempts to extract from them the name of the 'Creator', Luo elders in desperation offered 'Lubanga the Moulder', the spirit of spinal tuberculosis who 'moulded' men's backbones into fearful curves. For the original story, see Crazzolara in A. C. A. Wright, 'The Supreme Being among the Acholi of Uganda: Another Viewpoint', *Uganda Journal*, 7, 3, 1940, pp. 134–7.

In a just-published essay which came to my hand after the completion of this manuscript, Donatus Nwoga (*The Supreme God as Stranger in Igbo Religious Thought*, Ekwereazu: Hawk Press, 1984) suggests that it was Christian missionaries who similarly elevated Chukwu to the status of supreme being of the Igbo-speaking peoples. He argues that, a hundred years ago, 'Chukwu' was the name given by Igbo-speakers to the oracular spirit promoted by the people of Aro-Chukwu: a spirit that neither the Aro themselves nor the groups amongst whom they enjoyed influence thought of as anything more than the most powerful of a number of powerful spirits. According to Nwoga, it was only after the missionaries had taken this name, transformed its meaning and fed the result back to the Igbo that 'Chukwu' came to be used by the people themselves as the name of a supreme being. After a first hasty reading of this essay, my impression is that Nwoga has still a bit more to do before we can regard his case as conclusively proved. But he has certainly shattered for ever the dogmatic slumbers of many students of Igbo religion. Donatus Redivivus indeed!

53 Horton, 'A Hundred Years of Change'; Lienhardt, 'Dinka and Catholicism'.

54 For a more elaborate exposition and defence of this thesis, see R. Horton, 'African Conversion', *Africa*, 41, 2, 1971, pp. 85–108, and 'Rationality of Conversion'.

55 P'Bitek, *Religion of the Central Luo*, p. 88.

56 For milestones in the debate, see: M. Fortes, 'Pietas in Ancestor Worship: The Henry Myers Lecture, 1960', *Journal of the Royal Anthropological Institute*, 91, 2, 1961; I. Kopytoff, 'Ancestors as Elders in Africa: Further Thoughts', *Africa*, 43, 2, 1973, pp. 122–33; W. H. Sangree, 'Youths as Elders and Infants as Ancestors: The Complementarity of Alternate Generations, both Living and Dead, in

Tiriki, Kenya, and Irigwe, Nigeria,' *Africa*, 43, 1, 1974; E. L. Mendonsa, 'Elders, Office-Holders and Ancestors among the Sisala of Northern Ghana', *Africa*, 46, 1, 1976, pp. 56–65; J. C. Muller, 'Of Souls and Bones: The Living and the Dead among the Rukuba, Benue-Plateau State, Nigeria', *Africa*, 46, 3, 1976, pp. 258–73.

57 Fortes, 'Pietas in Ancestor Worship', and 'Some Reflections on Ancestor Worship in Africa', in M. Fortes and G. Dieterlen, eds., *African Systems of Thought*, London: Academic Press, 1965.

58 Beier, *Sacred Festivals*; Wescott and Morton-Williams, 'Symbolism and Ritual Context'; Barber, 'How Man Makes God'.

59 Idowu, *African Traditional Religion*, pp. 178–83 and Mbiti, *African Religions and Philosophy*, pp. 8–9, to take two examples, seem anxious to differentiate attitudes to the ancestors from attitudes to the supreme being.

60 The apathy of Azande toward the supreme being is well described by Evans-Pritchard, 'Zande Theology'. His remarks could well be used to characterize the attitudes of a dozen other peoples.

61 I shall not try to list the monographic material that either intentionally or unintentionally makes this point. To do so would be to include virtually every monograph that has successfully portrayed the indigenous religious heritage of an African people in the context of everyday life.

62 For changing perceptions of efficacy as important determinants of the rise and fall of cults in the indigenous religions, see J. Goody, 'Anomie in Ashanti?', *Africa*, 27, 4, 1957; Horton, 'The Kalabari World-View', and *Kalabari Sculpture*; Barber, 'How Man Makes God'; O. Okeke, 'Religious Change in Ikenanzizi'. Unpublished B.A. thesis, Port Harcourt: University of Port Harcourt, 1982.

63 See P'Bitek, *Religion of the Central Luo*. It may well have been P'Bitek's grounding in Acholi religious life which led him to place such heavy emphasis on the pragmatic element in his general remarks on African religions.

64 Horton, 'Spirit Possession in Kalabari Religion'; Barber, 'How Man Makes God'.

65 For a sample of views on this matter of leaders and members of neo-Christian Churches drawn from all over the African continent, see R. Horton, 'Professor Winch on Safari', *European Journal of Sociology*, 17, 1, 1976, p. 176.

66 Mbiti, *African Religions and Philosophy*, pp. 4–5; Metuh, *God and Man*, pp. 153–4.

67 For the Tiv conception of the after-life, see L. Bohannan and P. Bohannan, *The Tiv of Central Nigeria*, London: International African Institute, 1958, pp. 81–3.

68 The best description of an ancestral cult of this type that we have for sub-Saharan Africa is probably that which we get from Meyer Fortes's work on the Tallensi. See M. Fortes, *Oedipus and Job in West African Religion*. Cambridge: Cambridge University Press, 1959, 'Pietas in Ancestor Worship', and 'Reflections on Ancestor Worship'.

69 There seems to be no in-depth modern study of reincarnation beliefs available. It is clear that such beliefs are by no means universal in the indigenous traditions of sub-Saharan Africa. Nonetheless, they seem fairly widespread in the forest area of West Africa. And my own ideas about them have been largely formed by conversations with students, colleagues and friends of Igbo and Yoruba origin.

70 Metuh, *God and Man*, pp. 153–4.

71 For the classic justification of this proposition in terms of everyday usage see G. Ryle, *The Concept of Mind*, Harmondsworth: Penguin 1970, pp. 301–11.

72 Typical here is the way in which neurologists account for a whole range of perceptual, credal and behavioural abnormalities in terms of prior injury to the head. In each case, the link between abnormality and prior injury is established, first by deploying a theory of the neural mechanisms underlying *normal* operation of the function in question, and then by showing how the injury interfered with these mechanisms.

73 A prominent figure in this line of business is R. L. Gregory. See his: *Eye and Brain: The Psychology of Seeing*, London: Weidenfeld & Nicholson, 1966.

74 For a review, critique and diagnosis of similar attempts to ban causal explanations of veridical beliefs in the sciences, see D. Bloor, *Knowledge and Social Imagery*, London: Routledge & Kegan Paul, 1976, chs. 1–3.

75 In this matter, Mbiti resembles the men who refused to look down the telescope. Though he is certainly aware of the work of Wilson and P'Bitek (see Mbiti, *African Religions and Philosophy*), he has apparently decided to ignore it. Idowu, by contrast ('Study of Religion', pp. 11–12, *African Traditional Religion*, pp. 61–2) acknowledges the existence of reports of this kind, but tries to weaken their credibility by accusations of prejudice against their authors.

76 For this approach see V. W. Turner, *Chihamba*, pp. 88–96. Turner makes powerful use of Herman Melville's allegory of Captain Ahab and the Great White Whale in portraying modern man's fight with God.

77 For their bad reputation in this respect with leaders of other faiths, see E. R. Dodds, *Pagan and Christian in an Age of Anxiety*, London: Cambridge University Press, 1965, pp. 106, 120–2.

78 One could fairly give the prize for intellectual obscurantism in the modern West to theologians such as Otto, Barth, Bultmann and Tillich!

79 The following passage from Kepler (in W. Heisenberg, *Philosophic Problems of Nuclear Science*, London: Faber & Faber, 1952, p. 78) provides a good illustration:

> I have endeavoured to gain for human reason, aided by geometrical calculation, an insight into His way of creation; may the creator of the heavens themselves, the father of all reason, to whom our mortal senses owe their existence; may He who is himself immortal ... keep me in His grace and guard me from reporting anything about His work which cannot be justified before His magnificence or which may misguide our powers of reason, and may He cause us to aspire to the perfection of His works of creation by the dedication of our lives ...

80 One easily discovers striking similarities which provide useful points of contact for presenting one's message. But it is precisely these points of contact which make an agent in the Christianization process ponder seriously on the whole missiological and evangelical enterprise; whether in the light of his present knowledge of the religion of those he is to Christianize, dialogue rather than impatient attempt to convert his hearers should not be his guiding principle, and whether it is still right for him to consider all those who want to remain in their own religious persuasions as eternally damned. (Gaba, 'Man's Salvation', p. 400.)

81 The following passages convey both Idowu's basic ideological stance and the intensity of feeling behind it:

> The question at issue ... is briefly this. "Do primitive peoples have any concept or knowledge of God?" And since that question can no longer be answered in the negative,

how do we answer the supporting question of "What or which God, their own God or the real God?" The heresy began precisely at the point where the question was answered explicitly, unequivocally, that it must be their own God, that is, a god other than the supreme God as known in the personal experiences, theology or religio-cultural conception of the Western world. The mind of the Western scholar, or investigator, or still more to the point, theorist, has played a trick on him: he has rejected on the ground of prejudice and emotional resistance to truth the fact that the same God who is Lord of the universe is the one whose revelation is apprehended universally and therefore by the "primitive peoples" in their own way, and he immediately falls, consequently, into the trap of *making* God in his own image by thinking that, "I look down upon these peoples as an offensive scum of humanity; it follows, therefore, that the God whom I worship, or, at least, who is regarded as the God of my glorious and incomparable culture, must be of the same mind as I – He can have no time for an excrescence of their kind".

Thus, the world has been treated to meaningless terms like "the high gods of primitive peoples" or "wherever you go among these people, there is a supreme god". It would seem that the authors of this heresy have been so absorbed in the task of proving the difference between "their own God" and "the high gods of primitive peoples" that they have failed to see the glaring conclusion of their own premise, i.e. an artificial supreme god for each nation and a consequent artificial, universal polytheism. The reason for the racial confusion and injustice and unrelieved suffering throughout the world today is that there is a plurality of imagined, racially egocentric gods who are independent of one another and each of whom is seeking at the earliest opportunity to champion the cause of his own racial protégés in undoing other gods and their protégés. (Idowu, *African Traditional Religion*, pp. 61–2.)

Finally, in order to understand the basis of African Traditional Religion, the scholar must divest his mind of the obnoxious notion of a High God. As I have said repeatedly, this comes out of the refusal – deliberate refusal – on the part of foreign investigators to accept that Africans are as much entitled to a place with the Supreme God as they are ... Africa recognizes only one God, the Supreme, Universal God. Even though she has pictures of Him which are of various shades, calls Him by various names and approaches Him in various ways, He nevertheless remains one and the same God, the Creator of all the end of the earth. Man's problems – personal, domestic, social, political, relational, national, and international – will never be really solved until he has learnt to think of one God and one universe, and of his fellowmen as persons with identical basic values and spiritual urges like himself. (Idowu, 'Study of Religion', pp. 11–12.)

82 Several Nigerian friends have said to me that what they find most painful and difficult in Christian commitment is the idea that they, as Christians, may be saved, but that some of their most beloved relatives and friends, still non-Christians, may be damned.

83 H. W. Turner, 'The Way Forward', pp. 3–4, 13–14.

84 I cannot help thinking that Christian theologians have not really stretched themselves as far as they might have done in the matter of those who hold definitely non-monotheistic beliefs. There seems to have been concentration on the theological upgrading of members of other 'Great World Religions'. (The latter is a theologian's phrase for religions which have very large numbers of adherents and a theistic focus which can plausibly be represented as showing continuities with the Christian God.) This has left radical polytheists and atheists 'unredeemed', has perpetuated anxiety among Christian students of these other outlooks, and has encouraged continued distortion of their content in the effort to bring their adherents 'into the fold'. It seems to me that if the

theologians had devoted the amount of energy and ingenuity to the problem of polytheists and atheists that they have devoted to the problem of evil, we should by now be relieved of the agonized contortions performed by some of our Christian colleagues in the study of African religions. Perhaps they might consider as a starting point the statement which the novelist Morris West (*The World is Made of Glass*, London: Coronet Books 1984, p. 316), puts into the mouth of a Mother Superior faced with the request that she allow the burial in her convent cemetery of an unbeliever who has worked for her order: 'Gianni, my boy, it doesn't matter what we believe about God. It's what he knows about us. Your Magda will be very welcome here.'

85 H. W. Turner, 'The Way Forward'.
86 P. Rieff, *Freud: The Mind of the Moralist*, London: Methuen, 1965.
87 Fortes, *Oedipus and Job*.

7 AFRICAN TRADITIONAL THOUGHT AND WESTERN SCIENCE

1 'Destiny and the Unconscious in West Africa', *Africa*, 31, 2, 1961; 'The Kalabari World-View: an Outline and Interpretation', *Africa*, 32, 2, 1962; 'Ritual Man in Africa', *Africa*, 34, 2, 1964.

2 See, for instance, J. Beattie, 'Ritual and Social Change', *Man*, New Series, 1, 1, 1966.

3 See Beattie, ibid.

4 M. Fortes, *Oedipus and Job in West African Religion*, Cambridge: Cambridge University Press, 1959; J. Middleton; *Lugbara Religion*, London: Oxford University Press, 1960; G. Lienhardt, *Divinity and Experience: the Religion of the Dinka*, Oxford: Clarendon Press, 1961; Horton, for instance 'The Kalabari World-View'.

5 'An Ndembu Doctor in Practice', in A. Kiev, ed., Magic, Faith and Healing, London, Collier-Macmillan, 1964, pp. 233, 262. See also: V. W. Turner, *Ndembu Divination*, Rhodes-Livingstone Paper No. 31, Manchester: Manchester University Press, 1961, 'A Ndembu Doctor in Practice', in A. Kiev, ed., *Magic, Faith and Healing*, London: Collier-Macmillan, 1964.

6 M. Gluckman, *Politics, Law and Ritual in Tribal Society*, Oxford: Basil Blackwell, 1965. See especially ch. 6: 'Mystical Disturbance and Ritual Adjustment'.

7 A. Kiev, ed., *Magic, Faith and Healing*, passim.

8 Horton, 'Destiny and the Unconscious'.

9 E. E. Evans-Pritchard, *Theories of Primitive Religion*, London: Oxford University Press, 1965, p. 8.

10 See, for instance, Evans-Pritchard, ibid., p. 88.

11 E. E. Evans-Pritchard, *Nuer Religion*, Oxford: Clarendon Press, 1956; Lienhardt, *Divinity and Experience*.

12 Evans-Pritchard, *Theories of Primitive Religion*, p. 316.

13 R. Horton 'The Kalabari World-View'; 'A Hundred years of Change in Kalabari Religion', in J. Middleton, ed., *Black Africa*, New York: Collier-Macmillan, 1970; 'God, Man and the Land in a Northern Ibo Village-Group', *Africa*, 26, 1, 1956. M. Fortes, *The Web of Kinship among the Tallensi*, London: Oxford University Press, 1949, especially pp. 21–2 and p. 219.

14 Fortes, *Oedipus and Job*, p. 76.
15 R. E. Bradbury, 'Review of *Oedipus and Job in West African Religion*', in *Man*, September, 1959.
16 Such parallels arouse the more uncomfortable thought that in all the theorizing we sociologists have done about the working of traditional African societies, we may often have done little more than translate indigenous African theories about such workings.
17 Middleton, *Lugbara Religion*.
18 Just how little headway British social anthropologists appear to be making with traditional religious thought is betrayed by their tendency to confine themselves to the study of its political manipulation, and to leave psychologists the job of accounting for its substantive features. In this context, I should like to draw attention to the curiously menial role in which the modern British anthropologist has cast the psychologist – the role of the well-disciplined scavenger. On the one hand, the psychologist is expected to keep well away from any intellectual morsel currently considered digestible by the anthropologist. On the other hand, he is tossed all indigestible morsels, and is expected to relieve the anthropologist of the embarrassing smell they would create if left in his house uneaten.
19 See, for instance, *Scientific Change* (Symposium on the History of Science, University of Oxford, 9–15 July, 1961), A. C. Crombie, ed., London: Heinemann, 1968; especially the chapter on 'Chinese Science' and the subsequent interventions by Willy Hartner and Stephen Toulmin.
20 Western society today may be said to harbour science like a foreign god, powerful and mysterious. Our lives are changed by its handiwork but the population of the West is as far from understanding the nature of this strange power as a remote peasant of the Middle Ages may have been from understanding the theology of Thomas Aquinas. (J. Barzun, 'Introduction' to S. Toulmin, *Foresight and Understanding*, London: Hutchinson, 1961.
21 Coming from Africa, this is something of a *cri de coeur*. In the authoritarian political climate of emergent African nations, there are particular dangers that this may be the outcome of 'westernization'. For since the spirit of science, as I shall emphasize in part 2, is essentially anti-authoritarian, there is a great temptation to take the preoccupation with impersonal models as the essence of science, and to reject the real essence as inconvenient. Hence the need to insist so strongly on disentangling the two.
22 Philosophically minded readers will notice here some affinities with Karl Popper, who also makes the transition from a 'closed' to an 'open' predicament crucial for the take-off from tradition to science. For me, however, Popper obscures the issue by packing too many contrasts into his definitions of 'closed' and 'open'. Thus, for him, the transition from one predicament to the other implies not just a growth in the awareness of alternatives but also a transition from communalism to individualism, and from ascribed status to achieved status. But, as I hope to show in this essay, it is the awareness of alternatives which is crucial for the take-off into science. Not individualism or achieved status: for there are lots of societies where both of the latter are well developed, but which show no signs whatever of take-off. In the present context, therefore, my own narrower definition of 'closed' and 'open' seems more appropriate.
23 E. E. Evans-Pritchard, *Witchcraft, Oracles and Magic among the Azande*, Oxford: Clarendon Press, 1937, p. 195.

24 Ibid., p. 338.
25 Evans-Pritchard, *Theories of Primitive Religion*, p. 55.
26 C. Laye, *The Dark Child*, London: Collins, 1955. Quoted in J. Jahn, *Muntu: An Outline of Neo-African Culture*, London: Faber & Faber, 1961, p. 125. As an attempt to make an inventory of distinctive and universal features of African culture, Jahn's book seems to me highly tendentious. But its imaginative sketch of the assumptions underlying magical beliefs and practices is one of the most suggestive treatments of the subject I have seen.
27 Evans-Pritchard, *Witchcraft, Oracles and Magic*, p. 449.
28 R. Horton, *Kalabari Sculpture*, Lagos: Department of Antiquities, Federal Republic of Nigeria, 1965.
29 H. Lavondes, 'Magie et Language', *L'Homme*, 3, 3, 1963.
30 Ibid., p. 115.
31 From the piecemeal, situation-bound character of traditional idea-systems, some have been led to infer that the anthropologist must analyze them in an equally piecemeal situational manner, and not as systems. Thus in her recent *Purity and Danger* (London: Routledge & Kegan Paul, 1966), Mary Douglas talks about the error of pinning out entire traditional idea-systems like Lepidoptera, in abstraction from the real-life situations in which their various fragments actually occur. But abstraction is as abstraction does. Provided that comparison of total idea-systems leads to interesting results, it is surely as justifiable as any other kind of comparison. After all, what about the abstraction and comparison of social structures?
32 See E. Gellner, *Thought and Change*, London: Weidenfeld & Nicolson, 1964, p. 105 for a similar point exemplified in the philosophy of Descartes.
33 See, for instance, M. Fortes, 'Pietas in Ancestor Worship', *Journal of the Royal Anthropological Institute*, 91, part 2, 1961.
34 See R. Horton, 'The Kalabari *Ekine* Society: A Borderland of Religion and Art', *Africa*, 33, 2, 1963.
35 See Beattie, 'Ritual and Social Change'.
36 C. Achebe, *Things Fall Apart*, London: Heinemann, 1957.
37 The idea of secondary elaboration as a key feature of pre-scientific thought-systems was put forward with great brilliance and insight by Evans-Pritchard in his *Witchcraft, Oracles and Magic*. All subsequent discussions, including the present one, are heavily indebted to his lead.
38 T. Kuhn, *The Structure of Scientific Revolutions*, Chicago: University of Chicago Press, 1962.
39 Evans-Pritchard, *Witchcraft, Oracles and Magic*, passim.
40 S. F. Nadel, *Nupe Religion*, London: Routledge & Kegan Paul, 1956, especially ch. 6.
41 D. Forde, 'Spirits, Witches and Sorcerers in the Supernatural Economy of The Yako', *Journal of the Royal Anthropological Institute*, 88, 2, 1958.
42 Some similar comments on the themes of ignorance and uncertainty in relation to the scientific outlook are made by R. G. Armstrong in a brief but trenchant critique of 'The Notion of Magic' by M. Wax and R. Wax, *Current Anthropology*, 4, 5, December, 1963.
43 This observation may well prove to be a milestone in our understanding of traditional thought. It was first made some years ago by Mary Douglas, who has

developed many of its implications in her recent book *Purity and Danger*. Though we clearly disagree on certain wider implications, the present discussion is deeply indebted to her insights.

44 Middleton, *Lugbara Religion*.

45 This association of foreign lands with chaos and pollution seems to be a universal of pre-scientific thought systems. For this, see M. Eliade, *The Sacred and the Profane*, New York: Harvest Books, 1961, especially ch. 1.

46 In these rites of recreation, traditional African thought shows its striking affinities with pre-scientific thought in many other parts of the world. The worldwide occurrence and meaning of such rites was first dealt with by Mircea Eliade in his *Myth of the Eternal Return*, Princeton: Princeton University Press, 1954. A more recent treatment from which the present analysis has profited greatly is to be found in the chapter entitled 'Le Temps Retrouvé', in C. Lévi-Strauss, *La Pensée Sauvage*, Paris: Plon, 1962.

47 See M. Griaule, *Conversations with Ogotemmeli*, London: Oxford University Press, 1965; G. Dieterlen, 'The Dogon', in D. Forde, ed., *African Worlds*, London: Oxford University Press, 1954.

48 For some interesting remarks on this aspect of West African ritual dramas, see C. Tardits, 'Religion, Epic, History: Notes on the Underlying Functions of Cults in Benin Civilisations', *Diogenes*, 37, 1962.

49 Lévi-Strauss, I think, is making much the same point about rites of renewal when he talks of the continuous battle between pre-scientific classificatory systems and the non-repetitive changes involved in the passage of time. See Lévi-Strauss, *La Pensée Sauvage*.

50 C. P. Snow, *The Two Cultures and the Scientific Revolution*, Cambridge: Cambridge University Press, 1960, p. 10.

51 J. M. L. Abercrombie, *The Anatomy of Judgement*, London: Hutchinson, 1960; quoted on p. 131.

52 The discussion that follows leans heavily upon J. Goody and I. Watt, 'The Consequences of Literacy', *Comparative Studies in Society and History*, 5, 3, 1963. Goody and Watt are, I believe, among the first to have spelled out the probable importance of the transition from oral to written transmission of beliefs for the take-off from tradition into science. I have drawn heavily here upon their characterization of the contrasting predicaments of thinkers in oral and literate cultures; though my argument diverges somewhat from theirs in its later stages.

53 Ibid., pp. 311–19.

54 This point, I think, is relevant to an argument advanced against my analysis of magic. (John Beattie, personal communication.) The argument is that once a person learns another language, he becomes aware of alternative possibilities of dividing up the world by words and, on my premises, must inevitably adopt a non-magical outlook.

In rebuttal, I would say that where a person learns another people's language and thought only at the common-sense level, he is not exposed to a radically different way of dividing up the world by words. Indeed, he is liable to see most of the common-sense words and concepts of the alien language as having equivalents in his own. They are 'the same words' and 'the same thoughts'. It is only when he learns the alien language and thought at the theoretical level that he becomes aware of a radically different way of dividing the world.

55 For a brilliant sketch of the beginnings of the 'open' predicament in the Greek city-states, see K. Popper, *The Open Society and its Enemies*, London: G. Routledge & Sons, 1945. Although, as I said earlier, Popper's definition of 'closed' and 'open' differs somewhat from my own, much of what he says is relevant to my argument and has indeed provided inspiration for it.

56 For the importance of the confrontation between these three thought-traditions, see F. Heer, *The Mediaeval World*, London: Weidenfeld & Nicholson, 1962.

57 Take, for instance, the following passage from Xenophanes, quoted in S. Toulmin, *The Fabric of the Heavens*, London: Hutchinson, 1961:

Mortals consider that the gods are begotten as they are, and have clothes and voices and figures like theirs. The Ethiopians make their gods black and snub-nosed; the Thracians say theirs have blue eyes and red hair. Yes, and if oxen and horses or lions had hands, and could paint with their hands, and produce works of art as men do, horses would paint the gods with shapes like horses, and oxen like oxen, and make their bodies in the image of their several kinds.

58 For this see P. Hazard, *The European Mind 1680–1715*, Harmondsworth: Penguin, 1964 (especially ch. 4).

59 Quoted from 'The Vanity of Dogmatizing', in B. Willey, *The Seventeenth Century Background*, Harmondsworth: Penguin in association with Chatto & Windus 1962, p. 168.

60 See Popper, *Open Society and its Enemies*, for some of these reactions to pre-Socratic 'open' thinking.

61 See Heer, *The Mediaeval World*, for a vivid picture of the way in which the medieval world oscillated crazily between 'open' and 'closed' attitudes.

8 PARADOX AND EXPLANATION: A REPLY TO MR SKORUPSKI

1 'Science and Traditional Religious Thought'; Parts 1 and 2, *Philosophy of the Social Sciences*, 3, 1973, pp. 97–115; Parts 3 and 4, *Philosophy of the Social Sciences*, 3, 1973, pp. 209–30. All subsequent references to 'Skorupski' are to these articles.

2 R. Horton, 'Ritual Man in Africa', *Africa*, 34, 1964, pp. 85–103.

3 I agree with Skorupski that identification of the entities postulated by a low-level theory with those postulated by a high-level theory poses much the same problems as does identification of observables with the entities postulated by a low-level theory. (Skorupski, pp. 101–2).

4 Skorupski, p. 101.

5 I have avoided the more usual formulation: 'Identity of Indiscernibles'. As Skorupski has pointed out to me, the latter, which makes indiscernibility a sufficient and not merely a necessary condition of identity, is currently the subject of controversy amongst logicians.

6 W. Heisenberg, *Philosophic Problems of Nuclear Science*, London: Faber & Faber, 1952, 100–5.

7 R. Harré, *The Philosophies of Science*. Oxford: Oxford University Press, 1972, pp. 102–3.

8 For this idea of elliptical explanatory statements, see C. Hempel, 'Explanation in Science and History', in P. Nidditch, ed., *The Philosophy of Science*, Oxford: Oxford University Press, 1968, pp. 61–5.

9 Skorupski, p. 213.
10 The dominant preoccupation of the earlier pre-Socratics was that of trying to discover the ultimate 'stuff' of which all the diverse entities and phenomena of the
observable world were made up. For Parmenides and his followers, Zeno and
Melissus, this obsessive concern with the unity underlying the diversity of the
world raised in acute form the problem of how what was one could also be many.
The Parmenideans disposed of the problem by arguing that the One was the real
and that the Many was merely an illusion. Later on, Leucippus and Democritus
reached what is the essence of the modern solution when they suggested that the
diversities of the observed world were the outcome of a diversity of configurations
of things of a single kind: atoms. On this, see G. Kirk and J. Raven, *The Pre-
Socratic Philosophers*, Cambridge: Cambridge University Press, 1971,
pp. 263–306, 400–26.
11 A. J. Ayer, *The Origins of Pragmatism*. London: Macmillan, 1968, p. 333.
12 On this, see A. Danto, *What Philosophy Is*, Harmondsworth: Penguin, 1971,
pp. 119–23; P. Alexander, *Sensationalism and Scientific Explanation*. London:
Routledge & Kegan Paul, 1963, pp. 117, 129–31.
13 In the introductory part of his critique (pp. 102–3), Skorupski implies that he is
going to deploy his arguments in the reverse order. In actual fact, however, he
deploys the part–whole argument in earnest only after he has dealt with the question of contingent identity. So this is the order in which I take his arguments here.
14 I hope the reader will forgive the sudden switch from tables to chlorine gas. The
initial reference to tables serves to orientate, letting the reader know that the discussion is going to exhume Eddington's hoary paradox. The switch to chlorine gas
is a switch to a case which is in many ways simpler for purposes of argument.
15 On the importance of this last criterion, see D. Davidson, 'The Individuation of
Events', in N. Rescher, ed., *Essays in Honor of Carl G. Hempel*, Dordrecht:
Reidel, 1969, pp. 231–2. Though Davidson proposed this criterion in connection
with events rather than with entities, I think it can be extended to the latter in so
far as changes in entities are events.
16 This thought occurred to me after reading J. Stevenson, 'Sensations and Brain
Processes; a Reply to J. J. C. Smart', in C. Borst, ed., *The Mind/Brain Identity
Theory*, London: Macmillan, 1970, pp. 87–92. Stevenson (p. 89) suggests that the
usual forms of psychological–physiological identification leave us unsatisfied.
This is because they merely substitute for two entities, one psychic and one
physiological, a single entity which nonetheless has *both* psychic *and* physiological
properties.
17 For similar misgivings about assessment of theoretical identity, see N. Holmstrom, 'Some Comments on a Version of Physicalism', *Philosophical Studies*, 23,
1972, pp. 163–9.
18 Skorupski, p. 103.
19 Heisenberg, *Philosophic Problems*, pp. 54–5. The same point is made very force-
fully in N. Hanson, *Patterns of Discovery*, Cambridge: Cambridge University
Press, 1958, pp. 119–26. Hanson cites a number of working scientists from Democritus to Heisenberg who have enunciated this principle in one form or another.
20 I am grateful to Skorupski for helping me to formulate this passage succinctly –
though needless to say he flatly disagrees with it!
21 As will be evident from note 10, Parmenides was one of the first super-realists.

22 See A. Eddington, *The Nature of the Physical World*, Cambridge: Cambridge University Press, 1928; P. Feyerabend, 'Explanation, Reduction and Empiricism', in H. Fiegl and G. Maxwell, eds., *Minnesota Studies in the Philosophy of Science*, Vol. III, Minneapolis: University of Minnesota Press, 1962, pp. 28–97; G. Maxwell, 'The Ontological Status of Theoretical Entities', in Fiegl and Maxwell, eds., *Minnesota Studies*, pp. 3–27; W. Sellars, *Science, Perception and Reality*, London: Routledge & Kegan Paul, 1963, pp. 106–26.

23 S. Stebbing, *Philosophy and the Physicists*, London: Methuen, 1958, pp. 45–64.

24 Amongst the anti-religious group, we can count such figures as Comte, Mach, Russell and Ayer. Amongst the pro-religious, the best-known is probably Pierre Duhem.

25 A. Lavoisier, 'Reflexions on Phlogiston', *Memoires de l'Academie Royale des Sciences*, Paris, 1876. (Quoted by J. Partington, *A History of Chemistry*, Vol. III. London, 1962. Also by S. Toulmin and J. Goodfield, *The Architecture of Matter*, London: Hutchinson, 1962, p. 228.)

26 On this, see Toulmin and Goodfield, *Architecture of Matter*, pp. 252–3.

27 On the combination of paradox with explanatory fertility in the notion of quantum jumps, see Toulmin and Goodfield, ibid., pp. 280–2.

28 Apparently de Broglie and Schrodinger still hold to this theory. See M. Hesse, 'Models and Matter' and N. Hanson, 'Postscript', in S. Toulmin, *Quanta and Reality*, London: Hutchinson, 1962, pp. 49–57 and 85–93.

29 On this, see again Hesse and Hanson in *Quanta and Reality*.

30 For an account of Feynman's theories of time-reversals in the life-courses of elementary particles, see B. Hoffman, *The Strange Story of the Quantum*, Harmondsworth: Penguin, 1959, pp. 214–22. Though this is a popular exposition written for mathematical illiterates like myself, the writer would appear to be a reputable mathematical physicist! For thoughts on the paradox implicit in Feynman's ideas, see J. G. Whitrow, *The Natural Philosophy of Time*, London: Nelson, 1963, pp. 280–3.

31 For an exposition of these concepts, see R. Harré, *An Introduction to the Logic of the Sciences*, London: Macmillan, 1965, pp. 97–103.

32 Mindful of Skorupski's warning (Skorupski, p. 111), I have tried in the foregoing to avoid the usual layman's mistake of lumping what is merely bizarre or unpicturable in with what is genuinely paradoxical. The paradoxes I have pointed to here, together with the tolerant attitude to them of many physicists, have in fact been the subjects of minority criticism amongst physicists themselves. A good example of such minority criticism is to be found in M. Bunge, 'Analogy in Quantum Theory: from Insight to Nonsense', *British Journal for the Philosophy of Science*, 18, 1968, pp. 265–86. Bunge complains bitterly about the paradoxicality of many current formulations of quantum theory, and about the cheerful tolerance of such paradoxicality. He supports the argument of this essay by pointing to the over-extension of analogy as the chief source of paradox, but recommends that, whatever the usefulness of analogy in the development of a 'youthful' theory, it should be ruthlessly jettisoned once the theory is 'mature'. Against such views, philosophers of science such as Harré, Hesse and Masterman argue very convincingly that a theory which tries to jettison its guiding analogy is as good as dead. On this, see R. Harré, *The Principles of Scientific Thinking*, London: Macmillan, 1970; M. Hesse, *Models and Analogies in Science*. London 1963, and

'Models and Matter', in Toulmin, ed., *Quanta and Reality*; M. Masterman, 'The Nature of a Paradigm', in I. Lakatos and A. Musgrave, eds., *Criticism and the Growth of Knowledge*, Cambridge: Cambridge University Press, 1970, pp. 59–89.

As regards Skorupski's own attempts to sweep the paradoxes associated with theoretical schemes under the table, I must say I find them unimpressive. In the first place, his invocation of mathematics is of dubious value. Thus he says (p. 111): 'A physicist does not ask himself in vacuo whether the concept of a thing with wave-like and particle-like characteristics makes sense, he goes to the mathematics of the theory, whose coherence guarantees the coherence of the theory'. Now this surely won't do: for the first thing the physicist asks himself about a new mathematical formalism is whether its terms are 'physically intelligible'. Indeed, one of the current worries of the quantum physicists is that, in some areas, their formalism, though beautifully coherent, yields predictions that are physically nonsensical. (On this, see N. Hanson, *The Concept of the Positron*, Cambridge 1963, pp. 97–100, 211; and 'Postscript' in Toulmin, ed., *Quanta and Reality*, pp. 87–90). Again, it would seem that, whilst the mathematical formalization of a model enables us to give our predictions the numerical precision which is indispensable to their testability, this formalization, by itself, can generate no radically new predictions. Left with the formalism and no model, the result, as Hesse puts it, would be that 'we should have no expectations at all, and we should then be imprisoned for ever inside the range of our existing experiments'. (Hesse, 'Models and Matter', pp. 56–7). Secondly, in his note 38, Skorupski seems, in his quotation of Hanson, to agree after all with my idea that scientists, though not delighted by having to do so, will go along with a theory containing a modicum of paradox until something with greater predictive value turns up. And in this, he seems very near to giving in to my argument; for, as we shall see presently, such an attitude on the part of the scientists is not far from the attitude of those African religious thinkers we both deal with.

33 Hanson, *Patterns of Discovery*, pp. 119–35.
34 These terms are taken from the introduction to Claude Lévi-Strauss's *La Pensée Sauvage*, Paris: Plon, 1962. Like many anthropologists, Lévi-Strauss has an antiseptic view of science which ignores the extent of its dependence on the humble process of analogy. Hence he contrasts the pre-scientific thinker as *bricoleur* (roughly, 'handyman') with the scientist as *ingenieur* ('engineer'). In fact, his description of allegedly pre-scientific *bricolage* in the realm of ideas provides us with some excellent clues toward an understanding of model-building in the sciences.
35 E. Evans-Pritchard, *Nuer Religion*, Oxford: Clarendon Press, 1956; G. Lienhardt, *Divinity and Experience: the Religion of the Dinka*, Oxford: Clarendon Press, 1961.
36 Skorupski, p. 211.
37 Evans-Pritchard, *Nuer Religion*, pp. 124–5; Lienhardt, *Divinity and Experience*, p. 81.
38 Evans-Pritchard, *Nuer Religion*, pp. 48–52; Lienhardt, *Divinity and Experience*, p. 56.
39 Evans-Pritchard, *Nuer Religion*, pp. 123–4.
40 Ibid., p. 125.

41 E. Gellner, 'Concepts and Society', in B. Wilson, ed., *Rationality*, Oxford: Basil Blackwell, 1970, see especially pp. 36–9.
42 Evans-Pritchard, *Nuer Religion*, p. 124.
43 Ibid., p. 2.
44 Lienhardt, *Divinity and Experience*, pp. 28, 155.
45 Evans-Pritchard, *Nuer Religion*, pp. 1–2, 4, 9; Lienhardt, *Divinity and Experience*, p. 155.
46 Evans-Pritchard, *Nuer Religion*, pp. 1–2; Lienhardt, *Divinity and Experience*, pp. 46, 156.
47 Skorupski, p. 214.
48 Nuer philosophy is, as we have seen, essentially of a religious kind, and is dominated by the idea of *kwoth*, Spirit. As Spirit cannot be directly experienced by the senses, what we are considering is a conception. *Kwoth* would, indeed, be entirely indeterminate and could not be thought of by Nuer at all were it not that it is contrasted with the idea of *cak*, creation, in terms of which it can be defined by reference to effects and relations and by the use of symbols and metaphors. But these definitions are only schemata, as Otto puts it, and if we seek for elucidation beyond these terms, a statement of what Spirit is thought to be like in itself, we seek of course in vain. Nuer do not claim to know. They say that they are merely *doar*, simple people, and how can simple people know about such matters? What happens in the world is determined by Spirit and Spirit can be influenced by prayer and sacrifice. This much they know, but no more; and they say, very sensibly, that since the European is so clever perhaps he can tell them the answer to the question he asks. (Evans-Pritchard, *Nuer Religion*, pp. 315–16.)

Within the single world known to them (for they dwell little upon fancies of any "other world" of different constitution), the Dinka claim that they encounter "spirits" of various kinds, which they generally call *jok*. In this account I call them "powers". These "powers" are regarded as higher in the scale of being than men and other merely terrestrial creatures, and operate beyond the categories of space and time which limit human actions; but they are not imagined to form a separate "spirit-world" of their own, and their interest for Dinka is as ultra-human forces participating in human life and often affecting men for good and ill. They emerge in the interpretation of events, and hence the broad Dinka division into "that which is of men" and "that which is of powers" is in part a classification of events into two kinds. (Lienhardt, *Divinity and Experience*, p. 28.)

Dinka religion, then, is a relationship between men and ultra-human powers encountered by men, between the two parts of a radically divided world. As will be seen, it is rather phenomenological than theological, an interpretation of signs of ultra-human activity rather than a doctrine of the intrinsic nature of the powers behind those signs. (Ibid., p. 32.)

49 Evans-Pritchard, *Nuer Religion*, pp. 1–3; Lienhardt, *Divinity and Experience*, pp. 32–4.
50 Evans-Pritchard, *Nuer Religion*, pp. 304–10; Lienhardt, *Divinity and Experience*, pp. 46, 57–63, 156.
51 Skorupski, pp. 211–19.
52 Although Evans-Pritchard uses the word 'mystery' from time to time, there is no evidence of any corresponding concept (with anything like the Christian connotation) in Nuer thought. In the passage quoted in note 48, indeed, Evans-Pritchard himself seems to admit that the Nuer attitude to paradox is pragmatic rather than reverential or celebratory.
53 Skorupski, pp. 106–7.

54 Though she would probably not agree with the details of this interpretation, I got the basic idea from a conversation with Professor Dorothy Emmet.

55 For a very uncompromising exposition of this view, see D. Z. Phillips, *Faith and Philosophical Enquiry*. London: Routledge & Kegan Paul, 1970.

56 This point is made, with abundant documentation, in K. Thomas, *Religion and the Decline of Magic*, London: Weidenfeld & Nicholson, 1971.

57 Skorupski, pp. 107–11.

58 Clement of Alexandria had perceived that if Christianity was to be more than a religion for the uneducated it must come to terms with Greek philosophy and Greek science; simple-minded Christians must no longer "fear philosophy as children fear a scarecrow"; Tertullian's maxim, "nobis curiositate opus non est post Christum Iesum" was seen to be a fatal bar to the conversion of the intelligent. (E. R. Dodds, *Pagan and Christian in an Age of Anxiety*, Cambridge: Cambridge University Press, 1965, p. 106).

Had any cultivated pagan of the second century been asked to put in a few words the difference between his own view of life and the Christian one, he might have replied that it was the difference between *logismos* and *pistis*, between reasoned conviction and blind faith. To anyone brought up on classical Greek philosophy, *pistis* meant the lowest grade of cognition: it was the state of mind of the uneducated, who believe things on hearsay without being able to give reasons for their belief ... Later Porphyry seems to have repeated the same protest against "irrational and unexamined *pistis*"; and Julian exclaims, "There is nothing in your philosophy beyond the one word 'believe'!" But by Porphyry's time, and still more by Julian's, the situation had changed in two ways.

In the first place, Christians were now prepared, as we have noticed, to state a reasoned case. Athenagoras had already recognized the need for *logismos*; Origen was ready to refute the pagans point by point, borrowing for the purpose all the weapons in the arsenal of Greek philosophy. His contempt for *pistis* is hardly less than that of Celsus. "We accept it", he says "as useful for the multitude": it is the best that can be done for them, "since, partly owing to the necessities of life and partly owing to human weakness, very few people are enthusiastic about rational thought". (Ibid., pp. 120–2.)

59 Skorupski, pp. 109–10. For him, the fact that the immediate opponents of mystery-mongers like Tertullian were rationalizers *within* the church is evidence against my view of both rationalization and mystification as reactions to non-Christian competition. This, however, is like saying that, since the immediate opponents of British advocates of saturation-bombing during World War Two were fellow RAF Air-Marshals who advocated selective bombing, neither the saturation nor the selective policy were reactions to the German threat!

60 Newman was important here. So, too was Duhem, with his Bellarminian brand of positivism which at once enlarged and restricted the province of science.

61 See for instance P. Teilhard de Chardin, *The Future of Man*, translated by N. Denny, New York: Harper & Row, 1964; and A. Hardy, *The Living Stream*. London: Collins, 1966.

62 For a stimulating review of recent developments in this field, by one who clearly has strong hankerings towards a 're-spiritualization' of basic explanatory hypotheses, see A. Koestler, *The Roots of Coincidence*, London: Hutchinson, 1972.

63 See for example J. Piaget, *The Language and Thought of the Child*, London: Routledge & Kegan Paul, 1959, and *The Child's Conception of the World*, London: Routledge & Kegan Paul, 1965. For a recent summary of the work of Piaget and others on the early development of material-object schemata, see M. Vernon, *The Psychology of Perception*, Harmondsworth: Penguin, 1968, esp. pp. 18–40.

64 Emile Durkheim, in his *Elementary Forms of the Religious Life*, (English translation London: Allen & Unwin, 1915), tried to demonstrate that the basic
concepts of the material-object language are inculcated by society. As adherents
of a discipline of which he was one of the founding fathers, many sociologists have
accepted this part of his theorizing more or less unreflectively.

65 Piaget, *Language and Thought*, and Vernon, *Psychology of Perception*.

66 J. L. Austin, *Sense and Sensibilia*, Oxford: Clarendon Press, 1962.

67 One testimony to the fact that the structure of the 'observation' or the 'material-
object' language varies relatively little from culture to culture, particularly within
the Old World Culture Area, is the ease with which people learn to speak foreign
languages and to orientate themselves at the everyday level in the cultures of
those languages. (Orientation at the level of basic theory may, on the other hand,
take a lifetime.) Another testimony is provided by the professional linguists in
their use of a 'basic word list' (i.e. a list of 100–200 common material-object
terms) to assess lexical similarities between languages. For the use of such a list
implies the assumption that, in any language other than one's own, there are
100–200 common material-object terms whose meanings are to all intents and
purposes the same as those on one's list.

   Again, when one considers the history of Western culture alone, it is remarkable how little the everyday, 'material-object' language has been affected by the
revolutionary changes of theoretical schema which have taken place over the last
thousand years. As each change has loomed up, many of those not directly
involved in its promotion (especially, as we have seen, the poets) have protested
violently against the anticipated destruction of their everyday world. Yet the
everyday world has continued much as usual, protected by the stability of the
'material-object' or 'observation' language which gives it shape.

   This impressive fact about the 'observation' language in Western culture is all
too often neglected by that influential school of historians and philosophers of
science who take their lead from the pronouncements of Thomas Kuhn, Paul
Feyerabend and the late Norwood Russell Hanson. Members of this school are
apt to insist on the incommensurability of successive theoretical frameworks.
They point to the fact that both the apparatus designed to test a theory and the
results of manipulating this apparatus are described in language which is itself
'theory-laden' – i.e. impregnated with the concepts of this theory. From this, they
suggest, it follows that there is no neutral observation language which we can use
as the basis for a comparative assessment of any two theories. A favourite
corroborative quote of this school is the following:

Enter a laboratory; approach the table crowded with an assortment of apparatus, an electric
cell, silk-covered copper wire, small cups of Mercury, spools, a mirror mounted on an iron
bar; the experimenter is inserting into a small opening the metal ends of ebony-headed
pins; the iron bar oscillates, and the mirror attached to it throws a luminous band upon a
celluloid scale; the forward-backward motion of this spot enables the physicist to observe
the minute oscillations of the iron bar. But ask him what he is doing. Will he answer "I am
studying the oscillations of an iron bar which carries a mirror?" No, he will say he is
measuring the electrical resistance of the spools. If you are astonished, if you ask him what
his words mean, what relation they have with the phenomenon he has been observing and
which you have noted at the same time as he, he will answer that your question requires a
long explanation and that you should take a course in electricity. (P. Duhem, *La Théorie
Physique*, Paris, 1914, p. 218.)

Like so many pieces of 'key' evidence presented by philosophers of science, this one is double-edged. On the one hand, it does show very dramatically how the physicist tends to describe his experimental operations in language that is thoroughly 'theory-laden'. On the other hand, it shows, not only that what is going on *can* be described in terms of a theory-neutral observation language, but also that there is a sense in which the two languages are describing the same things. In this respect, it should give little comfort to the theoretical relativists who make use of it. For it highlights a crucial feature of all experimental set-ups which makes nonsense of relativist ideas. The point it makes is that although all set-ups involve artificial arrangements and simplifications, they are nonetheless regarded as extensions of that everyday world which is enshrined for us in our observation language. And in the final analysis, it is their status as extensions of the everyday world that guarantees their value. Physics, indeed, derives its very significance from an assumption of continuity between what goes on in the laboratory and what goes on in the great world outside. In many cases, it is true, it *is* only the artificial arrangements made in the laboratory that actually *do* make it possible to decide between one theory and another. But if these arrangements were regarded as so completely discontinuous with the world outside that the results of their manipulation could have no significance whatsoever for that world and for the theory-neutral propositions that describe it, then physics would become a meaningless activity.

In this context, it is interesting to note that Kuhn, in one of a very interesting series of second thoughts, admits that, where debate on the significance of an allegedly crucial series of experimental observations is being conducted by protagonists of radically different theories, one of the strategies which they are likely to adopt if they are genuinely interested in reaching agreement is precisely that of resorting as far as possible to shared everyday language, in the hope of bringing about an agreed version of 'the facts' which can be used in a critical comparison of the two theories (T. Kuhn, 'Reflections on my Critics', in Lakatos and Musgrave, eds., *Growth of Knowledge*, pp. 276–7).

Underlying all these problems, I think, is the basic paradox inherent in the thesis of theoretical identity. Where we are using a theory with confidence to solve particular puzzles within its acknowledged domain of application, we crawl out along one limb of the paradox, and use the operations of theoretical identification to enable us to describe what we observe directly in terms of our theory. Where, however, the theory is in doubt, we crawl out along the other limb, and remember the axiom that the explanans must always be something other than the explanandum. And it is in this phase that we try to re-describe the crucial phenomena in terms of a more neutral language which is continuous with the language of everyday.

68 Perhaps the most interesting illustration of this phenomenon is to be found in the sphere of causality.

To my mind, there is a clear connection between the fact that an infant builds up its causal schemata by manual manipulation of objects roughly commensurable with itself, and the fact that adult causal perception is more or less limited to contexts where the events concerned are spatio-temporally contiguous and roughly commensurable. (On these limitations, see A. Michotte, *The Perception of Causality*, London: Methuen, 1963; and M. Black, *Models and Metaphors*,

Ithaca: Cornell University Press, 1962.) Now, I as have argued elsewhere (R. Horton, 'African Traditional Thought and Western Science', *Africa*, 37, 1–2, 1967), one of the principal functions of theory is to transcend the limited causal sensitivity of everyday thought, and to spotlight connections which such thought could never apprehend. Yet the very theory whose function it is to transcend this limitation is itself affected by the pre-verbal schemata which give rise to it. In the sciences, for example, there is a strong tendency to accept only those theoretical models in which all postulated causal connections involve spatio-temporal contiguity between the events and entities featured in them. In this context, the prominence given to Newtonian dynamics in discussions of scientific method is misleading. For not only did Newton's contemporaries regard his idea of action at a distance as scandalous: he himself had misgivings about it. (On this, see Toulmin and Goodfield, *Architecture of Matter*, pp. 194–7). And, as a modern leader in the field has said, the whole of post-Newtonian physics can be regarded as an attempt to restore spatio-temporal contiguity as a guiding principle in the formulation of ideas about causal connections between theoretical entities. (M. Born, *Natural Philosophy of Cause and Chance*, Oxford: Clarendon Press, 1951, pp. 8–9, 16–17, 25–30, and *Physics in My Generation*, London: Pergamon Press, 1965, pp. 21–2, 96–8.)

In the sphere of religious ideas, the same thing would seem to be true. Thus, where the idea of a spiritual being is brought in to spotlight a link between a given event (say sickness) and some other antecedent event (say social disturbance), this being is thought of as present, not only when and where the event and its antecedent take place, but at all intermediate points in space and time. Indeed, one way in which we can make sense of ideas about spiritual omnipresence is by regarding them as responses to the requirement of spatio-temporal contiguity of cause and effect at the level of theoretical entities.

69 Fragment cited by Kirk and Raven, *Pre-Socratic Philosophers*, pp. 158–61.
70 Fragment cited by Kirk and Raven, ibid., pp. 144–5.
71 Fragment cited by Kirk and Raven, ibid., pp. 434–5.
72 Fragment cited by Kirk and Raven, ibid., pp. 429–30.
73 On the one hand, this schema is a reasoned revival of ancient Western doctrines concerning a spiritual substratum of the universe. On the other hand, it is a precursor of doctrines of 'spirits' and 'active principles' in chemistry, and of ether- and field-theories in physics. On this last topic, see S. Sambursky, *The Physics of the Stoics*, London: Hutchinson, 1971, and Toulmin and Goodfield, *Architecture of Matter*, pp. 51–2, 61, 101–5, 194–5.
74 R. Descartes, *Principia Philosophiae*, part 4, Ch. 204, (quoted by H. Kearney, *Science and Change 1500–1700*, London: Weidenfeld & Nicholson, 1971, p. 156).
75 P. Alexander, *Sensationalism*, pp. 136–7.

9 TRADITION AND MODERNITY REVISITED

1 R. Horton, 'African Traditional Thought and Western Science', *Africa*, 37, 1–2, 1967.
2 For responses which criticize the comparison itself as Eurocentric or otherwise ill-conceived, see: S. Tambiah, 'The Form and Meaning of Magical Acts', in R. Horton and R. Finnegan, eds., *Modes of Thought*, London: Faber & Faber,

1973, pp. 224–9; K. Wiredu, 'How not to Compare African Traditional Thought with Western Thought', in *Philosophy and an African Culture*, Cambridge: Cambridge University Press, 1980.

3 Perhaps the outstanding example here is that of Goody's work on the effect of the change from oral to written transmission of ideas upon a people's mode of thought. The original inspiration for his general thesis was his fieldwork in Northern Ghana. However, initially with Ian Watt and later by himself, he explored its applicability to the revolution in thought in sixth-century BC Greece. The verdict of at least some respectable classicists can be summed up by the terse comment of Moses Finlay, current doyen of Anglo-American classicists: 'Goody has said what needs to be said.' See J. Goody and I. Watt, 'The Consequences of Literacy', *Comparative Studies in Society and History*, 5, 3, 1963; J. Goody, *The Domestication of the Savage Mind*, Cambridge: Cambridge University Press, 1977. For the classisicists' accolade, see M. Finley, *The Use and Abuse of History*, London: Chatto & Windus, 1975, p. 112.

Another example is that of the work on witchcraft and sorcery pioneered by Evans-Pritchard and carried on by a long line of Africanist scholars. I think it would be fair to say that insights arising from this work and applied to earlier Europe have brought about at least a mini-revolution in our understanding of certain aspects of Western cognitive 'traditionalism'. For the pioneering inspiration, see E. Evans-Pritchard, *Witchcraft, Oracles and Magic among the Azande*, Oxford: Clarendon Press, 1937. For some idea of the fruitfulness of the interaction between Africanists and Europeanists on this topic, see M. Douglas, ed., *Witchcraft Accusations and Confessions*, London: Tavistock Publications, 1970. For two of the 'new wave' books on the intellectual history of earlier Europe that have resulted from this interaction, see A. Macfarlane, *Witchcraft in Tudor and Stuart England*. London: Routledge & Kegan Paul, 1970: K. Thomas, *Religion and the Decline of Magic*, London: Weidenfeld & Nicholson, 1971.

4 For more on the rationale of applying Africanist insights in the context of earlier Europe, see my 'African Thought-patterns: the Case for a Comparative Approach', *Ch'Indaba* (forthcoming).

5 The classic statement of this point is in C. Lévi-Strauss, *Tristes Tropiques*, Paris: Plon, 1955.

6 For Symbolist interpretations generally, see: T. Parsons, *The Structure of Social Action*, 2 vols., New York: Free Press, 1949, pp. 5, 420–5, 431, 721; E. Leach, *Political Systems of Highland Burma*, London: Bell, 1954, Introduction; E. Leach, 'Virgin birth', *Proceedings of the Royal Anthropological Institute for 1966*, London, 1967; R. Firth, 'Problem and Assumption in an Anthropological Study of Religion', *Journal of the Royal Anthropological Institute*, 89, 2, 1959; J. Beattie, *Other Cultures*, London: Routledge & Kegan Paul, 1964, pp. 202–40. For an influential 'Symbolist' critique of my ideas, see J. Beattie, 'Ritual and Social Change', *Man*, New Series, 1, 1966; 'On Understanding Ritual', in B. Wilson, ed., *Rationality*, Oxford: Basil Blackwell, 1970; 'Understanding African Traditional Religion', *Second Order*, 2, 2, 1973.

7 For 'Fideist' interpretations generally, see: P. Winch, 'Understanding a Primitive Society', *American Philosophical Quarterly*, 1, 1964; D. Z. Phillips, *Religion without Explanation*, Oxford: Basil Blackwell, 1977. For 'Fideist' critiques of my approach, see: P. Winch, 'Savage and Modern Minds', *Times Higher Education*

Supplement, 7 September, 1973, p. 13. M. Crick, *Explorations in Language and Meaning*, London: Malaby Press, 1976, pp. 157–8.

8 For critiques of the 'Symbolist' approach, see I. Jarvie and J. Agassi, 'The Problem of the Rationality of Magic', *British Journal of Sociology*, 8, 2, 1967; S. Lukes, 'Some Problems about Rationality', *European Journal of Sociology*, 8, 2, 1967; J. Peel, 'Understanding Alien Thought-Systems', *British Journal of Sociology*, 20, 1969; J. Skorupski, *Symbol and Theory*, Cambridge: Cambridge University Press, 1976. For critiques of the 'Fideist' approach, see I. Jarvie, *Concepts and Society*, London: Routledge & Kegan Paul, 1972, ch. 2; W. Mounce, 'Understanding a Primitive Society', *Philosophy*, 48, 1973; Skorupski, *Symbol and Theory*, and 'Review of D. Z. Phillips, *Religion without Explanation*', *Mind*, 88, 1979.

9 For my own critiques of these two schools, see the following. On 'Symbolists': 'Lévy-Bruhl, Durkheim and the Scientific Revolution' in Horton and Finnegan, *Modes of Thought*; 'Understanding African Traditional Thought: a Reply to Professor Beattie', *Second Order*, 56, 1, 1976. On 'Fideists': 'Professor Winch on Safari', *European Journal of Sociology*, 17, 1976.

10 For some of these answers, see Horton, 'Professor Winch on Safari', p. 176.

11 On this, see Horton, 'Durkheim and the Scientific Revolution ', pp. 283–300.

12 R. Horton, 'Paradox and Explanation: a Reply to Mr Skorupski', *Philosophy of the Social Sciences*, 3, 3–4, 1973.

13 Horton, 'Understanding African Traditional Thought', pp. 20–3.

14 R. Horton, 'Social Psychologies: African and Western', in M. Fortes and R. Horton, *Oedipus and Job in West African Religion*, Cambridge: Cambridge University Press, 1983.

15 For a sample of such criticism, see: B. Barnes, 'Paradigms: Scientific and Social', *Man*, New Series, 4, 1969, and 'The Comparison of Belief-Systems: Anomaly versus Falsehood', in Horton and Finnegan, *Modes of Thought*; Beattie, 'Understanding African Traditional Religion', p. 10; P. Feyerabend, *Against Method*, London: New Left Books, 1975, pp. 296–8; E. Gellner, *The Legitimation of Belief*, Cambridge: Cambridge University Press, 1974, pp. 149–67; D. Gjertsen, 'Closed and Open Belief Systems', *Second Order*, 7, 1–2, 1980; Goody, *Domestication of the Savage Mind*, pp. 42–3; B. Hallen, 'Robin Horton on Critical Philosophy and Traditional Thought', *Second Order*, 6, 1, 1977; M. Marwick, 'How Real Is the Charmed Circle?', *Africa*, 43, 1, 1973; and 'Witchcraft and the Epistemology of Science', Presidential Address to Section N of the British Association for the Advancement of Science, Stirling, 1974; Skorupski, 'Science and Traditional Religious Thought', pp. 189–204.

16 See for example Peel, 'Alien Thought Systems'; Skorupski, 'Science and Traditional Religious Thought', pp. 189–204.

17 See for example Feyerabend, *Against Method*, p. 298.

18 On this, see: Beattie, 'Understanding African Traditional Religion', p. 10; Gellner, *Legitimation of Belief*, p. 156; R. Frankenberg and J. Leeson, 'Choice of Healer in Lusaka', in J. Loudon ed., *Social Anthropology and Medicine*, London: Academic Press, 1976, pp. 226–7.

19 See Beattie, 'Understanding African Traditional Religion', p. 10; Goody, *Domestication of the Savage Mind*, p. 42.

20 See Barnes, 'Paradigms'; Gjertsen, 'Closed and Open Belief Systems'.

21 For more on this, see: R. Horton, 'African Conversion', *Africa*, 41, 2, 1971 and 'On the Rationality of Conversion', *Africa*, 45, 4, 1975.

22 On this, see: Feyerabend, *Against Method*; I. Lakatos, 'Falsification and the Methodology of Scientific Research Programmes', in J. Worrall and G. Currie, eds., *Imre Lakatos: Philosophical Papers*, vol. I, Cambridge: Cambridge University Press, 1977, L. Laudan, *Progress and its Problems*, Berkeley: University of California Press, 1977.

23 Gellner, *Legitimation of Belief*, pp. 157–8.

24 See for instance: M. Rudwick, *The History of the Natural Sciences as Cultural History* (Inaugural Lecture, Free University of Amsterdam), Amsterdam: Free University Press, 1975, pp, 30–1; Y. Elkana, 'The Distinctiveness and Universality of Science: Reflections on the Work of Professor Robin Horton', *Minerva*, 15, 2, 1977; Goody, *Domestication of the Savage Mind*, pp. 36–51, 149; G. Macdonald and P. Pettit, *Semantics and Social Science*, London: Routledge & Kegan Paul, 1981, p. 53.

25 Horton, 'Traditional Thought and Western Science', pp. 64–5.

26 Ibid., pp. 179–86. Goody's criticisms, in particular, read very oddly against the background of this section of the paper. For not only do I take the change from oral to written transmission of ideas as one of several factors behind the transition from 'closed' to 'open', I explicitly follow his lead in discussing *how* this change may affect modes of thought.

27 In Wilson, *Rationality*.

28 Ibid., p. 147.

29 M. Hesse, *The Structure of Scientific Inference*, London: Macmillan, 1974, ch. 1.

30 For post-1967 writing on this, see especially my 'Paradox and Explanation'.

31 On this see: Goody and Watt, 'Consequences of Literacy'; Goody, *Domestication of the Savage Mind*, pp. 26–9; G. I. Jones, 'Time and Oral Tradition', *Journal of African History*, 6, 2, 1965.

32 From this point of view, the classic monographs still remain those of the Oxford School, notably: E. Evans-Pritchard, *Nuer Religion*, Oxford: Clarendon Press, 1956; G. Lienhardt, *Divinity and Experience: The Religion of the Dinka*, Oxford: Clarendon Press, 1961; J. Middleton, *Lugbara Religion*, London: Oxford University Press, 1960; J. Buxton, *Religion and Healing in Mandari*, Oxford: Clarendon Press, 1973. As we go through this series, we find a steadily-increasing attention to ideational change. A seminal recent work from outside the Oxford School is M. L. Swantz, *Ritual and Symbol in Transitional Zaramo Society*, Lund: Gleerup, 1970. For my own small contributions on this topic, see: 'Types of Spirit Possession in Kalabari Religion', in J. Beattie and J. Middleton, eds., *Spirit Mediumship and Society in Africa*, London: Routledge & Kegan Paul, 1969 and 'On the Rationality of Conversion', part 1, *Africa*, 45, 3, 1975. Ironically, these contributions can be and have been cited as evidence against my 1967 thesis of traditional 'closure'!

33 T. Chappel, 'The Yoruba Cult of Twins in Historical Perspective', *Africa*, 44, 2, 1974.

34 A few of the early items in what is a growing tide of writing along these lines are: J. Peel, *Aladura: a Religious Movement among the Yoruba*, London: Oxford University Press, 1968; J. Fernandez, 'Fang Representations under Acculturation', in P. Curtin, ed., *Africa and the West*, Madison: University of Wisconsin

Press 1972; W. McGaffey, 'The West in Congolese Experience', in ibid.; J. Janzen, 'The Tradition of Renewal in Kongo Religion', in N. Booth, ed., *African Religions*, New York: Nok, 1977; R. Horton, 'A Hundred Years of Change in Kalabari Religion', in J. Middleton ed., *Black Africa*, New York: Macmillan, 1970, 'On the Rationality of Conversion'; H. Bucher, *Spirits and Power*, Cape Town: Oxford University Press, 1980.

35 On this, see: P. Hountondji, *Sur la 'Philosophie Africaine'*, Paris: Maspero, 1976, chs. 3, 8.

36 For the Kalabari example, see R. Horton, 'Kalabari Diviners and Oracles', *Odu*, New Series, 1, 1, 1964, pp. 12–13. For the Yoruba example, see Hallen, 'Critical Philosophy and Traditional Thought', pp. 84–6.

37 This aspect of modern ideational change emerges very clearly from the writings on 'conversion' cited in note 32.

38 S. Toulmin and J. Goodfield, *The Discovery of Time*, London: Hutchinson, 1956; J. Plumb, *The Death of the Past*. Harmondsworth: Penguin, 1969; P. Medawar, 'On the Effecting of All Things Possible', in his *The Hope of Progress*, London: Methuen, 1972; L. Sklair, *The Sociology of Progress*, London: Routledge & Kegan Paul, 1970, chs. 1–6; C. Webster, *The Great Instauration*, London: Duckworth, 1975.

39 J. S. Mill, *On Liberty*, first published in London, 1859.

40 Feyerabend, *Against Method*; Lakatos, 'Methodology of Scientific Research'; Laudan, *Progress and its Problems*.

41 Lakatos, 'Methodology of Scientific Research', p. 219.

42 For a sample of this criticism, see some of the biologists' contributions to A. Koestler and J. Smythies, eds., *Beyond Reductionism*, London: Hutchinson, 1972. See also R. Sheldrake, *A New Science of Life*, London: Blond & Briggs, 1981.

43 The continuity of respectable opposition to the Quantum Theory is well shown by the fact that the preface to David Bohm's iconoclastic *Causality and Chance in Modern Physics* (London: Routledge & Kegan Paul, 1957) was written by that great early opponent of the orthodoxy, Prince Louis de Broglie.

44 See for instance Horton: 'Paradox and Explanation'; 'Understanding African Traditional Thought'; 'Professor Winch on Safari'; 'Material-Object Language and Theoretical Language: Towards a Strawsonian Sociology of Thought', in S. C. Brown, ed., *Philosophical Disputes in the Social Sciences*, Hassocks: Harvester, 1979.

45 Nigerian students in my classes are always incredulous when I tell them that the majority of my Western friends and acquaintances live in the light of entirely non-spiritualistic views of the world.

46 For examples drawn from African as well as from Western cultures, see my 'Traditional Thought and Western Science', pp. 53–8.

47 For more on this, see ibid., pp. 66–9; and my 'Paradox and Explanation', pp. 250–3, 292–6.

48 I am indebted for this idea to John Skorupski. See his 'Science and Traditional Religious Thought', *Philosophy of the Social Sciences*, 3, 1973, p. 214.

49 On this, see: M. Born, *Natural Philosophy of Cause and Chance*, Oxford: Clarendon Press, 1951, pp. 8–9, 16–17, 25–30; *Physics in My Generation*, New York: Springer, 1969, pp. 21–2, 96–8.

50 For more on this, see my 'Paradox and Explanation', pp. 233–50, 290–2.

51 In thus setting primary theory in its technological, economic and social context, I am heavily indebted to: S. Hampshire, *Thought and Action*, London: Chatto & Windus, 1959, especially ch. 1; P. Strawson, *Individuals*, London: Methuen, 1959, especially chs. 1 and 3. These two books deserve to be far better known than they are to English-speaking 'sociologists of knowledge'. To the great detriment of their subject, the latter show an excessive fondness for the Teutonic mists, and an unwarranted contempt for the clearer air of home.

52 Hominid palaeontologists have pointed to two features of *pre-homo sapiens* hominid life for which at least a simple system of linguistic communication on primary-theory lines seems likely to have been a prerequisite. The first is the rather exact repetition of tool forms, which is hard to conceive of as having been executed in the absence of some sort of verbal instruction. The second is the hunting and killing of large and dangerous animals, which again is hard to conceive of as a possibility in the absence of co-operation directed by a verbally preconcerted plan. On this, see J. Monod, *Chance and Necessity*, London: Collins, 1972, pp. 125–7.

53 For an excellent exposition and defence of the thesis of a long period of overlap and two-way interaction between cultural and biological evolution, by one of the few social anthropologists willing to come to terms with the findings of human biology and palaeontology, see C. Geertz, 'The Growth of Culture and the Evolution of Mind' in his *The Interpretation of Culture*, London: Hutchinson, 1975. For biologists' expositions see: S. Washburn, 'Speculations on the Inter-relations of Tools and Biological Evolution' in J. Spuhler, ed., *The Evolution of Man's Capacity for Culture*, Detroit: Wayne State University Press, 1959; Monod, *Chance and Necessity*, pp. 120–30.

54 For relevant findings from recent research into the structure and physiology of primate and human central nervous systems, see: E. Lenneberg, *Biological Foun-dations of Language*, New York: Wiley, 1967; N. Geschwind, 'The Development of the Brain and the Evolution of Language', in his *Selected Papers on Language and the Brain*, Dordrecht: Reidel, 1974; C. Laughlin and E. d'Aquili, *Biogenetic Structuralism*, New York: Columbia University Press, 1974; G. Stent, *Paradoxes of Progress*, San Francisco: Freeman, 1978, chs. 2, 8, 10.

55 For the classic arguments here, see: N. Chomsky, 'Review of B. Skinner, *Verbal Behaviour*', *Language*, 35, January–March, 1959, and *Language and Mind*, New York: Harcourt Bruce Jovanovich, 1968; Lenneberg, *Biological Foundations of Language*.

56 For a general commentary on the fruitlessness and pigheadedness of the older debate between extremists on both sides, see M. Midgely, *Beast and Man*, Hassocks: Harvester, 1979. For more detailed accounts dealing with the intricate relationship between development guided by innate predisposition and behavioural change resulting from learning, see: K. Lorentz, *Evolution and the Modification of Behaviour*, Chicago: Chicago University Press, 1965; T. Bower, *Human Development*, San Francisco: W. H. Freeman, 1979.

57 On this, see my 'Paradox and Explanation', pp. 303–4. For a more elaborate treatment, see J. Ziman, *Reliable Knowledge*, Cambridge: Cambridge University Press, 1978, pp. 111–23. Ziman seems to shy away from acknowledging any element of innate predisposition in the formation of infant cognitive schemata. Nonetheless, he surely has to concede that, from birth onward, the infant

responds to his environment in a manner which is quite distinct from that of any other animal species. And this can only be because of some element of genetically based programming.

58 It seems to me that, had the 'Ordinary Language' philosophers cared to devote more thought to the relation between ordinary language and scientific language, they might well have replied to Russell along the lines adumbrated here.

59 Perhaps it is because my circle of near and dear has always included adherents of both types of 'hidden' world that the similarities between the two types have come to impress me more than the differences.

60 This general characterization of technological/economic/social trends in Western society from c. AD 1200 to the present day sums up the diagnoses, on the one hand, of a distinguished line of historical sociologists running from Karl Marx to Peter Berger, and on the other hand of such shrewd general commentators on Western society as Donald Schon and Alvin Toffler. See K. Marx and F. Engels, *The Manifesto of the Communist Party*, London, 1847, Section 18, 2; P. Berger, B. Berger and H. Kellner, *The Homeless Mind*, Harmondsworth: Penguin, 1973, especially chs.3, 4, 8; A. Toffler, *Future Shock*, London: Pan Books, 1970; D. Schon, *Beyond the Stable State*, London: Temple Smith, 1971.

61 In emphasizing the key importance of people's own concept of the sources and nature of knowledge, I follow Yehuda Elkana. See for example his *The Problem of Knowledge in Historical Perspective*, Athens: The University Press, 1973.

62 Note that it is secondary theory that is involved in this competition. Primary theoretical activity remains consensual, which is what we should expect given what I have said about its foundations.

63 It seems that this is as true of the Azande as it is of other 'traditionalists'. For their attempts to escape from a central inconsistency of their theory when this is thrust under their noses, see Evans-Pritchard, *Witchcraft, Oracles and Magic*, p. 25.

64 I stress *current* significance because it seems to me that, in such settings, as new problems and new theoretical developments aimed at resolving them come to the fore, bygone problems and the relevant theoretical developments fade out of collective awareness.

65 I have said a little about this more positive aspect of cognitive 'traditionalism' in my 'African Traditional Thought and Western Science', pp. 55–8. I expand on it considerably in 'Social Psychologies'.

66 I have a horrid suspicion that, given the right conditions, supposedly reputable scientists could lend support to total elimination of members of a rival school. The case of Lysenko and the Russian Darwinists comes to mind here.

67 The way in which inter-theoretic competition generates a continuous flow of new experience is well brought out by Lakatos in his discussion of so-called 'crucial experiments'. See his 'Methodology of Scientific Research Programmes', especially pp. 68–86.

68 On this, see S. Toulmin and J. Goodfield, *The Architecture of Matter*, London: Hutchinson, 1962, pp. 38–40.

69 Some readers may feel surprised that, having noted how inter-theoretic competition breaks the link between secondary theory and practical life, I do not go on to say something about the cognitive fruits of the resulting 'detachment'. The reason is that I think the supposed 'detachment' is largely spurious. Members of competing schools are often passionately committed to their respective bodies of

theory, and strongly antipathetic to the theories and persons of their opponents. It is not that 'detachment' gives theorists 'clearer' sight; but rather that the ever-expanding horizon of experience stimulates them to ceaseless cognitive effort.

70 One may well see cognitive 'modernism' as a sort of Pandora's Box. For not only does it contain possibilities of cognitive progress which have hitherto been beyond the traditionalist's grasp. It also contains an array of intellectual diseases which have no parallel in traditionalistic theorizing.

71 But see references to work supporting this contention in note 3.

72 In what follows, I am indebted (as in 1967!) to Goody and Watt, 'The Consequences of Literacy'.

73 E. Gellner, *Thought and Change*, London: Weidenfeld & Nicholson, 1964, pp. 64–8.

74 Ibid., pp. 64–73.

75 For sixteenth-century negativism, see: M. Montaigne, *Essays*, Great Books no. 25, Chicago: Chicago University Press, 1952; Toulmin and Goodfield, *Discovery of Time*, pp. 77–8.

76 On Bacon's position in relation to the revolution, see Webster, *The Great Instauration*.

77 On technological progress in medieval Europe, see L. White, *Mediaeval Technology and Social Change*, Oxford: Clarendon Press, 1962.

78 On this, see again Webster, *The Great Instauration*.

79 R. Jones, *Ancients and Moderns*, St. Louis: Washington University Press, 1936.

80 For the importance to late medieval thought of communities around the Western Mediterranean in which Jewish, Christian and Islamic cultural traditions were juxtaposed, see F. Heer, *The Mediaeval World*, London: Weidenfeld & Nicholson, 1961. For the importance to the thought of the nascent scientific revolution of the commercial cities of the Netherlands, see R. Mandrou, *From Humanism to Science*, Harmondsworth: Penguin, 1973, especially pp. 224–7.

81 As to why it has to be a 'world' language, see pp. 203 *et seq.* above.

82 This point is well made in M. Hollis, 'The Limits of Irrationality' and 'Reason and Ritual', in Wilson, ed., *Rationality*.

83 It is here, I think, that I have a disagreement with Hollis. See his 'The Epistemological Unity of Mankind' and my 'A Reply to Martin Hollis'; both in S. Brown ed., *Philosophical Disputes in the Social Sciences*, Hassocks: Harvester, 1979.

POSTSCRIPT

1 E. E. Evans-Pritchard, 'Lévy-Bruhl's Theory of Primitive Mentality', *Bulletin of the Faculty of Arts* (Cairo), 2, 1934, pp. 1–36.

2 J. Goody, *The Domestication of the Savage Mind*, Cambridge: Cambridge University Press, 1977, p. 38.

3 G. E. R. Lloyd, *Demystifying Mentalities*, Cambridge: Cambridge University Press, 1990, p. 6; S. J. Tambiah, *Magic, Science, Religion and the Scope of Rationality*, Cambridge: Cambridge University Press, 1991, p. 131.

4 For accusations of positivism, see: R. Devisch, 'Perspectives on Divination in Contemporary Sub-Saharan Africa' in W. van Binsbergen and M. Schoffeleers, eds., *Theoretical Explorations in African Religion*, London: Kegan Paul Inter-

national, 1985, pp. 51–67. P. Peek, 'Introduction', p. 11; R. Shaw, 'Splitting Truths from Darkness', p. 37; J. Fernandez, 'Afterword', pp. 215–17; all in P. Peek, ed., *African Divination Systems*, Bloomington; Indiana University Press, 1991. I was also reliably informed that the prevalent comment on my oral delivery of 'Back to Frazer?' (paper 4) was 'Too positivist'! For accusations of logical empiricism, see: H. Penner, 'Rationality, Ritual and Science' in J. Neusner, E. S. Frerichs and P. V. Flesher, eds., *Religion, Science and Magic*, New York: Oxford University Press, 1989, pp. 18–19; E. T. Lawson and R. N. McCauley, *Rethinking Religion*, Cambridge: Cambridge University Press, 1991, p. 36. Penner, Lawson and McCauley seem worried above all by my early contrast between 'observation' or 'common-sense' language on the one hand, and 'theoretical' language on the other. Looking back with the wisdom of hindsight, I can see that this was an element of the logical empiricist approach which I hung on to when I had abandoned other aspects of it. I can also see why I did this. It was because of a sense (now, I think, amply vindicated) that someone was in danger of throwing out a valuable baby with the empiricist bathwater. What was needed was a terminology which did justice to two equally important aspects of the situation: first, to the observation that there is a certain stratum of discourse that seems to go back to the dawn of human life and that seems closely geared to universals of human perception, and another stratum that seems to be a subsequent development elaborated to make up for the deficiencies of its more basic counterpart; and second, to the observation that both strata are equally theory-laden and indeed equally theoretical. This terminology I have endeavoured to supply with my distinction between 'primary theory' and 'secondary theory'. Such a post-positivist approach, however, does not eliminate the old problem which positivists and logical empiricists sought to solve with their notion of 'correspondence rules'. For there remains the very large question of how we are to see the relation between the-world-as-described-in-primary-theoretical-terms and the-world-as-described-in-secondary-theoretical-terms. This question is still intensively discussed by post-positivist philosophers. (See for instance: S. Kripke, 'Naming and Necessity' in D. Davidson and G. Harman, eds., *Semantics of Natural Language*, Dordrecht: Reidel, 1972; M. Hesse, *The Structure of Scientific Inference*, London: Macmillan, 1974; J. Skorupski, *Symbol and Theory*, Cambridge: Cambridge University Press, 1976, especially ch. 13, 'Paradox and Explanation'. As I see it, the achievement of my own 'Paradox and Explanation' (paper 8) is to show how this same persistent question generates similar paradoxes in both religious and scientific language.

5   It is significant that whilst positivist philosophers of science like Carnap and Ayer saw religion as poles apart from science, it is some of their post-positivist successors who have taken the lead in advocating versions of the Similarity Thesis. Here, see: M. Polanyi, *Personal Knowledge*, London: Routledge and Kegan Paul, 1973, pp. 287–9, 291, 294; P. Feyerabend, *Against Method*, London: New Left Books, 1975, pp. 295–8.

6   On this, see Lawson and McCauley, *Rethinking Religion*, p. 36; K. Nielsen, *An Introduction to the Philosophy of Religion*, London: Macmillan, 1982, p. 176; Tambiah, *Scope of Rationality*, p. 159.

7   J. Fernandez, *Persuasions and Performances*, Bloomington: Indiana University Press, 1986.

8 J. Habermas, *The Theory of Communicative Action*, Vol. II, Oxford: Polity Press, 1989, especially ch. 5.

9 Tambiah, *Scope of Rationality*, p. 6.

10 J. Grinevald, 'L'Ecologie Contre le Mythe Rationnel de l'Occident' in Y. Preis-werk and J. Vallet, eds., *La Pensée Métissé*, Paris: Presses Universitaires de France, 1990; Tambiah, *Scope of Rationality*, p. 109.

11 Lawson and McCauley, *Rethinking Religion*, especially pp. 155–8.

12 Devisch, 'Perspectives on Divination'.

13 On this, see Lawson and McCauley, *Rethinking Religion*, pp. 155–8.

14 Ibid.

15 For some recent instances of this, see: Peek, *African Divination Systems*. See especially 'Introduction', p. 11; Shaw, 'Splitting Truths from Darkness', p. 137; Fernandez, 'Afterword', p. 216. See also Tambiah, *Scope of Rationality*, p. 91.

16 For this version, see Feyerabend, *Against Method*, pp. 295–8.

17 R. Feyerabend, *Science in a Free Society*, London: New Left Books, 1978, p. 77.

18 J. Overing, 'Today I shall Call Him Mummy', in J. Overing, ed., *Reason and Morality*, London: Tavistock, 1985.

19 On the indigenous religions, see: I. Kopytoff, 'Revitalization and the Genesis of Cults in Pragmatic Religion', in I. Karp and C. S. Bird, eds., *Explorations in African Systems of Thought*, Bloomington: Indiana University Press, 1980; 'Suku Knowledge and Belief', *Africa*, 51, 3, 1981; A. D. Buckley, *Yoruba Medicine*, Oxford: Clarendon Press, 1985; Peek, *African Divination Systems*. The last is a strange volume. Most of the contributors make it clear in their fieldwork reports that explanation, prediction and control of current worldly problems is what sustains the divination process. Yet some still feel compelled to 'dress up' the subjects of these reports in the latest Parisian semeiological/semantic fashions in order to make them respectable. Here, see especially the pieces by Devisch ('Mediumistic Divination among the Northern Yaka of Zaire') and Parkin ('Simultaneity and Sequencing in the Oracular Speech of Kenyan Diviners'). For studies of religious change which bring out the contrast between the indigenous religions as shaped by the preoccupation with explanation, prediction and control of worldly events, and imported Christianity as shaped more by the preoccu-pation with communion with God for its own sake, see: J. Peel, *Aladura*, London: Oxford University Press, 1968, and 'The Pastor and the Babalawo', *Africa*, 60, 3, 1990; R. Hackett, *Religion in Calabar*, Berlin: Mouton de Gruyter, 1988.

20 See for instance: J. Parry, 'The Brahmanical Tradition and the Technology of the Intellect', in J. Overing, *Reason and Morality*.

21 P. Brown, *The World of Late Antiquity*, London: Thames and Hudson, 1989, and *The Cult of the Saints*, London: SCM Press, 1981; K. Jolly, 'Magic, Miracle and Popular Practice in the Early Mediaeval Period' in Neusner, Frerichs and Flesher, *Religion, Science and Magic*; J. Ravetz, 'The Varieties of Scientific Experience' in A. R. Peacocke, ed., *The Sciences and Theology in the Twentieth Century*, London: Oriel Press, 1981; K. Thomas, *Religion and the Decline of Magic*, London: Weidenfeld & Nicholson, 1971; C. Webster, *From Paracelsus to Newton*, Cambridge: Cambridge University Press, 1983; R. S. Westfall, *Science and Religion in the Seventeenth Century*, New Haven: Yale University Press, 1958, and *Force in Newton's Physics*, London: Macdonald, 1971; L. White, *Mediaeval Religion and Technology*, Berkeley: University of California Press, 1978; F. Yates,

Giordano Bruno and the Hermetic Tradition, London: Routledge & Kegan Paul, 1964, and *The Rosicrucian Enlightenment*, London: Routledge & Kegan Paul, 1972.

22 The interesting thing about historians of science is that, when they deal with Aristotle, Ptolemy, Priestley, Maxwell and all those others in earlier science, they are, by their own admission, dealing with various instances of 'failed science', instances which lack the cognitive power of contemporary theory. And yet, we never hear a whisper from them to urge that what was pushing these people was not the quest for explanation, prediction and control, but rather the desire to produce beautiful poetry or to solve semeiological puzzles. Why this lack of an approach so typical of social anthropology? After all, the situation is patently the same. In both cases, we are faced with systems apparently governed by the quest for explanation, prediction and control. In both cases, moreover, we are faced with systems whose cognitive efficacy, judged against the yardstick of contemporary science, often seems poor. Why the great urge in anthropology to say that things are not what they seem, whilst there is no corresponding urge in the historiography of the sciences? I think the answer is twofold. First, the historians of science are much more sophisticated than the anthropologists about putting ideas into context. Thus they judge an earlier theory in the light, not of present-day evidence, but of evidence available to its propounders. Judged in this light, much that would seem merely silly by present-day standards seems like a pretty good effort for its time. So the problem of casting aspersions on other people's ideas is not so acute as it is for the anthropologists. Secondly, the modern white liberal conscience has no problem with bashing its own forebears, but a considerable problem with being unkind to non-Westerners.

23 White, *Mediaeval Religion and Technology*, p. 239; Westfall, *Force in Newton's Physics*; Webster, *From Paracelsus to Newton*.

24 Yates, *Rosicrucian Enlightenment*, pp. 226–7, 232; Ravetz, 'Varieties of Scientific Experience', pp. 200–1.

25 For a very clear account of how the contrastive definition developed as a response to the challenge of the sciences, and for a lucid exposé of its deficiencies, see D. Jenkins, *The Bishop of Durham's Guide to the Debate about God*, Cambridge: Lutterworth Press, 1985. For an equally lucid analysis, which edges a little closer than does Jenkins to the similarity view, see D. Emmet, 'Prospects in the Philosophy of Religion' in D. Pailin, ed., *University of Manchester Faculty of Theology: Seventy-Fifth Anniversary Papers 1979*, Faculty of Theology, Victoria University of Manchester, 1979. The similarity view is also being explored by the Epiphany Philosophers, the study group of theologians, philosophers and scientists with which Emmet is closely associated. For contributions from a theologian/physicist, see: I. G. Barbour, *Myths, Models and Paradigms*, London: SCM Press, 1974; *Religion in an Age of Science* (The Gifford Lectures 1989–1991, Vol. I), London: SCM Press, 1990. For a much-praised contribution by a philosopher, see: J. M. Soskice, *Metaphor and Religious Language*, Oxford: Clarendon Press, 1985. For proposals for a new religion/science by a respected professional botanist, see: R. Sheldrake, *The Rebirth of Nature*, London: Century, 1990. For a theistic interpretation of cosmic evolution, see: H. Montefiore, *The Probability of God*, London: SCM Press, 1985.

26 On this, see: J. D. Y. Peel, 'History, Culture and the Comparative Method: a

West African Puzzle', in L. Holy, ed., *Comparative Anthropology*, Oxford: Basil Blackwell, 1987; W. Van Binsbergen, *Religious Change in Zambia: Exploratory Studies*, London: Kegan Paul International, 1981, especially pp. 38–42; R. L. Stirrat, 'Sacred Models', *Man*, 19, 2, 1984.

27 C. Geertz, 'Religion as a Cultural System', in M. Banton, ed., *Anthropological Approaches to the Study of Religion*, London: Tavistock, 1966.

28 R. Horton, 'Social Psychologies, African and Western', in M. Fortes and R. Horton, *Oedipus and Job in West African Religion*, Cambridge: Cambridge University Press, 1983.

29 E. E. Evans-Pritchard, 'The Intellectualist (English) Interpretation of Magic', *Bulletin of the Faculty of Arts* (Cairo), 1, 1933.

30 On this, see for instance: Goody, *Domestication of the Savage Mind*, pp. 36–51, 149.

31 I have developed and illustrated this point in more detail in a so-far unpublished manuscript entitled 'Karl Marx on Religion'.

32 For an outline of the importance of the earth-cult in pre-colonial West African societies, see: J. Goody, *Technology, Tradition and the State in West Africa*, London: Oxford University Press, , 1971.

33 Ibid.

34 Ibid.

35 N. Levtzion, *Ancient Ghana and Mali*. London: Methuen, 1973, pp. 115–16.

36 For an overall picture of the pre-colonial Asante state and its theoretical under-pinning, see I. Wilks, 'Ashanti Government', in D. Forde and P. Kaberry, eds., *West African Kingdoms in the Nineteenth Century*, London: Oxford University Press, , 1967.

37 On this, see: M. Fortes, 'Kinship and Marriage among the Ashanti', in A. R. Radcliffe-Brown and D. Forde, eds., *African Systems of Kinship and Marriage*, London: Oxford University Press, 1950; *Kinship and the Social Order*, London: Routledge & Kegan Paul, 1969, chs. 9–11. See also my own attempt at a synthesis in Horton, 'Social Psychologies'.

38 On this, see: I. Wilks, 'Aspects of Bureaucratization in Ashanti in the Nine-teenth Century', *Journal of African History*, 3, 2, 1966; 'Ashanti Government'.

39 R. Horton, 'African Conversion', *Africa*, 41, 2, 1971; and 'On the Rationality of Conversion', *Africa*, 45, 3–4, 1975.

40 See for instance: J. Argyle, *The Fon of Dahomey: a History and Ethnography of the Old Kingdom*, Oxford: Clarendon Press 1966, pp. 83–4.

41 This interpretation of Islamic militancy in West Africa remains controversial. Its critics offer in its place an interpretation which relies heavily on the alleged inherent militancy of the Islamic message. I hope to deal with these critics at length in a future publication. Meanwhile, suffice it to say that they beg the key question of why there was a turn to militancy in some areas but not in others. My interpretation provides a definite answer to this question.

42 Peel, 'The Pastor and the Babalawo', p. 363.

43 See: J. Beattie, 'On Understanding Ritual', in B. Wilson, ed., *Rationality*, Oxford: Basil Blackwell, 1970; M. Bloch, *From Blessing to Violence*, Cambridge: Cambridge University Press, 1986; especially chs. 1 and 8.

44 This example is based on the annual festival for the communal deity Fenibaso in the Kalabari village of Soku. For details, see: R. Horton, 'Types of Spirit

Possession in Kalabari Religion', in J. Beattie and J. Middleton, eds., *Spirit Mediumship and Society in Africa*, London: Routledge & Kegan Paul, 1969.

45 R. Horton, 'Understanding African Traditional Religion: a Reply to Professor Beattie', *Second Order*, 5, 1, 1976. See especially pp. 20–3.

46 On this, see: Bloch, *From Blessing to Violence*; Shaw in Peek, ed., *African Divination Systems*.

47 E. R. Leach, *Political Systems of Highland Burma*, London: Bell, 1954; J. Middleton, *Lugbara Religion*, London: Oxford University Press, 1960; V. Turner, *The Drums of Affliction*, Oxford: Clarendon Press, 1968; I. Lewis, *Ecstatic Religion*, Harmondsworth: Penguin, 1971; E. Mendonsa, *The Politics of Divination*, Berkeley: University of California Press, 1982.

48 Two important collections which give considerable attention to the power aspect are: J. Middleton and E. Winter, eds., *Witchcraft and Sorcery in East Africa*, London: Routledge & Kegan Paul, 1963; M. Douglas, ed., *Witchcraft Accusations and Confessions*, London: Tavistock, 1970.

49 For instance, M. Foucault, *Power/Knowledge*, Brighton: Harvester, 1980.

50 Bloch, *From Blessing to Violence*; R. Fardon, ed., *Knowledge and Power*, Edinburgh: Scottish Academic Press, 1985; Peek, ed., *African Divination Systems*, especially R. Shaw, 'Splitting Truths from Darkness', and S. R. Whyte, 'Knowledge and Power in Nyole Divination'.

51 R. Barnes, *Interests and the Growth of Knowledge*, London: Routledge & Kegan Paul, 1977. See especially pp. 33–7.

52 D. Lan, *Guns and Rain*, London: James Currey, 1985.

53 It seems significant in this context that John Skorupski, in his penetrating discussion of some prominent mid-twentieth-century anthropological theories of religion (*Symbol and Theory*, Cambridge: Cambridge University Press, 1976), saw the main focus of debate as being on the question of whether the generalizing/ theoretical strand of religious discourse should be interpreted literally or metaphorically. There is virtually nothing in his book about myth.

54 Lévi-Strauss, for instance, has nothing to say about the generalizing/theoretical strand.

55 On this, see: R. Bultmann, 'New Testament and Mythology', in H. W. Bartsch, ed., *Kerygma and Myth*, London: S.P.C.K., 1960.

56 On this, see: C. Lévi-Strauss, *La Pensée Sauvage*, Paris: Plon, 1962; G. S. Kirk, *Myth, Its Meaning and Functions*, Cambridge: Cambridge University Press, 1970; J. D. Y. Peel, 'Making History: the Past in the Ijesha Present', *Man*, New Series, 19, 1, 1984. Peel makes the important point that the mythic element infuses much of what Westerners most respect as 'academic history'.

57 For the complaint of 'coldness', see: Peel, 'History, Culture and the Comparative Method', pp. 107–8. For the complaint of 'thinness', see J. Skorupski, 'Comment on Professor Horton's "Paradox and Explanation"', *Philosophy of the Social Sciences*, 3, 1975, pp. 69–70.

58 A. Droogers, 'From Waste-Making to Recycling', in van Binsbergen and Schoffeleers, *Theoretical Explanations*, p. 118.

59 One of the basic modern theological classics on the communion aspect is undoubtedly Martin Buber's *I and Thou*, Edinburgh: T. & T. Clark, 1970. Another earlier classic on this aspect, by a man who was a theologian at heart even if not by profession, is William James's *Varieties of Religious Experience*, (Harmondsworth: Penguin, 1985).

60 S. Freud, *Totem and Taboo*, London: Routledge & Kegan Paul, 1950.

61 S. Freud, *The Future of an Illusion*, London: Hogarth Press, 1978.

62 Readers who have been taught to see Jung as more sympathetic to religion than Freud may be surprised that I pick Freud as my starting point here. My reason is that, although Freud may have been the less sympathetic of the two, he had more of a feeling than Jung for the reality to its adherents of the communion aspect of religion.

63 J. W. M. Whiting, 'Socialisation Process and Personality', in F. L. K. Hsu, ed., *Psychological Anthropology*, Homewood Illinois: Dorsey Press, 1961; M. Spiro and R. G. D'Andrade, 'A Cross-Cultural Study of Some Supernatural Beliefs', *American Anthropologist*, 60, 1958; M. Spiro, *Culture and Human Nature*, Chicago: Chicago University Press, 1987.

64 M. Fortes, 'Pietas in Ancestor Worship', *Journal of the Royal Anthropological Institute*, 91, part 2, 1961.

65 P. Brown, *World of Late Antiquity*, pp. 51–6; *The Making of Late Antiquity*, Cambridge Mass.: Harvard University Press, 1978. See especially pp. 83–9.

66 See: L. Bohannan and P. Bohannan, *The Tiv of Central Nigeria*, London: International African Institute, 1953. See pp. 81–2.

67 O. P'Bitek, *Religion of the Central Luo*, Nairobi: East African Literature Bureau, 1971.

68 M. Douglas, 'Heathen Darkness', in *Implicit Meanings*, London: Routledge & Kegan Paul, 1975.

69 For such critics, see note 6.

70 Relevant comments are to be found in: 'A definition of religion, and its uses' (paper 1): 'Back to Frazer?' (paper 4); 'Professor Winch on safari' (paper 5); 'Judaeo-Christian spectacles' (paper 6); 'African traditional thought and Western science' (paper 7); 'Paradox and explanation' (paper 8).

71 P. Brown, *World of Late Antiquity*.

72 Ibid., pp. 60–5.

73 Ibid., pp. 51–6.

74 E. R. Dodds, *Pagan and Christian in an Age of Anxiety*, Cambridge Mass.: Harvard University Press, 1965. Brown, P., *World of Late Antiquity*, pp. 82–3.

75 Peel, *Aladura*, passim.

76 The best introduction to eighteenth-century secularization is still probably the work of Paul Hazard. See: P. Hazard, *The European Mind 1680–1715*, Harmondsworth: Penguin, 1964; *European Thought in the Eighteenth Century*, Harmondsworth: Penguin, 1965. See also D. Willey, *The Eighteenth Century Background*, Harmondsworth: Penguin, 1962. For the nineteenth century, see M. Mandelbaum, 'Philosophic Movements in the Nineteenth Century'; F. M. Turner, 'Victorian Scientific Naturalism'; R. M. Young, 'Natural Theology, Victorian Periodicals and the Fragmentation of a Common Context'; all in C. Chant and J. Fauvel, eds., *Darwin to Einstein: Historical Studies on Science and Belief*, Harlow: Longman, 1980. For the new scientific theories, see: R. S. Westfall, *The Construction of Modern Science*, Cambridge: Cambridge University Press, 1971. T. Hankins, *Science and the Enlightenment*, Cambridge: Cambridge University Press, 1985.

77 For more on this, see my: 'African traditional thought and Western science' (paper 7), and 'Tradition and modernity revisited' (paper 9).

78 For a good account of the development of this form of religious life, see: Jenkins, *Bishop of Durham's Guide*.

79 For examples of this new trend, see note 25.

80 C. C. Gillispie, *The Edge of Objectivity*, Princeton: Princeton University Press, 1960; E. Gellner, *The Legitimation of Belief*, Cambridge: Cambridge University Press, 1974; Bloch, *Blessing to Violence*, and *Ritual, History and Power*, London: Athlone Press, 1989.

81 K. Popper, *Conjectures and Refutations*, London: Routledge & Kegan Paul, 1963; T. S. Kuhn, *The Structure of Scientific Revolutions*, Chicago: Chicago University Press, 1962; I. Lakatos, 'Falsification and the Methodology of Scientific Research Programmes', in J. Worrall and G. Currie, eds., *Imre Lakatos: Philosophical Papers*, Vol. I. Cambridge: Cambridge University Press, 1978.

82 On this, see: Ravetz, 'Varieties of Scientific Experience'; Webster, *Paracelsus to Newton*; Yates, *Rosicrucian Enlightenment*.

83 Lloyd, *Demystifying Mentalities*; P. Munz, *Our Knowledge of the Growth of Knowledge*, London: Routledge & Kegan Paul, 1985; J. R. Brown, *The Rational and the Social*, London: Routledge, 1989; F. M. Wuketits, ed., *Concepts and Approaches in Evolutionary Epistemology*, Dordrecht: Reidel, 1984.

84 On this, see: Parry, 'Brahmanical Tradition'.

85 On this, see: P. Brown, *World of Late Antiquity*, pp. 60–5; Horton, 'African Conversion', and 'Rationality of Conversion'.

86 I am indebted for this idea to E. Gellner, *Book, Plough and Sword*, London: Collins Harvill, 1988.

87 J. Overing, 'Translation as a Creative Process: the Power of a Name', in Holy, ed., *Comparative Anthropology*.

88 For the pernicious influence of this idea in the study of religion, see my 'Judaeo-Christian spectacles' (paper 6). For its equally pernicious influence in the historiography of science, see: D. Bloor, *Knowledge and Social Imagery*, London: Routledge & Kegan Paul, 1976.

89 For this label, see especially some of the contributions to Overing, ed., *Reason and Morality*.

90 One of my long-term ethnographic projects has been the study of the *Ekine* society of the Kalabari people of the Eastern Niger Delta. *Ekine* is best understood as a society of artists, and its performances as primarily aesthetic in intent. As the problem of interpreting Kalabari religious life drew me into more general reflections on Religion, I have a feeling that the problems of interpreting *Ekine* and its activities may draw me before long into similar general reflections on Art!

Bibliography

Abercrombie, J. M. L., *The Anatomy of Judgement*, London: Hutchinson, 1960.
Abrams, M. H., *The Mirror and the Lamp*, Oxford: Oxford University Press, 1953.
Natural Supernaturalism, New York: W. W. Norton, 1971.
Achebe, C., *Things Fall Apart*, London: Heinemann, 1957.
Arrow of God. London: Heinemann, 1954.
Agassi, J., 'Towards an Historiography of Science', *History and Theory*, Supplement 2, 1963.
Alexander, F., *Psychosomatic Medicine*, London: Allen & Unwin, 1952.
Alexander, P., *Sensationalism and Scientific Explanation*, London: Routledge & Kegan Paul, 1963.
Alexandre, P., ed., *French Perspectives in African Studies*, London: Oxford University Press, 1973.
Alquié, F., *The Philosophy of Surrealism*, Ann Arbor: University of Michigan Press, 1965.
Altizer, T. and Hamilton, J., *Radical Theology and the Death of God*, New York: Bobbs-Merrill, 1966.
Ardener, E., 'Review of Jarvie, I. C. *The Revolution in Anthropology*', *Man*, 95, 1965.
Argyle, W. J., *The Fon of Dahomey: a History and Ethnography of the Old Kingdom*, Oxford: Clarendon Press, 1966.
Arinze, F. A., *Sacrifice in Ibo Religion*, Ibadan: Ibadan University Press, 1970.
Armstrong, R. G., Critique of Wax, M. and Wax, R., '*The Notion of Magic*', *Current Anthropology*, 4, 5, 1963.
'Is Earth Senior to God? An Old West African Theological Controversy', *African Notes*, 9, 1, 1982.
Auger, P., 'The Regime of Castes in Populations of Ideas', *Diogenes*, 32, 1958.
Austin, J. L., *Sense and Sensibilia*, Oxford: Clarendon Press, 1962a
How To Do Things with Words, Oxford: Clarendon Press, 1962b.
Awolalu, J. O., *Yoruba Beliefs and Sacrificial Rites*, London: Longman, 1979.
Ayer, A. J., *Language, Truth and Logic*, London: Gollancz, 1936.
The Origins of Pragmatism, London: Macmillan, 1968.
Babayemi, S. O., 'The Ideological Base of Power of the Alaafin of Oyo and of his Chiefs', *Kiabara, Journal of the Humanities*, 4, 3, 1981.
Baëta, C., *Prophetism in Ghana*, London: SCM Press, 1962.
Banton, M., ed., *Anthropological Approaches to the Study of Religion*, London: Tavistock Publications, 1966.
Barber, K., 'How Man Makes God in West Africa: Yoruba Attitudes Towards the Orisa', *Africa*, 51, 3, 1981.

Barbour, I. G., *Myths, Models and Paradigms*, London: SCM Press, 1974.
Religion in an Age of Science, London: SCM Press, 1990.
Barley, N., *Symbolic Structures*, Cambridge: Cambridge University Press, 1983.
Barnes, S. B., 'Paradigms: Scientific and Social', *Man*, New Series, 4, 1969.
'The Comparison of Belief-Systems: Anomaly Versus Falsehood', in Horton and Finnegan, eds., *Modes of Thought*, 1973.
Scientific Knowledge and Sociological Theory, London: Routledge & Kegan Paul, 1974.
Interests and the Growth of Knowledge, London: Routledge & Kegan Paul, 1977.
Barraclough, G., *An Introduction to Contemporary History*, Harmondsworth: Penguin, 1967.
Bartsch, H. W., ed., *Kerygma and Myth*, London: S.P.C.K. 1960.
Barzun, J., 'Introduction' to Toulmin, *Foresight and Understanding*, 1961.
Bastide, R., 'Religions Africaines et Structures de Civilization', *Présence Africaine*, 66, 1968.
Beattie, J., *Other Cultures*, London: Cohen & West, 1964.
'Ritual and Social Change', *Man*, New Series 1, 1966.
'On Understanding Ritual', in Wilson, ed., *Rationality*, 1970.
'Understanding African Traditional Religion: a Comment on Horton', *Second Order*, 2, 2, 1973.
Beattie, J. and Middleton, J., eds., *Spirit Mediumship and Society in Africa*, London: Routledge & Kegan Paul, 1969.
Beier, U., *A Year of Sacred Festivals in One Yoruba Town*, Lagos: Nigeria Magazine Publications, 1959.
Benedict, R., *Patterns of Culture*, London: Routledge & Kegan Paul, 1935.
Berger, P., Berger, B. and Kellner, H., *The Homeless Mind*, Harmondsworth: Penguin, 1973.
Berlin, I., *Against the Current*, Oxford: Oxford University Press, 1981.
Bevan, E., *Symbolism and Belief*, London: Allen & Unwin, 1938.
Black, M., *Models and Metaphors*, Ithaca: Cornell University Press, 1962.
Black, S., *Mind and Body*, London: William Kimber, 1969.
Bloch, M., *From Blessing to Violence*, Cambridge: Cambridge University Press, 1986.
Ritual, History and Power, London: Athlone Press, 1989.
Bloor, D., *Knowledge and Social Imagery*, London: Routledge & Kegan Paul, 1976.
Bohannan, L. and Bohannan, P., *The Tiv of Central Nigeria*, London: International African Institute, 1958.
Bohm, D., *Causality and Chance in Modern Physics*, London: Routledge & Kegan Paul, 1957.
Booth, N. S., ed., *African Religions*, New York: Nok, 1977.
Born, M., *Natural Philosophy of Cause and Chance*, Oxford: Clarendon Press, 1951.
Physics in My Generation, London: Pergamon Press, 1965.
Borst, C. V., ed., *The Mind-Brain Identity Theory*, London: Macmillan, 1970.
Bourdillon, M. F. C. and Fortes, M., eds., *Sacrifice*, London: Academic Press, 1980.
Bower, T. G. R., *Human Development*, San Francisco: W. H. Freeman, 1979.
Bradbury, R. E., 'Review of Fortes, M. *Oedipus and Job in West African Religion*', *Man*, September, 1959.
Brain, J. L., 'Ancestors as Elders in Africa: Further Thoughts', *Africa*, 43, 2, 1973.
Bridgeman, P., *The Logic of Modern Physics*, New York: Macmillan, 1927.

Brown, J. R., *The Rational and the Social*, London: Routledge, 1989.

Brown, P., *The Making of Late Antiquity*, Cambridge Mass.: Harvard University Press, 1978.

The Cult of the Saints, London: SCM Press, 1981.

The World of Late Antiquity, London: Thames & Hudson, 1989.

Brown, S. C., ed., *Philosophical Disputes in the Social Sciences*, Hassocks: Harvester, 1979.

Buber, M., *I and Thou*, Edinburgh: T. & T. Clark, 1970.

Bucher, M., *Spirits and Power: an Analysis of Shona Cosmology*, Cape Town: Oxford University Press, 1980.

Buckley, A. D., *Yoruba Medicine*, Oxford: Clarendon Press, 1985.

Bultmann, R., 'New Testament and Mythology', in Bartsch, ed., *Kerygma and Myth*, 1960.

Bunge, M., 'Analogy in Quantum Theory: from Insight to Nonsense', *British Journal for the Philosophy of Science*, 18, 1968.

Burtt, E. A., *The Metaphysical Foundations of Modern Science*, London: Routledge & Kegan Paul, 1967.

Bushnell, J., 'La Virgen de Guadelupe as Surrogate Mother in San Juan Atingo', *American Anthropologist*, 60, 2, 1958.

Buxton, J., *Religion and Healing in Mandari*, Oxford: The Clarendon Press, 1973.

Cannon, W. B., 'Voodoo Death', *American Anthropologist*, 44, 1942. (Reprinted in Lessa and Vogt, eds., *Reader in Comparative Religion*.)

Carnap, R., *The Unity of Science*, London: Kegan Paul, 1934.

Philosophy and Logical Syntax, London: Kegan Paul, 1935.

Carr, E. H., *What is History?*, Harmondsworth: Penguin, 1964.

Cattell, R., 'The Personality and Motivation of the Researcher from Measurements of Contemporaries and from Biography', in Taylor and Barron, F., eds., *Scientific Creativity*, 1963.

Chant, C. and Fauvel, J., eds., *Darwin to Einstein: Historical Studies on Science and Belief*, Harlow: Longman, 1980.

Chappel, T., 'The Yoruba Cult of Twins in Historical Perspective', *Africa*, 44, 2, 1974.

Chomsky, N., 'Review of Skinner, B., *Verbal Behaviour*', *Language*, 35, January–March, 1959.

Language and Mind, New York: Harcourt Brace Jovanovich, 1967.

Reflections on Language, London: Collins Fontana, 1976.

Chukwukere, I., '*Chi* in Igbo Religion and Thought: The God in Every Man', *Anthropos*, 77, 3–4, 1983.

Clark, K. *Landscape into Art*, Harmondsworth: Penguin, 1956.

Civilization, London: J. Murray, 1969.

Cohen, A., *Two-Dimensional Man*, London: Routledge & Kegan Paul, 1974.

Crick, M., *Explorations in Language and Meaning: Towards a Semantic Anthropology*, London: Malaby Press, 1976.

Crombie, A. C., ed., *Scientific Change*, London: Heinemann, 1968.

Cupitt, D., *Taking Leave of God*, London: SCM Press, 1980.

The Sea of Faith, London: BBC Publications, 1984.

The Long-Legged Fly, London: SCM Press, 1987.

Curtin, P., ed., *Africa and the West*, Madison: University of Wisconsin Press, 1972.

Danto, A., *What Philosophy Is*, Harmondsworth: Penguin, 1971.

Davidson, D., 'The Individuation of Events', in Rescher, N., ed., *Essays in Honor of Carl G. Hempel*, 1969.

Davidson, D. and Harman, G., eds., *Semantics of Natural Languages*, Dordrecht: Reidel, 1972.

Davis, J., ed., *Religious Organization and Religious Experience*, London: Academic Press, 1982.

Descartes, R., *Principia Philosophiae*, Paris, 1644.

Devisch, R., 'Perspectives on Divination in Contemporary Sub-Saharan Africa', in Van Binsbergen and Schoffeleers, eds., *Theoretical Explorations*, 1985.

'Mediumistic Diviners among the Northern Yaka of Zaire', in Peek, ed., *African Divination Systems*, 1991.

Dickson, K. and Ellingworth, P., eds., *Biblical Revelation and African Beliefs*, London: Lutterworth Press, 1969.

Dieterlen, G., 'The Dogon', in Forde, ed., *African Worlds*, 1954.

Dillistone, P. W., *The Power of Symbols*, London: SCM Press, 1986.

Dodds, E. R., *Pagan and Christian in an Age of Anxiety*, Cambridge: Cambridge University Press, 1965.

Douglas, M., *Purity and Danger*, London: Routledge & Kegan Paul, 1966.

ed., *Witchcraft Accusations and Confessions*, London: Tavistock Publications, 1970.

Implicit Meanings, London: Routledge & Kegan Paul, 1975.

Douglas, M. and Kaberry, P., eds., *Man in Africa*, London: Tavistock Publications, 1969.

Droogers, A., 'From Waste-Making to Re-cycling' in Van Binsbergen and Schoffeleers, eds., *Theoretical Explorations*, 1985.

Duhem, P., *La Theorie Physique*, Paris, 1914.

The Aim and Structure of Physical Theory, Princeton: Princeton University Press, 1954.

Dumont, L., *Homo Hierarchicus*, Paris: Gallimard, 1966.

Durkheim, E., *De la Division du Travail Social*, Paris: Alcan, 1983. (Trans. G. Simpson, *The Division of Labour in Society*, New York: Macmillan, 1933.)

Les Formes Elémentaires de la Vie Religieuse, Paris: Alcan, 1912a. (Trans. J. Swain, *Elementary Forms of the Religious Life*, London: Allen & Unwin, 1915.)

'Review of *Les Fonctions Mentales dans les Societes Inférieures* and *Les Formes Elémentaires de la Vie Religieuse*', *Année Sociologique 1909–1912*, 12, 1912b.

Durkheim, E. and Mauss, M., 'De Quelques Formes Primitives de Classification: Contribution a l'Etude des Représentations Collectives', *Année Sociologique 1901–1902*, 1903. (Trans. J. Needham, *Primitive Classification*, London: Cohen & West, 1963.)

Eddington, A., *The Nature of the Physical World*, Cambridge: Cambridge University Press, 1928.

Eliade, M., *The Myth of the Eternal Return*, Princeton: Princeton University Press, 1954.

The Sacred and the Profane, New York: Harvest Books, 1961.

Elkana, Y., *The Problem of Knowledge in Historical Perspective*, Athens: The University Press, 1973.

'The Distinctiveness and Universality of Science: Reflections on the work of Professor Robin Horton', *Minerva*, 15, 2, 1977.

Emmet, D., 'Prospects in the Philosophy of Religion', in Pailin, ed., *Anniversary Papers*, 1979.

Evans-Pritchard, E. E., 'The Intellectualist (English) Interpretation of Magic', *Bulletin of the Faculty of Arts*, Egyptian University, Cairo, 1, 1933.

'Lévy-Bruhl's Theory of Primitive Mentality', *Bulletin of the Faculty of Arts*, Egyptian University, Cairo, 2, 1934.

Witchcraft, Oracles and Magic Among the Azande, Oxford: Clarendon Press 1937.

The Sanusi of Cyrenaica, Oxford: Clarendon Press, 1949.

Social Anthropology, London: Cohen & West, 1951.

Nuer Religion, Oxford: Clarendon Press, 1956.

Essays in Social Anthropology, London: Faber & Faber, 1962.

Theories of Primitive Religion, Oxford: Clarendon Press, 1965.

The Zande Trickster, Oxford: Clarendon Press, 1967.

Evans-Pritchard, E. E. et al., eds., *The Institutions of Primitive Society*, Oxford: Basil Blackwell, 1954.

Ezeanya, S. N., 'The Place of the Supreme God in the Traditional Religion of the Igbo', *West African Religion*, 1, 1963.

'God, Spirits, and the Spirit World', in Dickson and Ellingworth, eds., *Biblical Revelation*, 1969.

Fardon, R., ed., *Knowledge and Power*, Edinburgh: Scottish Academic Press, 1985.

Fashole-Luke, E., Gray, R., Hastings, A. and Tasie, G., eds., *Christianity in Independent Africa*, London: Rex Collings, 1978.

Fernandez, J., 'Fang Representations under Acculturation', in Curtin, P., ed., *Africa and the West*, 1972.

'African Religious Movements', *Annual Review of Anthropology*, 1978.

Persuasions and Performances, Bloomington: Indiana University Press, 1986.

'Afterword', in Peek, ed., *African Divination Systems*, 1991.

Feyerabend, P., 'Explanation, Reduction and Empiricism', in Fiegl and Maxwell, eds., *Minnesota Studies*, 1962.

'Consolations for the Specialist', in Lakatos and Musgrave, eds., *Growth of Knowledge*, 1970.

Against Method, London: New Left Books, 1975.

Science in a Free Society, London: New Left Books, 1978.

Fiegl, H. and Maxwell, G., eds., *Minnesota Studies in the Philosophy of Science*, 3, Minneapolis: University of Minnesota Press, 1962.

Finley, M., *The Use and Abuse of History*, London: Chatto & Windus, 1975.

Firth, R., 'Religious Belief and Personal Adjustment', *Journal of the Royal Anthropological Institute*, 78, 1950.

ed., *Man and Culture*, London: Routledge & Kegan Paul, 1957.

'Problem and Assumption in an Anthropological Study of Religion', *Journal of the Royal Anthropological Institute*, 89, 1959.

Symbols: Public and Private, London: Allen & Unwin, 1973.

Fisher, H., 'Conversion Reconsidered: Some Historical Aspects of Religious Conversion in Black Africa', *Africa*, 43, 1, 1973.

Forde, D., ed., *African Worlds*, London: Oxford University Press, 1954.

The Context of Belief, Liverpool: Liverpool University Press, 1958a.

'Spirits, Witches and Sorcerers in the Supernatural Economy of the Yako', *Journal of the Royal Anthropological Institute*, 88, 1958b.

Forde, D. and Kaberry, P., eds., *West African Kingdoms in the Nineteenth Century*, London: Oxford University Press, 1967.

Fortes, M., *The Web of Kinship among the Tallensi*, London: Oxford University Press, 1949.

'Kinship and Marriage among the Ashanti', in Radcliffe-Brown and Forde, eds., *African Systems*, 1950.

Oedipus and Job in West African Religion, Cambridge: Cambridge University Press, 1959.

'Pietas in Ancestor Worship', *Journal of the Royal Anthropological Institute*, 91, 2, 1961.

'Some Reflections on Ancestor-Worship in Africa', in Fortes and Dieterlen, eds., *African Systems of Thought*, 1965.

Kinship and the Social Order, London: Routledge & Kegan Paul, 1969.

'Preface. Anthropologists and Theologians: Common Interests and Divergent Approaches', in Bourdillon and Fortes, eds., *Sacrifice*, 1980.

Fortes, M. and Dieterlen, G., eds., *African Systems of Thought*, London: Academic Press, 1965.

Fortes, M. and Horton, R., *Oedipus and Job in West African Religion*, Cambridge: Cambridge University Press, 1983.

Foucault, M., *Power/Knowledge*, Brighton: Harvester, 1980.

Frankenberg, R. and Leeson, J., 'Choice of Healer in Lusaka', in Loudon, ed., *Social Anthropology and Medicine*, 1976.

Frazer, J. G., *The Golden Bough*, Abridged Edition, London: Macmillan, 1967.

Freud, S., *Totem and Taboo*, London: Routledge & Kegan Paul, 1950.

The Future of an Illusion, London: Hogarth Press, 1978.

Gaba, C. R., *Scriptures of an African People*, New York: Nok, 1973.

'Man's Salvation: Its Nature and Meaning in African Traditional Religion', in Fashole-Luke, Gray, Hastings and Tasie, eds., *Christianity in Independent Africa*, 1978.

Geertz, C., 'Religion as a Cultural System', in Banton, ed., *Anthropological Approaches*, 1966.

The Interpretation of Culture, London: Hutchinson, 1975.

Geertz, C. and Miller, J., 'Dialogue with Clifford Geertz', in Miller ed., *States of Mind*, 1983.

Gellner, E., 'Concepts and Society', *Transactions of the Fifth World Congress of Sociology*, 1, Louvain: International Sociological Association, 1962. (Reprinted in Wilson, ed., *Rationality*.)

Thought and Change, London: Weidenfeld & Nicholson, 1964.

'The New Idealism: Cause and Meaning in the Social Sciences', in Lakatos and Musgrave, eds., *Philosophy of Science*, 1968.

The Legitimation of Belief, Cambridge: Cambridge University Press, 1974.

Book, Plough and Sword, London: Collins Harvill, 1988.

Gerth, H. and Wright Mills, C., eds., *From Max Weber: Essays in Sociology*, London: Routledge & Kegan Paul, 1948.

Geschwind, N., *Selected Papers on Language and the Brain*, Dordrecht: Reidel, 1974.

Gillispie, C. C., *The Edge of Objectivity*, Princeton: Princeton University Press, 1960.

Gjertsen, D., 'Closed and Open Belief Systems', *Second Order*, 7, 1–2, 1980.

Glanvil, J., *The Vanity of Dogmatizing*, London, 1661.

Gluckman, M., *Order and Rebellion in Tribal Africa*, London: Cohen & West, 1963.

Politics, Law and Ritual in Tribal Society, Oxford: Basil Blackwell, 1965.

Gluckman, M. and Devons, E., eds., *Closed Systems and Open Minds*, Edinburgh and London: Oliver & Boyd, 1964.

Goldschmidt, W., *Comparative Functionalism*, Berkeley: University of California Press, 1966.

Goody, J., 'Anomie in Ashanti?', *Africa*, 27, 4, 1957.

'Religion and Ritual: the Definitional Problem', *British Journal of Sociology*, 12, 1961.

Technology, Tradition and the State, London: Oxford University Press, 1971.

The Domestication of the Savage Mind, Cambridge: Cambridge University Press, 1977.

Goody, J. and Watt, I., 'The Consequences of Literacy', *Comparative Studies in Society and History*, 5, 3, 1963.

Gregory, R. L., *Eye and Brain: The Psychology of Seeing*, London: Weidenfeld & Nicholson, 1966.

Griaule, M., *Conversations with Ogotemmeli*, London: Oxford University Press, 1965.

Grinevald, J., 'L'Ecologie Contre le Mythe Rationnel de l'Occident', in Preiswerk and Vallet, eds., *Pensée Métissé*, 1990.

Gutting, G. ed., *Paradigms and Revolutions*, Notre Dame, Indiana: University of Notre Dame Press, 1980.

Habermas, J., *The Theory of Communicative Action*, Vol. II, Oxford: Polity Press, 1989.

Hackett, R., *Religion in Calabar*, Berlin: Mouton de Gruyter, 1988.

Hallen, B., 'Robin Horton on Critical Philosophy and Traditional Thought', *Second Order*, 6, 1, 1977.

Halliday, J. L., *Psychosocial Medicine: a Study of the Sick Society*, New York: W. W. Norton, 1948.

Hampshire, S., *Thought and Action*, London: Chatto & Windus, 1959.

Hankins, T., *Science and the Enlightenment*, Cambridge: Cambridge University Press, 1989.

Hanson, N. R., *Patterns of Discovery*, Cambridge: Cambridge University Press, 1958.

'Postscript', to Toulmin, ed., *Quanta and Reality*, 1962.

The Concept of the Positron, Cambridge: Cambridge University Press, 1963.

Hardy, A., *The Living Stream*, London: Collins, 1965.

Harré, R., *Theories and Things*, London: Sheed & Ward, 1961.

An Introduction to the Logic of the Sciences, London: Macmillan, 1965.

The Principles of Scientific Thinking, London: Macmillan, 1970.

The Philosophies of Science, Oxford: Oxford University Press, 1972.

Hayes, V. C., ed., *Australian Essays in World Religions*, Adelaide: Australian Association for the Study of Religions, 1977.

Hazard, P., *The European Mind 1680–1715*, Harmondsworth: Penguin, 1964.

European Thought in the Eighteenth Century, Harmondsworth: Penguin, 1965.

Heer, F., *The Mediaeval World*, London: Weidenfeld & Nicholson, 1961.

Heisenberg, W., *Philosophic Problems of Nuclear Science*, London: Faber & Faber, 1952.

Hempel, C., 'Explanation in Science and History', in Nidditch, ed., *Philosophy of Science*, 1962.

Herskovitz, M., *Dahomey*, 2 vols., New York: J. J. Agustin, 1938.

Hesse, M., *Science and the Human Imagination*, London: SCM Press, 1954.

'Models and Matter', in Toulmin, S., ed., *Quanta and Reality*, 1962.

Models and Analogies in Science, London: Sheed & Ward, 1963.

The Structure of Scientific Inference, London: Macmillan, 1974.

Hoffman, B., *The Strange Story of the Quantum*, Harmondsworth: Penguin, 1959.

Hollis, M., 'Reason and Ritual', *Philosophy*, 43, 165, 1967a. (Reprinted in Wilson, ed., *Rationality*.)

'The Limits of Irrationality', *European Journal of Sociology*, 7, 1967b. (Reprinted in Wilson, ed., *Rationality*.)

'The Epistemological Unity of Mankind', in Brown, ed., *Philosophical Disputes*, 1979.

Hollis, M. and Lukes, S., eds., *Rationality and Relativism*, Oxford: Basil Blackwell, 1982.

Holmstrom, N., 'Some Comments on a Version of Physicalism', *Philosophical Studies*, 23, 1972.

Holy, L., ed., *Comparative Anthropology*, Oxford: Basil Blackwell, 1987.

Homans, G., *The Human Group*, London, 1951.

Horton, R., 'The Ohu System of Slavery in a Northern Ibo Village-Group', *Africa*, 24, 4, 1954.

'God, Man and the Land in a Northern Ibo Village-Group', *Africa*, 26, 1, 1956.

The Gods as Guests, Lagos: Nigeria Magazine Special Publications, No. 3, 1960a.

'A Definition of Religion, and Its Uses', *Journal of the Royal Anthropological Institute*, 90, 2, 1960b.

'Destiny and the Unconscious in West Africa', *Africa*, 21, 2, 1961.

'The Kalabari World-View: an Outline and an Interpretation', *Africa*, 32, 1, 1962.

'The Kalabari Ekine Society: a Borderland of Religion and Art', *Africa*, 33, 2, 1963a.

'Boundaries of Explanation in Social Anthropology', *Man*, 63, 6, 1963b.

'Kalabari Diviners and Oracles', *Odu*, New Series, 1, 1, 1964a.

'Ritual Man in Africa', *Africa*, 34, 1964b.

'Destiny and the Unconscious in West Africa', *Africa*, 34, 1964c.

Kalabari Sculpture, Lagos: Department of Antiquities, Federal Republic of Nigeria, 1965a.

'Duminea: a Festival for the Water Spirits', *Nigeria Magazine*, 86, 1965b.

'Igbo: an Ordeal for Aristocrats', *Nigeria Magazine*, 90, 1966a.

'Conference: the High God in West Africa', *Odu*, New Series, 2, 2, 1966b.

'Ikaki: the Tortoise Masquerade', *Nigeria Magazine*, 94, 1967a.

'African Traditional Thought and Western Science', *Africa*, 37, 1–2, 1967b.

'Neo-Tylorianism: Sound Sense or Sinister Prejudice?', *Man*, New Series, 3, 4, 1968.

'Types of Spirit Possession in Kalabari Religion', in Beattie and Middleton, eds., *Spirit Mediumship*, 1969a.

'Ikpataka Dogi: a Kalabari Funeral Rite', *African Notes*, 5, 3, 1969b.

'From Fishing Village to City State', in Douglas and Kaberry, eds., *Man in Africa*, 1969c.

'A Hundred Years of Change in Kalabari Religion', in Middleton, ed., *Black Africa*, 1970a.

'The Romantic Illusion: Roger Bastide on Africa and the West', *Odu*, New Series, 3, 1970b.

'African Conversion', *Africa*, 41, 2, 1971.

'Spiritual Beings and Elementary Particles: a Reply to Mr Pratt', *Second Order*, 1, 1, 1972.

'Lévy-Bruhl, Durkheim and the Scientific Revolution', in Horton and Finnegan, eds., *Modes of Thought*, 1973a.

'Paradox and Explanation: a Reply to Mr Skorupski', *Philosophy of the Social Sciences*, 3, 3–4, 1973b.

'On the Rationality of Conversion', *Africa*, 45, 3–4, 1975.

'Professor Winch on Safari', *European Journal of Sociology*, 17, 1976a.

'Understanding African Traditional Thought: a Reply to Professor Beattie', *Second Order*, 5, 1, 1976b.

'Material-Object Language and Theoretical Language: Towards a Strawsonian Sociology of Thought', in Brown, ed., *Philosophical Disputes*, 1979a.

'A Reply to Martin Hollis', in Brown, ed., *Philosophical Disputes*, 1979b.

'Tradition and Modernity Revisited', in Hollis and Lukes, eds., *Rationality and Relativism*, 1982.

'Social Psychologies: African and Western', in Fortes and Horton, *Oedipus and Job*, 1983.

'Judaeo-Christian Spectacles: Boon or Bane to the Study of African Religions?', *Cahiers d'Etudes Africaines*, 96, 24–4, 1984.

Horton, R. and Finnegan, R., eds., *Modes of Thought*, London: Faber & Faber, 1973.

Hountondji, P., *Sur La 'Philosophie Africaine'*, Paris: Maspero, 1976.

Hoyle, F., *The Black Cloud*, Harmondsworth: Penguin, 1960.

Hsu, F. L. K., ed., *Psychological Anthropology*, Homewood: Dorsey Press, 1961.

Huxley, A., *Brave New World*, London, 1930.

Brave New World Revisited, London, 1958.

Huxley, J., *Religion Without Revelation*, London, 1957.

ed., *Ritualization of Behaviour in Man and Animals, Philosophical Transactions of the Royal Society*, Series B, No. 251, 1966.

Idowu, E. B., *Olodumare: God in Yoruba Belief*, London: Longman, 1962.

'The Study of Religion, with Special Reference to African Traditional Religion', *Orita: Ibadan Journal of Religious Studies*, 1, 1, 1967.

African Traditional Religion: a Definition, London: SCM Press, 1973.

Isichei, E., *Igbo Worlds: an Anthology of Oral Histories and Historical Descriptions*, London: Macmillan, 1977.

Jahn, J., *Muntu: an Outline of Neo-African Culture*, London: Faber & Faber, 1961.

James, W., *Varieties of Religious Experience*, London: Longmans Green, 1902. (Reprinted 1985, Harmondsworth: Penguin.)

Janzen, J., 'The Tradition of Renewal in Kongo Religion', in Booth, ed., *African Religions*, 1977.

Jarvie, I. C., *The Revolution in Anthropology*, London: Routledge & Kegan Paul, 1964.

Concepts and Society, London: Routledge & Kegan Paul, 1972.

Jarvie, I. C. and Agassi, J., 'The Problem of the Rationality of Magic', *British Journal of Sociology*, 18, 1967.

Jenkins, D., *The Bishop of Durham's Guide to the Debate about God*, Cambridge: Lutterworth Press, 1985.

Jolly, K. 'Magic, Miracle and Popular Practice in the Early Mediaeval Period', in Neusner, Frerichs and Flesher, eds., *Religion, Science and Magic*, 1991.

Jones, G. I., 'Time and Oral Tradition', *Journal of African History*, 6, 2, 1965.

Jones, R., *Ancients and Moderns*, St Louis: Washington University Press, 1936.

Joske, W. D., *Material Objects*, London: Macmillan, 1967.

Karp, I. and Bird, C. S., *Explorations in African Systems of Thought*, Bloomington: Indiana University Press, 1980.

Kearney, H., *Science and Change 1500–1700*, London: Weidenfeld & Nicholson, 1971.

Kekes, J., 'Towards a Theory of Rationality', *Philosophy of the Social Sciences*, 3, 1973.

Kermode, F., *The Romantic Image*, London: Collins Fontana, 1971.

Kiev, A., ed., *Magic, Faith and Healing*, London: Collier-Macmillan, 1964.

Kirk, G. S., *Myth: Its Meaning and Functions*, Cambridge: Cambridge University Press, 1970.

Kirk, G. S. and Raven, J., *The Pre-Socratic Philosophers*, Cambridge: Cambridge University Press, 1971.

Kneale, W. C., *Probability and Induction*, Oxford: Clarendon Press, 1952.

Koestler, A., *The Roots of Coincidence*, London: Hutchinson, 1972.

Koestler, A. and Smythies, J., eds., *Beyond Reductionism*, London: Hutchinson, 1972.

Kopytoff, I., 'Ancestors as Elders in Africa', *Africa*, 41, 2, 1971.

'Revitalization and the Genesis of Cults in Pragmatic Religion', in Karp and Bird, eds., *Explorations*, 1980.

'Suku Knowledge and Belief', *Africa*, 51, 3, 1981.

Kripke, S., 'Naming and Necessity', in Davidson and Harman, eds., *Semantics*, 1972.

Kuhn, T. S., *The Structure of Scientific Revolutions*, Chicago: Chicago University Press, 1962.

Lakatos, I., 'Falsification and the Methodology of Scientific Research Programmes', in Lakatos and Musgrave, eds., *Criticism and the Growth of Knowledge*, 1970.

Lakatos, I. and Musgrave, A., eds., *Problems in the Philosophy of Science*, Amsterdam: North Holland, 1968.

eds., *Criticism and the Growth of Knowledge*, Cambridge: Cambridge Univesity Press, 1970.

Lan, D., *Guns and Rain*, London: James Currey, 1985.

Langer, S. *Philosophy in a New Key*, Cambridge Mass.: Harvard University Press, 1951.

Laslett, P. and Runciman, W., eds., *Philosophy, Politics and Society*, Vol. II, Oxford: Basil Blackwell, 1963.

Laudan, L., *Progress and Its Problems*, Berkeley: University of California Press, 1977.

Laughlin, C. and d'Aquili, E., *Biogenetic Structuralism*, New York: Columbia University Press, 1974.

Lavoisier, A., 'Reflexions on Phlogiston', *Memoires de l'Academie Royale des Sciences*, Paris, 1876.

Lavondes, H., 'Magie at Langage', *L'Homme*, 3, 3, 1963.

Lawson, E. T. and McCauley, R. N., *Rethinking Religion*, Cambridge: Cambridge University Press, 1991.

Laye, C., *The Dark Child*, London: Collins, 1955.

Leach, E. R. *Political Systems of Highland Burma*, London: Bell, 1954.

Rethinking Anthropology, London: The Athlone Press, 1961.

'Ritualization in Man in Relation to Conceptual and Social Development', in J. Huxley, ed., *Ritualization of Behaviour in Man and Animals, Philosophical Transactions of the Royal Society*, Series B, 251, 1966.

'Virgin Birth', *Proceedings of the Royal Anthropological Institute 1966*, 1967.

'Ritual', in *International Encyclopedia of the Social Sciences*, 13, New York, 1968.

Leiris, M. and Delange, J., *African Art*, London: Braziller, 1968.

Lenneberg, E., *Biological Foundations of Language*, New York: Wiley, 1967.

Lessa, W. A. and Vogt, E. Z., eds., *A Reader in Comparative Religion*, New York: Harper & Row, 1965.

Lévi-Strauss, C., *Tristes Tropiques*, Paris: Plon, 1955.

La Pensée Sauvage, Paris: Plon, 1962.

Levtzion, N., *Ancient Ghana and Mali*, London: Methuen, 1973.

Lévy-Bruhl, L., *Les Fonctions Mentales dans les Societés Inférieures*, Paris: Alcan, 1910.

La Mentalité Primitive, Paris: Alcan, 1922.

L'Ame Primitive, Paris: Alcan, 1927.

Le Surnaturel et la Nature dans la Mentalité Primitive, Paris: Alcan, 1931.

La Mythologie Primitive, Paris: Alcan, 1935.

L'Expérience Mystique et les Symboles Chez les Primitifs, Paris: Alcan, 1938.

Les Carnets de Lucien Lévy-Bruhl, Paris: Presses Universitaires de France, 1949.

Lewis, I. M., *Ecstatic Religion*, Harmondsworth: Penguin, 1971.

ed., *Islam in Tropical Africa*, London: Oxford University Press, 1966.

Lienhardt, G., 'Modes of Thought', in Evans-Pritchard E. et al., eds., *Institutions of Primitive Society*, 1954.

Divinity and Experience: the Religion of the Dinka, Oxford: Clarendon Press, 1961.

'The Dinka and Catholicism', in Davis, *Religious Organization*, 1982.

Linton, R., *The Cultural Background of Personality*, New York: Appleton-Century, 1945.

Lloyd, G., *Polarity and Analogy: Two Types of Argumentation in Early Greek Thought*, Cambridge: Cambridge University Press, 1966.

Demystifying Mentalities, Cambridge: Cambridge University Press, 1990.

Lorentz, K., *Evolution and the Modification of Behaviour*, Chicago: Chicago University Press, 1965.

Loudon, J., ed., *Social Anthropology and Medicine*, London: Academic Press, 1976.

Lukes, S., 'Some Problems about Rationality', *European Journal of Sociology*, 8, 1967. (Reprinted in Wilson, ed., *Rationality*.)

Emile Durkheim, New York: Harper & Row, 1972.

'On the Social Determination of Truth', in Horton and Finnegan, eds., *Modes of Thought*, 1973.

Lumsden, C. J. and Wilson, E. O., *Genes, Mind and Culture*, Cambridge Mass.: Harvard University Press, 1981.

Macdonald, G. and Pettit, P., *Semantics and Social Science*, London: Routledge & Kegan Paul, 1981.

Macfarlane, A., *Witchcraft in Tudor and Stuart England*, London: Routledge & Kegan Paul, 1970.

Mach, E., *The Analysis of Sensations*, Chicago: Open Court Publishing Company, 1914.

Macintyre, A., 'A Mistake about Causality in the Social Sciences', in Laslett and Runciman, eds., *Philosophy, Politics and Society*, 1963.

'The Idea of a Social Science', *Aristotelian Society Supplement*, 41, 1967. (Reprinted in Wilson, ed., *Rationality*.)

Macquarrie, J., *The Scope of Demythologizing*, London: SCM Press, 1960.

God and Secularity, London: Lutterworth Press, 1968.

Malinowski, B., 'Magic, Science and Religion', in Needham, ed., *Science, Religion and Reality*, 1928.

A Scientific Theory of Culture, Chapel Hill: University of North Carolina Press, 1944.

Mandelbaum, M., 'Philosophic Movements in the Nineteenth Century', in Chant and Fauvel, eds., *Darwin to Einstein*, 1980.

Mandrou, R., *From Humanism to Science*, Harmondsworth: Penguin, 1973.

Marett, R. R., *The Threshold of Religion*, London: Methuen, 1914.

Marwick, M., 'How Real Is the Charmed Circle?', *Africa*, 43, 1, 1973.

'Witchcraft and the Epistemology of Science', Presidential Address to Section N of the British Association for the Advancement of Science, 1974.

Marx, K., *The Manifesto of the Communist Party*, London, 1847.

Masterman, M., 'The Nature of a Paradigm', in Lakatos and Musgrave, eds., *Growth of Knowledge*, 1970.

Maxwell, G., 'The Ontological Status of Theoretical Entities', in Fiegl and Maxwell, eds., *Minnesota Studies*, 1962.

Mbiti, J. S., *African Religions and Philosophy*, London: Heinemann, 1969.

Concepts of God in Africa, London: SPCK, 1970.

McGaffey, W., 'The West in Congolese Experience', in Curtin, ed., *Africa and the West*, 1972.

Medawar, P., *The Hope of Progress*, London: Methuen, 1972.

Mellor, D., 'Physics and Furniture', in Rescher, N., ed., *Studies in the Philosophy of Science*, 1969.

Mendonsa, E., 'Elders, Office-Holders and Ancestors among the Sisala of Northern Ghana', *Africa*, 46, 1, 1976.

The Politics of Divination, Berkeley: University of California Press, 1982.

Metuh, E. I., *God and Man in African Religion*, London: Geoffrey Chapman, 1981.

Michotte, A., *The Perception of Causality*, London: Methuen, 1963.

Middleton, J., *Lugbara Religion*, London: Oxford University Press, 1960.

ed., *Black Africa: its People and their Cultures Today*, New York: Macmillan, 1970.

Middleton, J. and Winter, E., eds., *Witchcraft and Sorcery in East Africa*, London: Routledge & Kegan Paul, 1963.

Midgley, M., *Beast and Man*, Hassocks: Harvester, 1979.

Mill, J. S., *On Liberty*, London, 1859.

Miller, J., ed., *States of Mind*, London: BBC Publications, 1983.

Monod, J., *Chance and Necessity*, London: Collins, 1972.

Montaigne, M., *Essays*, Great Books No. 25, Chicago: Chicago University Press, 1952.

Montefiore, H., *The Probability of God*, London: SCM Press, 1985.

Morton-Williams, P., 'The Yoruba Ogboni Cult in Oyo', *Africa*, 30, 4, 1960.

'An Outline of the Cosmology and Cult Organization of the Oyo Yoruba', *Africa*, 34, 3, 1964.

Mounce, W. O., 'Understanding a Primitive Society', *Philosophy*, 48, 186, 1973.

Muller, J. C., 'Of Souls and Bones: The Living and the Dead among the Rukuba, Benue-Plateau State, Nigeria', *Africa*, 46, 3, 1976.

Munz, P., *Our Knowledge of the Growth of Knowledge*, London: Routledge & Kegan Paul, 1985.

Murdoch, I., *Sartre*, New Haven: Yale University Press, 1963.

Nadeau, H., *History of Surrealism*, London: Cape, 1968.

Nadel, S. F., *Nupe Religion*, London: Routledge & Kegan Paul, 1954.

Needham, J., ed., *Science, Religion and Reality*, London: Sheldon Press 1928.

Neusner, J., Frerichs, E. S. and Flesher, P. V., eds., *Religion, Science and Magic*, New York: Oxford University Press, 1991.

Nidditch, P., ed., *The Philosophy of Science*, Oxford: Oxford University Press, 1967.

Nielsen, K., An Introduction to the Philosophy of Religion, London: Macmillan, 1982.

Nwoga, D., *The Supreme God as Stranger in Igbo Religious Thought*, Ikwereazu: Hawk Press, 1984.

Nwokamma, K., 'The Rise of the Cassava Goddess in Western Ikwerre', unpublished final-year research essay, Dept. of Philosophy and Religious Studies, University of Port Harcourt, 1989.

Oakley, F., 'Christian Theology and the Newtonian Science: the Rise of the Concept of the Laws of Nature', *Church History*, 30, 1961.

Okeke, O., 'Religious Change in Ikenanzizi', unpublished final-year research essay, Dept. of History, University of Port Harcourt, 1982.

Otto, R., *The Idea of the Holy*, London: Oxford University Press, 1928.

Overing, J., 'Today I Shall Call Him Mummy', in Overing, ed., *Reason and Morality*, 1985.

ed., *Reason and Morality*, London: Tavistock Publications, 1985.

'Translation as a Creative Process: the Power of a Name', in Holy, ed., *Comparative Anthropology*, 1987.

Packard, V., *The Hidden Persuaders*, Harmondsworth: Penguin, 1957.

Pailin, D., ed., *University of Manchester Faculty of Theology: Seventy-Fifth Anniversary Papers*, Faculty of Theology: Victoria University of Manchester, 1979.

Parkin, D., 'Simultaneity and Sequencing in the Oracular Speech of Kenyan Diviners', in Peek, ed., *African Divination Systems*, 1991.

Parrinder, G., *African Traditional Religion*, London: Sheldon Press, 1954.

Parry, J., 'The Brahmanical Tradition and the Technology of the Intellect' in Overing, ed., *Reason and Morality*, 1985.

Parsons, T., *The Structure of Social Action*, 2 Vols., New York: Free Press, 1949.

The Social System, London: Tavistock Publications, 1952.

Partington, J., *A History of Chemistry*, Vol. III, London, 1962.

Pauw, B., *Religion in a Tswana Chiefdom*, London: Oxford University Press, 1960.

P'bitek, O., *Religion of the Central Luo*, Nairobi: East African Literature Bureau, 1971a.

African Religions in Western Scholarship, Nairobi: East African Literature Bureau, 1971b.

Peacocke, A. R., ed., *The Sciences and Theology in the Twentieth Century*, London: Oriel Press, 1981.

Pearson, K., *The Grammar of Science*, London: A. & C. Black, 1911.

Peek, P., ed., *African Divination Systems*, Bloomington: Indiana University Press, 1991.

Peel, J. D. Y., 'Understanding Alien Thought-Systems', *British Journal of Sociology*, 20, 1968a.

Aladura, London: Oxford University Press, 1968b.

'Making History: the Past in the Ijesha Present', *Man*, New Series, 19, 1, 1984.

'History, Culture and the Comparative Method: a West African Puzzle', in Holy, ed., *Comparative Anthropology*, 1987.

'The Pastor and the Babalawo', *Africa*, 60, 3, 1990.

Penner, H., 'Rationality, Ritual and Science', in Neusner, Frerichs and Flesher, eds., *Religion, Science and Magic*, 1989.

Perls, F., Hefferline, R. and Goodman, P., *Gestalt Therapy*, New York: Julian Press, 1951.

Phillips, D. Z., *Faith and Philosophical Enquiry*, London: Routledge & Kegan Paul, 1970.

Religion Without Explanation, Oxford: Basil Blackwell, 1977.

Piaget, J., *The Language and Thought of the Child*, London: Routledge & Kegan Paul, 1959.

The Child's Conception of the World, London: Routledge & Kegan Paul, 1965.

Picton, J., 'Concerning God and Man in Igbira', *African Notes*, 5, 1, 1968.

Piddington, R., 'Malinowski's Theory of Needs', in Firth, ed., *Man and Culture*, 1957.

Plumb, J., 'The Historian's Dilemma', in Plumb, ed., *Crisis in the Humanities*, 1964.

ed., *Crisis in the Humanities*, Harmondsworth: Penguin, 1964.

The Death of the Past, Harmondsworth: Penguin, 1969.

Polanyi, M., *Personal Knowledge*, Chicago: University of Chicago Press, 1958.

Popper, K., *The Open Society and Its Enemies*, London: Routledge & Kegan Paul, 1945.

Conjectures and Refutations, London: Routledge & Kegan Paul, 1963.

Preiswerk, Y. and Vallet, J., eds., *La Pensée Métissé*, Paris: Presses Universitaires de France, 1990.

Quine, W. V., *From a Logical Point of View*, Cambridge Mass.: Harvard University Press, 1953.

Word and Object, Cambridge Mass.: MIT Press, 1960.

Radcliffe-Brown, A. R., *Structure and Function in Primitive Society*, London: Cohen & West, 1952.

Radcliffe-Brown, A. R. and Forde, D., eds., *African Systems of Kinship and Marriage*, London: Oxford University Press, 1950.

Ranger, T. and Kimambo, I., *The Historical Study of African Religion*, London: Heinemann, 1972.

Ravetz, J., 'The Varieties of Scientific Experience', in Peacocke, ed., *Sciences and Theology*, 1981.

Rescher, N., ed., *Essays in Honor of Carl G. Hempel*, Dordrecht: Reidel, 1969a.

ed., *Studies in the Philosophy of Science*, American Philosophical Society Monographs No. 3, Oxford, 1969b.

Richards, A. I., 'African Systems of Thought: an Anglo-French Dialogue', *Man*, New Series, 2, 1967.

Rieff, P., *Freud: the Mind of the Moralist*, London: Methuen, 1965.

Rigby, P. J., 'Sociological Factors in the Contact of the Gogo of Central Tanzania with Islam', in Lewis, ed., *Islam in Tropical Africa*, 1966.

Roszak, T., *The Making of a Counter-Culture*, London: Faber & Faber, 1970.

Rowley, H. H., *Prophecy and Religion in Ancient China and Israel*, London, 1956.

Rudwick, M., *The History of the Natural Sciences as Cultural History* (Inaugural Lecture, Free University of Amsterdam), Amsterdam: Free University Press, 1975.

Ryle, G., *The Concept of Mind*, Harmondsworth: Penguin, 1970.

Sahlins, M., *Islands of History*, Chicago: Chicago University Press, 1985.

Sambursky, S., *The Physics of the Stoics*, London: Hutchinson, 1971.

Sangree, W. H., 'Youths as Elders and Infants as Ancestors: The Complementarity of Alternate Generations, both Living and Dead, in Tiriki, Kenya, and Irigwe, Nigeria', *Africa*, 43, 1, 1974.

Sargant, W., *Battle for the Mind*, London: Pan Books, 1958.

Schmidt, W., *The Origin and Growth of Religion: Facts and Theories*, London: Methuen, 1931.

Schon, D., *Beyond the Stable State*, London: Temple Smith, 1971.

Searle, J. R., *Speech Acts*, Cambridge: Cambridge University Press, 1969.

Sellars, W., *Science, Perception and Reality*, London: Routledge & Kegan Paul, 1963.

Shaw, R., 'Splitting Truths from Darkness', in Peek, ed., *African Divination Systems*, 1991.

Sheldrake, R., *A New Science of Life*, London: Blond & Briggs, 1981.

The Rebirth of Nature, London: Century, 1990.

Sklair, L., *The Sociology of Progress*, London: Routledge & Kegan Paul, 1970.

Skorupski, J., 'Science and Traditional Religious Thought', *Philosophy of the Social Sciences*, 3, 1973.

'What is Magic?', *Cambridge Review*, January, 1975a.

'Comment on Professor Horton's "Paradox and Explanation"', *Philosophy of the Social Sciences*, 3, 1975b.

Symbol and Theory, Cambridge: Cambridge University Press, 1976.

'Review of Phillips, D. Z., *Religion Without Explanation*', *Mind*, 88, 1979.

Skultans, V., *Intimacy and Ritual*, London: Routledge & Kegan Paul, 1974.

Smart, N., *The Phenomenon of Religion*, London: Macmillan, 1973.

Snow, C. P., *The Two Cultures and the Scientific Revolution*, Cambridge: Cambridge University Press, 1960.

Soskice, J. M., *Metaphor and Religious Language*, Oxford: Clarendon Press, 1985.

Sperber, D., *Rethinking Symbolism*, Cambridge: Cambridge University Press, 1975.

Spiro, M., 'Religion: Problems of Definition and Explanation' in Banton, ed., *Anthropological Approaches*, 1966.

'Virgin Birth, Parthenogenesis and Physiological Paternity: an Essay in Cultural Interpretation', *Man*, New Series, 3, 1968.

Culture and Human Nature, Chicago: Chicago University Press, 1987.

Spiro, M. and d'Andrade, R., 'A Cross-Cultural Study of Some Supernatural Beliefs', *American Anthropologist*, 60, 1958.

Spuhler, J., ed., *The Evolution of Man's Capacity for Culture*, Detroit: Wayne State University Press, 1959.

Stebbing, S., *Philosophy and the Physicists*, London: Methuen, 1937.

Stent, G., *Paradoxes of Progress*, San Francisco: W. H. Freeman, 1978.

Stevenson, J., 'Sensations and Brain Processes: a Reply to J. J. C. Smart', in Borst, ed., *Mind-Brain Identity*, 1970.

Stirrat, R. L., 'Sacred Models', *Man*, 19, 2, 1984.

Strawson, P., *Individuals*, London: Methuen, 1960.

The Bounds of Sense, London: Methuen, 1966.

Logico-Linguistic Papers, London: Methuen, 1971.

Sundkler, B., *Bantu Prophets in South Africa*, London: Oxford University Press, 1961.

Swantz, M. L., *Ritual and Symbol in Traditional Zaramo Society*, Lund: Gleerup, 1970.

Tambiah, S. J., 'The Form and Meaning of Magical Acts', in Horton and Finnegan, eds., *Modes of Thought*, 1973.

'A Performative Approach to Ritual', *Proceedings of the British Academy*, 45, 1981.

Magic, Science, Religion and the Scope of Rationality, Cambridge: Cambridge University Press, 1991.

Tardits, C., 'Religion, Epic, History: Notes on the Underlying Functions of Cults in Benin Civilizations', *Diogenes*, 37, 1962.

Tawney, R. H., *Religion and the Rise of Capitalism*, Harmondsworth: Penguin, 1938.

Taylor, C., 'Rationality', in Hollis and Lukes, eds., *Rationality and Relativism*, 1982.

Taylor, C. and Barron, F., eds., *Scientific Creativity*, New York: Wiley, 1963.

Taylor, J. V., *The Primal Vision*, London: SCM Press, 1963.

Teilhard de Chardin, P., *The Future of Man*, New York: Harper & Row, 1964.

Thomas, K., *Religion and the Decline of Magic*, London: Weidenfeld & Nicholson, 1971.

Toffler, A., *Future Shock*, London: Pan Books, 1970.

Toulmin, S., *Foresight and Understanding*, London: Hutchinson, 1961a.

The Fabric of the Heavens, London: Hutchinson, 1961b.

ed., *Quanta and Reality*, London: Hutchinson, 1962.

Toulmin, S. and Goodfield, J., *The Architecture of Matter*, London: Hutchinson, 1962.

The Discovery of Time, London: Hutchinson, 1965.

Turner, F. M., 'Victorian Scientific Naturalism', in Chant and Fauvel, eds., *Darwin to Einstein*, 1980.

Turner, H. W., 'A Methodology for Modern African Religious Movements', *Comparative Studies in Society and History*, 7, 3, 1966.

African Independent Church, 2 Vols., Oxford: Clarendon Press, 1967.

'A Model for the Structure of Religion in Relation to the Secular', *Cahiers des Religions Africaines*, 3, 6, 1969.

'The Primal Religions of the World and Their Study', in Hayes, ed., *Australian Essays, 1977*.

'The Way Forward in the Religious Study of African Primal Religions', *Journal of Religion in Africa*, 12, 1, 1981.

Turner, S. P., *Sociological Explanation as Translation*, Cambridge: Cambridge University Press, 1980.

Turner, V. W., *Ndembu Divination*, Rhodes-Livingstone Paper No. 31, Manchester: Manchester University Press, 1961.

Chihamba: the White Spirit, Rhodes-Livingstone Paper No. 38, Manchester: Manchester University Press, 1962.

'A Ndembu Doctor in Practice', in Kiev, ed., *Magic, Faith and Healing*, 1964.

The Forest of Symbols, Ithaca: Cornell University Press, 1967.

The Drums of Affliction, Oxford: Clarendon Press, 1968.

Tylor, E. B., *Primitive Culture*, London: John Murray, 1871.

Ubah, C. N., 'The Supreme Being, Divinities and Ancestors in Igbo Traditional Religion: Evidence from Otanchara and Otanzu', *Africa*, 52, 2, 1982.

Van Binsbergen, W., *Religious Change in Zambia*: Exploratory Studies, London: Kegan Paul International, 1981.

Van Binsbergen, W. and Schoffeleers, M., eds., *Theoretical Explorations in African Religion*, London: Kegan Paul International, 1985.

Van Buren, P., *The Secular Meaning of the Gospel*, London: Macmillan, 1963.

Vernon, M., *The Psychology of Perception*, Harmondsworth: Penguin, 1968.

Wach, J., *Sociology of Religion*, London: Kegan Paul, Trench, Trubner, 1947.

Wallace, A. F. C., 'Revitalization Movements', *American Anthropologist*, 58, 2, 1956.

Washburn, S., 'Speculations on the Inter-relations of Tools and Biological Evolution', in Spuhler, ed., *Man's Capacity for Culture*, 1959.

Watson, W., *On Understanding Physics*, Cambridge: Cambridge University Press, 1938.

Weber, M., 'The Social Psychology of World Religions', in Gerth and Wright Mills, eds., *Essays in Sociology*, 1948.

Webster, C., *The Great Instauration*, London: Duckworth, 1975.

From Paracelsus to Newton, Cambridge: Cambridge University Press, 1983.

Wescott, J. and Morton-Williams, P., 'The Symbolism and Ritual Context of the Yoruba Laba Shango', *Journal of the Royal Anthropological Institute*, 92, 1, 1962.

West, M., *The World Is Made of Glass*, London: Coronet Books, 1984.

Westfall, R. S., *Science and Religion in the Seventeenth Century*, New Haven: Yale University Press, 1958.

Force in Newton's Physics, London: Macdonald, 1971a.

The Construction of Modern Science, Cambridge: Cambridge University Press, 1971b.

White, L., *Mediaeval Technology and Social Change*, Oxford: Clarendon Press, 1962.

'Mediaeval Uses of Air', *Scientific American*, 223, 2, 1970.

Mediaeval Religion and Technology, Berkeley: University of California Press, 1978.

Whiting, J. W. M., 'Socialization Process and Personality', in Hsu, F. L. K., ed., *Psychological Anthropology*, 1961.

Whitrow, J. G., *The Natural Philosophy of Time*, London: Nelson, 1963.

Whyte, S. R., 'Knowledge and Power in Nyole Divination', in Peek, ed., *African Divination Systems*, 1991.

Wilks, I., 'Aspects of Bureaucratization in Ashanti in the Nineteenth Century', *Journal of African History*, 3, 2, 1966.

'Ashanti Government', in Forde and Kaberry, eds., *West African Kingdoms*, 1967.

Willey, B., *Seventeenth Century Background*, Harmondsworth: Penguin, 1962.

Eighteenth Century Background, Harmondsworth: Penguin, 1967.

Wilson, B., ed., *Rationality*, Oxford: Basil Blackwell, 1970.

Wilson, E. O., *Sociobiology*, Cambridge Mass.: Harvard University Press, 1975.

Wilson, M., *Rituals of Kinship among the Nyakyusa*, Oxford: Oxford University Press, 1957.

Communal Rituals of the Nyakyusa, Oxford: Oxford University Press, 1959.

Winch, P., *The Idea of a Social Science, and Its Relation to Philosophy*, London: Routledge & Kegan Paul, 1958.

'Understanding a Primitive Society', *American Philosophical Quarterly*, 1, 1964. (Reprinted in Wilson, ed., *Rationality*.)

'Savage and Modern Minds', *Times Higher Education Supplement*, September 7th, 1973.

Wiredu, K., *Philosophy and an African Culture*, Cambridge: Cambridge University Press 1980.

Worral, J. and Currie, G., *Imre Lakatos: Philosophical Papers*, Vol. I, Cambridge: Cambridge University Press, 1978.

Worsley, P., *The Trumpet Shall Sound*, London: McGibbon & Kee, 1956.

Wright, A. C. A., 'The Supreme Being among the Acholi of Uganda: Another Viewpoint', *Uganda Journal*, 7, 3, 1940.

Wuketits, F. M., ed., *Concepts and Approaches in Evolutionary Epistemology*, Dordrecht: Reidel, 1984.

Wyllie, R. W., 'On the Rationality of the Devout Opposition', *Journal of Religion in Africa*, 11, 2, 1980.

Yates, F., *Giordano Bruno and the Hermetic Tradition*, London: Routledge & Kegan Paul, 1964.

The Rosicrucian Enlightenment, London: Routledge & Kegan Paul, 1972.

Young, M., 'The Divine Kingship of the Jukun: a Re-evaluation of Some Theories', *Africa*, 36, 2, 1966.

Young, R. M., 'Natural Theology, Victorian Periodicals and the Fragmentation of a Common Context', in Chant and Fauvel, eds., *Darwin to Einstein*, 1980.

Zahan, D., 'Towards a History of the Yatenga Mossi', in Alexandre, ed., *French Perspectives*, 1973.

Ziman, J., *Reliable Knowledge*, Cambridge: Cambridge University Press, 1978.

Zinkernagel, P., *Conditions for Description*, London: Routledge & Kegan Paul, 1962.

Zuesse, E. M., *Ritual Cosmos: The Sanctification of Life in African Religion*, Athens: Ohio University Press, 1979.

Index

DATE DUE

MAR 4 - 1999		
DEC 1 1 2001		